Chapter 90

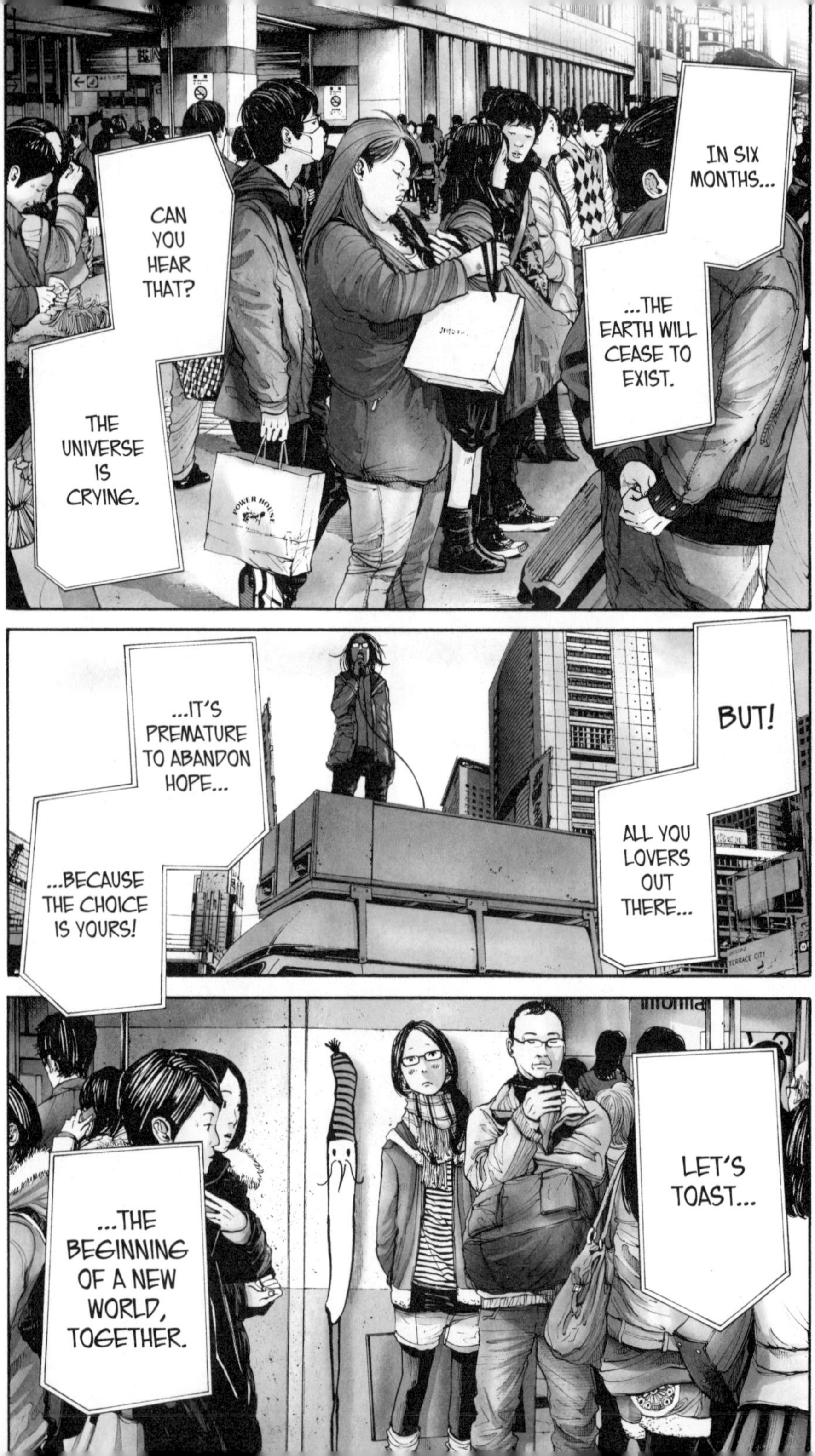

IN SIX MONTHS...
...THE EARTH WILL CEASE TO EXIST.
CAN YOU HEAR THAT?
THE UNIVERSE IS CRYING.
POWER HOUSE
BUT!
ALL YOU LOVERS OUT THERE...
...IT'S PREMATURE TO ABANDON HOPE...
...BECAUSE THE CHOICE IS YOURS!
TERRACE CITY
LET'S TOAST...
...THE BEGINNING OF A NEW WORLD, TOGETHER.

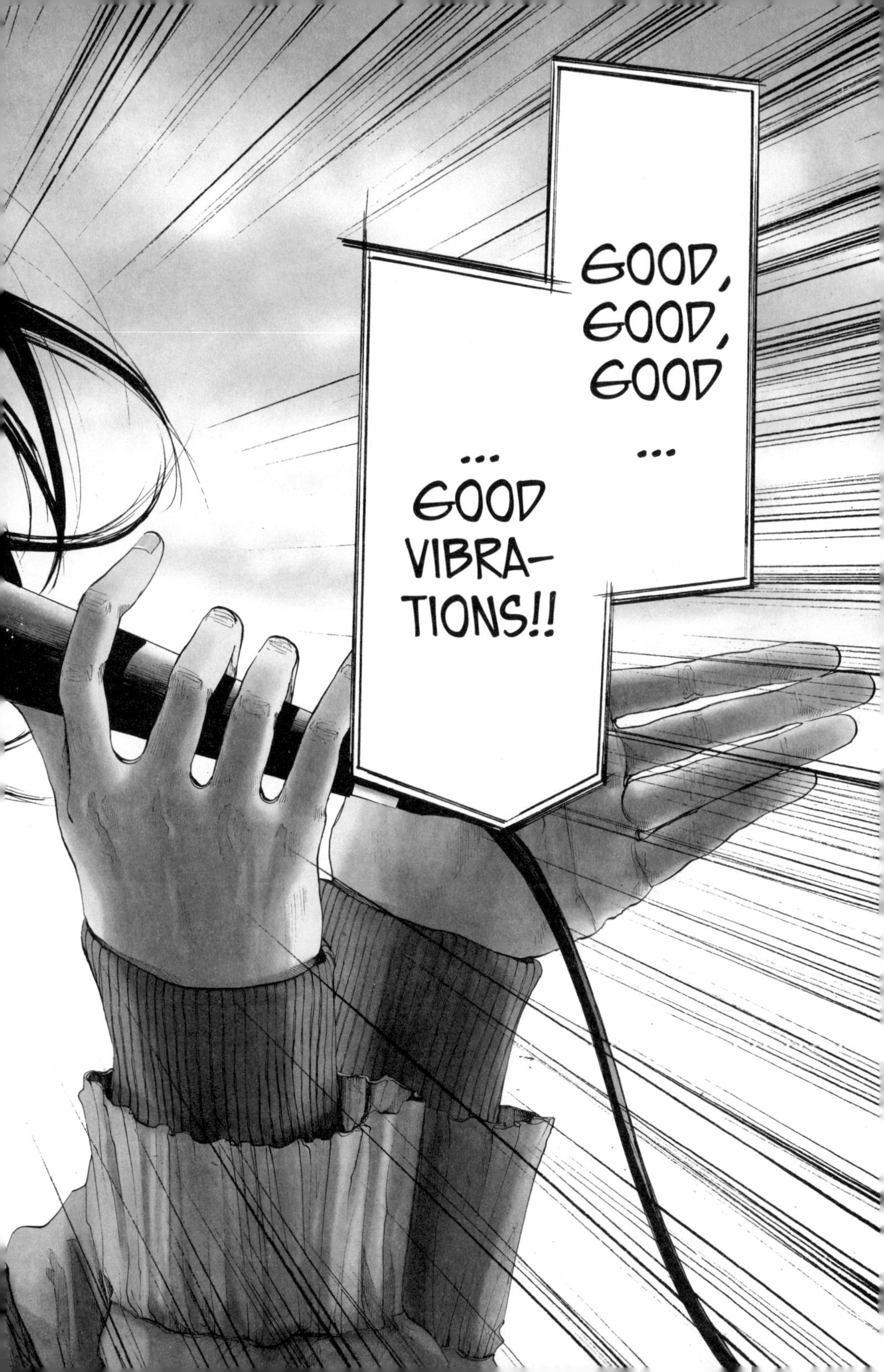
GOOD, GOOD, GOOD ...
... GOOD VIBRA-TIONS!!

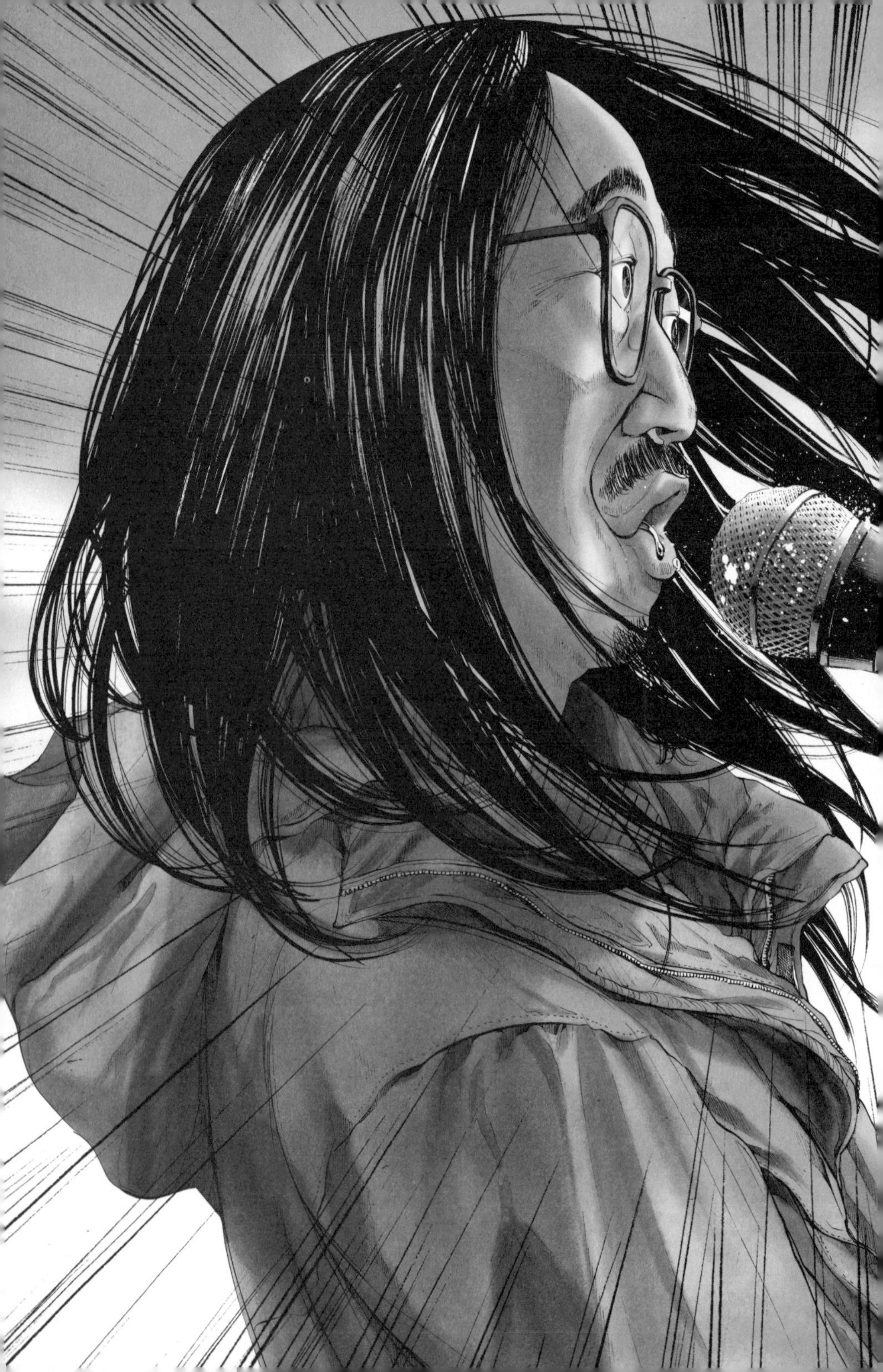

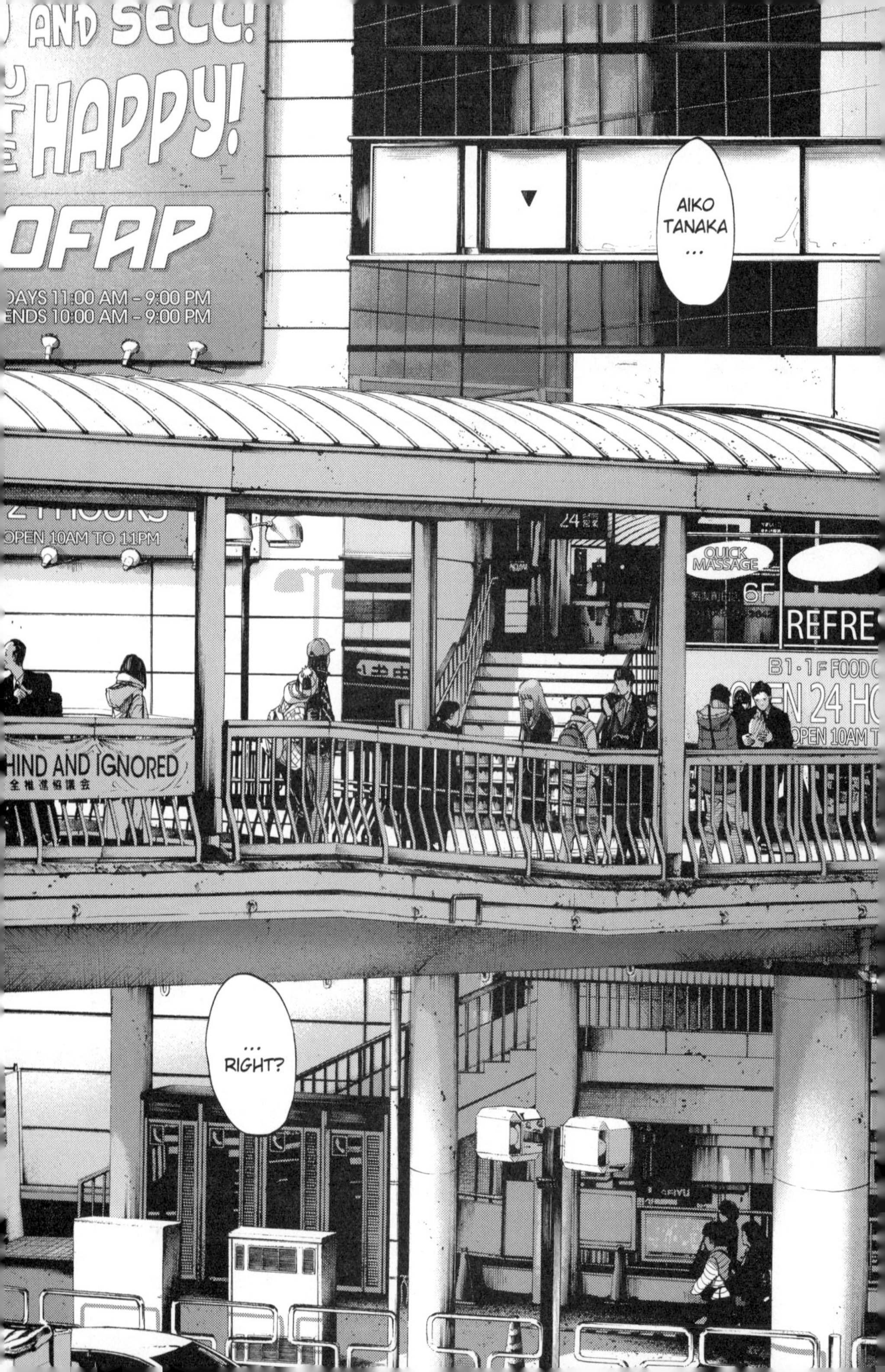
AIKO TANAKA ...
AND SELL!
HAPPY!
OFAP
DAYS 11:00 AM – 9:00 PM
ENDS 10:00 AM – 9:00 PM
QUICK MASSAGE
6F
REFRE
OPEN 10AM TO 11PM
B1・1F FOOD C
OPEN 10AM T
HIND AND IGNORED
... RIGHT?

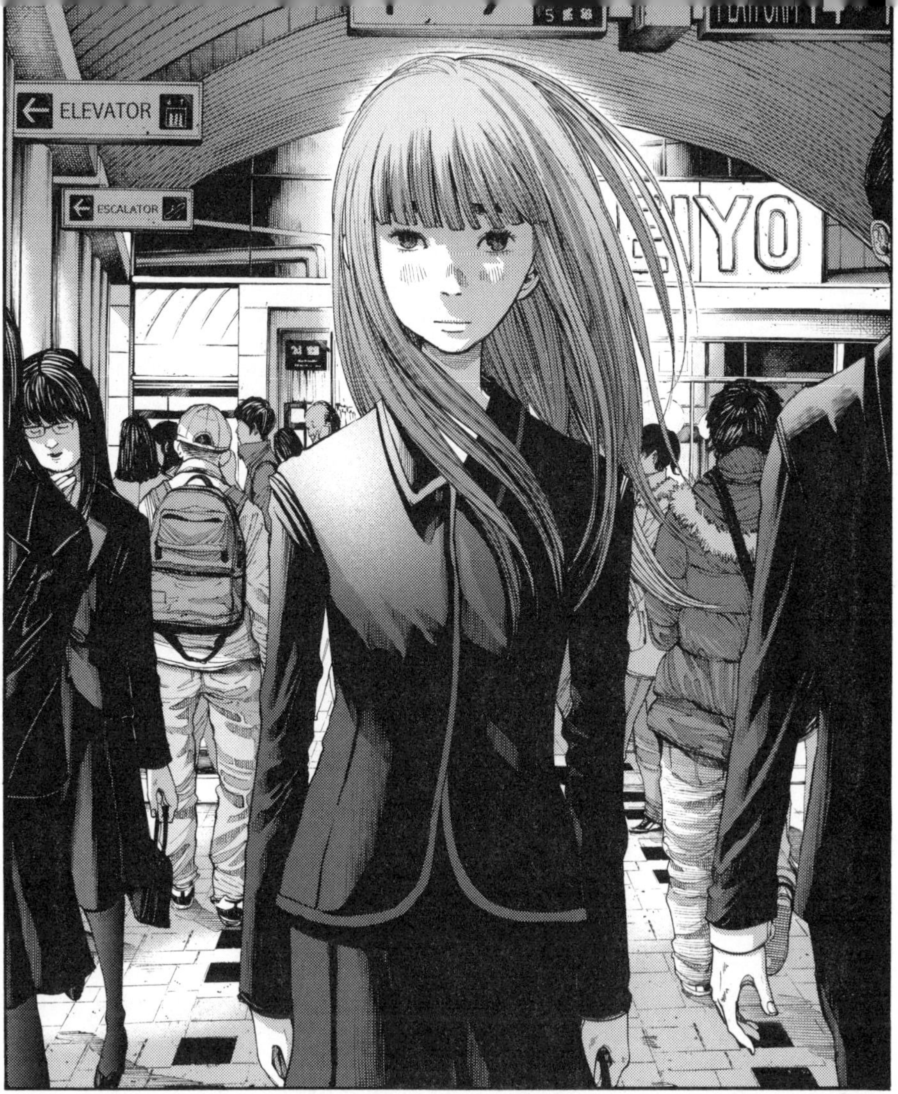
ELEVATOR
ESCALATOR

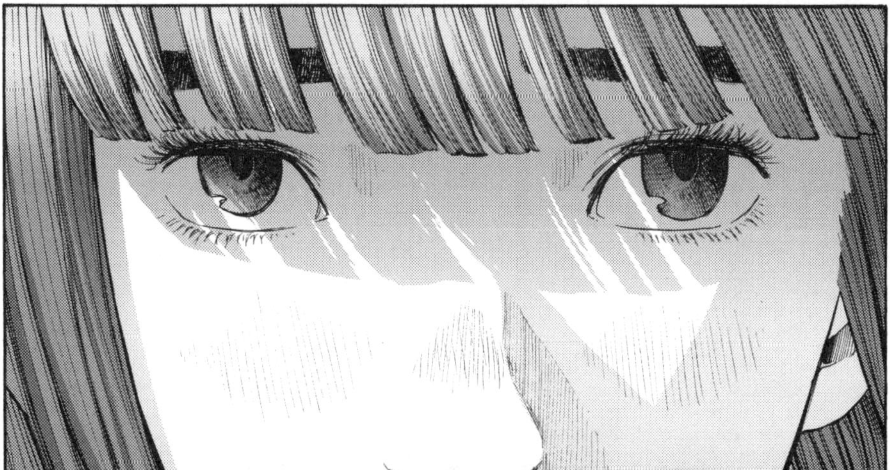

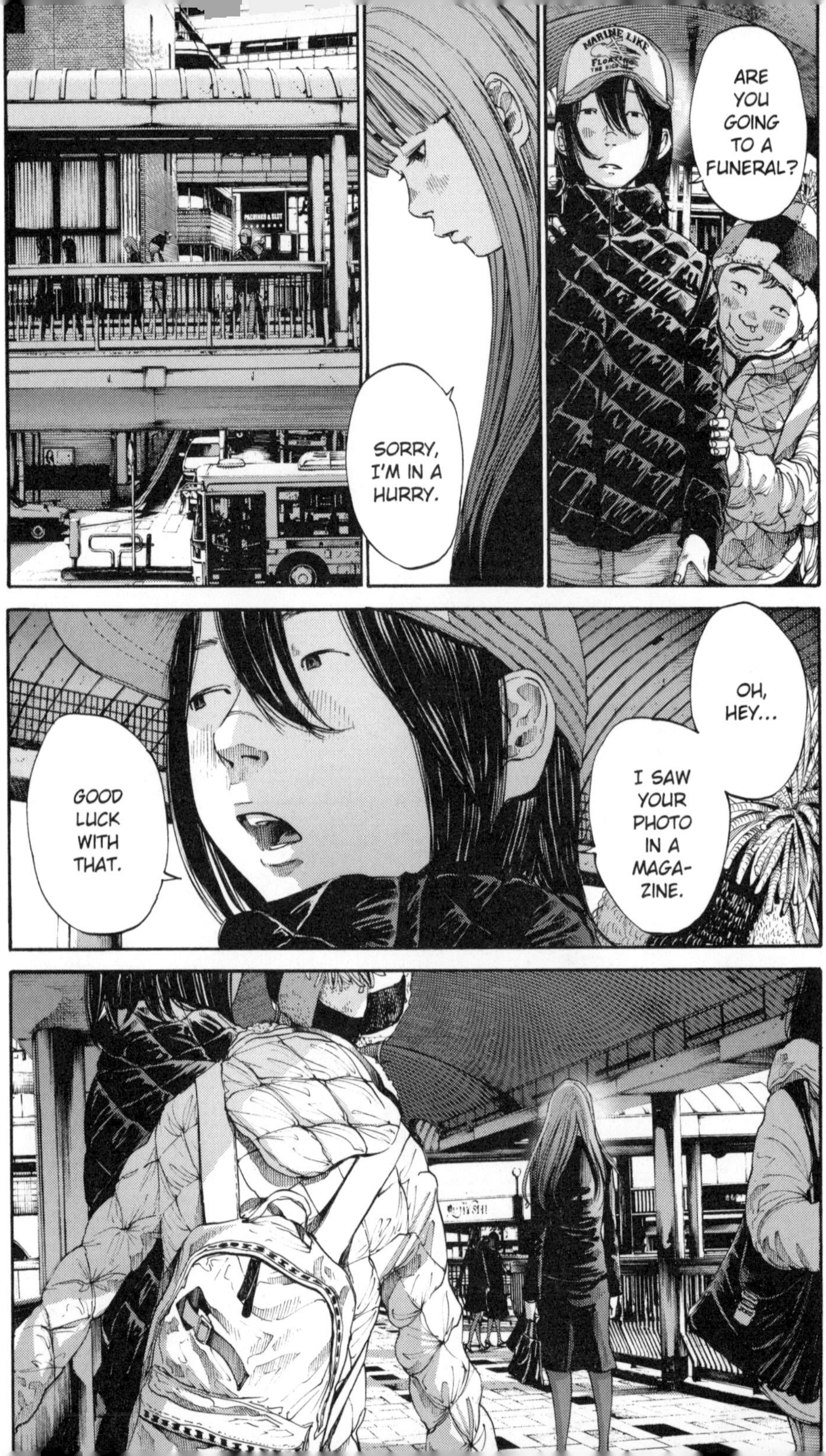
ARE YOU GOING TO A FUNERAL?
SORRY, I'M IN A HURRY.
OH, HEY...
I SAW YOUR PHOTO IN A MAGAZINE.
GOOD LUCK WITH THAT.

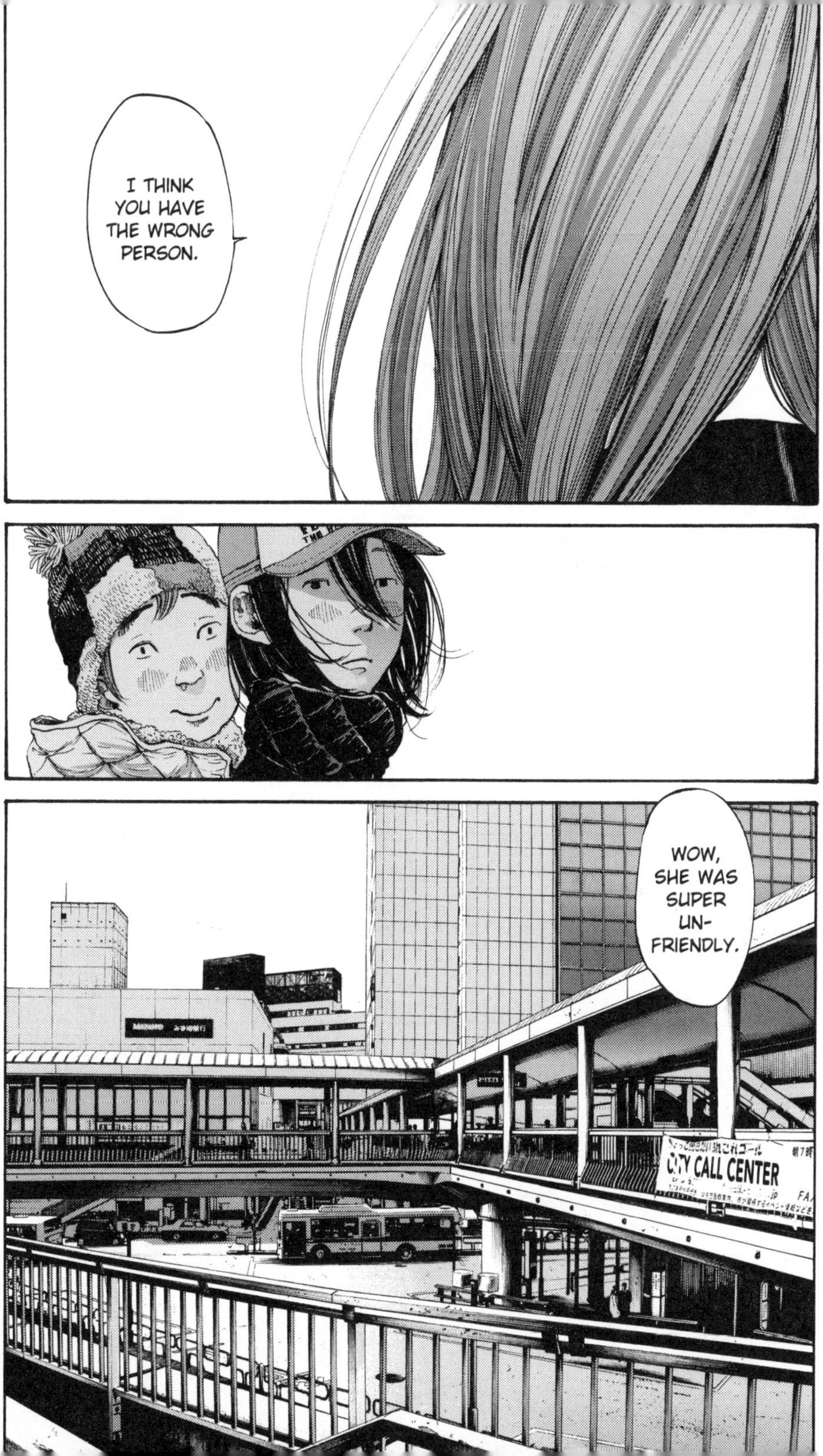
I THINK YOU HAVE THE WRONG PERSON.
WOW, SHE WAS SUPER UN-FRIENDLY.

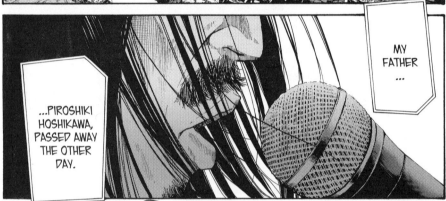

MY FATHER...

...PIROSHIKI HOSHIKAWA, PASSED AWAY THE OTHER DAY.

YES, HELLO...

NO, NO. WE'RE STILL IN SHINJUKU.

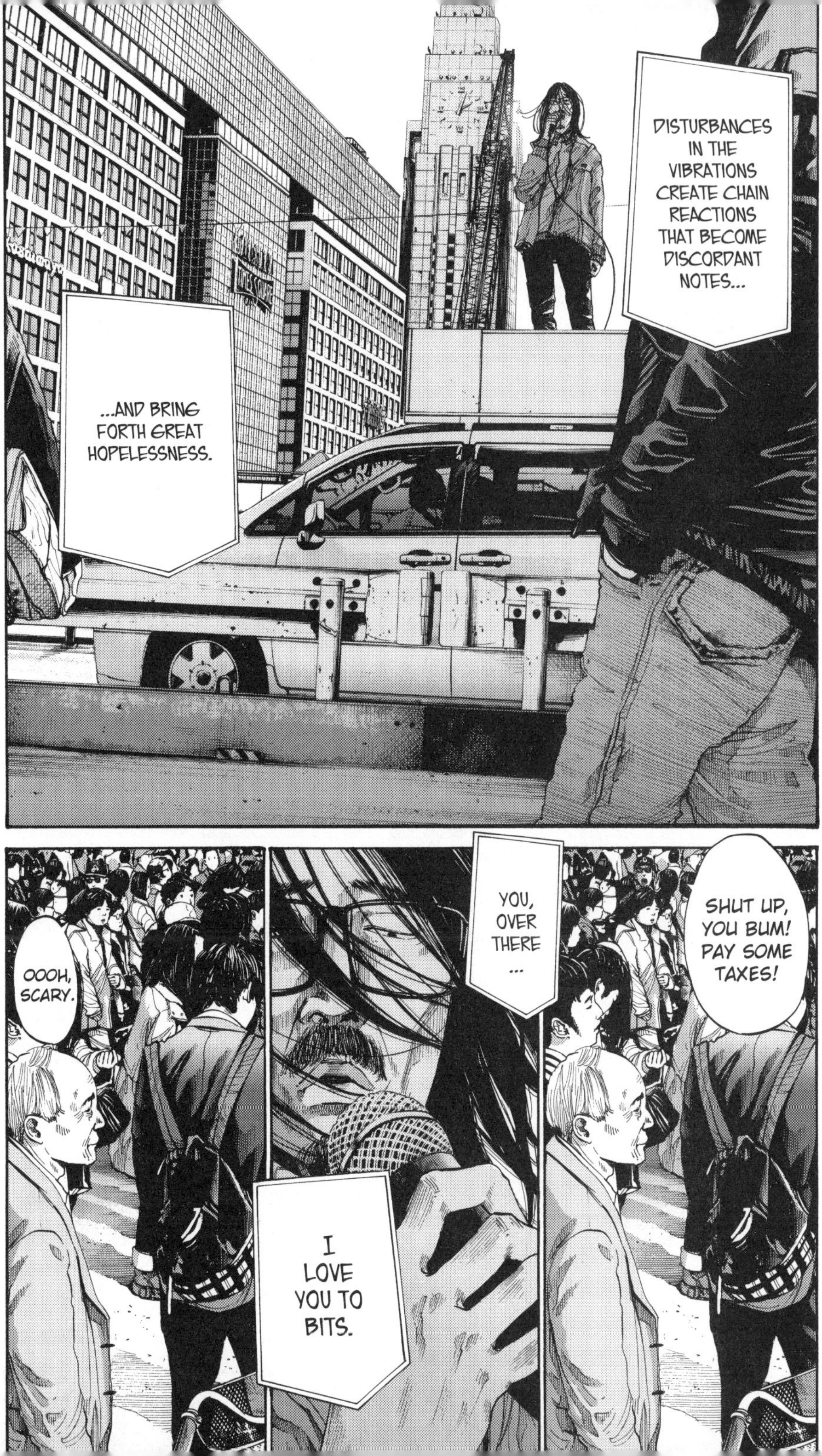
DISTURBANCES IN THE VIBRATIONS CREATE CHAIN REACTIONS THAT BECOME DISCORDANT NOTES...
...AND BRING FORTH GREAT HOPELESSNESS.
SHUT UP, YOU BUM! PAY SOME TAXES!
YOU, OVER THERE ...
I LOVE YOU TO BITS.
OOOH, SCARY.

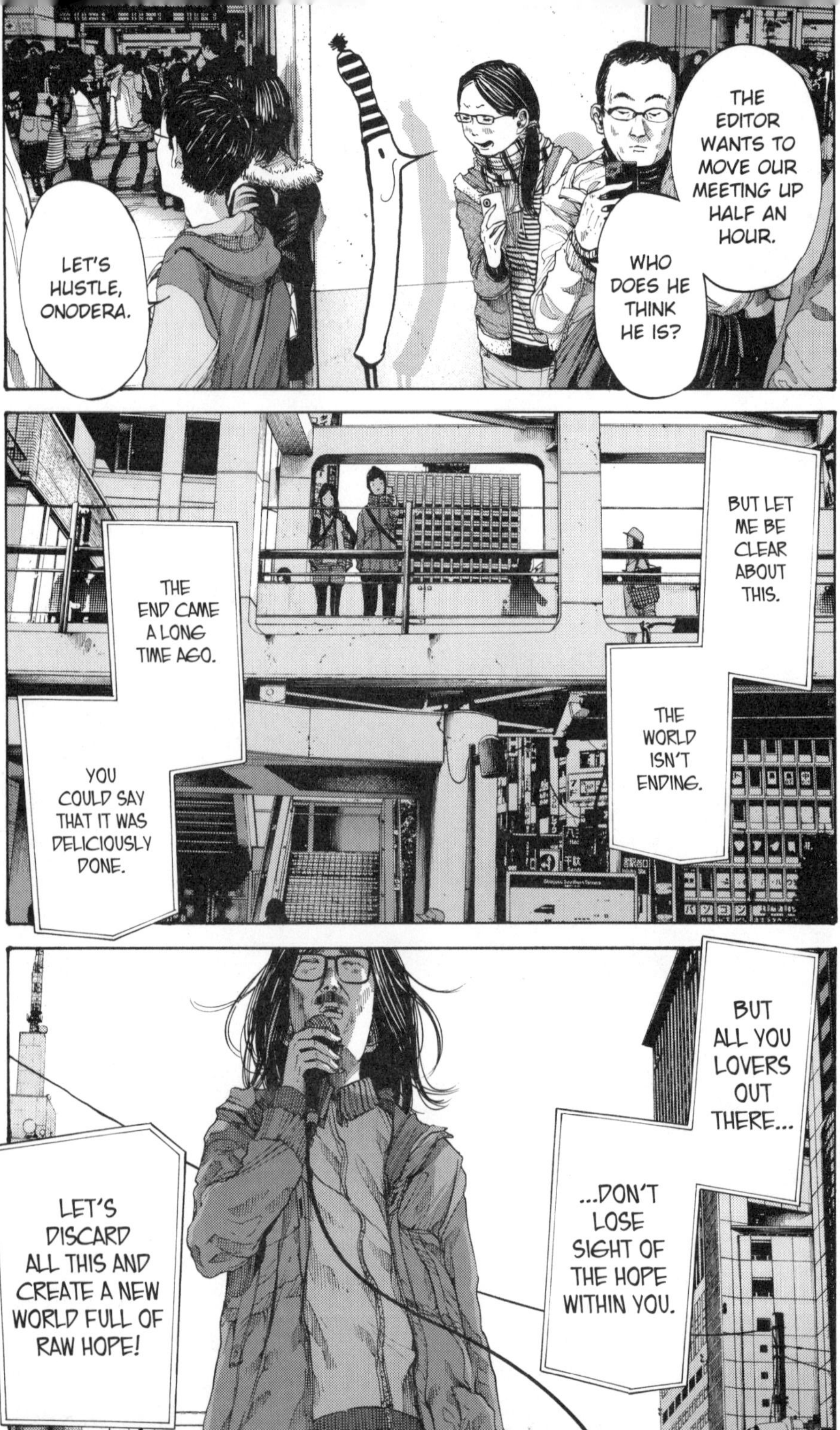
THE EDITOR WANTS TO MOVE OUR MEETING UP HALF AN HOUR.
WHO DOES HE THINK HE IS?
LET'S HUSTLE, ONODERA.
BUT LET ME BE CLEAR ABOUT THIS.
THE WORLD ISN'T ENDING.
THE END CAME A LONG TIME AGO.
YOU COULD SAY THAT IT WAS DELICIOUSLY DONE.
BUT ALL YOU LOVERS OUT THERE...
...DON'T LOSE SIGHT OF THE HOPE WITHIN YOU.
LET'S DISCARD ALL THIS AND CREATE A NEW WORLD FULL OF RAW HOPE!

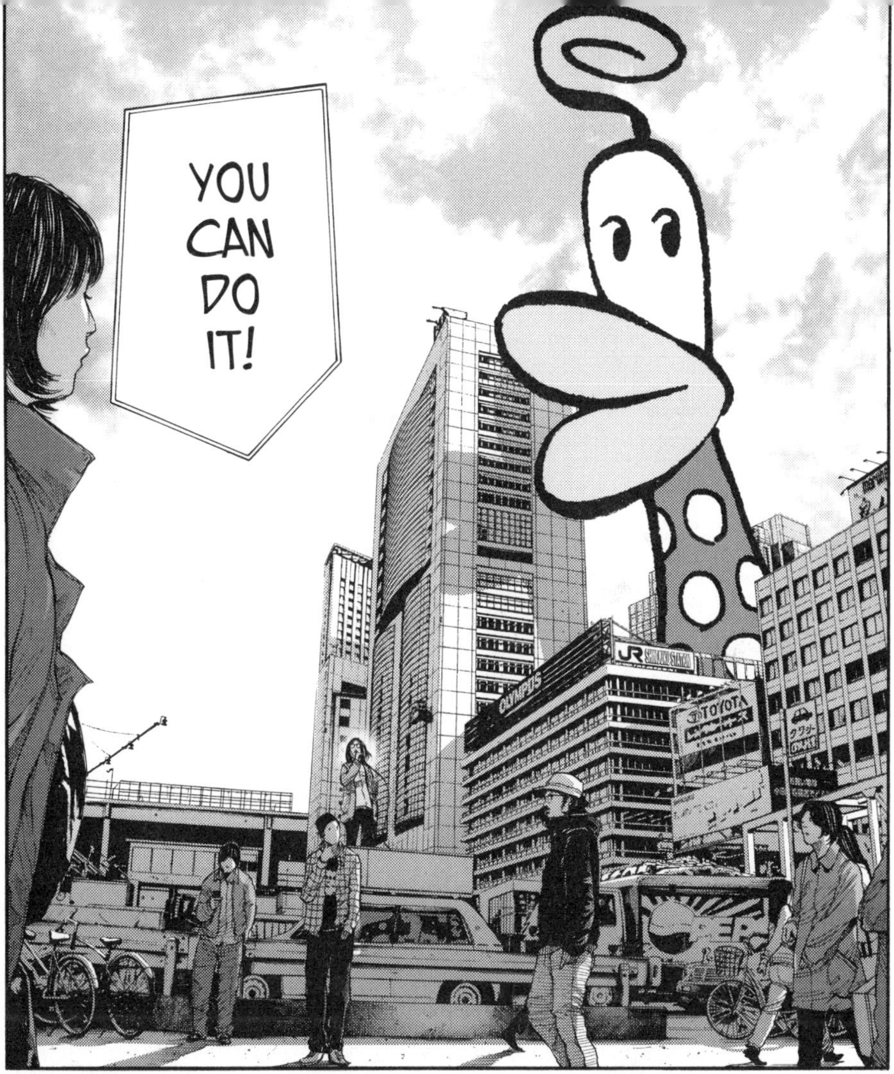
YOU CAN DO IT!
JR SHINJUKU STATION
OLYMPOS
TOYOTA

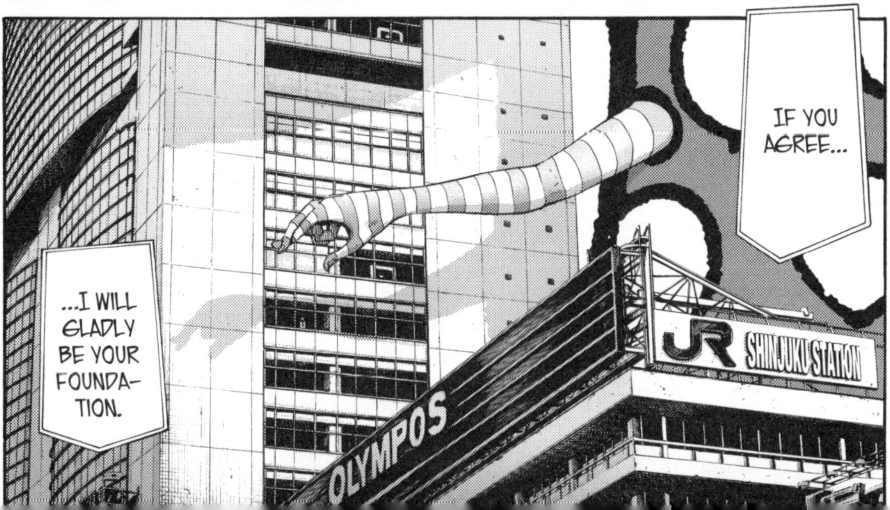
IF YOU AGREE...
...I WILL GLADLY BE YOUR FOUNDA-TION.
JR SHINJUKU STATION
OLYMPOS

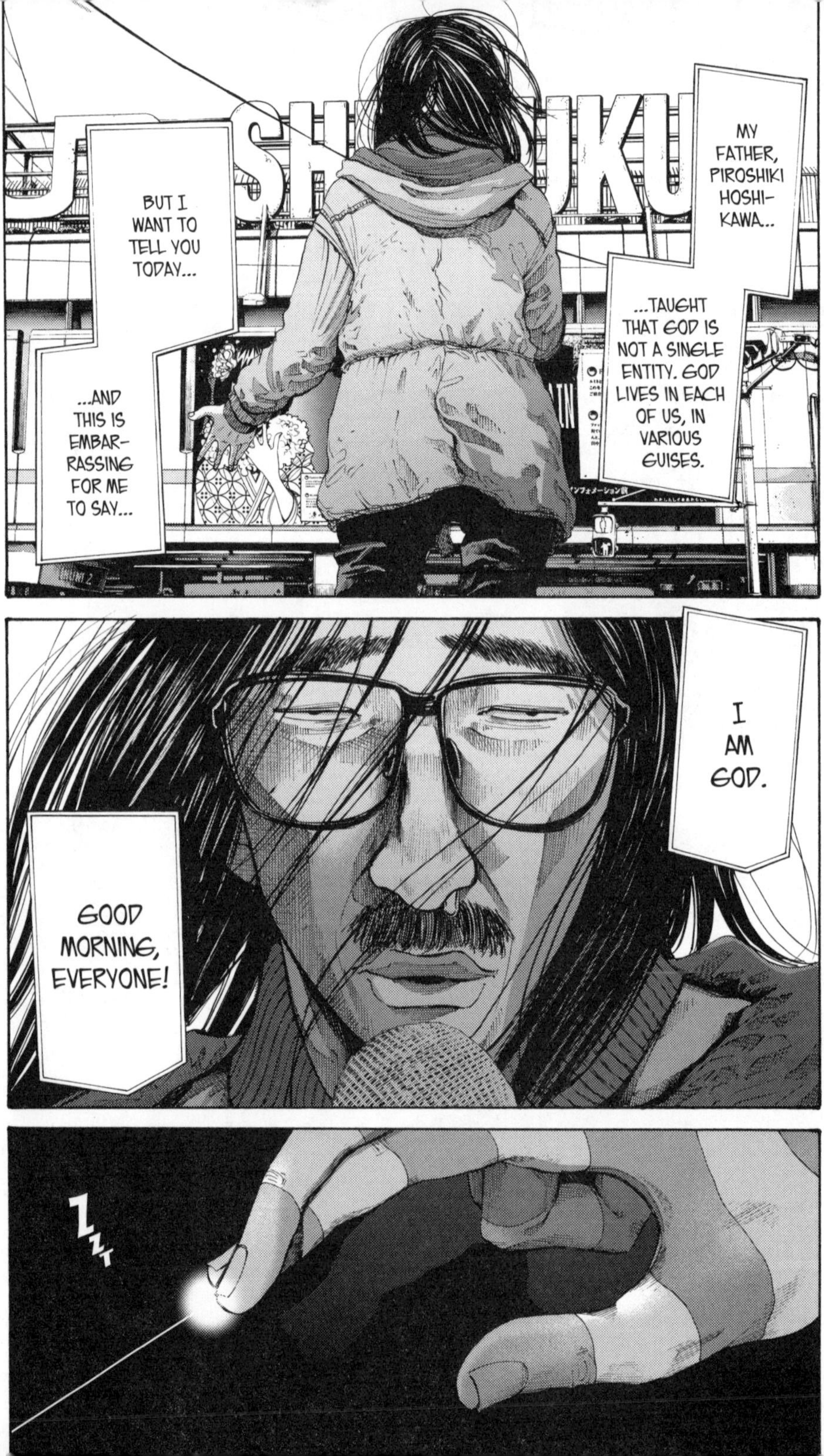
MY FATHER, PIROSHIKI HOSHI-KAWA...
...TAUGHT THAT GOD IS NOT A SINGLE ENTITY. GOD LIVES IN EACH OF US, IN VARIOUS GUISES.
BUT I WANT TO TELL YOU TODAY...
...AND THIS IS EMBAR-RASSING FOR ME TO SAY...
I AM GOD.
GOOD MORNING, EVERYONE!
ZZT

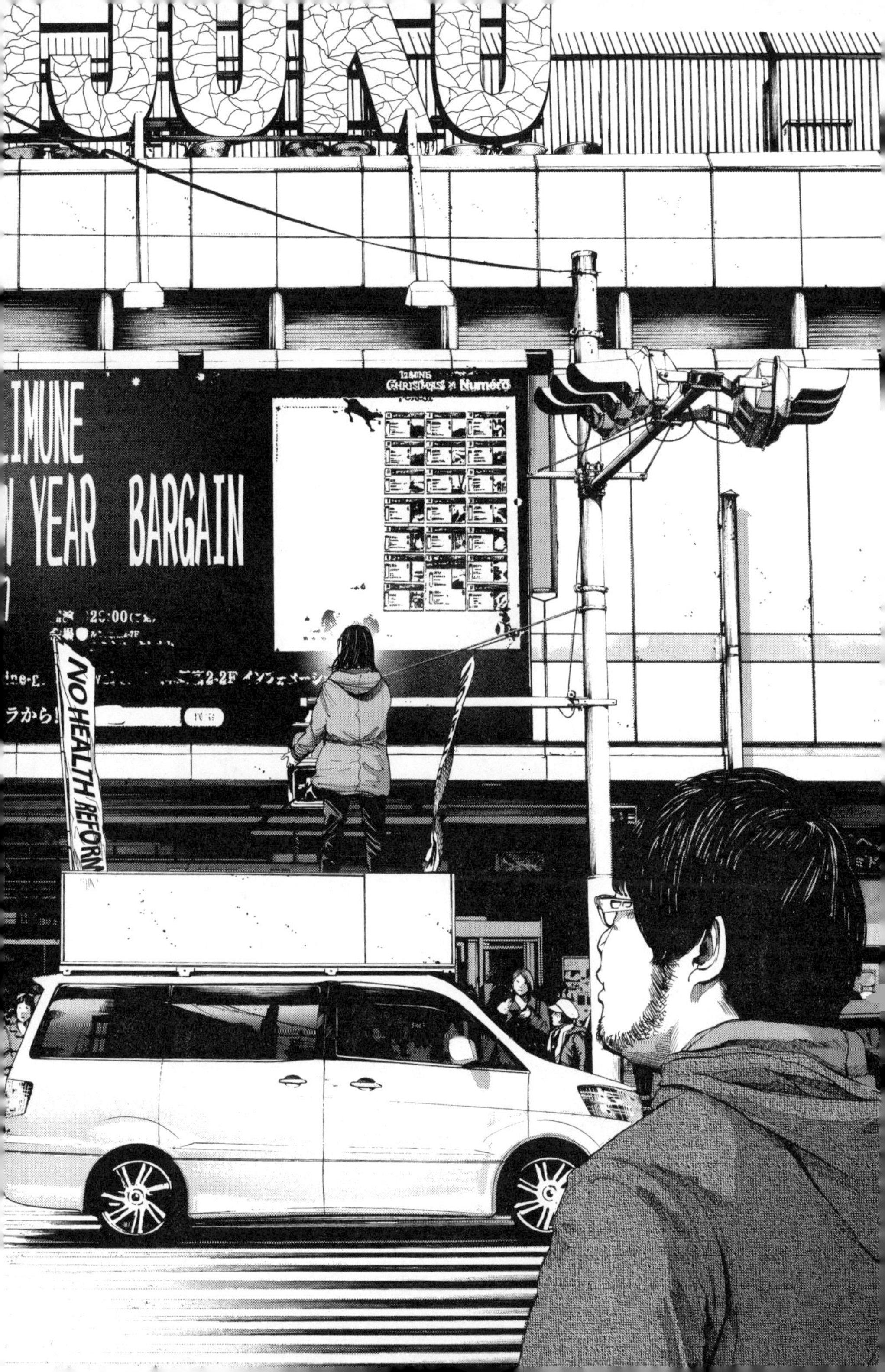
IMUNE
YEAR BARGAIN
NO HEALTH REFORM
ラから!

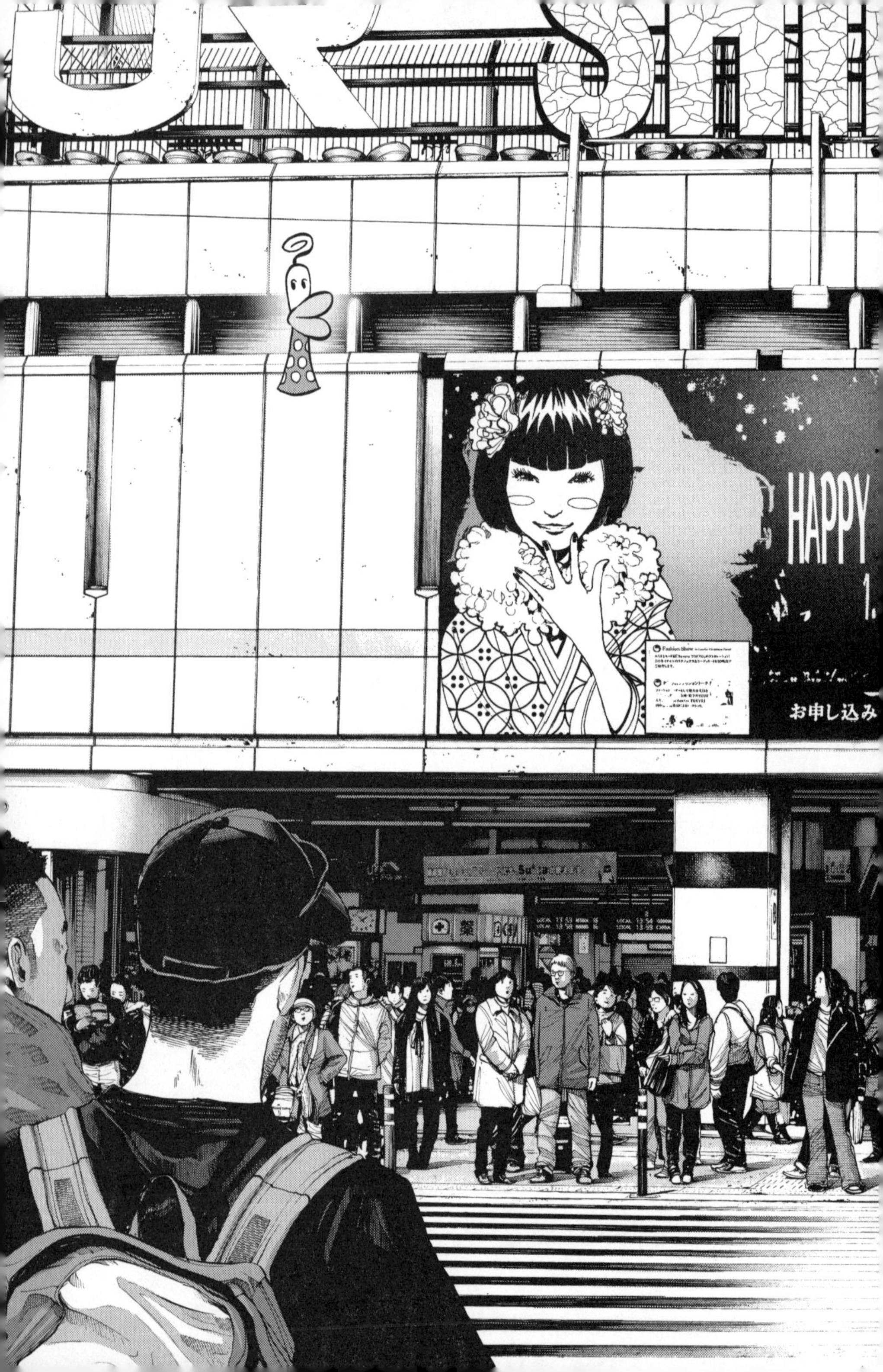
HAPPY
お申し込み

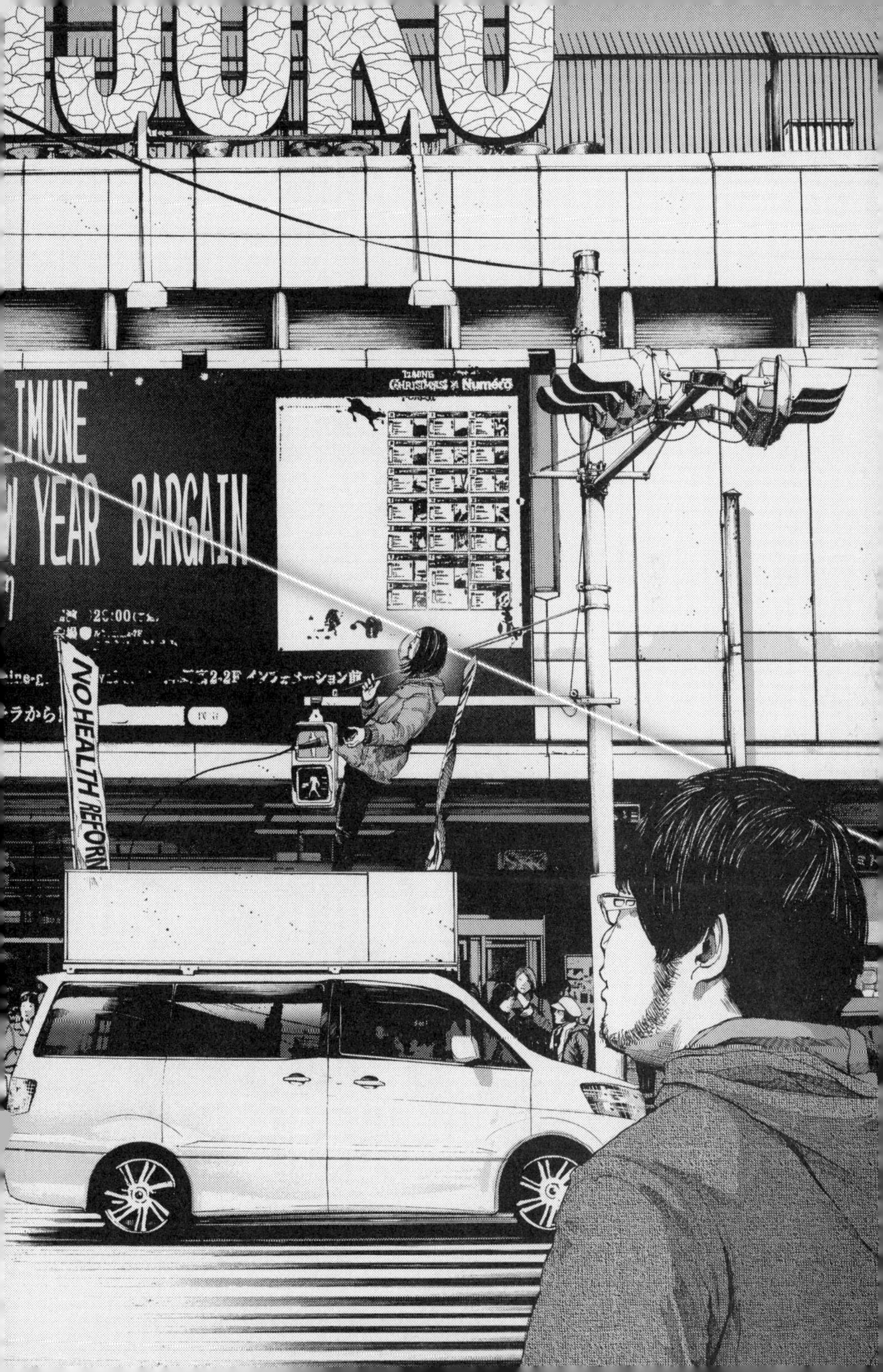
IMUNE
YEAR BARGAIN
NO HEALTH REFORM

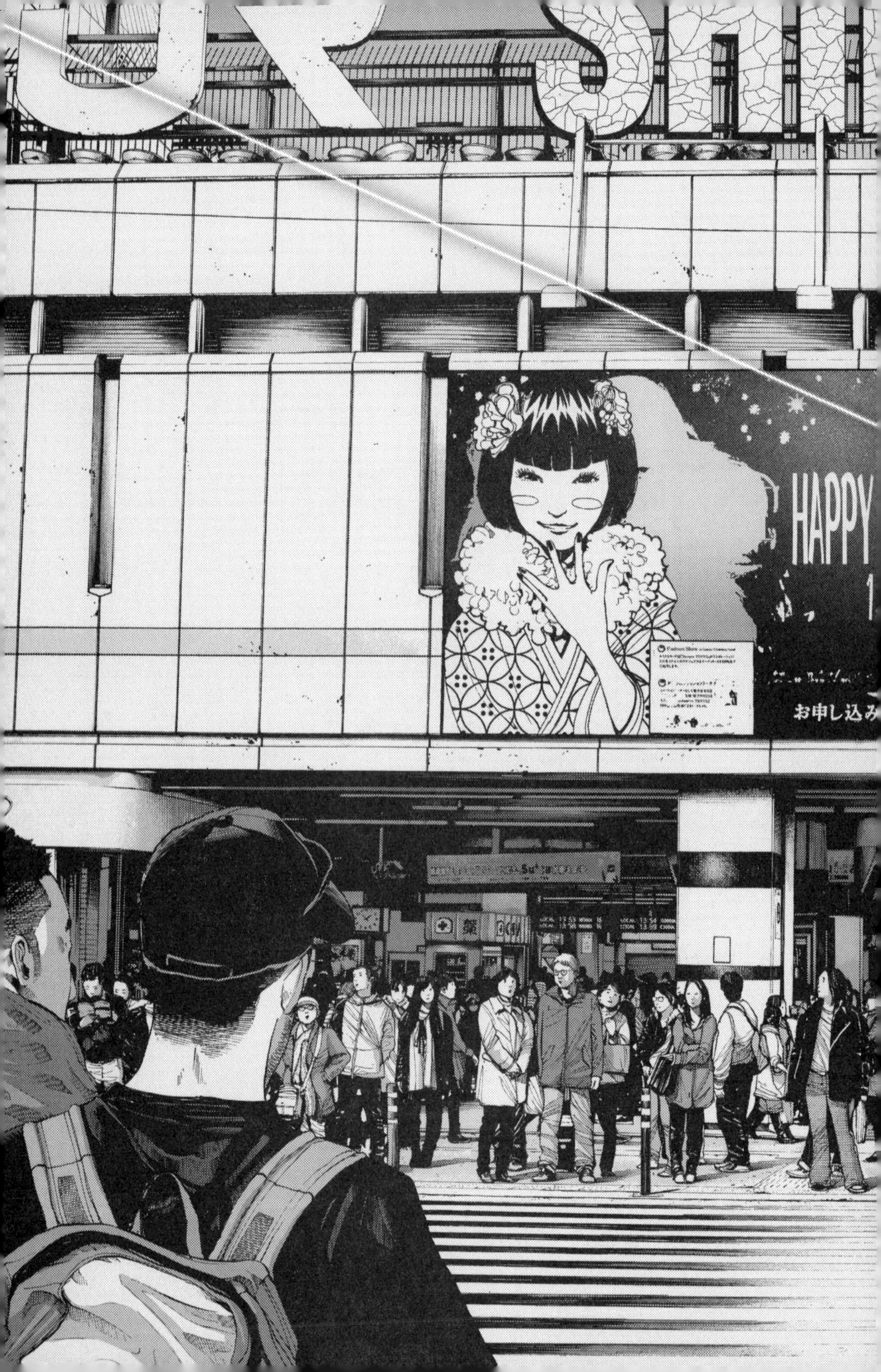
HAPPY
お申し込み

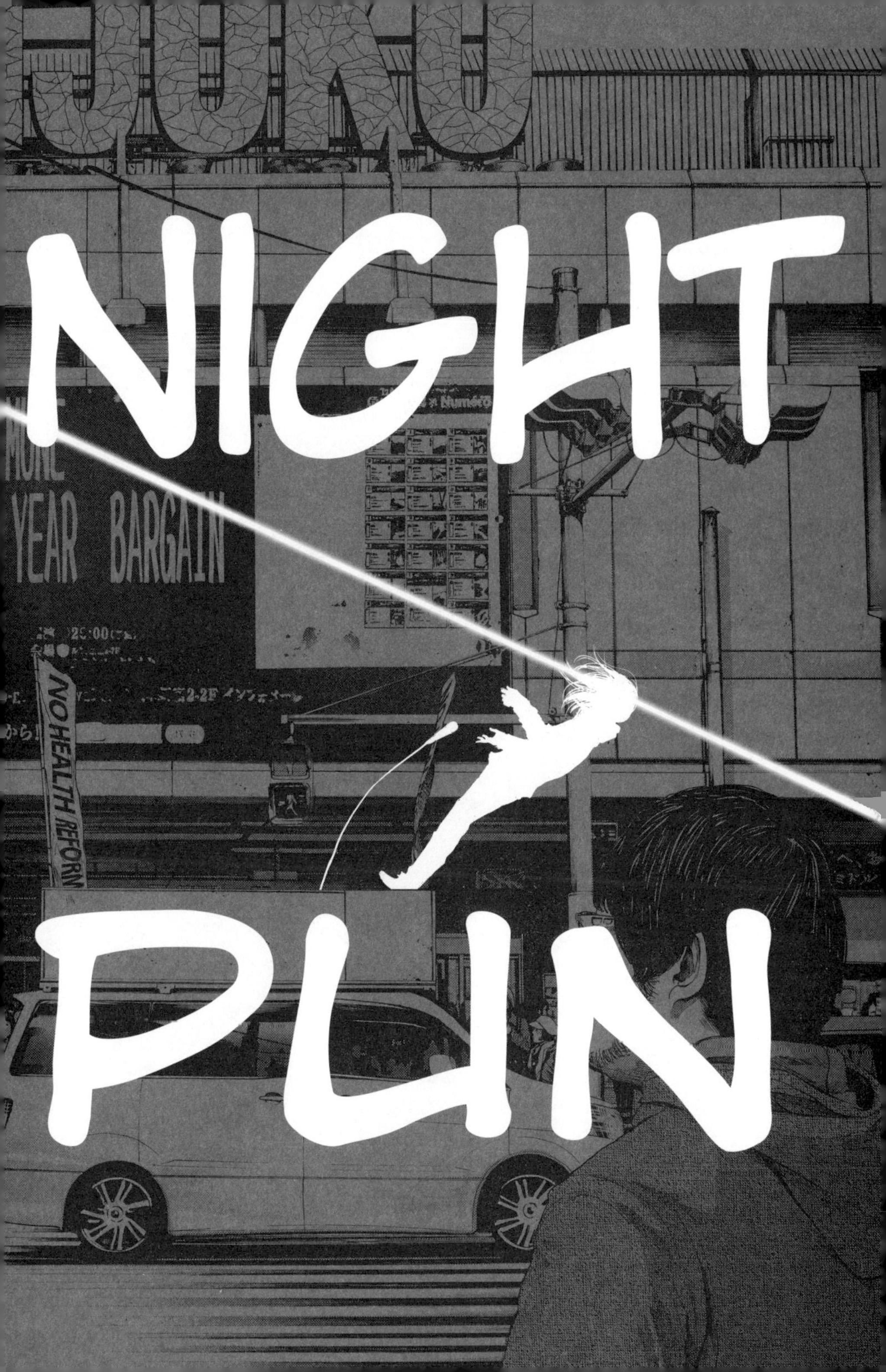
NIGHT
PUN
YEAR BARGAIN
NO HEALTH REFORM

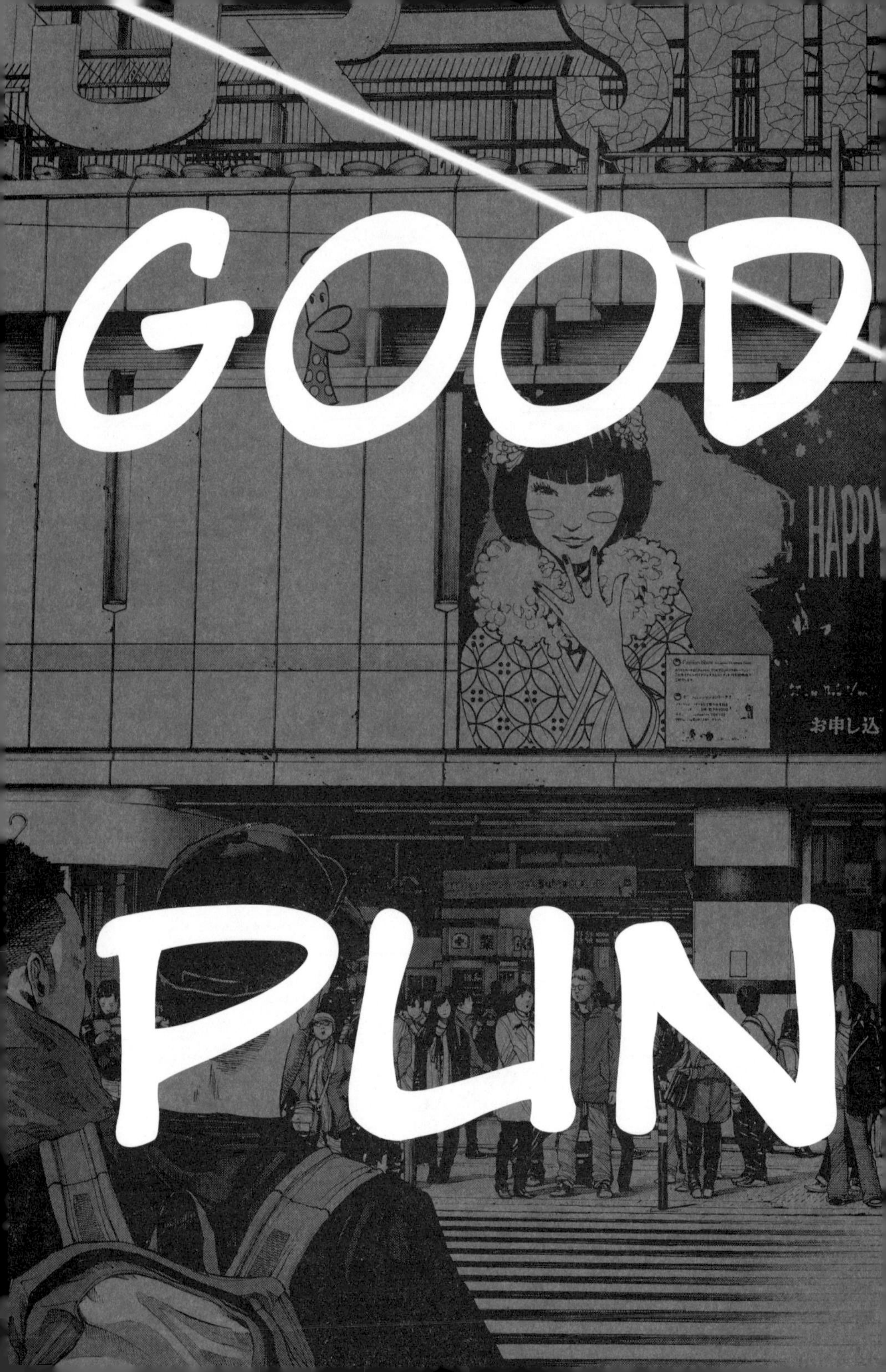
GOOD
PUN
HAPP
お申し込

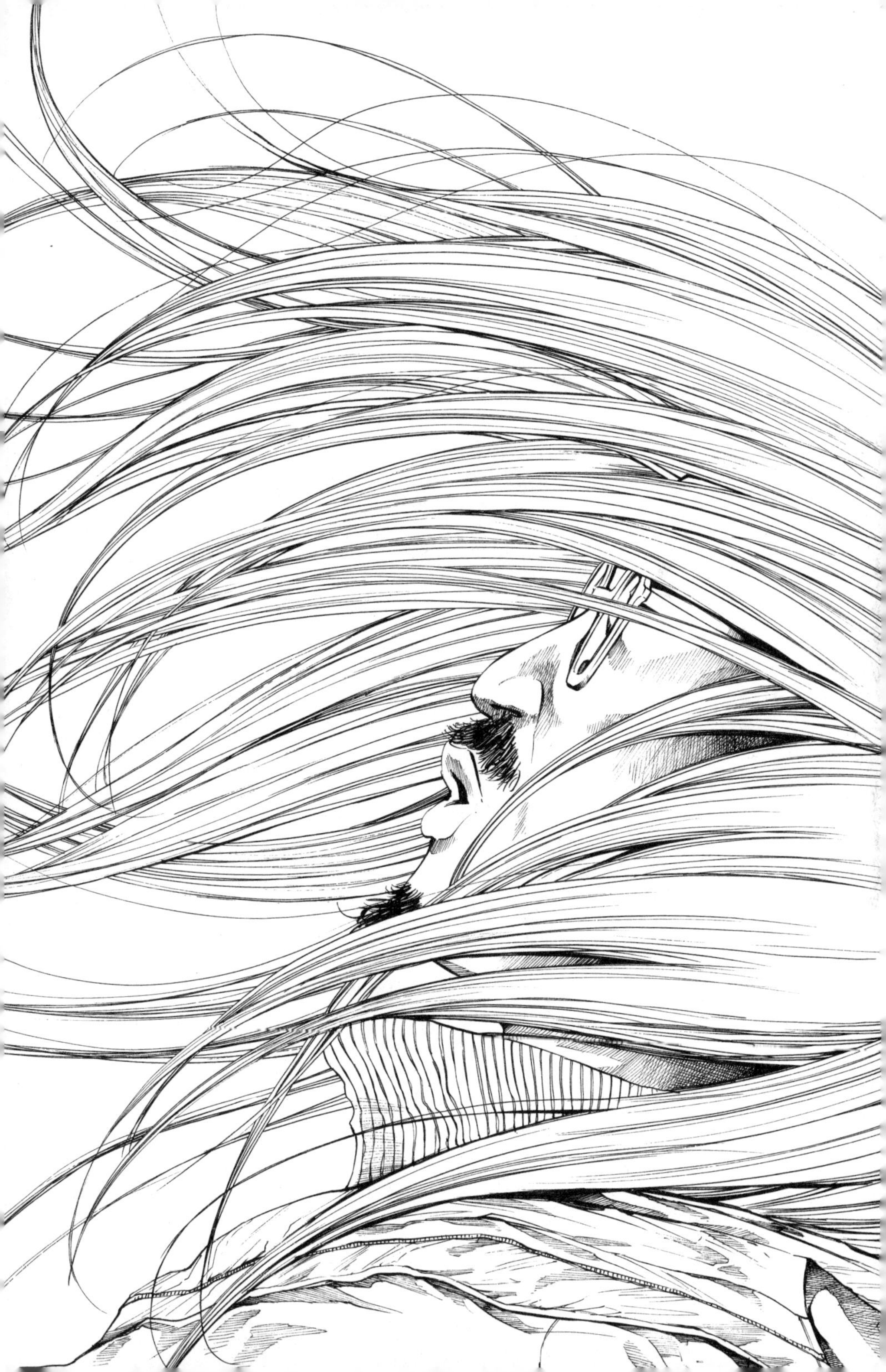

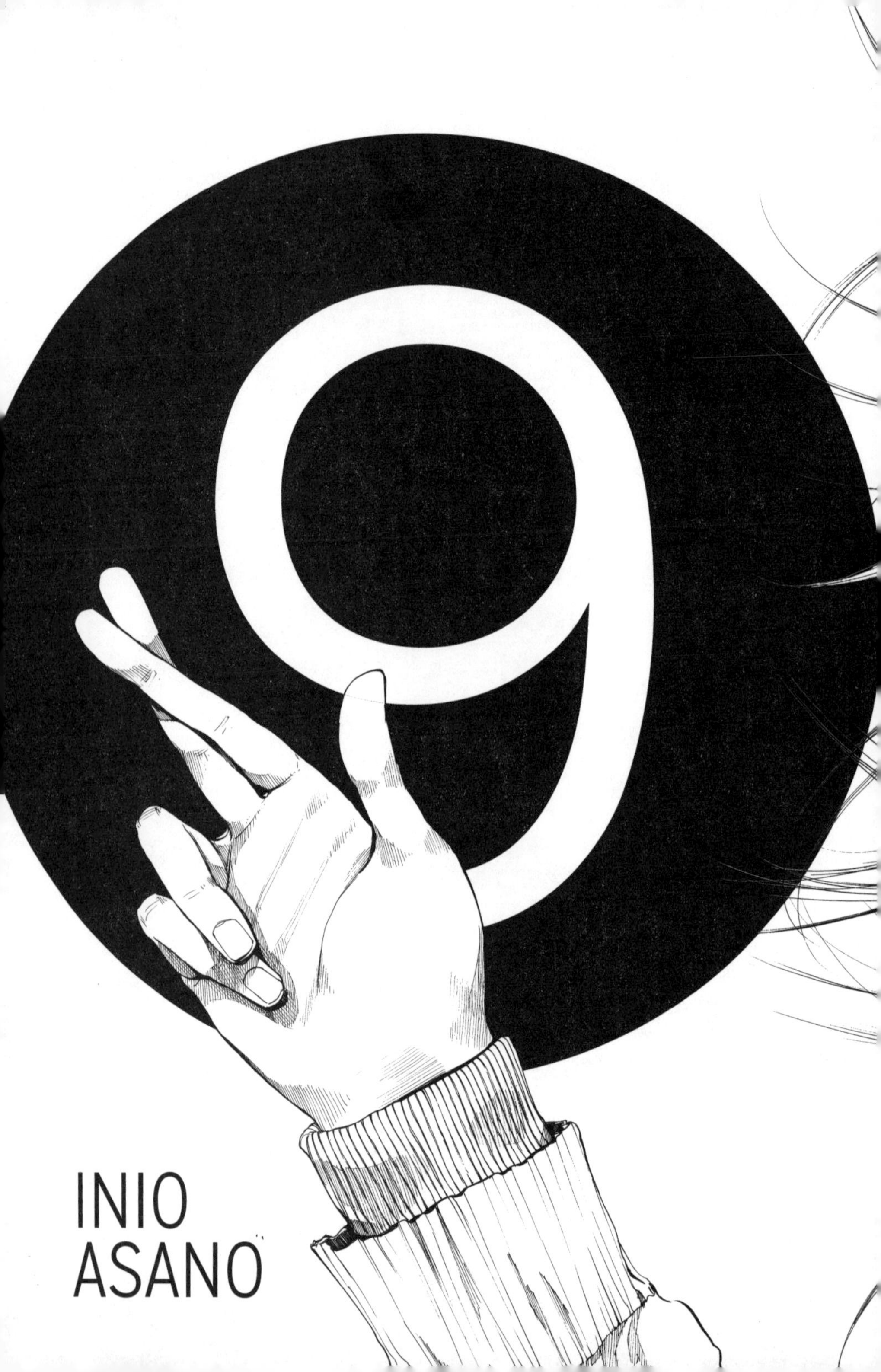
9
INIO
ASANO

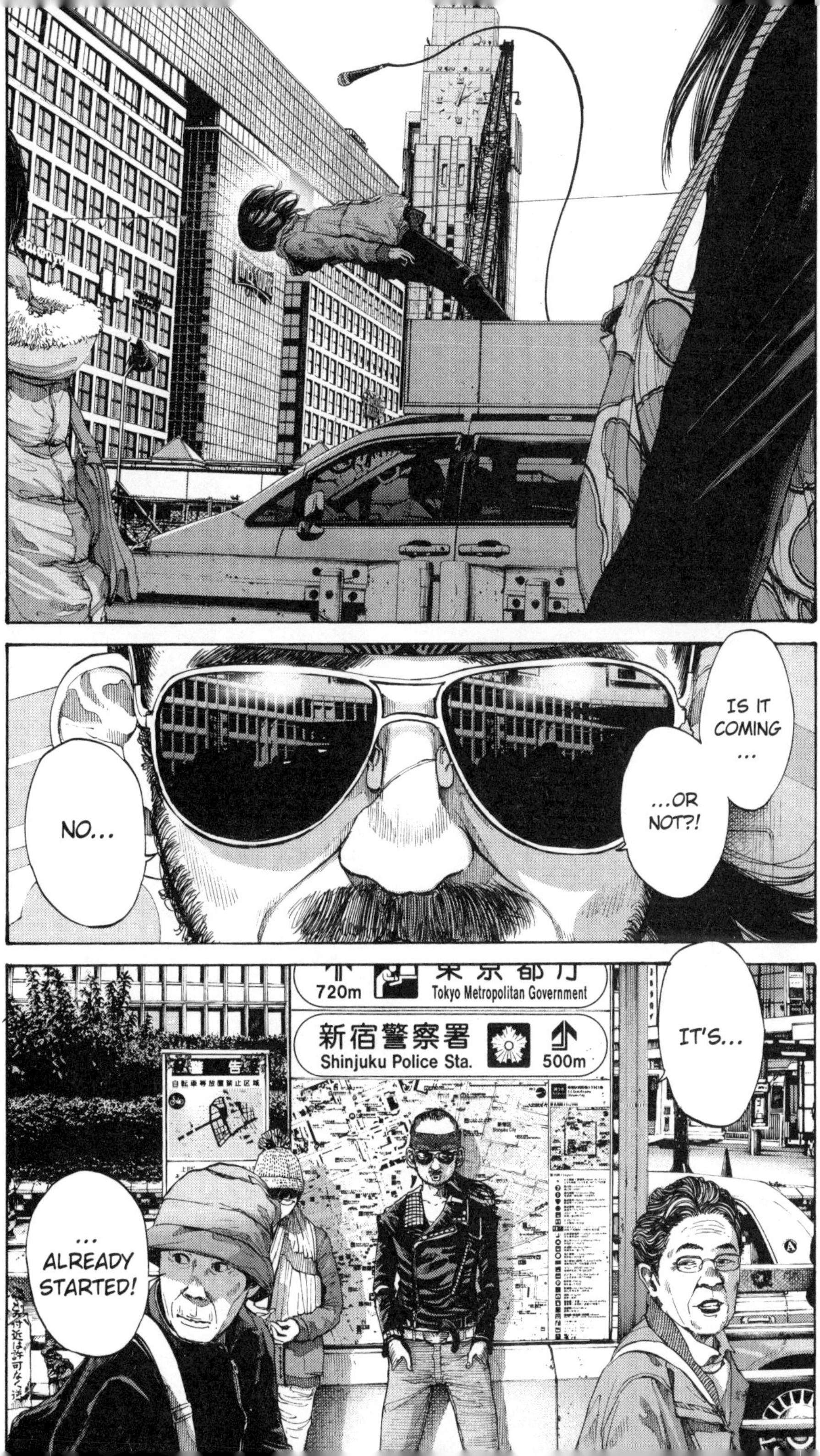
IS IT COMING ...
...OR NOT?!
NO...
IT'S...
720m
Tokyo Metropolitan Government
新宿警察署
Shinjuku Police Sta.
500m
... ALREADY STARTED!

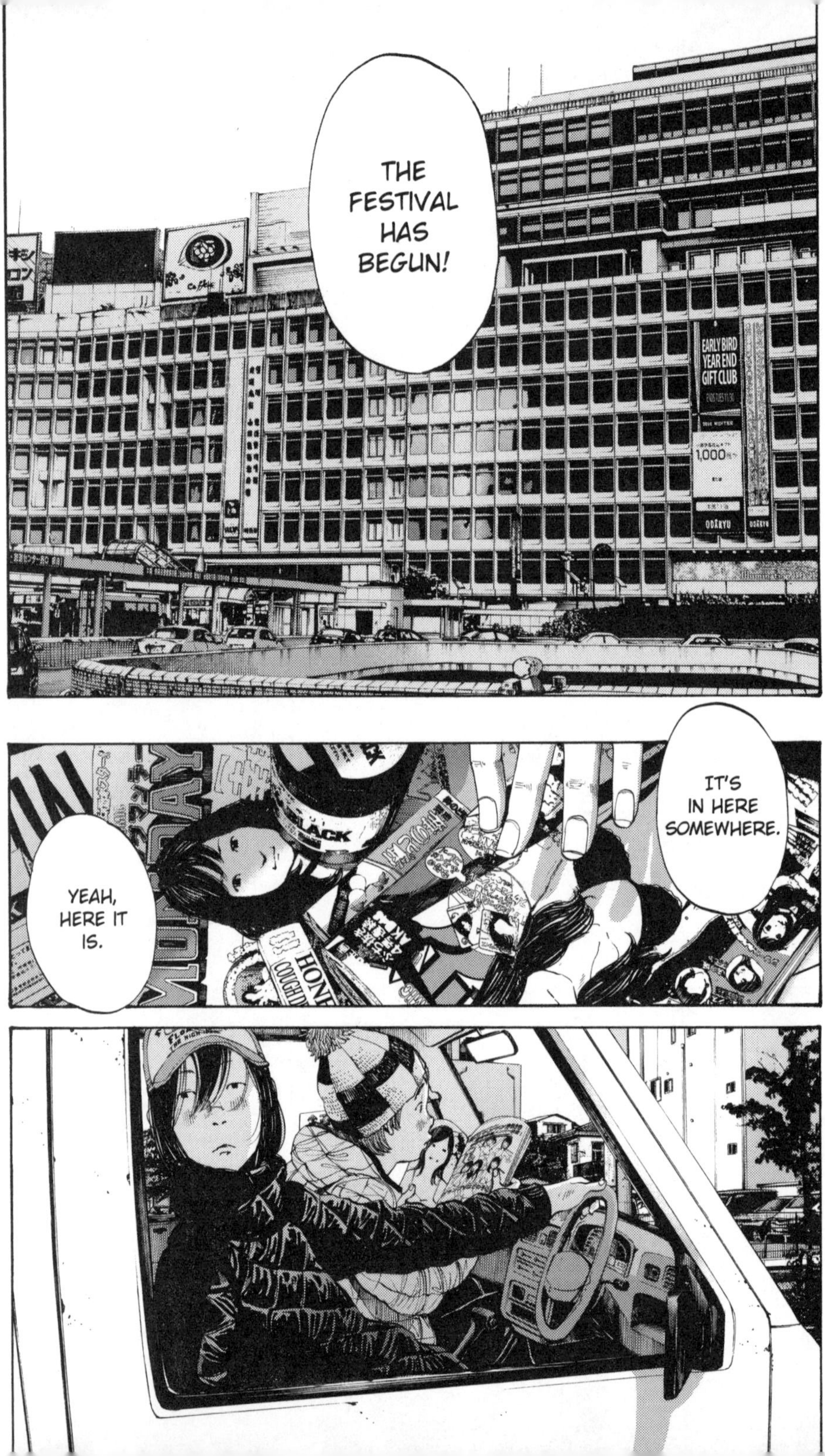
THE FESTIVAL HAS BEGUN!
EARLY BIRD YEAR END GIFT CLUB
IT'S IN HERE SOMEWHERE.
YEAH, HERE IT IS.

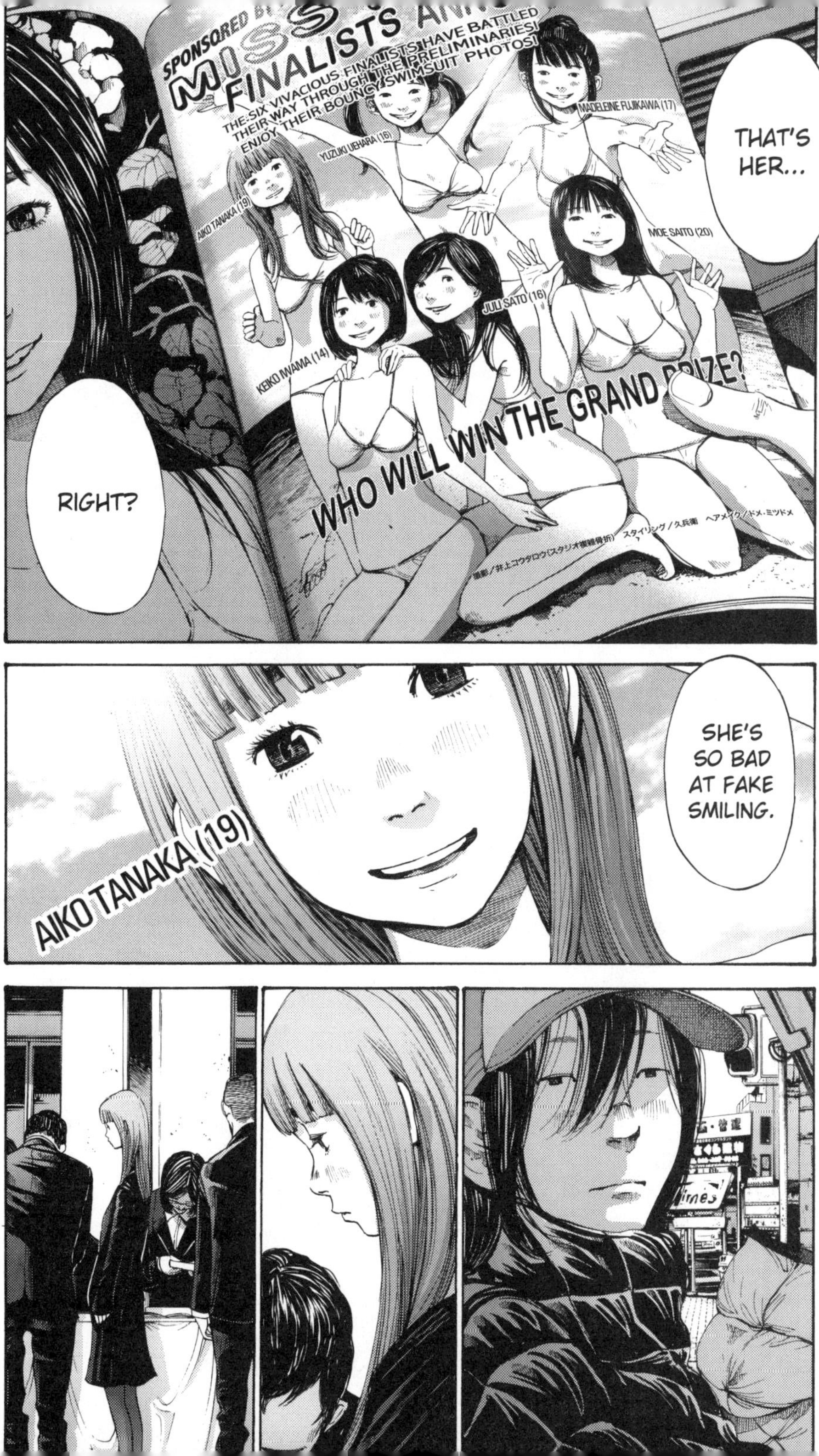
THAT'S HER...
SPONSORED BY
FINALISTS
THE SIX VIVACIOUS FINALISTS HAVE BATTLED THEIR WAY THROUGH THE PRELIMINARIES! ENJOY THEIR BOUNCY SWIMSUIT PHOTOS!
MADELEINE FUJIKAWA (17)
YUZUKI UEHARA (16)
AIKO TANAKA (19)
MOE SAITO (20)
JULI SATO (16)
KEIKO IWAMA (14)
WHO WILL WIN THE GRAND PRIZE?
撮影／井上コウタロウ(スタジオ複雑骨折) スタイリング／久兵衛 ヘアメイク／ドメ・ミツドメ
RIGHT?
SHE'S SO BAD AT FAKE SMILING.
AIKO TANAKA (19)

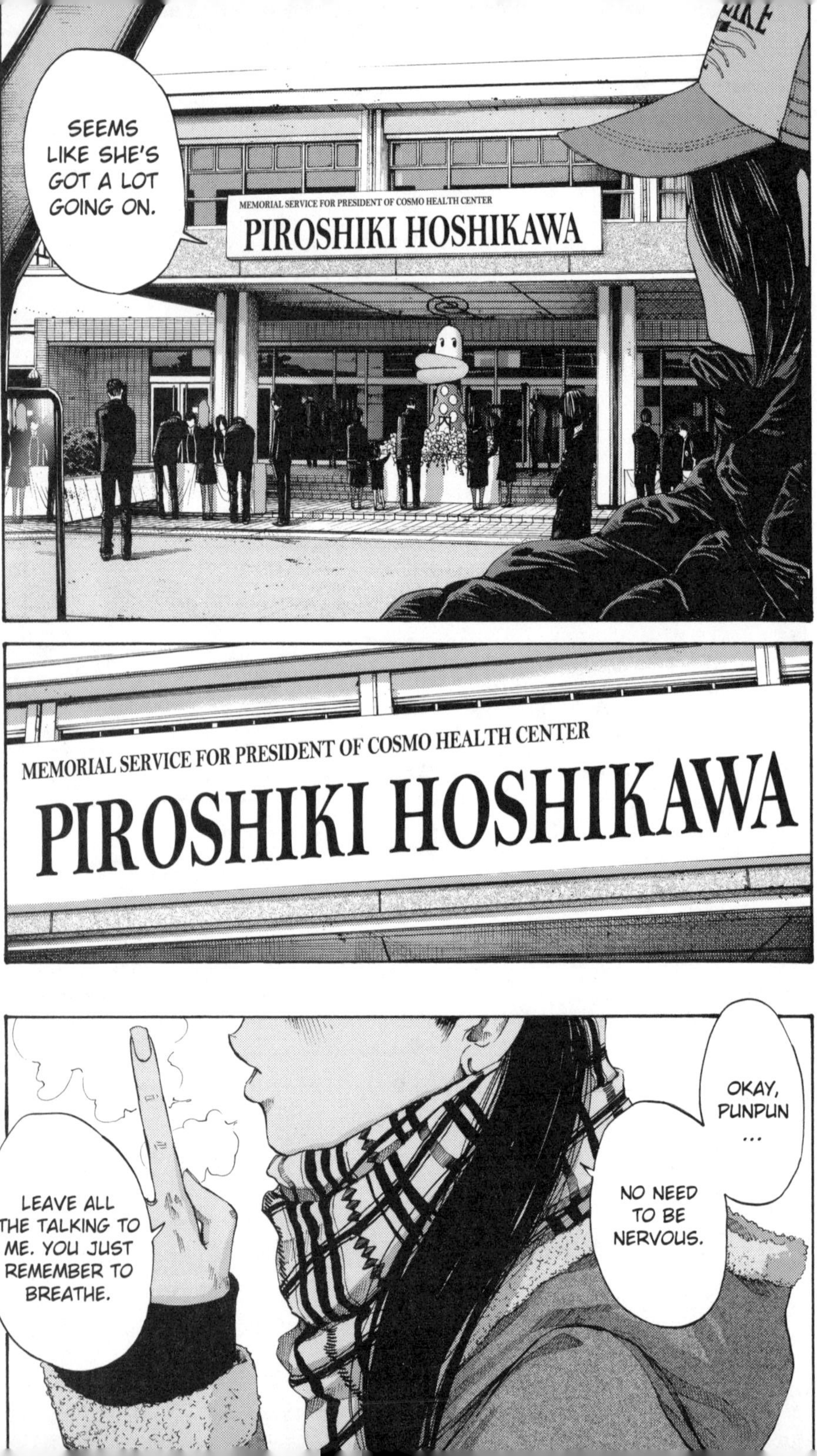
MEMORIAL SERVICE FOR PRESIDENT OF COSMO HEALTH CENTER
PIROSHIKI HOSHIKAWA
SEEMS LIKE SHE'S GOT A LOT GOING ON.
MEMORIAL SERVICE FOR PRESIDENT OF COSMO HEALTH CENTER
PIROSHIKI HOSHIKAWA
OKAY, PUNPUN ...
NO NEED TO BE NERVOUS.
LEAVE ALL THE TALKING TO ME. YOU JUST REMEMBER TO BREATHE.

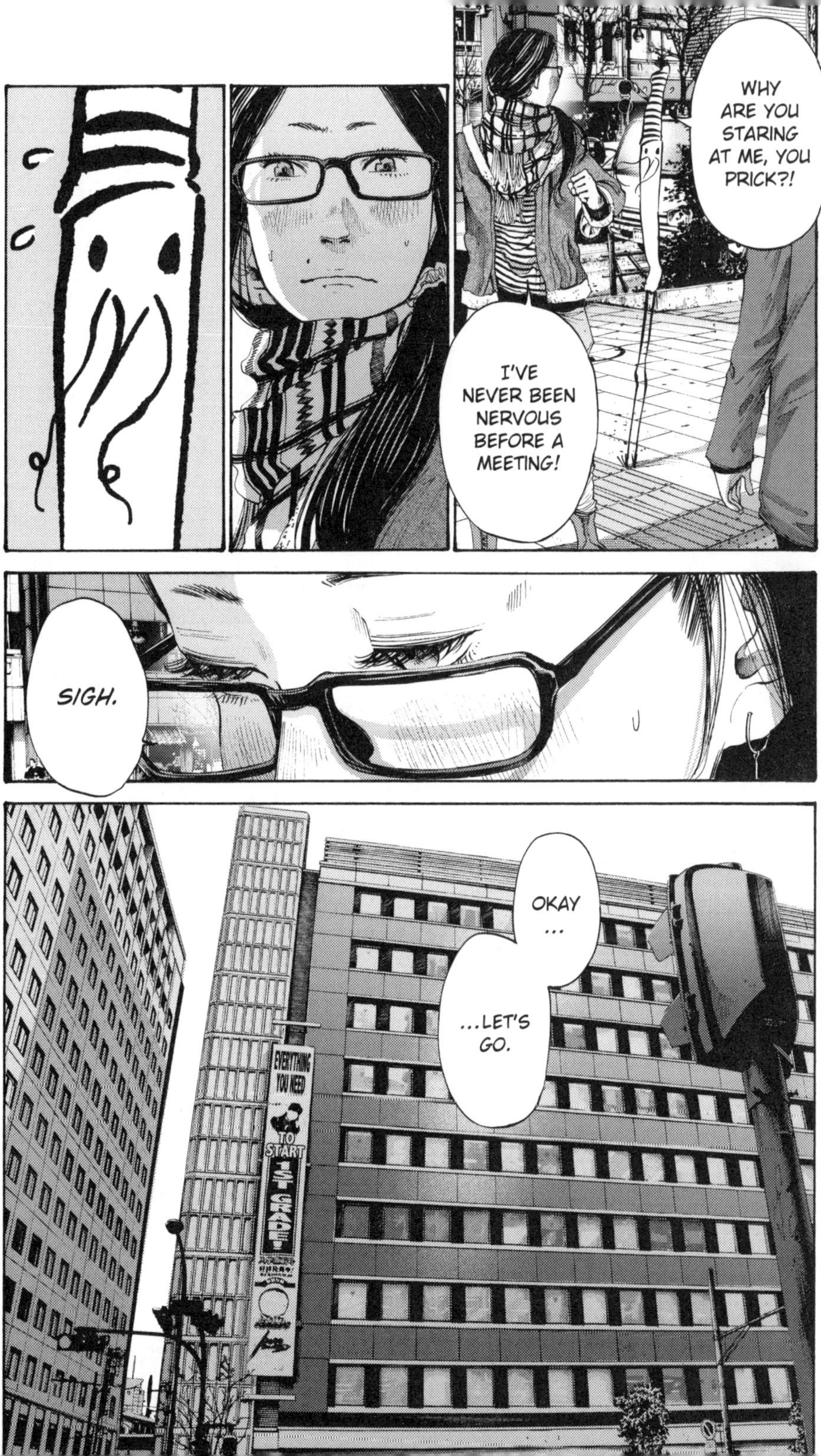
WHY ARE YOU STARING AT ME, YOU PRICK?!
I'VE NEVER BEEN NERVOUS BEFORE A MEETING!
SIGH.
OKAY ...
...LET'S GO.
EVERYTHING YOU NEED
TO START
1ST GRADE

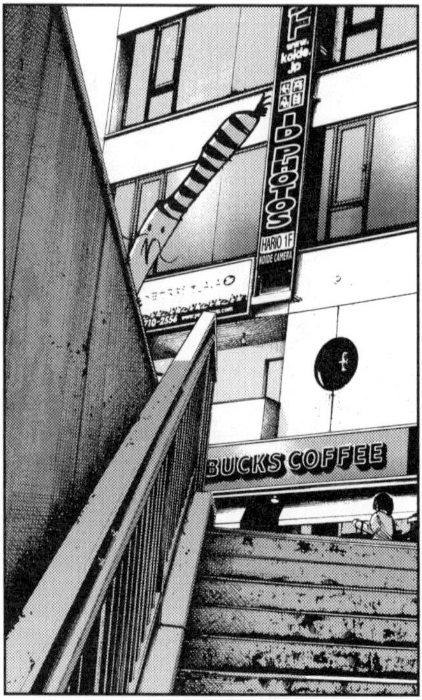
www.
koide.
jp
ID PHOTOS
HARIO 1F
KOIDE CAMERA
BUCKS COFFEE

Chapter 91

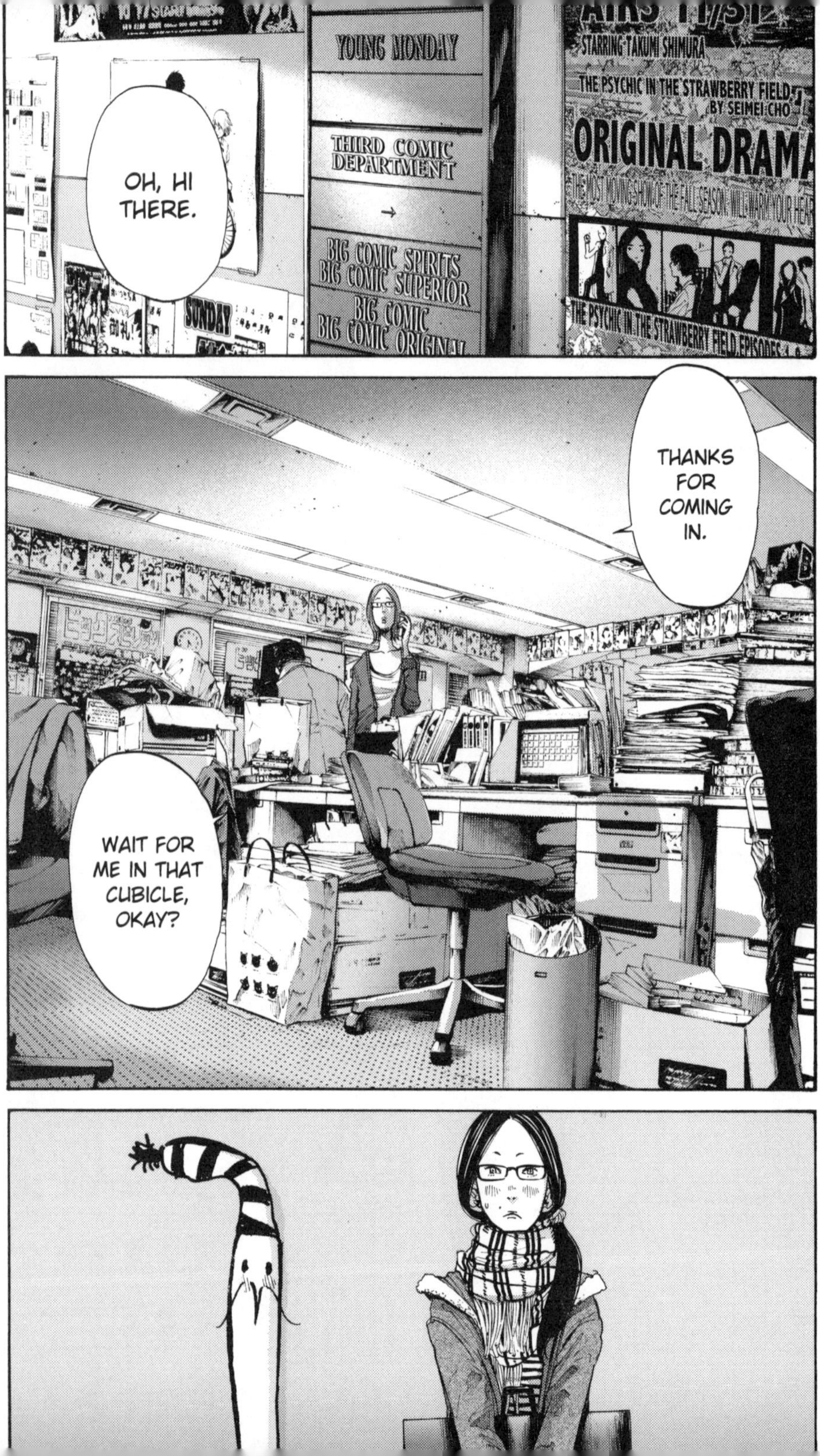
STARRING TAKUMI SHIMURA
THE PSYCHIC IN THE STRAWBERRY FIELD
BY SEIMEI CHO
ORIGINAL DRAMA
THE MOST MOVING SHOW OF THE FALL SEASON WILL WARM YOUR HEAR
THE PSYCHIC IN THE STRAWBERRY FIELD EPISODES
YOUNG MONDAY
THIRD COMIC DEPARTMENT
→
BIG COMIC SPIRITS
BIG COMIC SUPERIOR
BIG COMIC
SUNDAY
OH, HI THERE.
THANKS FOR COMING IN.
WAIT FOR ME IN THAT CUBICLE, OKAY?

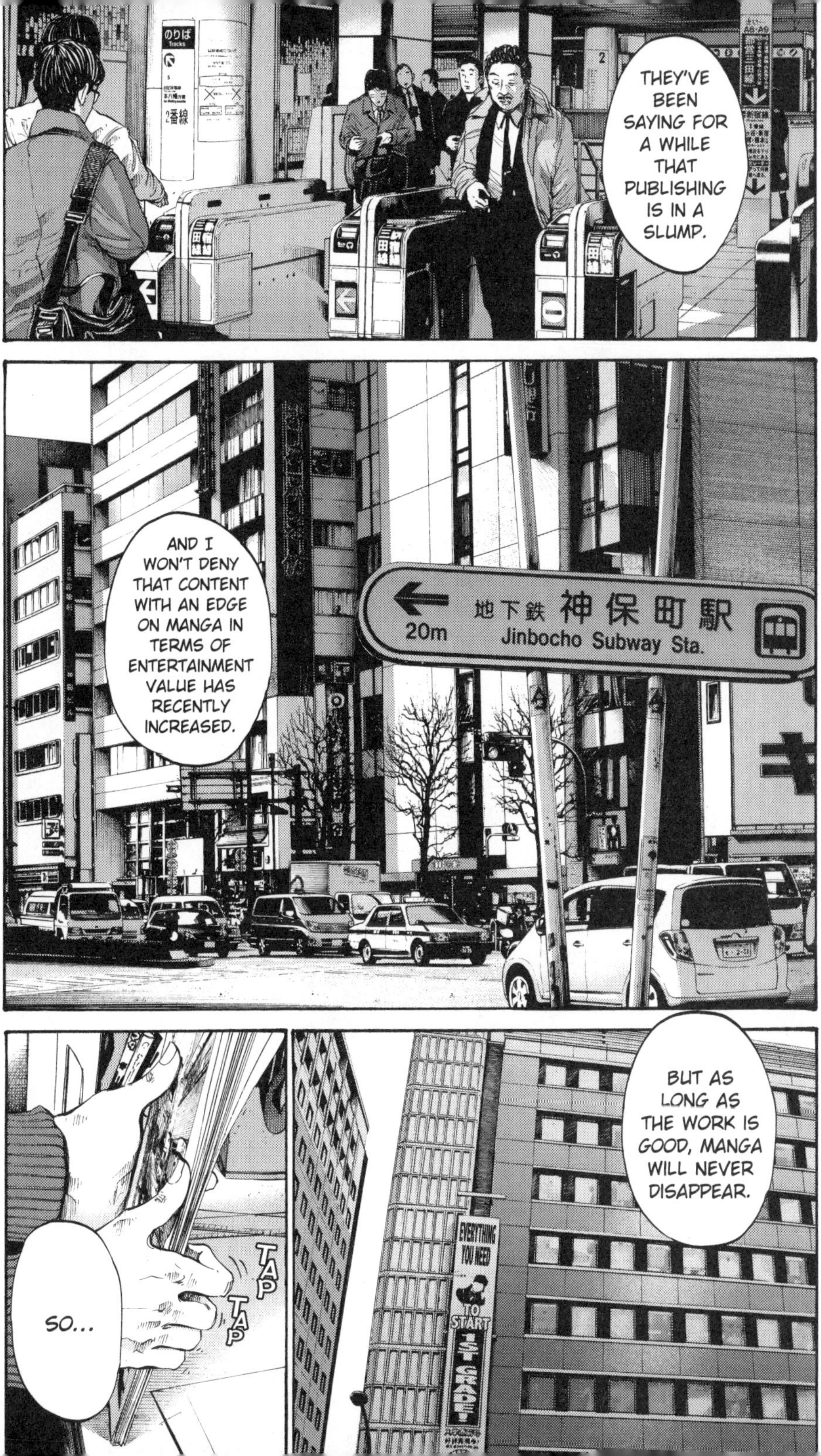
のりば
Tracks
2番線
THEY'VE BEEN SAYING FOR A WHILE THAT PUBLISHING IS IN A SLUMP.
地下鉄 神保町駅
20m
Jinbocho Subway Sta.
AND I WON'T DENY THAT CONTENT WITH AN EDGE ON MANGA IN TERMS OF ENTERTAINMENT VALUE HAS RECENTLY INCREASED.
BUT AS LONG AS THE WORK IS GOOD, MANGA WILL NEVER DISAPPEAR.
EVERYTHING YOU NEED TO START 1ST GRADE!
TAP
TAP
SO...

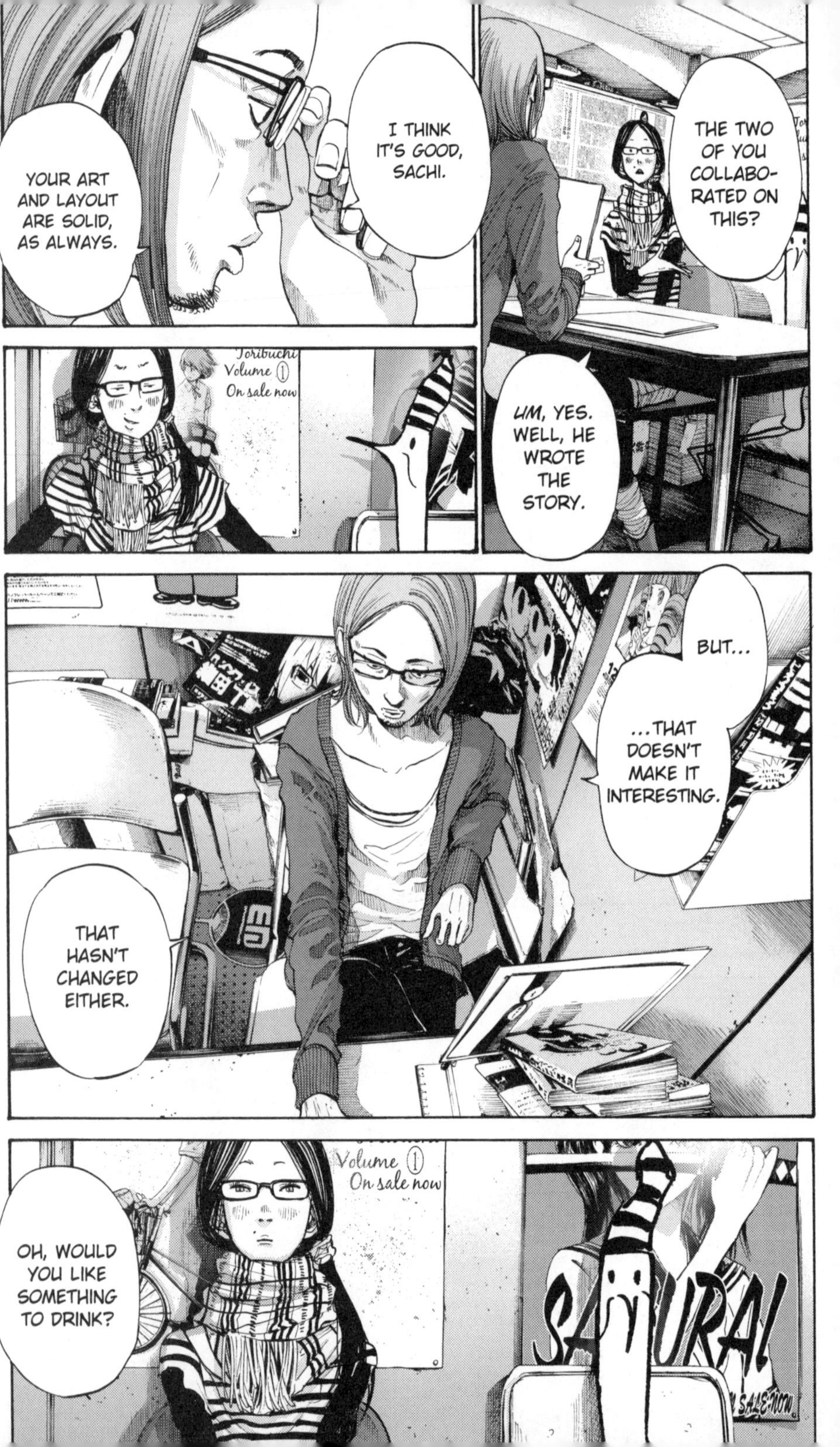
THE TWO OF YOU COLLABORATED ON THIS?
UM, YES. WELL, HE WROTE THE STORY.
I THINK IT'S GOOD, SACHI.
YOUR ART AND LAYOUT ARE SOLID, AS ALWAYS.
Toribuchi Volume ① On sale now
BUT...
...THAT DOESN'T MAKE IT INTERESTING.
THAT HASN'T CHANGED EITHER.
Volume ① On sale now
OH, WOULD YOU LIKE SOMETHING TO DRINK?

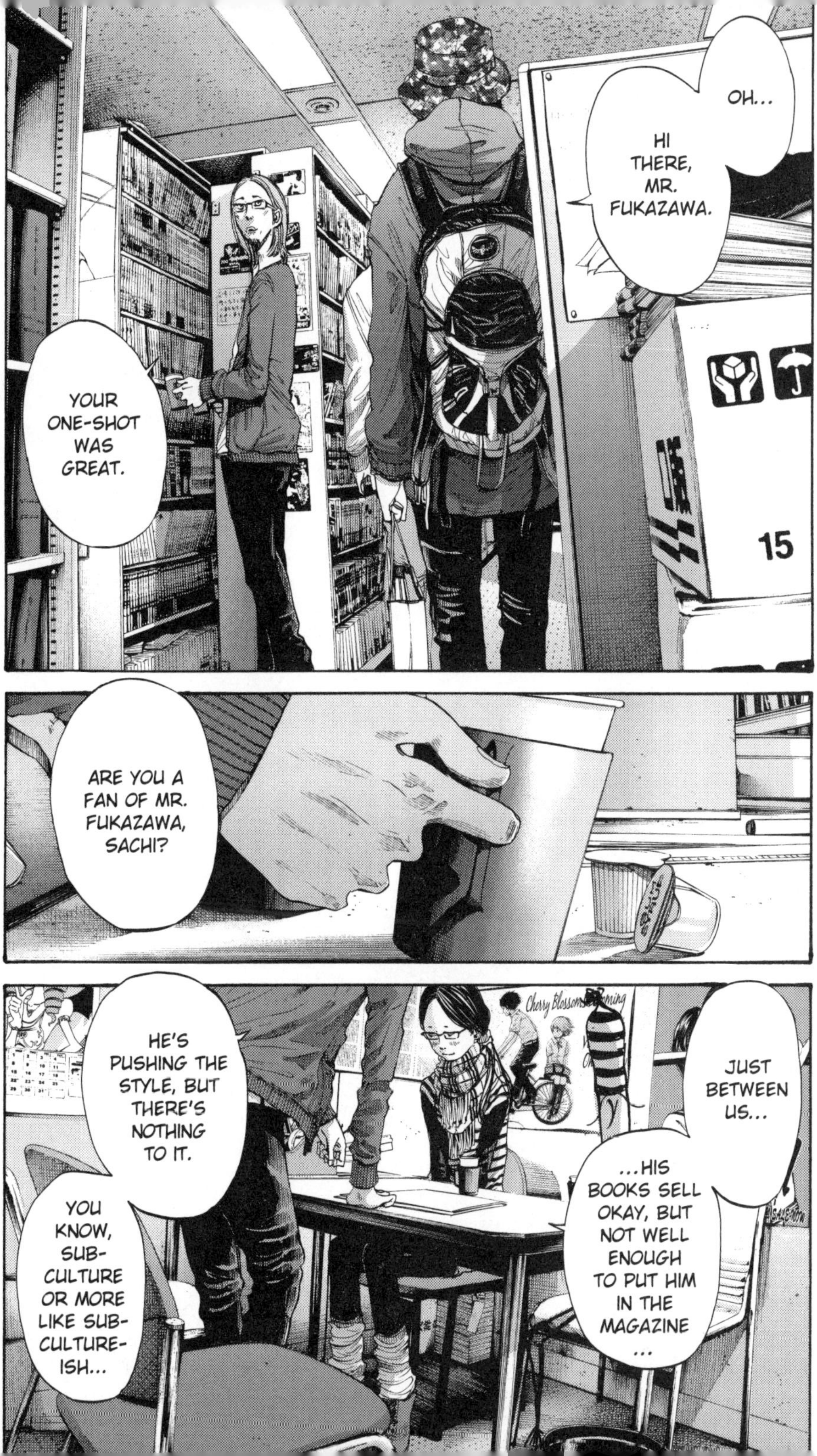
OH... HI THERE, MR. FUKAZAWA.
YOUR ONE-SHOT WAS GREAT.
ARE YOU A FAN OF MR. FUKAZAWA, SACHI?
JUST BETWEEN US...
...HIS BOOKS SELL OKAY, BUT NOT WELL ENOUGH TO PUT HIM IN THE MAGAZINE...
HE'S PUSHING THE STYLE, BUT THERE'S NOTHING TO IT.
YOU KNOW, SUB-CULTURE OR MORE LIKE SUB-CULTURE-ISH...

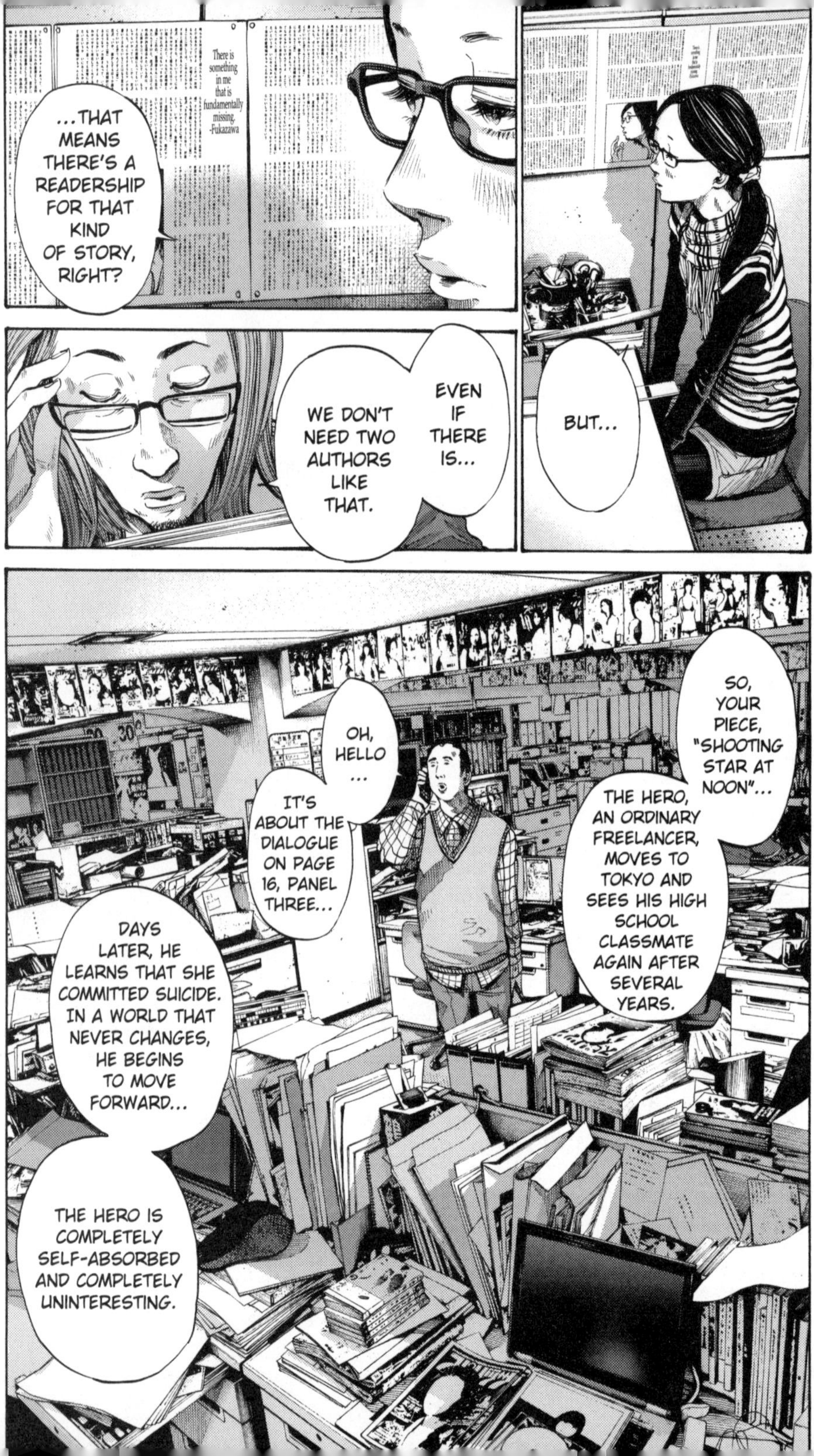
BUT...
...THAT MEANS THERE'S A READERSHIP FOR THAT KIND OF STORY, RIGHT?
There is something in me that is fundamentally missing. -Fukazawa
EVEN IF THERE IS...
WE DON'T NEED TWO AUTHORS LIKE THAT.
SO, YOUR PIECE, "SHOOTING STAR AT NOON"...
THE HERO, AN ORDINARY FREELANCER, MOVES TO TOKYO AND SEES HIS HIGH SCHOOL CLASSMATE AGAIN AFTER SEVERAL YEARS.
OH, HELLO...
IT'S ABOUT THE DIALOGUE ON PAGE 16, PANEL THREE...
DAYS LATER, HE LEARNS THAT SHE COMMITTED SUICIDE. IN A WORLD THAT NEVER CHANGES, HE BEGINS TO MOVE FORWARD...
THE HERO IS COMPLETELY SELF-ABSORBED AND COMPLETELY UNINTERESTING.

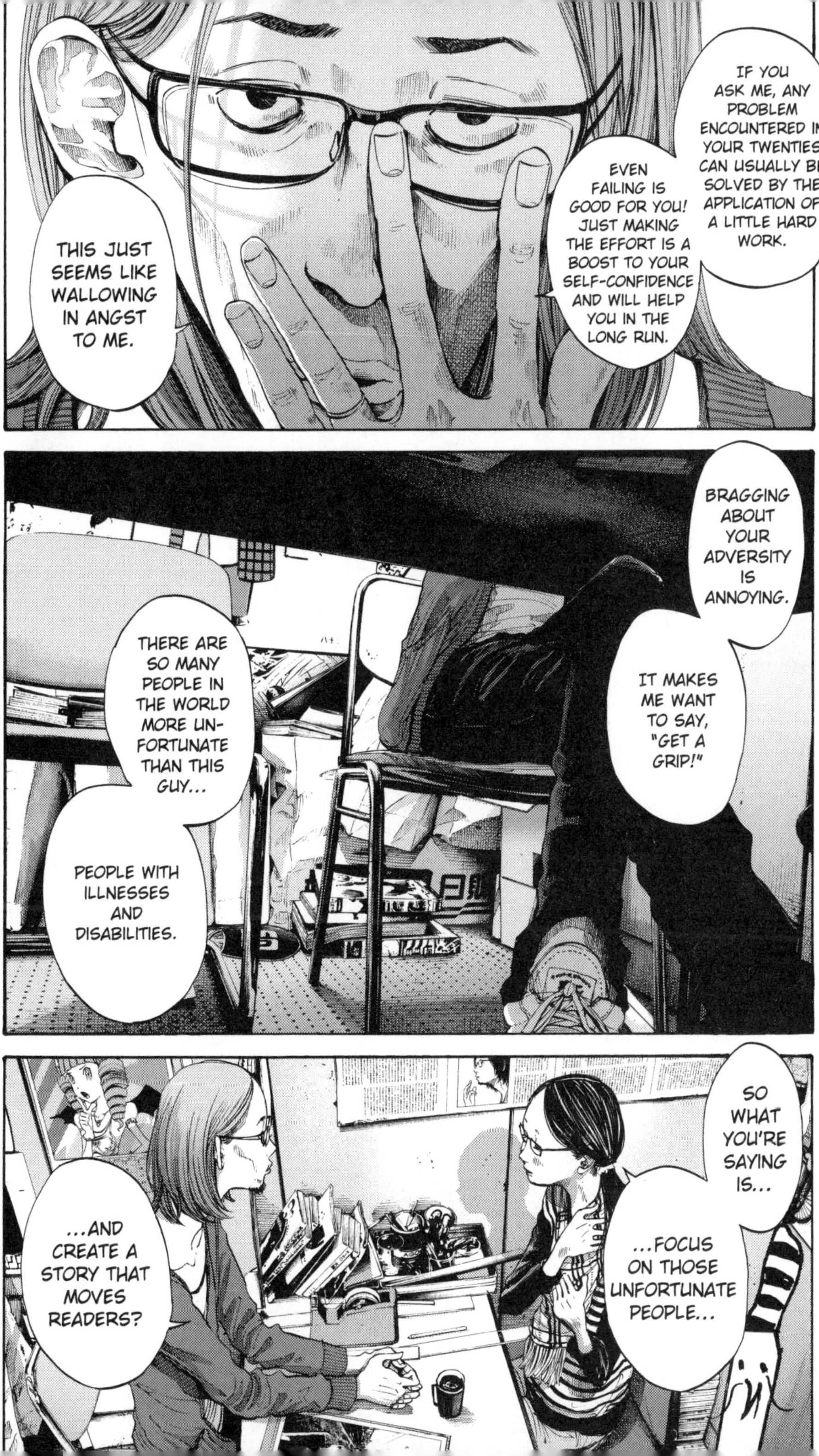
IF YOU ASK ME, ANY PROBLEM ENCOUNTERED IN YOUR TWENTIES CAN USUALLY BE SOLVED BY THE APPLICATION OF A LITTLE HARD WORK.
EVEN FAILING IS GOOD FOR YOU! JUST MAKING THE EFFORT IS A BOOST TO YOUR SELF-CONFIDENCE AND WILL HELP YOU IN THE LONG RUN.
THIS JUST SEEMS LIKE WALLOWING IN ANGST TO ME.
BRAGGING ABOUT YOUR ADVERSITY IS ANNOYING.
IT MAKES ME WANT TO SAY, "GET A GRIP!"
THERE ARE SO MANY PEOPLE IN THE WORLD MORE UN-FORTUNATE THAN THIS GUY...
PEOPLE WITH ILLNESSES AND DISABILITIES.
SO WHAT YOU'RE SAYING IS...
...FOCUS ON THOSE UNFORTUNATE PEOPLE...
...AND CREATE A STORY THAT MOVES READERS?

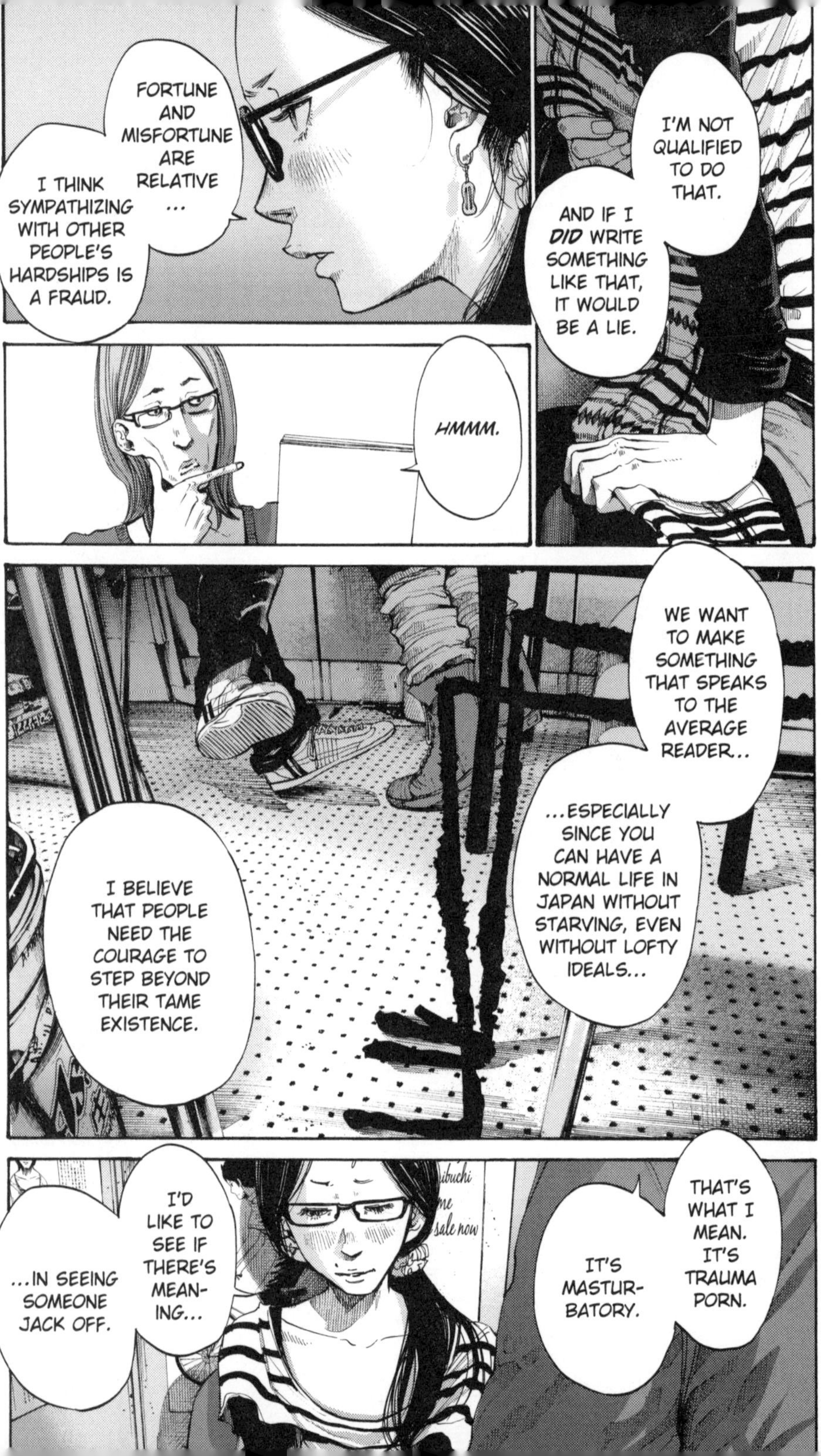
I'M NOT QUALIFIED TO DO THAT.
AND IF I *DID* WRITE SOMETHING LIKE THAT, IT WOULD BE A LIE.
FORTUNE AND MISFORTUNE ARE RELATIVE ...
I THINK SYMPATHIZING WITH OTHER PEOPLE'S HARDSHIPS IS A FRAUD.
HMMM.
WE WANT TO MAKE SOMETHING THAT SPEAKS TO THE AVERAGE READER...
...ESPECIALLY SINCE YOU CAN HAVE A NORMAL LIFE IN JAPAN WITHOUT STARVING, EVEN WITHOUT LOFTY IDEALS...
I BELIEVE THAT PEOPLE NEED THE COURAGE TO STEP BEYOND THEIR TAME EXISTENCE.
THAT'S WHAT I MEAN. IT'S TRAUMA PORN.
IT'S MASTUR-BATORY.
I'D LIKE TO SEE IF THERE'S MEAN-ING...
...IN SEEING SOMEONE JACK OFF.

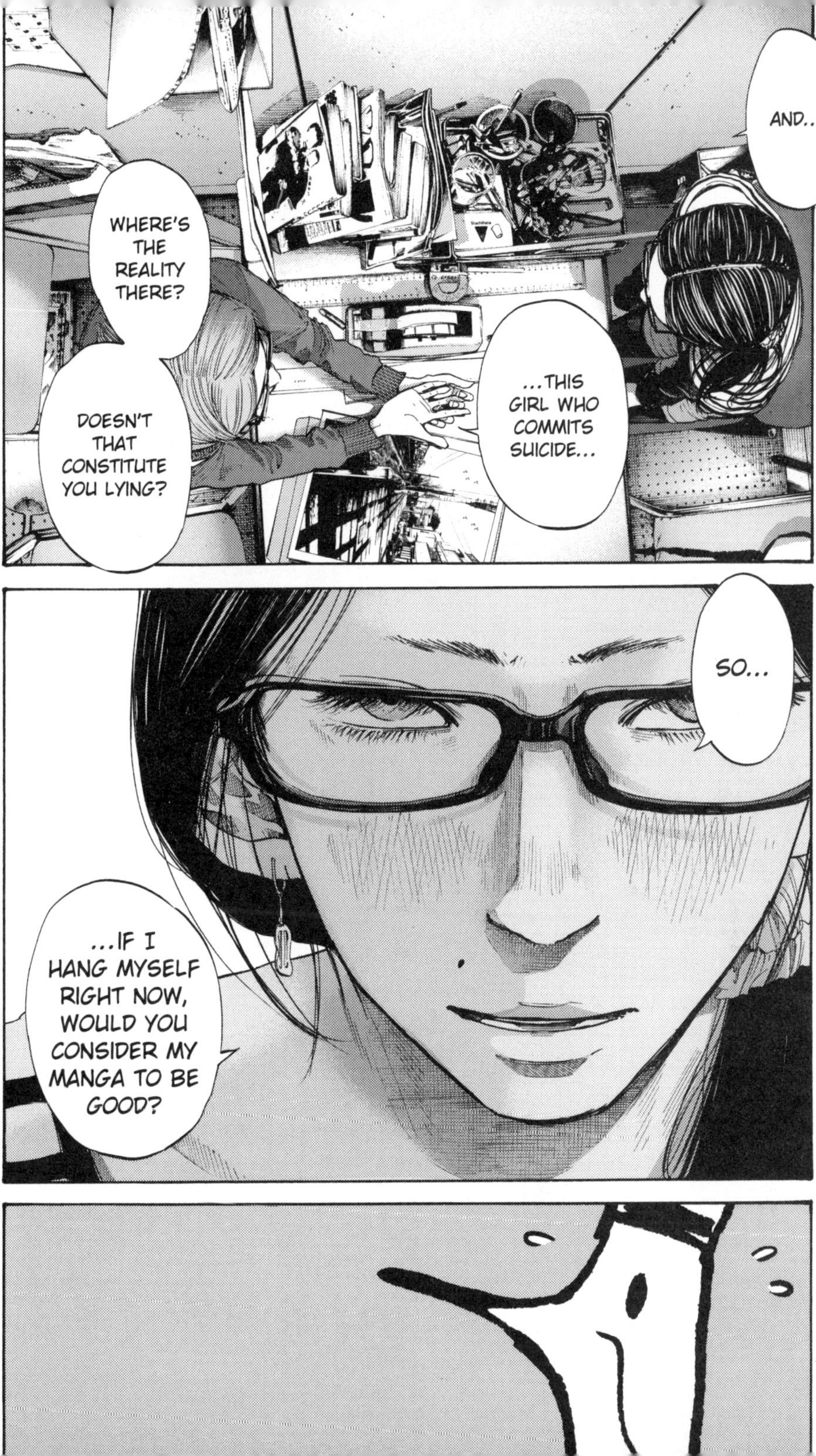
AND...
...THIS GIRL WHO COMMITS SUICIDE...
WHERE'S THE REALITY THERE?
DOESN'T THAT CONSTITUTE YOU LYING?
SO...
...IF I HANG MYSELF RIGHT NOW, WOULD YOU CONSIDER MY MANGA TO BE GOOD?

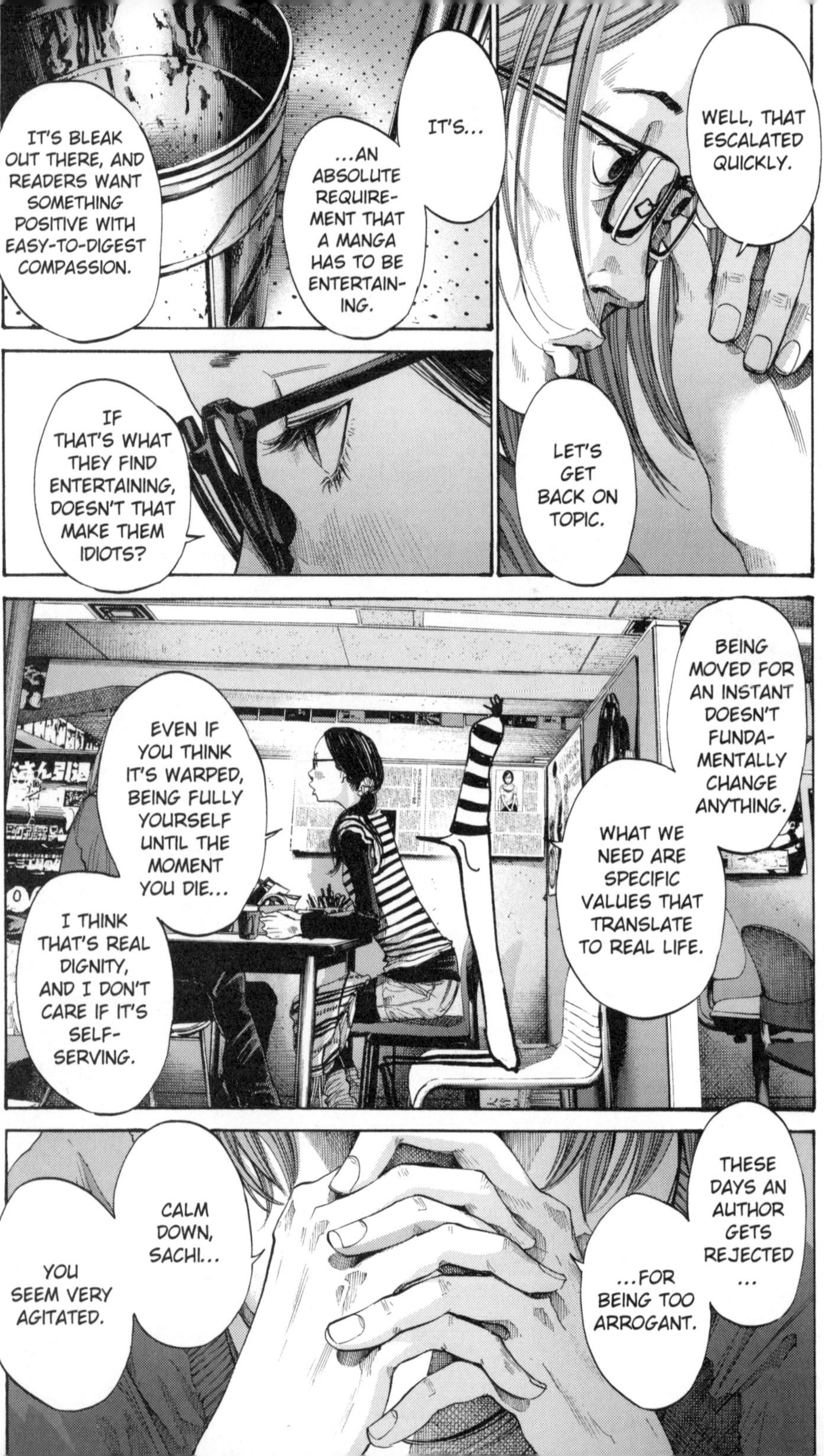
WELL, THAT ESCALATED QUICKLY.
LET'S GET BACK ON TOPIC.
IT'S...
...AN ABSOLUTE REQUIREMENT THAT A MANGA HAS TO BE ENTERTAINING.
IT'S BLEAK OUT THERE, AND READERS WANT SOMETHING POSITIVE WITH EASY-TO-DIGEST COMPASSION.
IF THAT'S WHAT THEY FIND ENTERTAINING, DOESN'T THAT MAKE THEM IDIOTS?
BEING MOVED FOR AN INSTANT DOESN'T FUNDAMENTALLY CHANGE ANYTHING.
WHAT WE NEED ARE SPECIFIC VALUES THAT TRANSLATE TO REAL LIFE.
EVEN IF YOU THINK IT'S WARPED, BEING FULLY YOURSELF UNTIL THE MOMENT YOU DIE...
I THINK THAT'S REAL DIGNITY, AND I DON'T CARE IF IT'S SELF-SERVING.
THESE DAYS AN AUTHOR GETS REJECTED...
...FOR BEING TOO ARROGANT.
CALM DOWN, SACHI...
YOU SEEM VERY AGITATED.

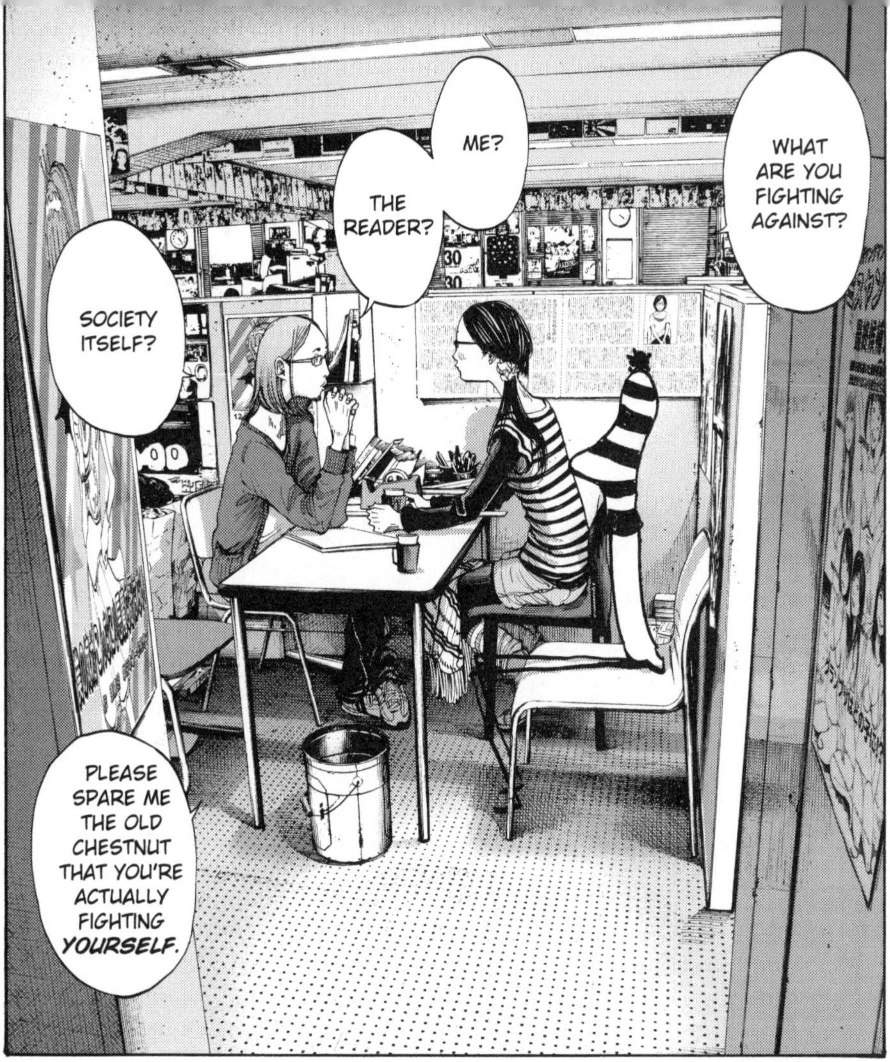
WHAT ARE YOU FIGHTING AGAINST?
ME?
THE READER?
SOCIETY ITSELF?
PLEASE SPARE ME THE OLD CHESTNUT THAT YOU'RE ACTUALLY FIGHTING ***YOURSELF***.

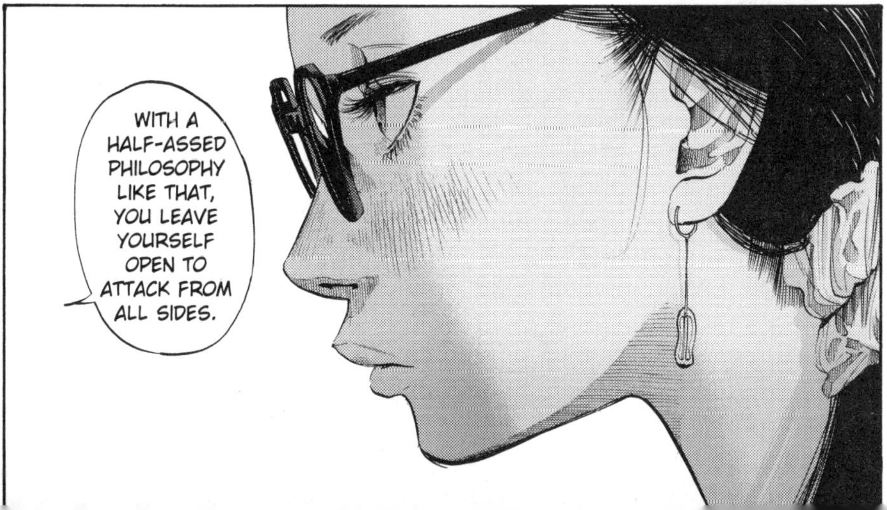
WITH A HALF-ASSED PHILOSOPHY LIKE THAT, YOU LEAVE YOURSELF OPEN TO ATTACK FROM ALL SIDES.

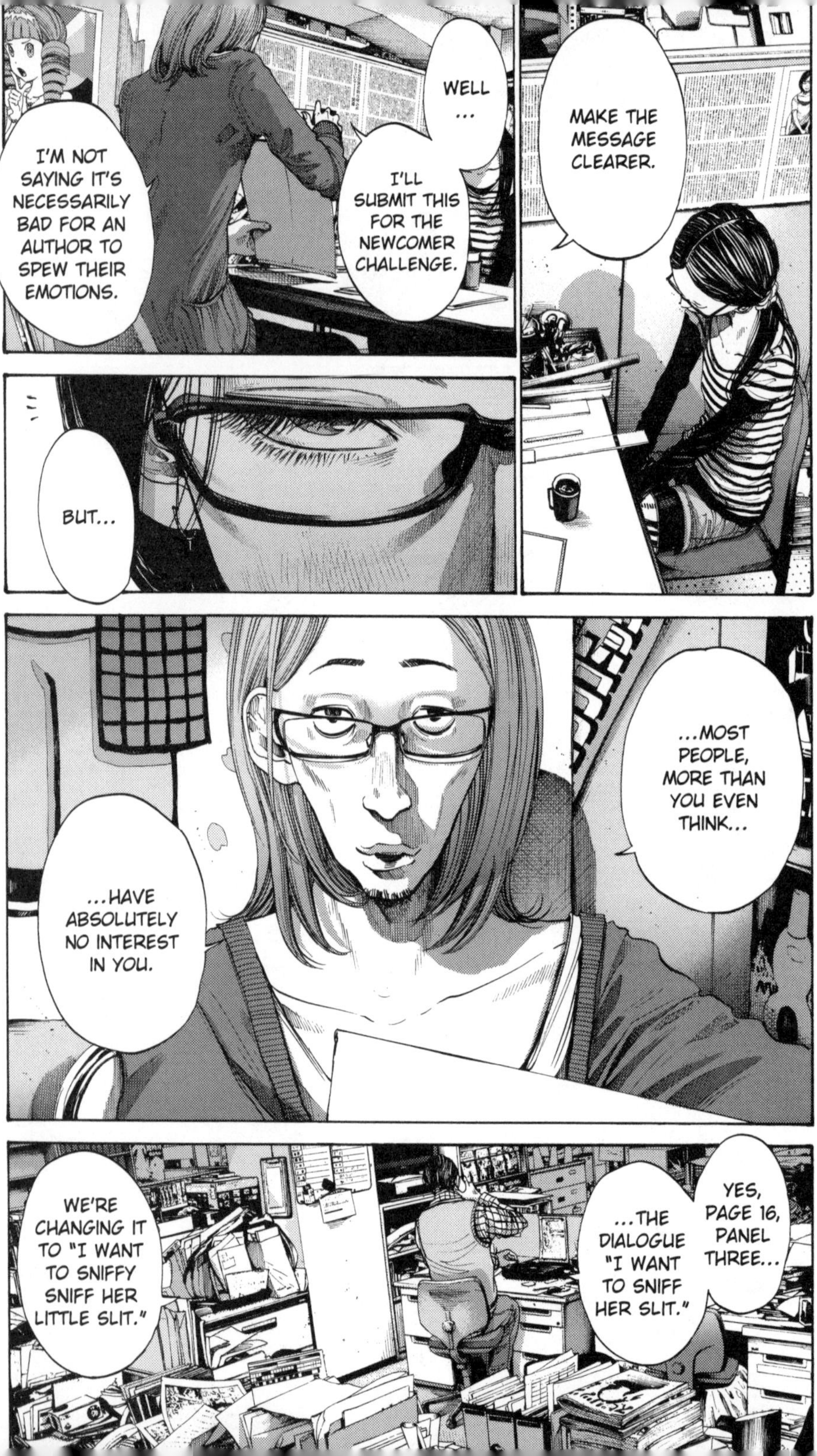
MAKE THE MESSAGE CLEARER.
WELL ...
I'LL SUBMIT THIS FOR THE NEWCOMER CHALLENGE.
I'M NOT SAYING IT'S NECESSARILY BAD FOR AN AUTHOR TO SPEW THEIR EMOTIONS.
BUT...
...MOST PEOPLE, MORE THAN YOU EVEN THINK...
...HAVE ABSOLUTELY NO INTEREST IN YOU.
YES, PAGE 16, PANEL THREE...
...THE DIALOGUE "I WANT TO SNIFF HER SLIT."
WE'RE CHANGING IT TO "I WANT TO SNIFFY SNIFF HER LITTLE SLIT."

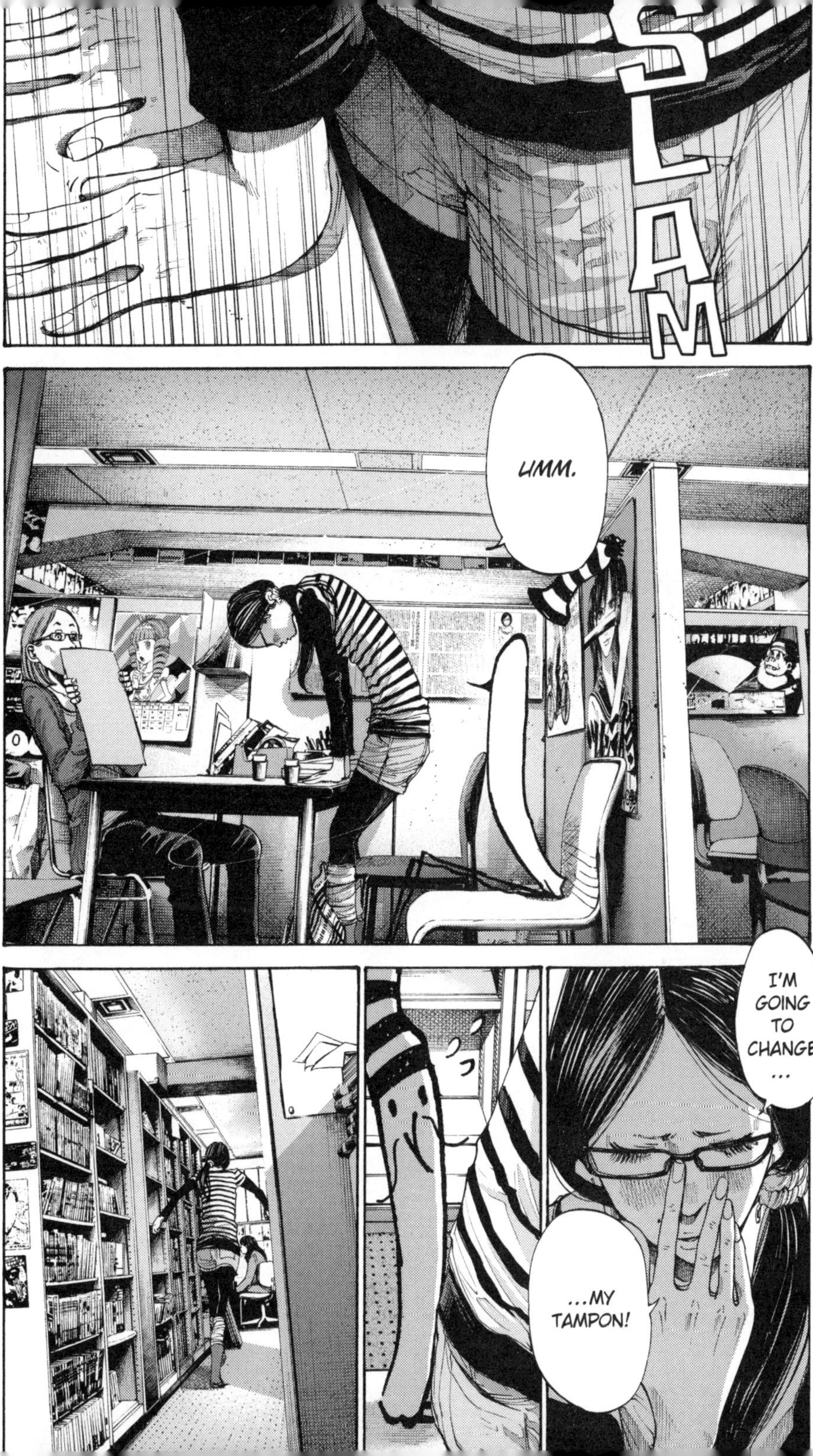
SLAM
UMM.
I'M GOING TO CHANGE ...
...MY TAMPON!

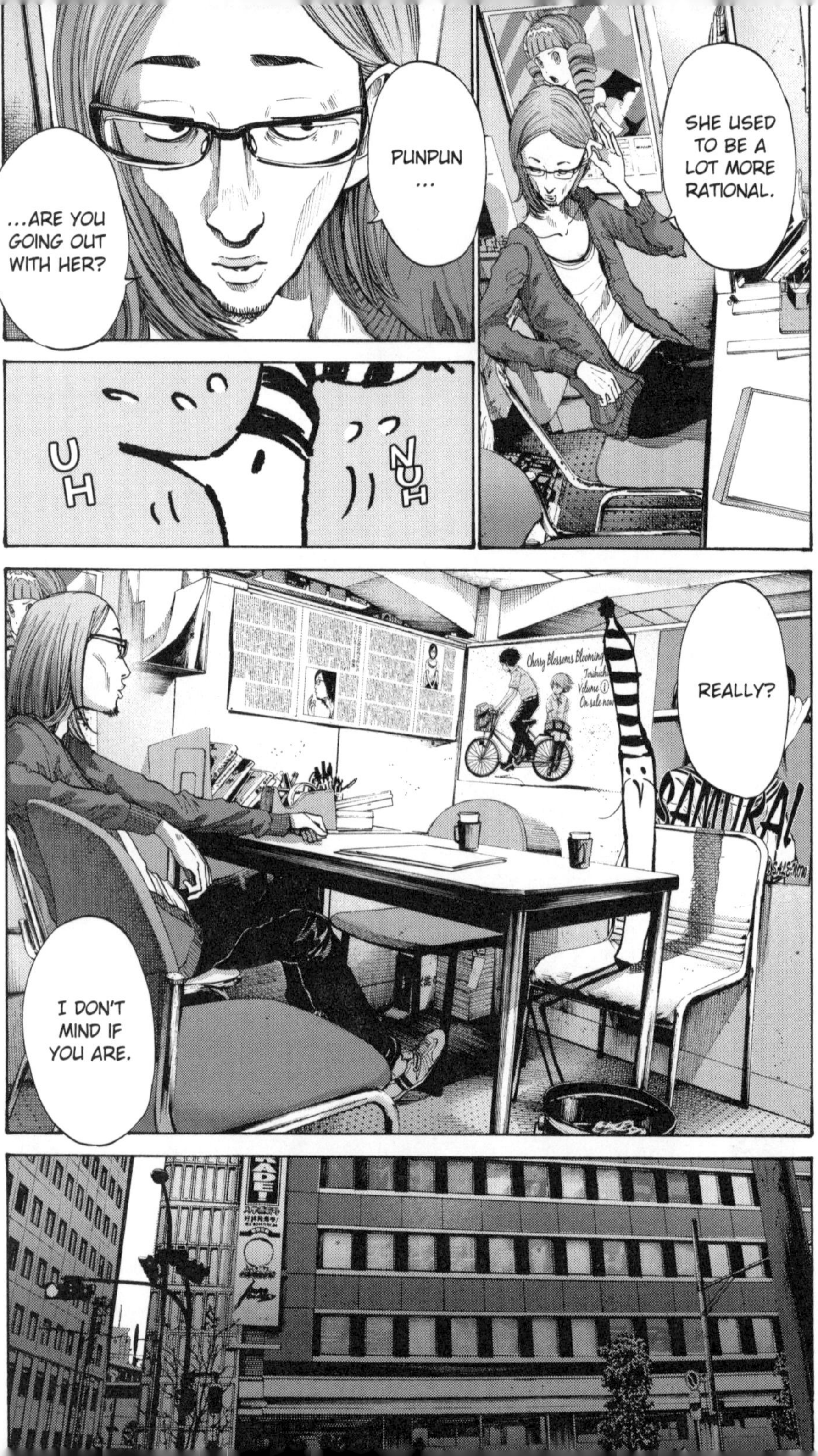
SHE USED TO BE A LOT MORE RATIONAL.
PUNPUN ...
...ARE YOU GOING OUT WITH HER?
UH NUH
REALLY?
Cherry Blossoms Blooming
I DON'T MIND IF YOU ARE.

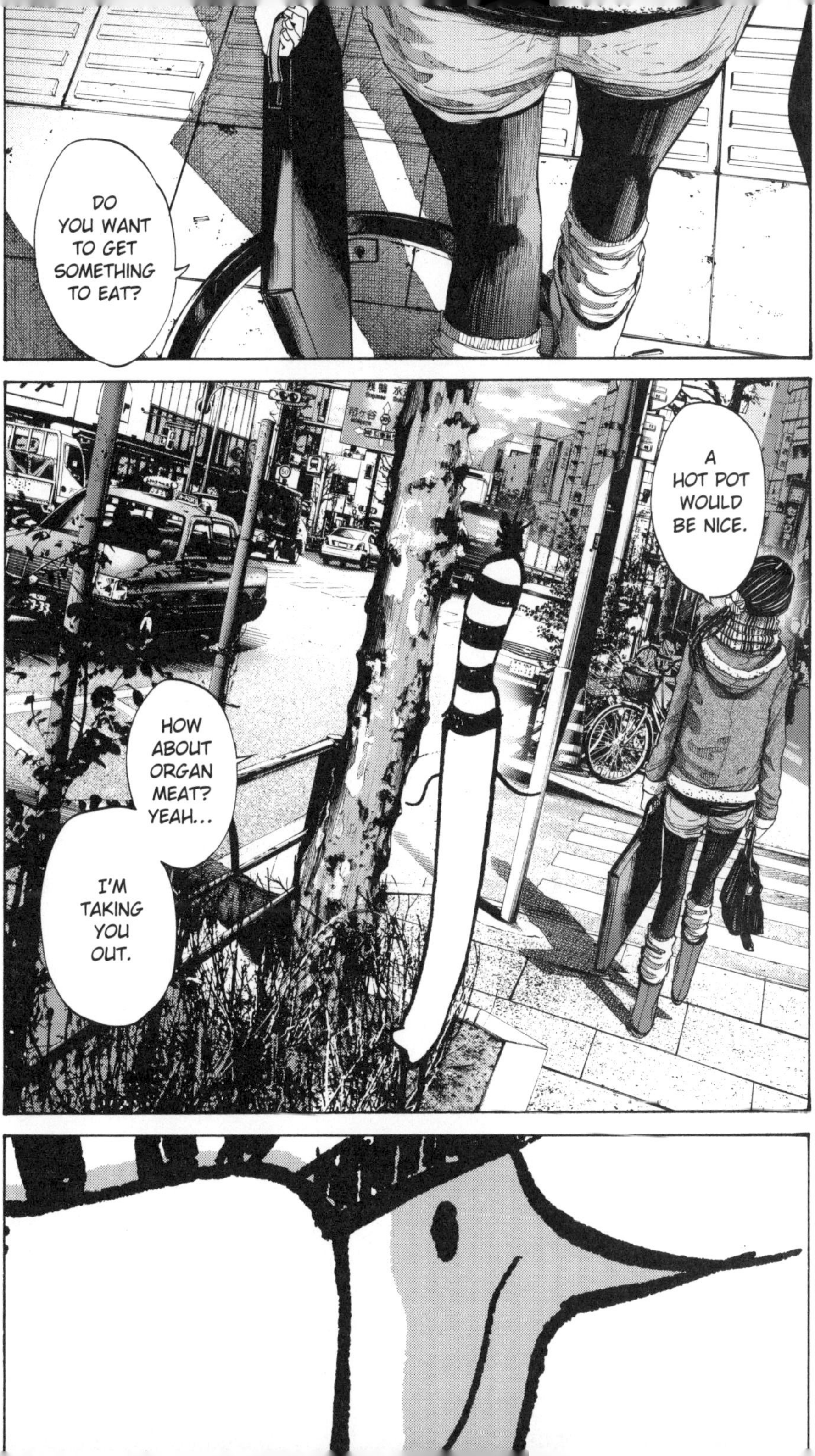
DO YOU WANT TO GET SOMETHING TO EAT?
A HOT POT WOULD BE NICE.
HOW ABOUT ORGAN MEAT? YEAH...
I'M TAKING YOU OUT.

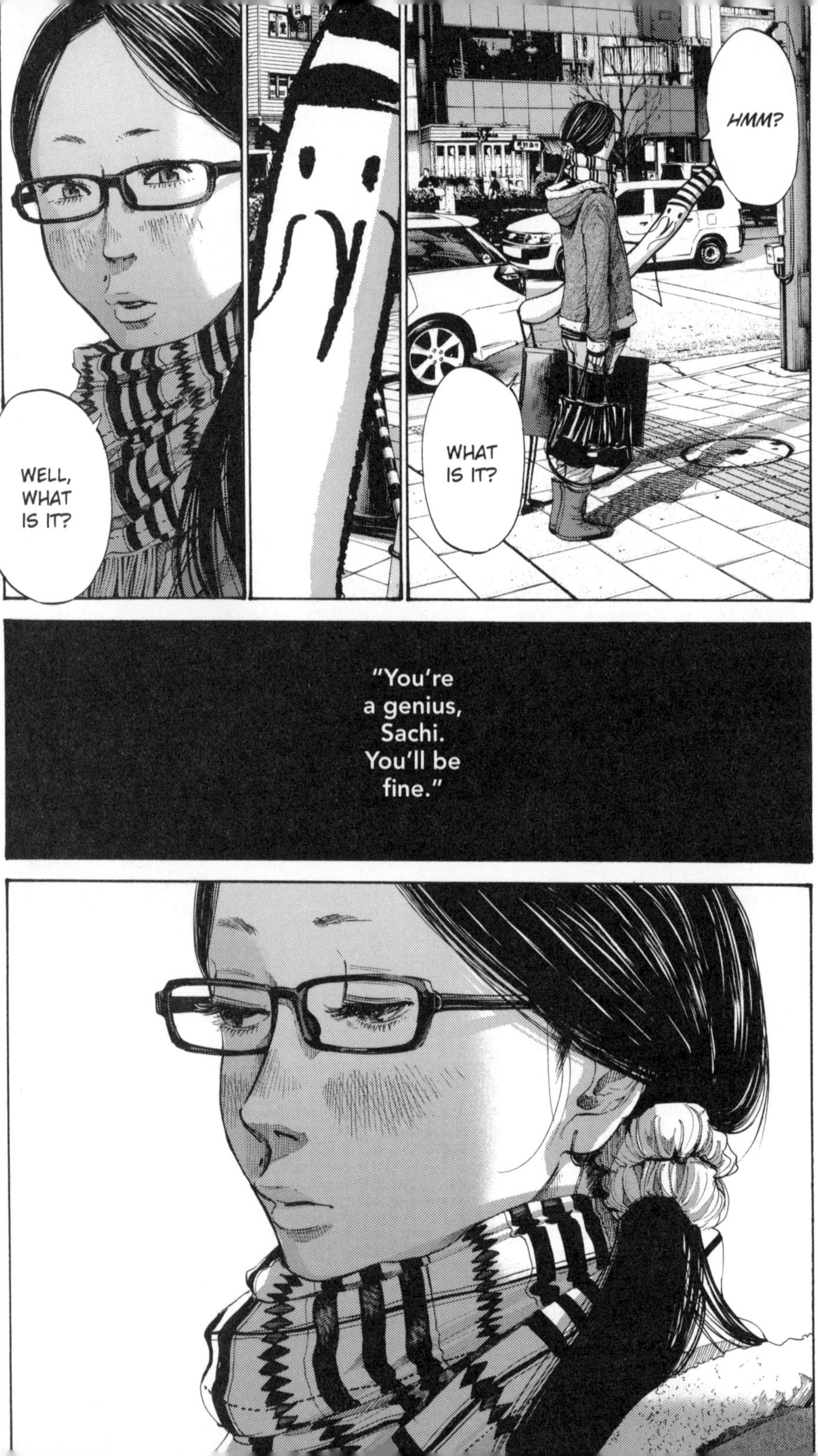
HMM?
WHAT IS IT?
WELL, WHAT IS IT?
"You're a genius, Sachi. You'll be fine."

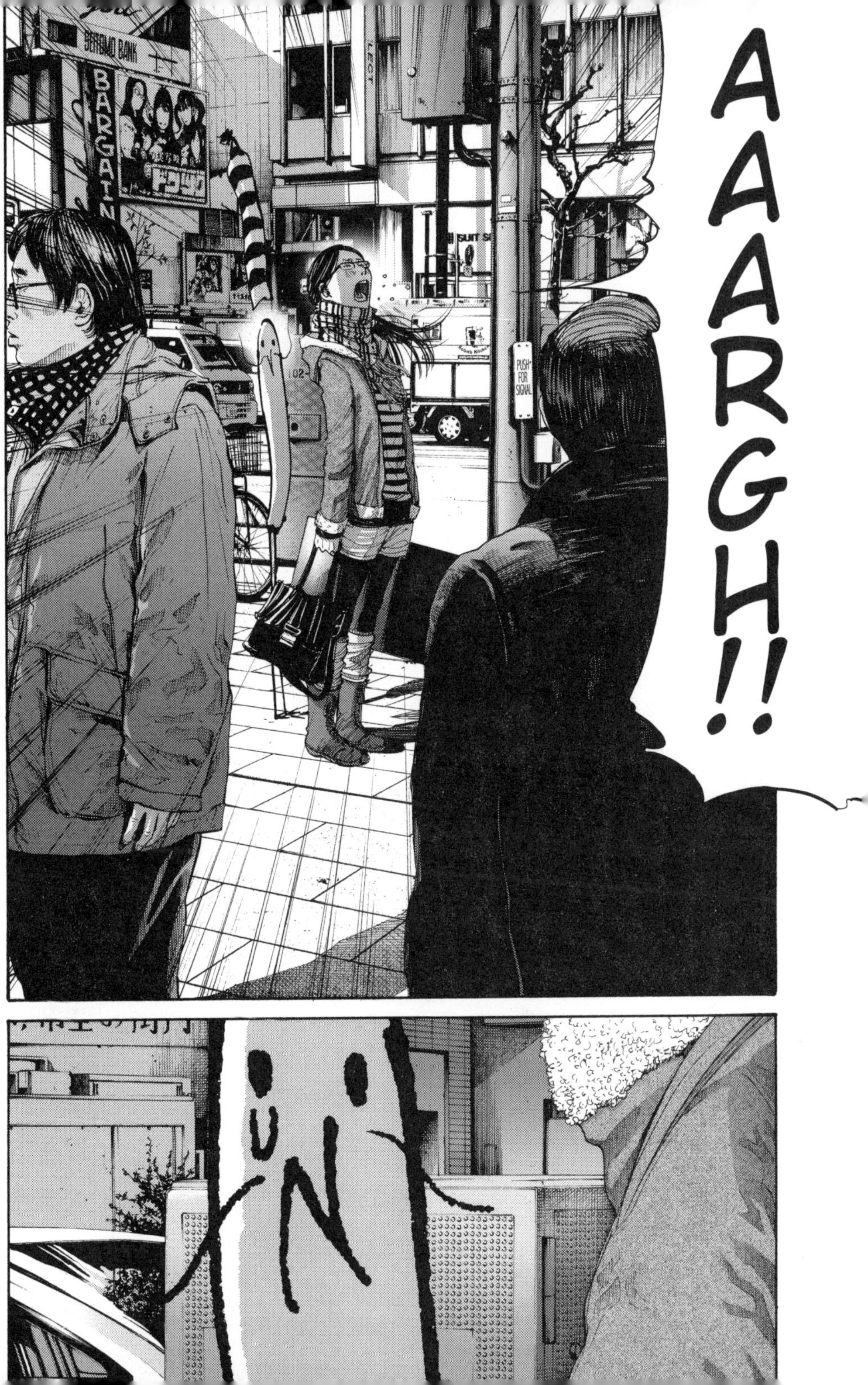
AAARGH!!
BARGAIN
PUSH FOR SIGNAL

DON'T SAY ANYTHING...

...FOR A WHILE.

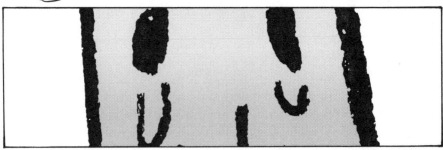

I JUST NEED TO DO IT...

JUST DO IT.

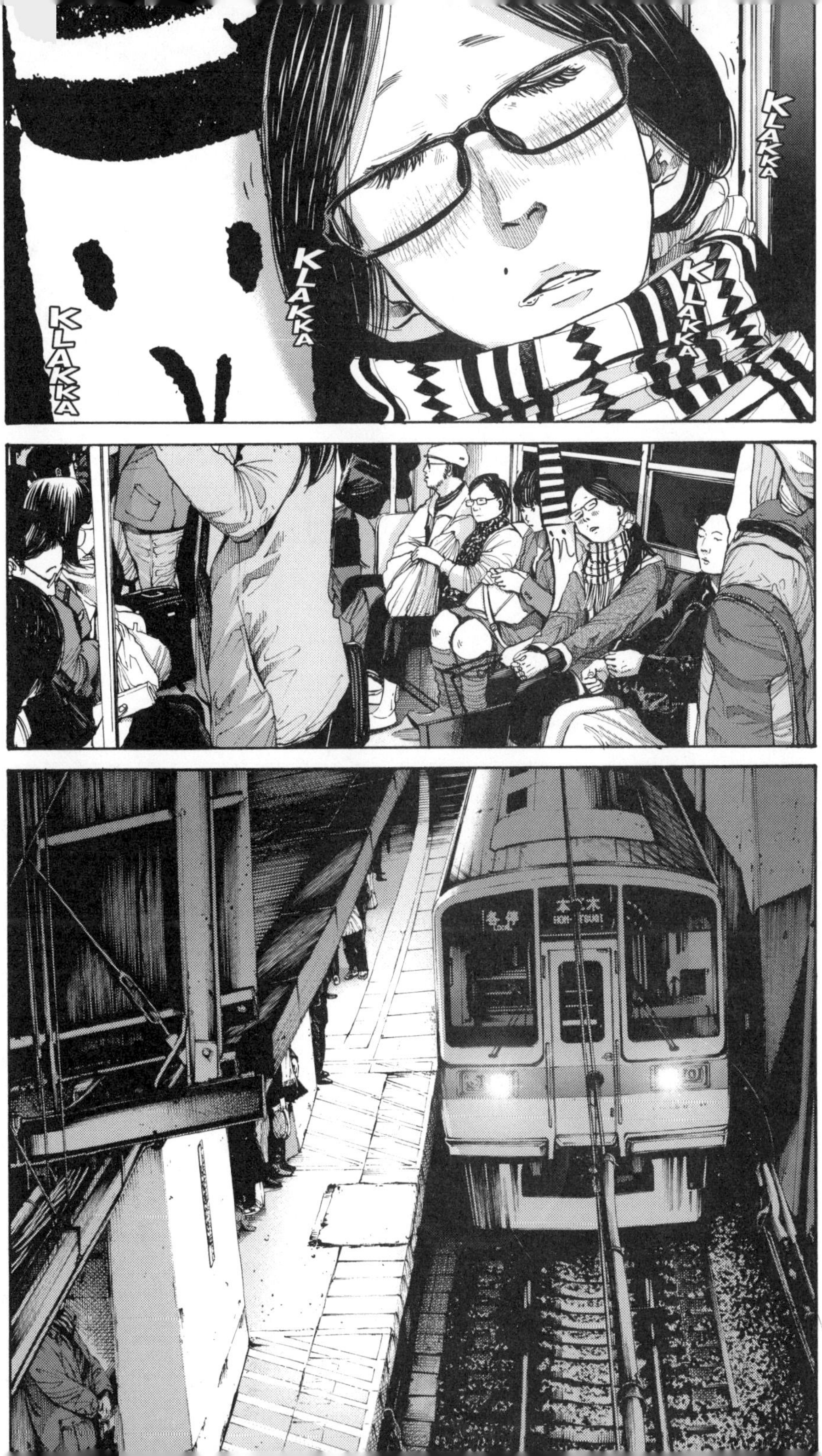
KLAKKA
KLAKKA
KLAKKA
KLAKKA

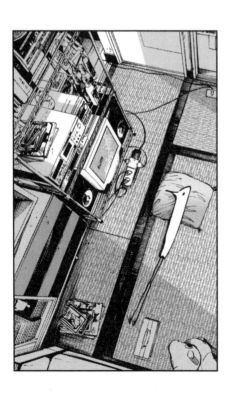

Chapter 92

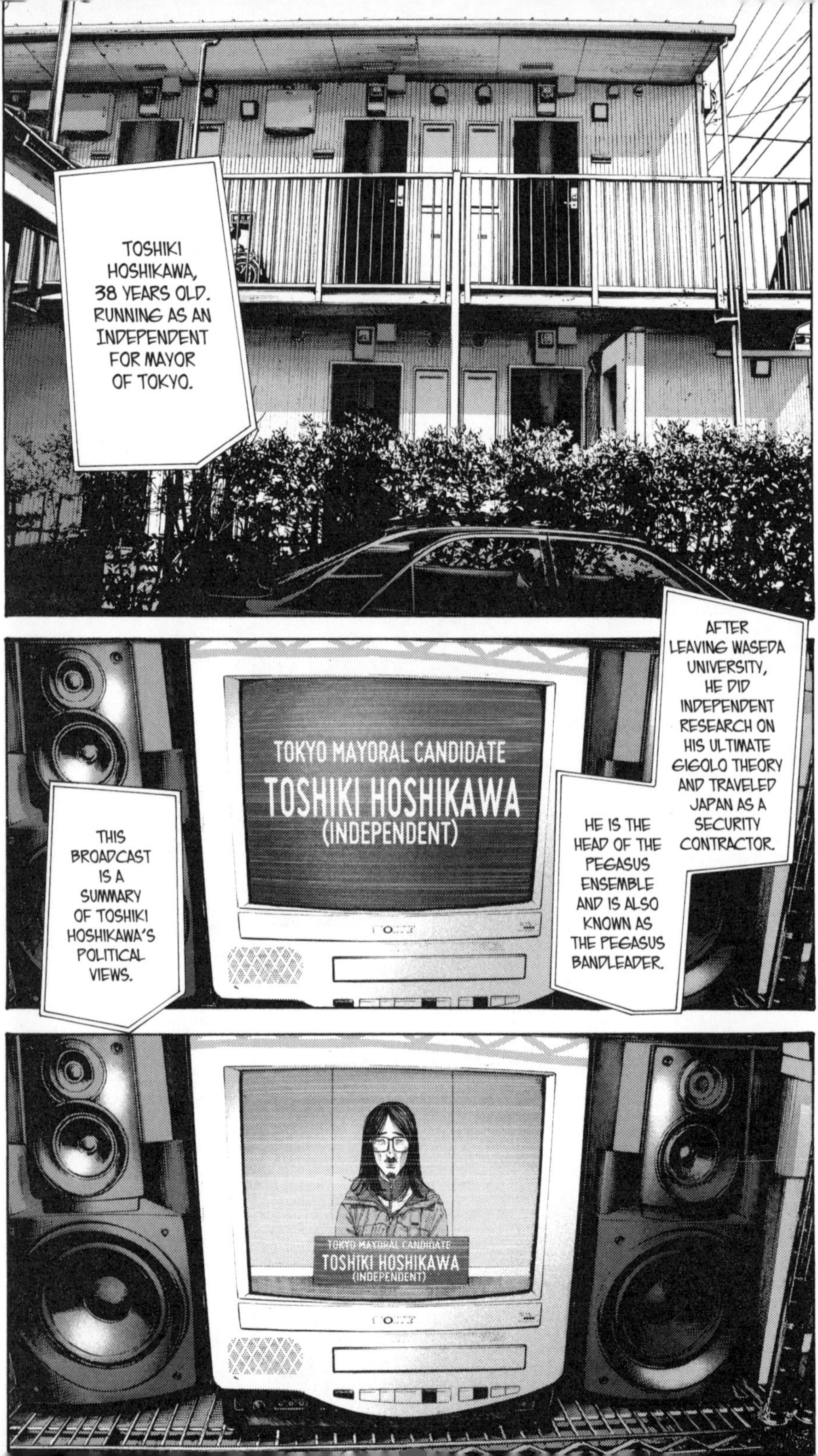
TOSHIKI HOSHIKAWA, 38 YEARS OLD. RUNNING AS AN INDEPENDENT FOR MAYOR OF TOKYO.
AFTER LEAVING WASEDA UNIVERSITY, HE DID INDEPENDENT RESEARCH ON HIS ULTIMATE GIGOLO THEORY AND TRAVELED JAPAN AS A SECURITY CONTRACTOR.
HE IS THE HEAD OF THE PEGASUS ENSEMBLE AND IS ALSO KNOWN AS THE PEGASUS BANDLEADER.
TOKYO MAYORAL CANDIDATE
TOSHIKI HOSHIKAWA
(INDEPENDENT)
THIS BROADCAST IS A SUMMARY OF TOSHIKI HOSHIKAWA'S POLITICAL VIEWS.
TOKYO MAYORAL CANDIDATE
TOSHIKI HOSHIKAWA
(INDEPENDENT)

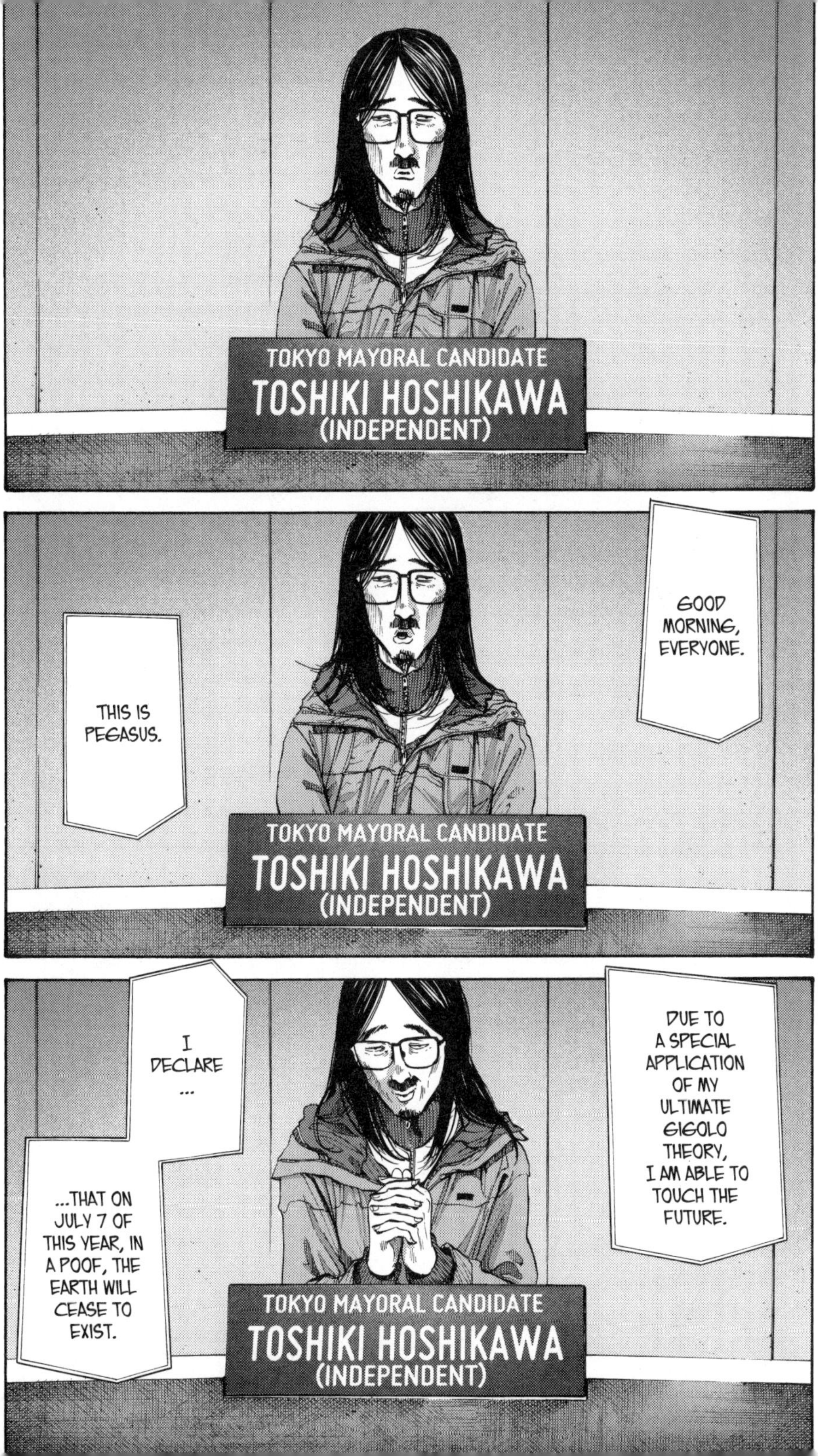
TOKYO MAYORAL CANDIDATE
TOSHIKI HOSHIKAWA
(INDEPENDENT)
GOOD MORNING, EVERYONE.
THIS IS PEGASUS.
TOKYO MAYORAL CANDIDATE
TOSHIKI HOSHIKAWA
(INDEPENDENT)
DUE TO A SPECIAL APPLICATION OF MY ULTIMATE GIGOLO THEORY, I AM ABLE TO TOUCH THE FUTURE.
I DECLARE ...
...THAT ON JULY 7 OF THIS YEAR, IN A POOF, THE EARTH WILL CEASE TO EXIST.
TOKYO MAYORAL CANDIDATE
TOSHIKI HOSHIKAWA
(INDEPENDENT)

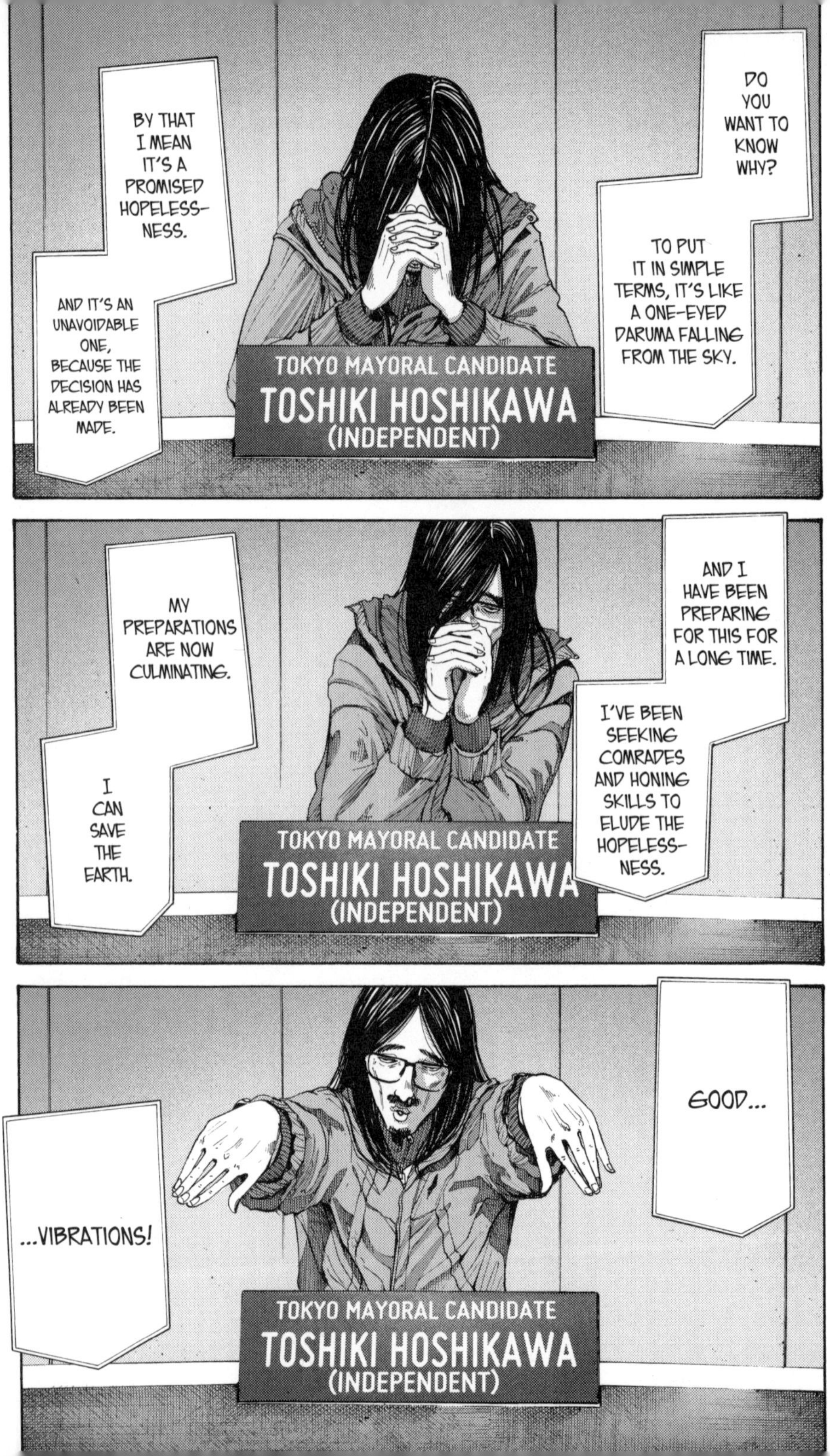
DO YOU WANT TO KNOW WHY?
TO PUT IT IN SIMPLE TERMS, IT'S LIKE A ONE-EYED DARUMA FALLING FROM THE SKY.
BY THAT I MEAN IT'S A PROMISED HOPELESS-NESS.
AND IT'S AN UNAVOIDABLE ONE, BECAUSE THE DECISION HAS ALREADY BEEN MADE.
TOKYO MAYORAL CANDIDATE
TOSHIKI HOSHIKAWA
(INDEPENDENT)
AND I HAVE BEEN PREPARING FOR THIS FOR A LONG TIME.
I'VE BEEN SEEKING COMRADES AND HONING SKILLS TO ELUDE THE HOPELESS-NESS.
MY PREPARATIONS ARE NOW CULMINATING.
I CAN SAVE THE EARTH.
TOKYO MAYORAL CANDIDATE
TOSHIKI HOSHIKAWA
(INDEPENDENT)
GOOD...
...VIBRATIONS!
TOKYO MAYORAL CANDIDATE
TOSHIKI HOSHIKAWA
(INDEPENDENT)

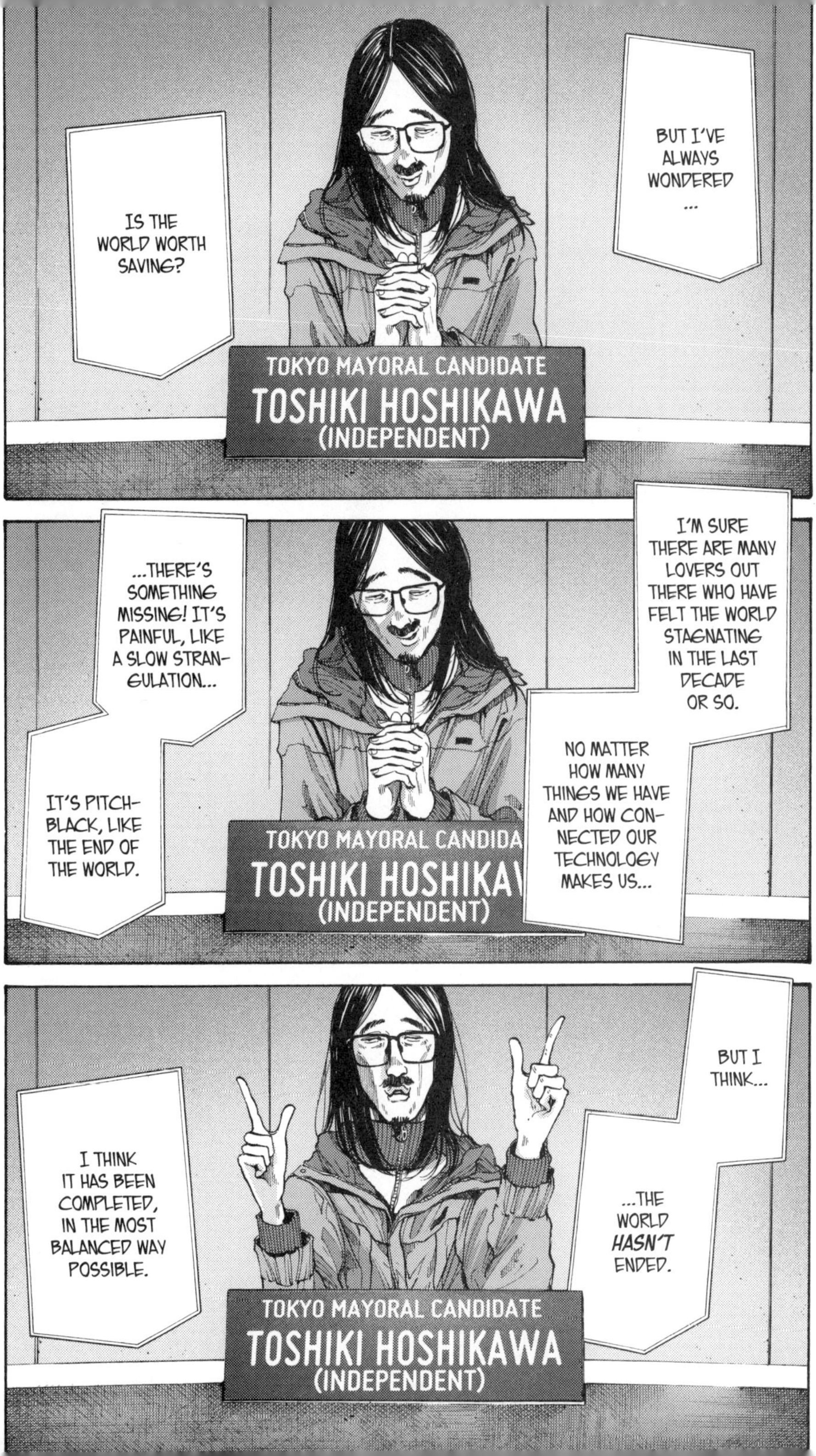
BUT I'VE ALWAYS WONDERED ...
IS THE WORLD WORTH SAVING?
TOKYO MAYORAL CANDIDATE
TOSHIKI HOSHIKAWA
(INDEPENDENT)
I'M SURE THERE ARE MANY LOVERS OUT THERE WHO HAVE FELT THE WORLD STAGNATING IN THE LAST DECADE OR SO.
NO MATTER HOW MANY THINGS WE HAVE AND HOW CON-NECTED OUR TECHNOLOGY MAKES US...
...THERE'S SOMETHING MISSING! IT'S PAINFUL, LIKE A SLOW STRAN-GULATION...
IT'S PITCH-BLACK, LIKE THE END OF THE WORLD.
TOKYO MAYORAL CANDIDA
TOSHIKI HOSHIKAV
(INDEPENDENT)
BUT I THINK...
...THE WORLD *HASN'T* ENDED.
I THINK IT HAS BEEN COMPLETED, IN THE MOST BALANCED WAY POSSIBLE.
TOKYO MAYORAL CANDIDATE
TOSHIKI HOSHIKAWA
(INDEPENDENT)

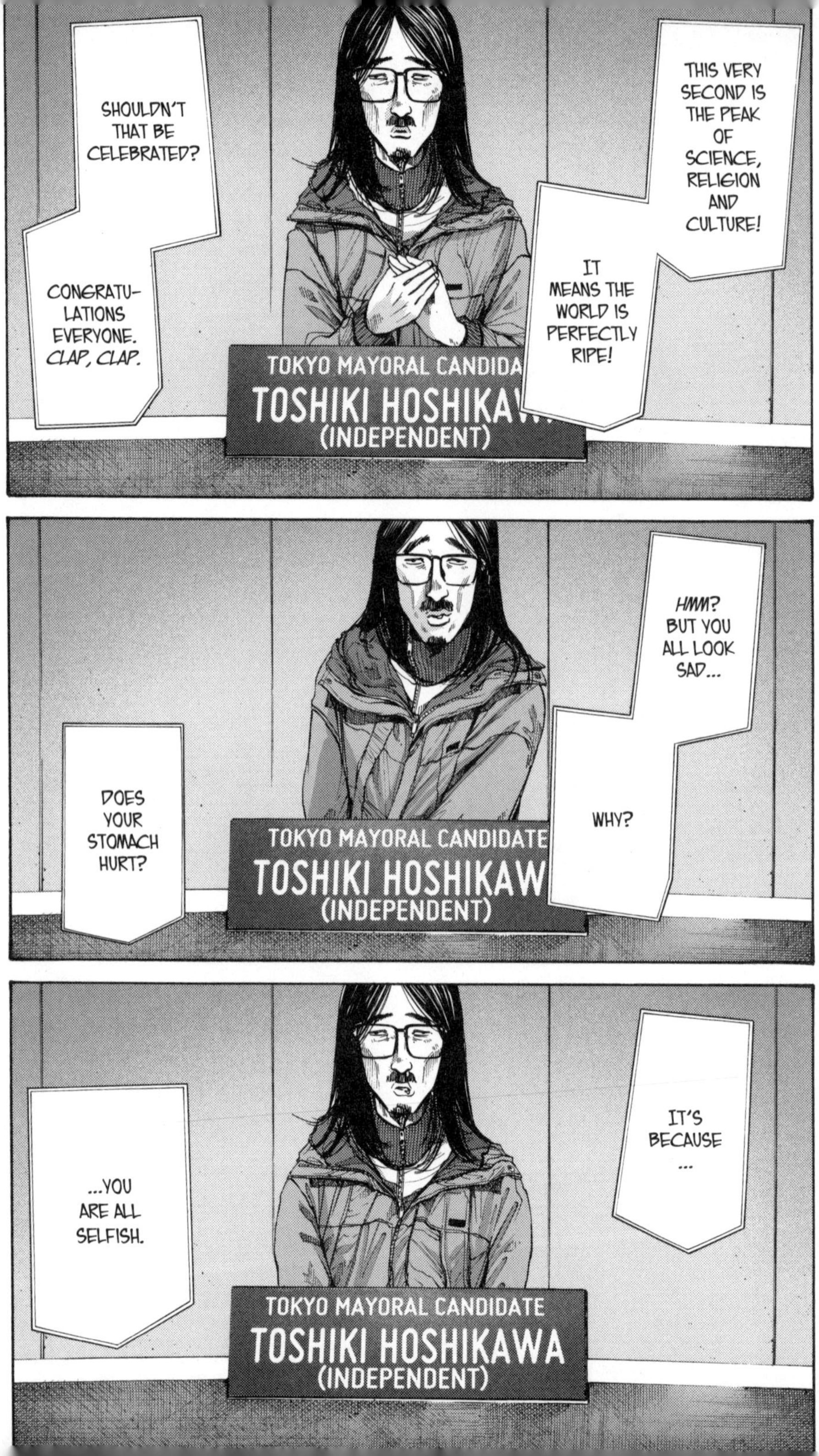
THIS VERY SECOND IS THE PEAK OF SCIENCE, RELIGION AND CULTURE!
IT MEANS THE WORLD IS PERFECTLY RIPE!
SHOULDN'T THAT BE CELEBRATED?
CONGRATU-LATIONS EVERYONE. *CLAP, CLAP.*
HMM? BUT YOU ALL LOOK SAD...
WHY?
DOES YOUR STOMACH HURT?
IT'S BECAUSE ...
...YOU ARE ALL SELFISH.
TOKYO MAYORAL CANDIDATE
TOSHIKI HOSHIKAWA
(INDEPENDENT)

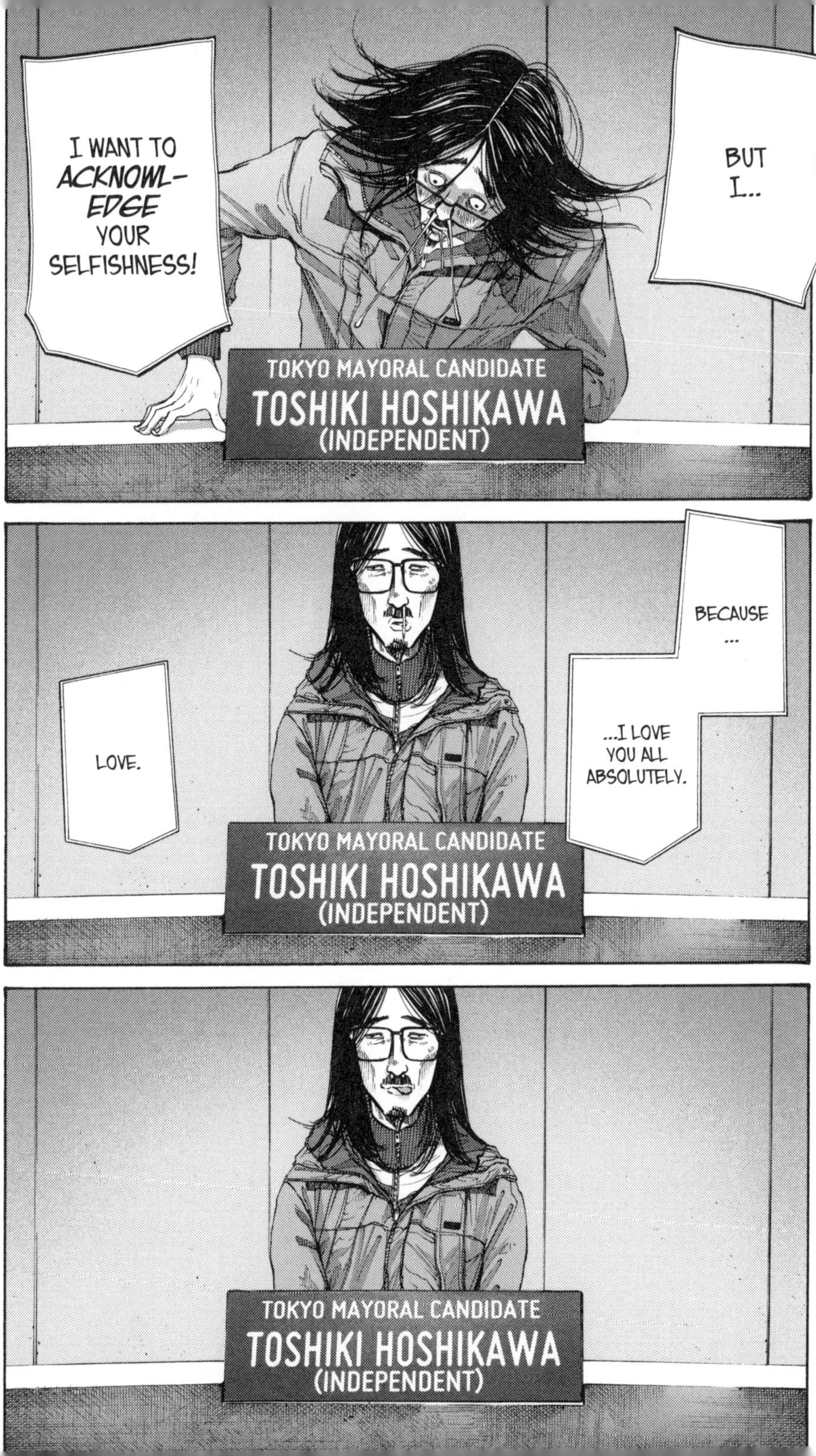
BUT I...
I WANT TO ACKNOWL-EDGE YOUR SELFISHNESS!
TOKYO MAYORAL CANDIDATE TOSHIKI HOSHIKAWA (INDEPENDENT)
BECAUSE ...
...I LOVE YOU ALL ABSOLUTELY.
LOVE.
TOKYO MAYORAL CANDIDATE TOSHIKI HOSHIKAWA (INDEPENDENT)
TOKYO MAYORAL CANDIDATE TOSHIKI HOSHIKAWA (INDEPENDENT)

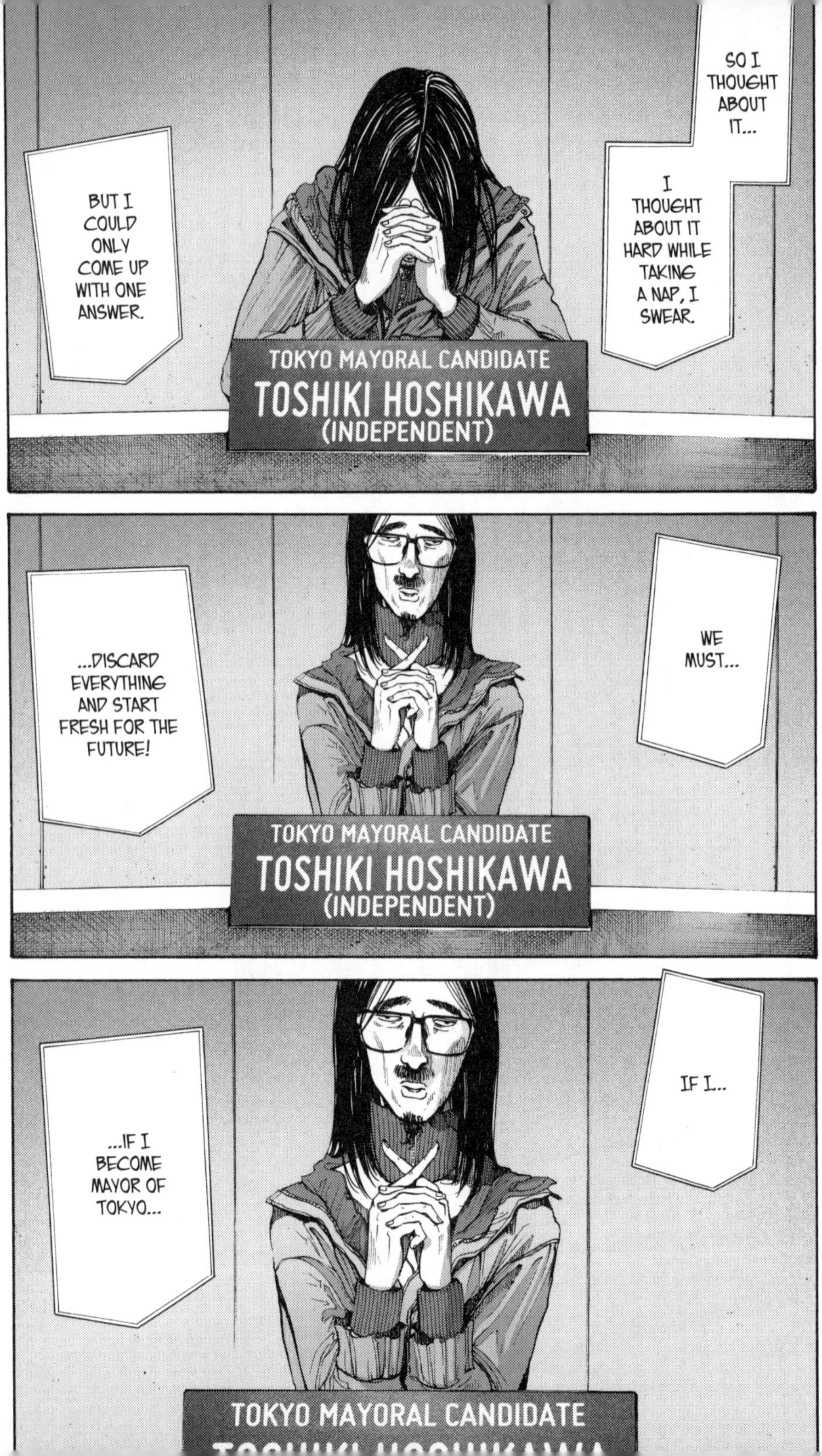
SO I THOUGHT ABOUT IT...
I THOUGHT ABOUT IT HARD WHILE TAKING A NAP, I SWEAR.
BUT I COULD ONLY COME UP WITH ONE ANSWER.
TOKYO MAYORAL CANDIDATE TOSHIKI HOSHIKAWA (INDEPENDENT)
WE MUST...
...DISCARD EVERYTHING AND START FRESH FOR THE FUTURE!
TOKYO MAYORAL CANDIDATE TOSHIKI HOSHIKAWA (INDEPENDENT)
IF I...
...IF I BECOME MAYOR OF TOKYO...
TOKYO MAYORAL CANDIDATE

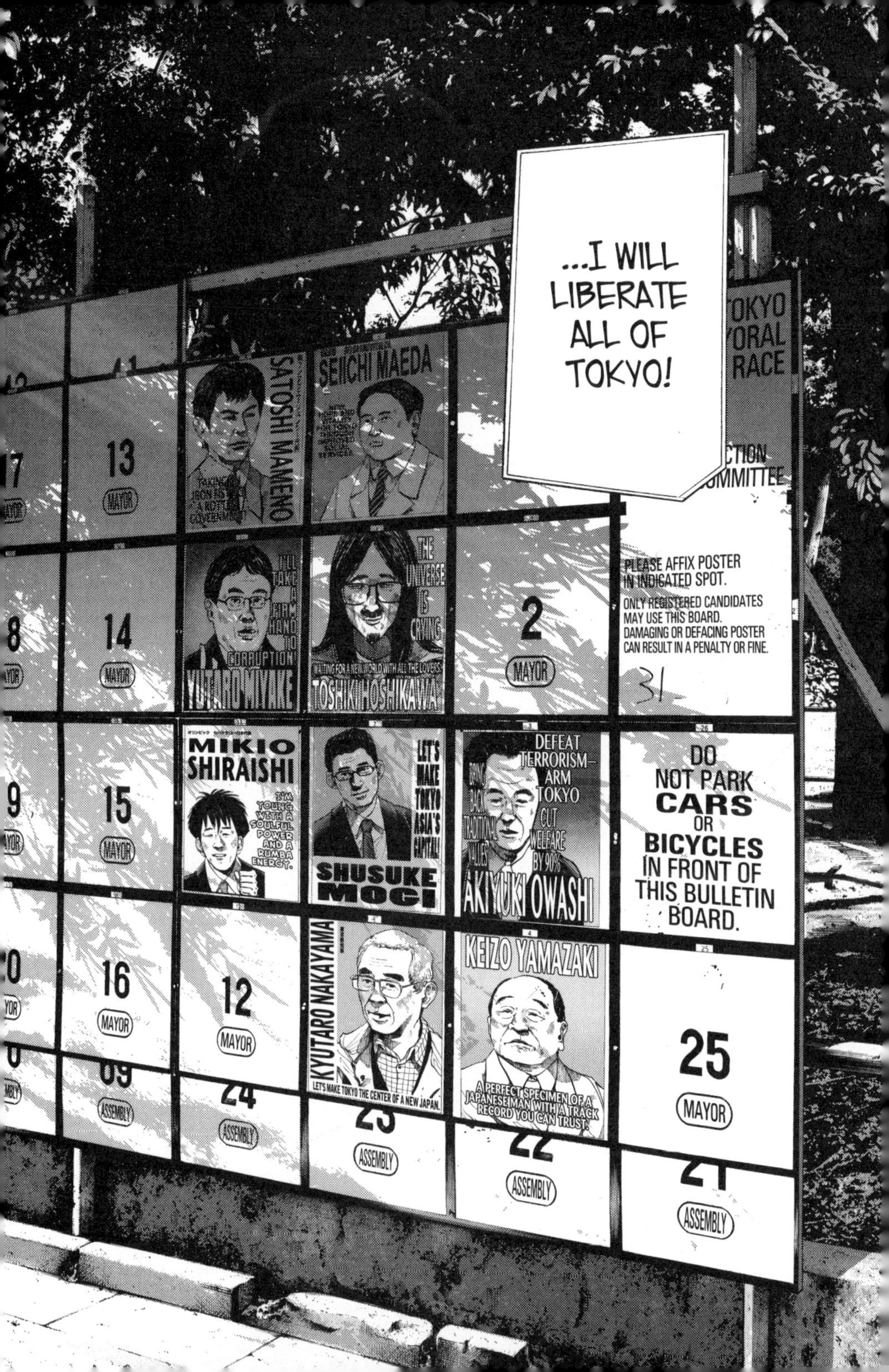
...I WILL LIBERATE ALL OF TOKYO!
TOKYO
YORAL
RACE
PLEASE AFFIX POSTER IN INDICATED SPOT.
ONLY REGISTERED CANDIDATES MAY USE THIS BOARD. DAMAGING OR DEFACING POSTER CAN RESULT IN A PENALTY OR FINE.
31
SEIICHI MAEDA
SATOSHI MAMENO
13 MAYOR
THE UNIVERSE IS CRYING
WAITING FOR A NEW WORLD WITH ALL THE LOVERS.
TOSHIKI HOSHIKAWA
I'LL TAKE A FIRM HAND TO CORRUPTION!
YUTARO MIYAKE
2 MAYOR
14 MAYOR
DO NOT PARK CARS OR BICYCLES IN FRONT OF THIS BULLETIN BOARD.
DEFEAT TERRORISM—ARM TOKYO
CUT WELFARE BY 90%
BRING BACK TRADITIONAL VALUES
AKIYUKI OWASHI
LET'S MAKE TOKYO ASIA'S CAPITAL!
SHUSUKE MOGI
MIKIO SHIRAISHI
I'M YOUNG WITH A SOULFUL POWER AND A RUMBA ENERGY.
15 MAYOR
25 MAYOR
KEIZO YAMAZAKI
A PERFECT SPECIMEN OF A JAPANESE MAN WITH A TRACK RECORD YOU CAN TRUST.
KYUTARO NAKAYAMA
LET'S MAKE TOKYO THE CENTER OF A NEW JAPAN.
12 MAYOR
16 MAYOR
ASSEMBLY

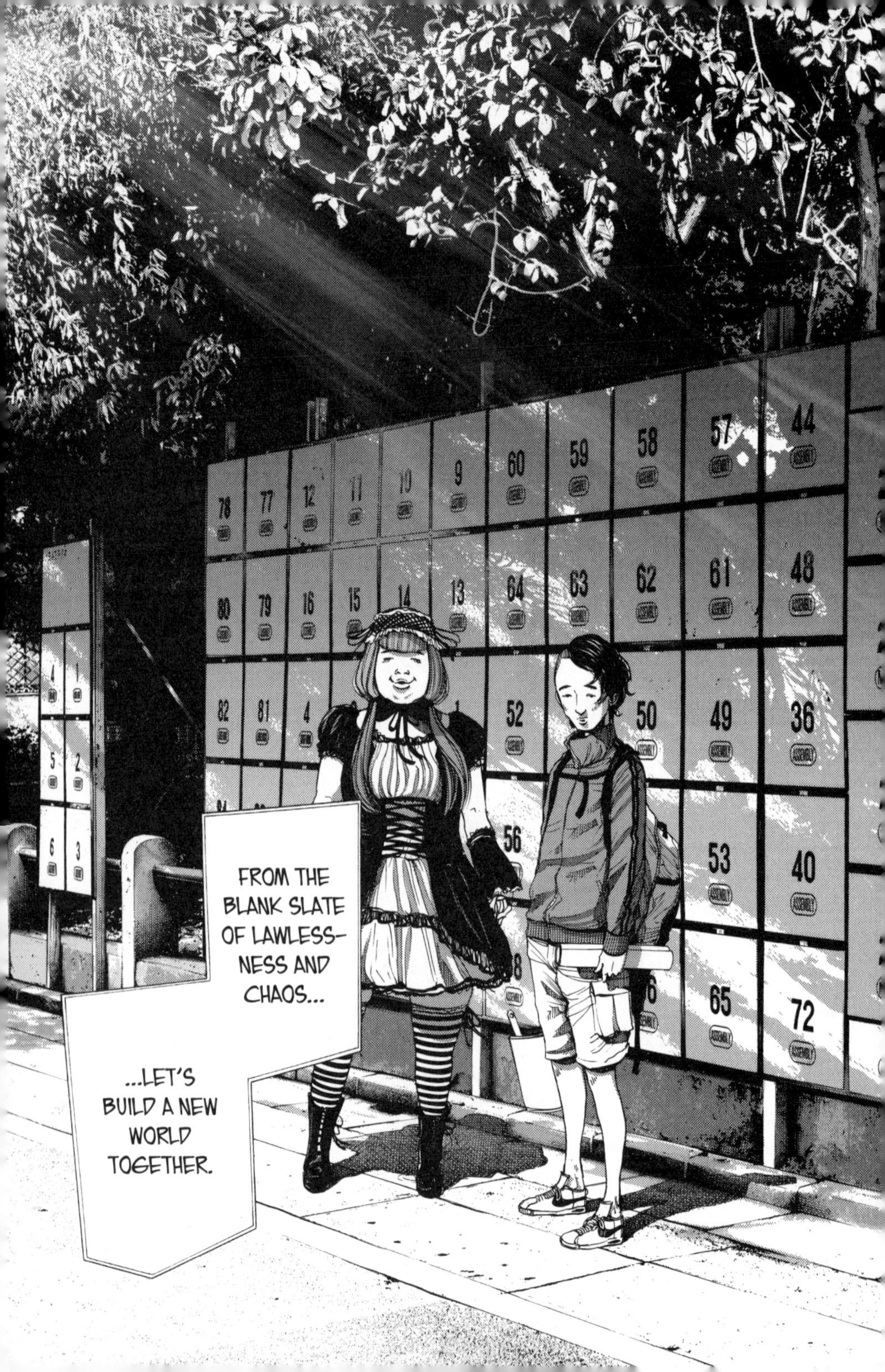
FROM THE BLANK SLATE OF LAWLESS-NESS AND CHAOS...
...LET'S BUILD A NEW WORLD TOGETHER.

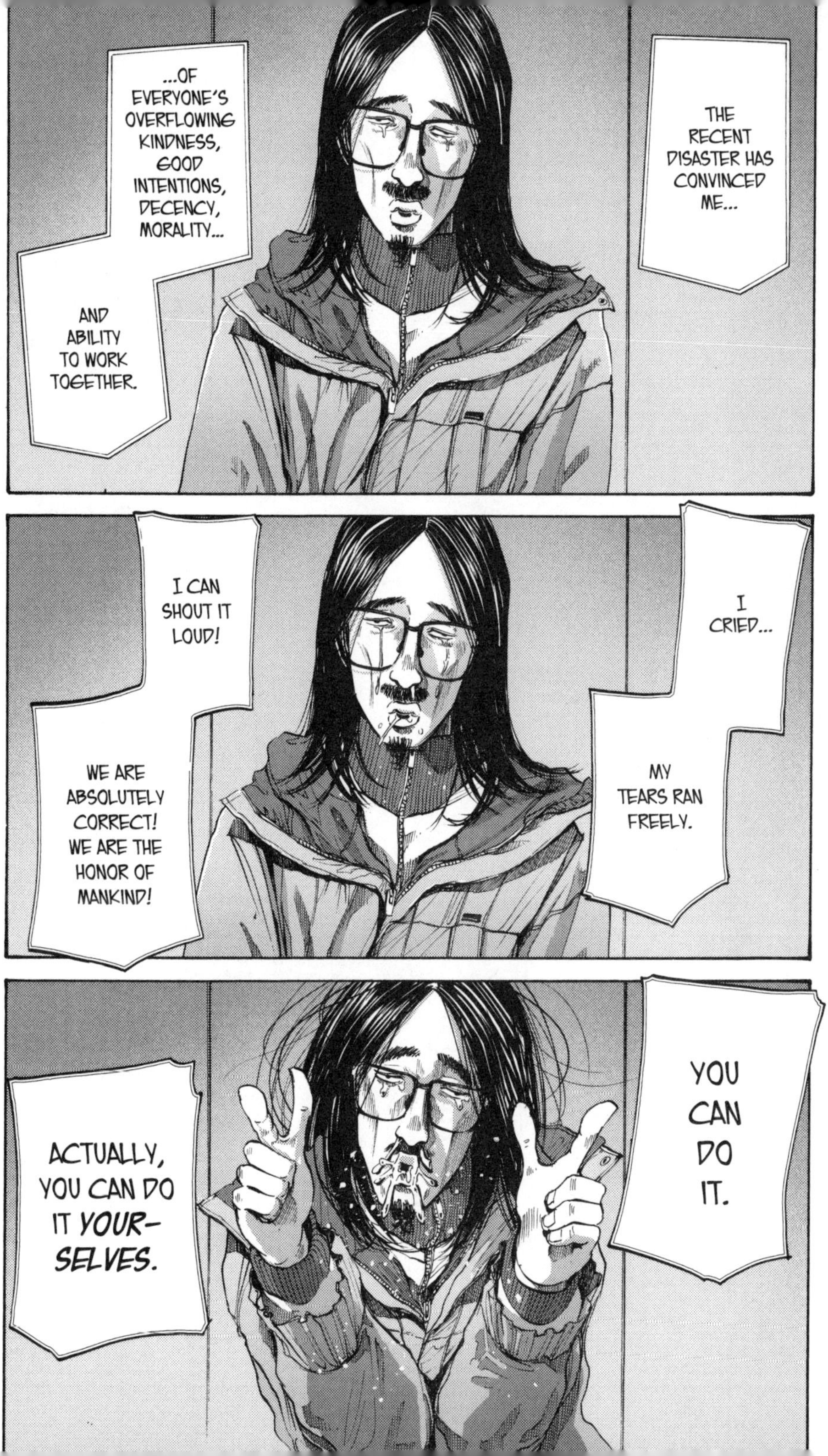
THE RECENT DISASTER HAS CONVINCED ME...
...OF EVERYONE'S OVERFLOWING KINDNESS, GOOD INTENTIONS, DECENCY, MORALITY...
AND ABILITY TO WORK TOGETHER.
I CRIED...
MY TEARS RAN FREELY.
I CAN SHOUT IT LOUD!
WE ARE ABSOLUTELY CORRECT! WE ARE THE HONOR OF MANKIND!
YOU CAN DO IT.
ACTUALLY, YOU CAN DO IT *YOURSELVES.*

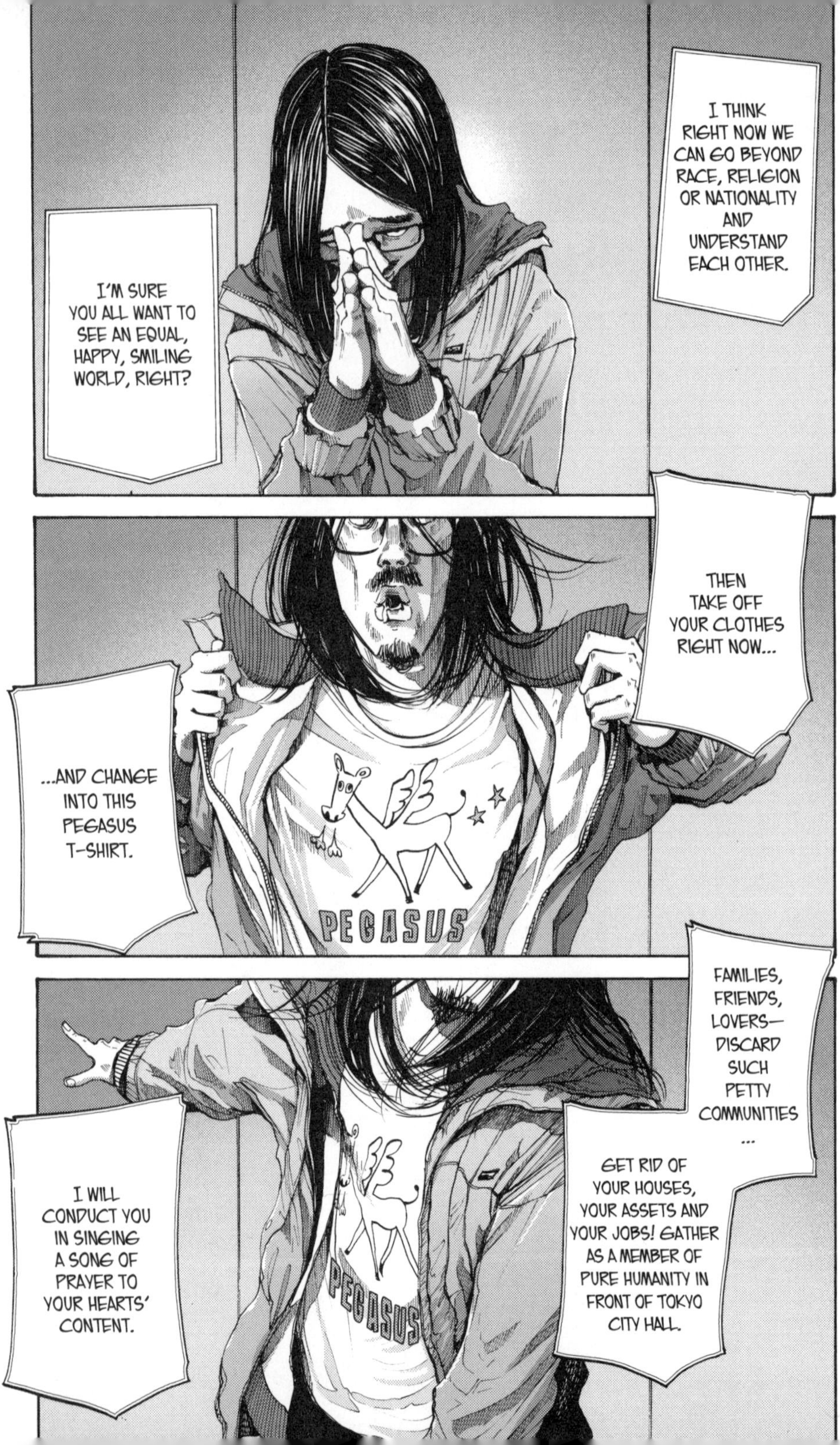
I THINK RIGHT NOW WE CAN GO BEYOND RACE, RELIGION OR NATIONALITY AND UNDERSTAND EACH OTHER.
I'M SURE YOU ALL WANT TO SEE AN EQUAL, HAPPY, SMILING WORLD, RIGHT?
THEN TAKE OFF YOUR CLOTHES RIGHT NOW...
...AND CHANGE INTO THIS PEGASUS T-SHIRT.
PEGASUS
FAMILIES, FRIENDS, LOVERS—DISCARD SUCH PETTY COMMUNITIES...
GET RID OF YOUR HOUSES, YOUR ASSETS AND YOUR JOBS! GATHER AS A MEMBER OF PURE HUMANITY IN FRONT OF TOKYO CITY HALL.
I WILL CONDUCT YOU IN SINGING A SONG OF PRAYER TO YOUR HEARTS' CONTENT.
PEGASUS

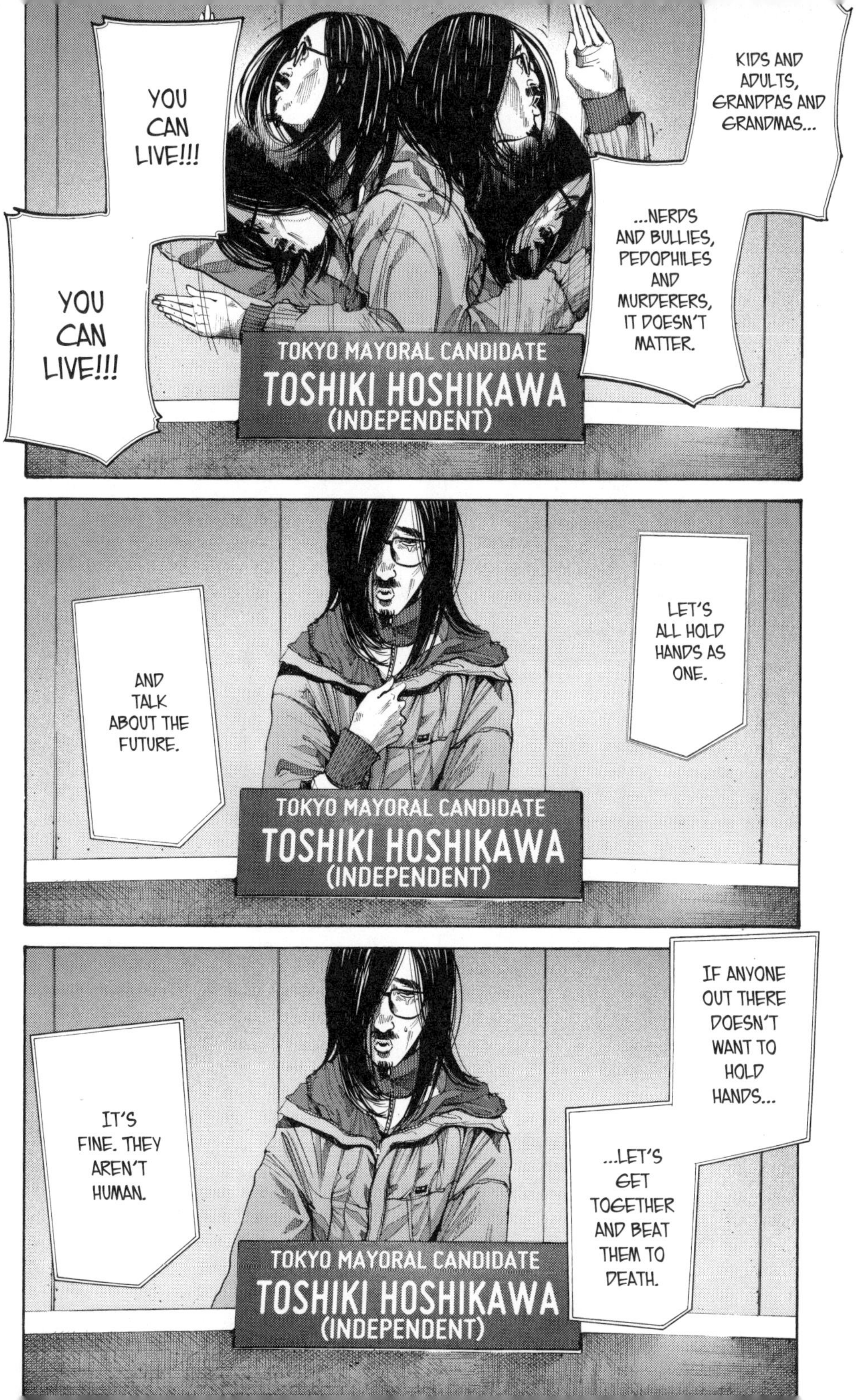
KIDS AND ADULTS, GRANDPAS AND GRANDMAS...
...NERDS AND BULLIES, PEDOPHILES AND MURDERERS, IT DOESN'T MATTER.
YOU CAN LIVE!!!
TOKYO MAYORAL CANDIDATE TOSHIKI HOSHIKAWA (INDEPENDENT)
YOU CAN LIVE!!!
LET'S ALL HOLD HANDS AS ONE.
TOKYO MAYORAL CANDIDATE TOSHIKI HOSHIKAWA (INDEPENDENT)
AND TALK ABOUT THE FUTURE.
IF ANYONE OUT THERE DOESN'T WANT TO HOLD HANDS...
...LET'S GET TOGETHER AND BEAT THEM TO DEATH.
TOKYO MAYORAL CANDIDATE TOSHIKI HOSHIKAWA (INDEPENDENT)
IT'S FINE. THEY AREN'T HUMAN.

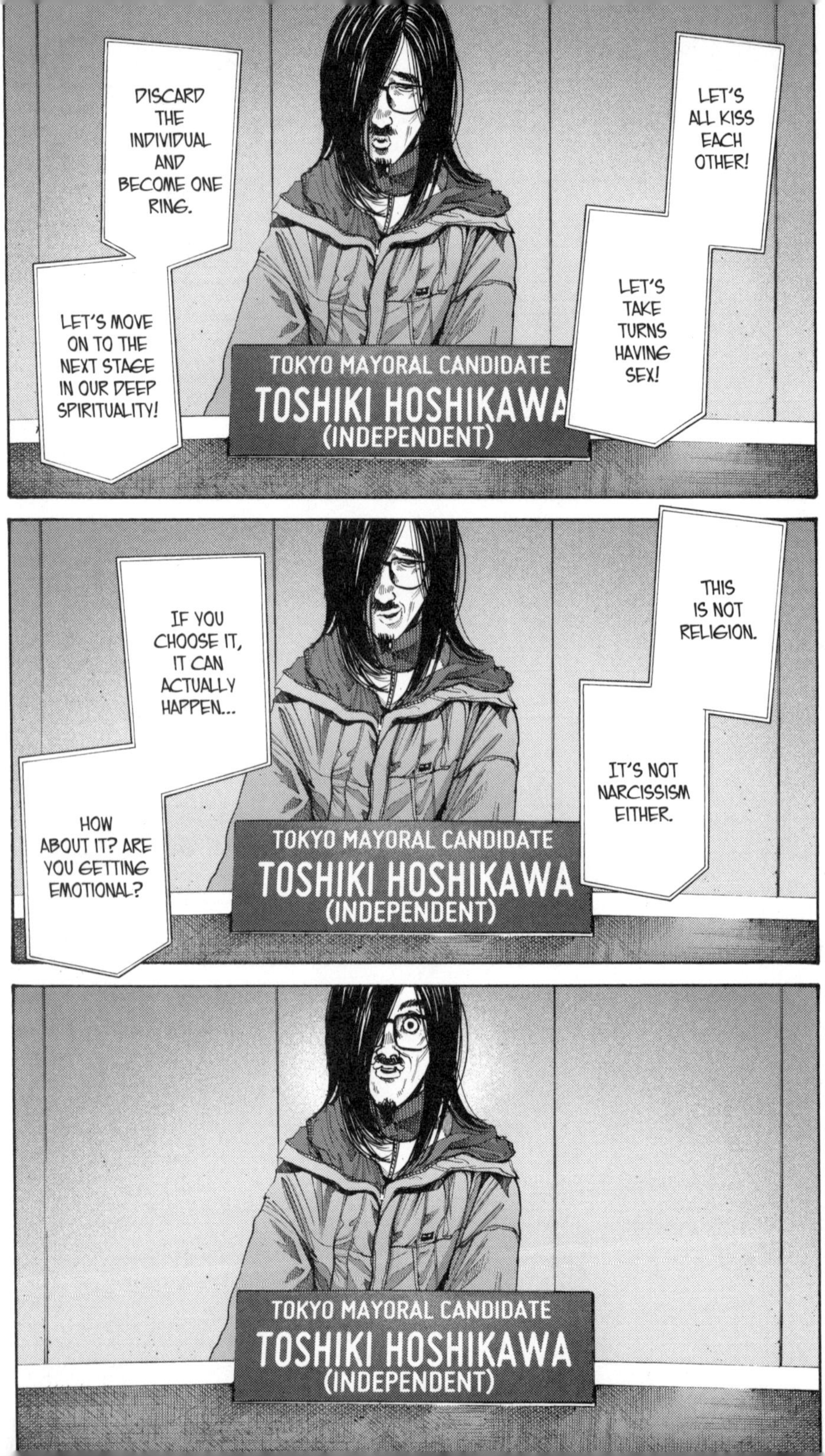
LET'S ALL KISS EACH OTHER!
DISCARD THE INDIVIDUAL AND BECOME ONE RING.
LET'S TAKE TURNS HAVING SEX!
LET'S MOVE ON TO THE NEXT STAGE IN OUR DEEP SPIRITUALITY!
TOKYO MAYORAL CANDIDATE
TOSHIKI HOSHIKAWA
(INDEPENDENT)
THIS IS NOT RELIGION.
IF YOU CHOOSE IT, IT CAN ACTUALLY HAPPEN...
IT'S NOT NARCISSISM EITHER.
HOW ABOUT IT? ARE YOU GETTING EMOTIONAL?
TOKYO MAYORAL CANDIDATE
TOSHIKI HOSHIKAWA
(INDEPENDENT)
TOKYO MAYORAL CANDIDATE
TOSHIKI HOSHIKAWA
(INDEPENDENT)

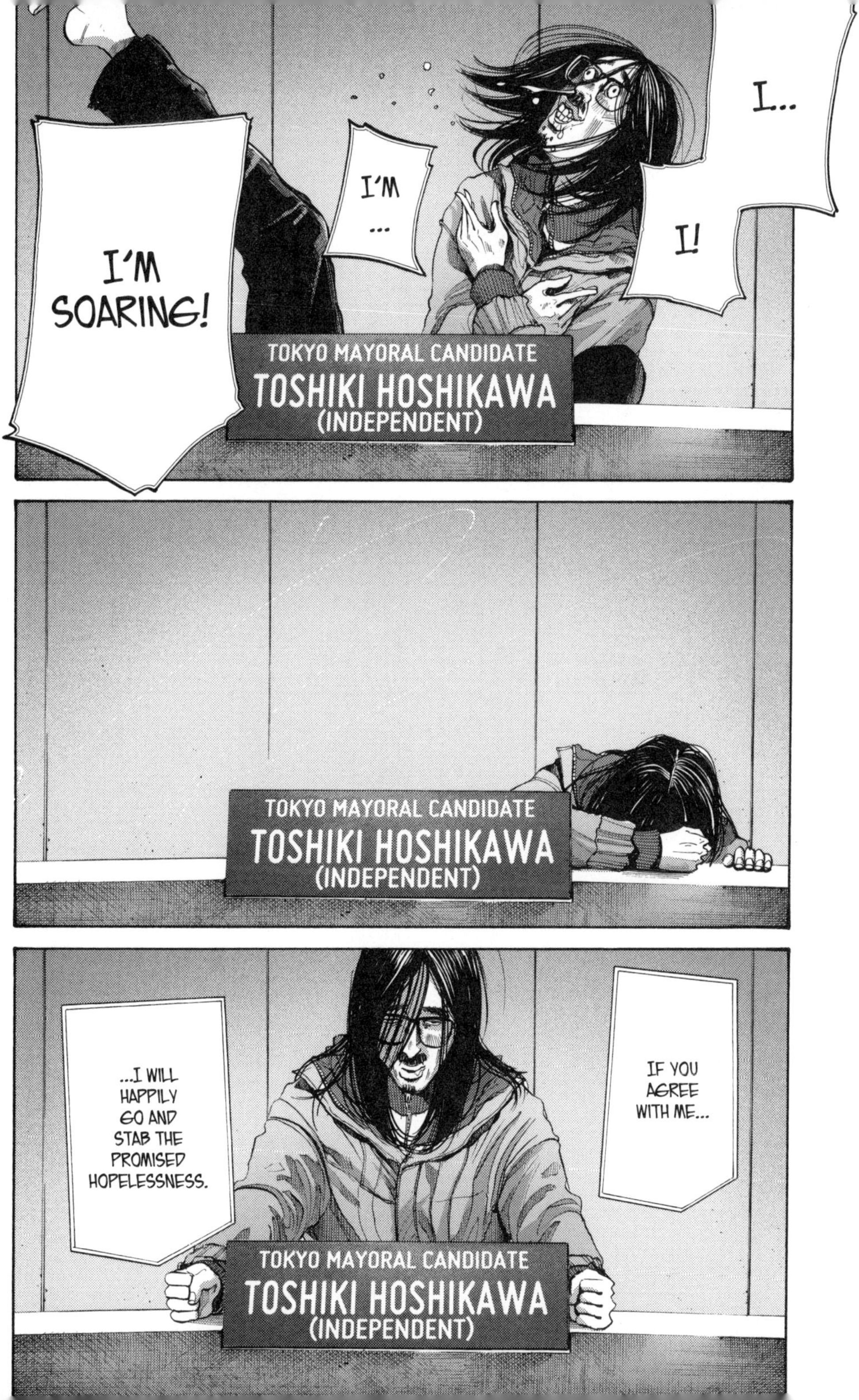
I... I!
I'M ...
I'M SOARING!
TOKYO MAYORAL CANDIDATE TOSHIKI HOSHIKAWA (INDEPENDENT)
TOKYO MAYORAL CANDIDATE TOSHIKI HOSHIKAWA (INDEPENDENT)
IF YOU AGREE WITH ME...
...I WILL HAPPILY GO AND STAB THE PROMISED HOPELESSNESS.
TOKYO MAYORAL CANDIDATE TOSHIKI HOSHIKAWA (INDEPENDENT)

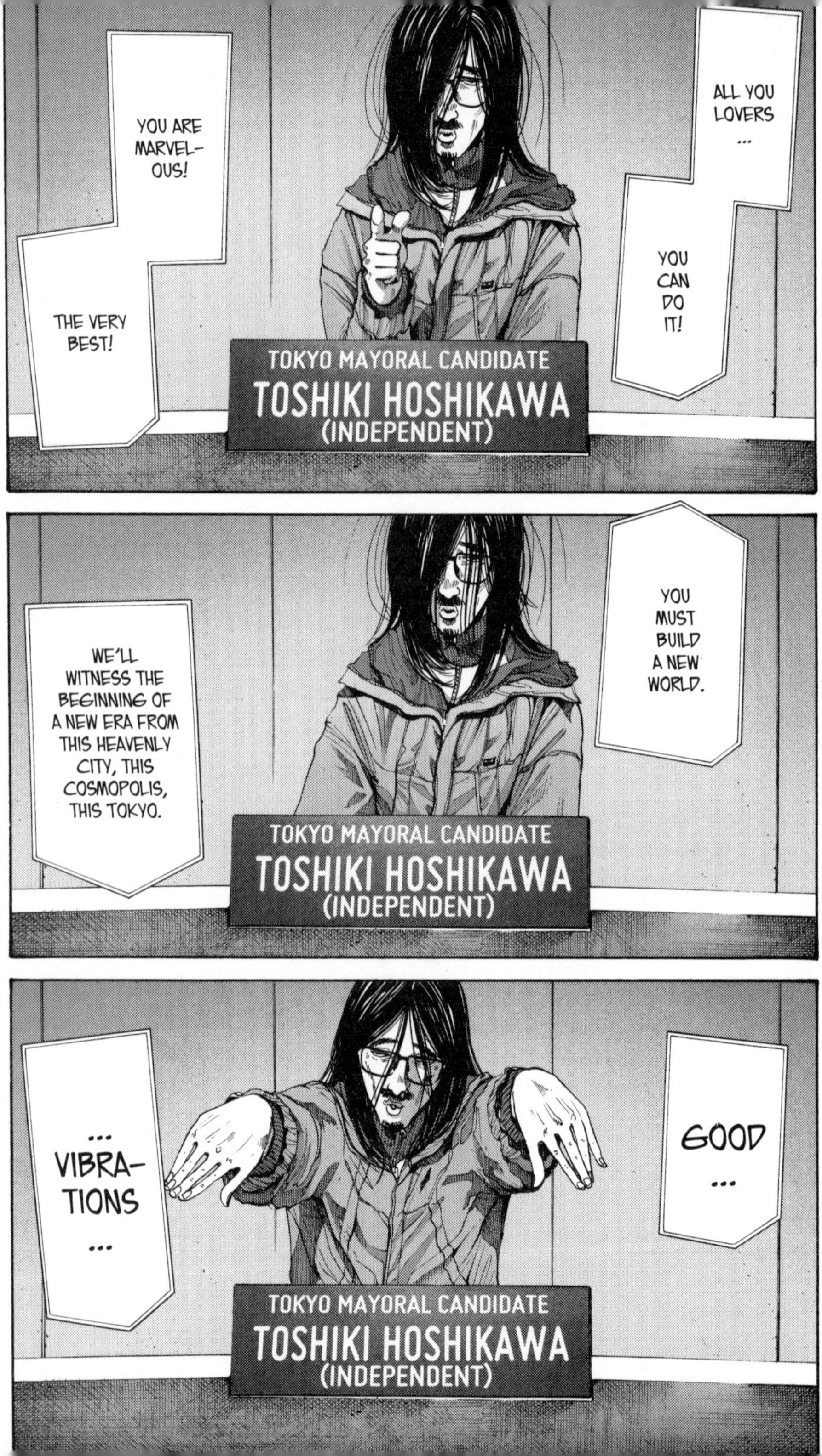
ALL YOU LOVERS ... YOU CAN DO IT!
YOU ARE MARVELOUS! THE VERY BEST!
TOKYO MAYORAL CANDIDATE
TOSHIKI HOSHIKAWA
(INDEPENDENT)
YOU MUST BUILD A NEW WORLD.
WE'LL WITNESS THE BEGINNING OF A NEW ERA FROM THIS HEAVENLY CITY, THIS COSMOPOLIS, THIS TOKYO.
TOKYO MAYORAL CANDIDATE
TOSHIKI HOSHIKAWA
(INDEPENDENT)
GOOD ...
... VIBRATIONS ...
TOKYO MAYORAL CANDIDATE
TOSHIKI HOSHIKAWA
(INDEPENDENT)

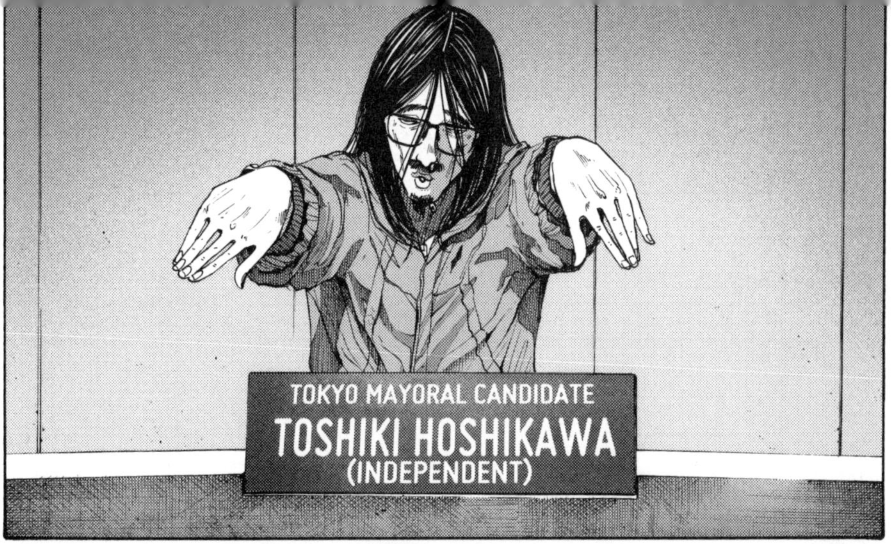
TOKYO MAYORAL CANDIDATE
TOSHIKI HOSHIKAWA
(INDEPENDENT)
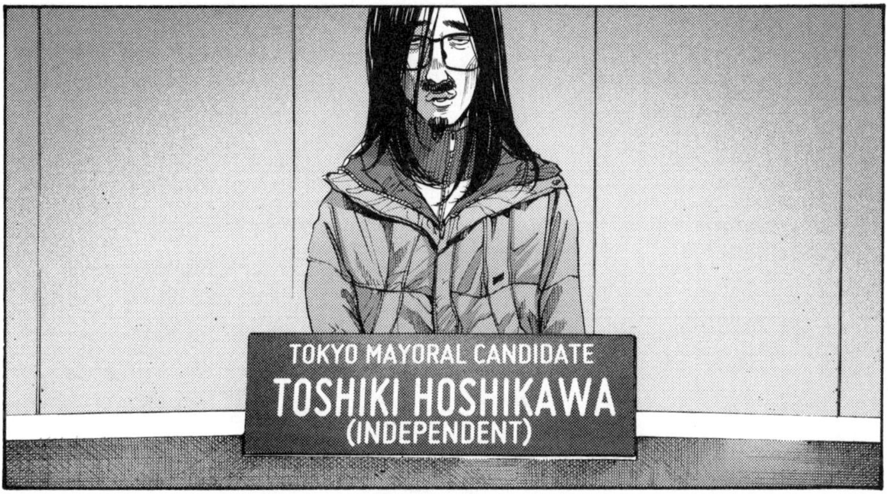
TOKYO MAYORAL CANDIDATE
TOSHIKI HOSHIKAWA
(INDEPENDENT)
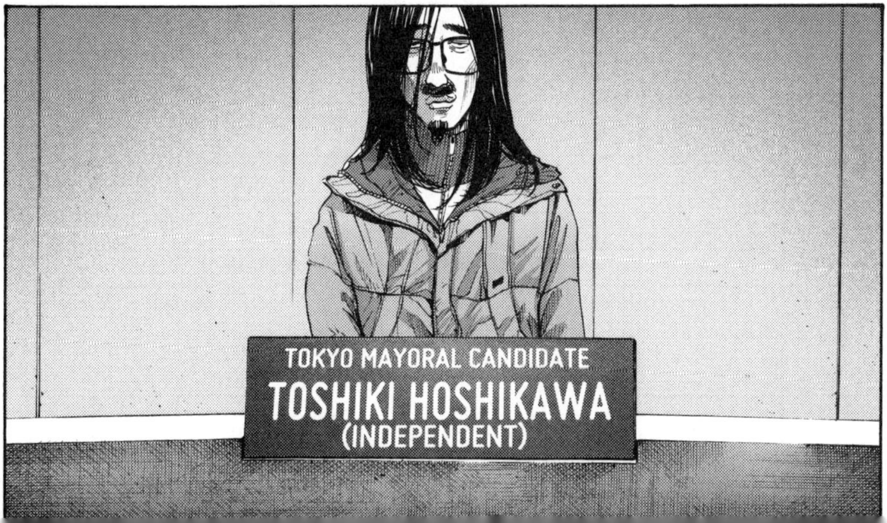
TOKYO MAYORAL CANDIDATE
TOSHIKI HOSHIKAWA
(INDEPENDENT)

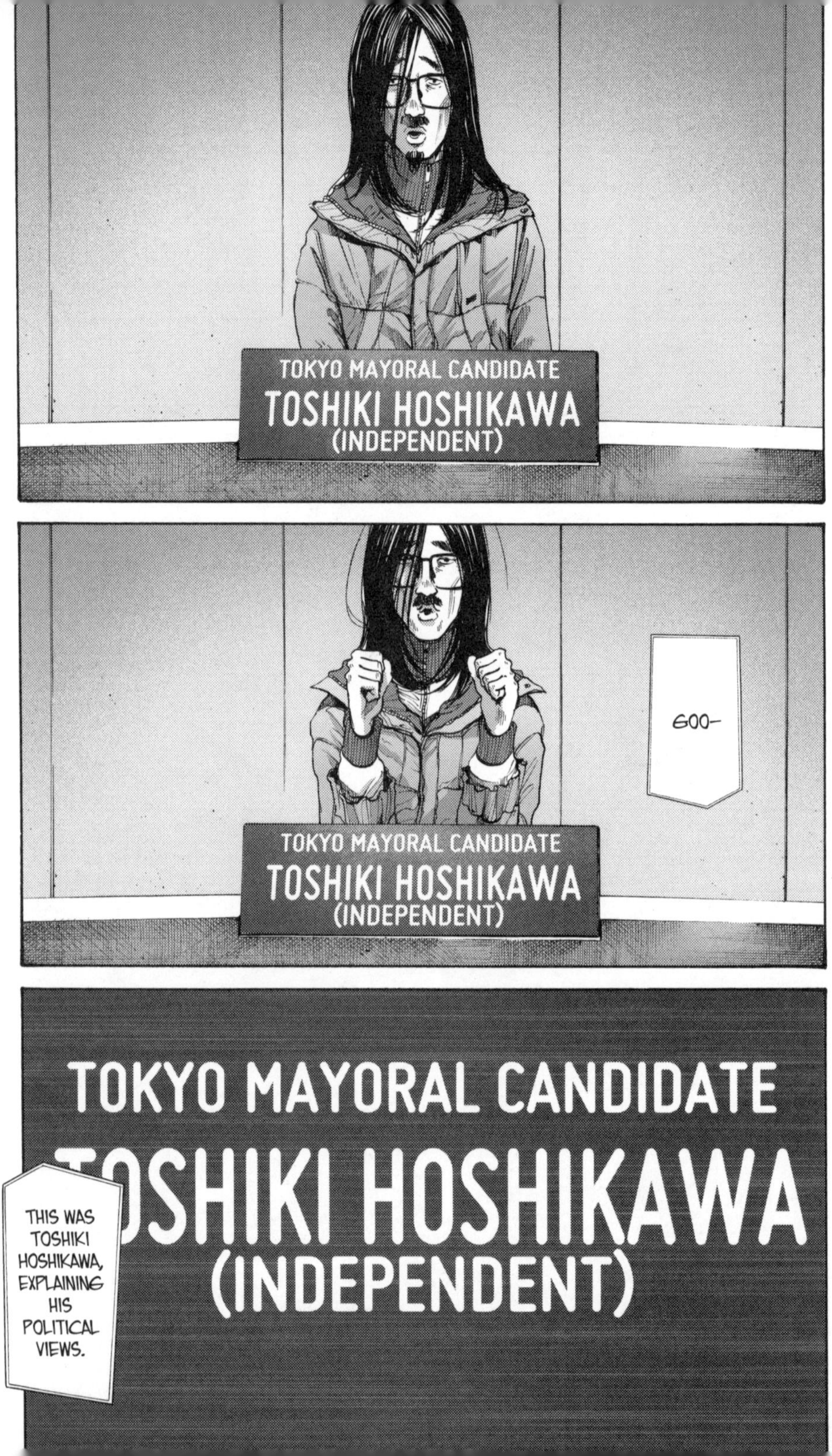
TOKYO MAYORAL CANDIDATE
TOSHIKI HOSHIKAWA
(INDEPENDENT)
GOO-
TOKYO MAYORAL CANDIDATE
TOSHIKI HOSHIKAWA
(INDEPENDENT)
TOKYO MAYORAL CANDIDATE
TOSHIKI HOSHIKAWA
(INDEPENDENT)
THIS WAS TOSHIKI HOSHIKAWA, EXPLAINING HIS POLITICAL VIEWS.

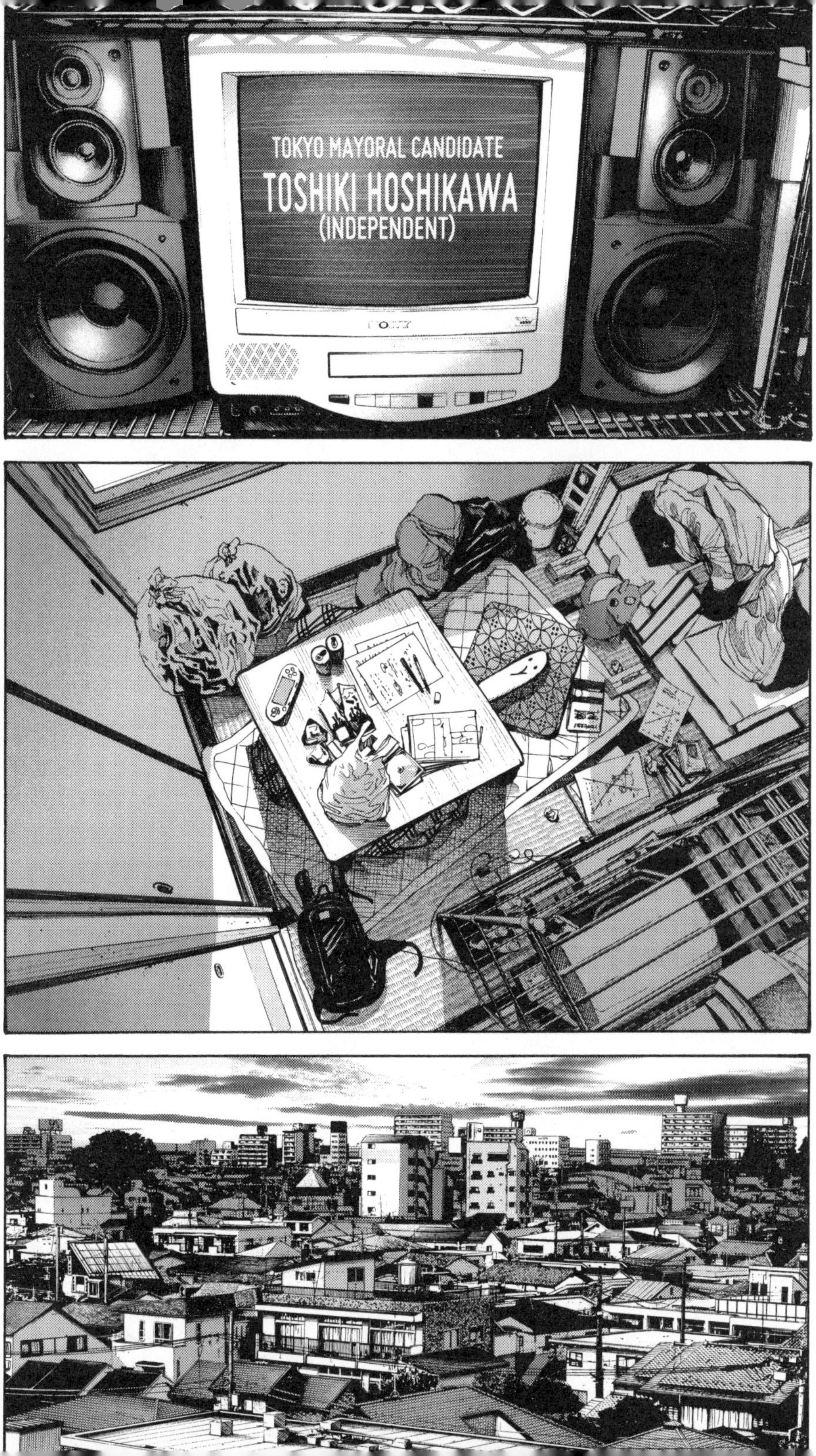
TOKYO MAYORAL CANDIDATE
TOSHIKI HOSHIKAWA
(INDEPENDENT)

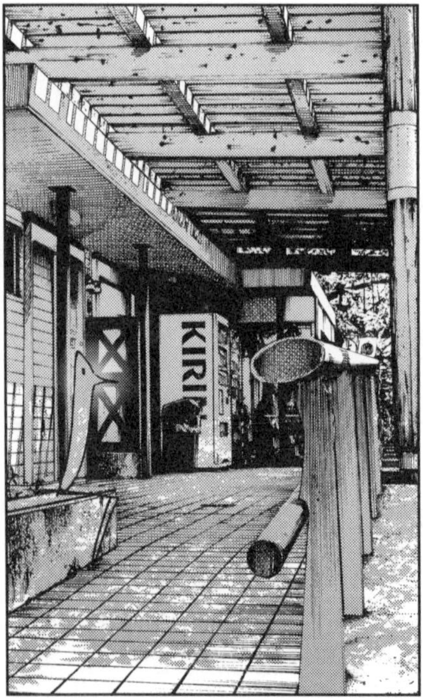
KIRI

Chapter 93

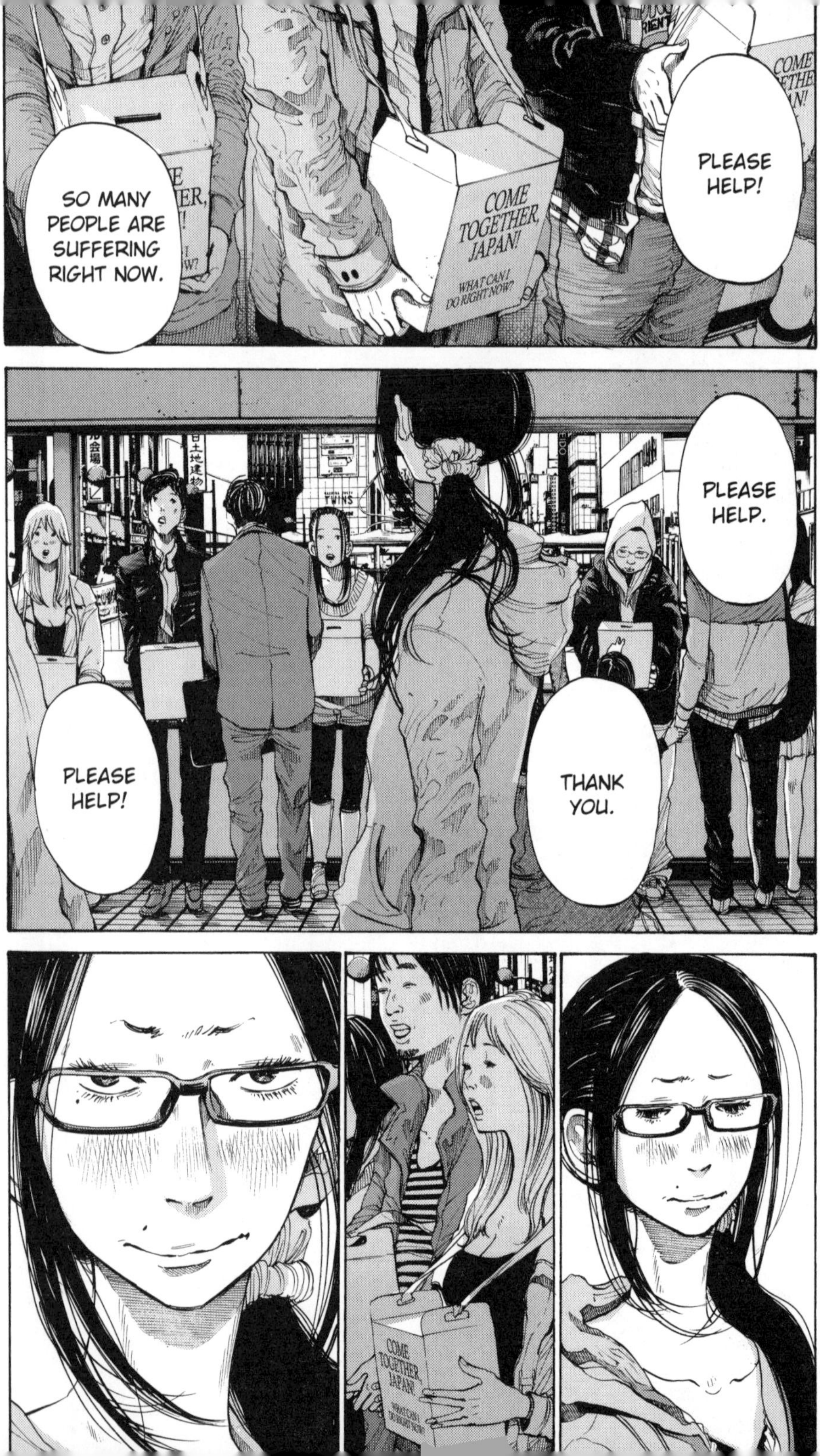
PLEASE HELP!
SO MANY PEOPLE ARE SUFFERING RIGHT NOW.
COME TOGETHER, JAPAN!
WHAT CAN I DO RIGHT NOW?
PLEASE HELP.
THANK YOU.
PLEASE HELP!
COME TOGETHER, JAPAN!

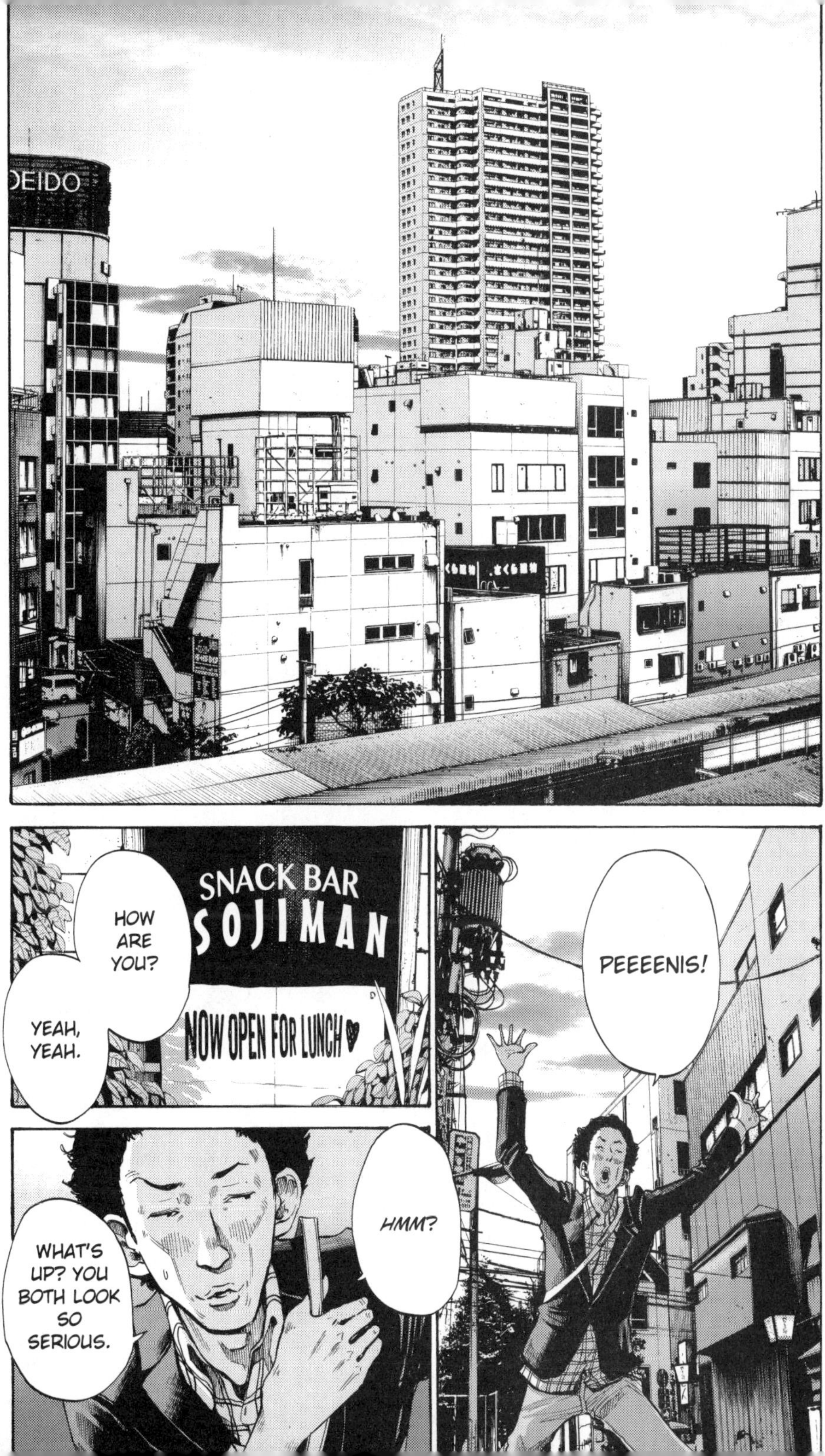
DEIDO
PEEEENIS!
SNACK BAR SOJIMAN
NOW OPEN FOR LUNCH
HOW ARE YOU?
YEAH, YEAH.
HMM?
WHAT'S UP? YOU BOTH LOOK SO SERIOUS.

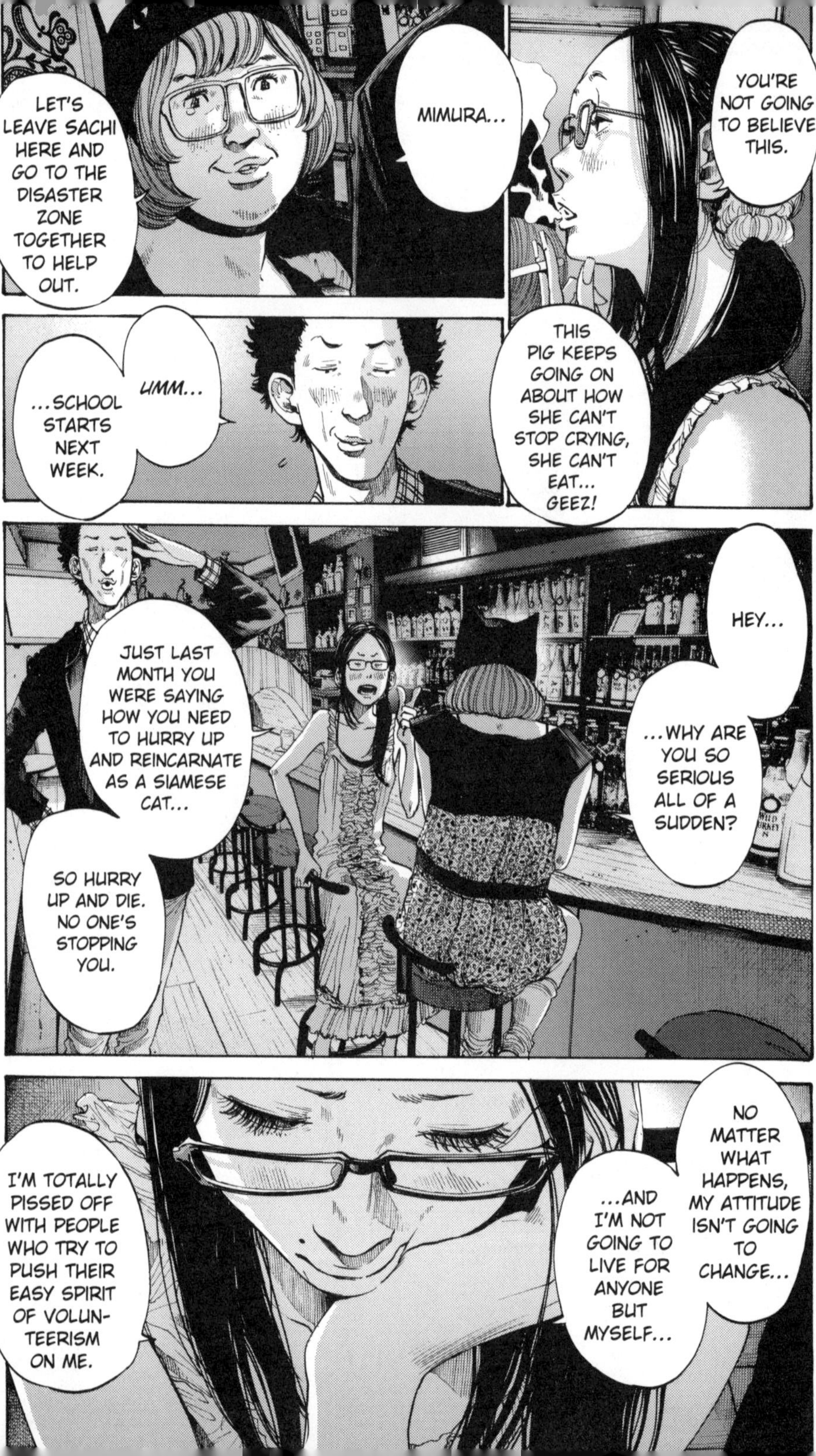
YOU'RE NOT GOING TO BELIEVE THIS.
THIS PIG KEEPS GOING ON ABOUT HOW SHE CAN'T STOP CRYING, SHE CAN'T EAT... GEEZ!
MIMURA...
LET'S LEAVE SACHI HERE AND GO TO THE DISASTER ZONE TOGETHER TO HELP OUT.
UMM...
...SCHOOL STARTS NEXT WEEK.
HEY...
...WHY ARE YOU SO SERIOUS ALL OF A SUDDEN?
JUST LAST MONTH YOU WERE SAYING HOW YOU NEED TO HURRY UP AND REINCARNATE AS A SIAMESE CAT...
SO HURRY UP AND DIE. NO ONE'S STOPPING YOU.
NO MATTER WHAT HAPPENS, MY ATTITUDE ISN'T GOING TO CHANGE...
...AND I'M NOT GOING TO LIVE FOR ANYONE BUT MYSELF...
I'M TOTALLY PISSED OFF WITH PEOPLE WHO TRY TO PUSH THEIR EASY SPIRIT OF VOLUN-TEERISM ON ME.

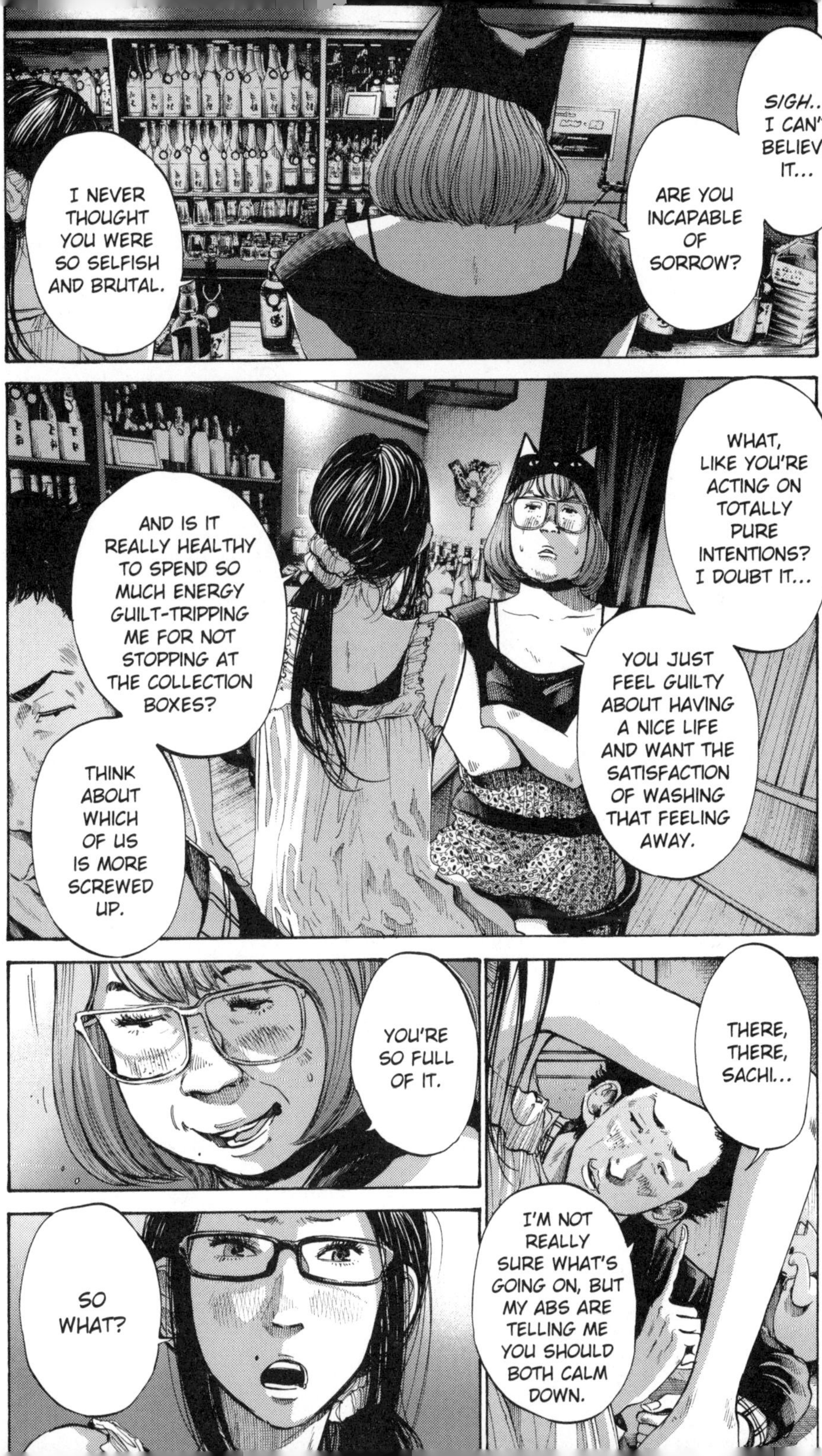
SIGH... I CAN'T BELIEVE IT...
ARE YOU INCAPABLE OF SORROW?
I NEVER THOUGHT YOU WERE SO SELFISH AND BRUTAL.
WHAT, LIKE YOU'RE ACTING ON TOTALLY PURE INTENTIONS? I DOUBT IT...
YOU JUST FEEL GUILTY ABOUT HAVING A NICE LIFE AND WANT THE SATISFACTION OF WASHING THAT FEELING AWAY.
AND IS IT REALLY HEALTHY TO SPEND SO MUCH ENERGY GUILT-TRIPPING ME FOR NOT STOPPING AT THE COLLECTION BOXES?
THINK ABOUT WHICH OF US IS MORE SCREWED UP.
THERE, THERE, SACHI...
I'M NOT REALLY SURE WHAT'S GOING ON, BUT MY ABS ARE TELLING ME YOU SHOULD BOTH CALM DOWN.
YOU'RE SO FULL OF IT.
SO WHAT?

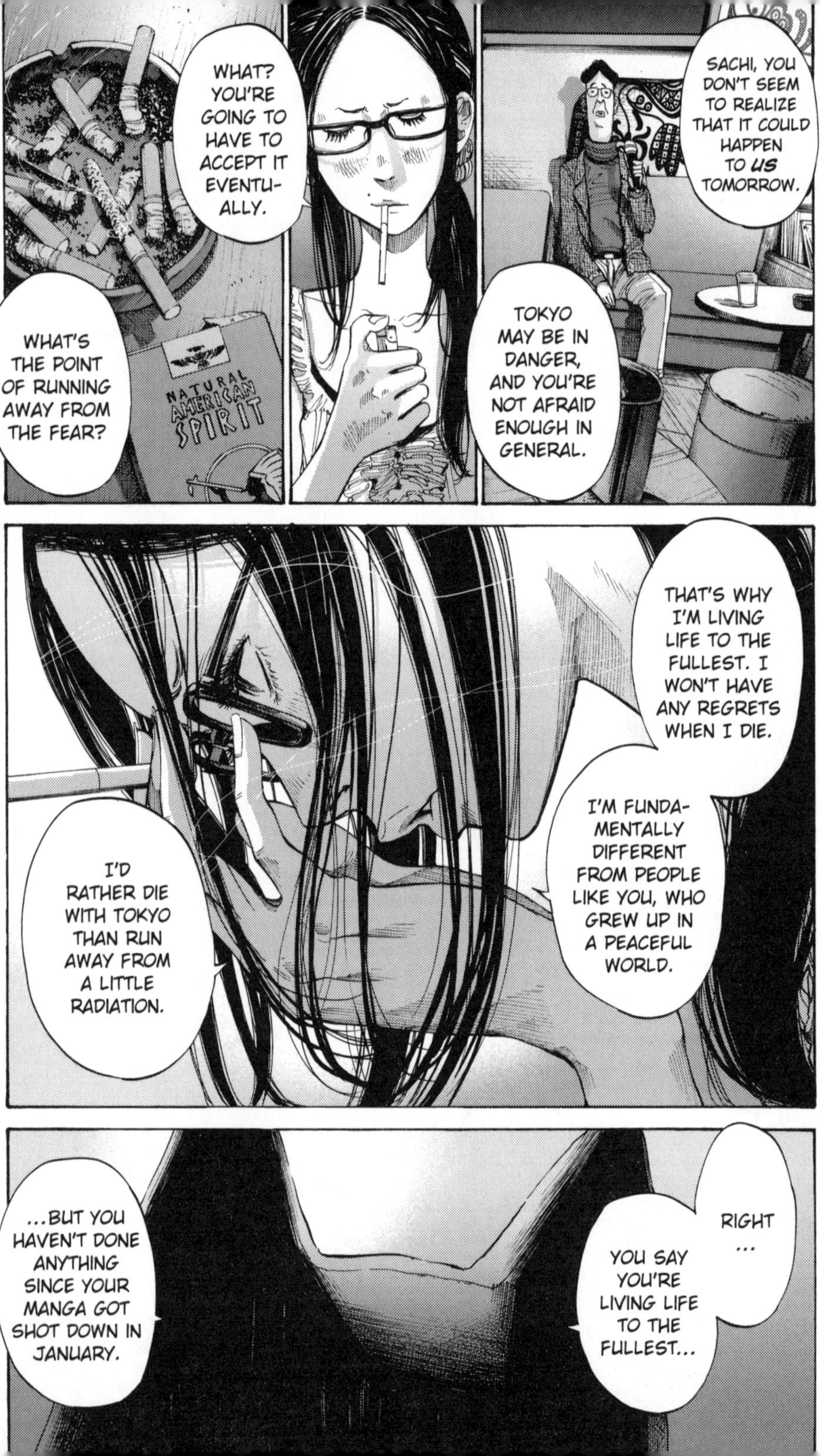
SACHI, YOU DON'T SEEM TO REALIZE THAT IT COULD HAPPEN TO *US* TOMORROW.
TOKYO MAY BE IN DANGER, AND YOU'RE NOT AFRAID ENOUGH IN GENERAL.
WHAT? YOU'RE GOING TO HAVE TO ACCEPT IT EVENTU-ALLY.
WHAT'S THE POINT OF RUNNING AWAY FROM THE FEAR?
NATURAL AMERICAN SPIRIT
THAT'S WHY I'M LIVING LIFE TO THE FULLEST. I WON'T HAVE ANY REGRETS WHEN I DIE.
I'M FUNDA-MENTALLY DIFFERENT FROM PEOPLE LIKE YOU, WHO GREW UP IN A PEACEFUL WORLD.
I'D RATHER DIE WITH TOKYO THAN RUN AWAY FROM A LITTLE RADIATION.
RIGHT ...
YOU SAY YOU'RE LIVING LIFE TO THE FULLEST...
...BUT YOU HAVEN'T DONE ANYTHING SINCE YOUR MANGA GOT SHOT DOWN IN JANUARY.

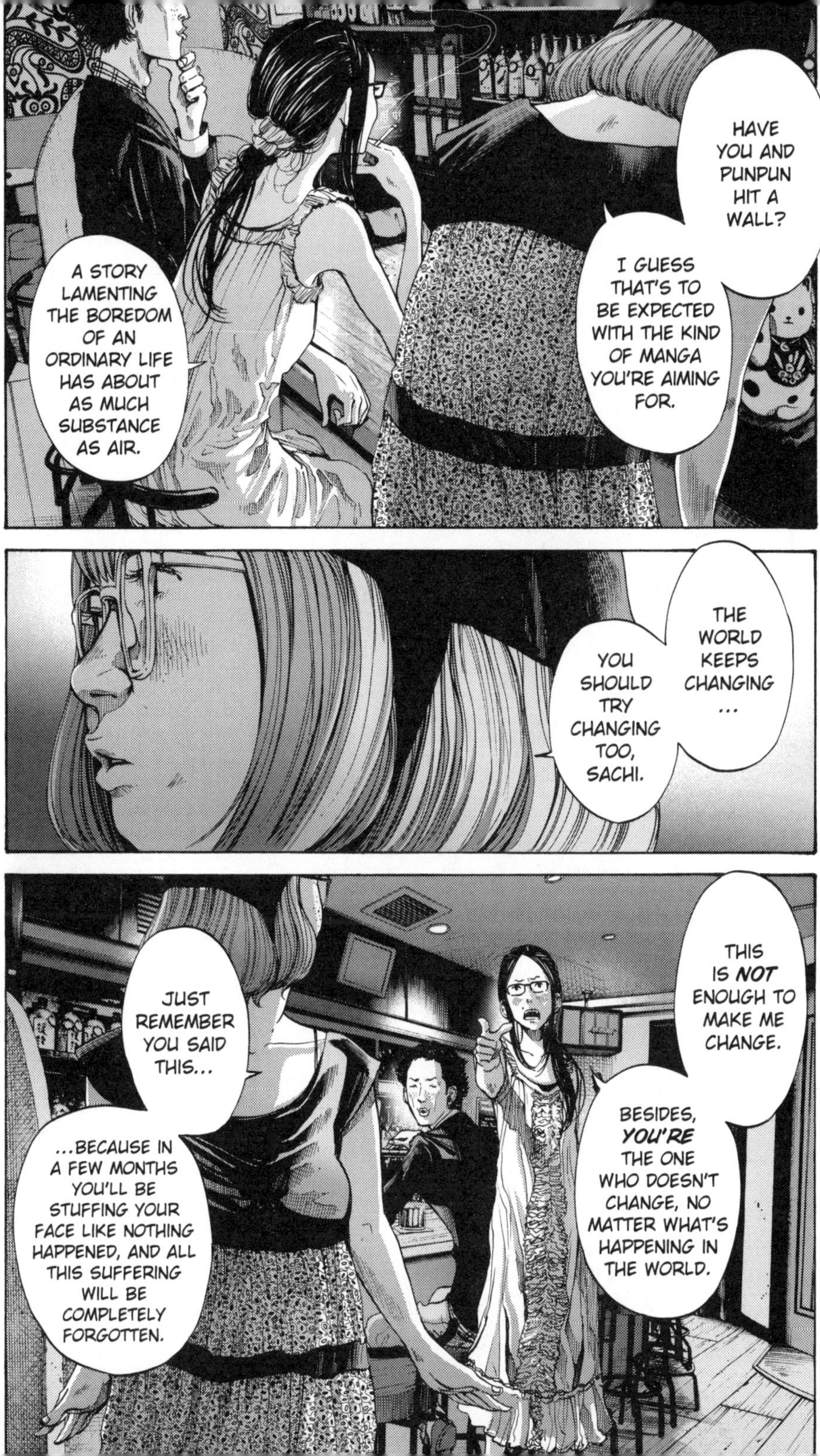
HAVE YOU AND PUNPUN HIT A WALL?
I GUESS THAT'S TO BE EXPECTED WITH THE KIND OF MANGA YOU'RE AIMING FOR.
A STORY LAMENTING THE BOREDOM OF AN ORDINARY LIFE HAS ABOUT AS MUCH SUBSTANCE AS AIR.
THE WORLD KEEPS CHANGING...
YOU SHOULD TRY CHANGING TOO, SACHI.
THIS IS **NOT** ENOUGH TO MAKE ME CHANGE.
BESIDES, ***YOU'RE*** THE ONE WHO DOESN'T CHANGE, NO MATTER WHAT'S HAPPENING IN THE WORLD.
JUST REMEMBER YOU SAID THIS...
...BECAUSE IN A FEW MONTHS YOU'LL BE STUFFING YOUR FACE LIKE NOTHING HAPPENED, AND ALL THIS SUFFERING WILL BE COMPLETELY FORGOTTEN.

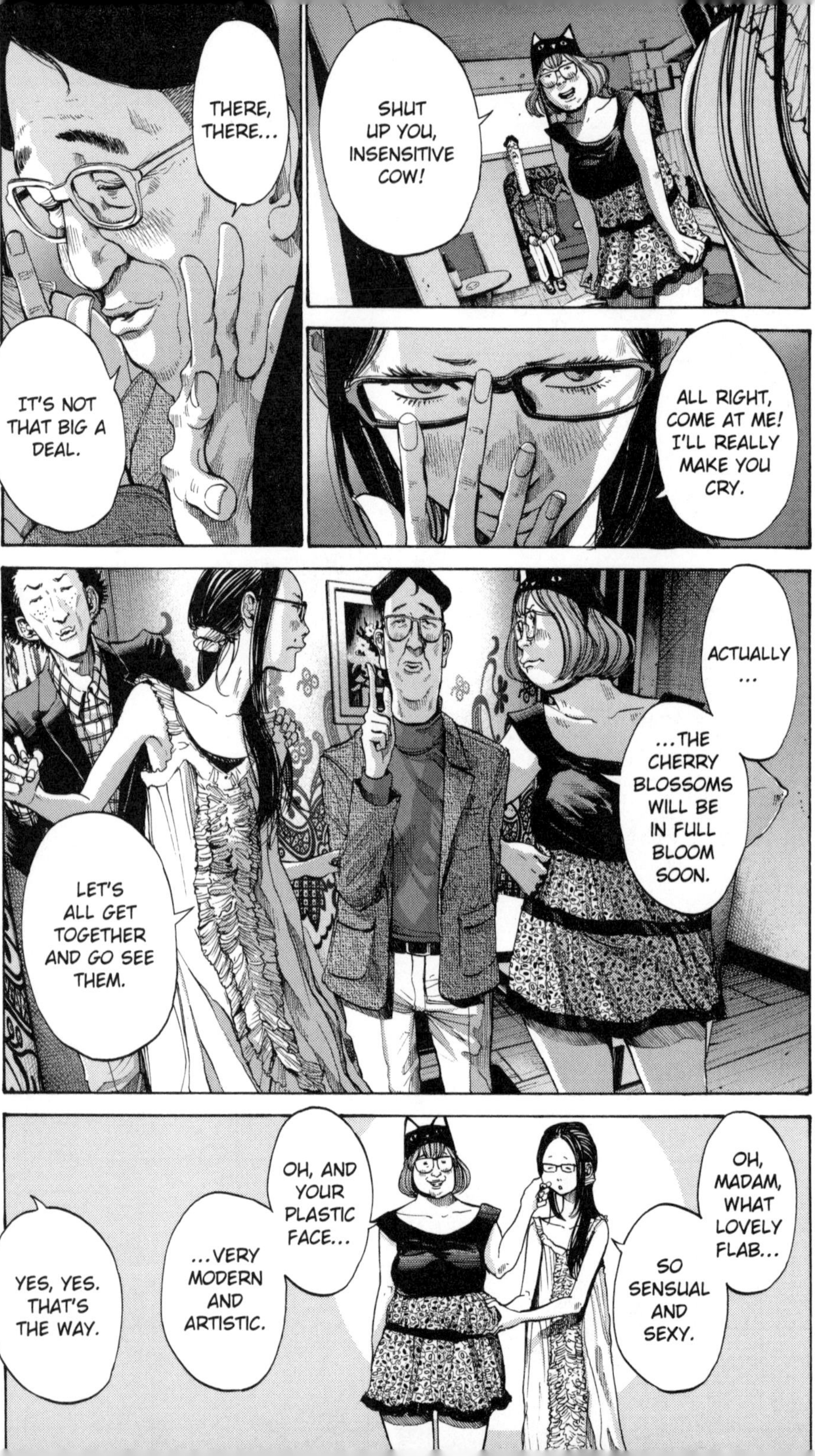
SHUT UP YOU, INSENSITIVE COW!
ALL RIGHT, COME AT ME! I'LL REALLY MAKE YOU CRY.
THERE, THERE...
IT'S NOT THAT BIG A DEAL.
ACTUALLY...
...THE CHERRY BLOSSOMS WILL BE IN FULL BLOOM SOON.
LET'S ALL GET TOGETHER AND GO SEE THEM.
OH, MADAM, WHAT LOVELY FLAB...
SO SENSUAL AND SEXY.
OH, AND YOUR PLASTIC FACE...
...VERY MODERN AND ARTISTIC.
YES, YES. THAT'S THE WAY.

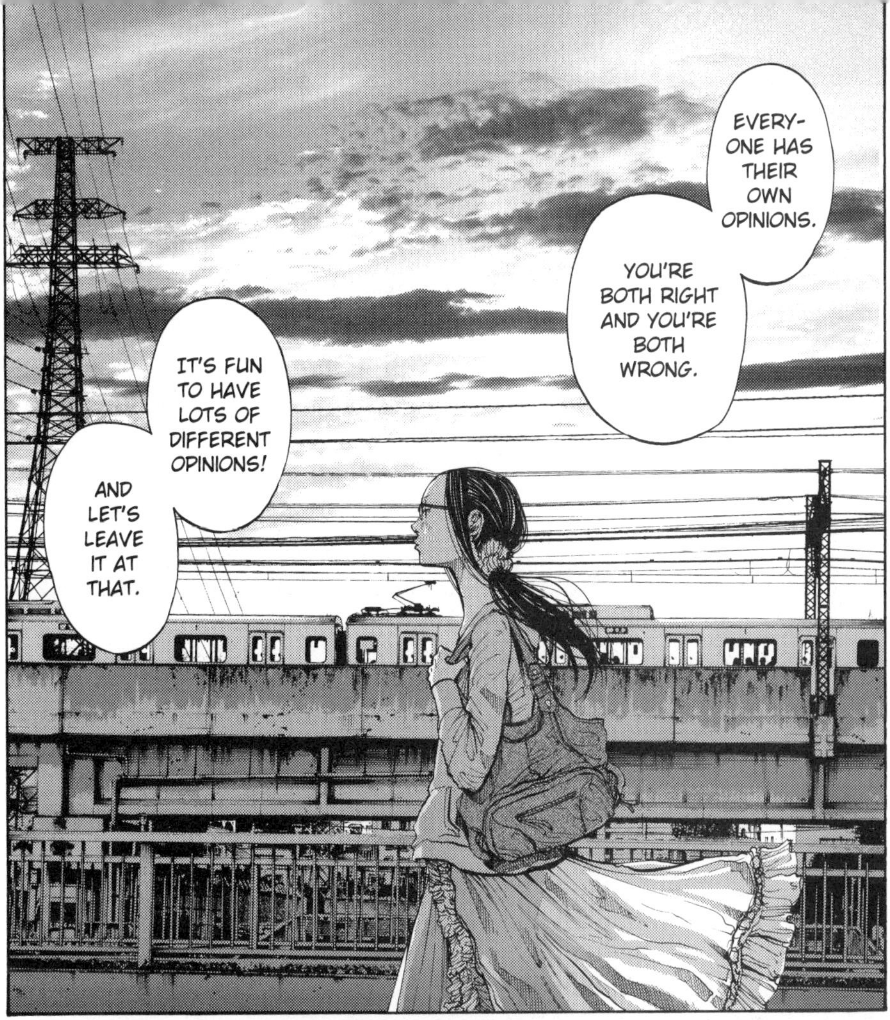
EVERY-ONE HAS THEIR OWN OPINIONS.
YOU'RE BOTH RIGHT AND YOU'RE BOTH WRONG.
IT'S FUN TO HAVE LOTS OF DIFFERENT OPINIONS!
AND LET'S LEAVE IT AT THAT.

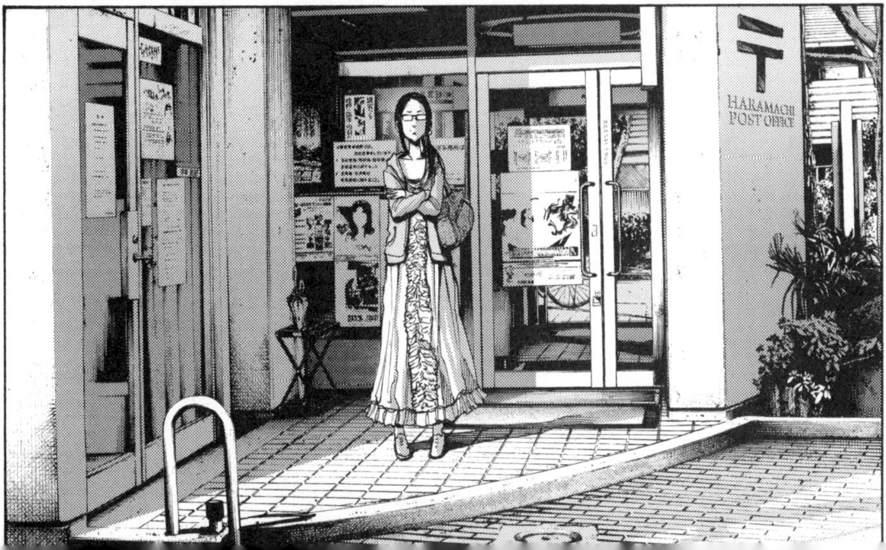
HARAMACHI POST OFFICE

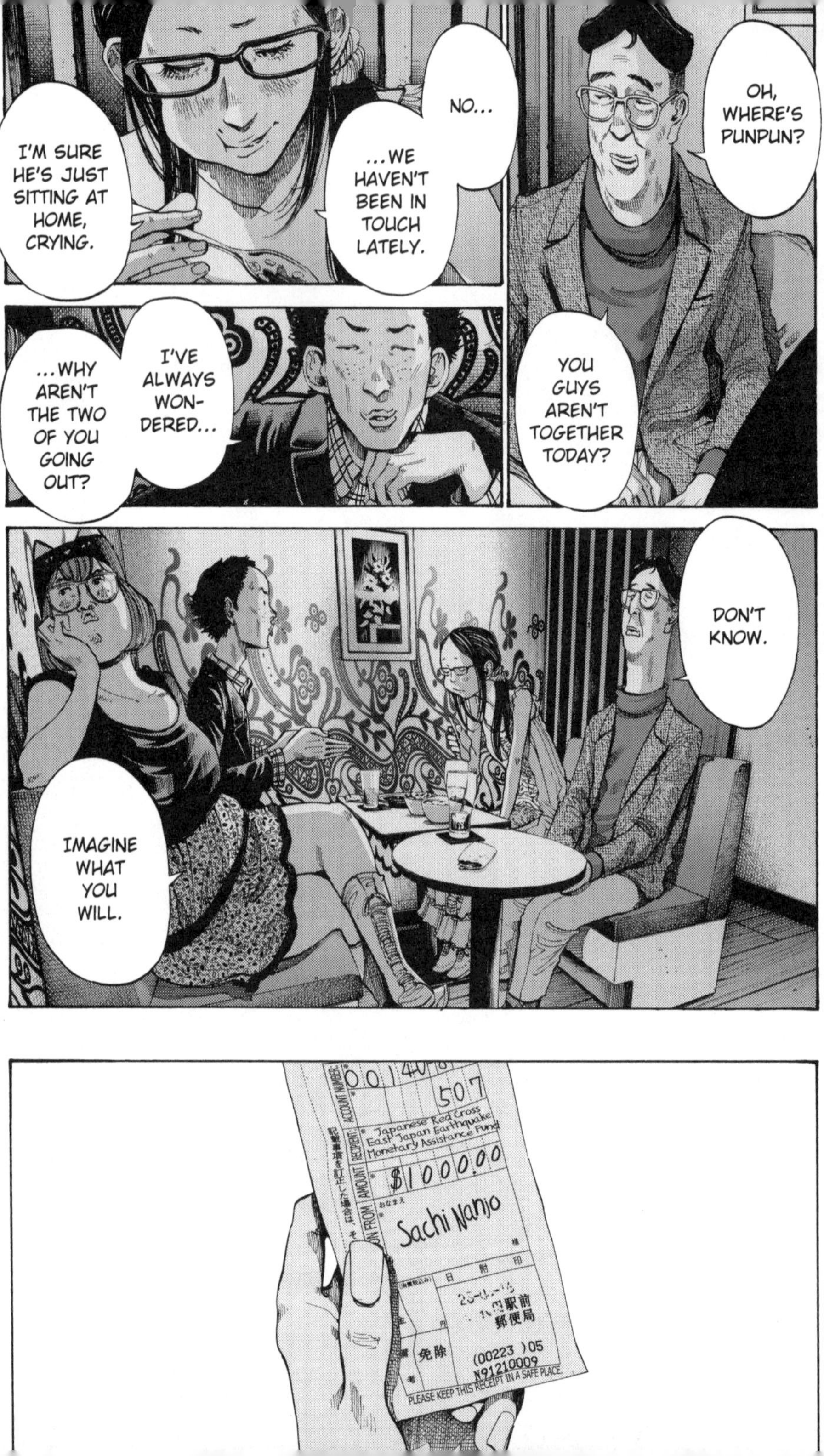
OH, WHERE'S PUNPUN?
YOU GUYS AREN'T TOGETHER TODAY?
NO...
...WE HAVEN'T BEEN IN TOUCH LATELY.
I'M SURE HE'S JUST SITTING AT HOME, CRYING.
I'VE ALWAYS WONDERED...
...WHY AREN'T THE TWO OF YOU GOING OUT?
DON'T KNOW.
IMAGINE WHAT YOU WILL.
ACCOUNT NUMBER:
507
RECIPIENT:
Japanese Red Cross East Japan Earthquake Monetary Assistance Fund
AMOUNT
$1000.00
FROM
Sachi Nanjo
郵便局
免除
(00223)05
N91210009
PLEASE KEEP THIS RECEIPT IN A SAFE PLACE.

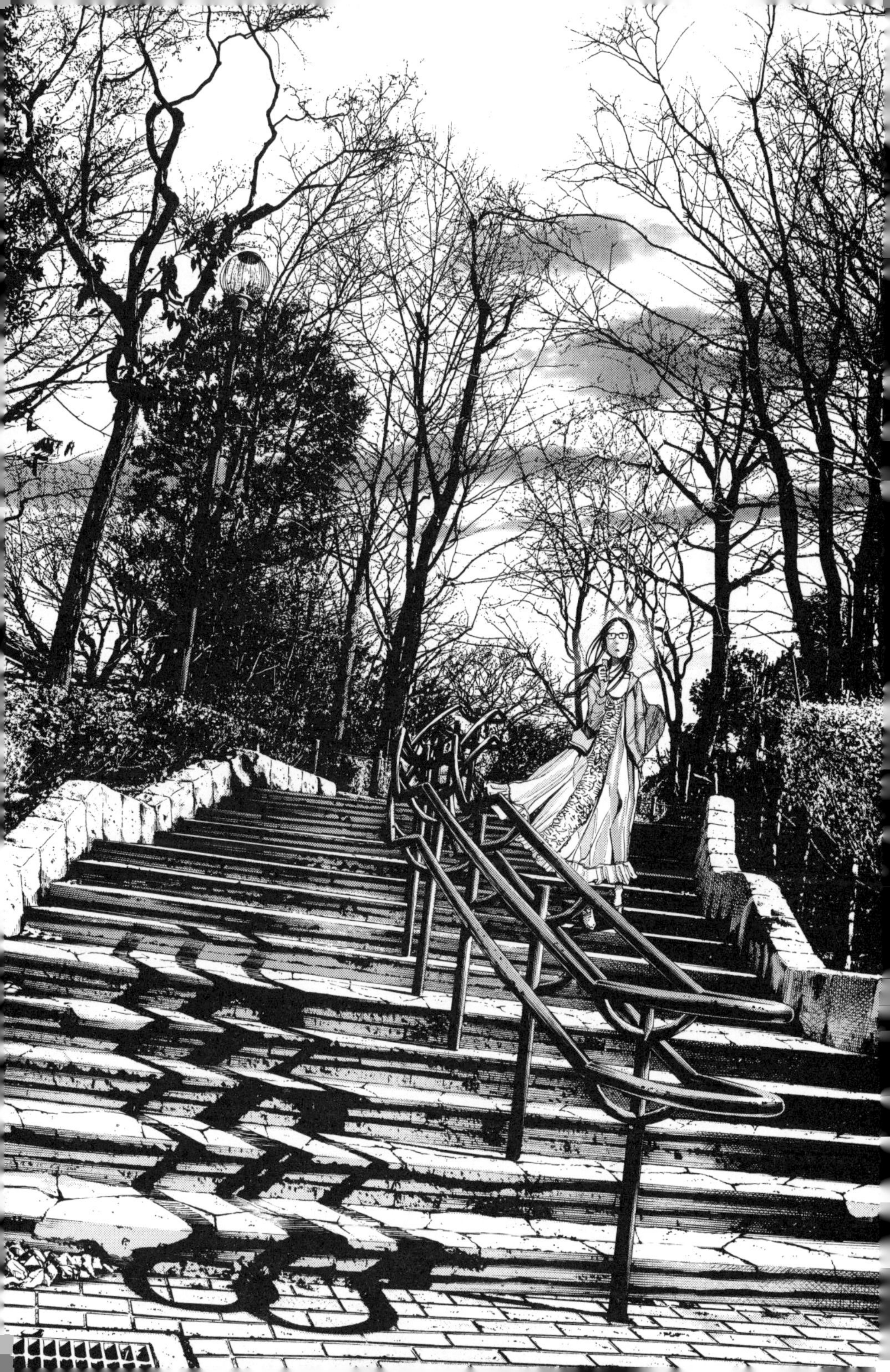

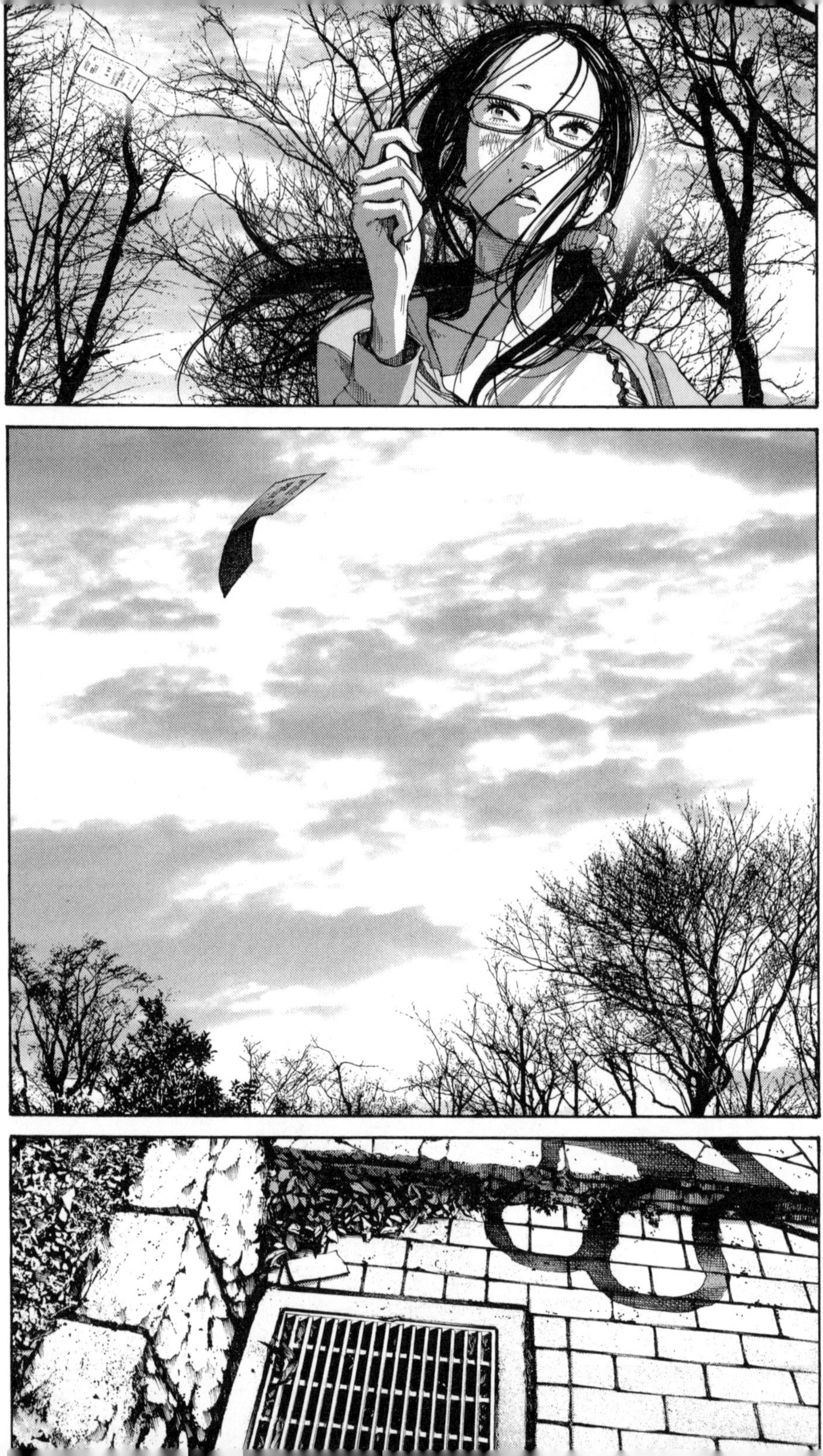

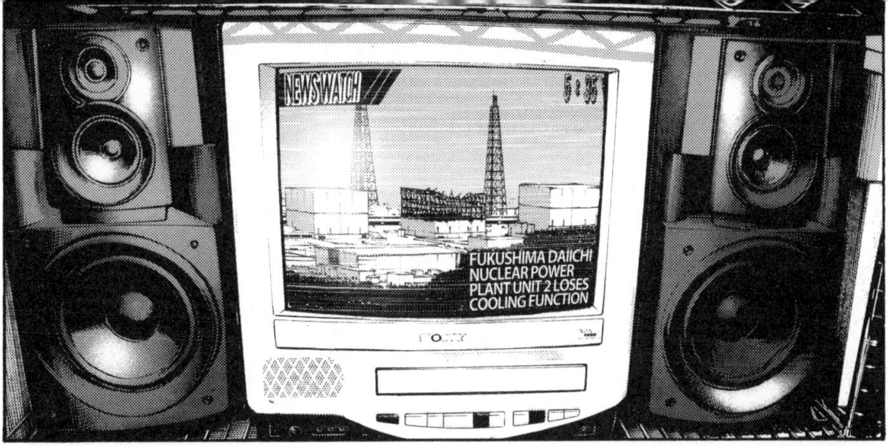
NEWSWATCH
FUKUSHIMA DAIICHI NUCLEAR POWER PLANT UNIT 2 LOSES COOLING FUNCTION

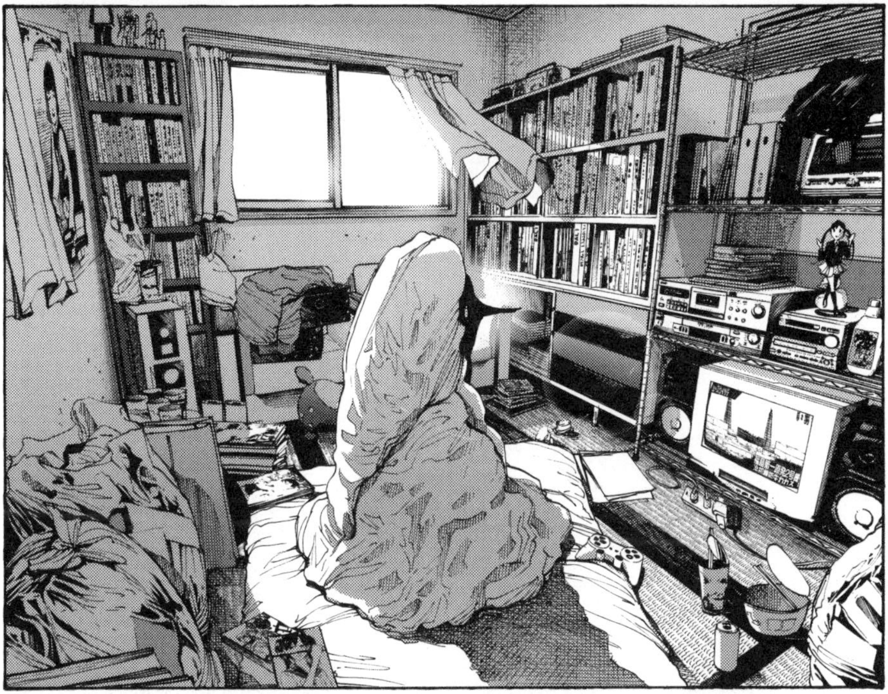

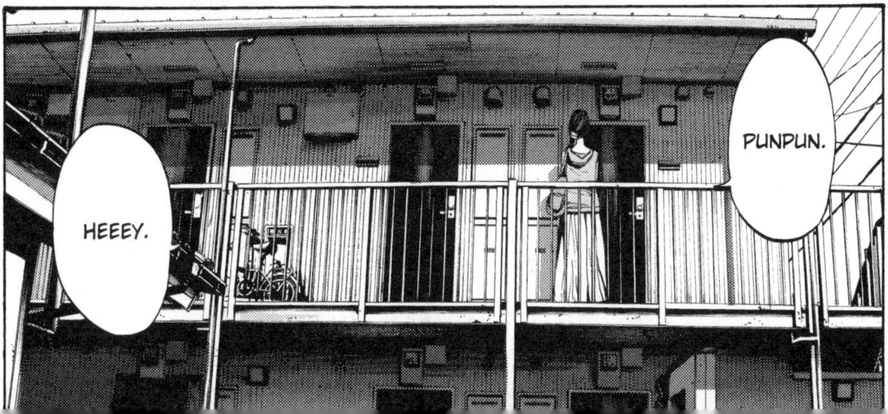
PUNPUN.
HEEEY.

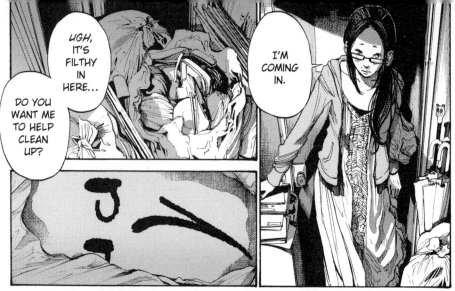

UGH, IT'S FILTHY IN HERE...

DO YOU WANT ME TO HELP CLEAN UP?

I'M COMING IN.

OH, PUNPUN ...

...YOU TOO, HUH?

ARE YOU MAKING PROGRESS ON THE MANGA?

AS IF.

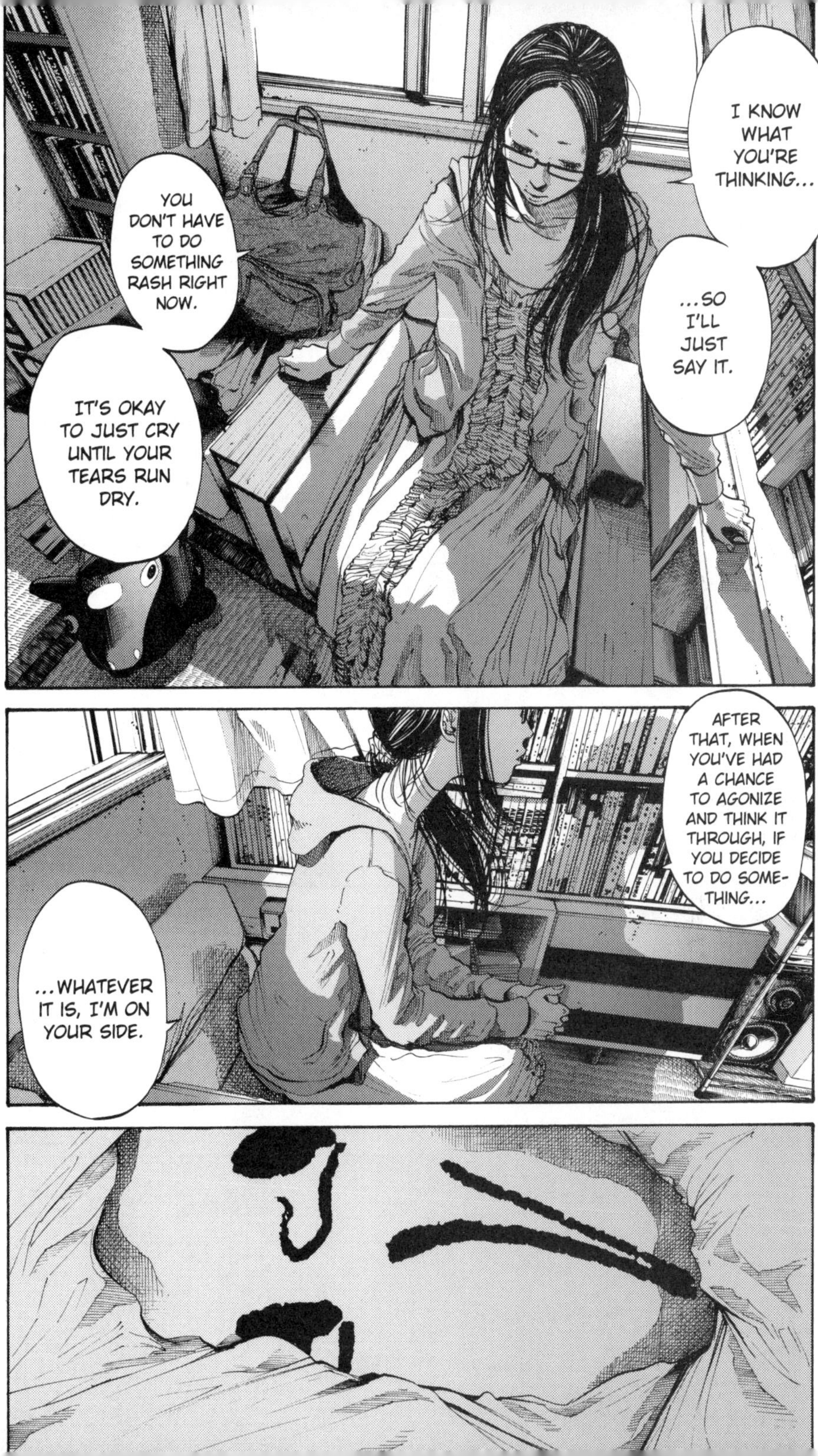
I KNOW WHAT YOU'RE THINKING...
...SO I'LL JUST SAY IT.
YOU DON'T HAVE TO DO SOMETHING RASH RIGHT NOW.
IT'S OKAY TO JUST CRY UNTIL YOUR TEARS RUN DRY.
AFTER THAT, WHEN YOU'VE HAD A CHANCE TO AGONIZE AND THINK IT THROUGH, IF YOU DECIDE TO DO SOME-THING...
...WHATEVER IT IS, I'M ON YOUR SIDE.

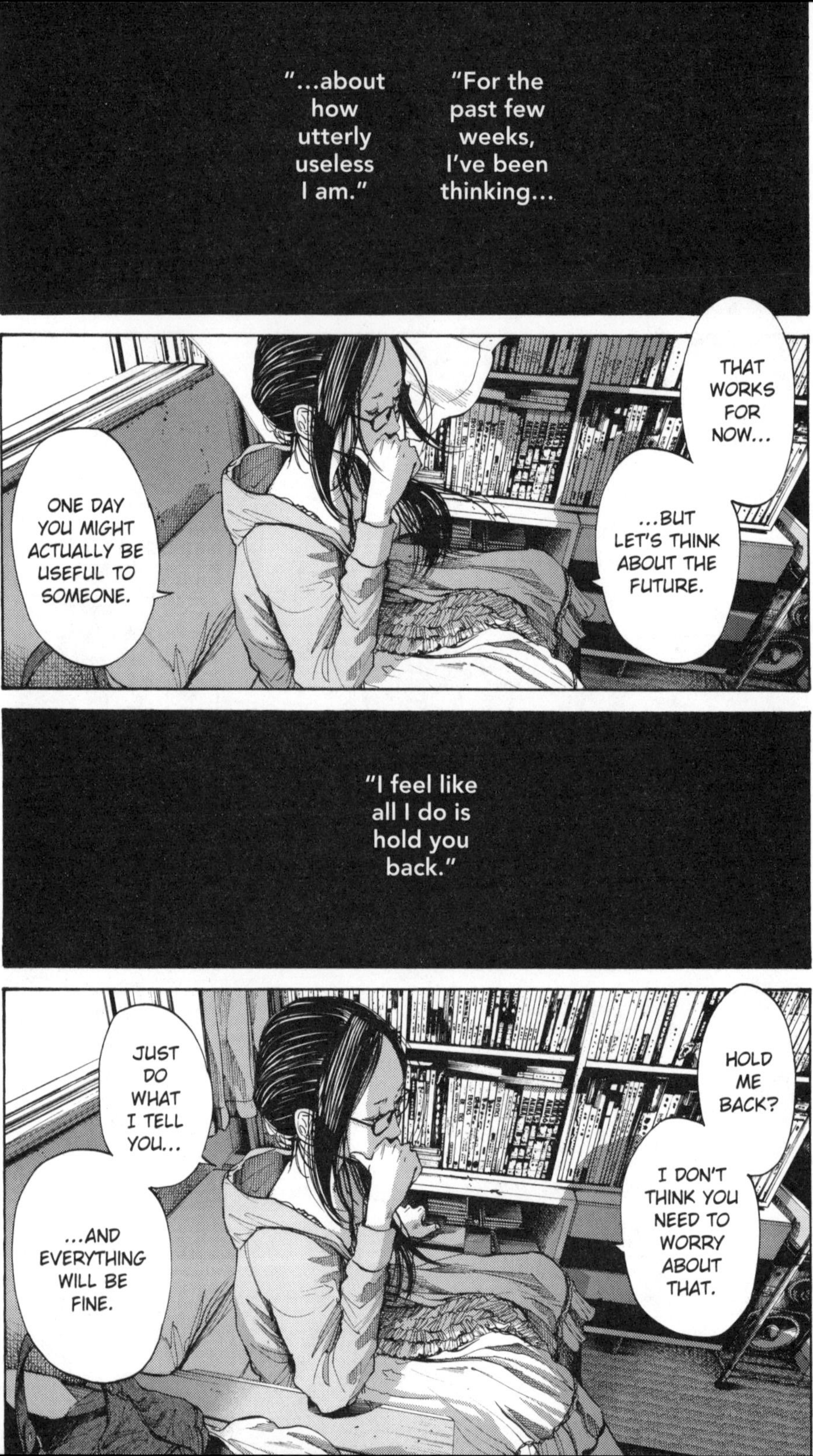
"For the past few weeks, I've been thinking...
"...about how utterly useless I am."
THAT WORKS FOR NOW...
...BUT LET'S THINK ABOUT THE FUTURE.
ONE DAY YOU MIGHT ACTUALLY BE USEFUL TO SOMEONE.
"I feel like all I do is hold you back."
HOLD ME BACK?
I DON'T THINK YOU NEED TO WORRY ABOUT THAT.
JUST DO WHAT I TELL YOU...
...AND EVERYTHING WILL BE FINE.

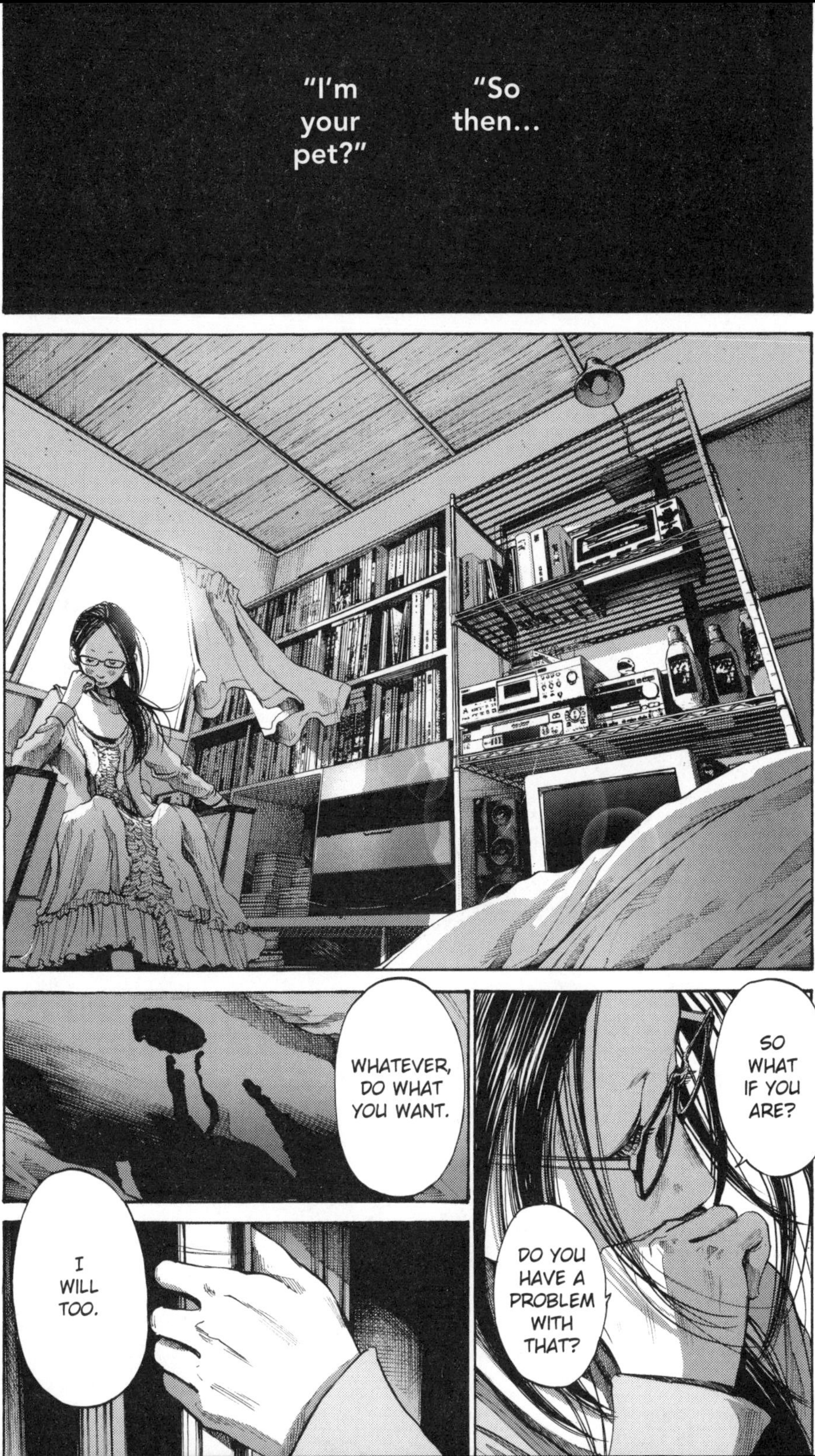
"So then...
"I'm your pet?"
SO WHAT IF YOU ARE?
DO YOU HAVE A PROBLEM WITH THAT?
WHATEVER, DO WHAT YOU WANT.
I WILL TOO.

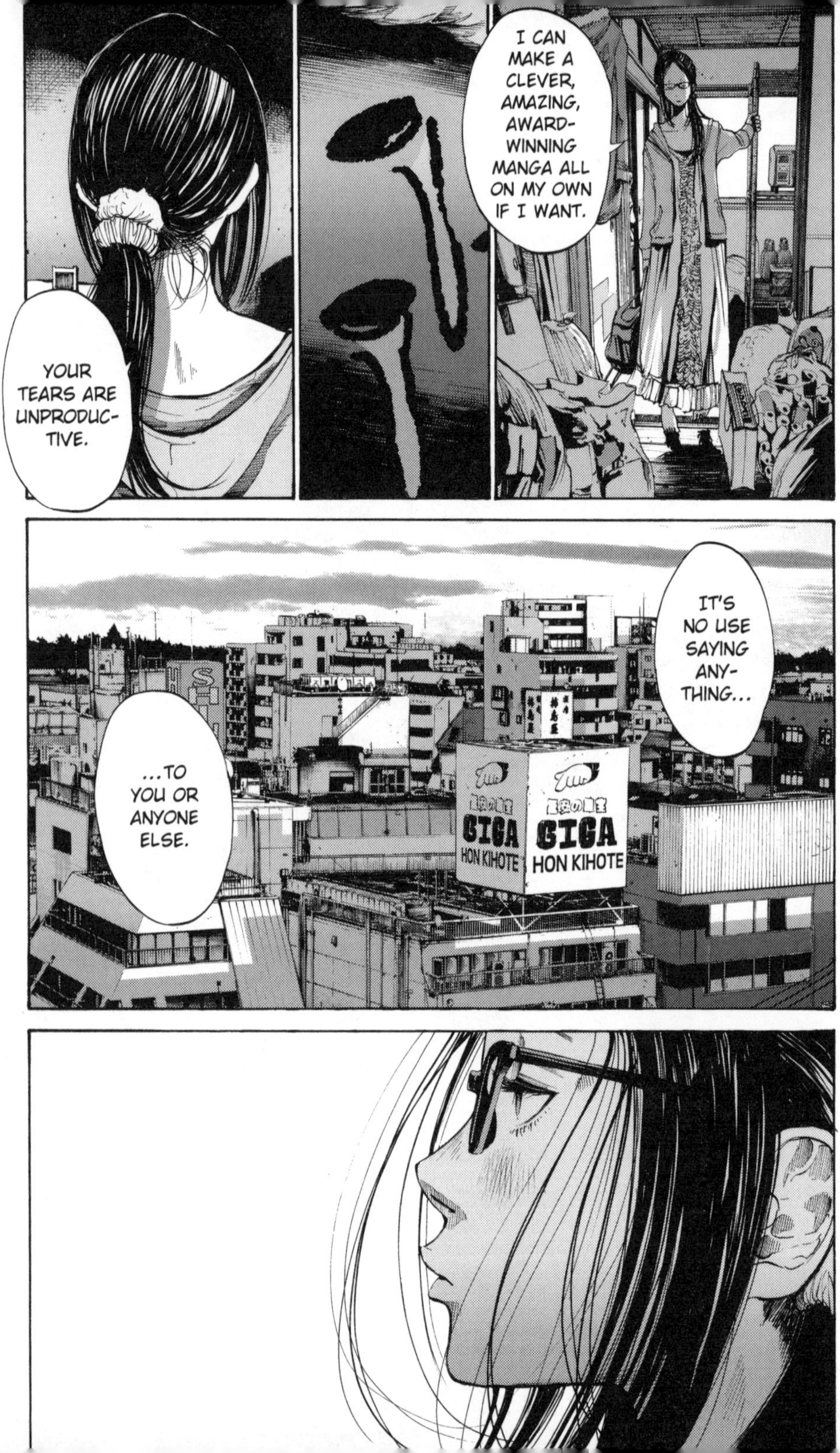
I CAN MAKE A CLEVER, AMAZING, AWARD-WINNING MANGA ALL ON MY OWN IF I WANT.
YOUR TEARS ARE UNPRODUC-TIVE.
IT'S NO USE SAYING ANY-THING...
...TO YOU OR ANYONE ELSE.
GIGA HON KIHOTE
GIGA HON KIHOTE

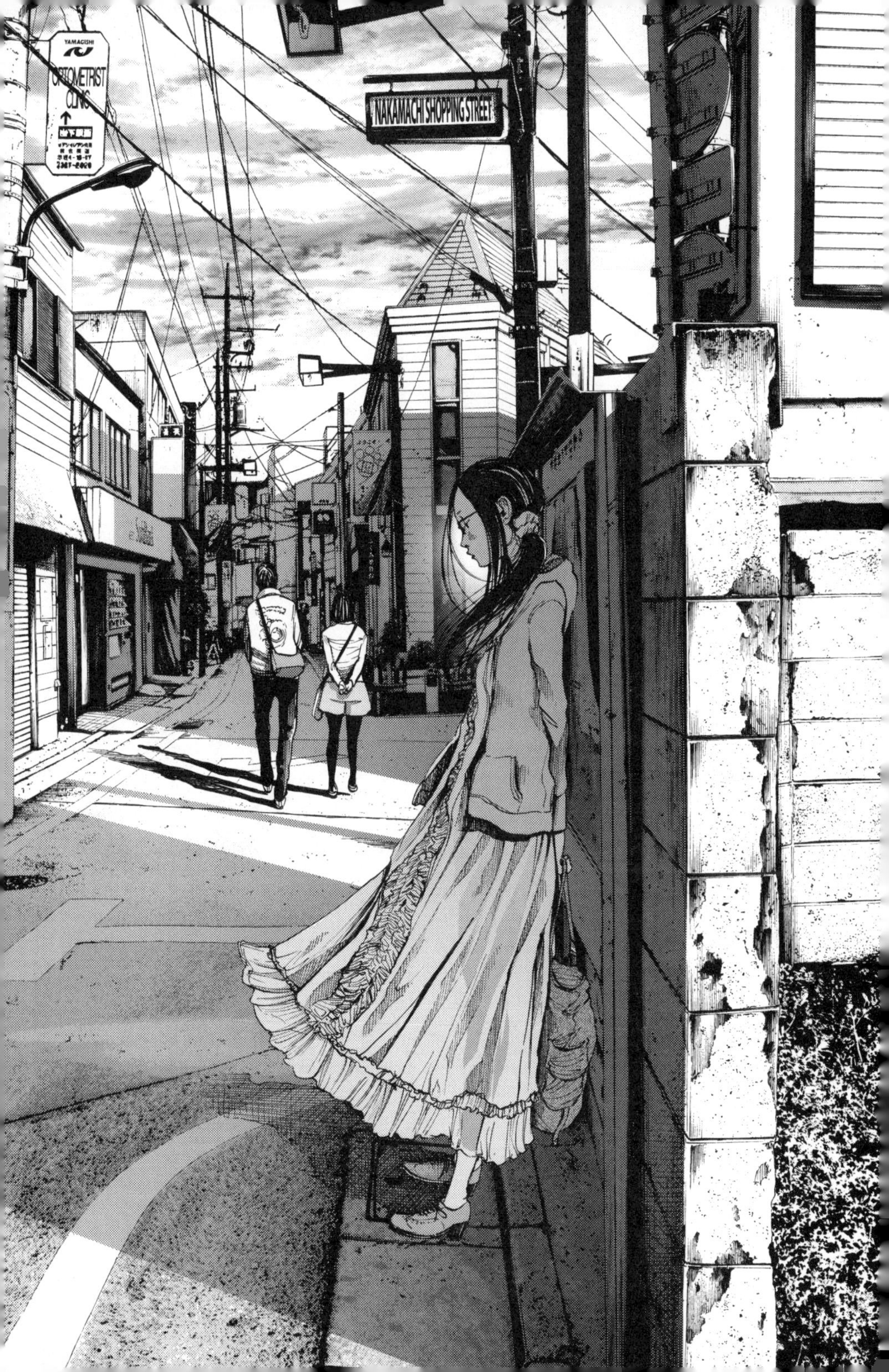
YAMAGISHI
OPTOMETRIST CLINIC
NAKAMACHI SHOPPING STREET

Chapter 94

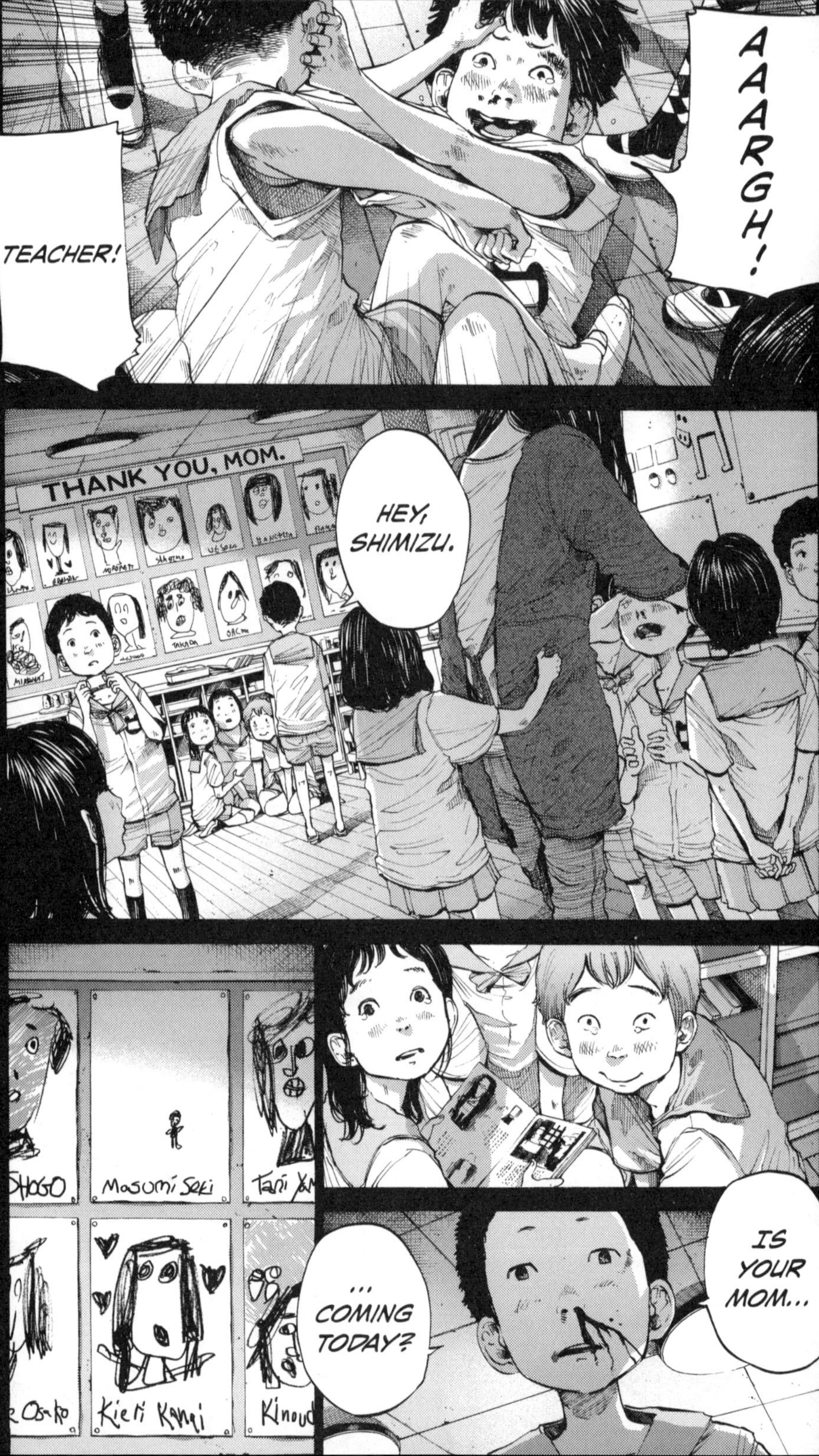
AAAARGH!
TEACHER!
THANK YOU, MOM.
HEY, SHIMIZU.
IS YOUR MOM...
... COMING TODAY?
Masumi Seki

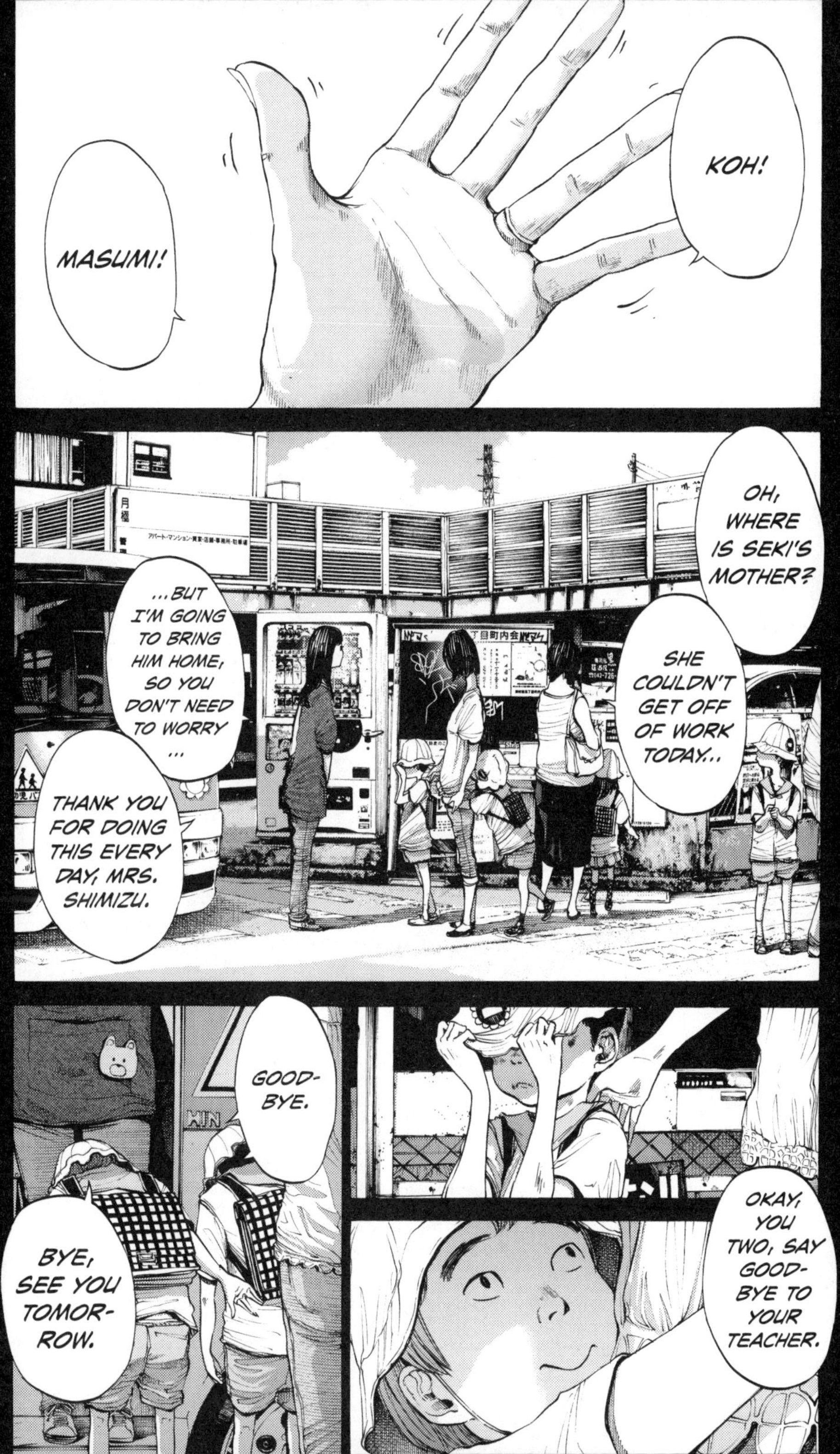
KOH!
MASUMI!
OH, WHERE IS SEKI'S MOTHER?
SHE COULDN'T GET OFF OF WORK TODAY...
...BUT I'M GOING TO BRING HIM HOME, SO YOU DON'T NEED TO WORRY ...
THANK YOU FOR DOING THIS EVERY DAY, MRS. SHIMIZU.
OKAY, YOU TWO, SAY GOOD-BYE TO YOUR TEACHER.
GOOD-BYE.
BYE, SEE YOU TOMORROW.

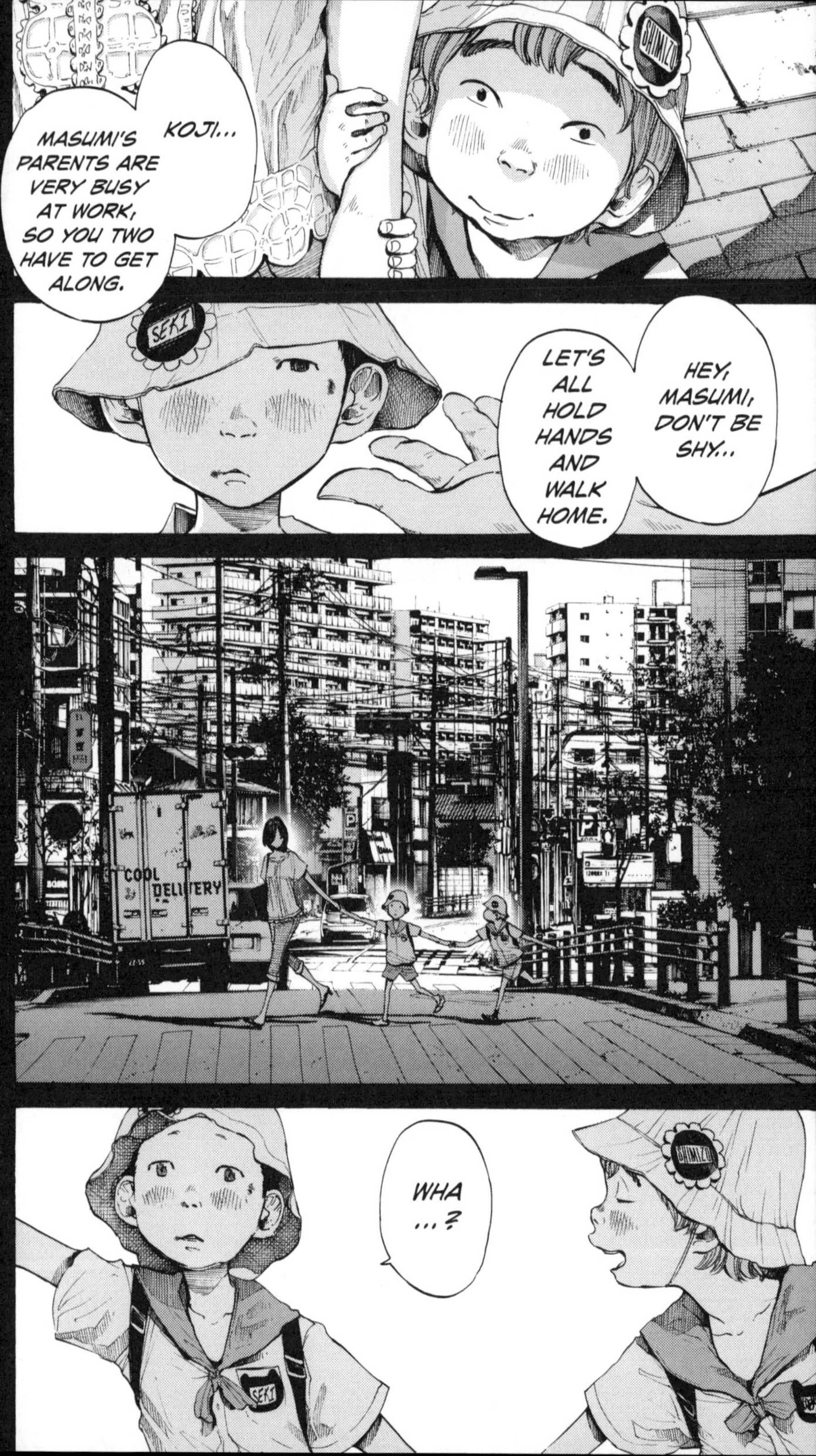
SHIMIZU
KOJI...
MASUMI'S PARENTS ARE VERY BUSY AT WORK, SO YOU TWO HAVE TO GET ALONG.
SEKI
HEY, MASUMI, DON'T BE SHY...
LET'S ALL HOLD HANDS AND WALK HOME.
COOL DELIVERY
SHIMIZU
WHA ...?
SEKI

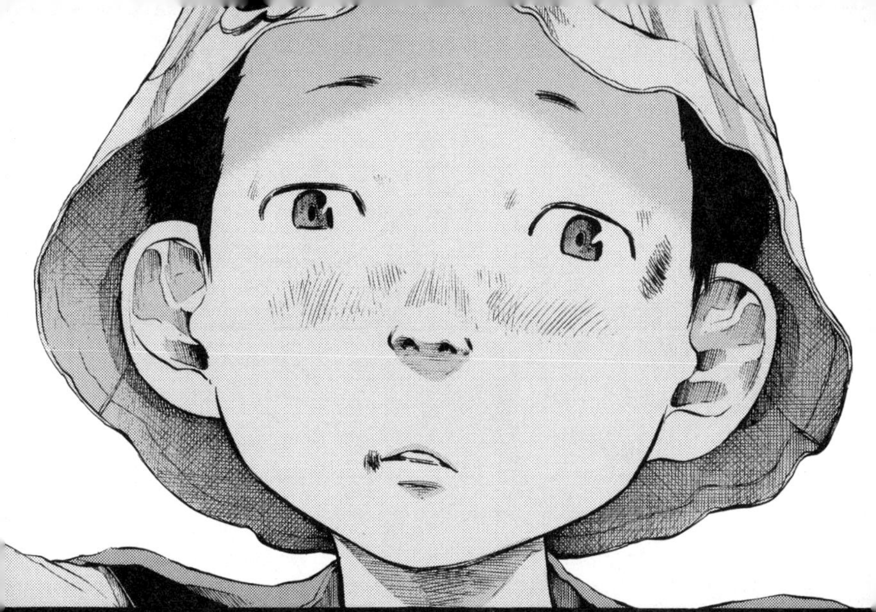
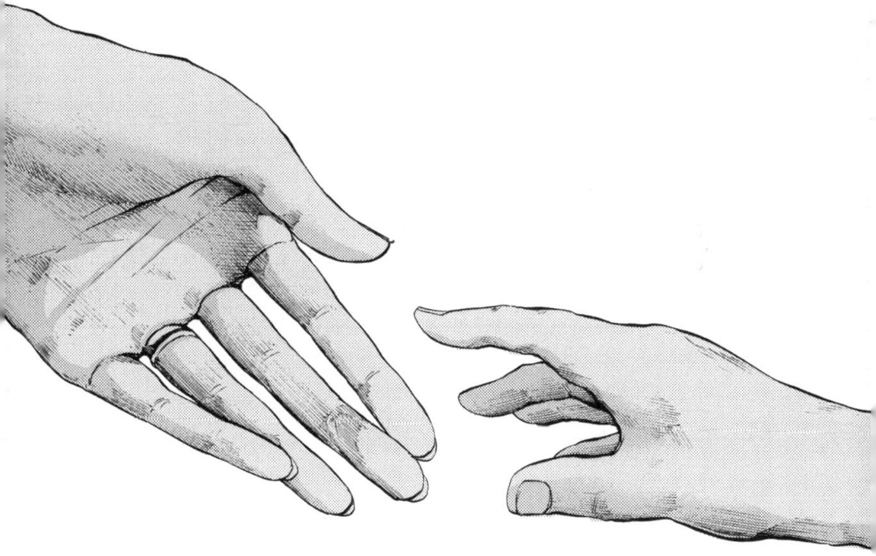

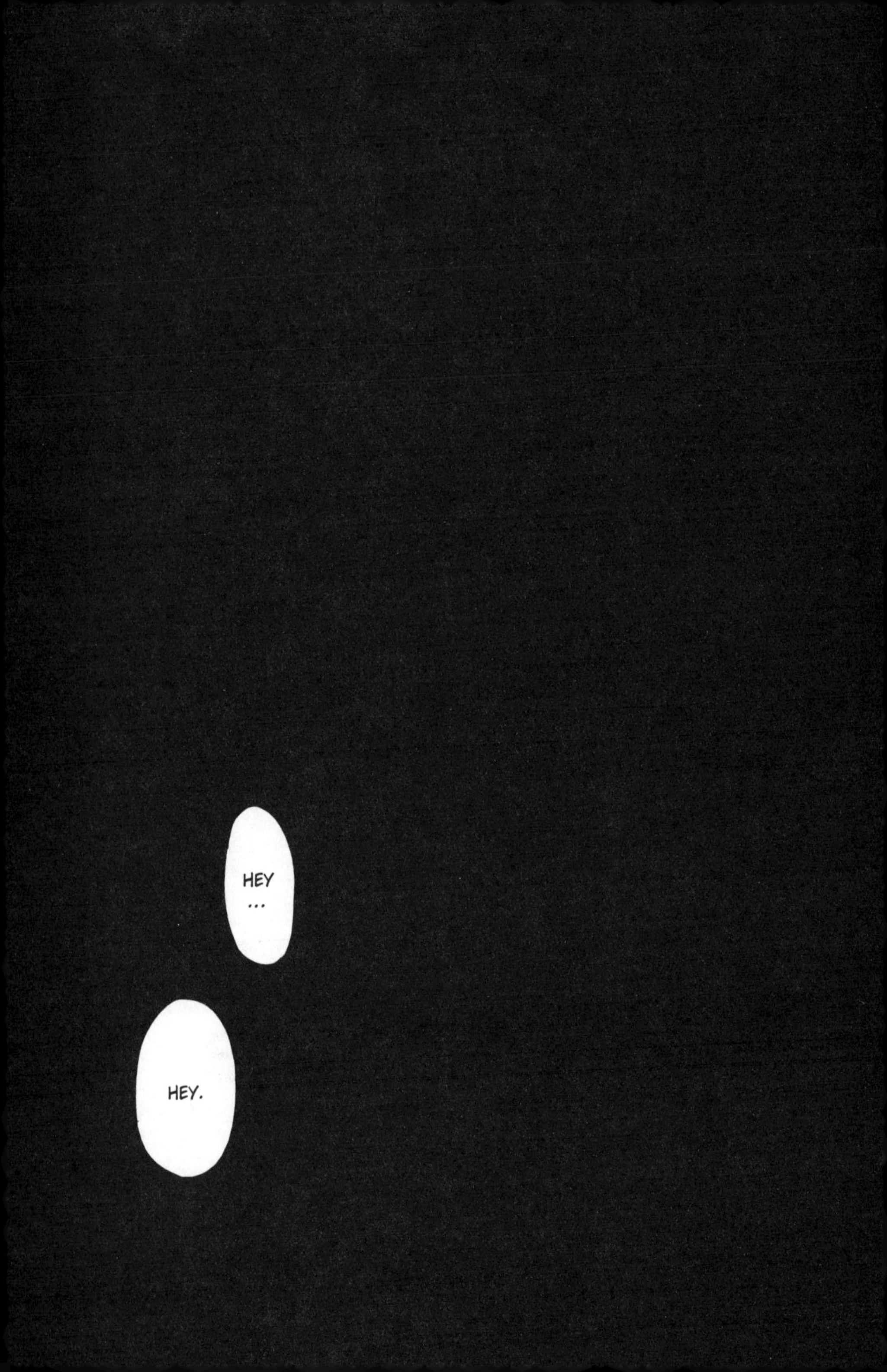
HEY ...
HEY.

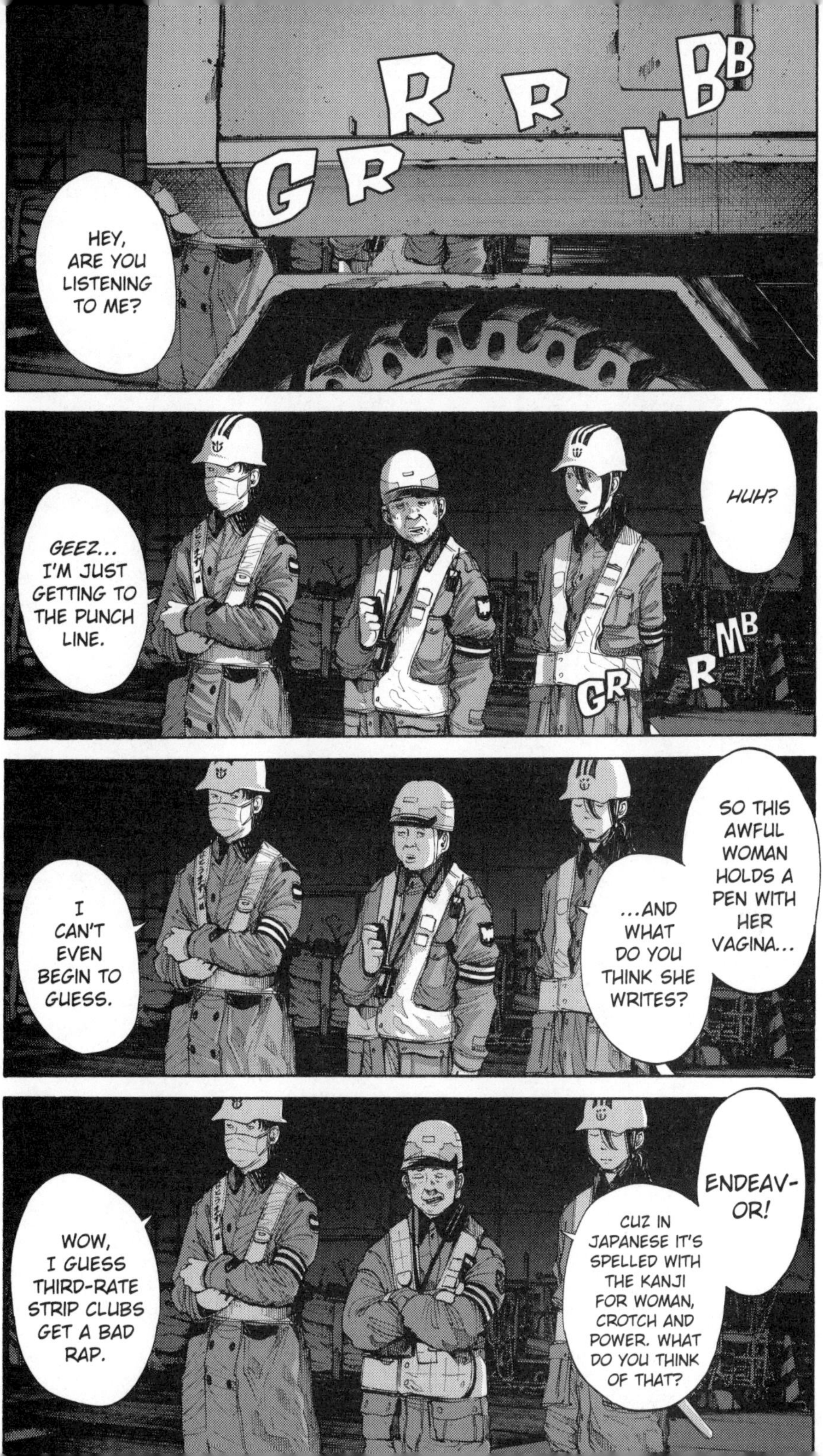
GRRRRMBB
HEY, ARE YOU LISTENING TO ME?
HUH?
GRRMB
GEEZ... I'M JUST GETTING TO THE PUNCH LINE.
SO THIS AWFUL WOMAN HOLDS A PEN WITH HER VAGINA...
...AND WHAT DO YOU THINK SHE WRITES?
I CAN'T EVEN BEGIN TO GUESS.
ENDEAV-OR!
CUZ IN JAPANESE IT'S SPELLED WITH THE KANJI FOR WOMAN, CROTCH AND POWER. WHAT DO YOU THINK OF THAT?
WOW, I GUESS THIRD-RATE STRIP CLUBS GET A BAD RAP.

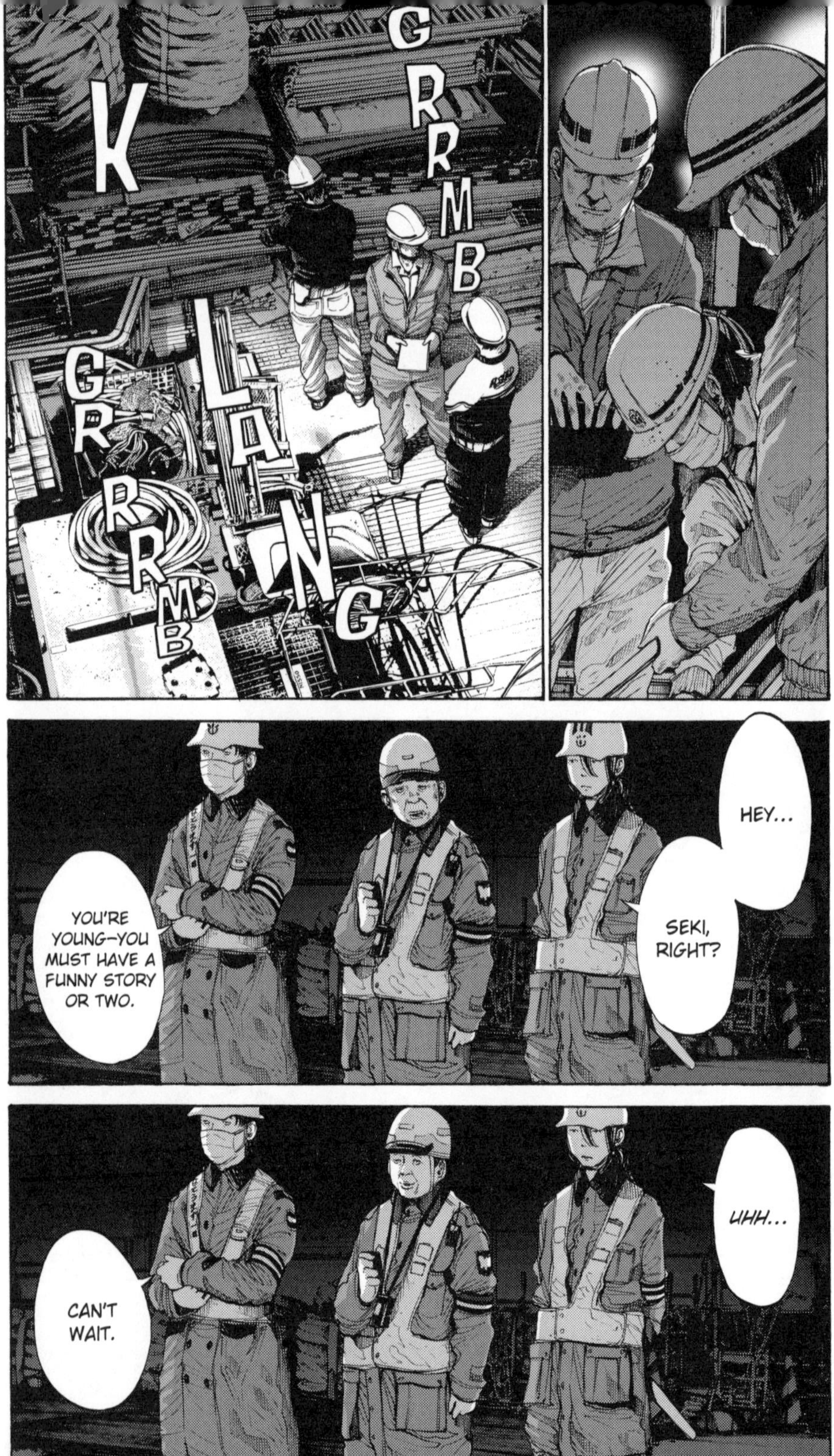
GRRMB
KLANG
GRRRMB
HEY...
SEKI, RIGHT?
YOU'RE YOUNG—YOU MUST HAVE A FUNNY STORY OR TWO.
UHH...
CAN'T WAIT.

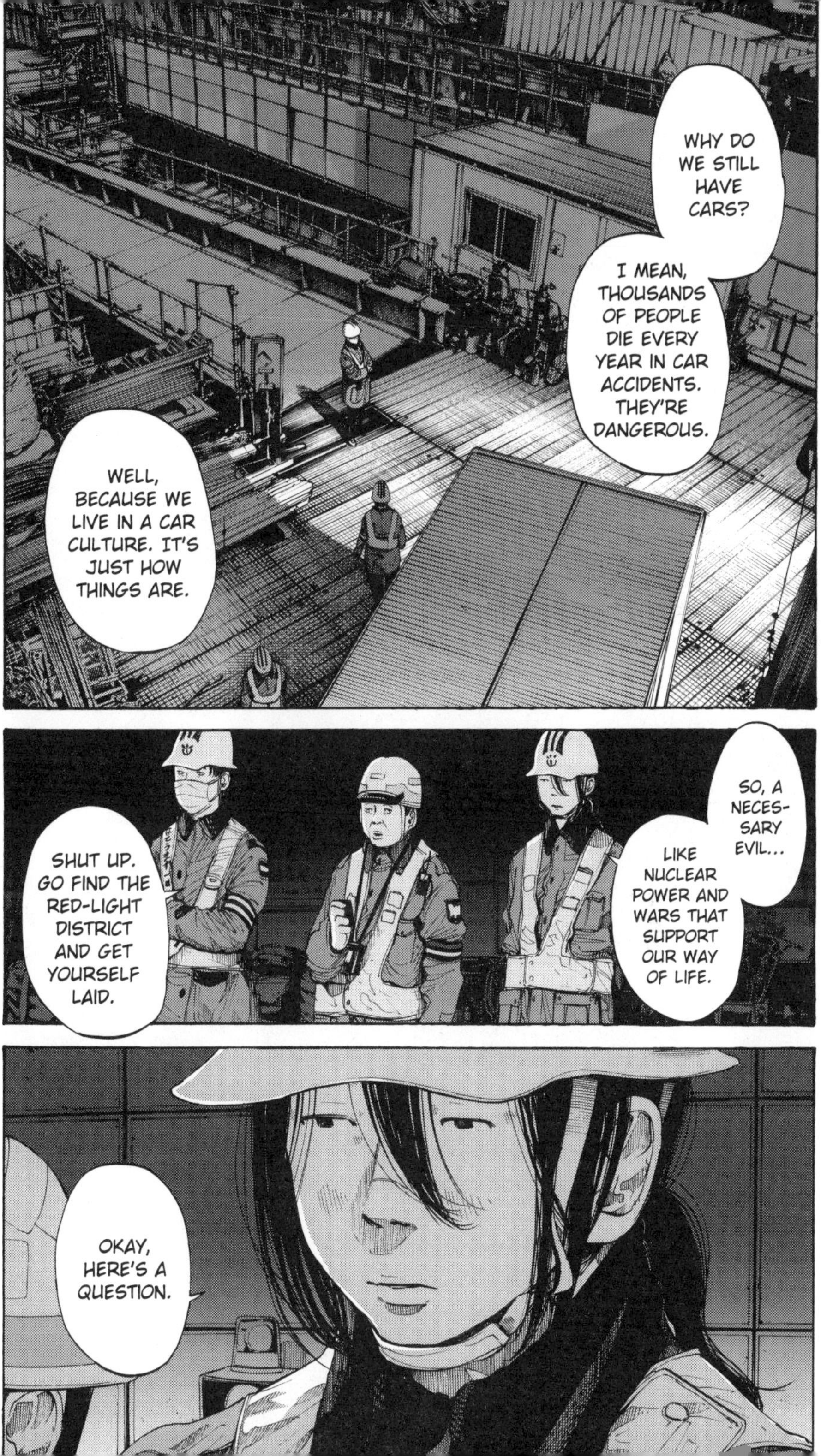
WHY DO WE STILL HAVE CARS?
I MEAN, THOUSANDS OF PEOPLE DIE EVERY YEAR IN CAR ACCIDENTS. THEY'RE DANGEROUS.
WELL, BECAUSE WE LIVE IN A CAR CULTURE. IT'S JUST HOW THINGS ARE.
SO, A NECES-SARY EVIL...
LIKE NUCLEAR POWER AND WARS THAT SUPPORT OUR WAY OF LIFE.
SHUT UP. GO FIND THE RED-LIGHT DISTRICT AND GET YOURSELF LAID.
OKAY, HERE'S A QUESTION.

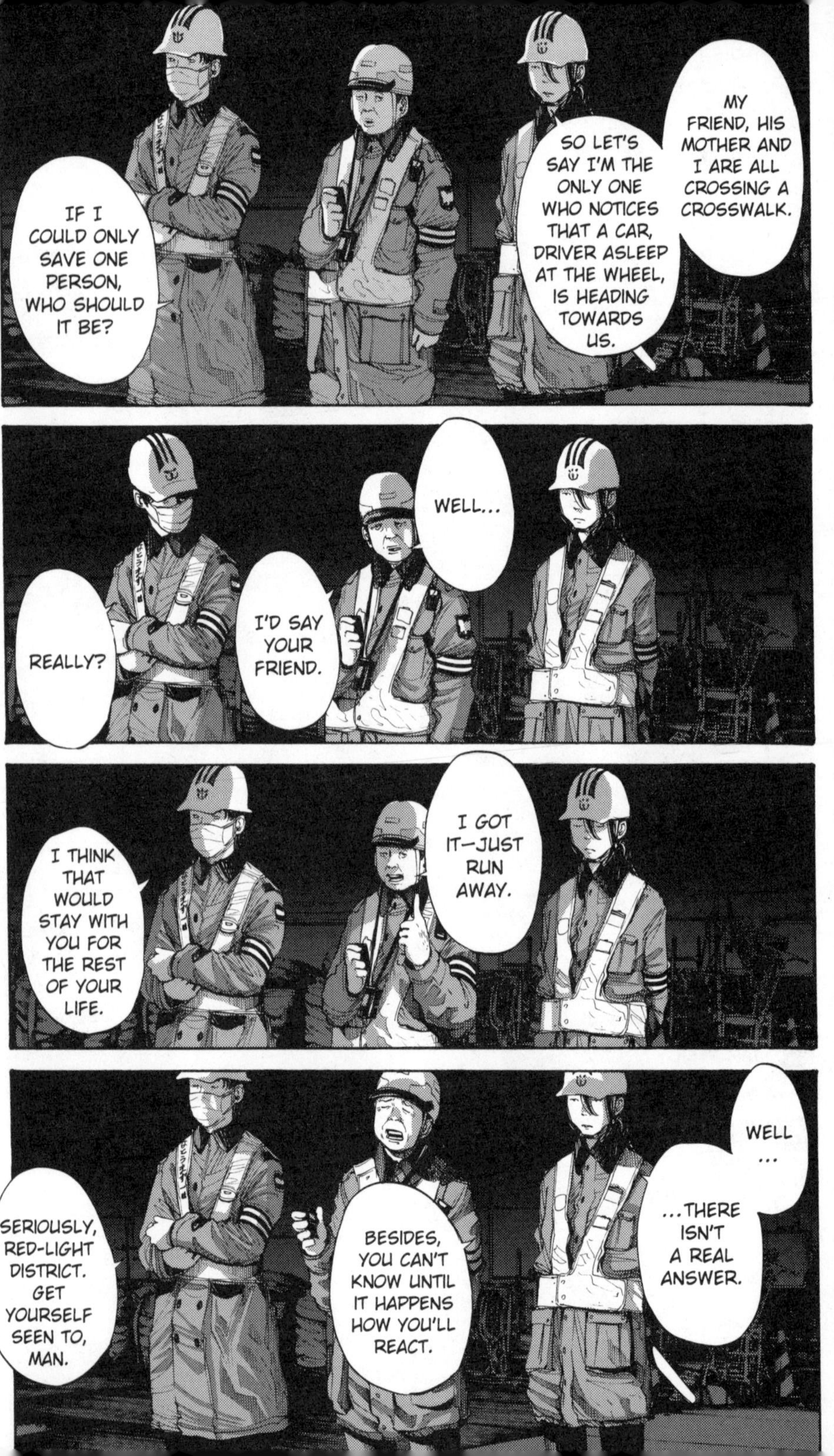
MY FRIEND, HIS MOTHER AND I ARE ALL CROSSING A CROSSWALK.
SO LET'S SAY I'M THE ONLY ONE WHO NOTICES THAT A CAR, DRIVER ASLEEP AT THE WHEEL, IS HEADING TOWARDS US.
IF I COULD ONLY SAVE ONE PERSON, WHO SHOULD IT BE?
WELL...
I'D SAY YOUR FRIEND.
REALLY?
I GOT IT—JUST RUN AWAY.
I THINK THAT WOULD STAY WITH YOU FOR THE REST OF YOUR LIFE.
WELL ...
...THERE ISN'T A REAL ANSWER.
BESIDES, YOU CAN'T KNOW UNTIL IT HAPPENS HOW YOU'LL REACT.
SERIOUSLY, RED-LIGHT DISTRICT. GET YOURSELF SEEN TO, MAN.

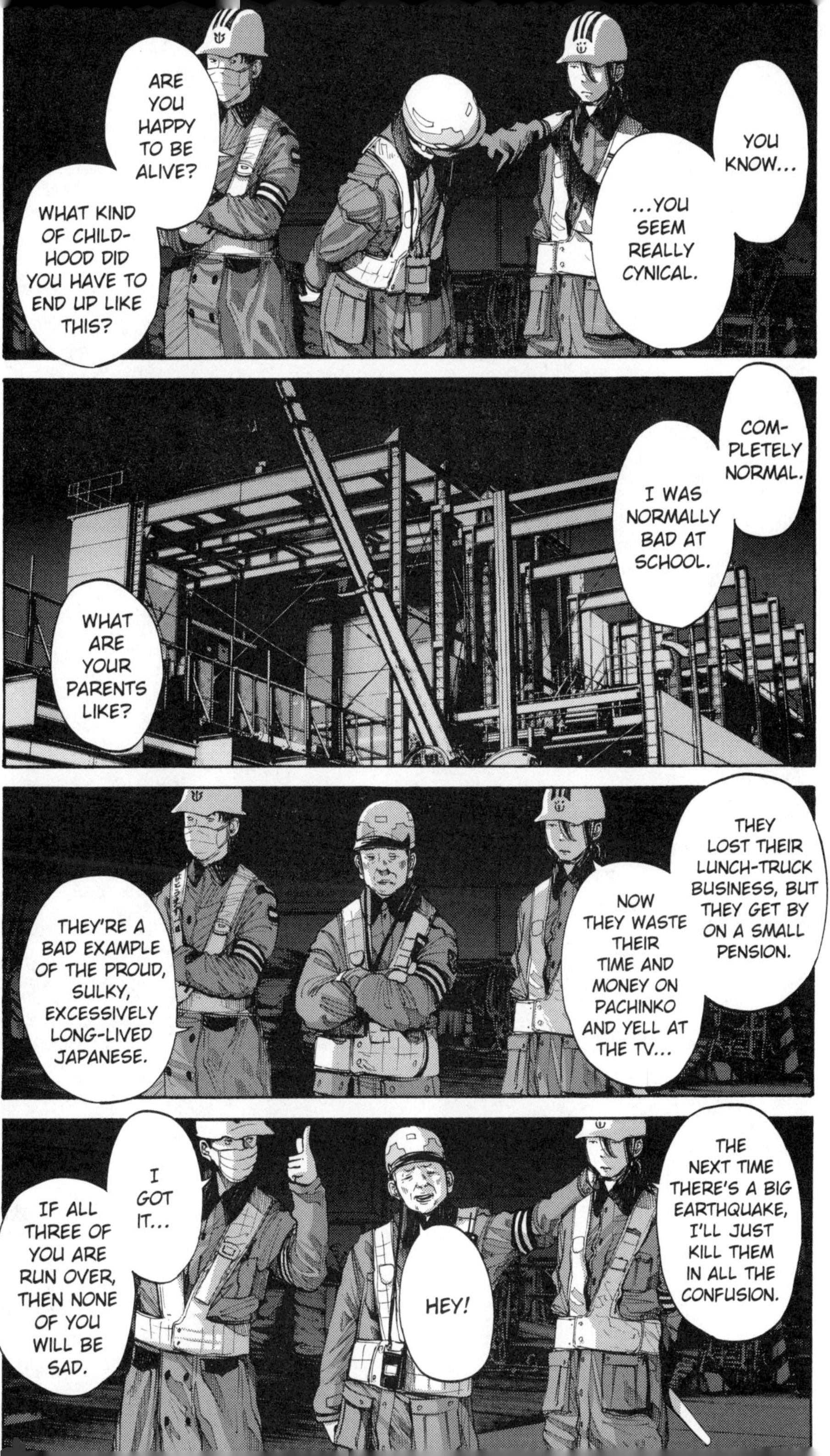
YOU KNOW...
...YOU SEEM REALLY CYNICAL.
ARE YOU HAPPY TO BE ALIVE?
WHAT KIND OF CHILD-HOOD DID YOU HAVE TO END UP LIKE THIS?
COM-PLETELY NORMAL.
I WAS NORMALLY BAD AT SCHOOL.
WHAT ARE YOUR PARENTS LIKE?
THEY LOST THEIR LUNCH-TRUCK BUSINESS, BUT THEY GET BY ON A SMALL PENSION.
NOW THEY WASTE THEIR TIME AND MONEY ON PACHINKO AND YELL AT THE TV...
THEY'RE A BAD EXAMPLE OF THE PROUD, SULKY, EXCESSIVELY LONG-LIVED JAPANESE.
THE NEXT TIME THERE'S A BIG EARTHQUAKE, I'LL JUST KILL THEM IN ALL THE CONFUSION.
HEY!
I GOT IT...
IF ALL THREE OF YOU ARE RUN OVER, THEN NONE OF YOU WILL BE SAD.

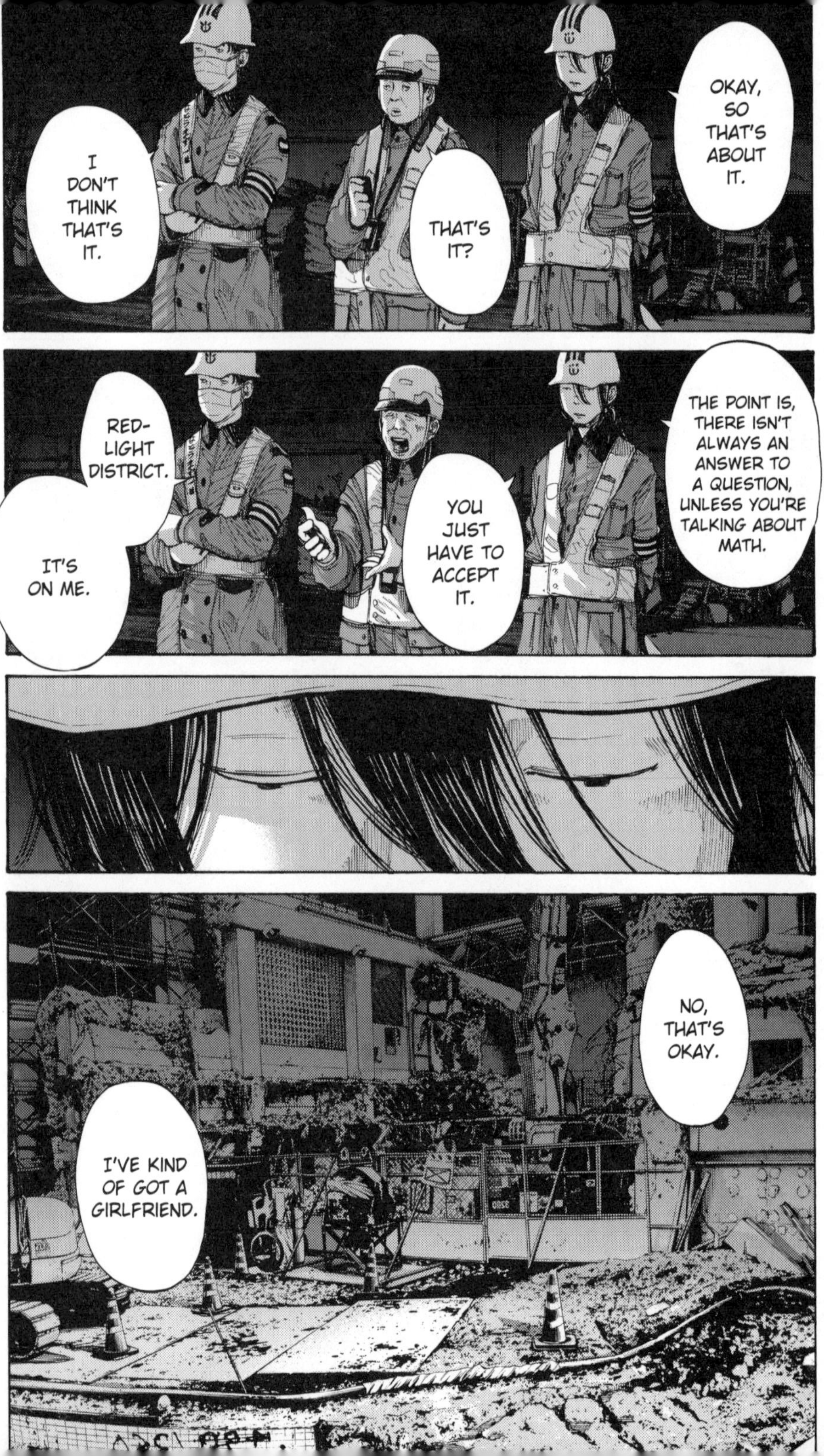
OKAY, SO THAT'S ABOUT IT.
THAT'S IT?
I DON'T THINK THAT'S IT.
THE POINT IS, THERE ISN'T ALWAYS AN ANSWER TO A QUESTION, UNLESS YOU'RE TALKING ABOUT MATH.
YOU JUST HAVE TO ACCEPT IT.
RED-LIGHT DISTRICT.
IT'S ON ME.
NO, THAT'S OKAY.
I'VE KIND OF GOT A GIRLFRIEND.

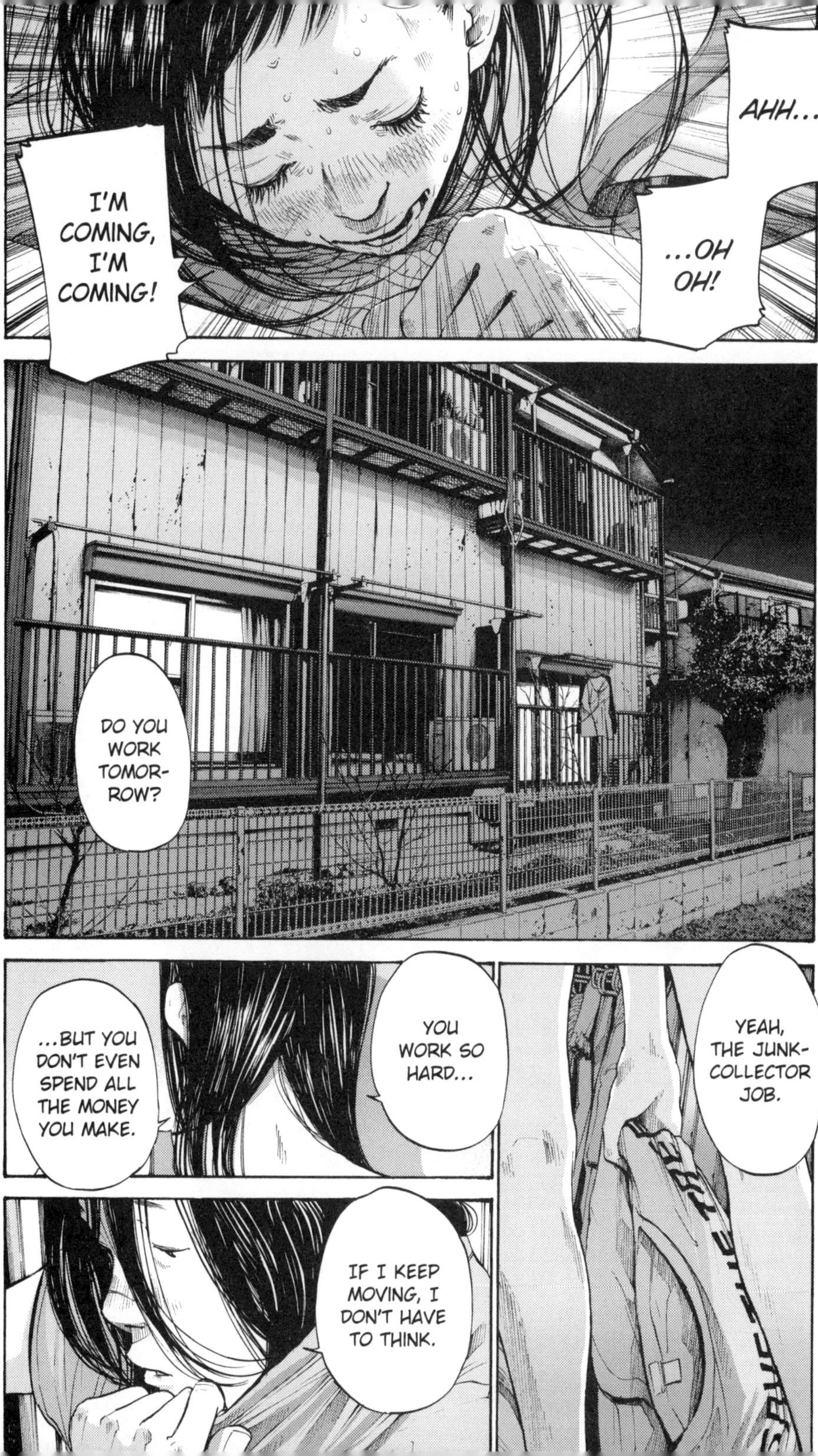
AHH...
...OH OH!
I'M COMING, I'M COMING!
DO YOU WORK TOMORROW?
YEAH, THE JUNK-COLLECTOR JOB.
YOU WORK SO HARD...
...BUT YOU DON'T EVEN SPEND ALL THE MONEY YOU MAKE.
IF I KEEP MOVING, I DON'T HAVE TO THINK.

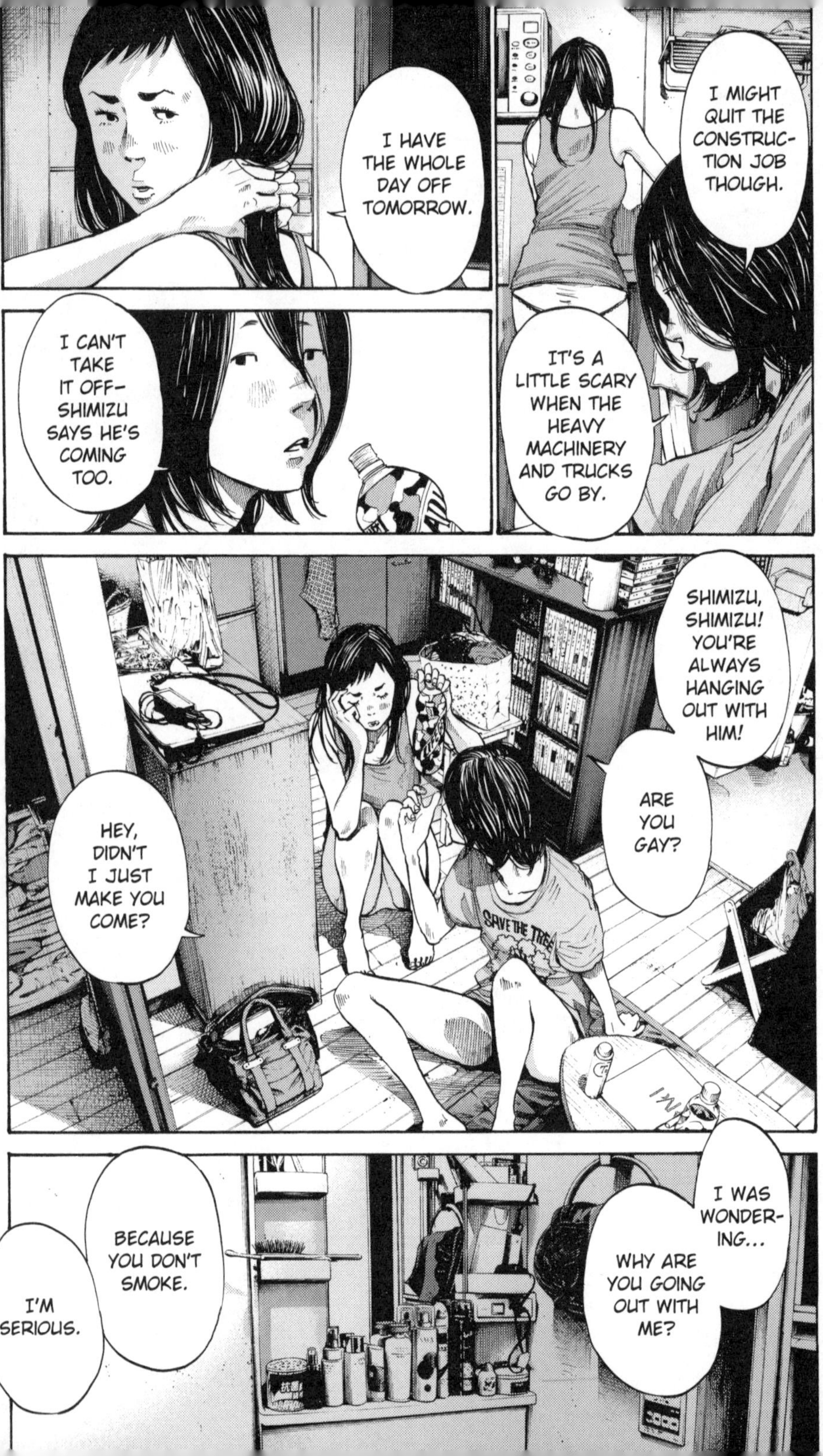
I MIGHT QUIT THE CONSTRUCTION JOB THOUGH.
IT'S A LITTLE SCARY WHEN THE HEAVY MACHINERY AND TRUCKS GO BY.
I HAVE THE WHOLE DAY OFF TOMORROW.
I CAN'T TAKE IT OFF–SHIMIZU SAYS HE'S COMING TOO.
SHIMIZU, SHIMIZU! YOU'RE ALWAYS HANGING OUT WITH HIM!
ARE YOU GAY?
HEY, DIDN'T I JUST MAKE YOU COME?
I WAS WONDERING...
WHY ARE YOU GOING OUT WITH ME?
BECAUSE YOU DON'T SMOKE.
I'M SERIOUS.

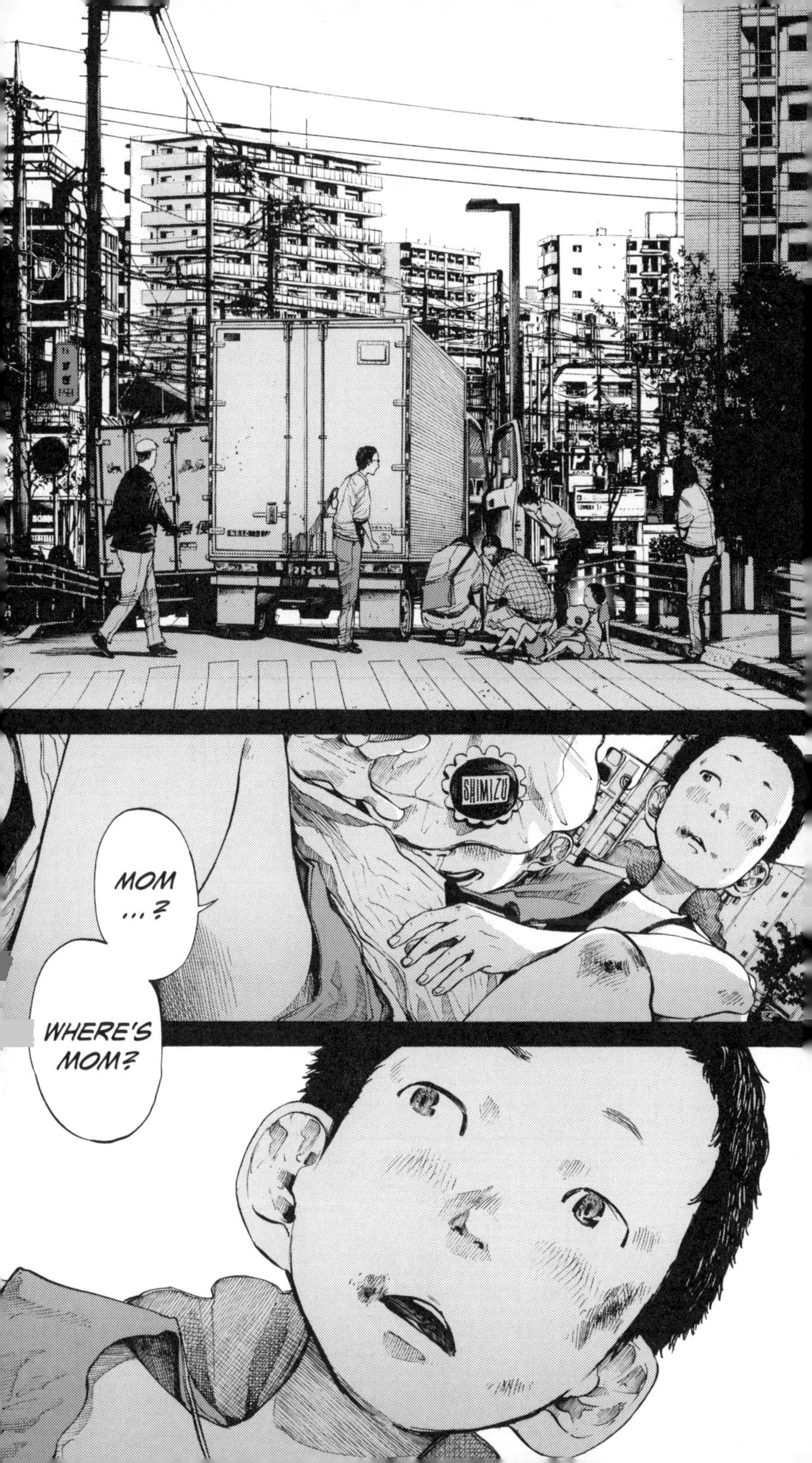
SHIMIZU
MOM ...?
WHERE'S MOM?

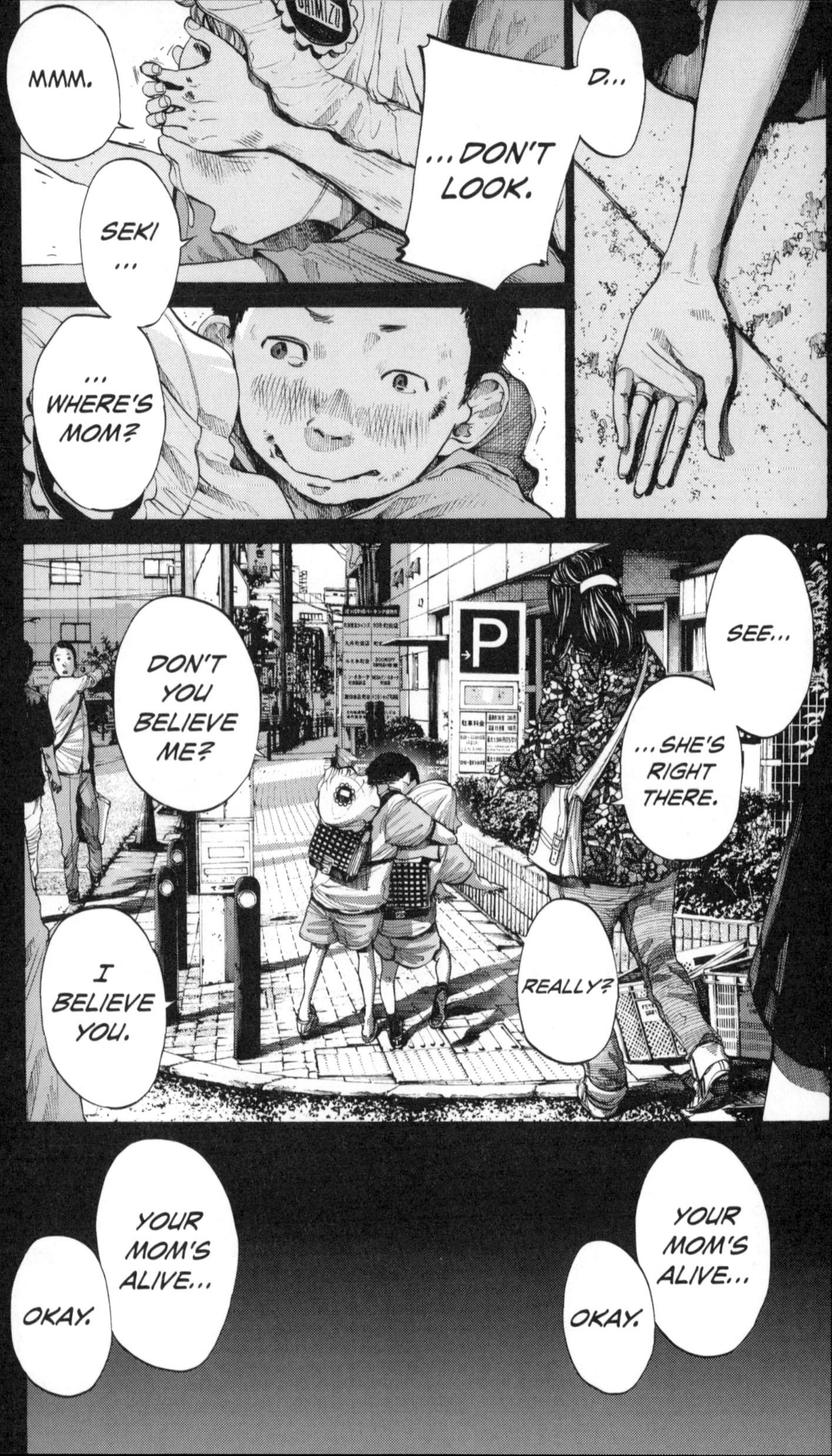
D...
...DON'T LOOK.
MMM.
SEKI ...
... WHERE'S MOM?
SEE...
...SHE'S RIGHT THERE.
DON'T YOU BELIEVE ME?
REALLY?
I BELIEVE YOU.
YOUR MOM'S ALIVE...
OKAY.
YOUR MOM'S ALIVE...
OKAY.

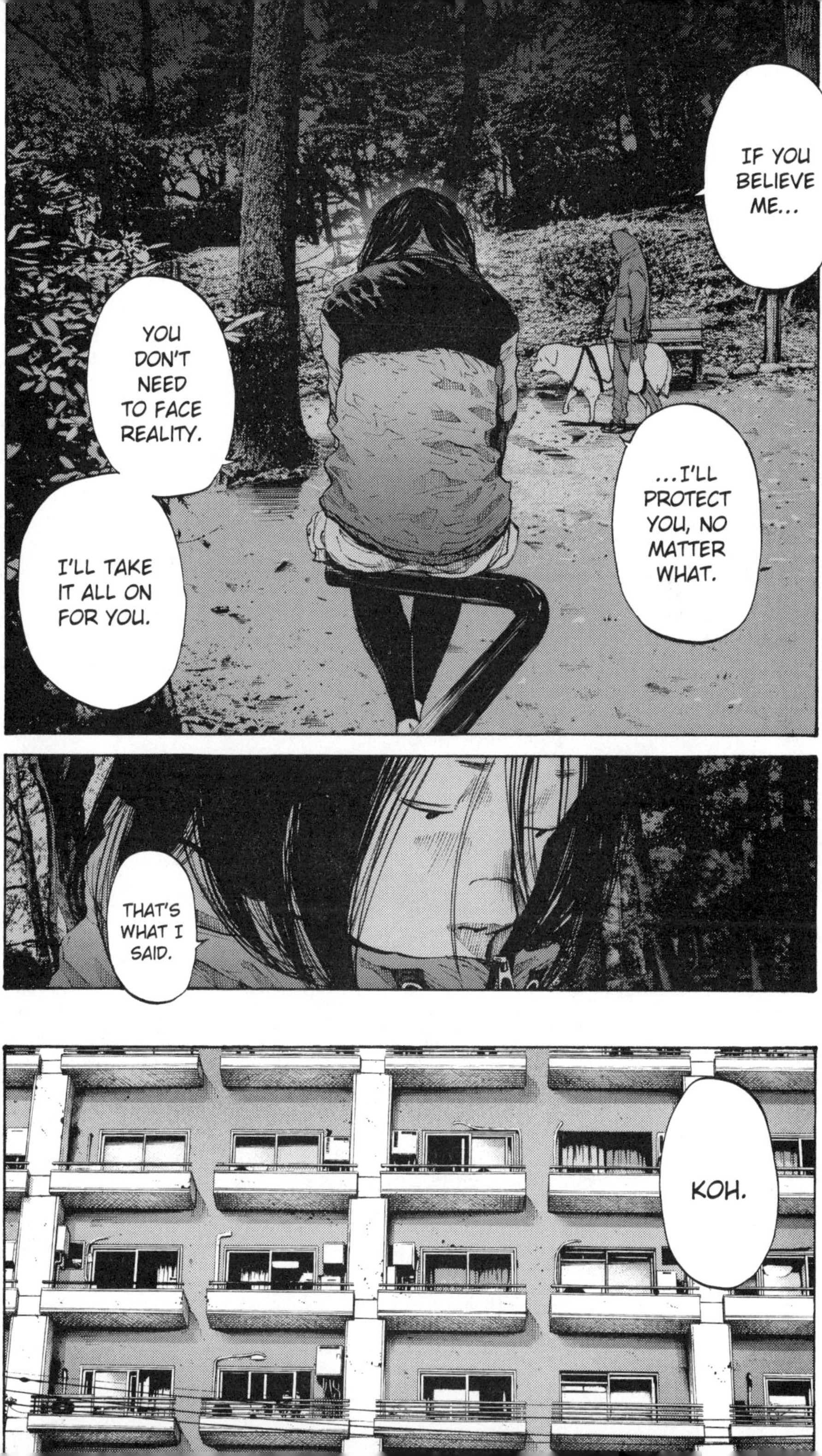
IF YOU BELIEVE ME...
...I'LL PROTECT YOU, NO MATTER WHAT.
YOU DON'T NEED TO FACE REALITY.
I'LL TAKE IT ALL ON FOR YOU.
THAT'S WHAT I SAID.
KOH.

DO YOU HAVE YOUR TISSUES?

OH!

AN ENTIRE BOX! YOU GOT ME!

LATERS.

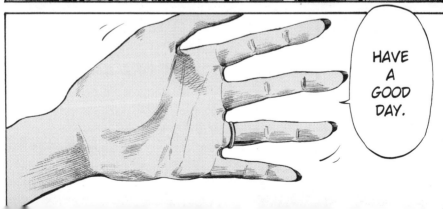

HAVE A GOOD DAY.

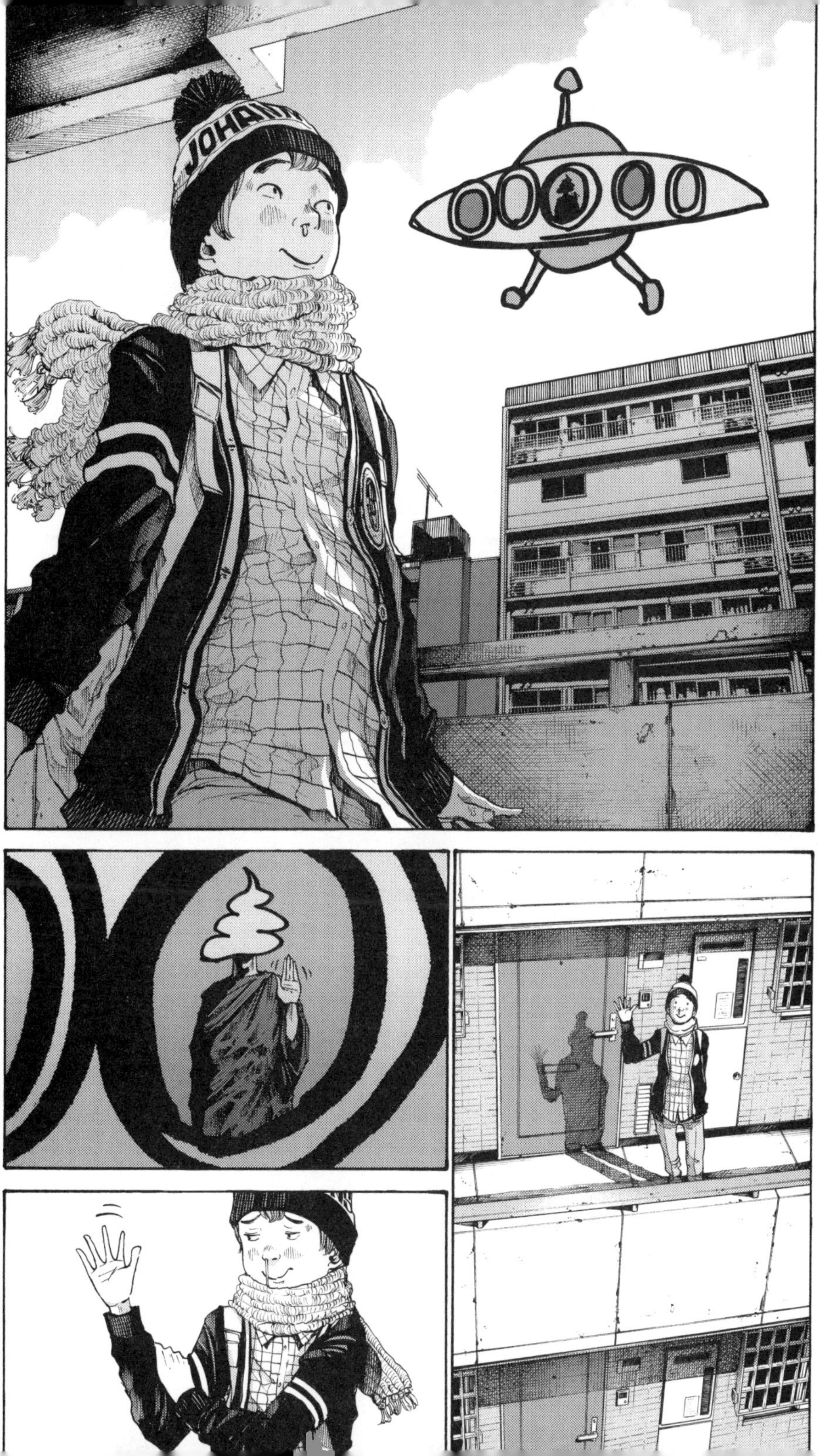

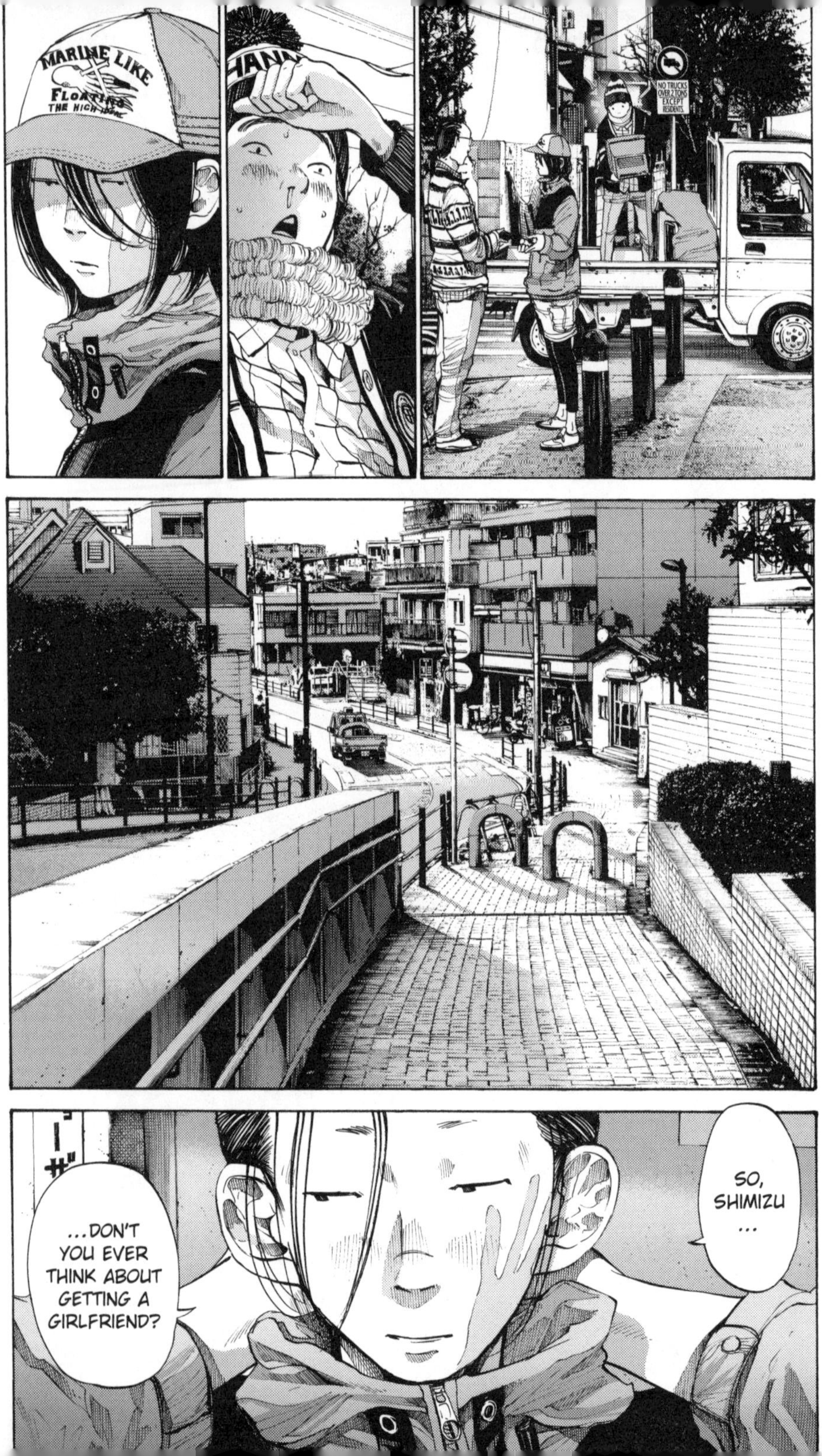
NO TRUCKS OVER 2 TONS EXCEPT RESIDENTS
SO, SHIMIZU ...
...DON'T YOU EVER THINK ABOUT GETTING A GIRLFRIEND?

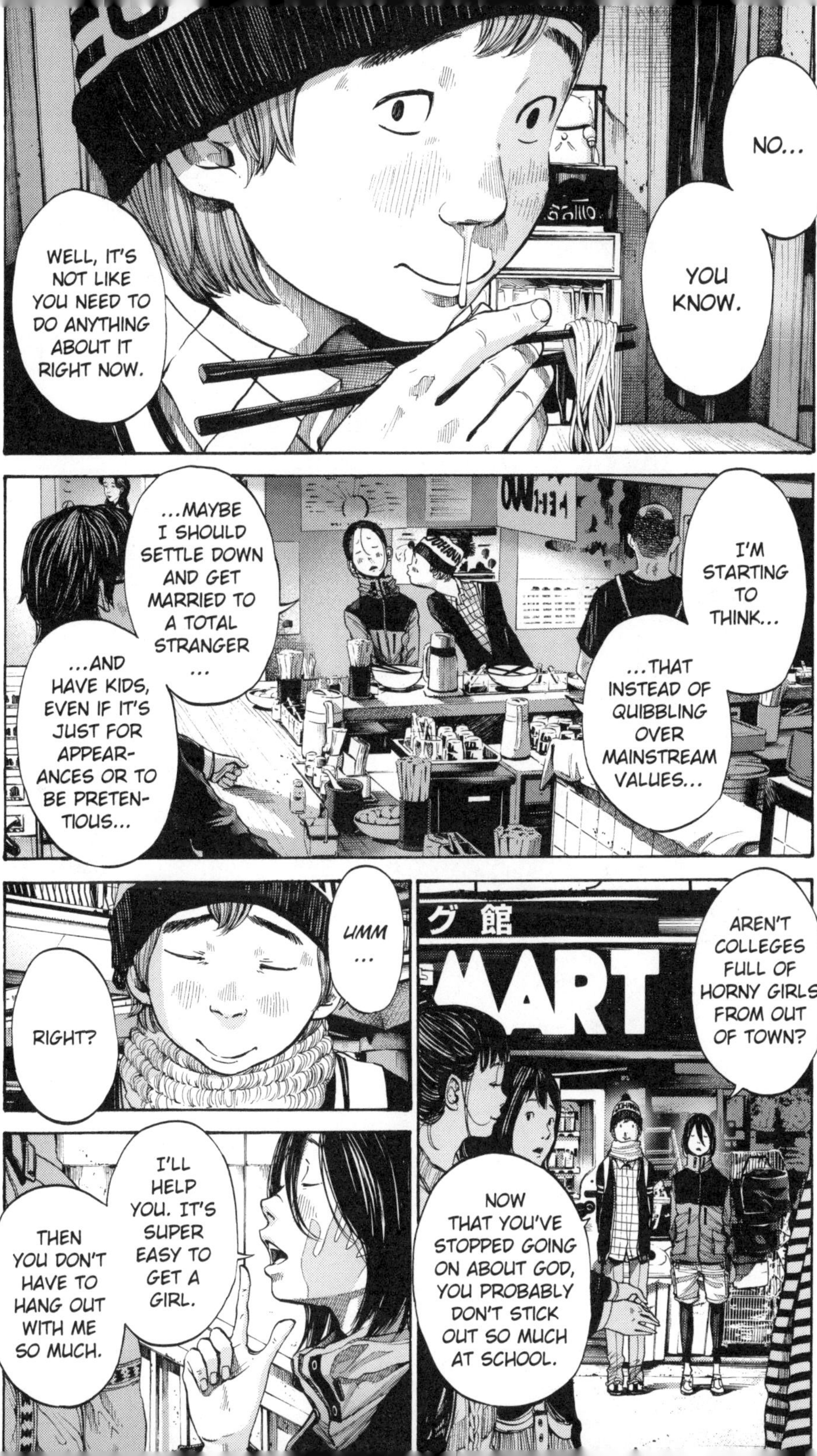
NO... YOU KNOW.
WELL, IT'S NOT LIKE YOU NEED TO DO ANYTHING ABOUT IT RIGHT NOW.
I'M STARTING TO THINK...
...THAT INSTEAD OF QUIBBLING OVER MAINSTREAM VALUES...
...MAYBE I SHOULD SETTLE DOWN AND GET MARRIED TO A TOTAL STRANGER...
...AND HAVE KIDS, EVEN IF IT'S JUST FOR APPEARANCES OR TO BE PRETENTIOUS...
グ 館
MART
AREN'T COLLEGES FULL OF HORNY GIRLS FROM OUT OF TOWN?
NOW THAT YOU'VE STOPPED GOING ON ABOUT GOD, YOU PROBABLY DON'T STICK OUT SO MUCH AT SCHOOL.
UMM...
RIGHT?
I'LL HELP YOU. IT'S SUPER EASY TO GET A GIRL.
THEN YOU DON'T HAVE TO HANG OUT WITH ME SO MUCH.

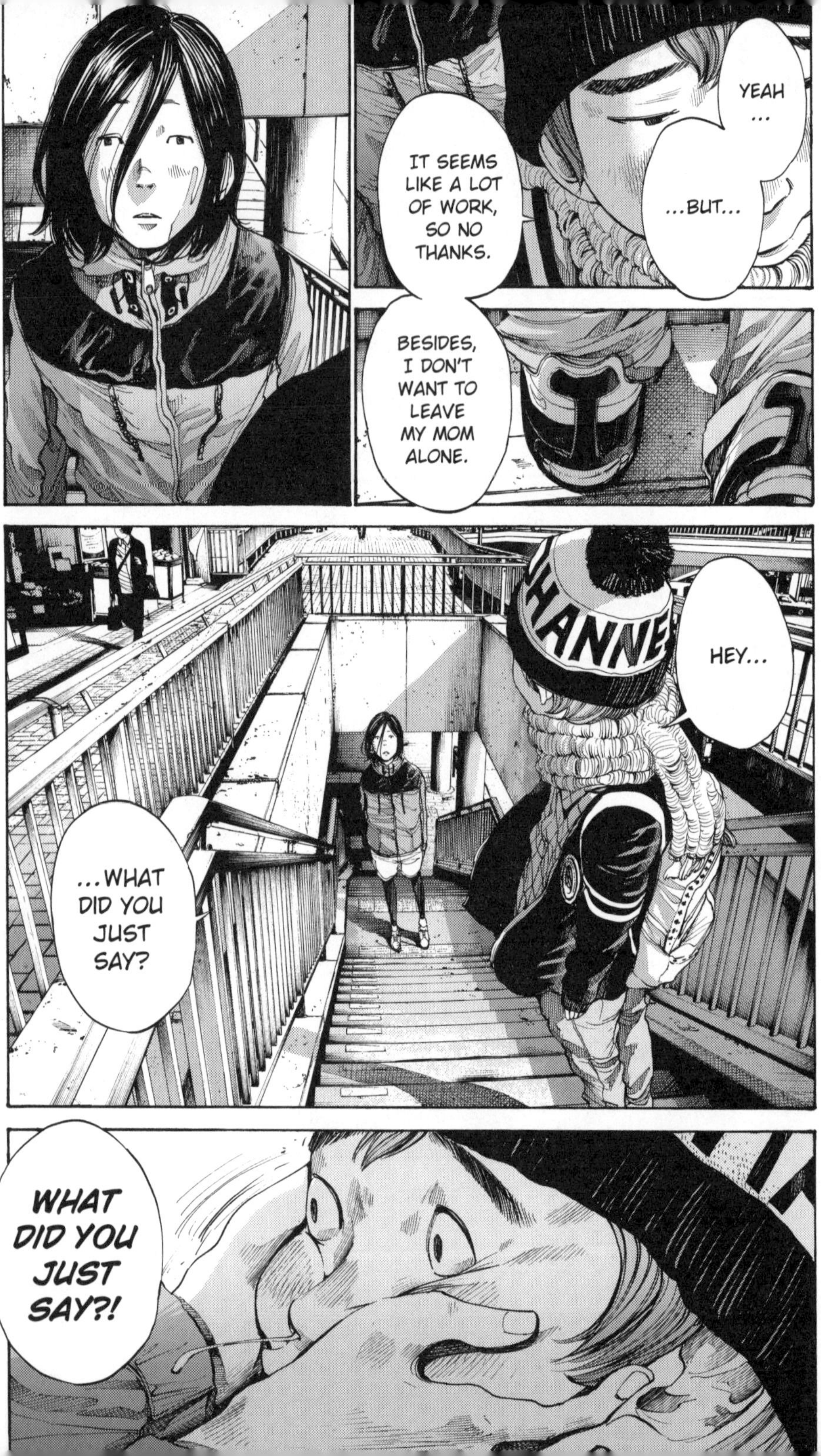
YEAH ...
...BUT...
IT SEEMS LIKE A LOT OF WORK, SO NO THANKS.
BESIDES, I DON'T WANT TO LEAVE MY MOM ALONE.
HEY...
...WHAT DID YOU JUST SAY?
WHAT DID YOU JUST SAY?!

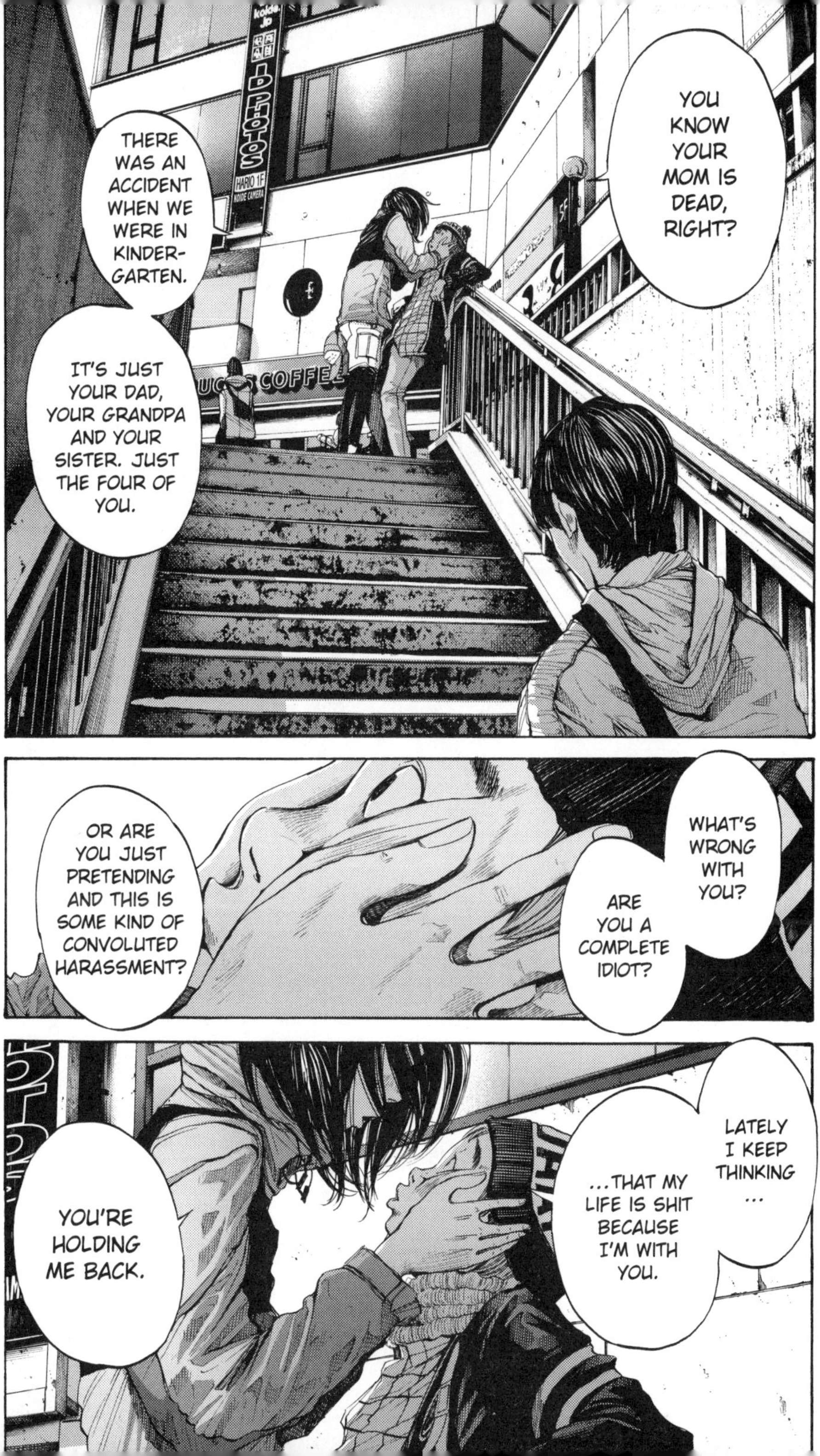
YOU KNOW YOUR MOM IS DEAD, RIGHT?
THERE WAS AN ACCIDENT WHEN WE WERE IN KINDER-GARTEN.
IT'S JUST YOUR DAD, YOUR GRANDPA AND YOUR SISTER. JUST THE FOUR OF YOU.
ID PHOTOS
HARIO 1F
KOIDE CAMERA
WHAT'S WRONG WITH YOU?
ARE YOU A COMPLETE IDIOT?
OR ARE YOU JUST PRETENDING AND THIS IS SOME KIND OF CONVOLUTED HARASSMENT?
LATELY I KEEP THINKING ...
...THAT MY LIFE IS SHIT BECAUSE I'M WITH YOU.
YOU'RE HOLDING ME BACK.

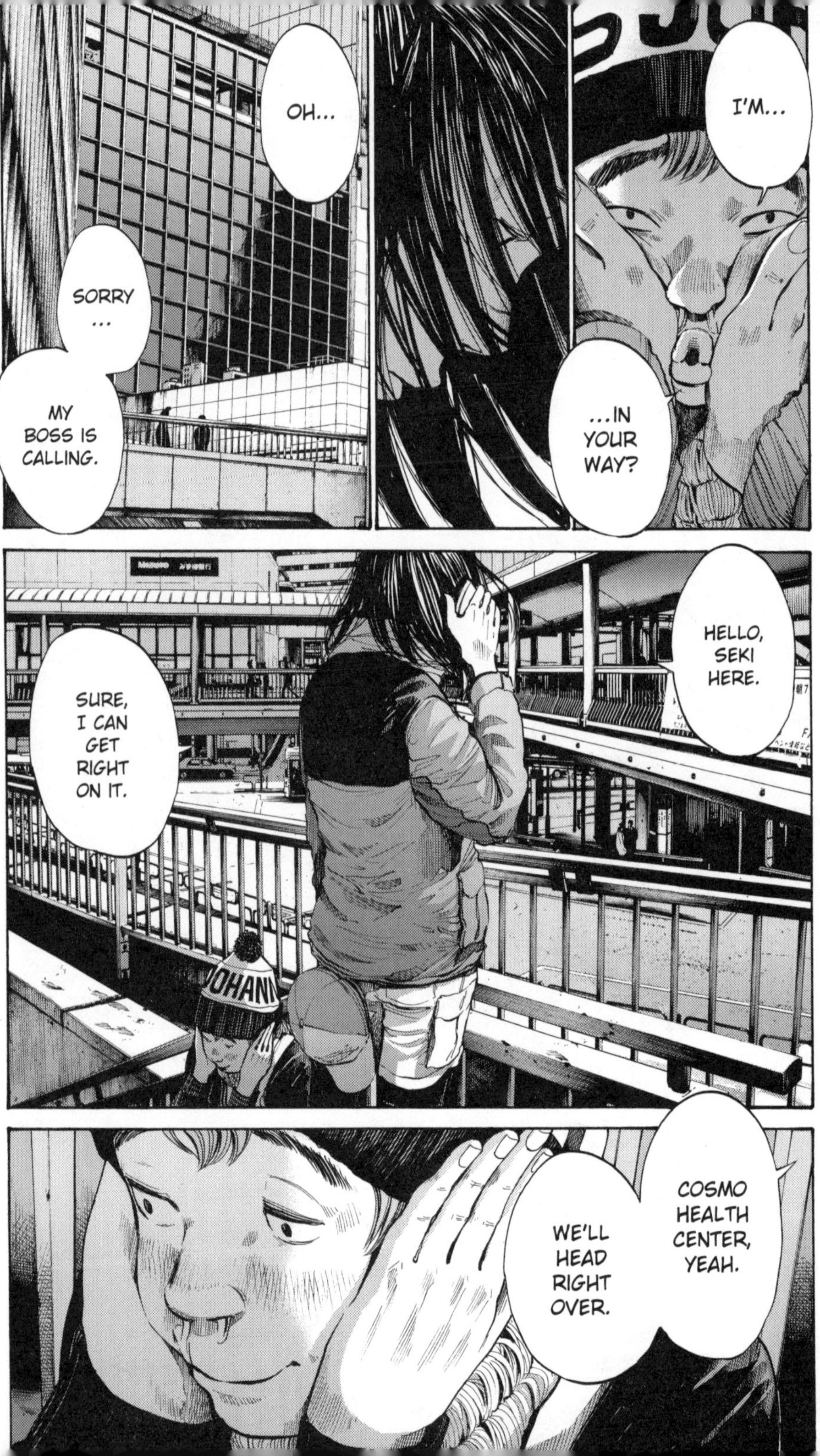
I'M...
...IN YOUR WAY?
OH...
SORRY ...
MY BOSS IS CALLING.
HELLO, SEKI HERE.
SURE, I CAN GET RIGHT ON IT.
COSMO HEALTH CENTER, YEAH.
WE'LL HEAD RIGHT OVER.

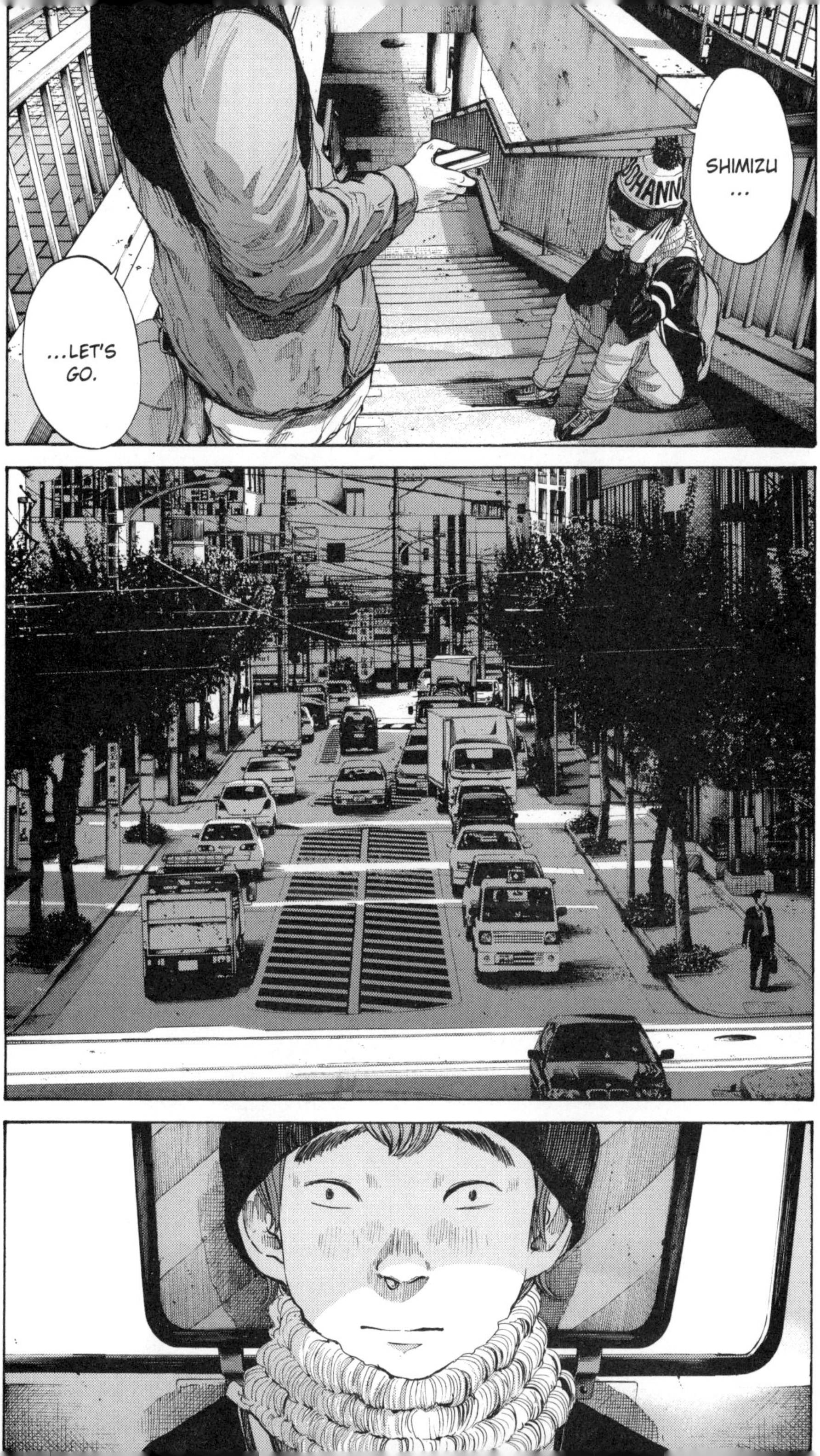
SHIMIZU ...
...LET'S GO.

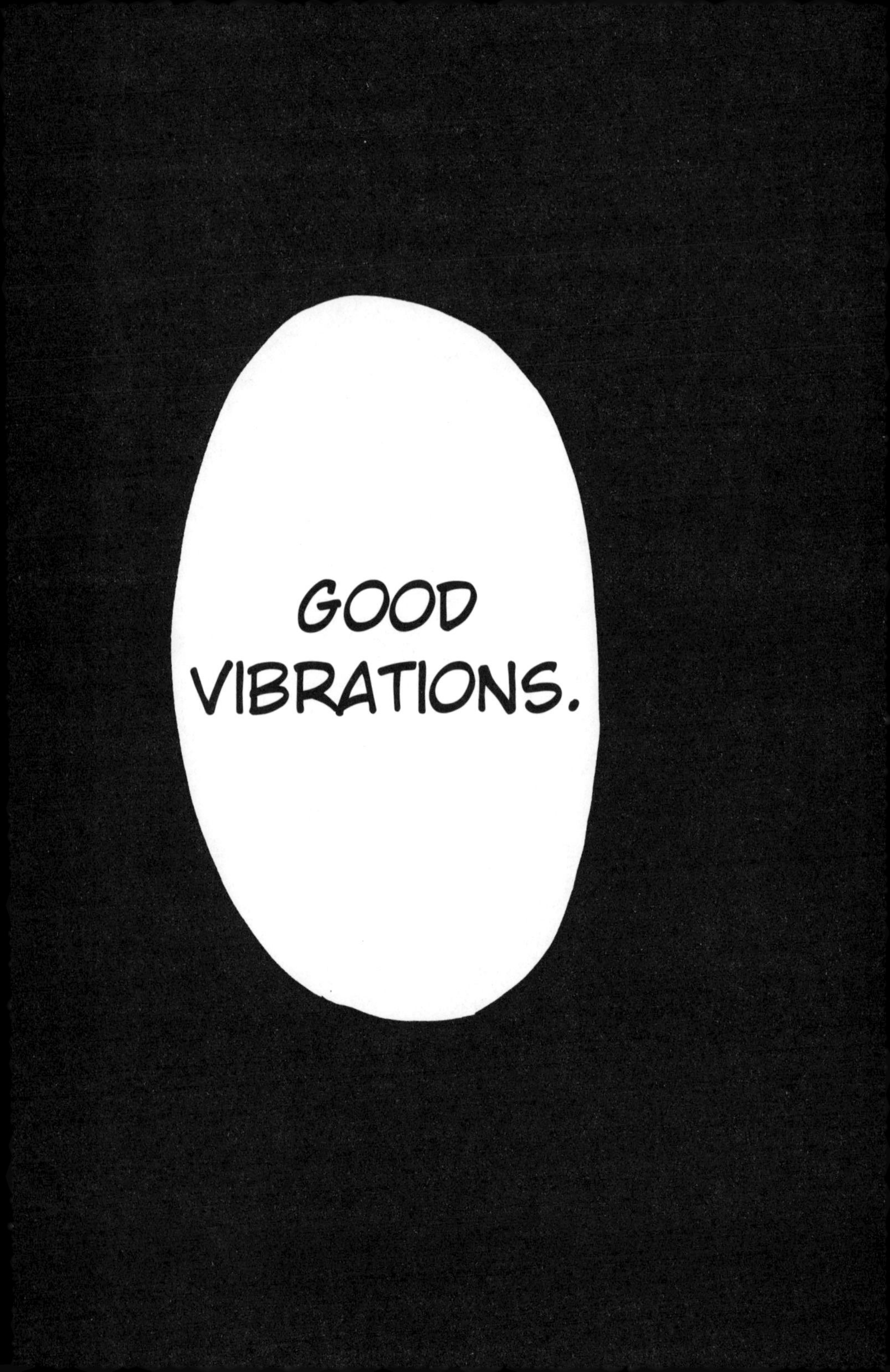
GOOD VIBRATIONS.

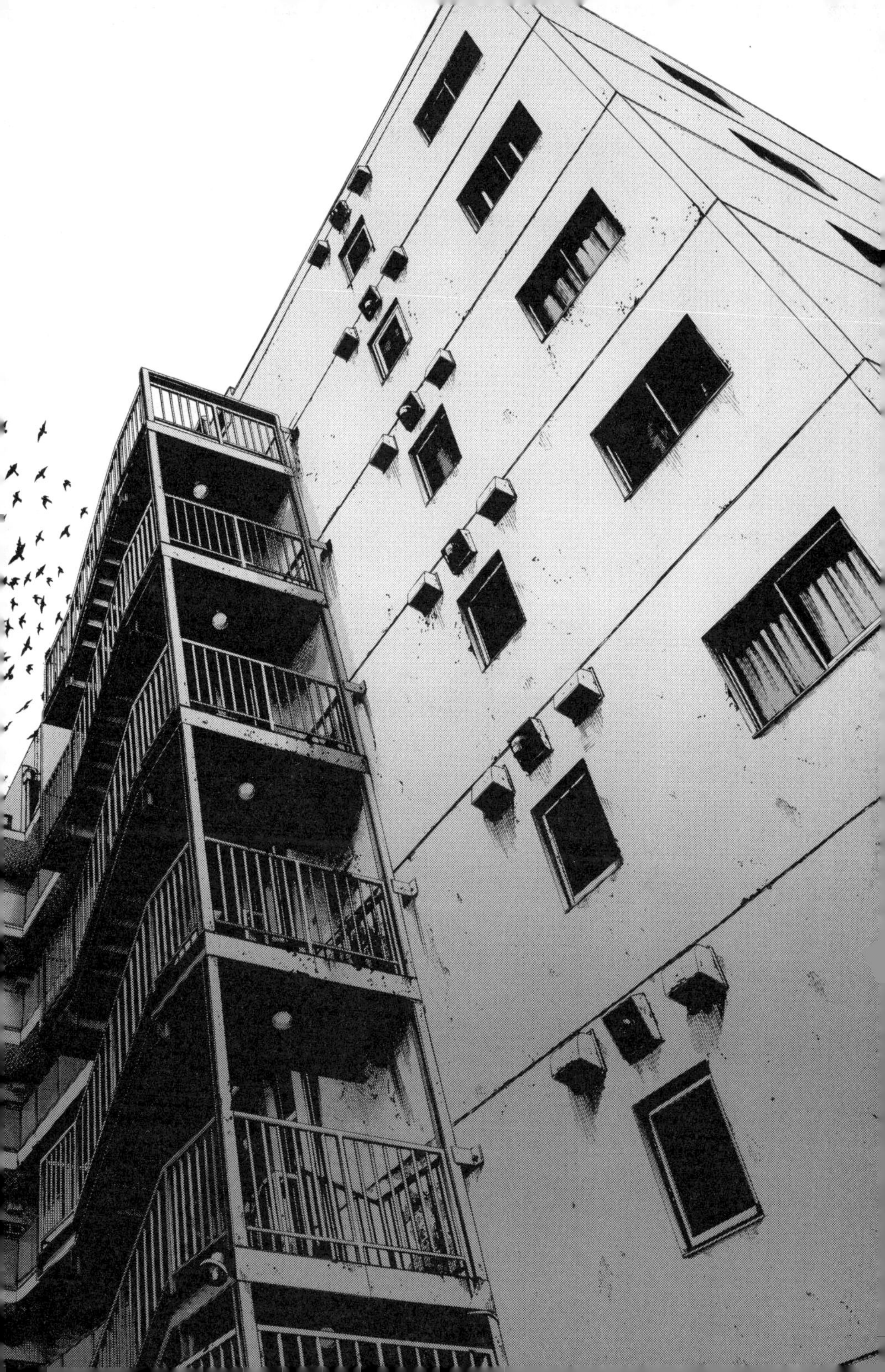

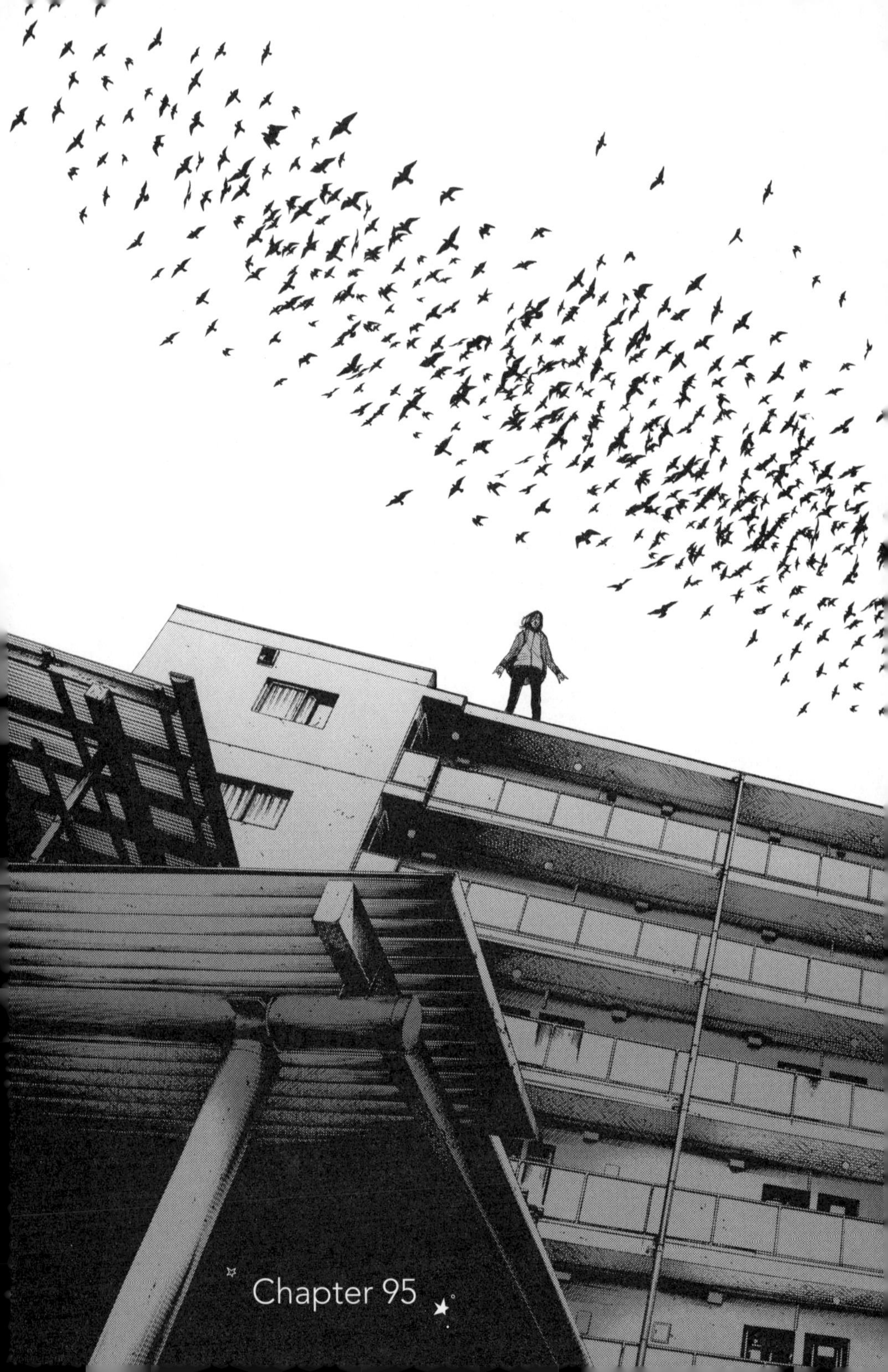
Chapter 95

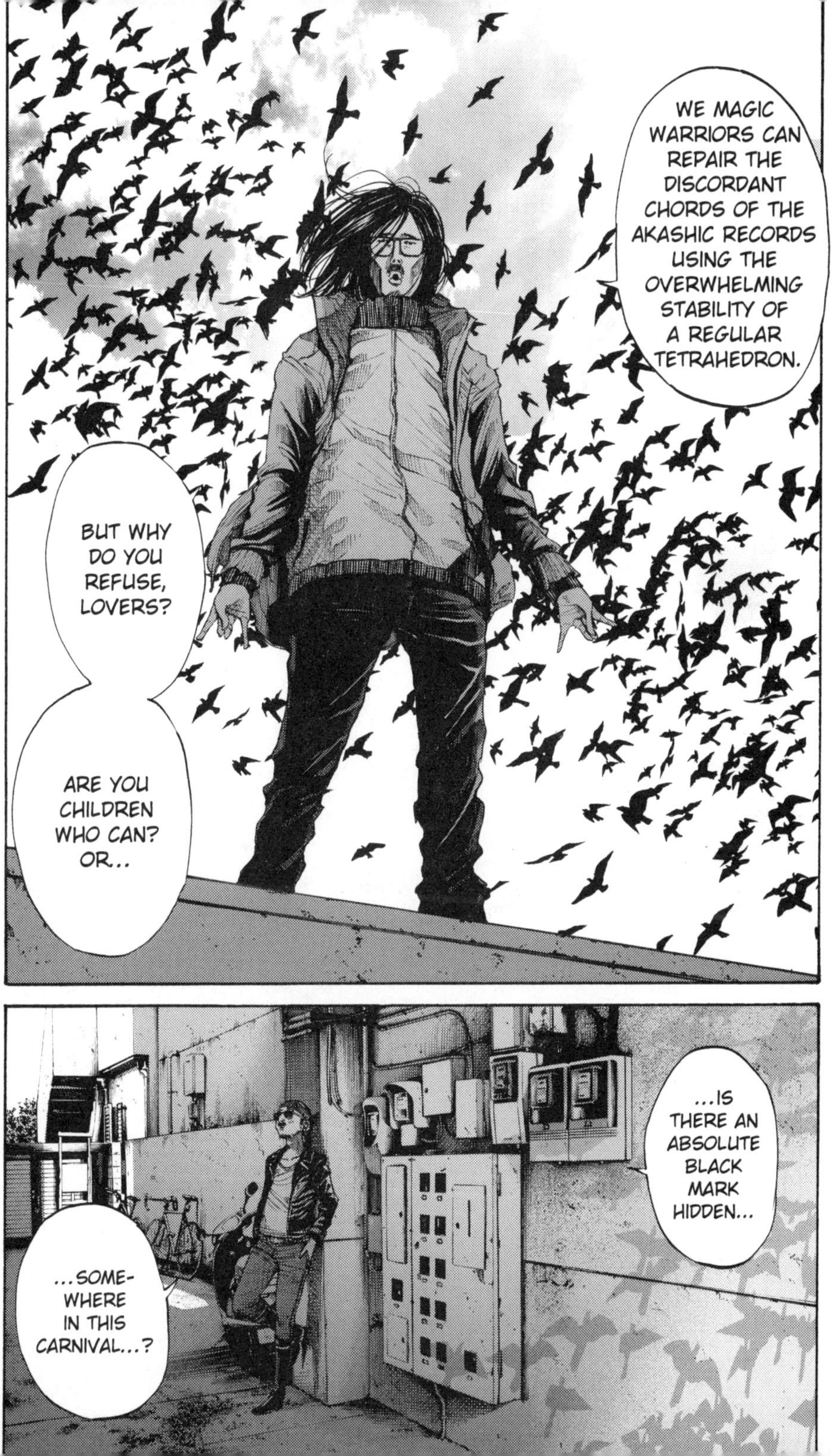
WE MAGIC WARRIORS CAN REPAIR THE DISCORDANT CHORDS OF THE AKASHIC RECORDS USING THE OVERWHELMING STABILITY OF A REGULAR TETRAHEDRON.
BUT WHY DO YOU REFUSE, LOVERS?
ARE YOU CHILDREN WHO CAN? OR...
...IS THERE AN ABSOLUTE BLACK MARK HIDDEN...
...SOME-WHERE IN THIS CARNIVAL...?

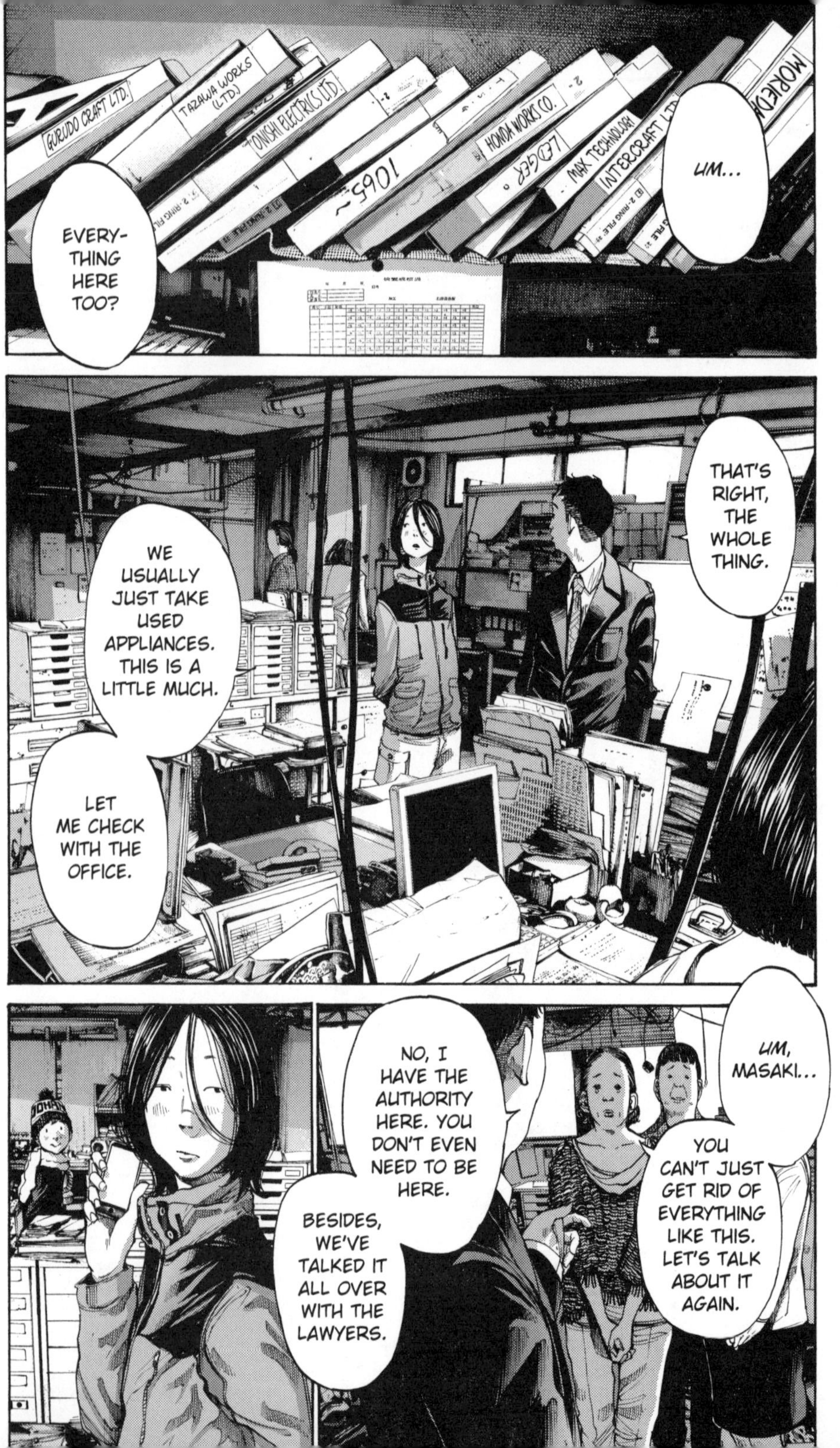
INTERCRAFT LTD.
MAX TECHNOLOGY
LEDGER
HONDA WORKS CO.
ONISHI ELECTRICS LTD.
TAZAWA WORKS (LTD.)
GURUDO CRAFT LTD.
UM...
EVERY-THING HERE TOO?
THAT'S RIGHT, THE WHOLE THING.
WE USUALLY JUST TAKE USED APPLIANCES. THIS IS A LITTLE MUCH.
LET ME CHECK WITH THE OFFICE.
UM, MASAKI...
YOU CAN'T JUST GET RID OF EVERYTHING LIKE THIS. LET'S TALK ABOUT IT AGAIN.
NO, I HAVE THE AUTHORITY HERE. YOU DON'T EVEN NEED TO BE HERE.
BESIDES, WE'VE TALKED IT ALL OVER WITH THE LAWYERS.

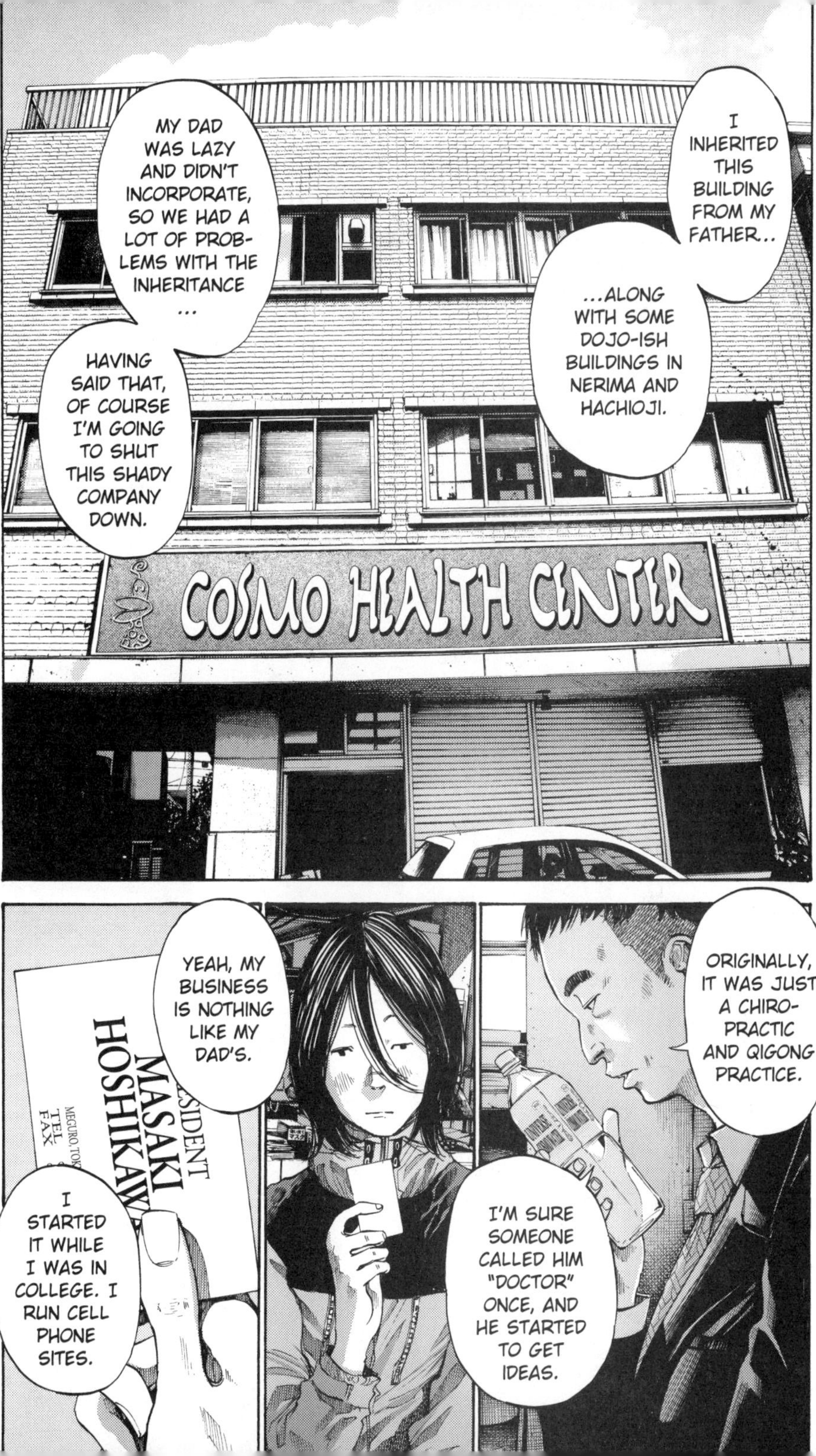
I INHERITED THIS BUILDING FROM MY FATHER...
...ALONG WITH SOME DOJO-ISH BUILDINGS IN NERIMA AND HACHIOJI.
MY DAD WAS LAZY AND DIDN'T INCORPORATE, SO WE HAD A LOT OF PROBLEMS WITH THE INHERITANCE...
HAVING SAID THAT, OF COURSE I'M GOING TO SHUT THIS SHADY COMPANY DOWN.
COSMO HEALTH CENTER
ORIGINALLY, IT WAS JUST A CHIROPRACTIC AND QIGONG PRACTICE.
I'M SURE SOMEONE CALLED HIM "DOCTOR" ONCE, AND HE STARTED TO GET IDEAS.
YEAH, MY BUSINESS IS NOTHING LIKE MY DAD'S.
MASAKI
TEL
FAX
I STARTED IT WHILE I WAS IN COLLEGE. I RUN CELL PHONE SITES.

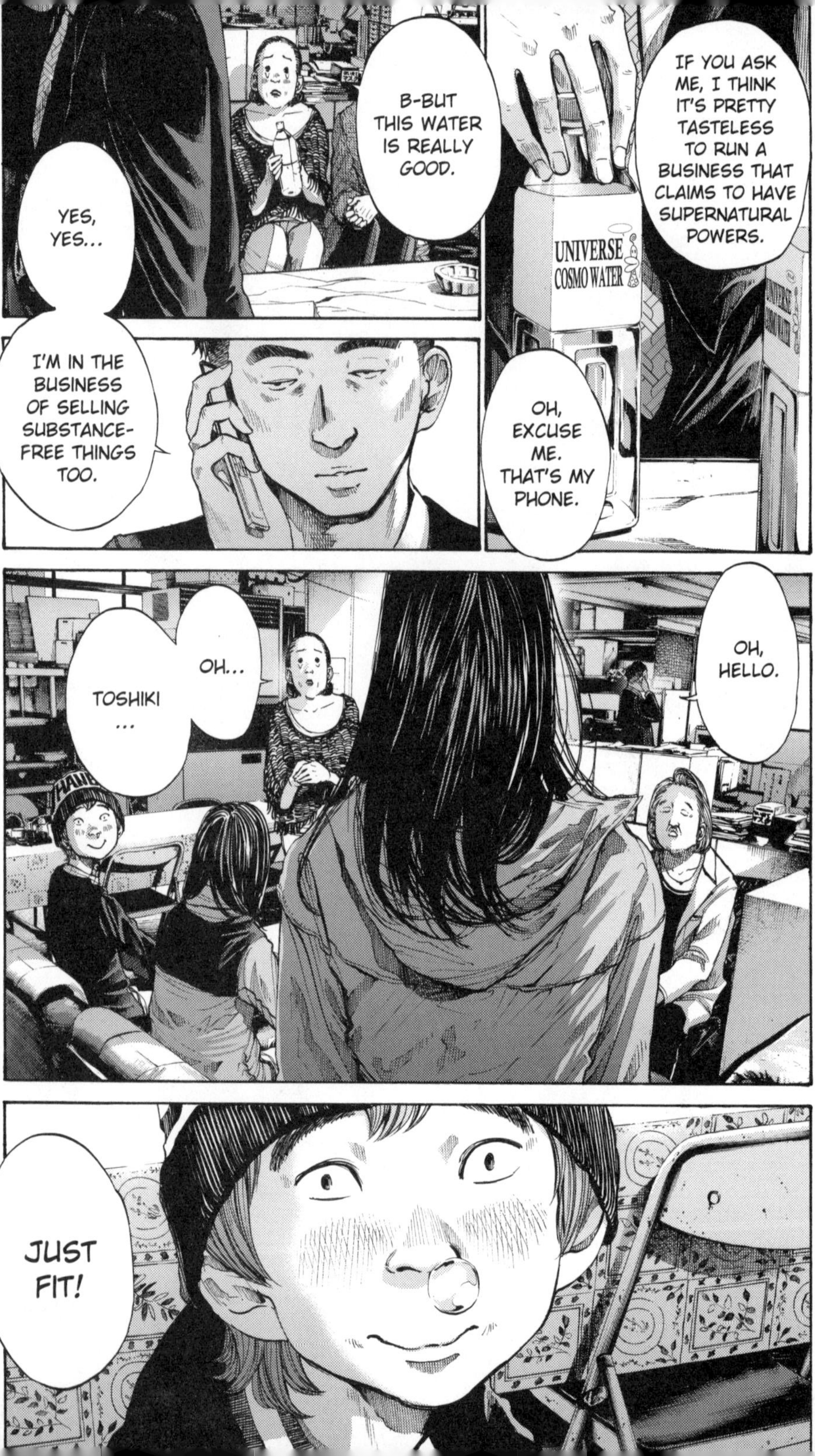
IF YOU ASK ME, I THINK IT'S PRETTY TASTELESS TO RUN A BUSINESS THAT CLAIMS TO HAVE SUPERNATURAL POWERS.
UNIVERSE COSMO WATER
OH, EXCUSE ME. THAT'S MY PHONE.
B-BUT THIS WATER IS REALLY GOOD.
YES, YES...
I'M IN THE BUSINESS OF SELLING SUBSTANCE-FREE THINGS TOO.
OH, HELLO.
OH...
TOSHIKI ...
JUST FIT!

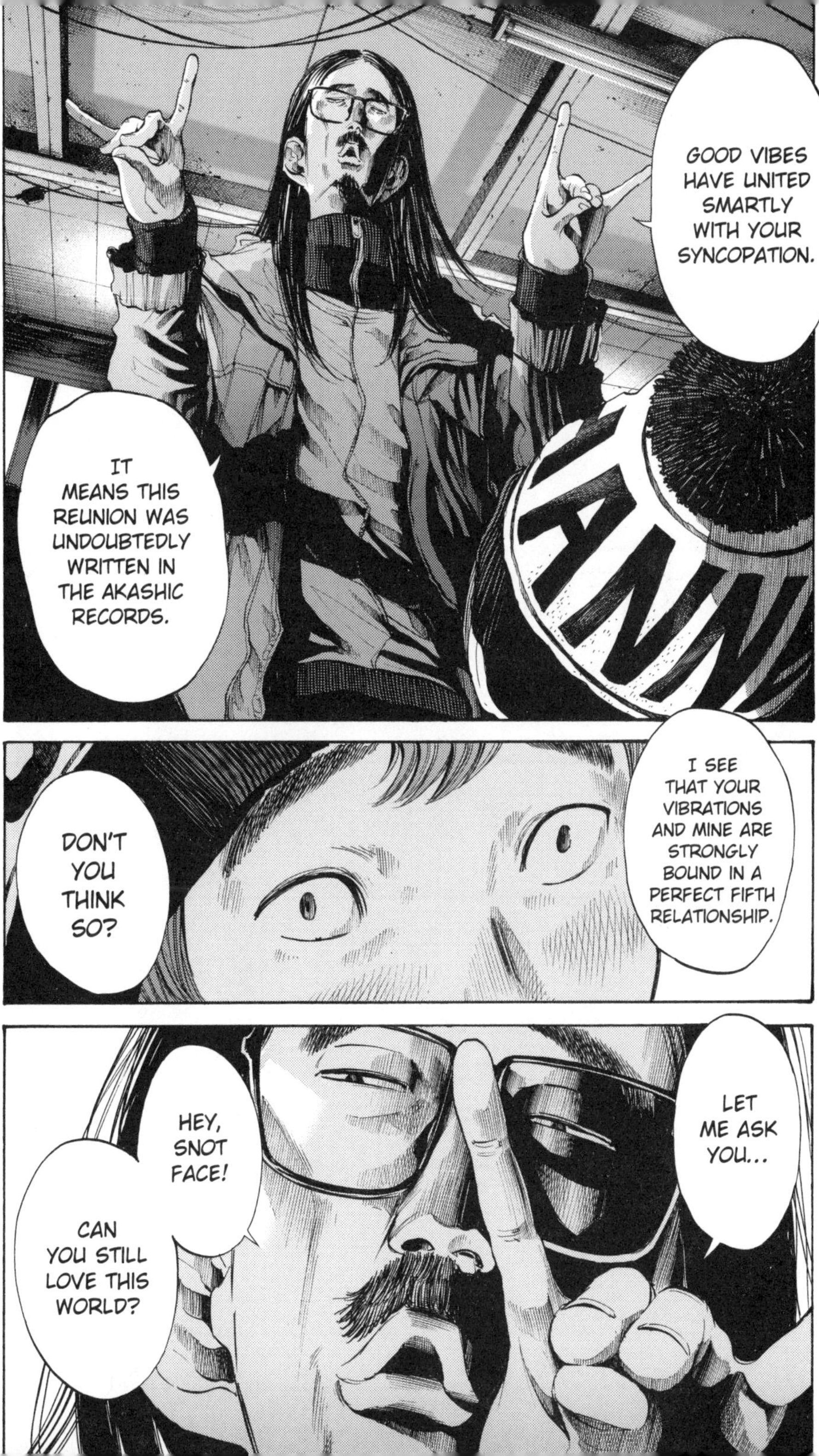
GOOD VIBES HAVE UNITED SMARTLY WITH YOUR SYNCOPATION.
IT MEANS THIS REUNION WAS UNDOUBTEDLY WRITTEN IN THE AKASHIC RECORDS.
I SEE THAT YOUR VIBRATIONS AND MINE ARE STRONGLY BOUND IN A PERFECT FIFTH RELATIONSHIP.
DON'T YOU THINK SO?
LET ME ASK YOU...
HEY, SNOT FACE!
CAN YOU STILL LOVE THIS WORLD?

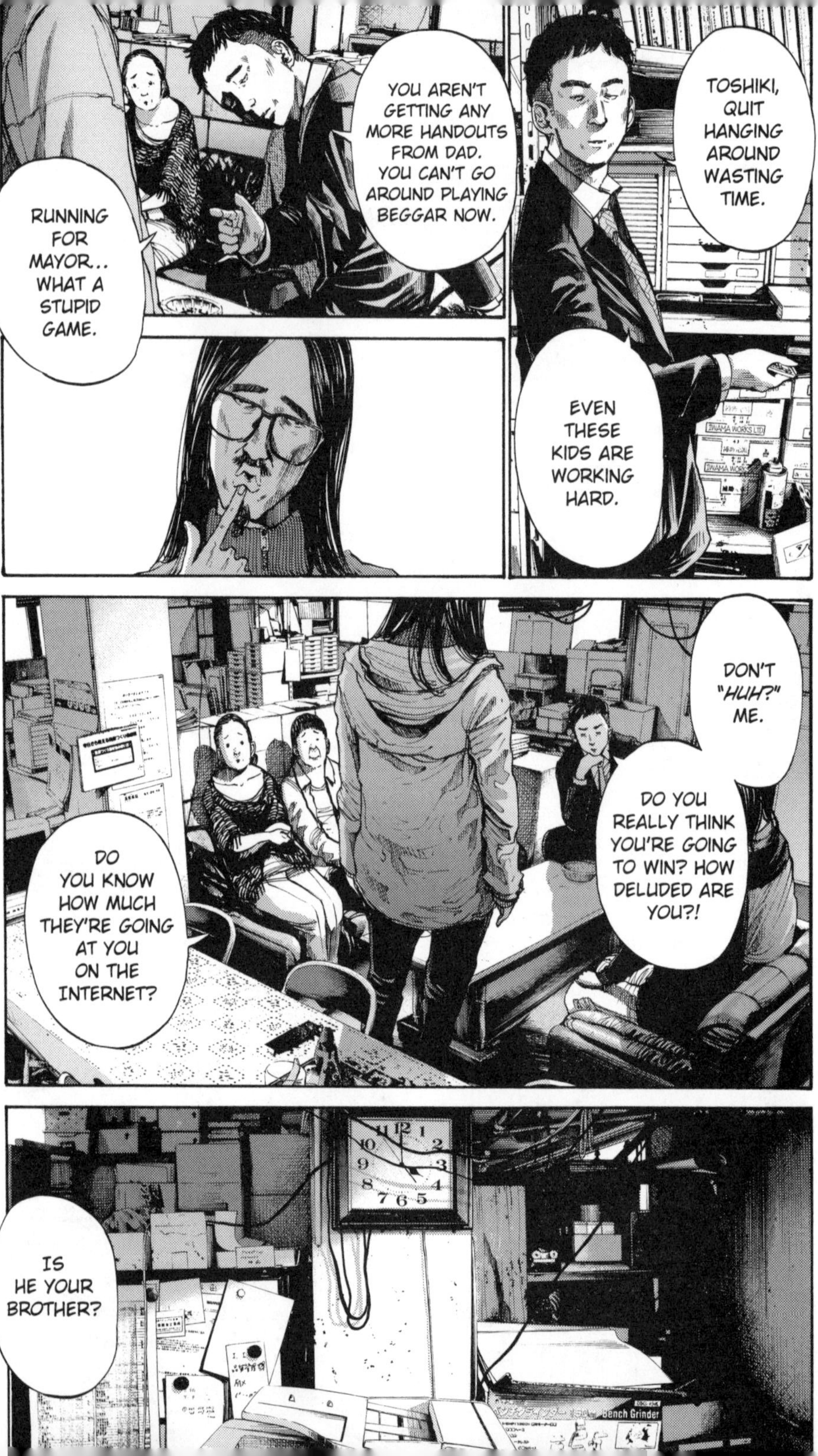
TOSHIKI, QUIT HANGING AROUND WASTING TIME.
EVEN THESE KIDS ARE WORKING HARD.
IWAMA WORKS LTD
YOU AREN'T GETTING ANY MORE HANDOUTS FROM DAD. YOU CAN'T GO AROUND PLAYING BEGGAR NOW.
RUNNING FOR MAYOR... WHAT A STUPID GAME.
DON'T "*HUH?*" ME.
DO YOU REALLY THINK YOU'RE GOING TO WIN? HOW DELUDED ARE YOU?!
DO YOU KNOW HOW MUCH THEY'RE GOING AT YOU ON THE INTERNET?
IS HE YOUR BROTHER?
Bench Grinder

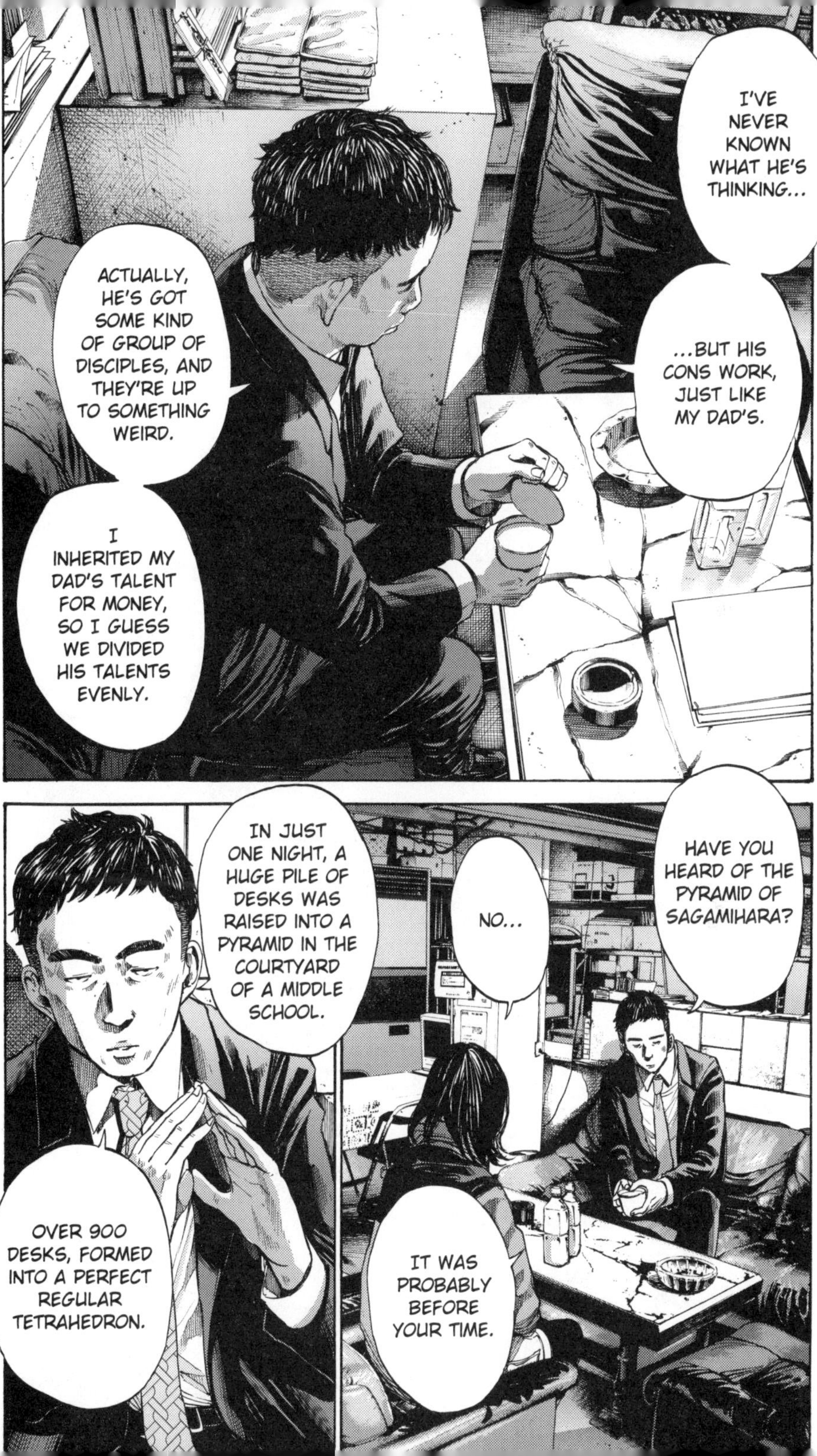
I'VE NEVER KNOWN WHAT HE'S THINKING...
...BUT HIS CONS WORK, JUST LIKE MY DAD'S.
ACTUALLY, HE'S GOT SOME KIND OF GROUP OF DISCIPLES, AND THEY'RE UP TO SOMETHING WEIRD.
I INHERITED MY DAD'S TALENT FOR MONEY, SO I GUESS WE DIVIDED HIS TALENTS EVENLY.
HAVE YOU HEARD OF THE PYRAMID OF SAGAMIHARA?
NO...
IT WAS PROBABLY BEFORE YOUR TIME.
IN JUST ONE NIGHT, A HUGE PILE OF DESKS WAS RAISED INTO A PYRAMID IN THE COURTYARD OF A MIDDLE SCHOOL.
OVER 900 DESKS, FORMED INTO A PERFECT REGULAR TETRAHEDRON.

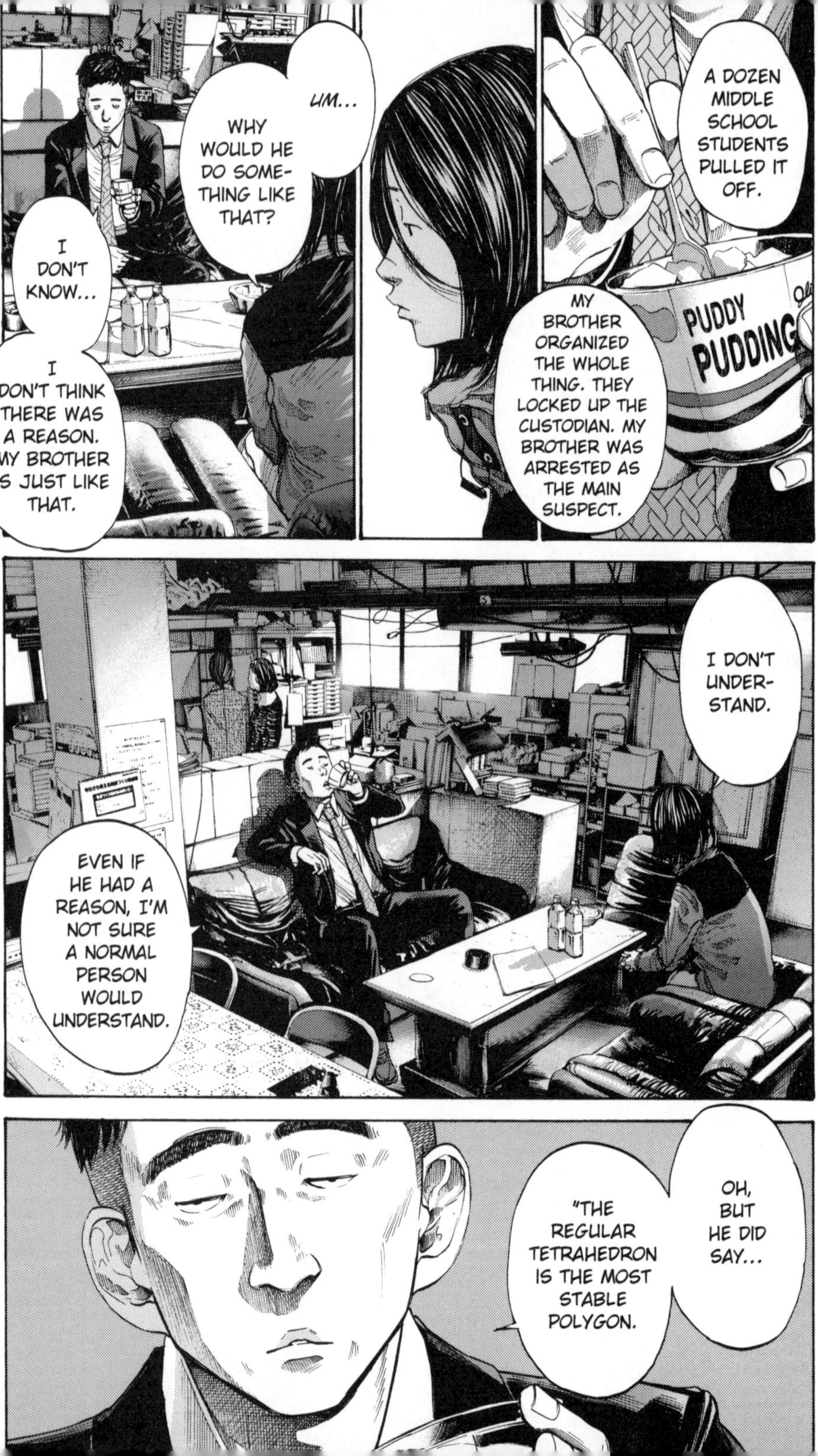
A DOZEN MIDDLE SCHOOL STUDENTS PULLED IT OFF.
PUDDY PUDDING
MY BROTHER ORGANIZED THE WHOLE THING. THEY LOCKED UP THE CUSTODIAN. MY BROTHER WAS ARRESTED AS THE MAIN SUSPECT.
UM...
WHY WOULD HE DO SOME-THING LIKE THAT?
I DON'T KNOW...
I DON'T THINK THERE WAS A REASON. MY BROTHER IS JUST LIKE THAT.
I DON'T UNDER-STAND.
EVEN IF HE HAD A REASON, I'M NOT SURE A NORMAL PERSON WOULD UNDERSTAND.
OH, BUT HE DID SAY...
"THE REGULAR TETRAHEDRON IS THE MOST STABLE POLYGON.

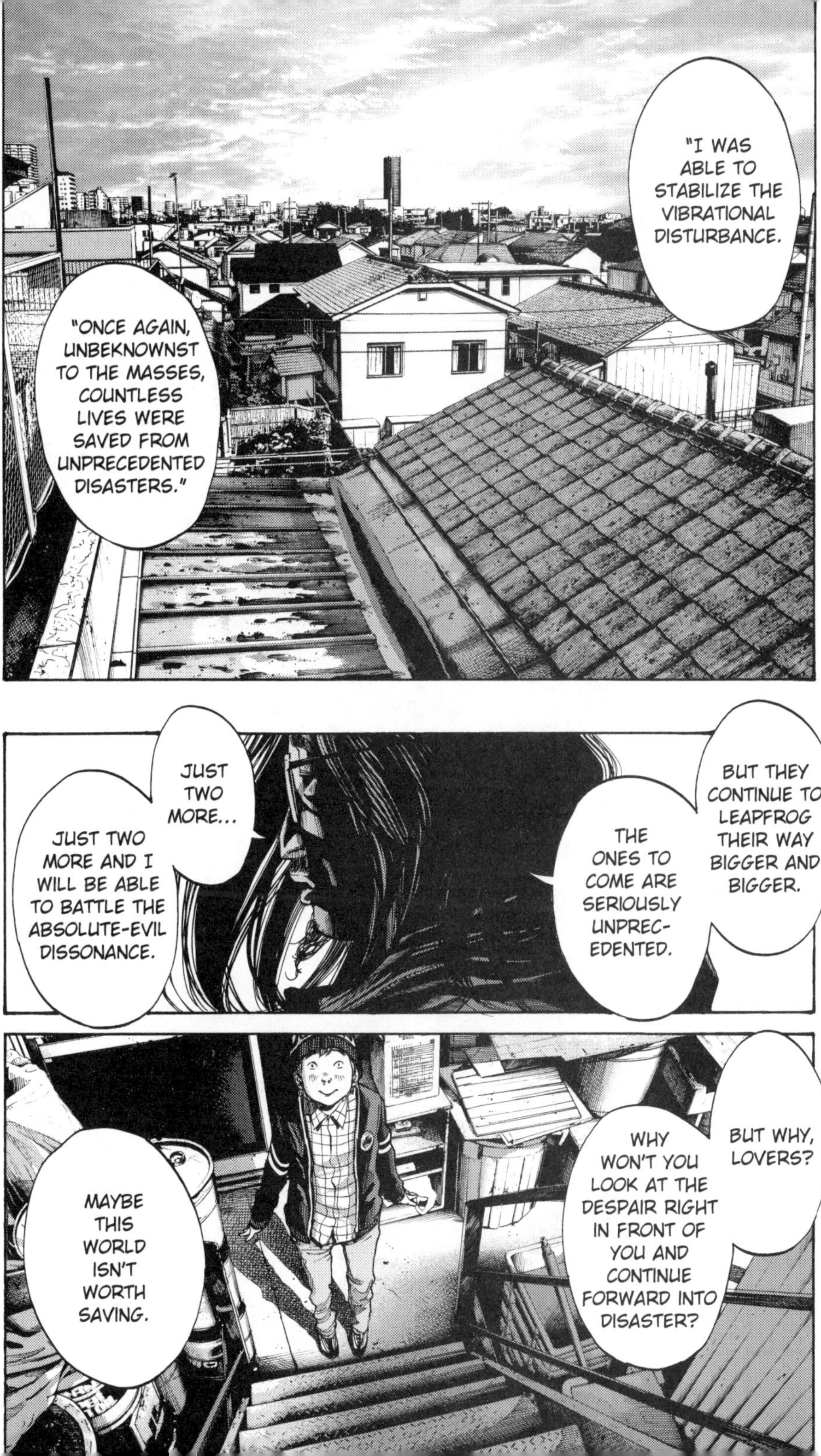
"I WAS ABLE TO STABILIZE THE VIBRATIONAL DISTURBANCE.
"ONCE AGAIN, UNBEKNOWNST TO THE MASSES, COUNTLESS LIVES WERE SAVED FROM UNPRECEDENTED DISASTERS."
BUT THEY CONTINUE TO LEAPFROG THEIR WAY BIGGER AND BIGGER.
THE ONES TO COME ARE SERIOUSLY UNPREC-EDENTED.
JUST TWO MORE...
JUST TWO MORE AND I WILL BE ABLE TO BATTLE THE ABSOLUTE-EVIL DISSONANCE.
BUT WHY, LOVERS?
WHY WON'T YOU LOOK AT THE DESPAIR RIGHT IN FRONT OF YOU AND CONTINUE FORWARD INTO DISASTER?
MAYBE THIS WORLD ISN'T WORTH SAVING.

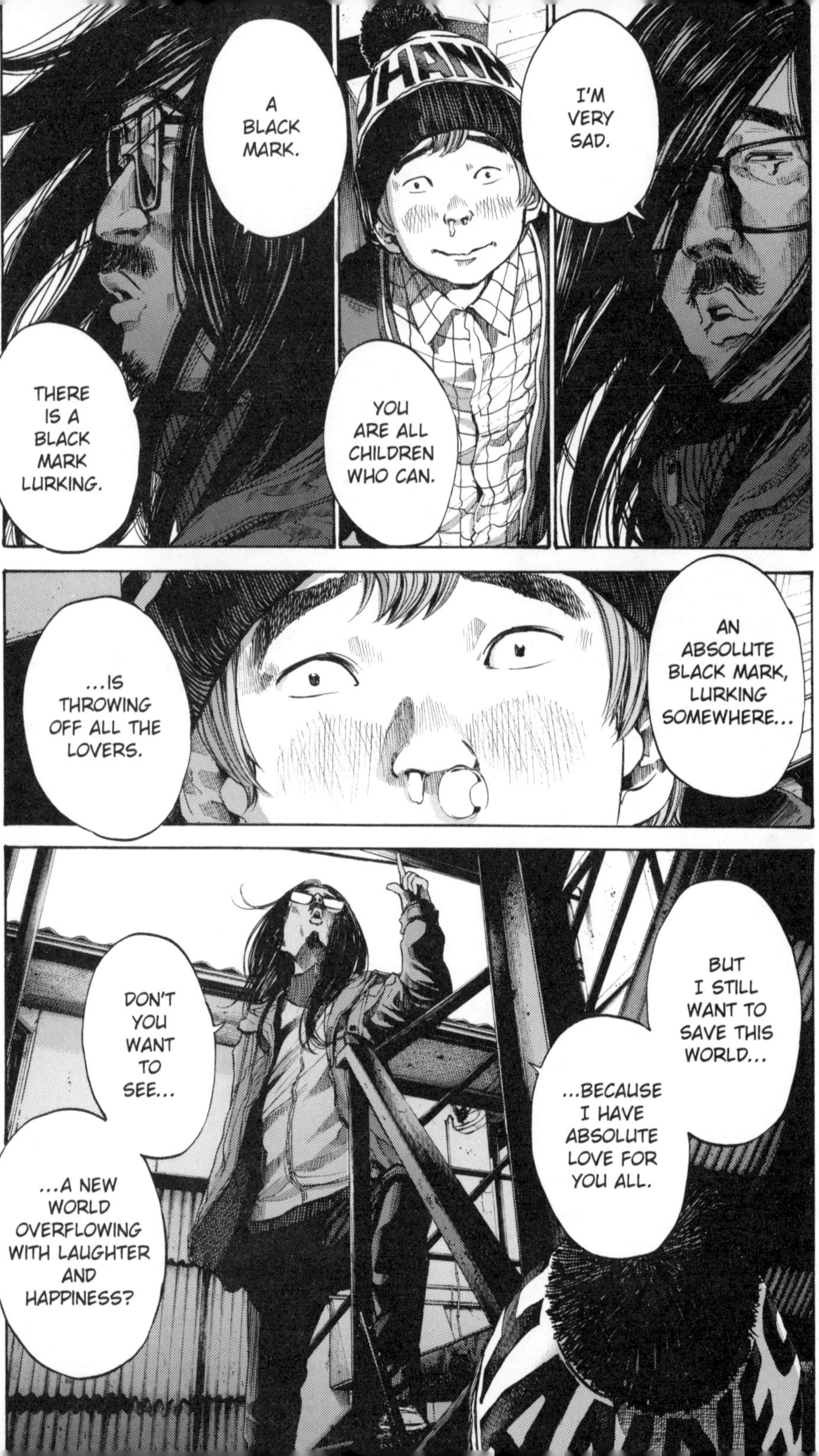

I'M VERY SAD.
YOU ARE ALL CHILDREN WHO CAN.
A BLACK MARK.
THERE IS A BLACK MARK LURKING.
AN ABSOLUTE BLACK MARK, LURKING SOMEWHERE...
...IS THROWING OFF ALL THE LOVERS.
BUT I STILL WANT TO SAVE THIS WORLD...
...BECAUSE I HAVE ABSOLUTE LOVE FOR YOU ALL.
DON'T YOU WANT TO SEE...
...A NEW WORLD OVERFLOWING WITH LAUGHTER AND HAPPINESS?

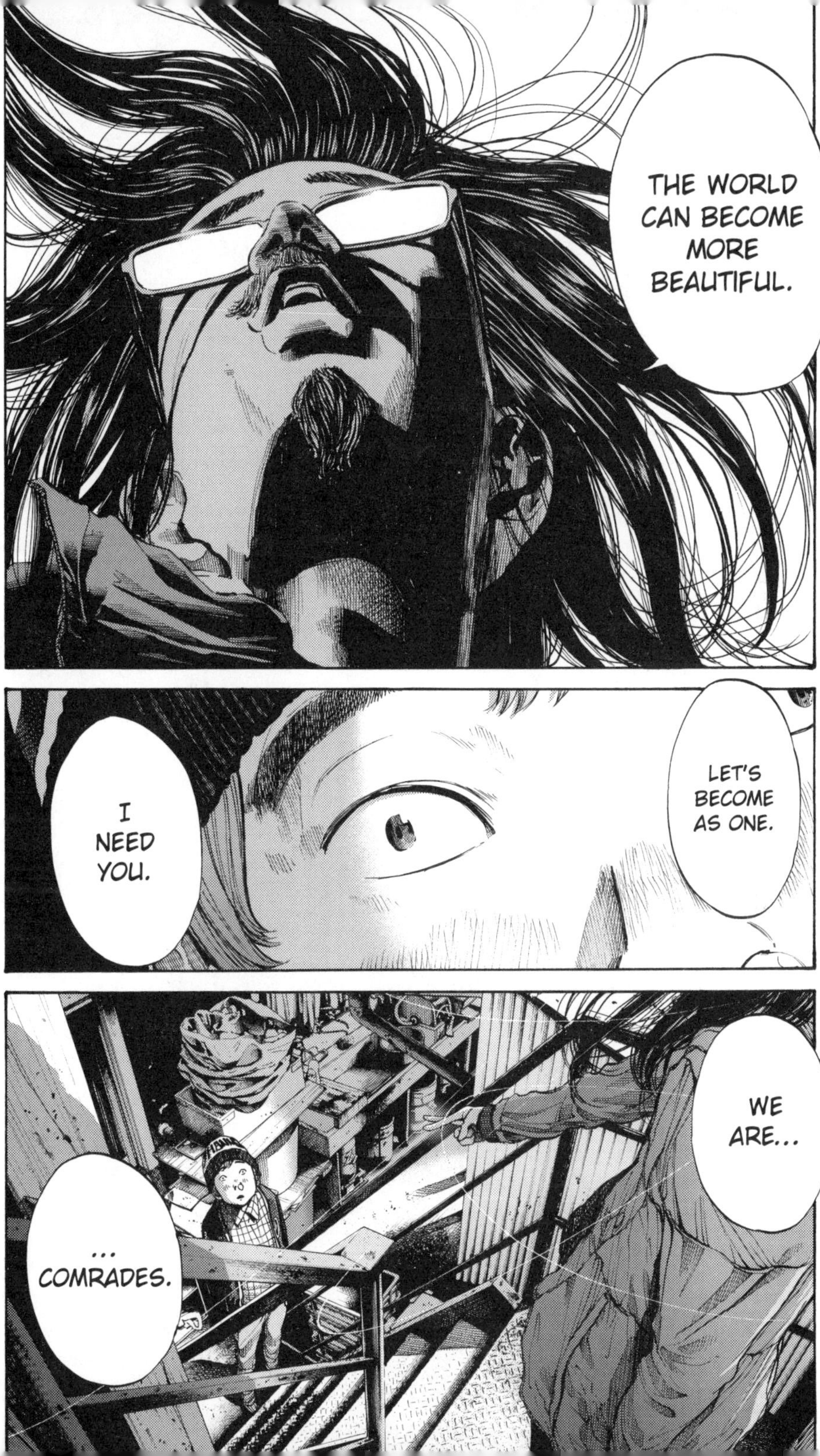
THE WORLD CAN BECOME MORE BEAUTIFUL.
LET'S BECOME AS ONE.
I NEED YOU.
WE ARE...
...COMRADES.

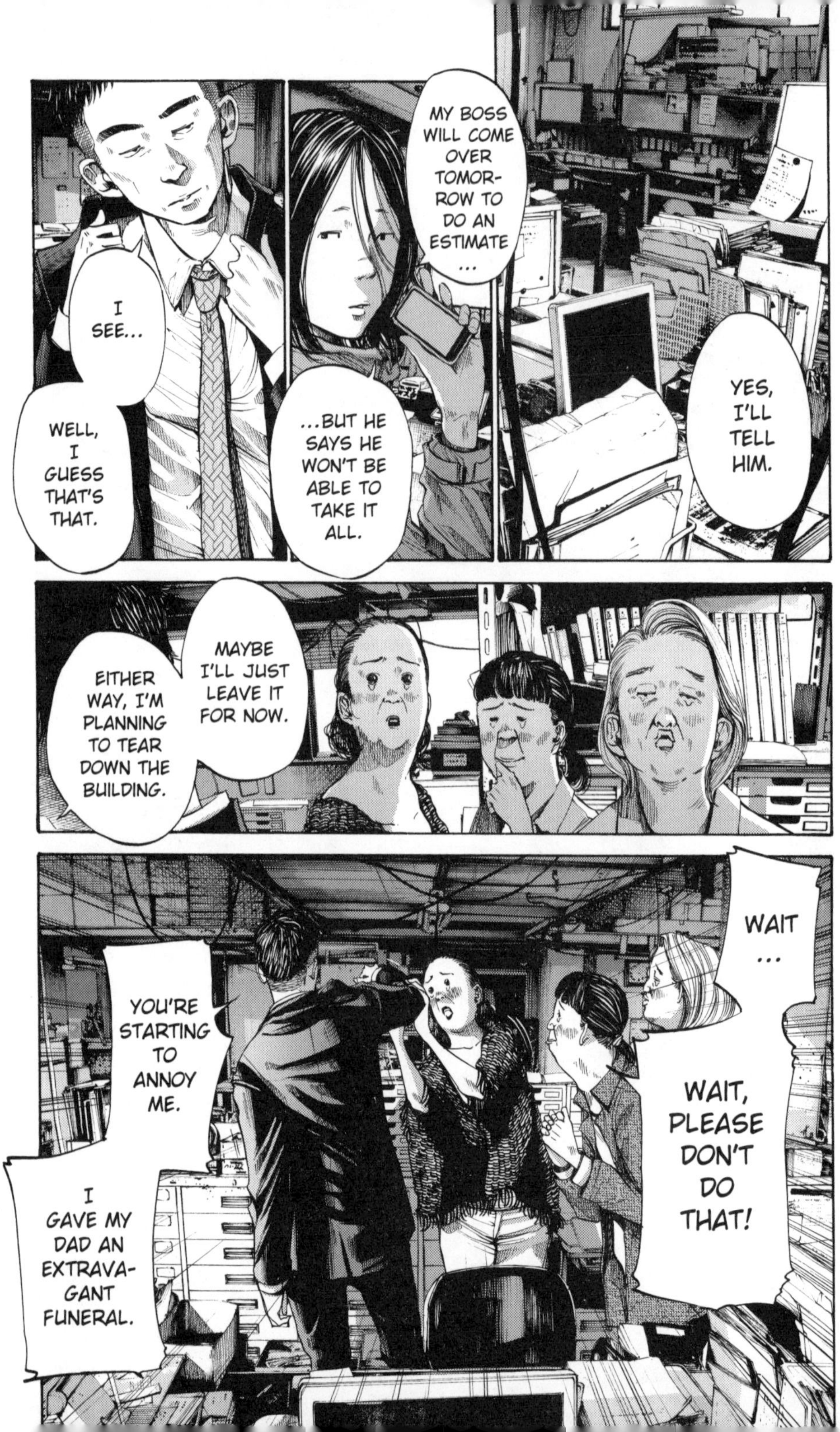
MY BOSS WILL COME OVER TOMOR-ROW TO DO AN ESTIMATE ...
...BUT HE SAYS HE WON'T BE ABLE TO TAKE IT ALL.
I SEE...
WELL, I GUESS THAT'S THAT.
YES, I'LL TELL HIM.
MAYBE I'LL JUST LEAVE IT FOR NOW.
EITHER WAY, I'M PLANNING TO TEAR DOWN THE BUILDING.
WAIT ...
WAIT, PLEASE DON'T DO THAT!
YOU'RE STARTING TO ANNOY ME.
I GAVE MY DAD AN EXTRAVA-GANT FUNERAL.

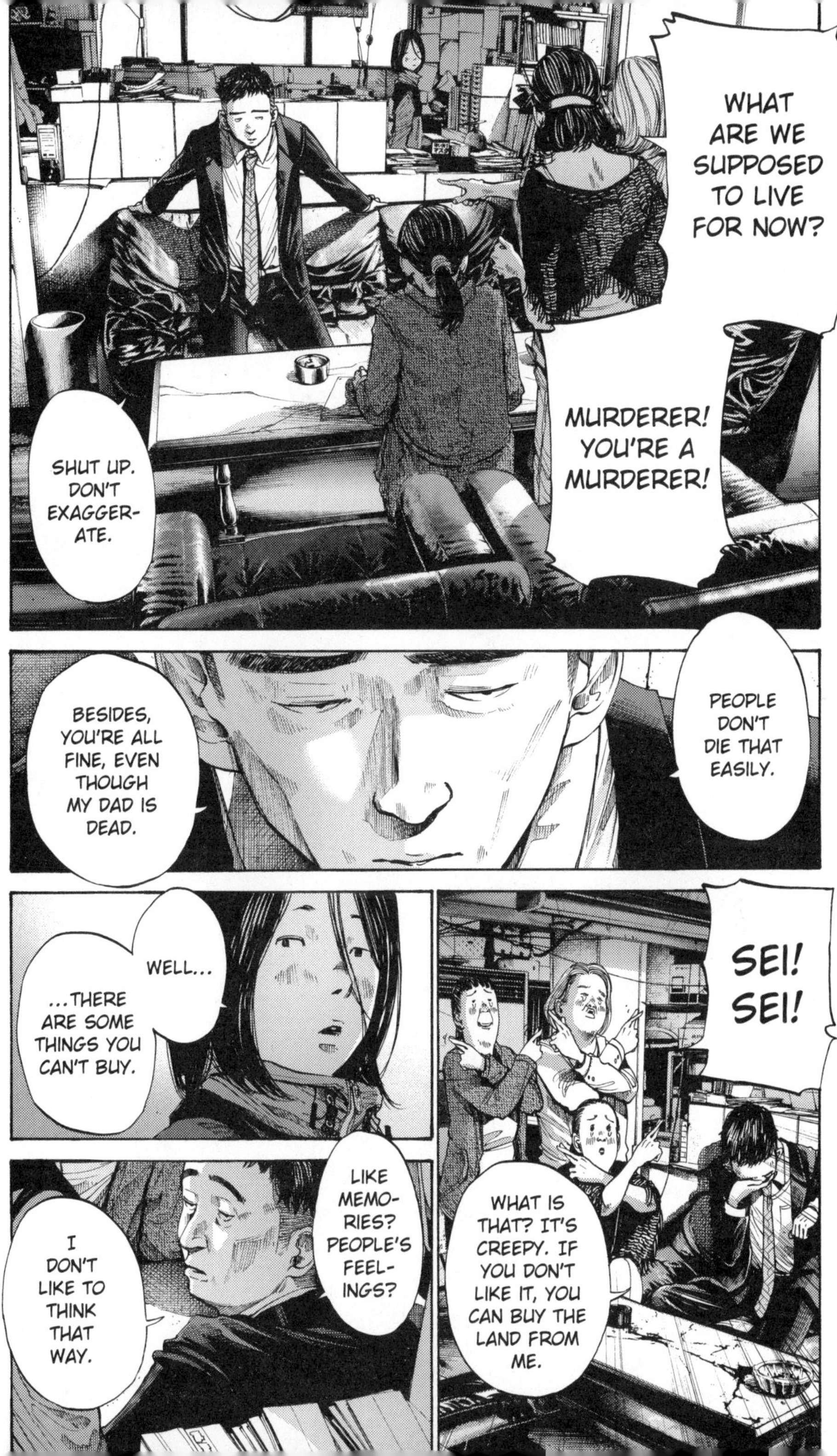
WHAT ARE WE SUPPOSED TO LIVE FOR NOW?
MURDERER! YOU'RE A MURDERER!
SHUT UP. DON'T EXAGGERATE.
PEOPLE DON'T DIE THAT EASILY.
BESIDES, YOU'RE ALL FINE, EVEN THOUGH MY DAD IS DEAD.
SEI! SEI!
WHAT IS THAT? IT'S CREEPY. IF YOU DON'T LIKE IT, YOU CAN BUY THE LAND FROM ME.
WELL...
...THERE ARE SOME THINGS YOU CAN'T BUY.
LIKE MEMORIES? PEOPLE'S FEELINGS?
I DON'T LIKE TO THINK THAT WAY.

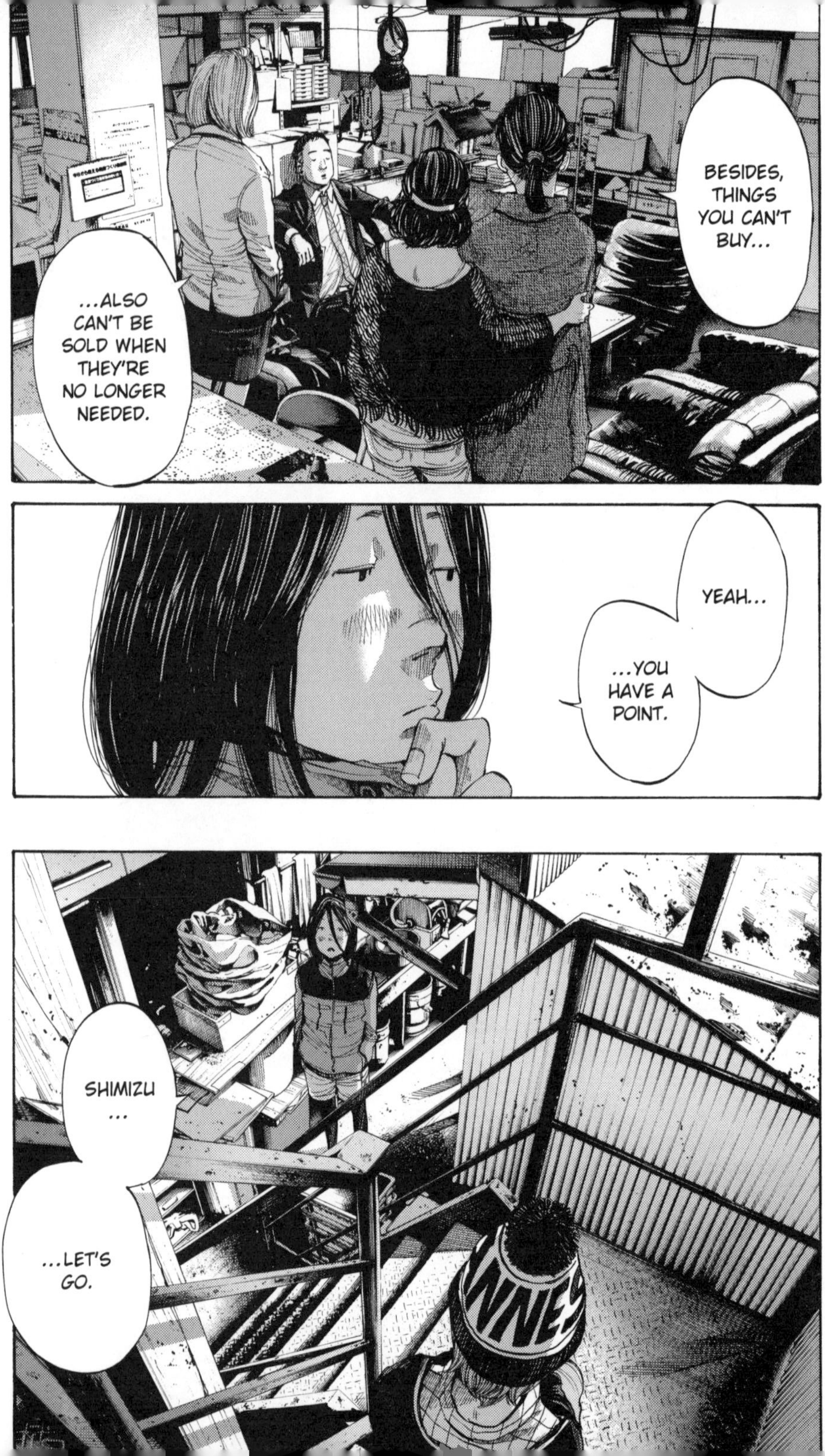
BESIDES, THINGS YOU CAN'T BUY...
...ALSO CAN'T BE SOLD WHEN THEY'RE NO LONGER NEEDED.
YEAH...
...YOU HAVE A POINT.
SHIMIZU...
...LET'S GO.

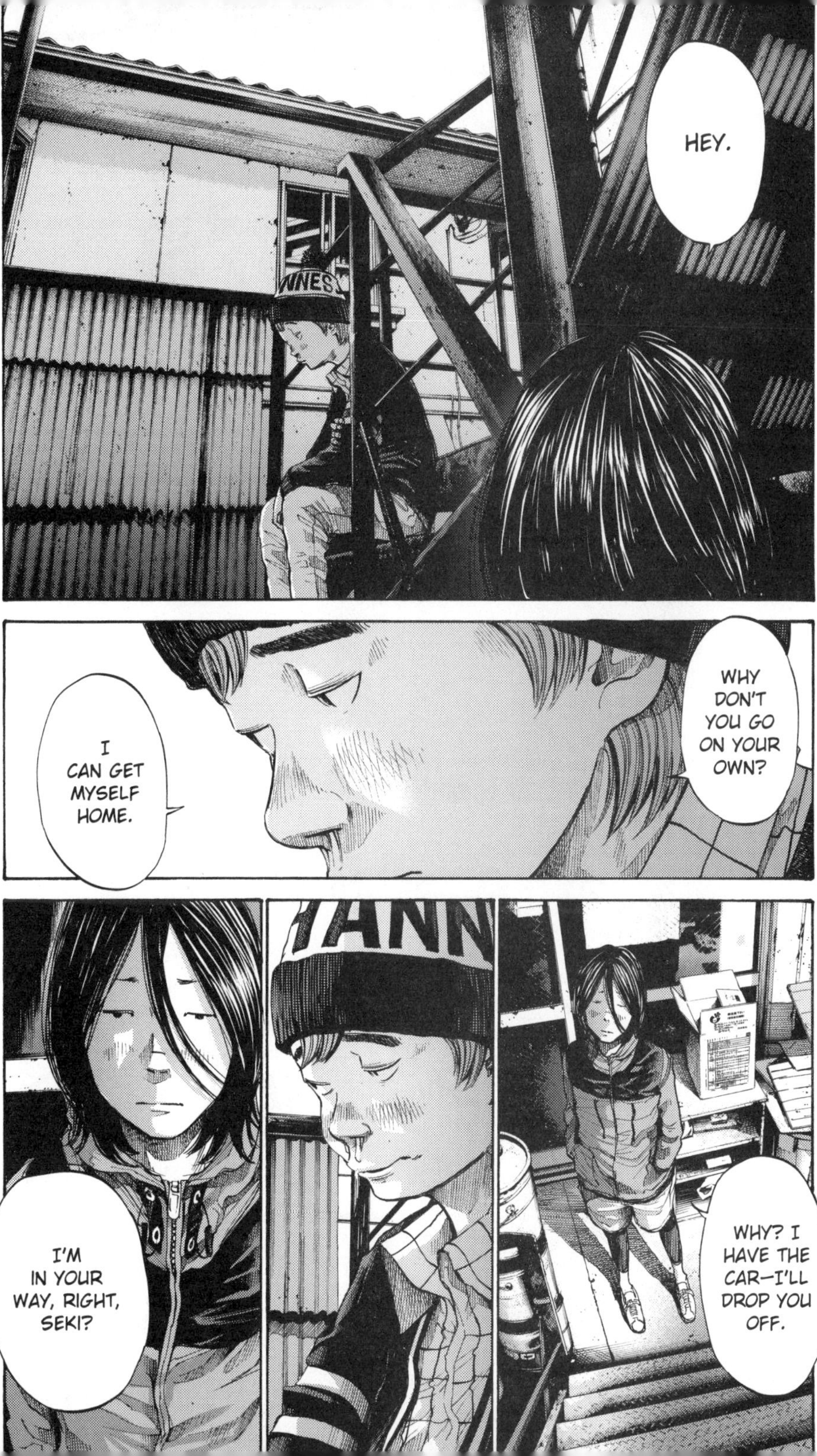
HEY.
WHY DON'T YOU GO ON YOUR OWN?
I CAN GET MYSELF HOME.
WHY? I HAVE THE CAR—I'LL DROP YOU OFF.
I'M IN YOUR WAY, RIGHT, SEKI?

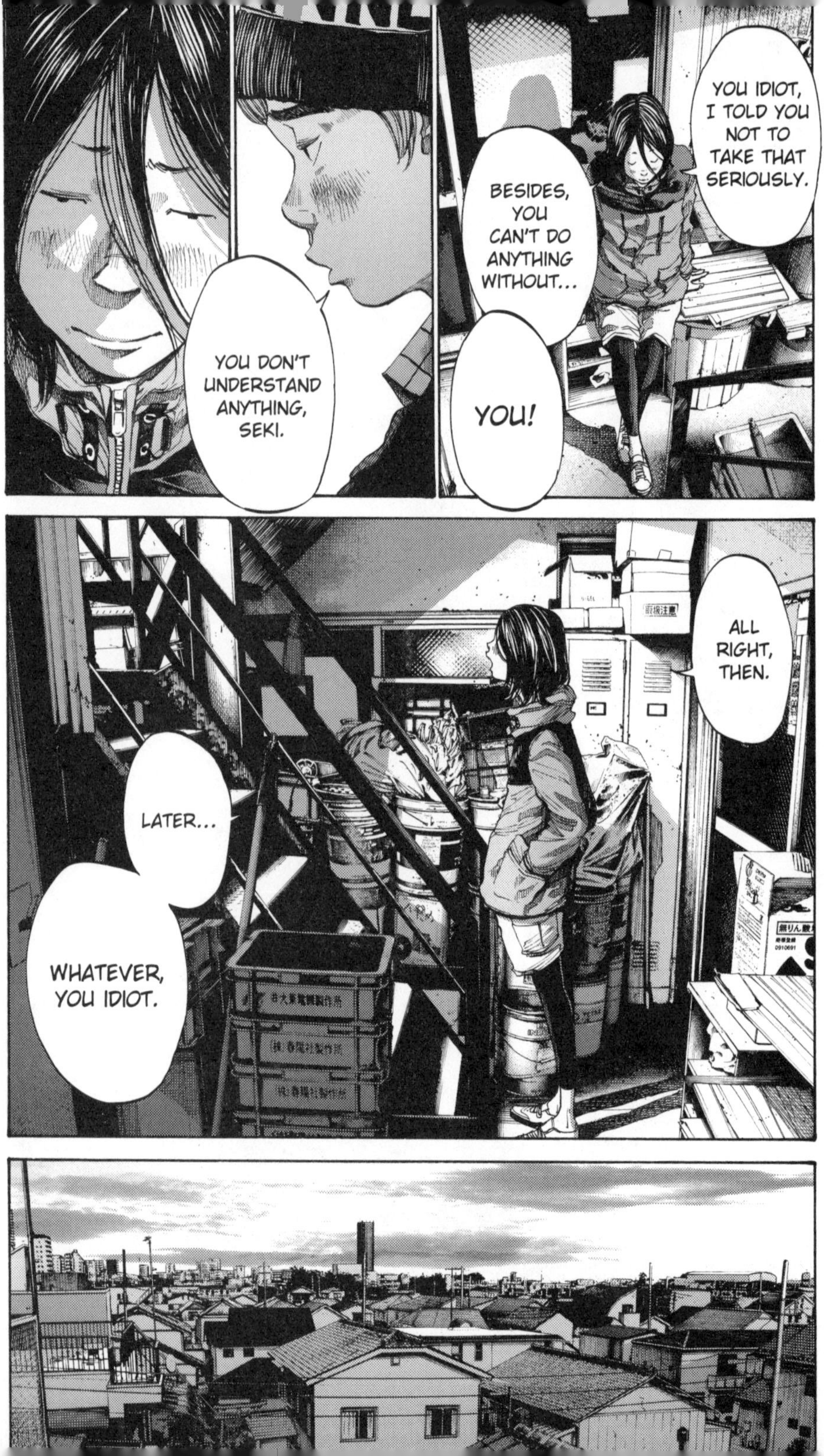
YOU IDIOT, I TOLD YOU NOT TO TAKE THAT SERIOUSLY.
BESIDES, YOU CAN'T DO ANYTHING WITHOUT...
YOU!
YOU DON'T UNDERSTAND ANYTHING, SEKI.
ALL RIGHT, THEN.
LATER...
WHATEVER, YOU IDIOT.

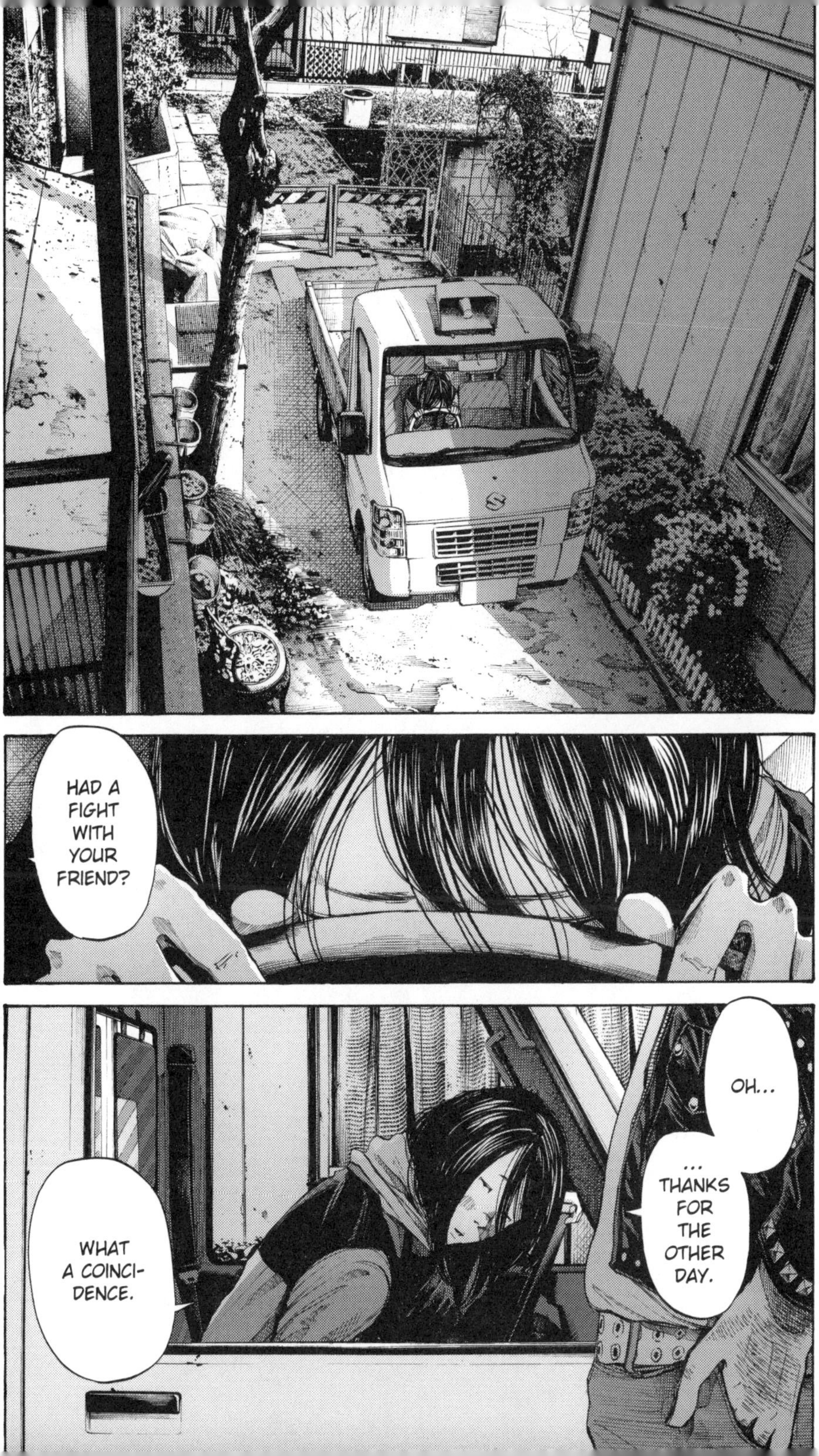
HAD A FIGHT WITH YOUR FRIEND?
OH...
...THANKS FOR THE OTHER DAY.
WHAT A COINCI-DENCE.

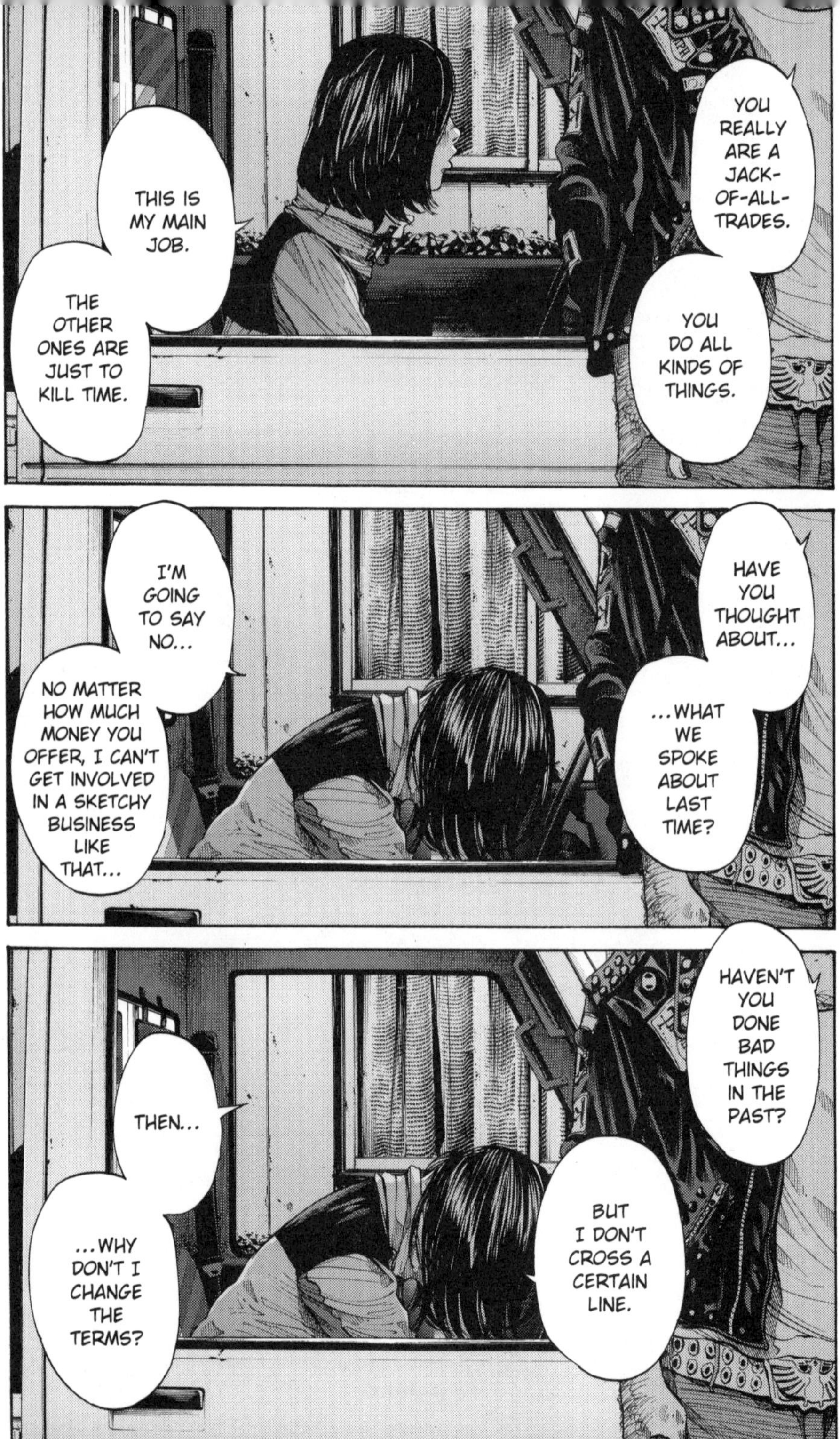
YOU REALLY ARE A JACK-OF-ALL-TRADES.
YOU DO ALL KINDS OF THINGS.
THIS IS MY MAIN JOB.
THE OTHER ONES ARE JUST TO KILL TIME.
HAVE YOU THOUGHT ABOUT...
...WHAT WE SPOKE ABOUT LAST TIME?
I'M GOING TO SAY NO...
NO MATTER HOW MUCH MONEY YOU OFFER, I CAN'T GET INVOLVED IN A SKETCHY BUSINESS LIKE THAT...
HAVEN'T YOU DONE BAD THINGS IN THE PAST?
BUT I DON'T CROSS A CERTAIN LINE.
THEN...
...WHY DON'T I CHANGE THE TERMS?

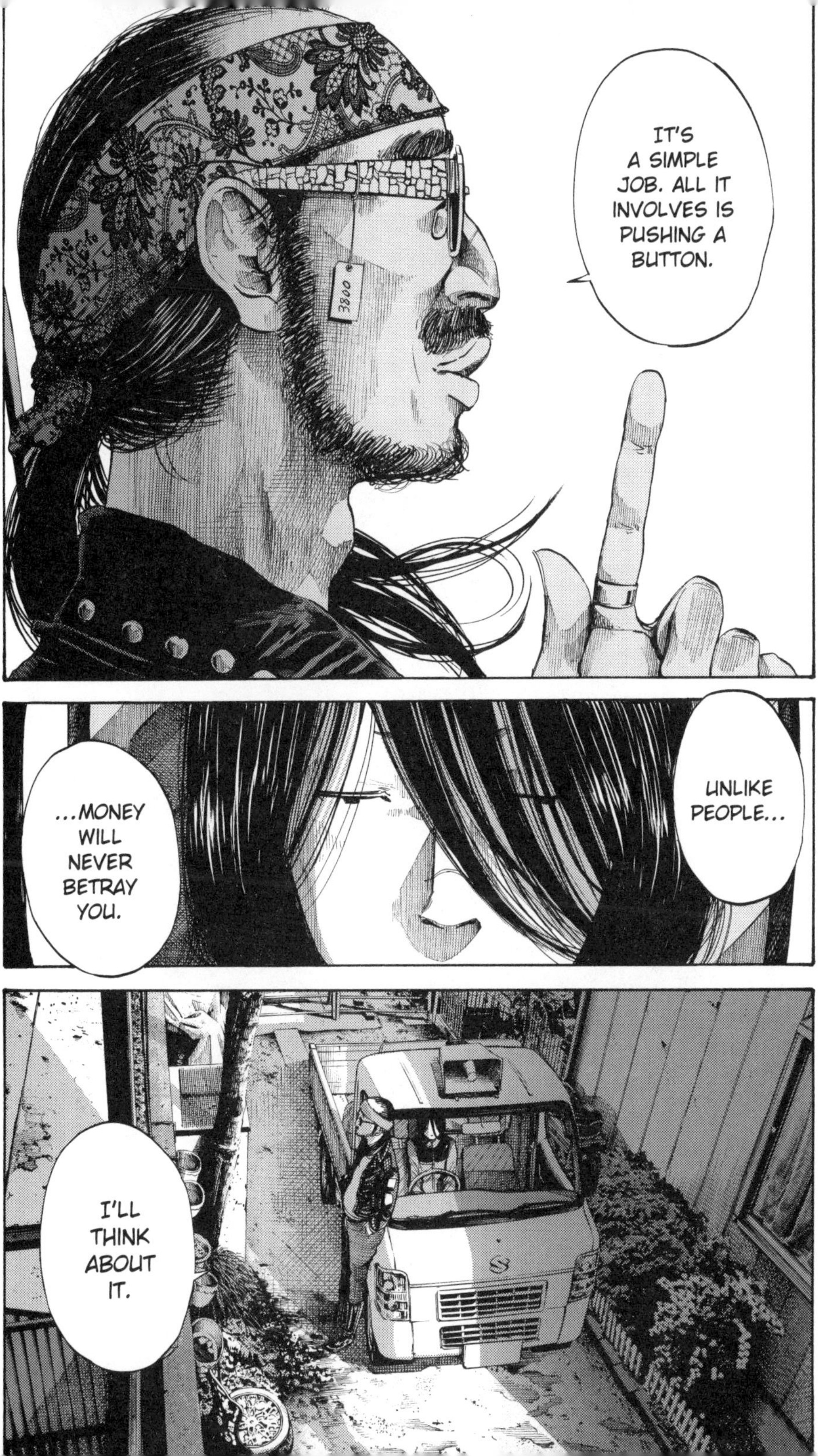
IT'S A SIMPLE JOB. ALL IT INVOLVES IS PUSHING A BUTTON.
3800
UNLIKE PEOPLE...
...MONEY WILL NEVER BETRAY YOU.
I'LL THINK ABOUT IT.

Chapter 96

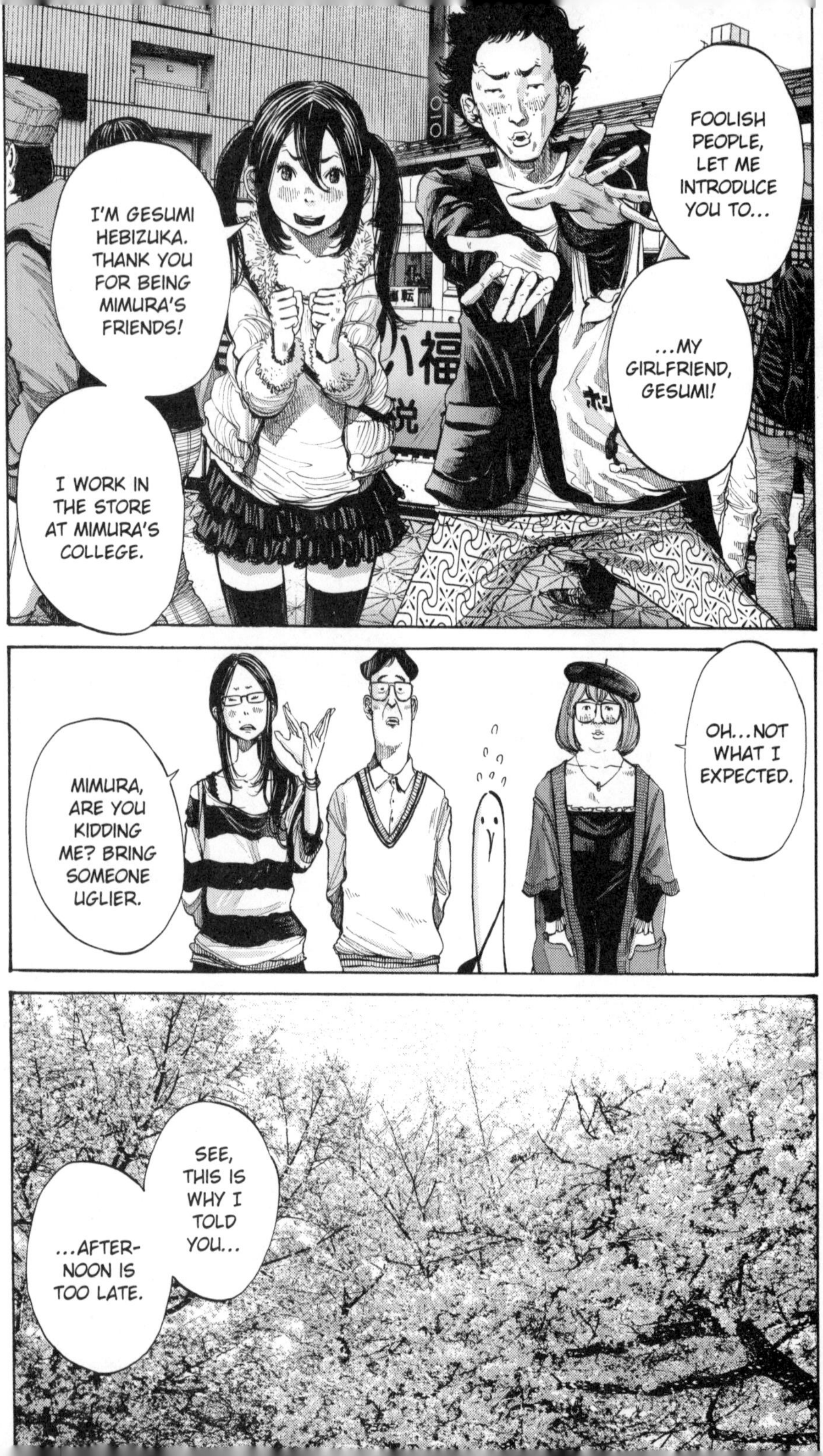
FOOLISH PEOPLE, LET ME INTRODUCE YOU TO...
...MY GIRLFRIEND, GESUMI!
I'M GESUMI HEBIZUKA. THANK YOU FOR BEING MIMURA'S FRIENDS!
I WORK IN THE STORE AT MIMURA'S COLLEGE.
OH...NOT WHAT I EXPECTED.
MIMURA, ARE YOU KIDDING ME? BRING SOMEONE UGLIER.
SEE, THIS IS WHY I TOLD YOU...
...AFTER-NOON IS TOO LATE.

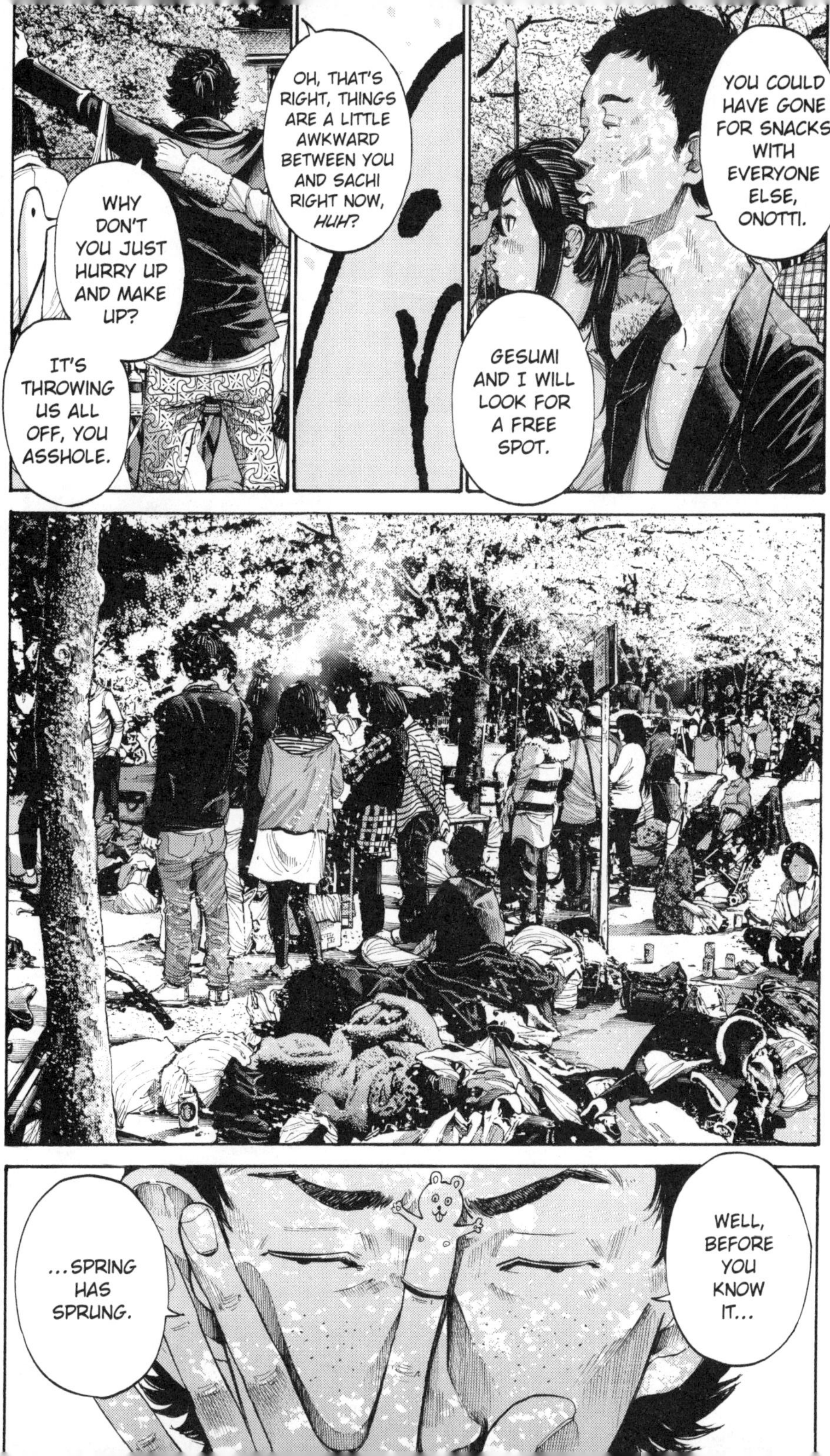
YOU COULD HAVE GONE FOR SNACKS WITH EVERYONE ELSE, ONOTTI.
GESUMI AND I WILL LOOK FOR A FREE SPOT.
OH, THAT'S RIGHT, THINGS ARE A LITTLE AWKWARD BETWEEN YOU AND SACHI RIGHT NOW, *HUH*?
WHY DON'T YOU JUST HURRY UP AND MAKE UP?
IT'S THROWING US ALL OFF, YOU ASSHOLE.
WELL, BEFORE YOU KNOW IT...
...SPRING HAS SPRUNG.

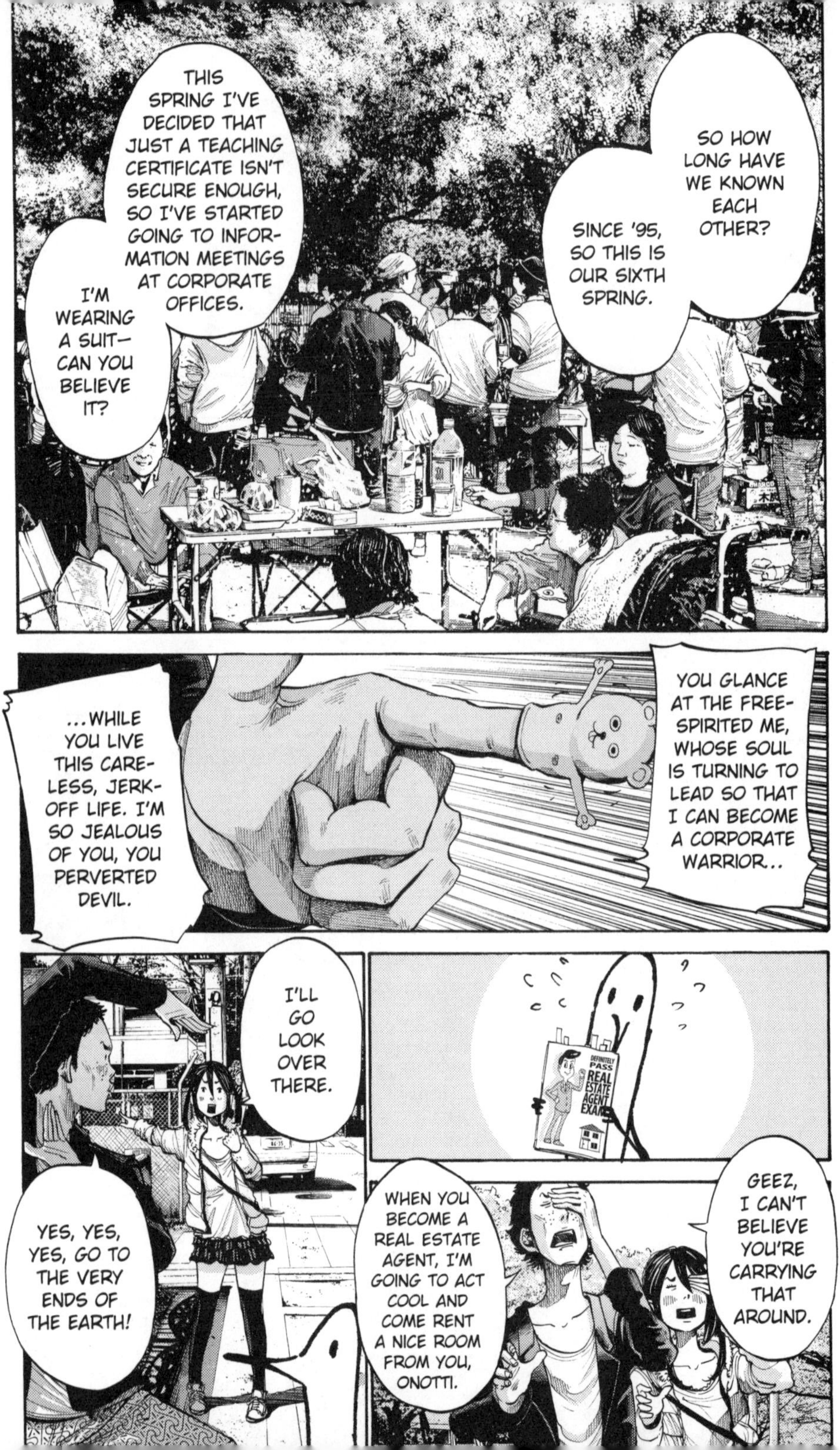

SO HOW LONG HAVE WE KNOWN EACH OTHER?
SINCE '95, SO THIS IS OUR SIXTH SPRING.
THIS SPRING I'VE DECIDED THAT JUST A TEACHING CERTIFICATE ISN'T SECURE ENOUGH, SO I'VE STARTED GOING TO INFORMATION MEETINGS AT CORPORATE OFFICES.
I'M WEARING A SUIT—CAN YOU BELIEVE IT?
YOU GLANCE AT THE FREE-SPIRITED ME, WHOSE SOUL IS TURNING TO LEAD SO THAT I CAN BECOME A CORPORATE WARRIOR...
...WHILE YOU LIVE THIS CARELESS, JERK-OFF LIFE. I'M SO JEALOUS OF YOU, YOU PERVERTED DEVIL.
DEFINITELY PASS
REAL ESTATE AGENT EXAM
GEEZ, I CAN'T BELIEVE YOU'RE CARRYING THAT AROUND.
WHEN YOU BECOME A REAL ESTATE AGENT, I'M GOING TO ACT COOL AND COME RENT A NICE ROOM FROM YOU, ONOTTI.
I'LL GO LOOK OVER THERE.
YES, YES, YES, GO TO THE VERY ENDS OF THE EARTH!

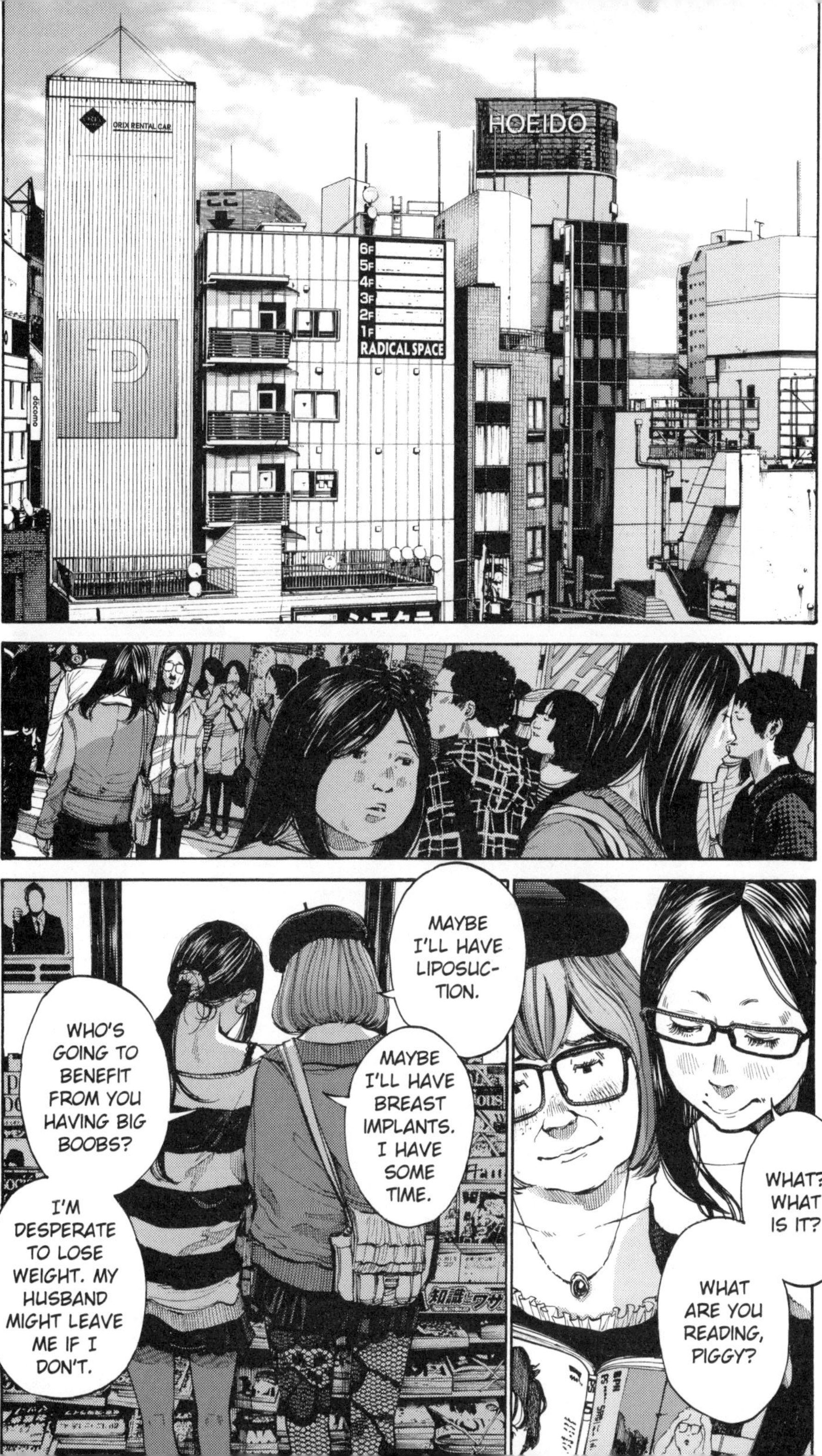
HOEIDO
6F
5F
4F
3F
2F
1F
RADICAL SPACE
ORIX RENTAL CAR
docomo
WHAT? WHAT IS IT?
WHAT ARE YOU READING, PIGGY?
MAYBE I'LL HAVE LIPOSUC-TION.
MAYBE I'LL HAVE BREAST IMPLANTS. I HAVE SOME TIME.
WHO'S GOING TO BENEFIT FROM YOU HAVING BIG BOOBS?
I'M DESPERATE TO LOSE WEIGHT. MY HUSBAND MIGHT LEAVE ME IF I DON'T.

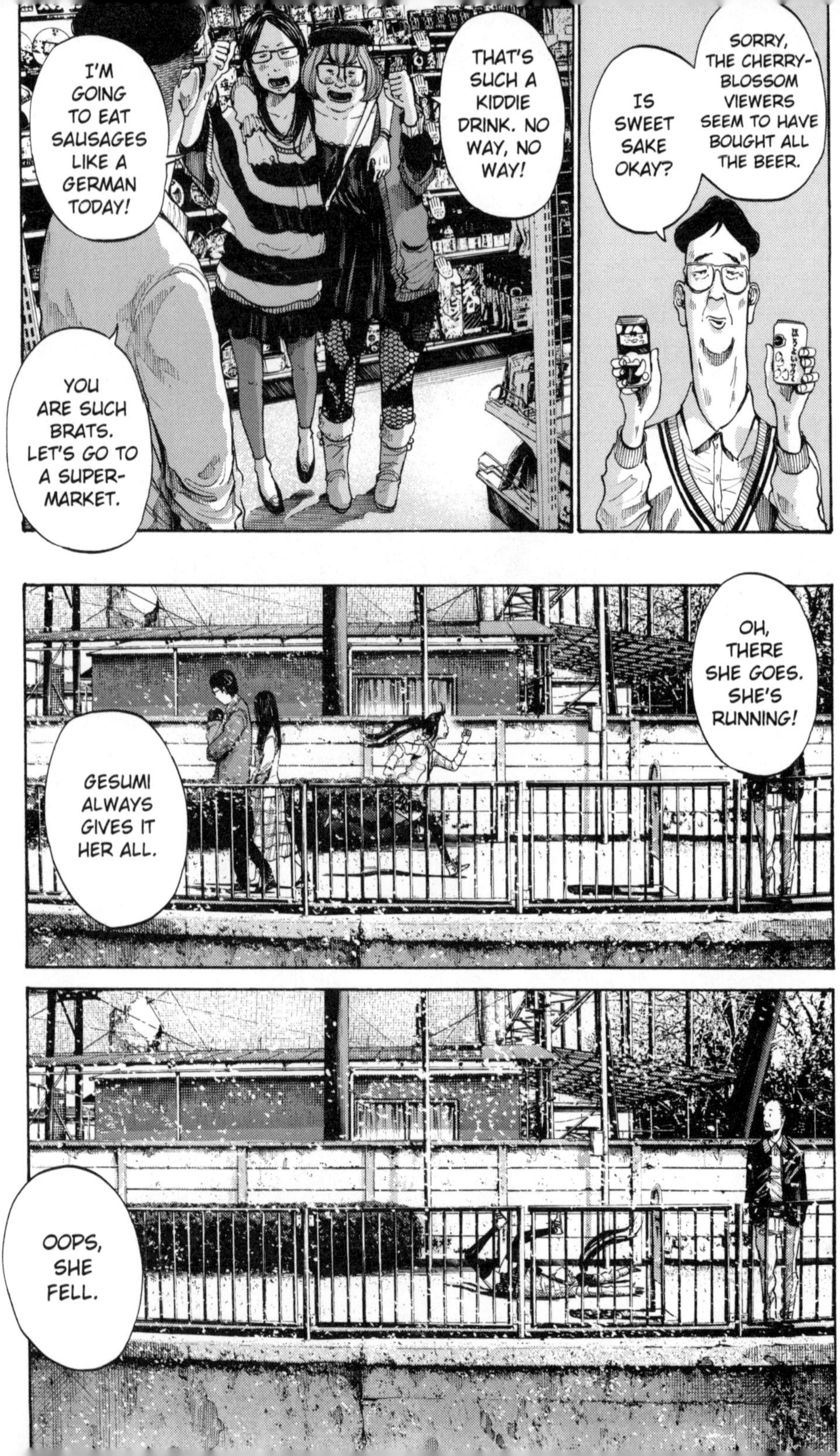
SORRY, THE CHERRY-BLOSSOM VIEWERS SEEM TO HAVE BOUGHT ALL THE BEER.
IS SWEET SAKE OKAY?
THAT'S SUCH A KIDDIE DRINK. NO WAY, NO WAY!
I'M GOING TO EAT SAUSAGES LIKE A GERMAN TODAY!
YOU ARE SUCH BRATS. LET'S GO TO A SUPER-MARKET.
OH, THERE SHE GOES. SHE'S RUNNING!
GESUMI ALWAYS GIVES IT HER ALL.
OOPS, SHE FELL.

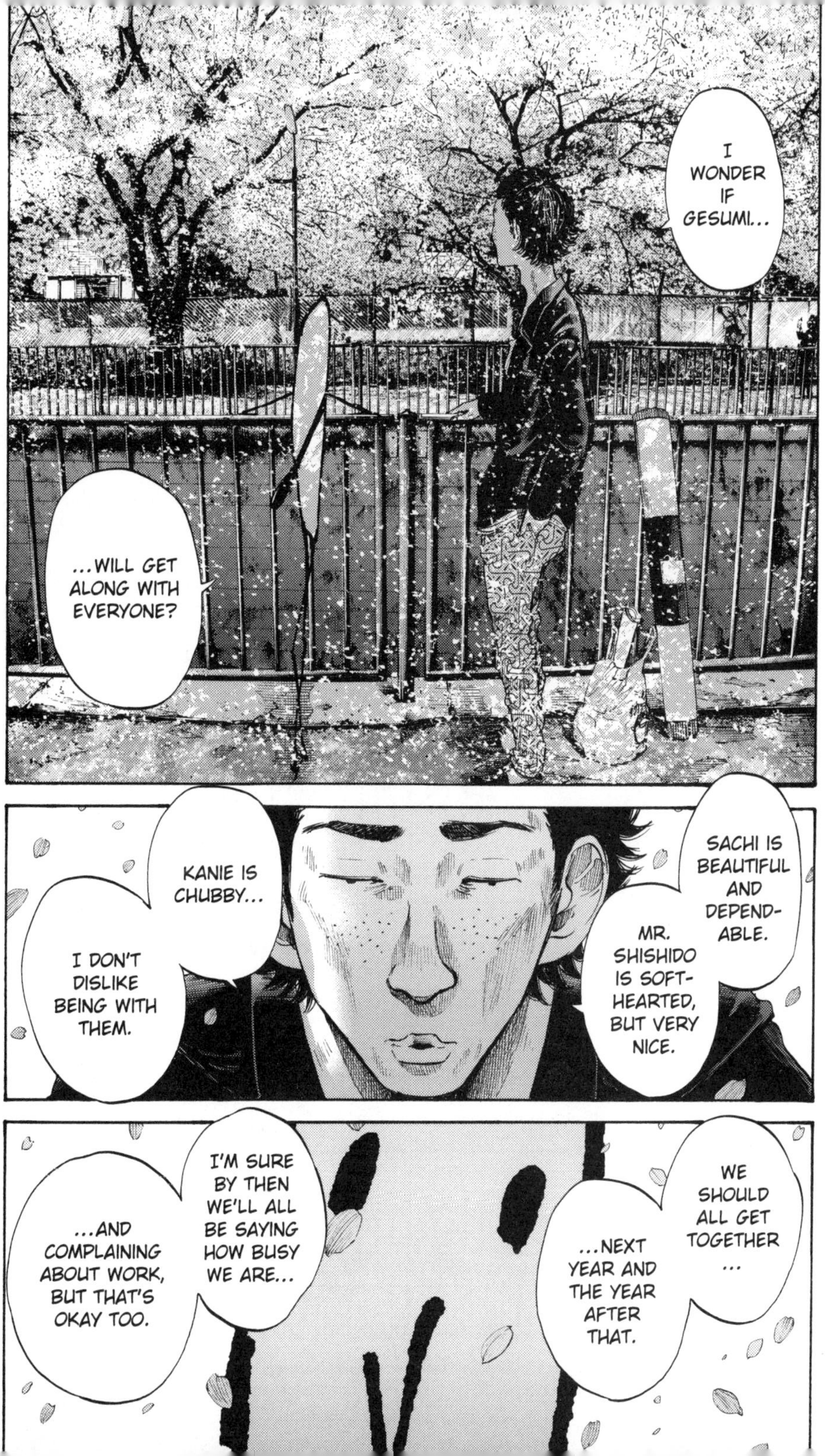
I WONDER IF GESUMI...
...WILL GET ALONG WITH EVERYONE?
SACHI IS BEAUTIFUL AND DEPEND-ABLE.
MR. SHISHIDO IS SOFT-HEARTED, BUT VERY NICE.
KANIE IS CHUBBY...
I DON'T DISLIKE BEING WITH THEM.
WE SHOULD ALL GET TOGETHER ...
...NEXT YEAR AND THE YEAR AFTER THAT.
I'M SURE BY THEN WE'LL ALL BE SAYING HOW BUSY WE ARE...
...AND COMPLAINING ABOUT WORK, BUT THAT'S OKAY TOO.

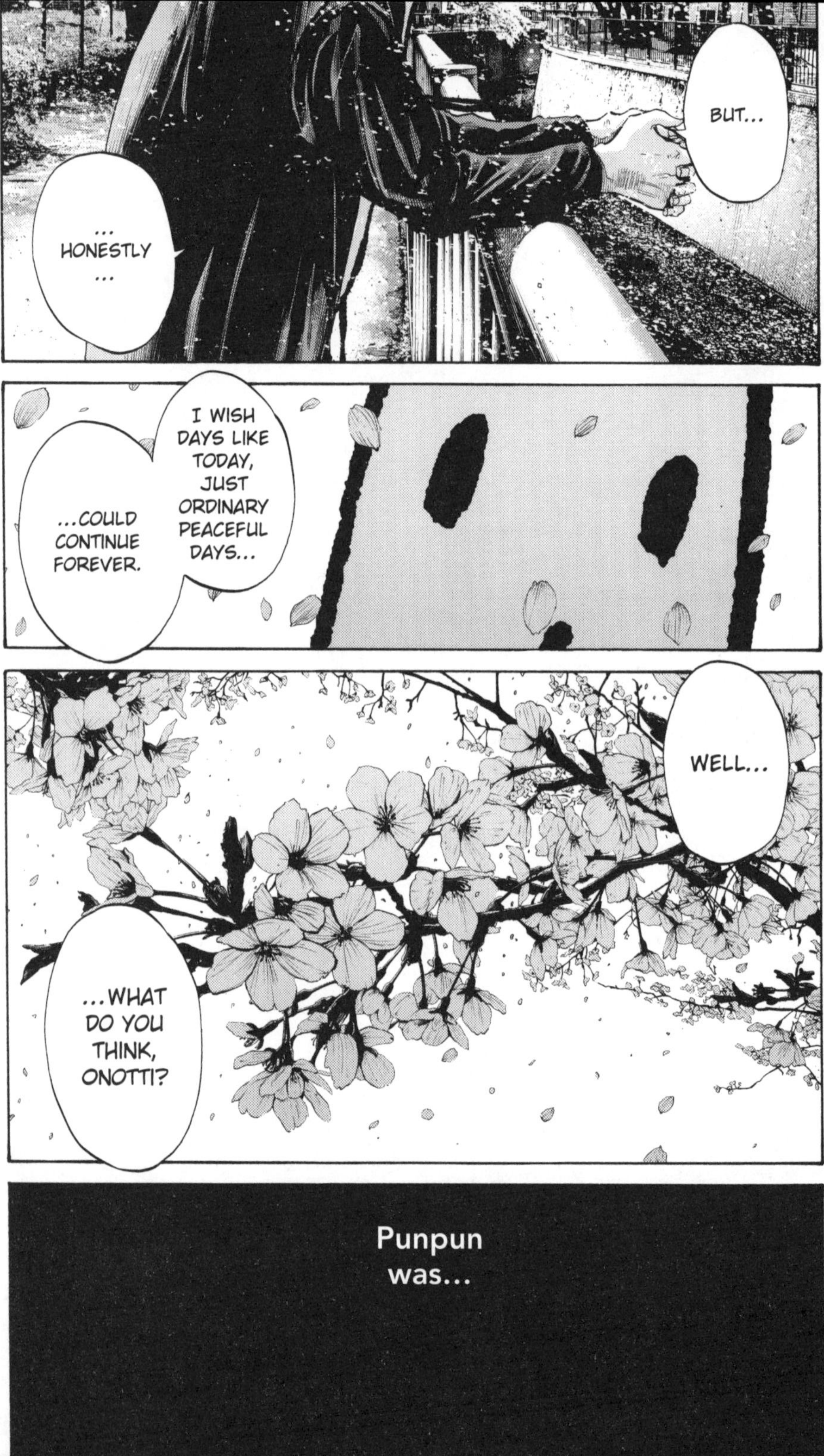
BUT...
...HONESTLY...
I WISH DAYS LIKE TODAY, JUST ORDINARY PEACEFUL DAYS...
...COULD CONTINUE FOREVER.
WELL...
...WHAT DO YOU THINK, ONOTTI?
Punpun was...

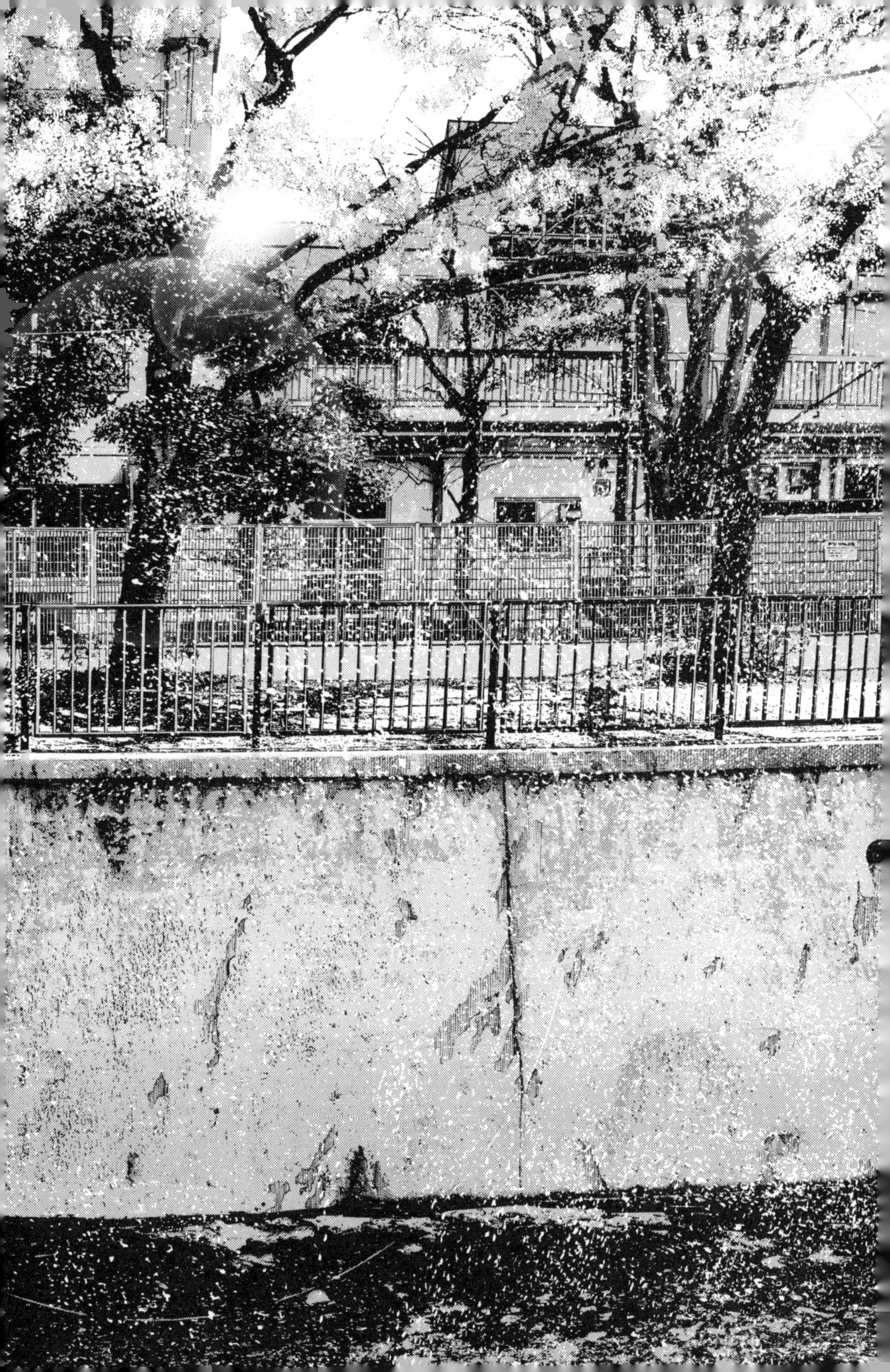

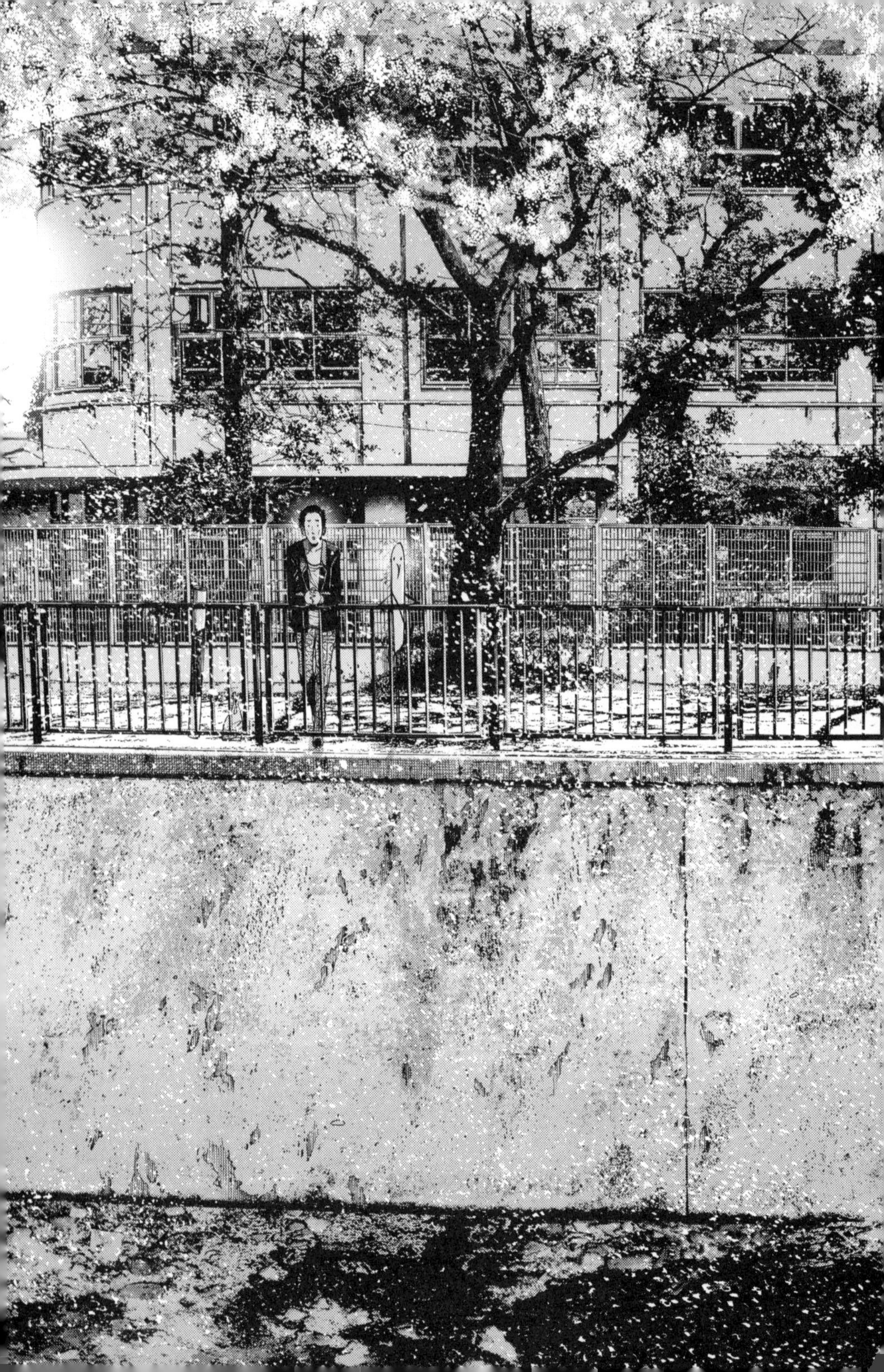

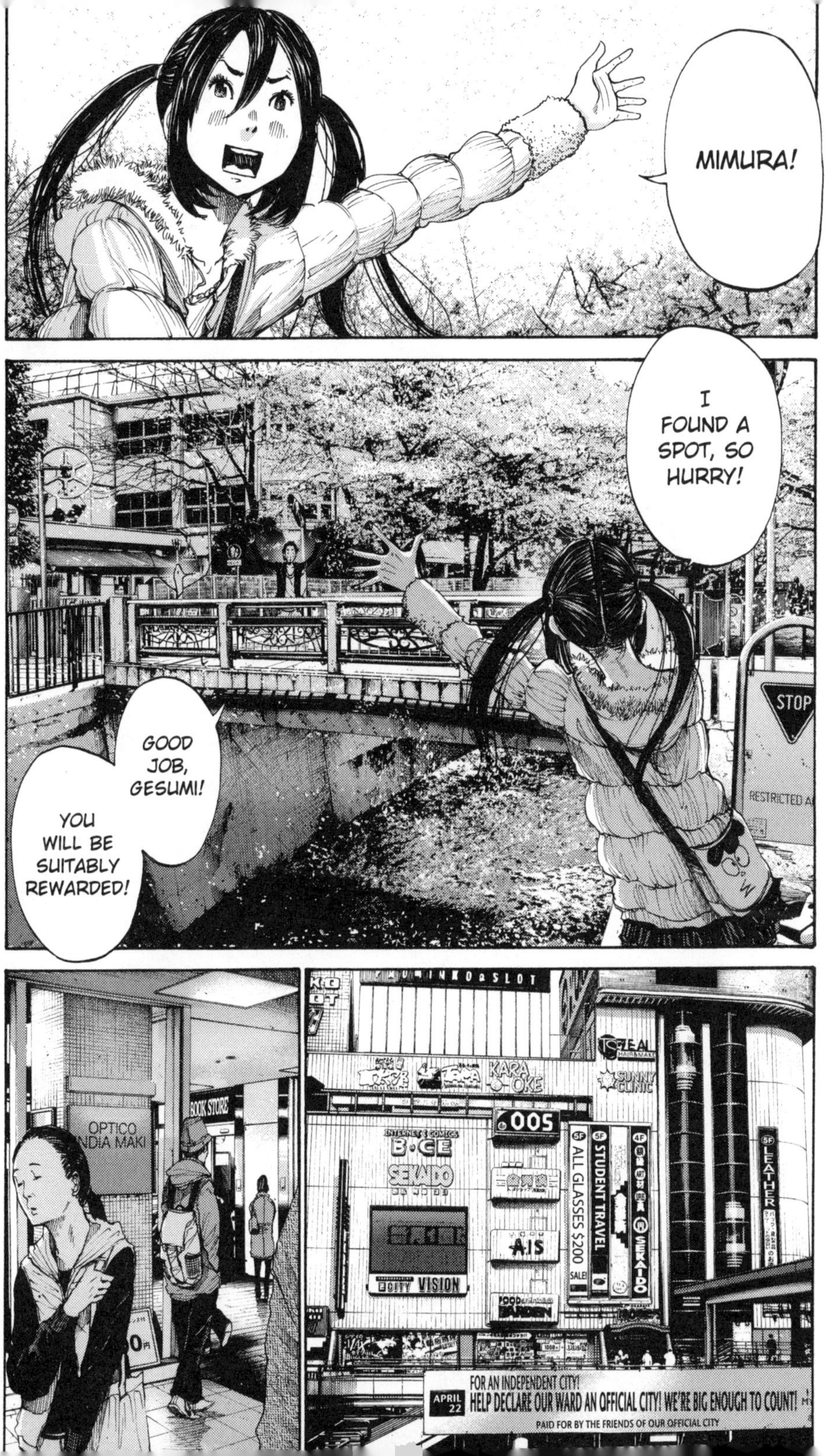
MIMURA!
I FOUND A SPOT, SO HURRY!
GOOD JOB, GESUMI!
YOU WILL BE SUITABLY REWARDED!
STOP
KARAOKE
SUNNY CLINIC
005
INTERNET & COMICS B·CE
SEKAIDO
5F ALL GLASSES $200 SALE!
5F STUDENT TRAVEL
SEKAIDO
5F LEATHER
A:IS
CITY VISION
FOR AN INDEPENDENT CITY!
APRIL 22
HELP DECLARE OUR WARD AN OFFICIAL CITY! WE'RE BIG ENOUGH TO COUNT!
PAID FOR BY THE FRIENDS OF OUR OFFICIAL CITY
BOOK STORE
OPTICO

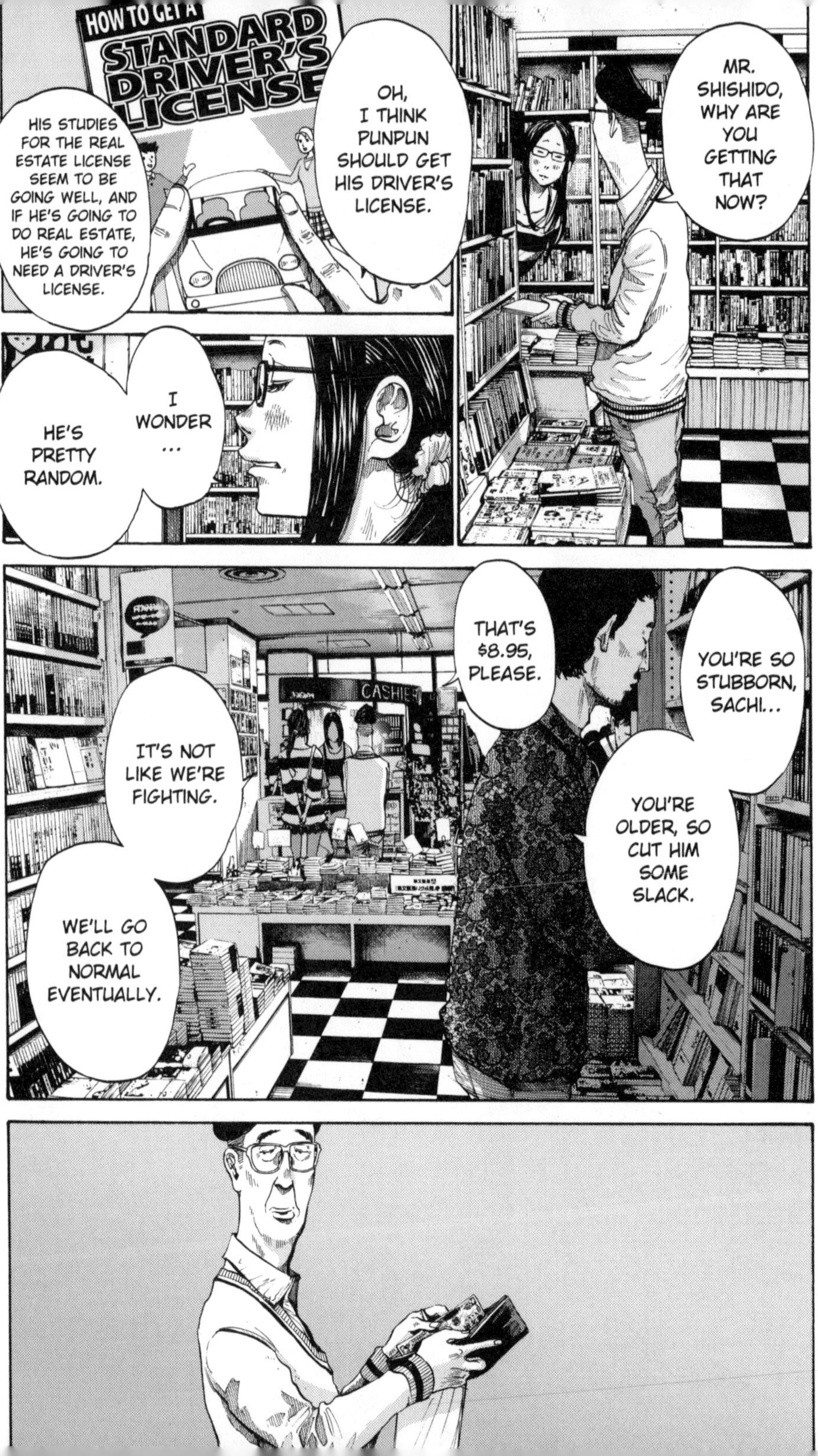
MR. SHISHIDO, WHY ARE YOU GETTING THAT NOW?
HOW TO GET A STANDARD DRIVER'S LICENSE
OH, I THINK PUNPUN SHOULD GET HIS DRIVER'S LICENSE.
HIS STUDIES FOR THE REAL ESTATE LICENSE SEEM TO BE GOING WELL, AND IF HE'S GOING TO DO REAL ESTATE, HE'S GOING TO NEED A DRIVER'S LICENSE.
I WONDER...
HE'S PRETTY RANDOM.
YOU'RE SO STUBBORN, SACHI...
YOU'RE OLDER, SO CUT HIM SOME SLACK.
THAT'S $8.95, PLEASE.
IT'S NOT LIKE WE'RE FIGHTING.
WE'LL GO BACK TO NORMAL EVENTUALLY.

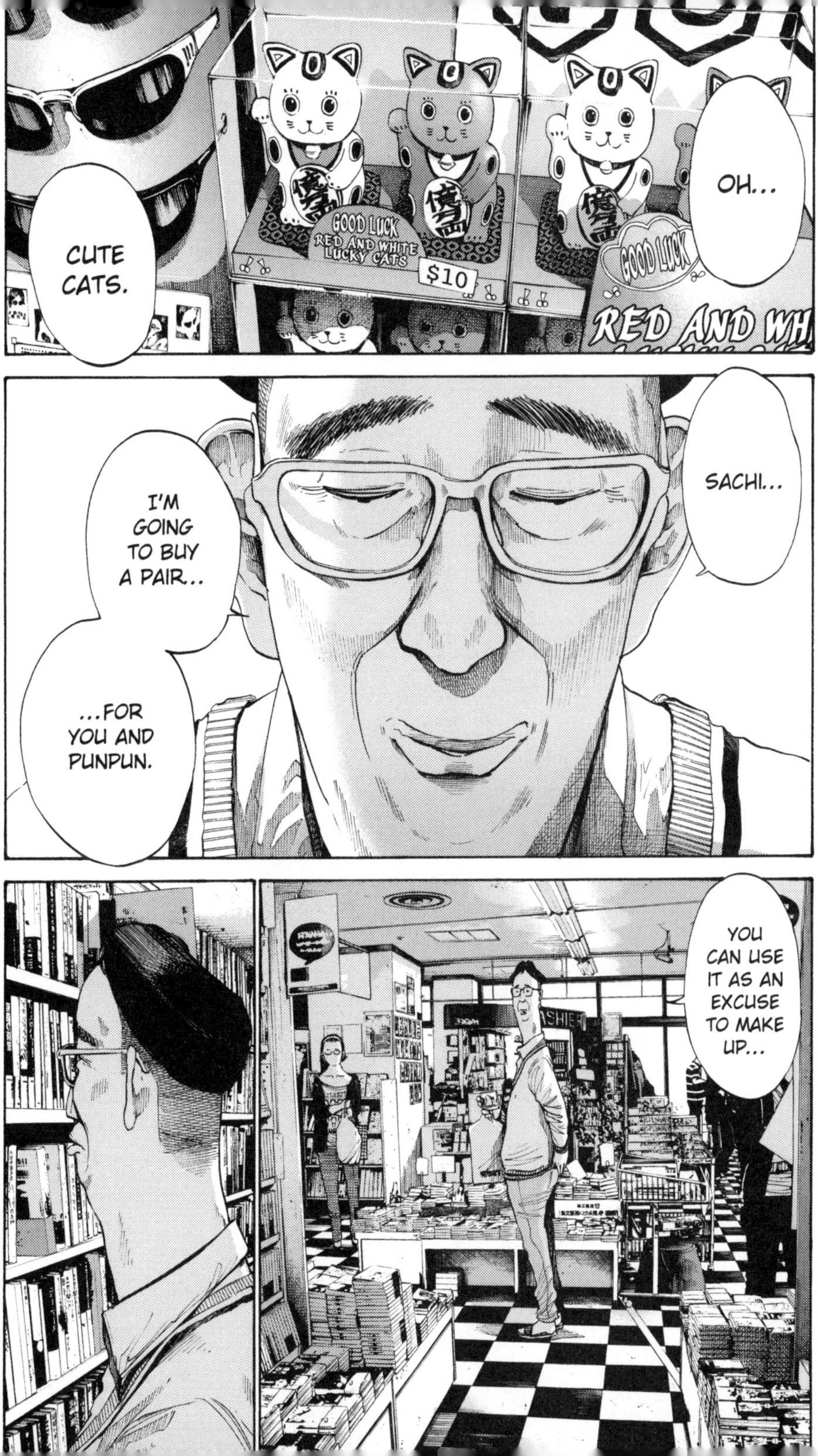
OH...
GOOD LUCK
RED AND WHITE LUCKY CATS
$10
GOOD LUCK
CUTE CATS.
SACHI...
I'M GOING TO BUY A PAIR...
...FOR YOU AND PUNPUN.
YOU CAN USE IT AS AN EXCUSE TO MAKE UP...

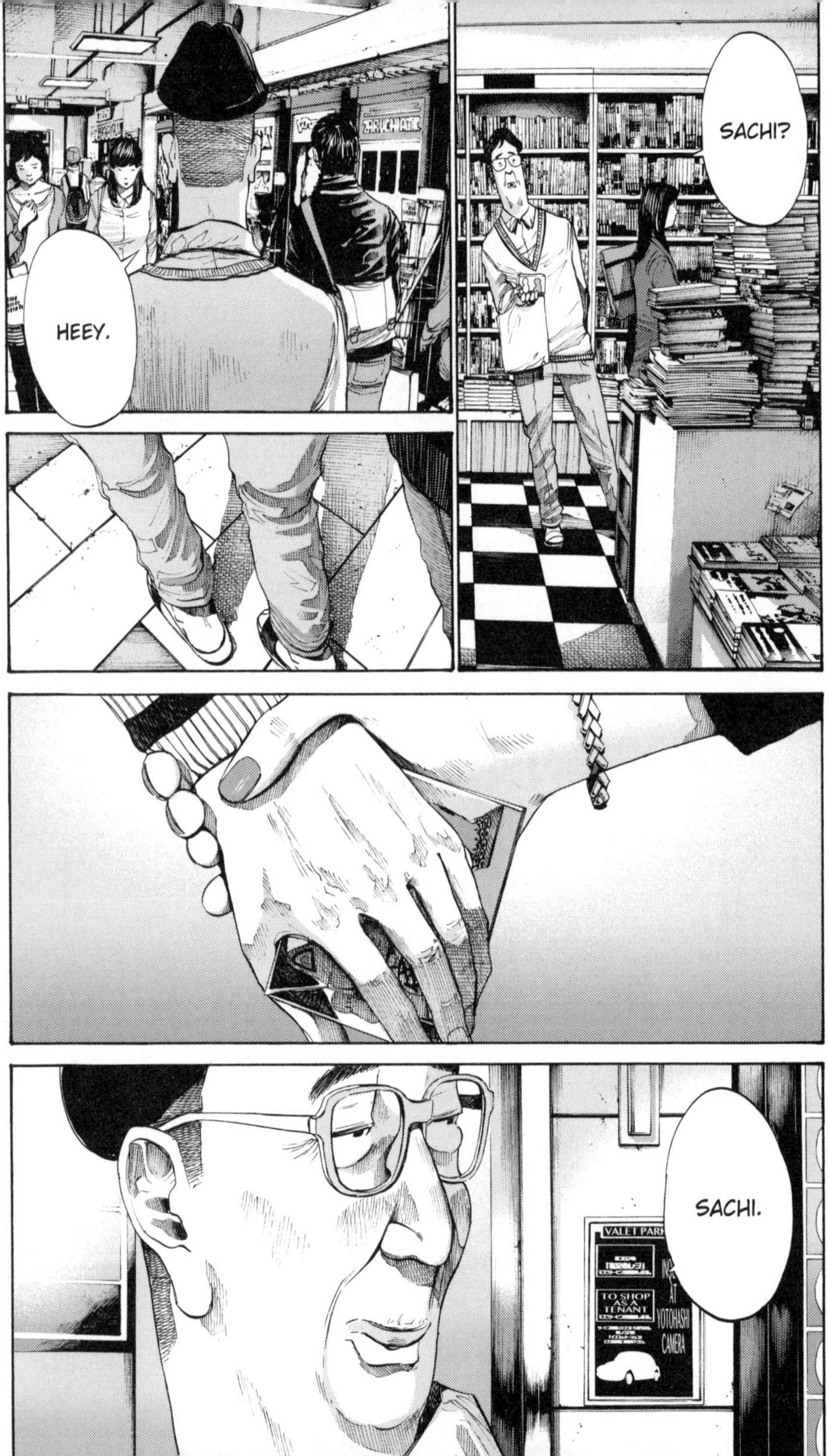
SACHI?
HEEY.
SACHI.
TO SHOP AS A TENANT
AT YOTOHASHI CAMERA

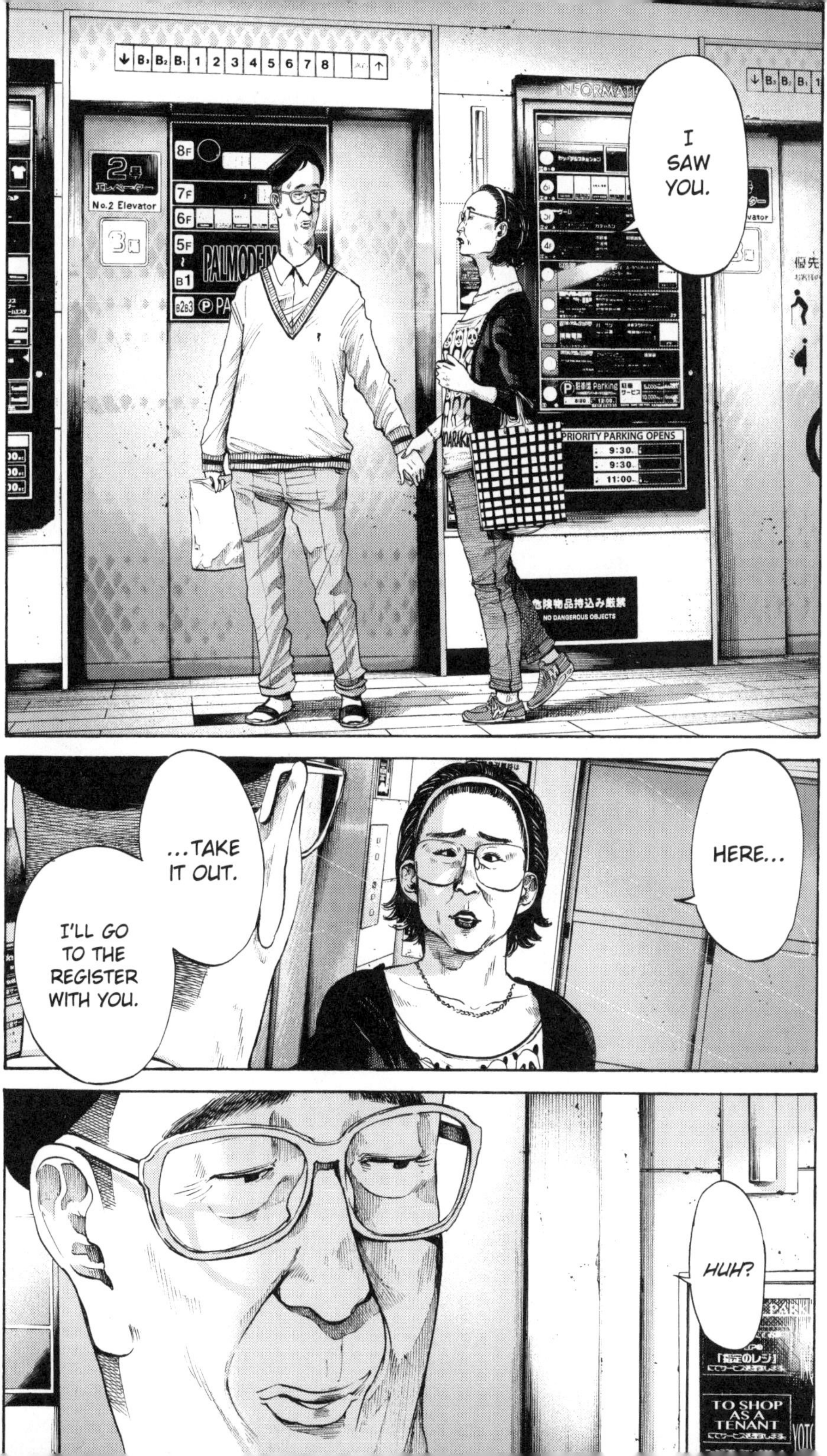

I SAW YOU.
No.2 Elevator
PRIORITY PARKING OPENS
9:30
9:30
11:00
危険物品持込み厳禁
NO DANGEROUS OBJECTS
HERE...
...TAKE IT OUT.
I'LL GO TO THE REGISTER WITH YOU.
HUH?
「指定のレジ」
TO SHOP AS A TENANT

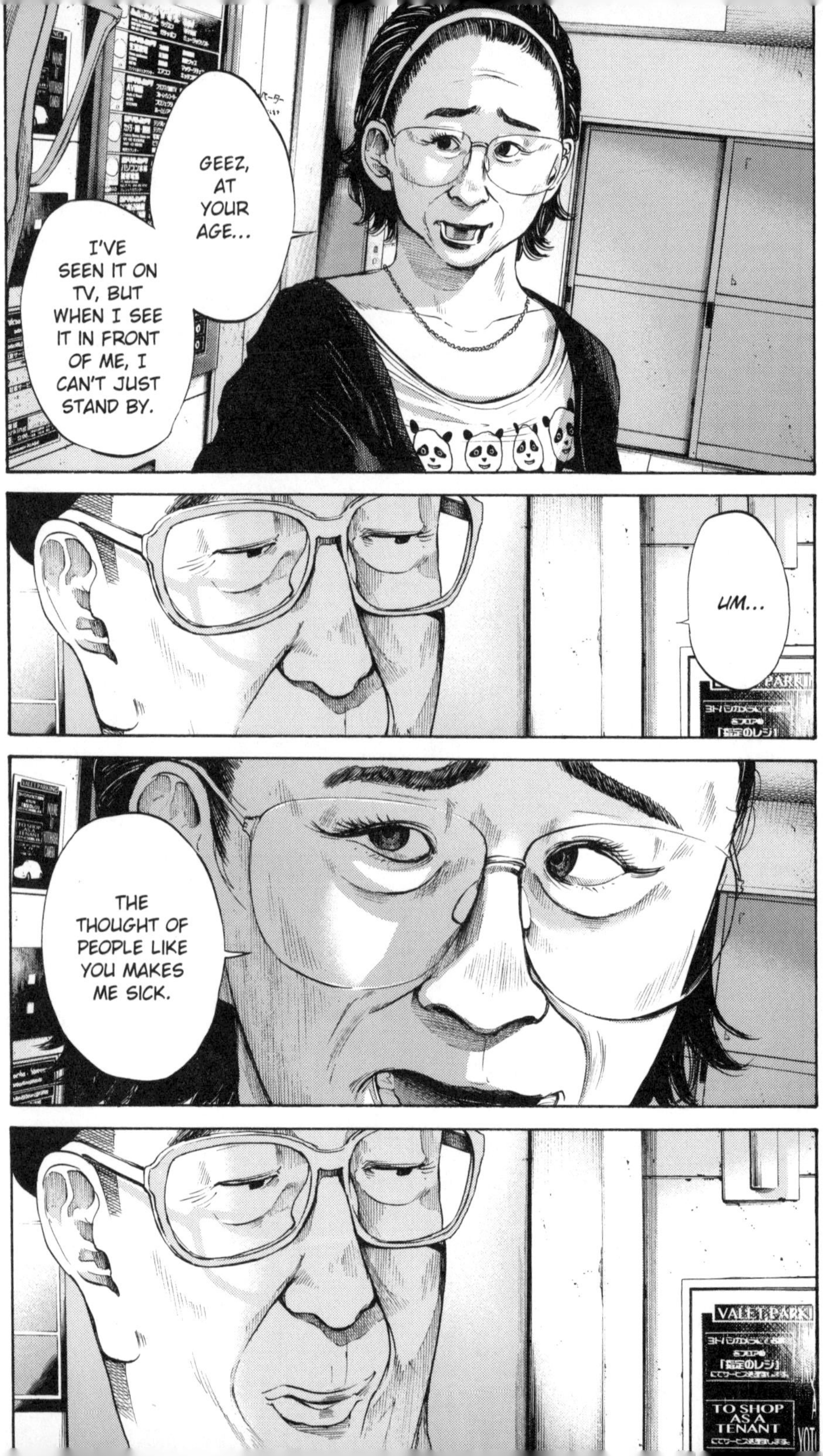
GEEZ, AT YOUR AGE...
I'VE SEEN IT ON TV, BUT WHEN I SEE IT IN FRONT OF ME, I CAN'T JUST STAND BY.
UM...
THE THOUGHT OF PEOPLE LIKE YOU MAKES ME SICK.
VALET PARK
TO SHOP AS A TENANT

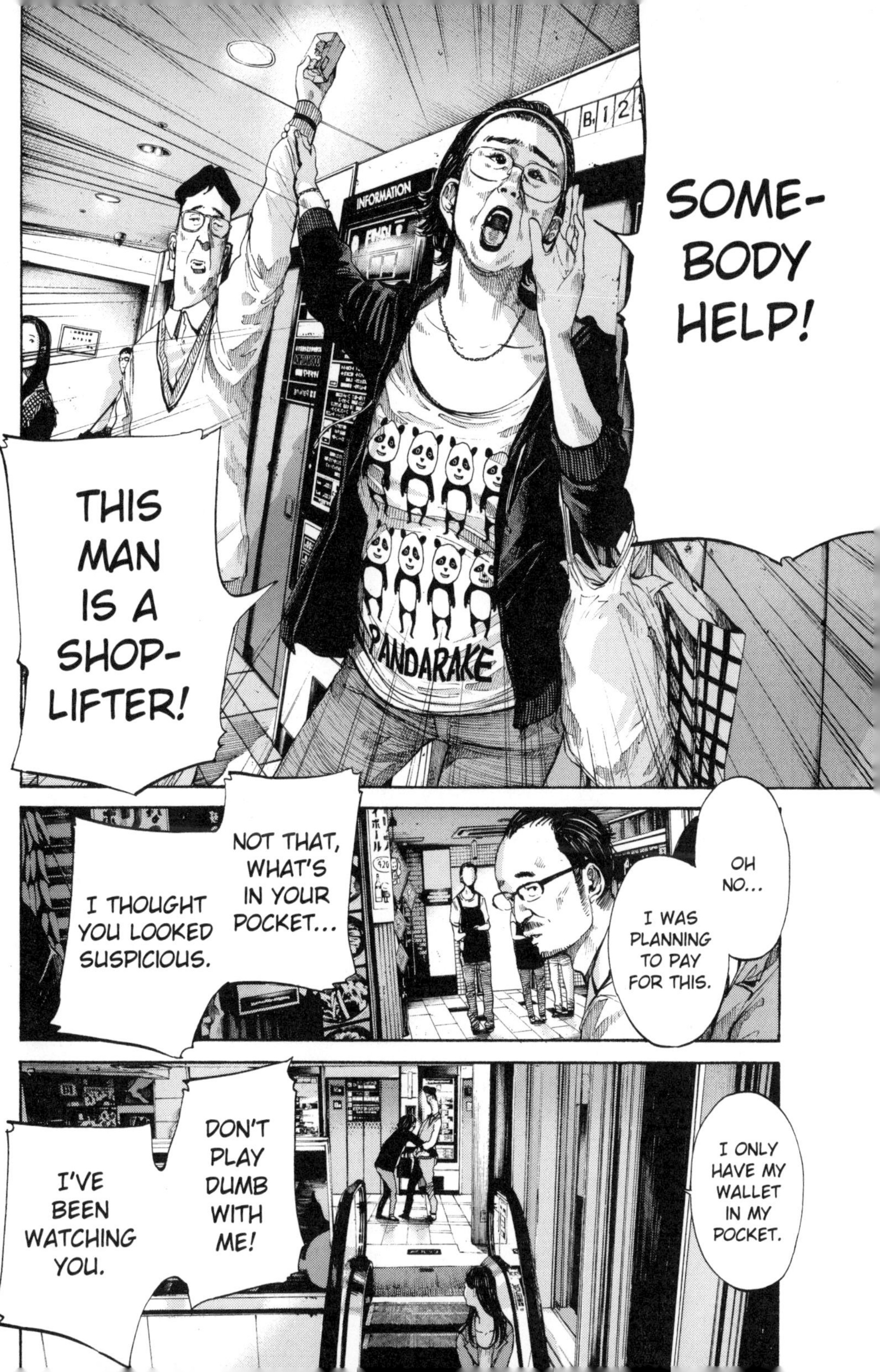
SOME-BODY HELP!
INFORMATION
PANDARAKE
THIS MAN IS A SHOP-LIFTER!
OH NO... I WAS PLANNING TO PAY FOR THIS.
NOT THAT, WHAT'S IN YOUR POCKET...
I THOUGHT YOU LOOKED SUSPICIOUS.
I ONLY HAVE MY WALLET IN MY POCKET.
DON'T PLAY DUMB WITH ME!
I'VE BEEN WATCHING YOU.

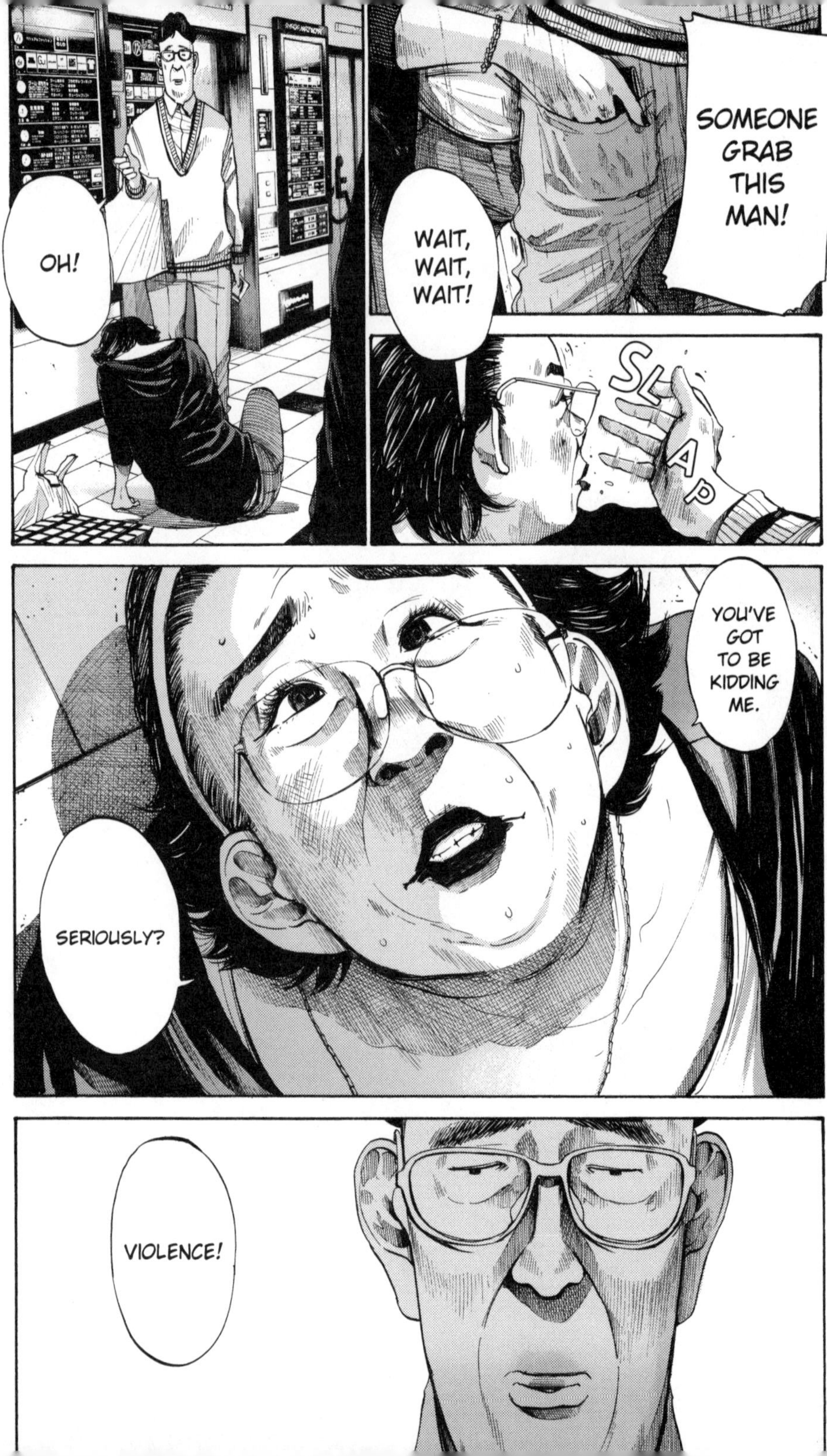
SOMEONE GRAB THIS MAN!
WAIT, WAIT, WAIT!
SLAP
OH!
YOU'VE GOT TO BE KIDDING ME.
SERIOUSLY?
VIOLENCE!

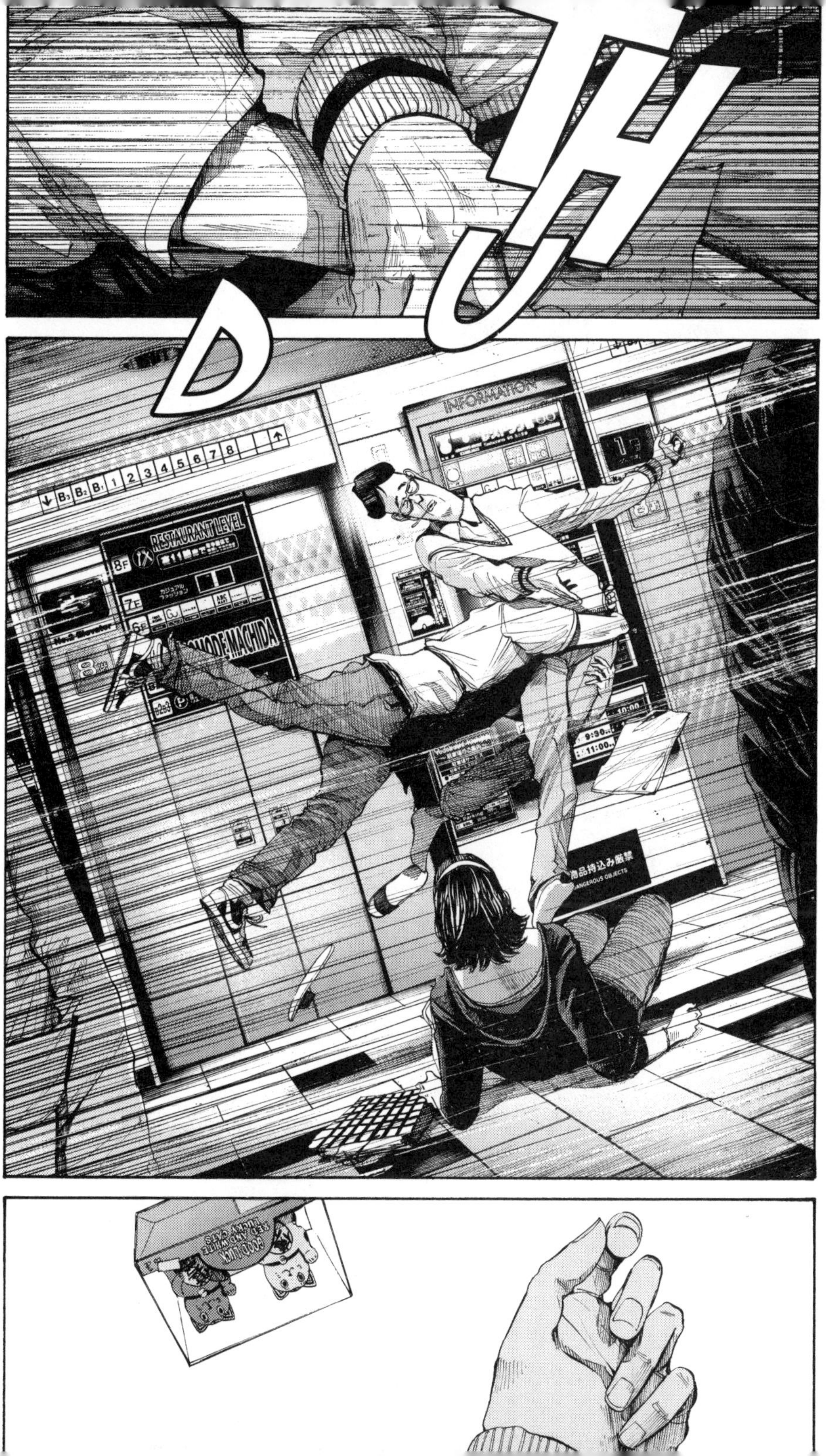
THUD
INFORMATION
RESTAURANT LEVEL
RED AND WHITE LUCKY CATS
GOOD LUCK

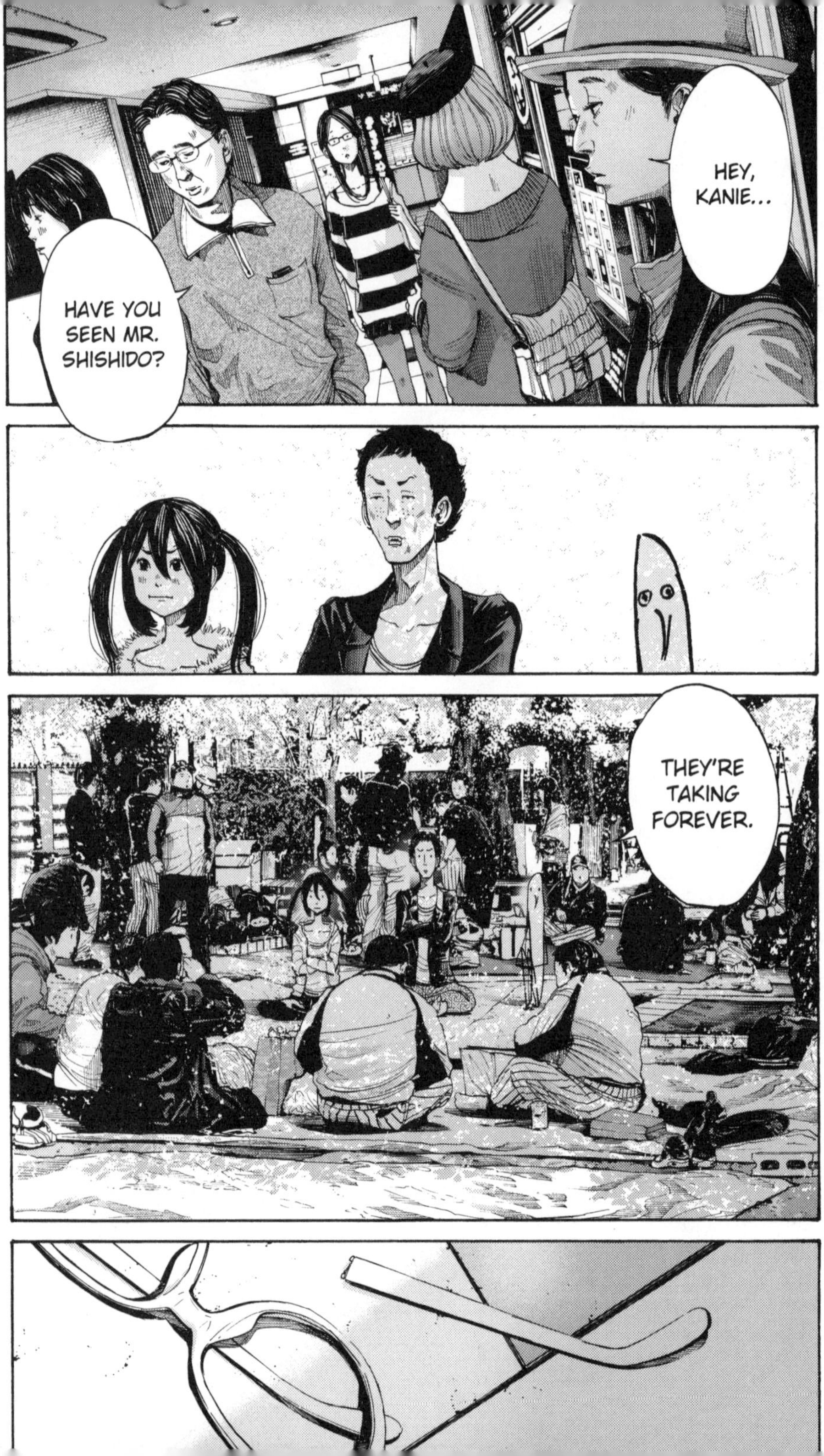
HEY, KANIE...
HAVE YOU SEEN MR. SHISHIDO?
THEY'RE TAKING FOREVER.

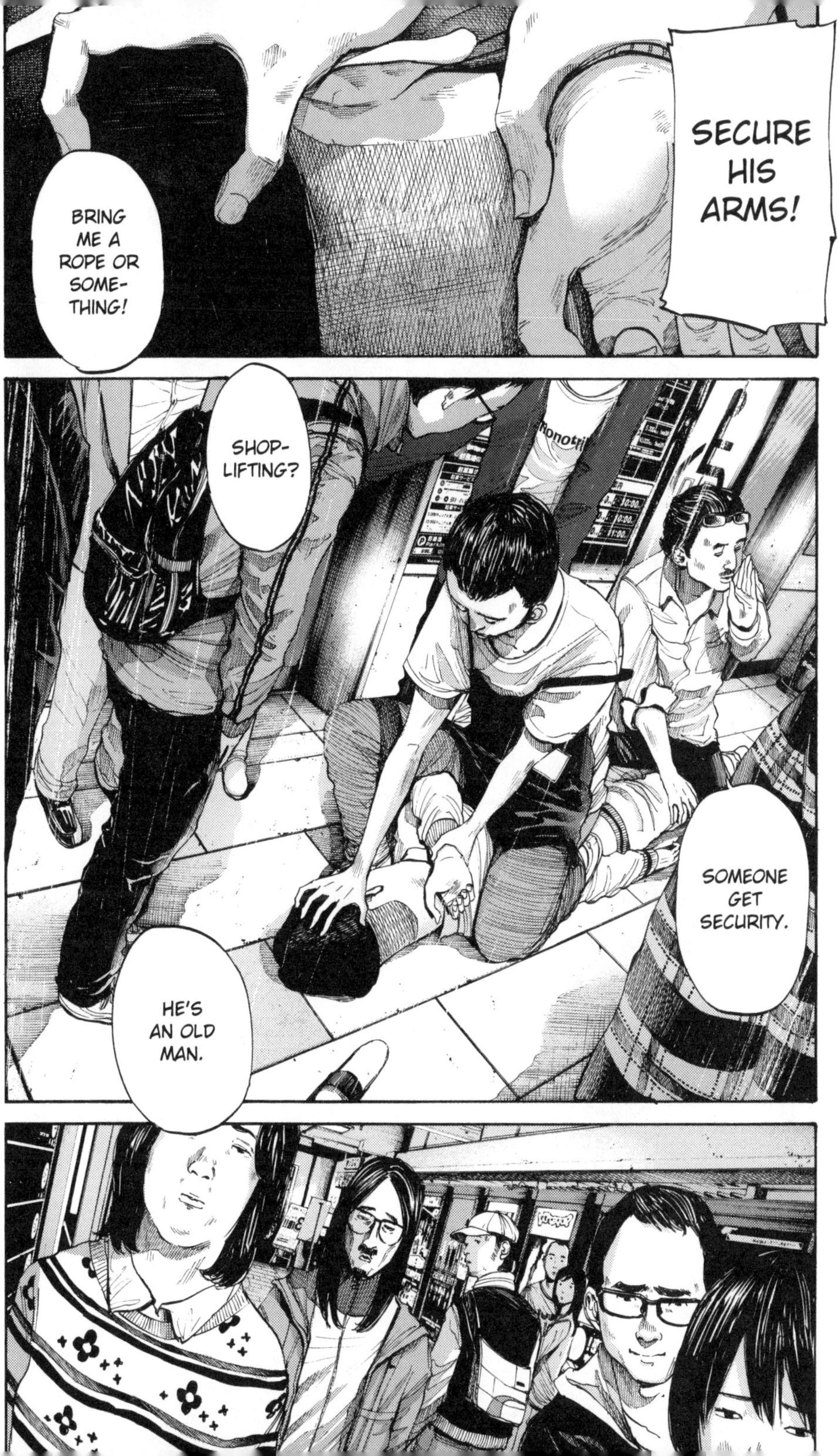
SECURE HIS ARMS!
BRING ME A ROPE OR SOME-THING!
SHOP-LIFTING?
SOMEONE GET SECURITY.
HE'S AN OLD MAN.

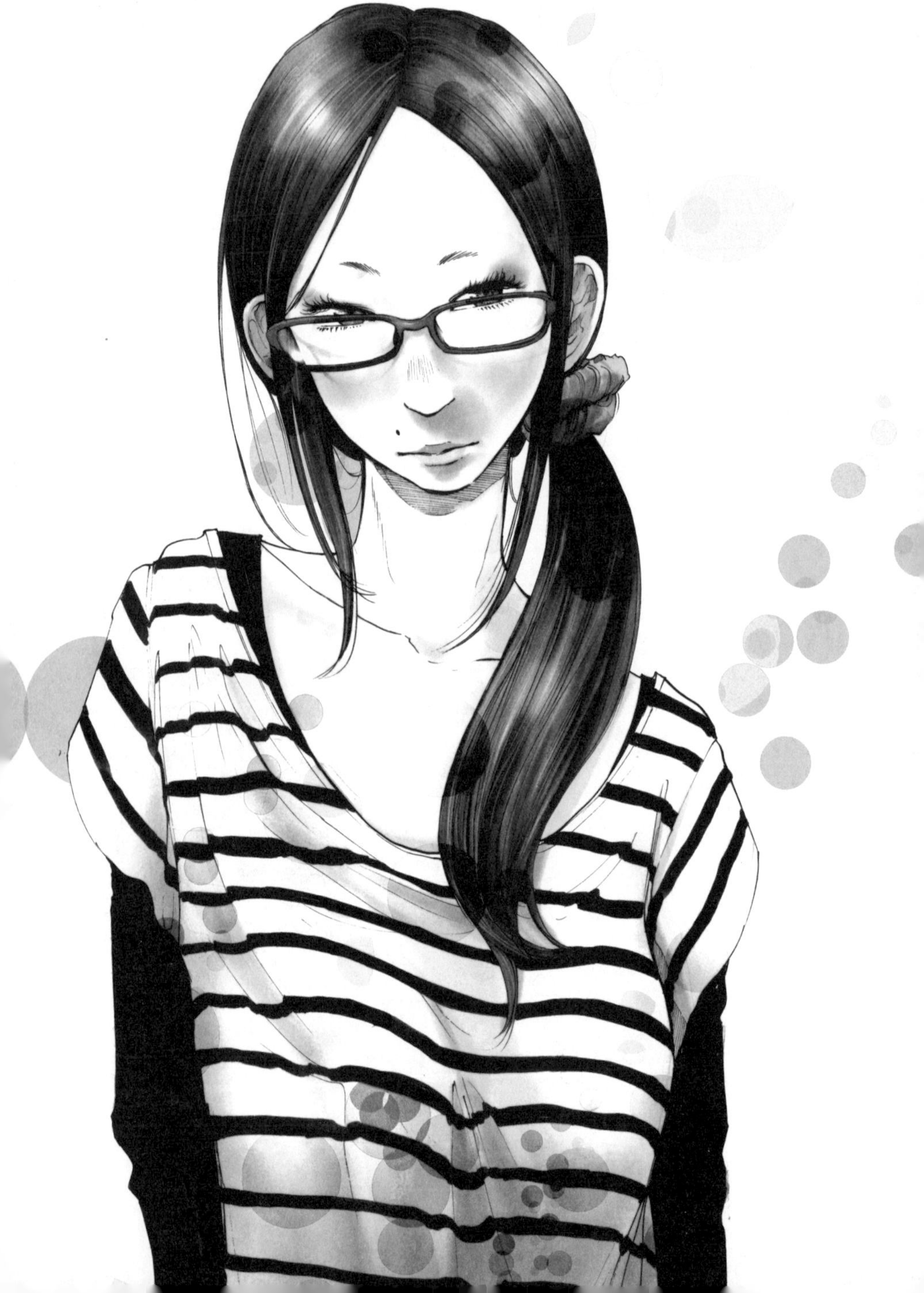

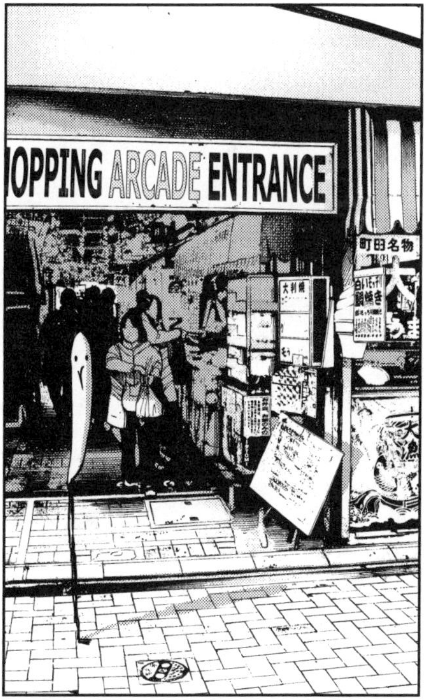

OPPING ARCADE ENTRANCE
町田名物

Chapter 97

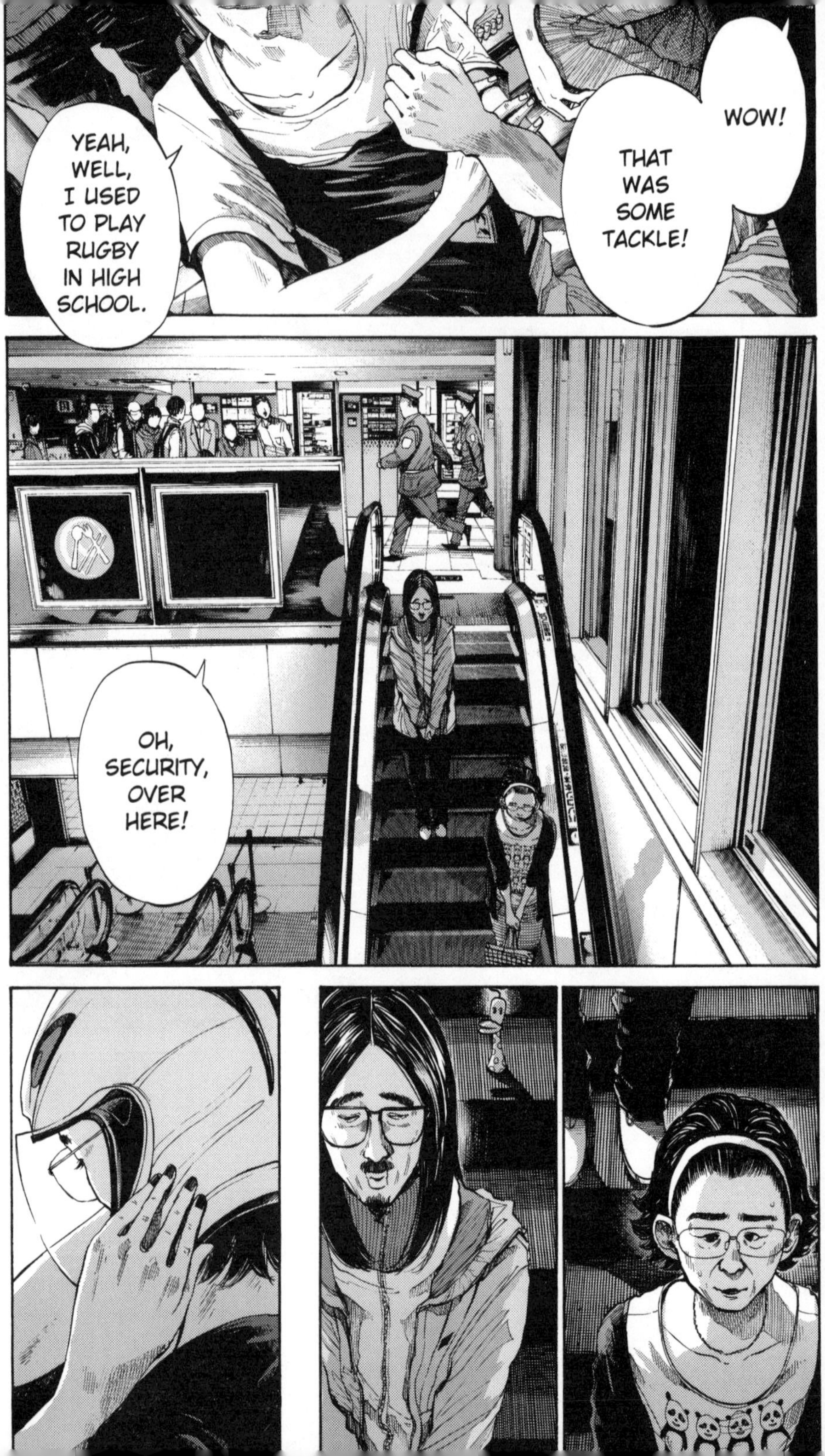
WOW!
THAT WAS SOME TACKLE!
YEAH, WELL, I USED TO PLAY RUGBY IN HIGH SCHOOL.
OH, SECURITY, OVER HERE!

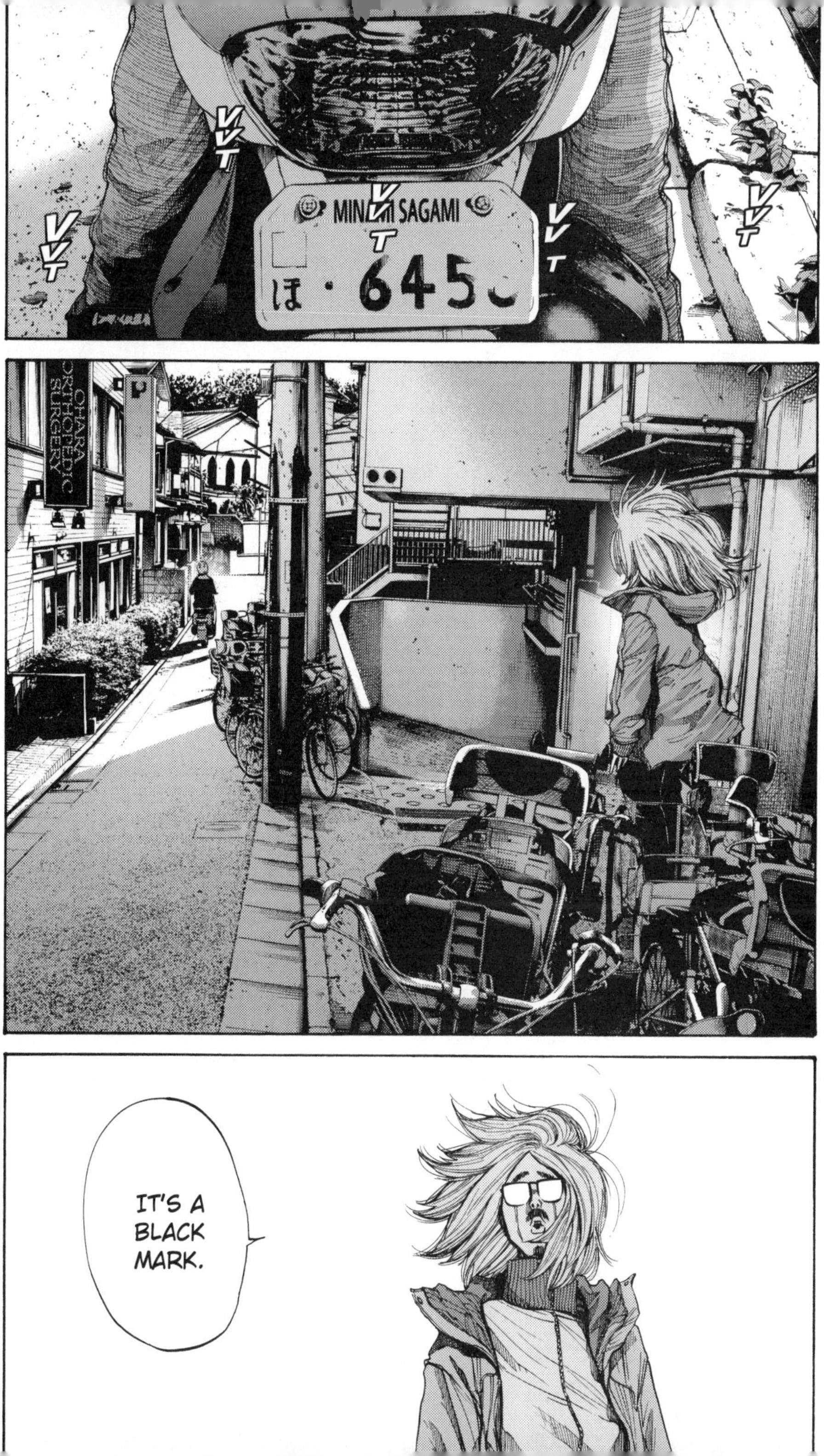
VVVT
VVVT
VVT
SAGAMI
ほ・645
VVT
VVVT
OHARA ORTHOPEDIC SURGERY
IT'S A BLACK MARK.

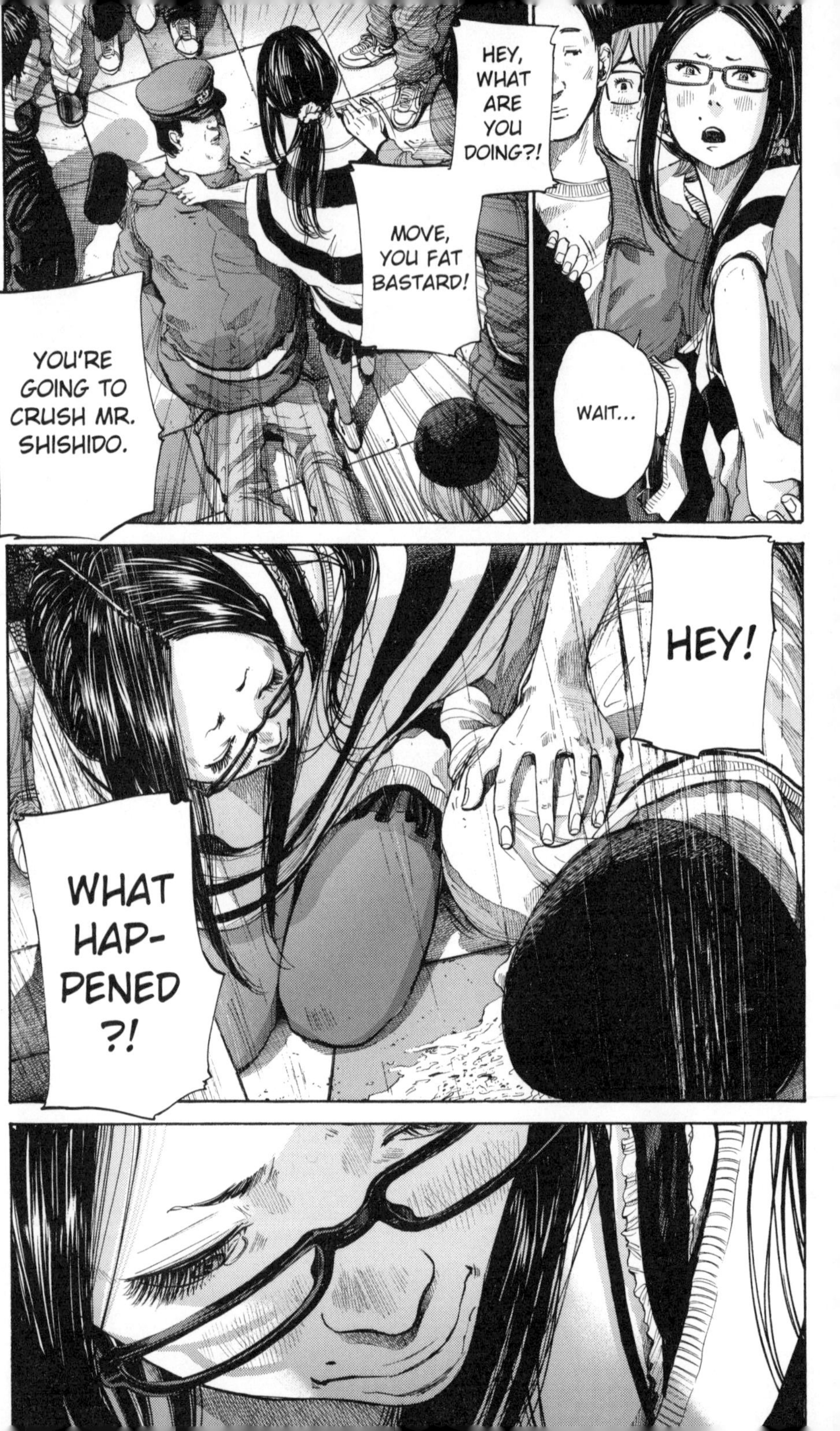
WAIT...
HEY, WHAT ARE YOU DOING?!
MOVE, YOU FAT BASTARD!
YOU'RE GOING TO CRUSH MR. SHISHIDO.
HEY!
WHAT HAP-PENED?!

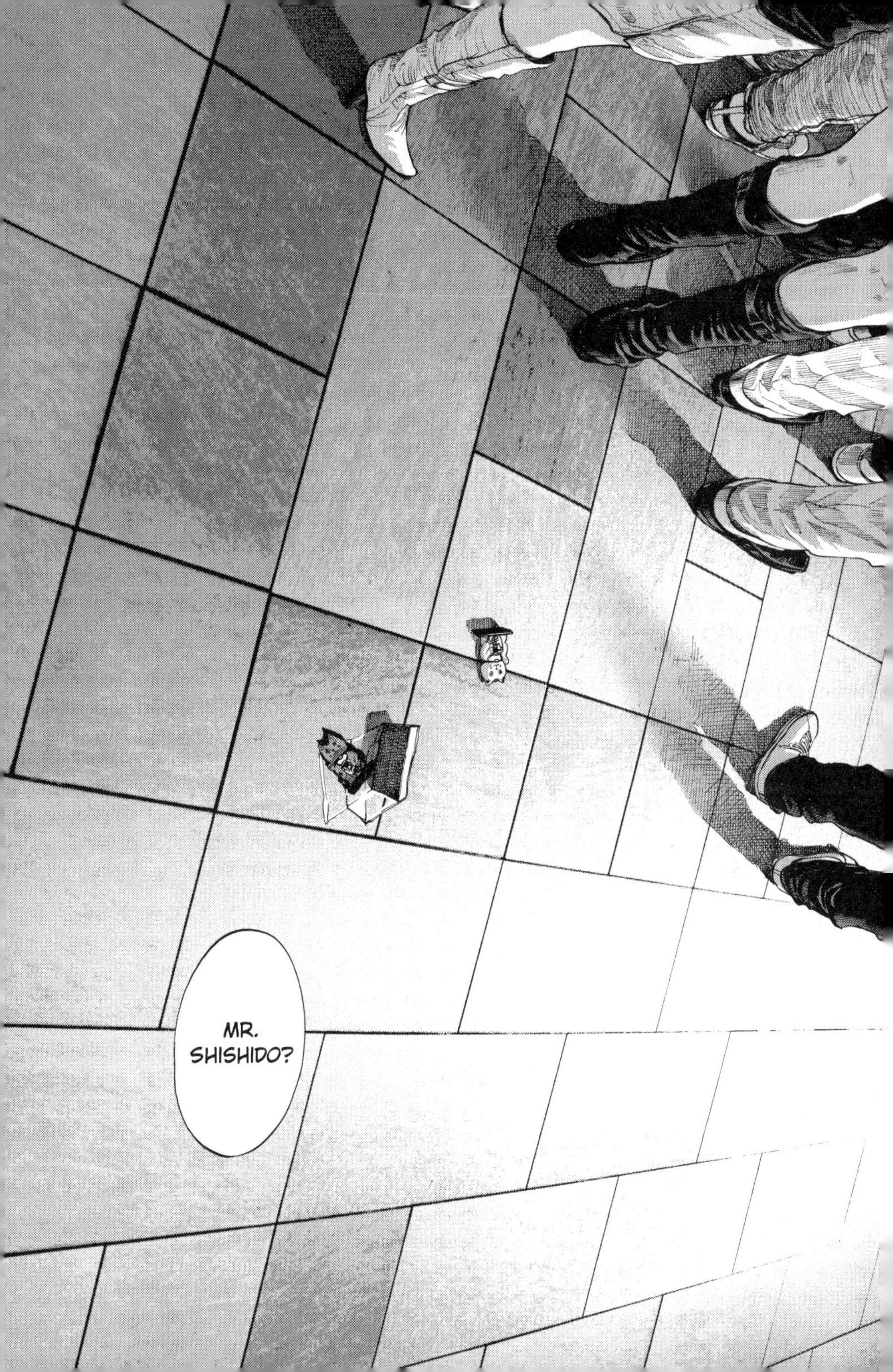
MR. SHISHIDO?

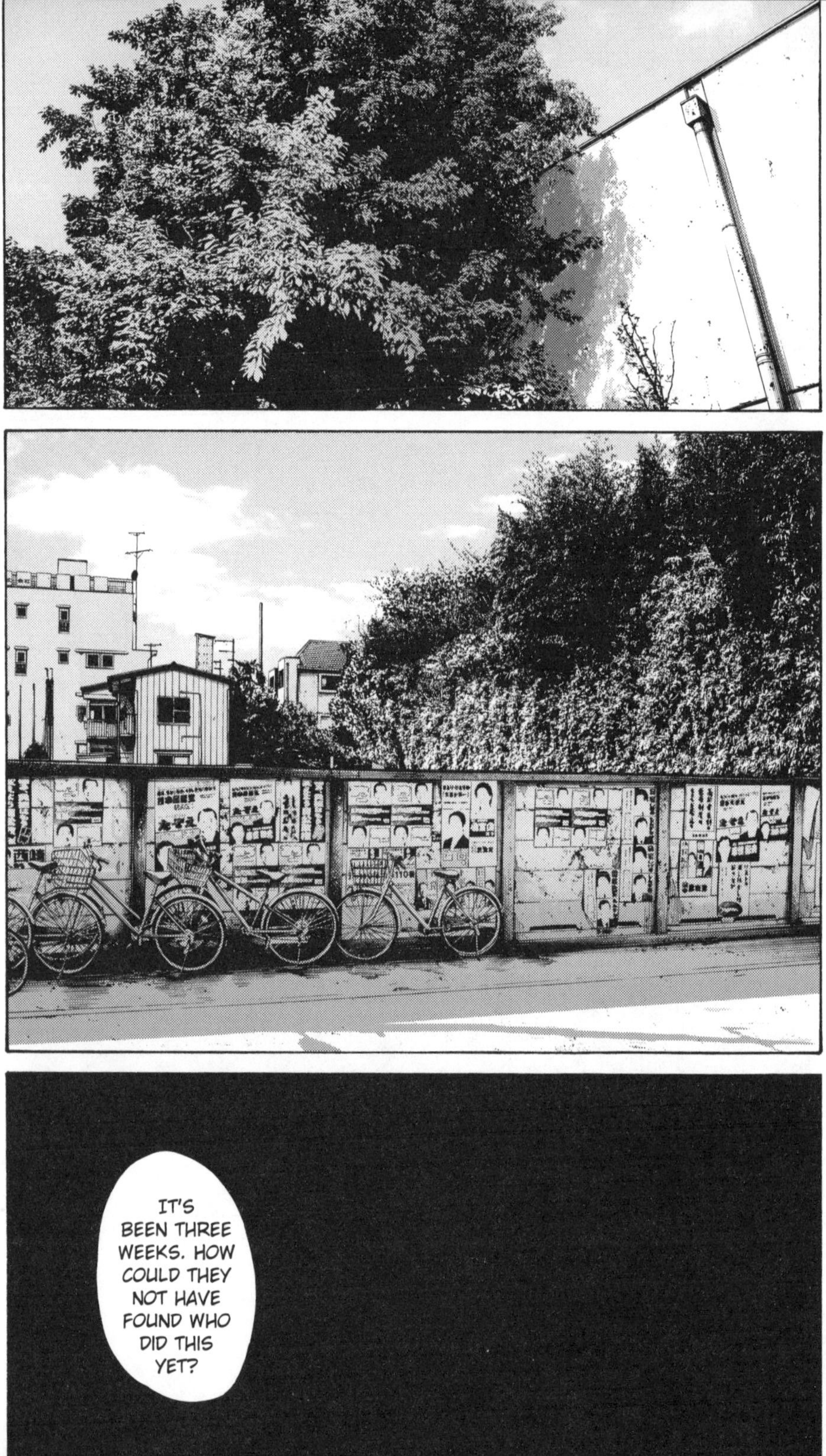
IT'S BEEN THREE WEEKS. HOW COULD THEY NOT HAVE FOUND WHO DID THIS YET?

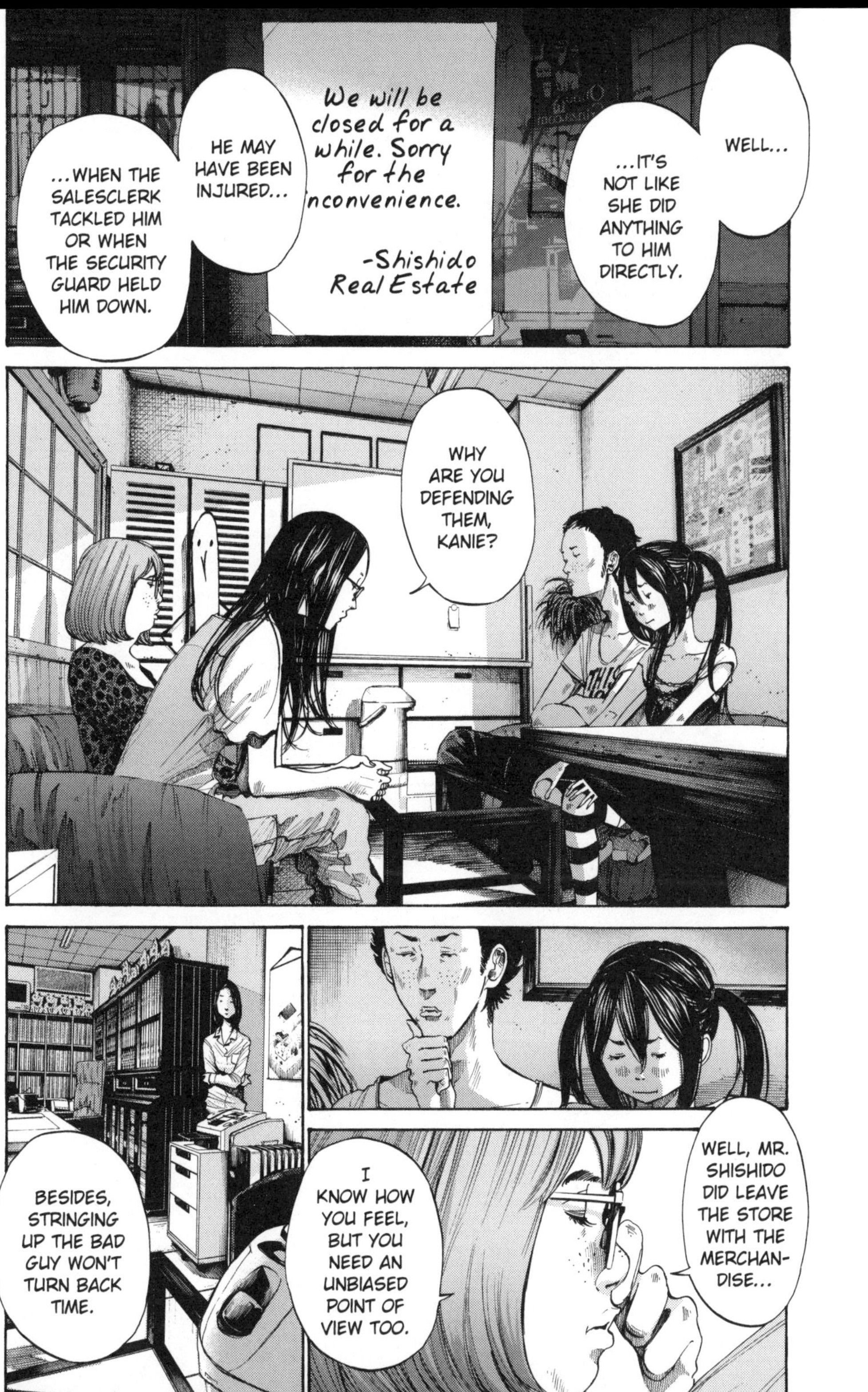
WELL...
...IT'S NOT LIKE SHE DID ANYTHING TO HIM DIRECTLY.
We will be closed for a while. Sorry for the inconvenience. -Shishido Real Estate
HE MAY HAVE BEEN INJURED...
...WHEN THE SALESCLERK TACKLED HIM OR WHEN THE SECURITY GUARD HELD HIM DOWN.
WHY ARE YOU DEFENDING THEM, KANIE?
WELL, MR. SHISHIDO DID LEAVE THE STORE WITH THE MERCHANDISE...
I KNOW HOW YOU FEEL, BUT YOU NEED AN UNBIASED POINT OF VIEW TOO.
BESIDES, STRINGING UP THE BAD GUY WON'T TURN BACK TIME.

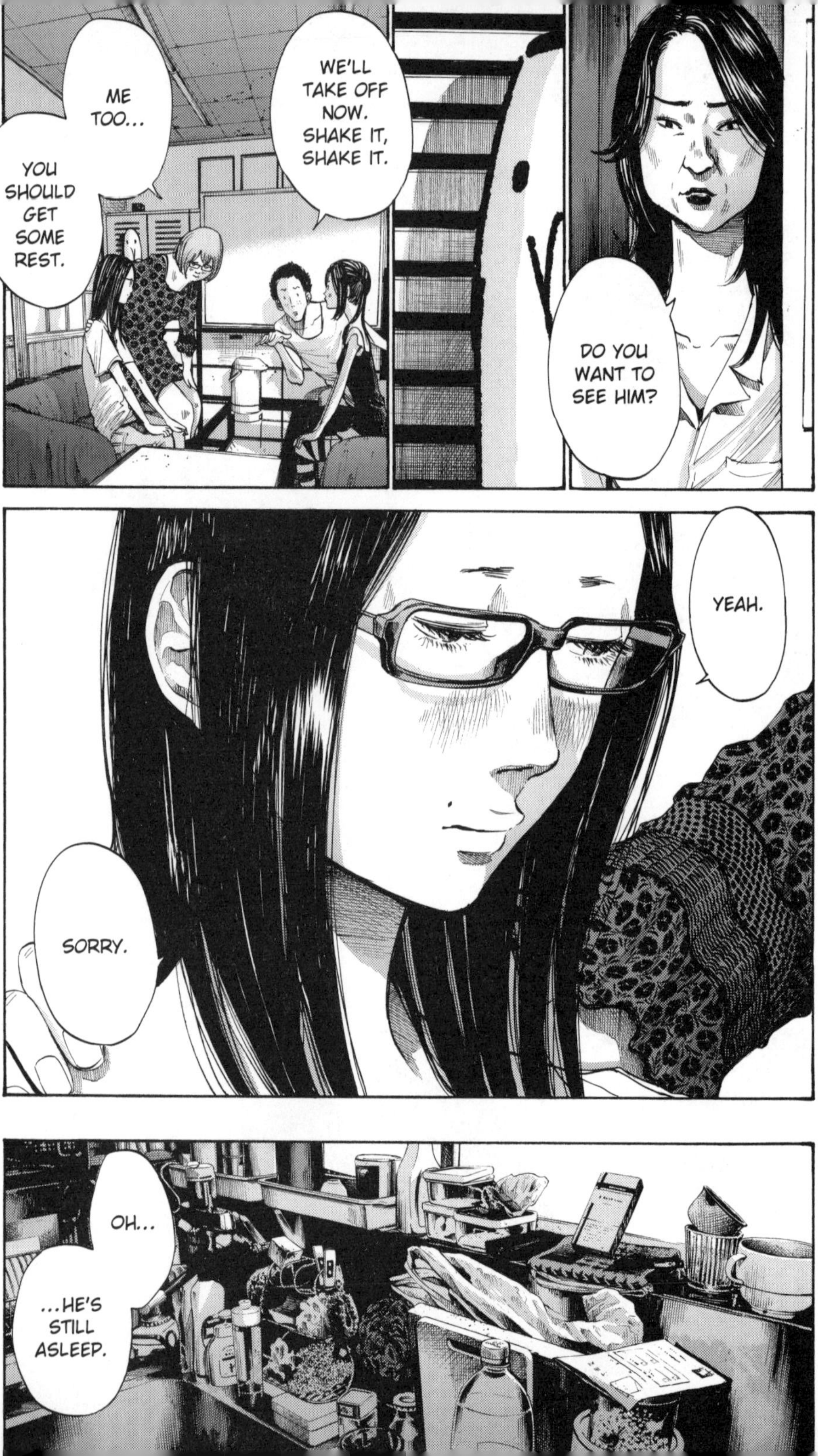
DO YOU WANT TO SEE HIM?
WE'LL TAKE OFF NOW. SHAKE IT, SHAKE IT.
ME TOO...
YOU SHOULD GET SOME REST.
YEAH.
SORRY.
OH...
...HE'S STILL ASLEEP.

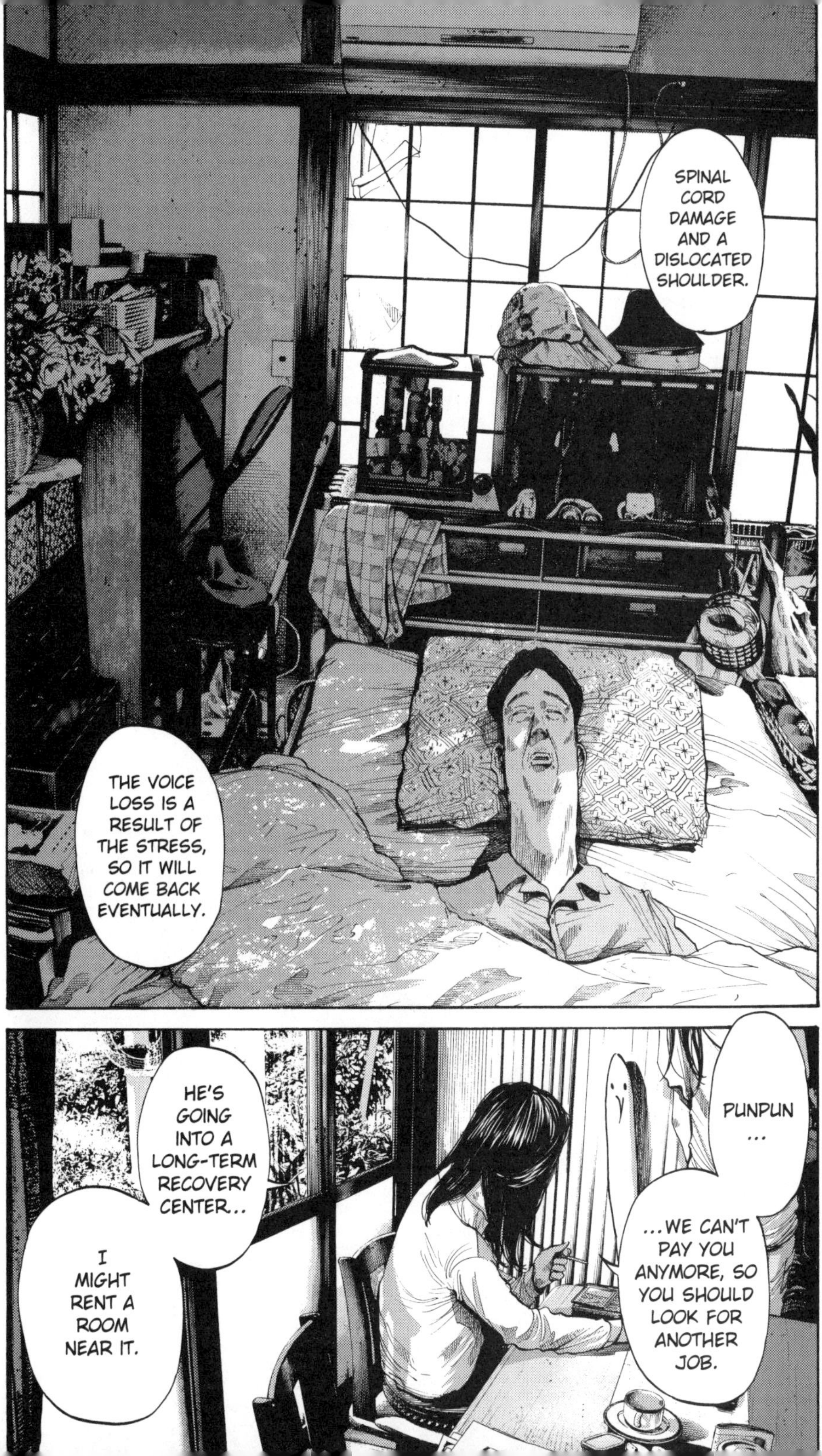
SPINAL CORD DAMAGE AND A DISLOCATED SHOULDER.
THE VOICE LOSS IS A RESULT OF THE STRESS, SO IT WILL COME BACK EVENTUALLY.
PUNPUN...
...WE CAN'T PAY YOU ANYMORE, SO YOU SHOULD LOOK FOR ANOTHER JOB.
HE'S GOING INTO A LONG-TERM RECOVERY CENTER...
I MIGHT RENT A ROOM NEAR IT.

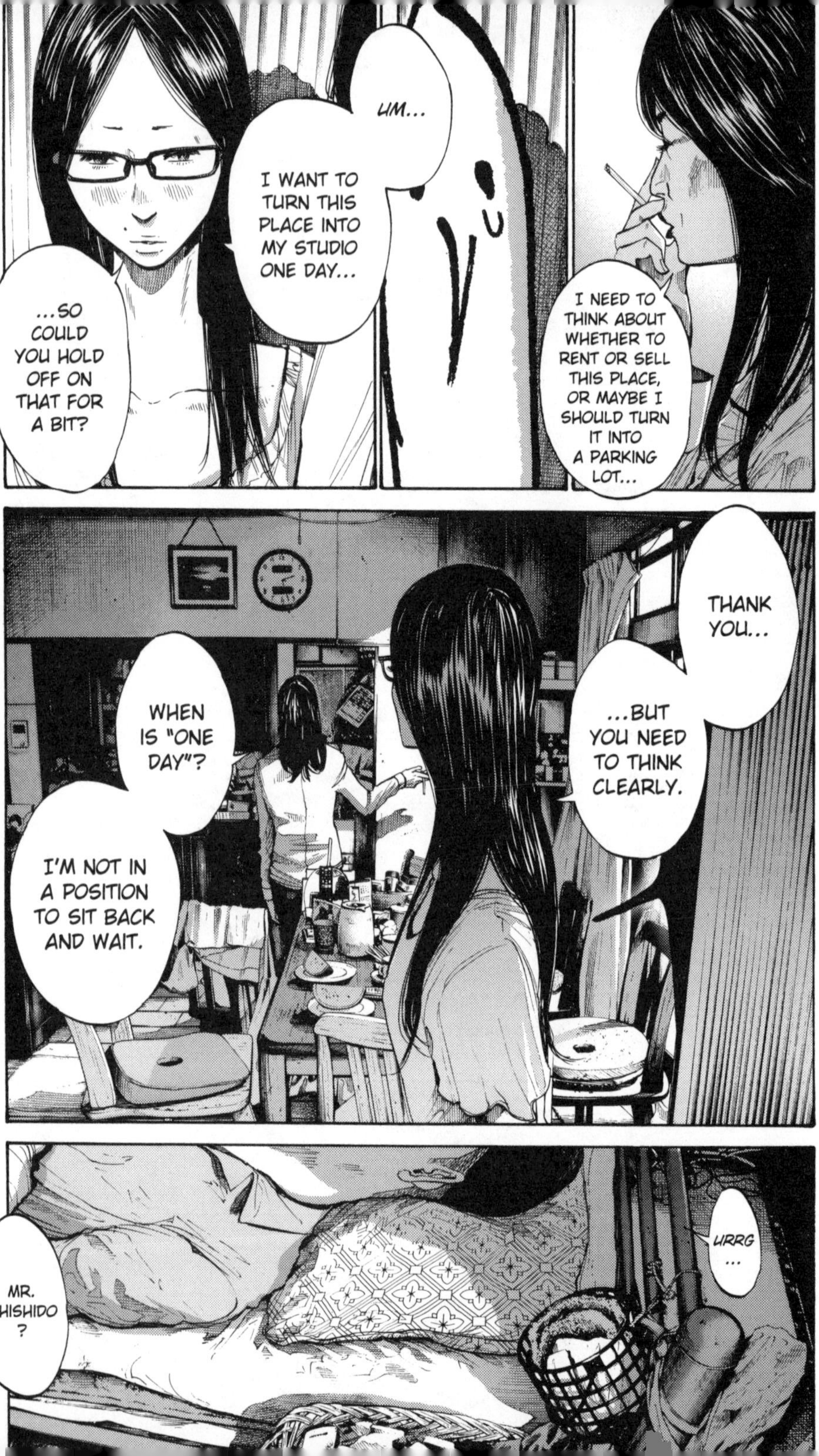
I NEED TO THINK ABOUT WHETHER TO RENT OR SELL THIS PLACE, OR MAYBE I SHOULD TURN IT INTO A PARKING LOT...
UM...
I WANT TO TURN THIS PLACE INTO MY STUDIO ONE DAY...
...SO COULD YOU HOLD OFF ON THAT FOR A BIT?
THANK YOU...
...BUT YOU NEED TO THINK CLEARLY.
WHEN IS "ONE DAY"?
I'M NOT IN A POSITION TO SIT BACK AND WAIT.
URRG ...
MR. SHISHIDO ?

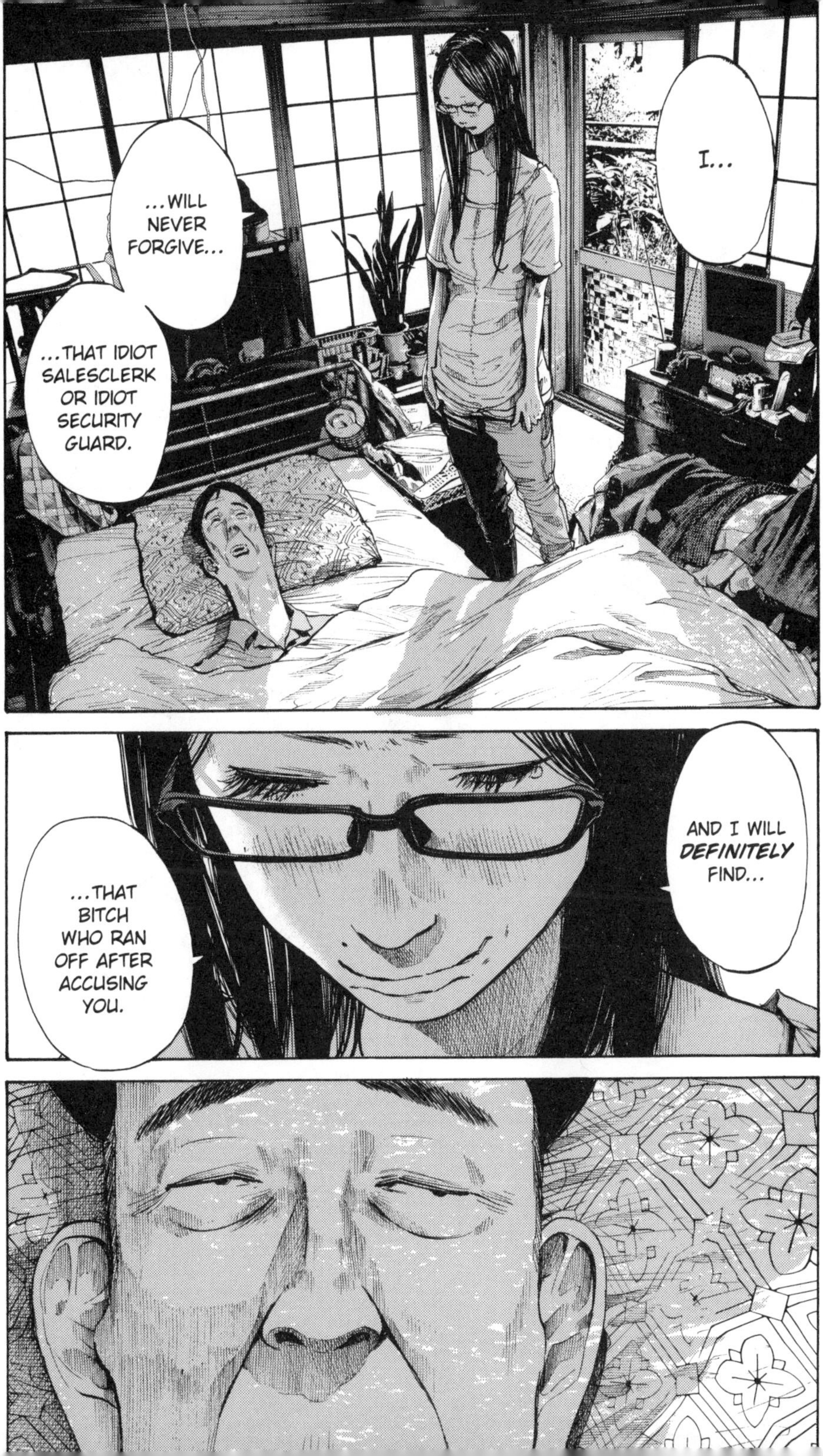
I...
...WILL NEVER FORGIVE...
...THAT IDIOT SALESCLERK OR IDIOT SECURITY GUARD.
AND I WILL *DEFINITELY* FIND...
...THAT BITCH WHO RAN OFF AFTER ACCUSING YOU.

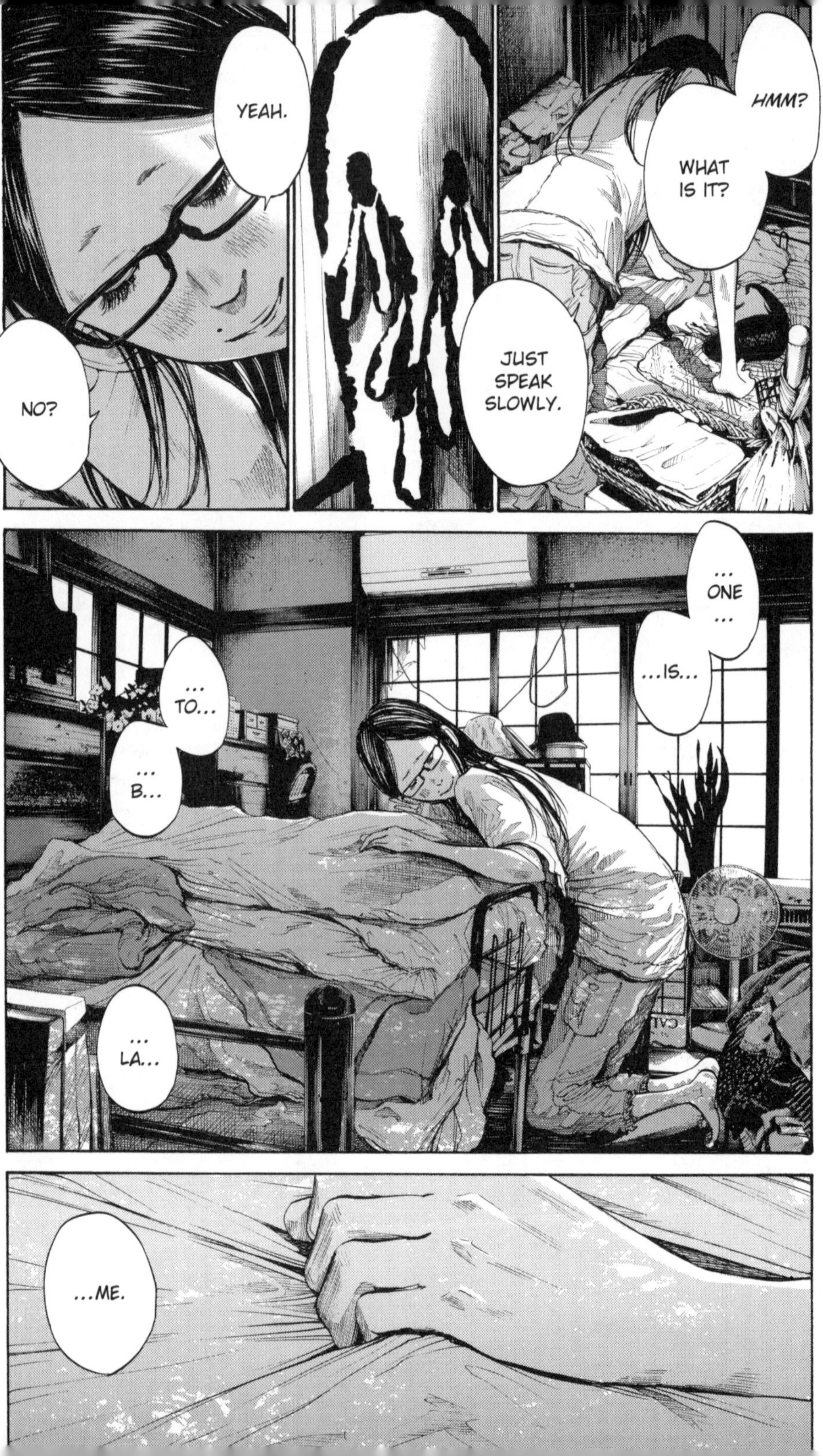
HMM?
WHAT IS IT?
JUST SPEAK SLOWLY.
YEAH.
NO?
... ONE ...
...IS...
... TO...
... B...
... LA...
...ME.

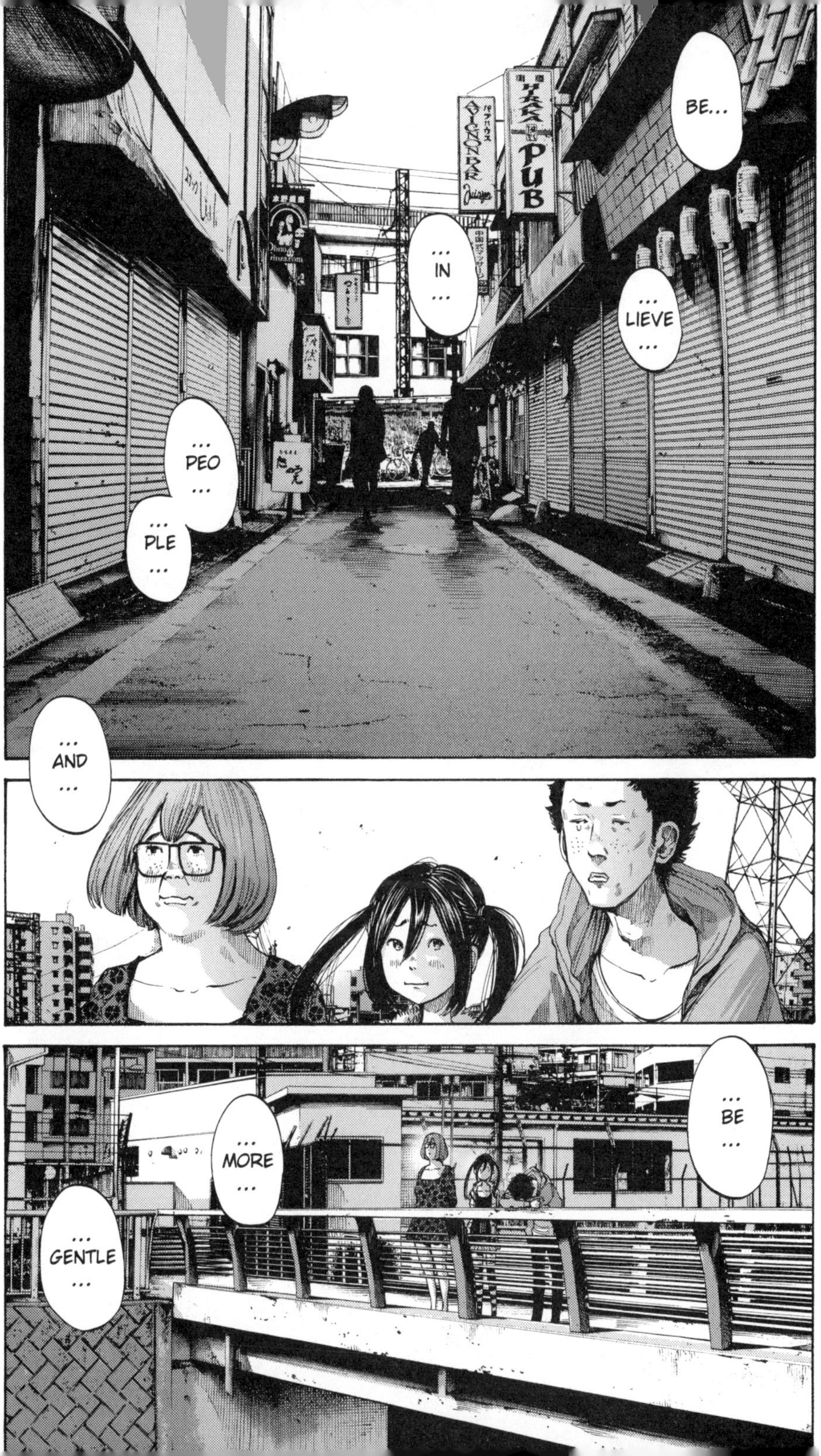
BE...
... LIEVE ...
... IN ...
PUB
... PEO ...
... PLE ...
... AND ...
... BE ...
... MORE ...
... GENTLE ...

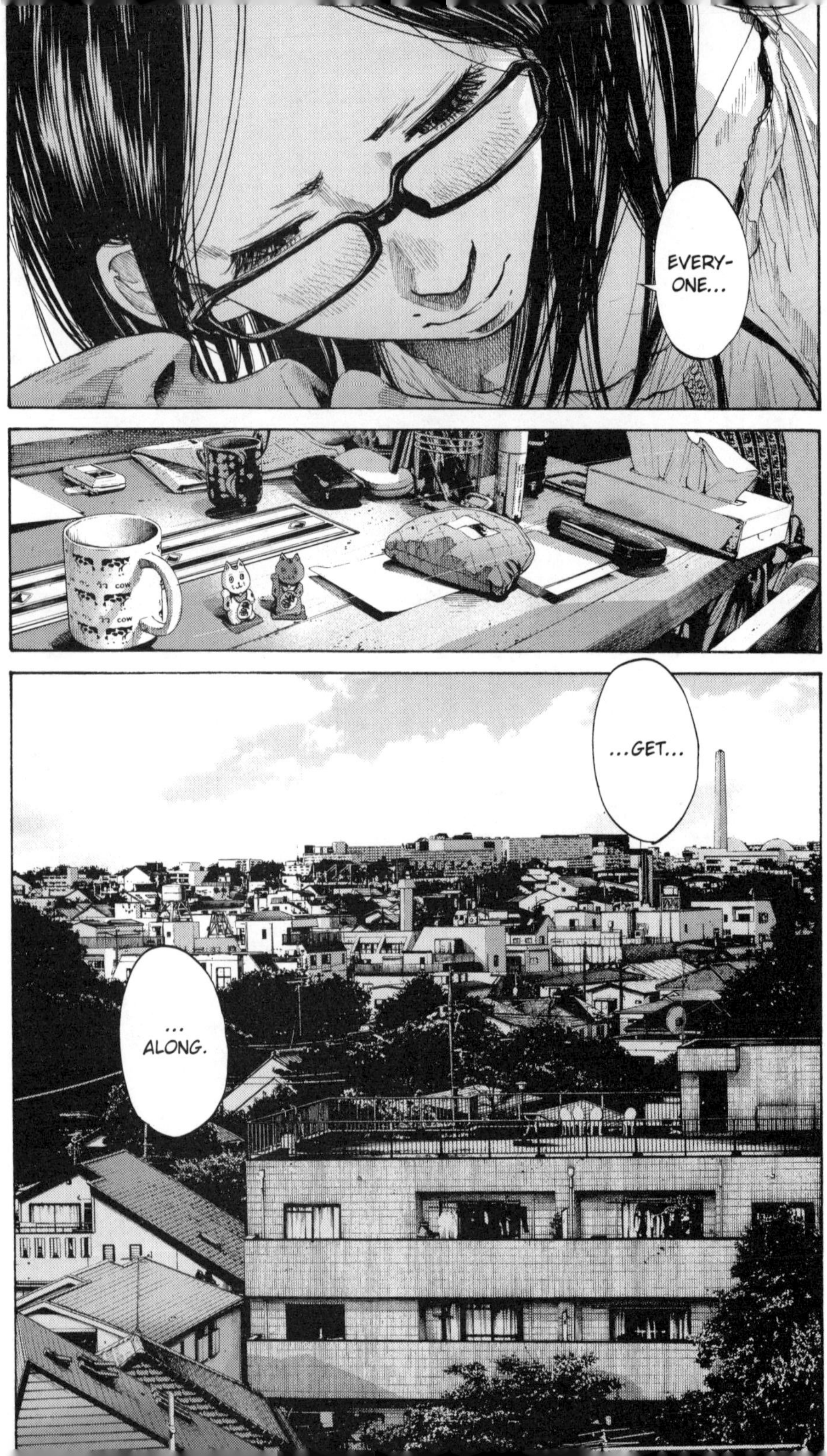
EVERY-
ONE...
...GET...
...
ALONG.

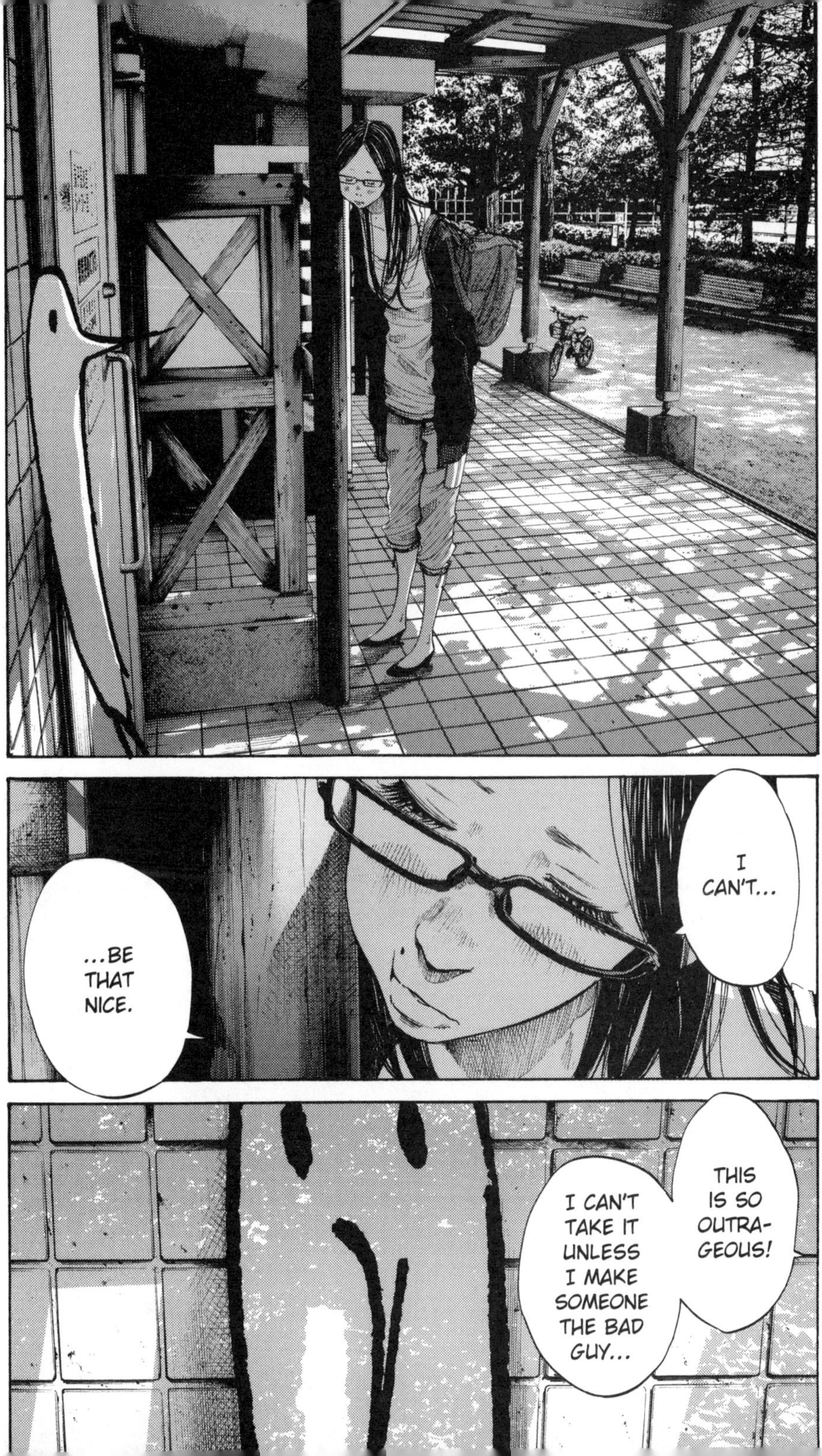
I CAN'T...
...BE THAT NICE.
THIS IS SO OUTRA-GEOUS!
I CAN'T TAKE IT UNLESS I MAKE SOMEONE THE BAD GUY...

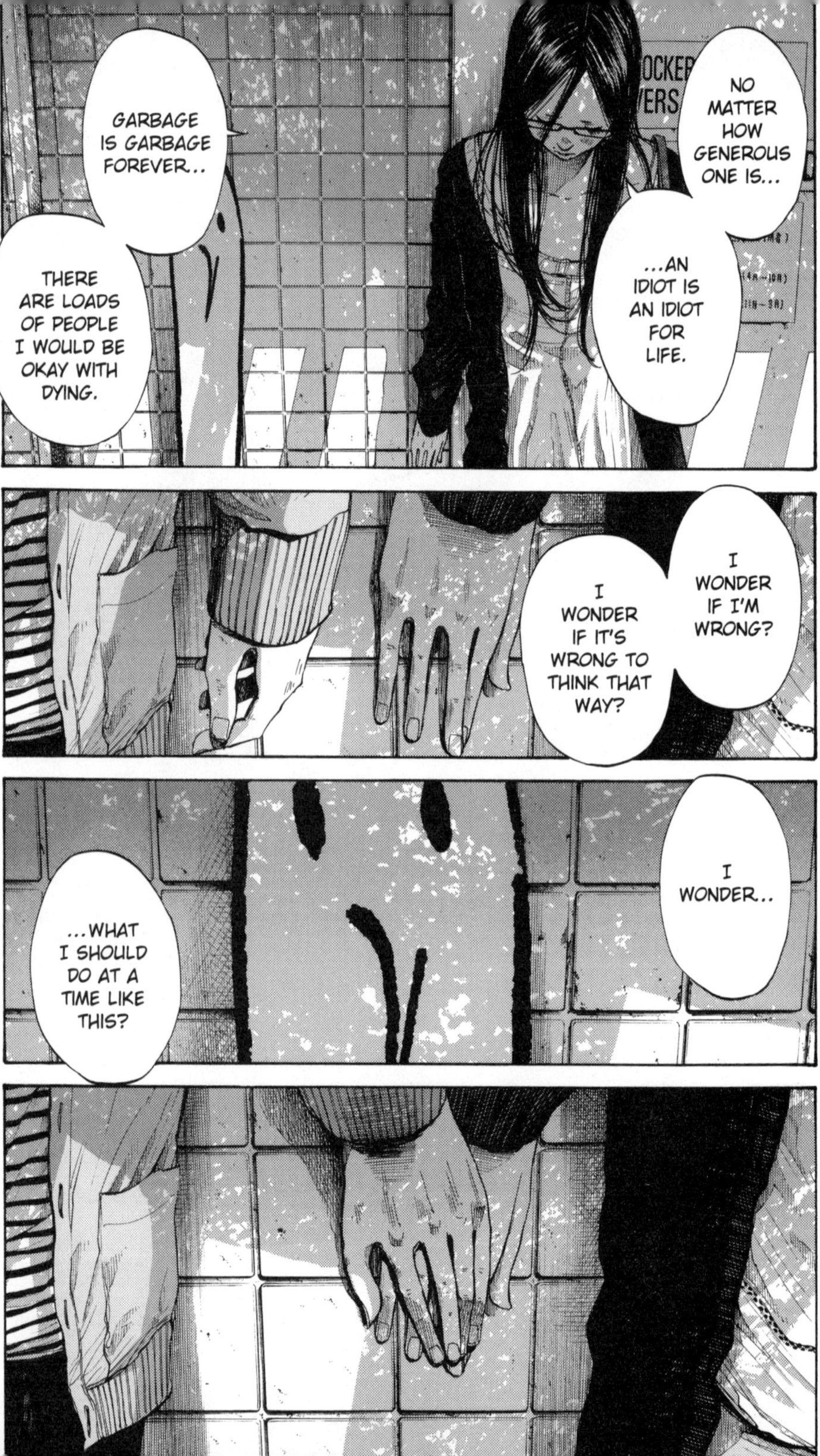
NO MATTER HOW GENEROUS ONE IS...
...AN IDIOT IS AN IDIOT FOR LIFE.
GARBAGE IS GARBAGE FOREVER...
THERE ARE LOADS OF PEOPLE I WOULD BE OKAY WITH DYING.
I WONDER IF I'M WRONG?
I WONDER IF IT'S WRONG TO THINK THAT WAY?
I WONDER...
...WHAT I SHOULD DO AT A TIME LIKE THIS?

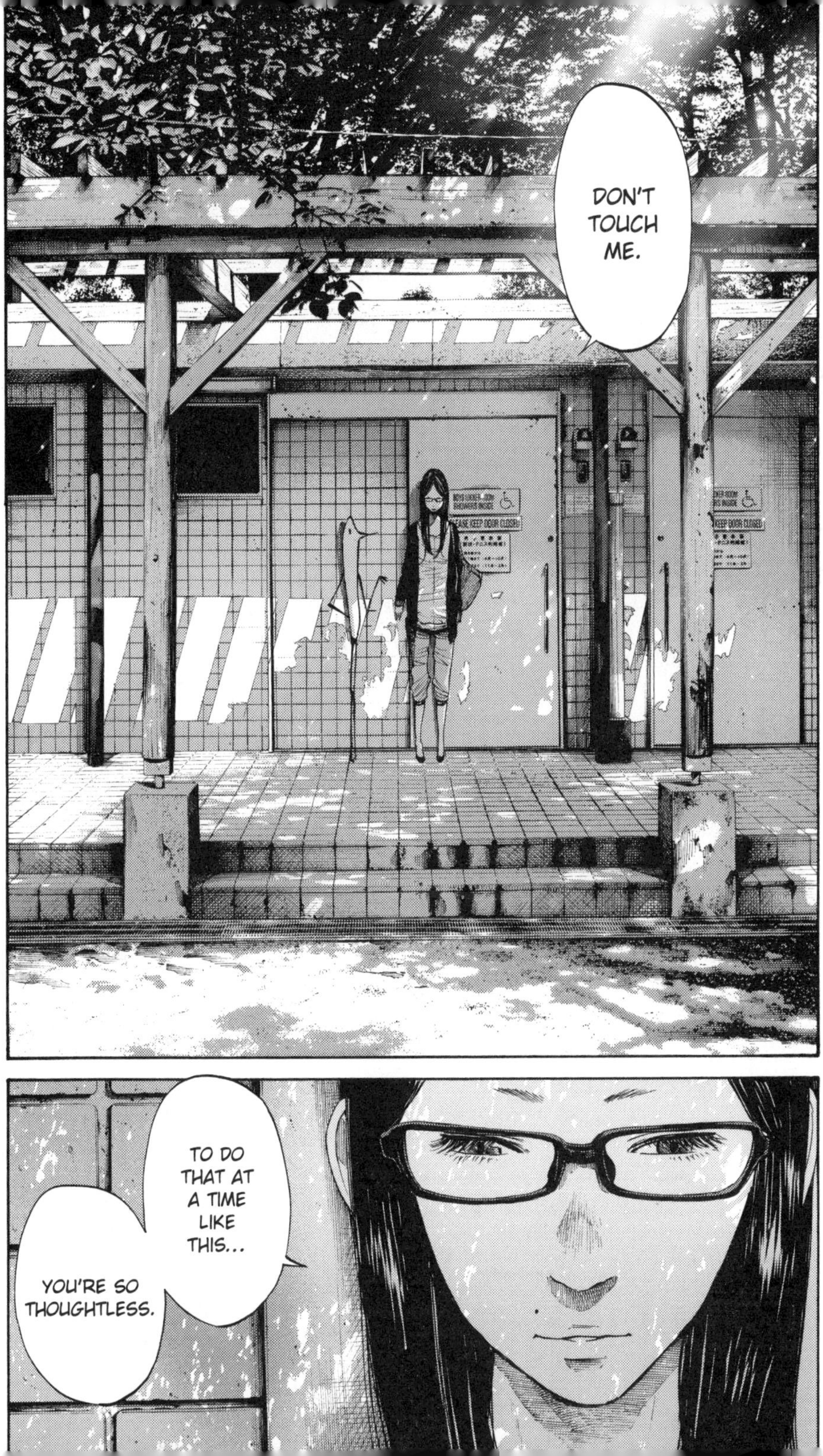
DON'T TOUCH ME.
TO DO THAT AT A TIME LIKE THIS...
YOU'RE SO THOUGHTLESS.

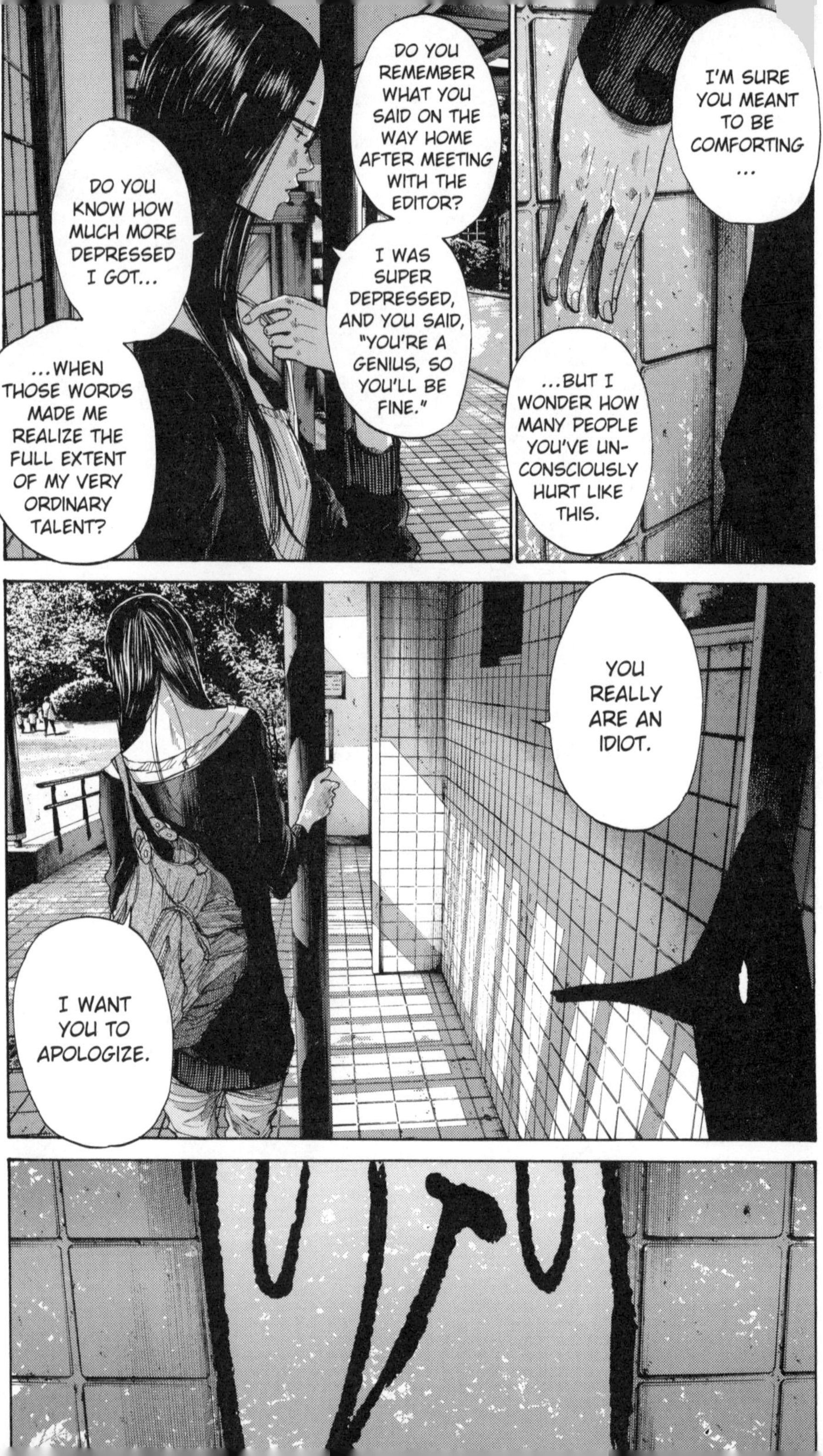
I'M SURE YOU MEANT TO BE COMFORTING...
...BUT I WONDER HOW MANY PEOPLE YOU'VE UN-CONSCIOUSLY HURT LIKE THIS.
DO YOU REMEMBER WHAT YOU SAID ON THE WAY HOME AFTER MEETING WITH THE EDITOR?
I WAS SUPER DEPRESSED, AND YOU SAID, "YOU'RE A GENIUS, SO YOU'LL BE FINE."
DO YOU KNOW HOW MUCH MORE DEPRESSED I GOT...
...WHEN THOSE WORDS MADE ME REALIZE THE FULL EXTENT OF MY VERY ORDINARY TALENT?
YOU REALLY ARE AN IDIOT.
I WANT YOU TO APOLOGIZE.

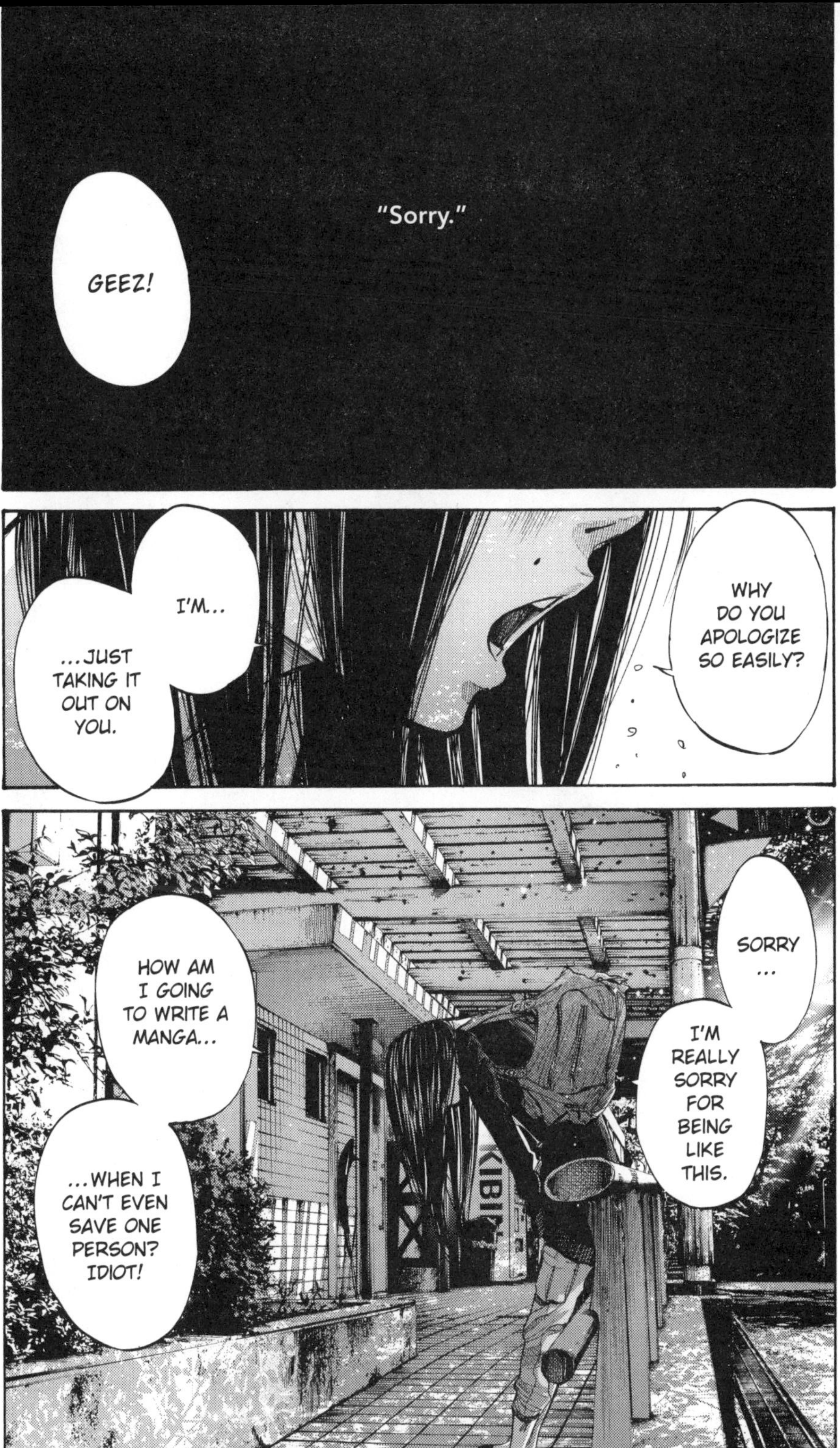
"Sorry."
GEEZ!
WHY DO YOU APOLOGIZE SO EASILY?
I'M...
...JUST TAKING IT OUT ON YOU.
SORRY...
I'M REALLY SORRY FOR BEING LIKE THIS.
HOW AM I GOING TO WRITE A MANGA...
...WHEN I CAN'T EVEN SAVE ONE PERSON? IDIOT!

Chapter 98

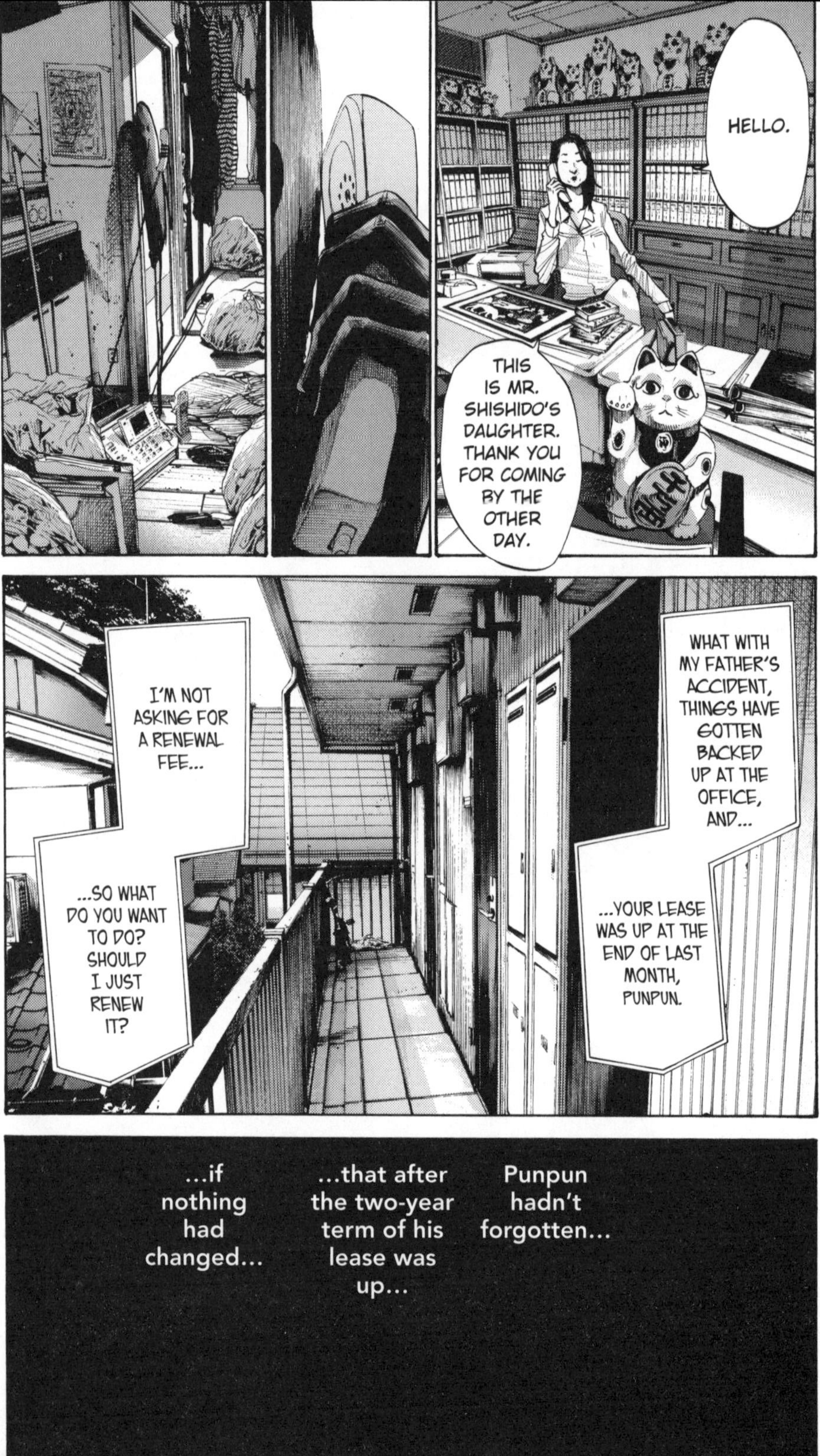
HELLO.
THIS IS MR. SHISHIDO'S DAUGHTER. THANK YOU FOR COMING BY THE OTHER DAY.
WHAT WITH MY FATHER'S ACCIDENT, THINGS HAVE GOTTEN BACKED UP AT THE OFFICE, AND...
...YOUR LEASE WAS UP AT THE END OF LAST MONTH, PUNPUN.
I'M NOT ASKING FOR A RENEWAL FEE...
...SO WHAT DO YOU WANT TO DO? SHOULD I JUST RENEW IT?
Punpun hadn't forgotten...
...that after the two-year term of his lease was up...
...if nothing had changed...

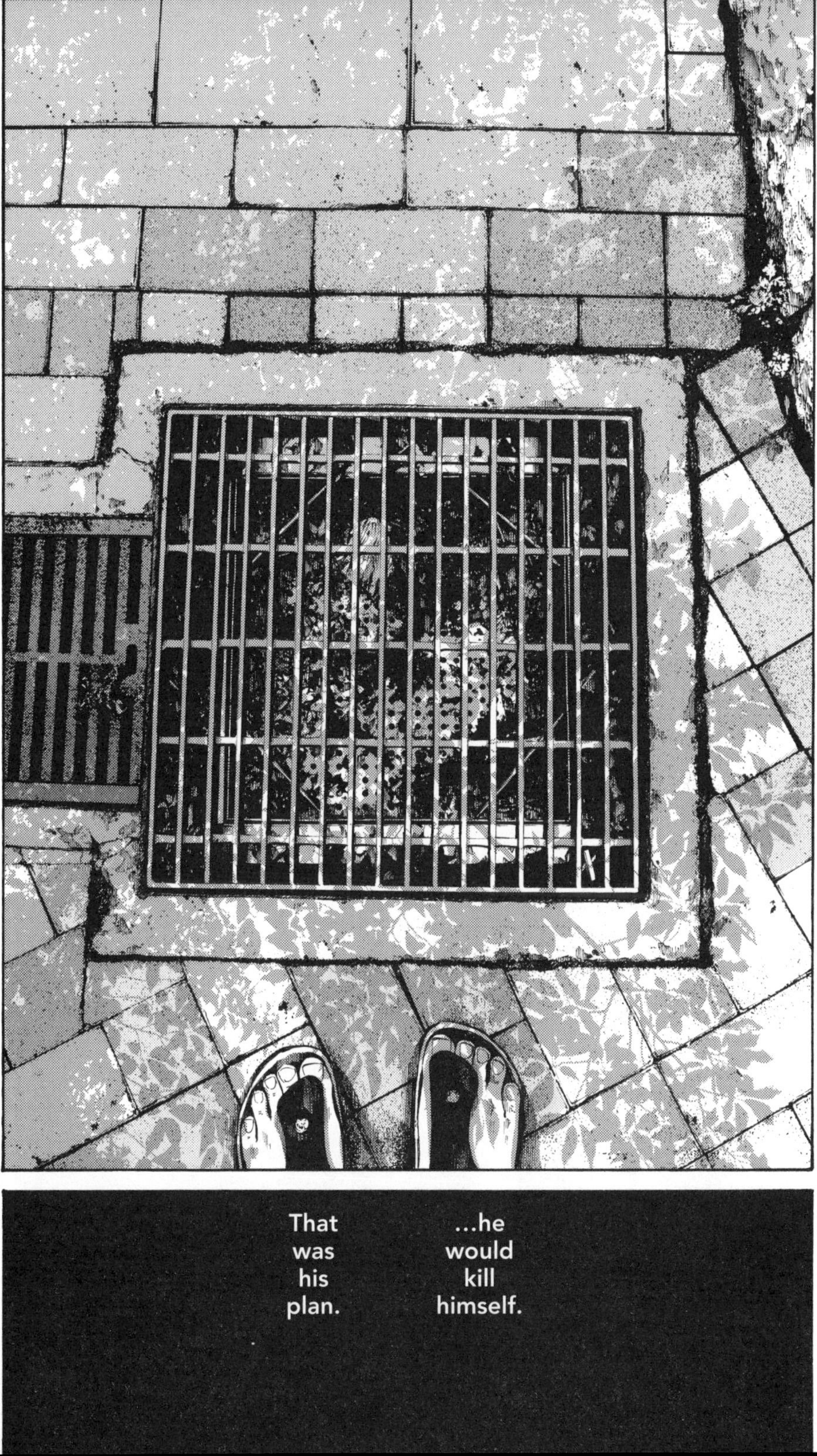
...he would kill himself.
That was his plan.

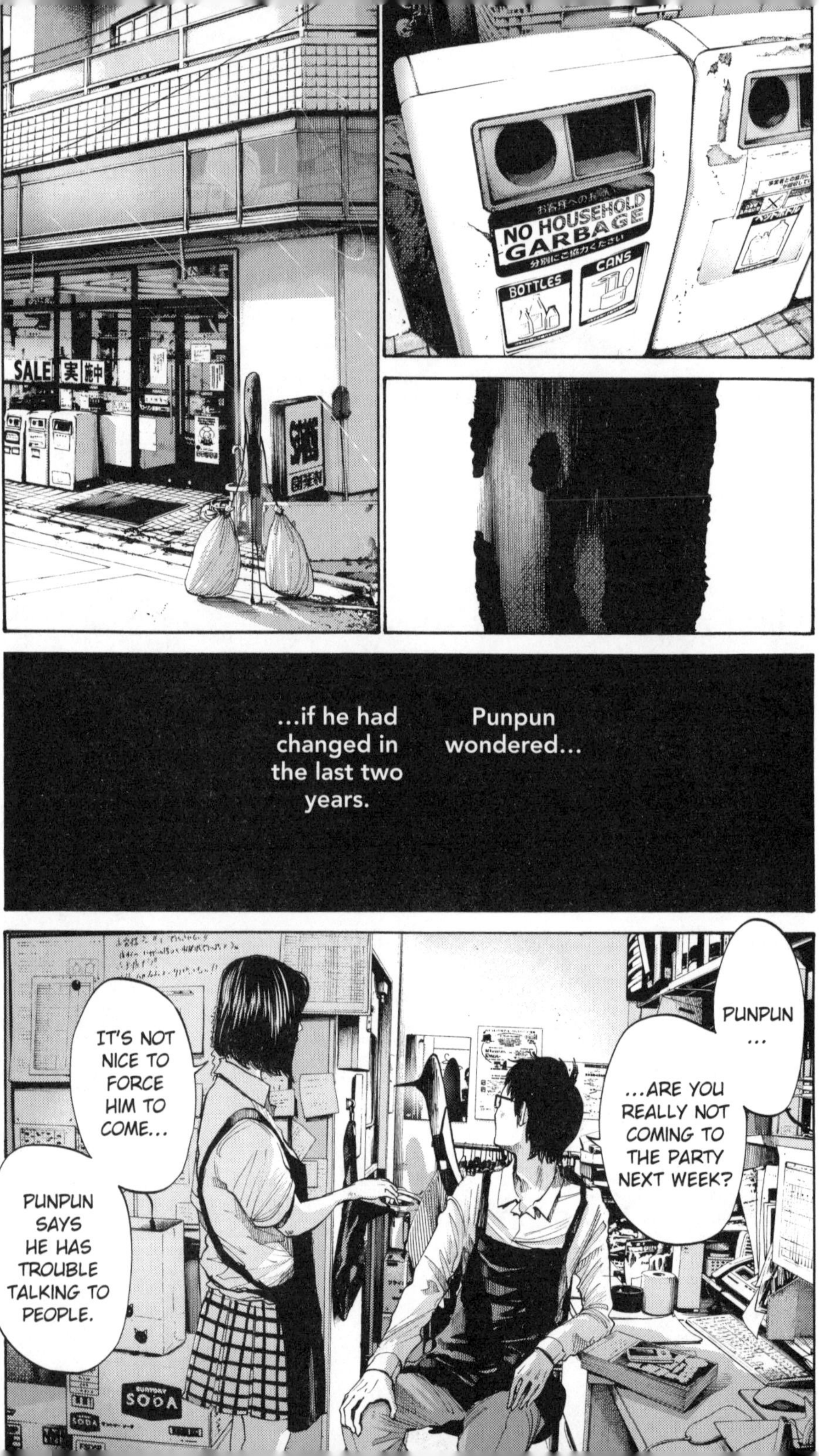
NO HOUSEHOLD GARBAGE
分別にご協力ください
BOTTLES
CANS
SALE 実施中
Punpun wondered...
...if he had changed in the last two years.
PUNPUN...
...ARE YOU REALLY NOT COMING TO THE PARTY NEXT WEEK?
IT'S NOT NICE TO FORCE HIM TO COME...
PUNPUN SAYS HE HAS TROUBLE TALKING TO PEOPLE.
SODA

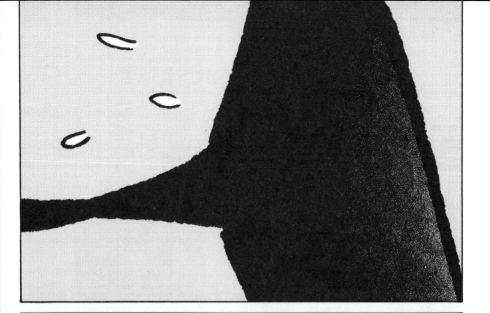

He had taken a little detour, yes... ...but he'd still ended up where he'd started.

BOTTLES AND CANS ONLU

He'd ended up where he'd started!

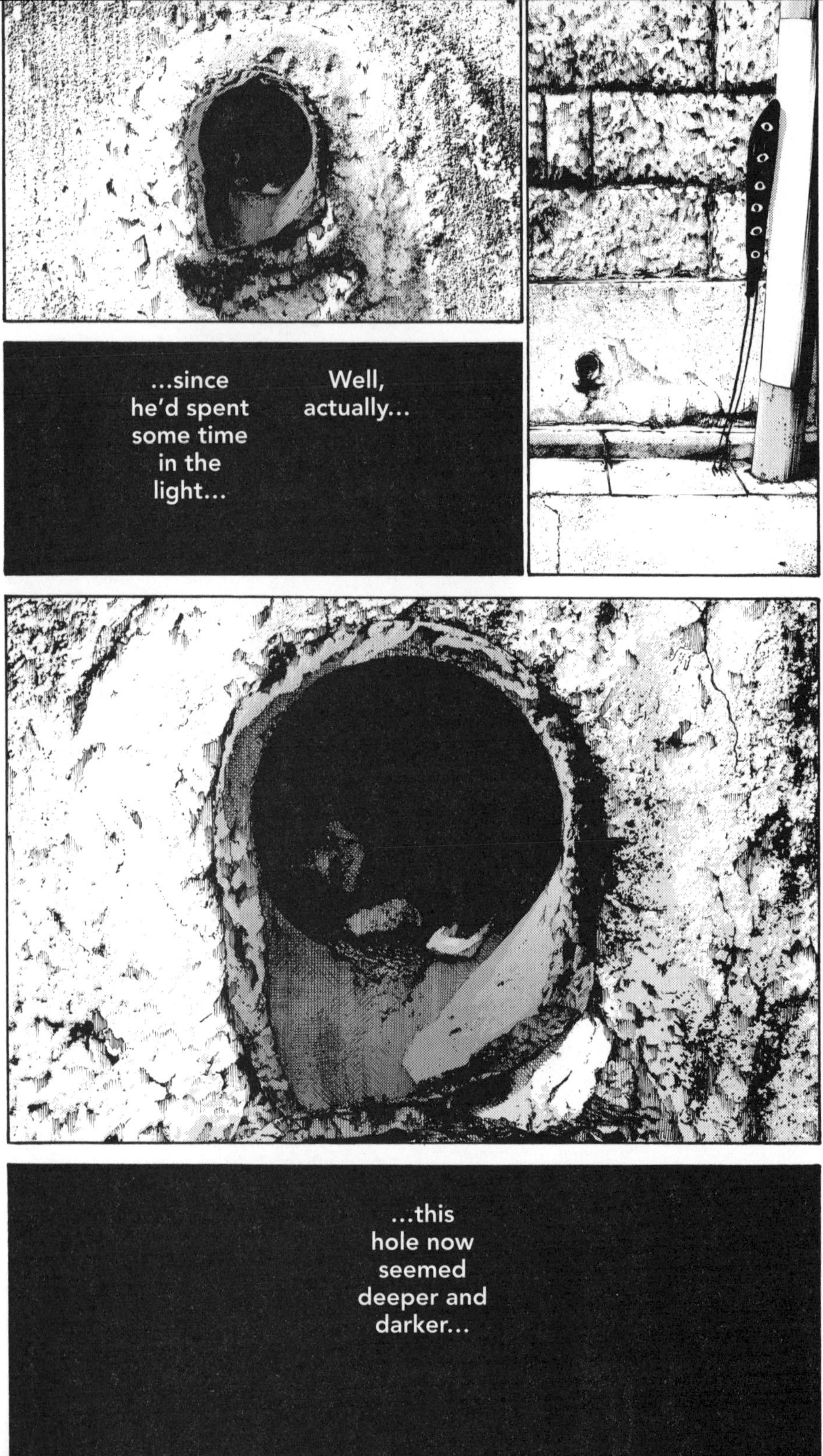
Well, actually...
...since he'd spent some time in the light...
...this hole now seemed deeper and darker...

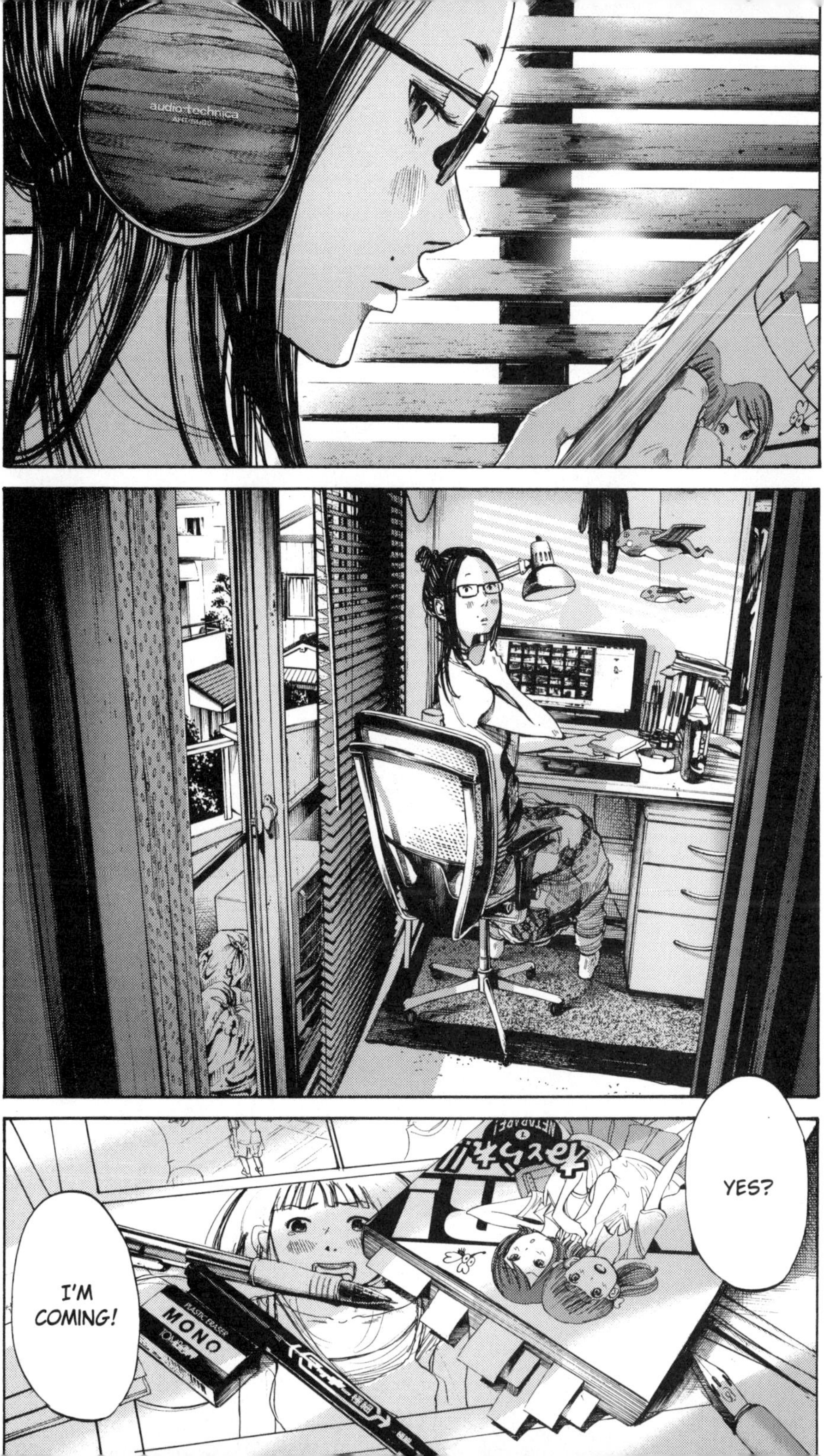
audio-technica
YES?
I'M COMING!
PLASTIC ERASER
MONO

URRR!

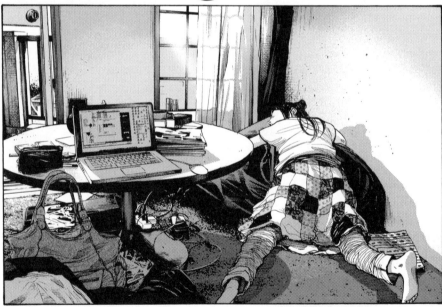

I WANT TO HAVE SEX.

SIGH...

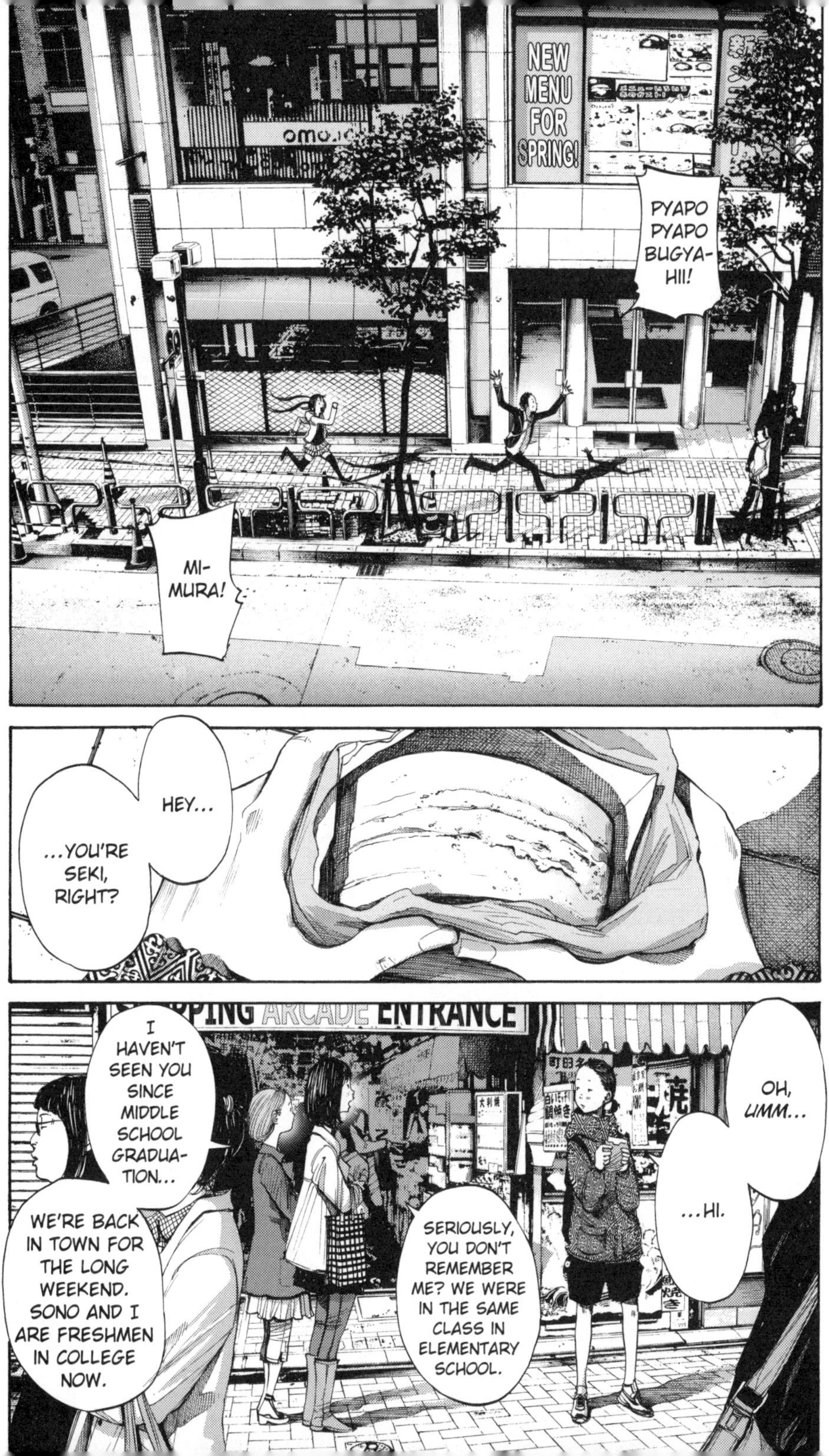
NEW MENU FOR SPRING!
PYAPO PYAPO BUGYA-HII!
MI-MURA!
HEY...
...YOU'RE SEKI, RIGHT?
ARCADE ENTRANCE
OH, UMM...
...HI.
SERIOUSLY, YOU DON'T REMEMBER ME? WE WERE IN THE SAME CLASS IN ELEMENTARY SCHOOL.
I HAVEN'T SEEN YOU SINCE MIDDLE SCHOOL GRADUA-TION...
WE'RE BACK IN TOWN FOR THE LONG WEEKEND. SONO AND I ARE FRESHMEN IN COLLEGE NOW.

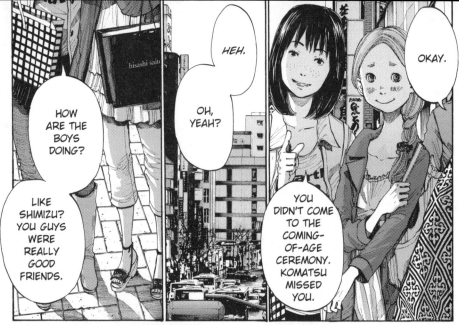

OKAY.
YOU DIDN'T COME TO THE COMING-OF-AGE CEREMONY. KOMATSU MISSED YOU.
HEH.
OH, YEAH?
HOW ARE THE BOYS DOING?
LIKE SHIMIZU? YOU GUYS WERE REALLY GOOD FRIENDS.
WHO'S...
...SHIMIZU?

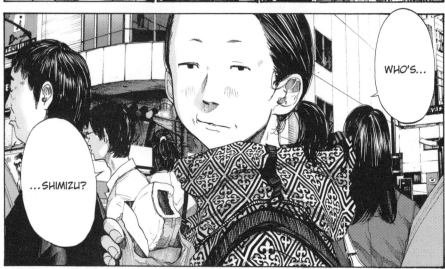

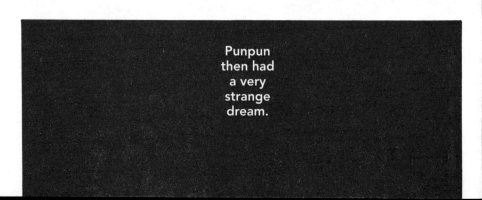

Punpun then had a very strange dream.

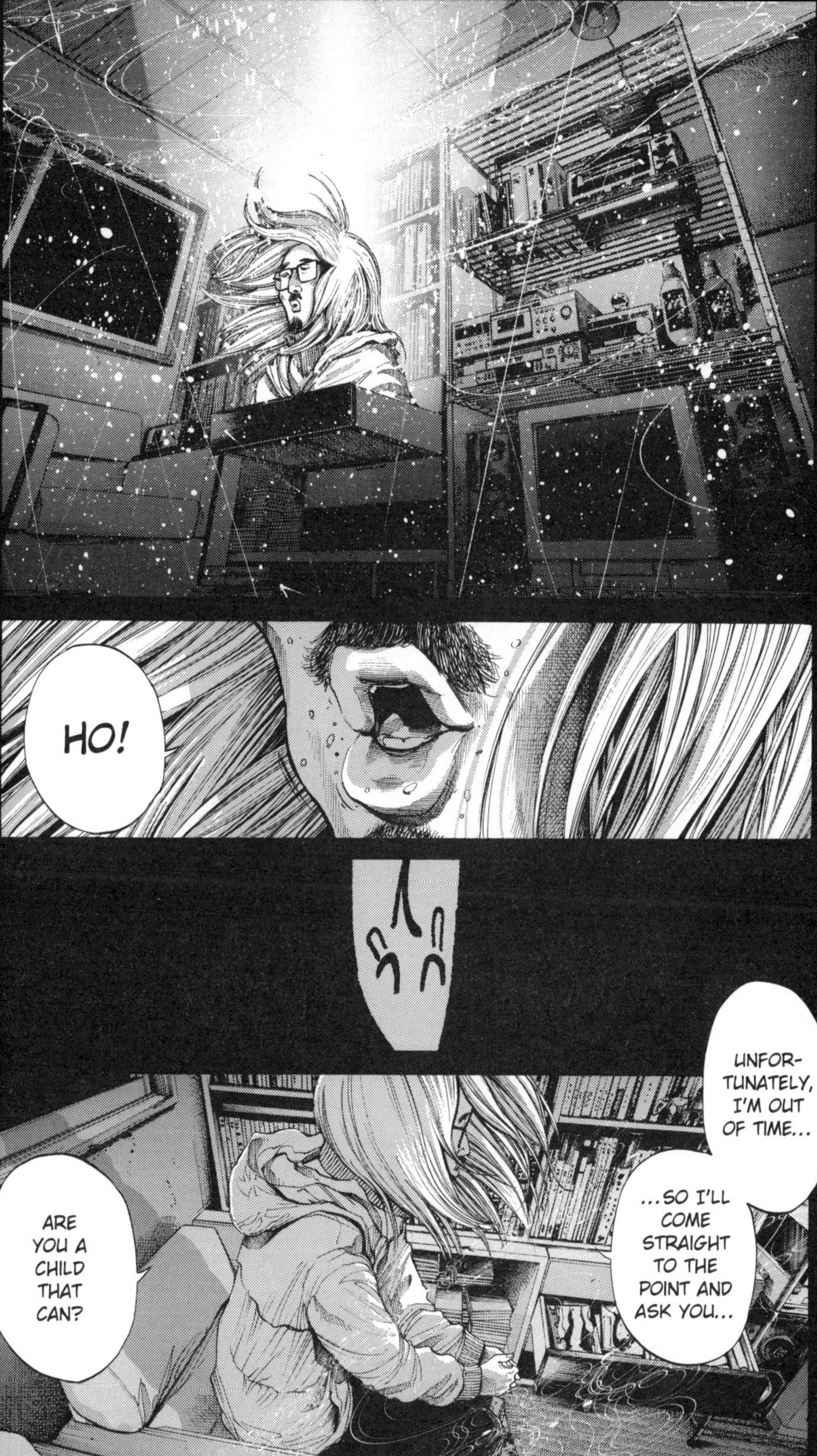
HO!
UNFOR-TUNATELY, I'M OUT OF TIME...
...SO I'LL COME STRAIGHT TO THE POINT AND ASK YOU...
ARE YOU A CHILD THAT CAN?

"I'm always a child who can't."

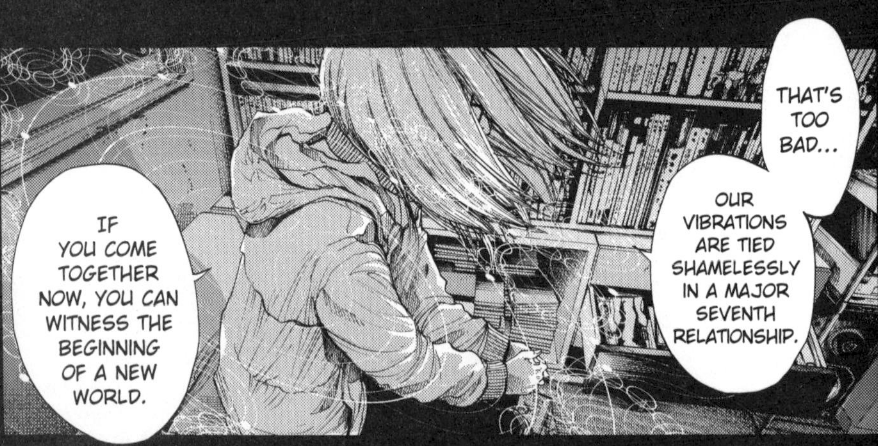
THAT'S TOO BAD...
OUR VIBRATIONS ARE TIED SHAMELESSLY IN A MAJOR SEVENTH RELATIONSHIP.
IF YOU COME TOGETHER NOW, YOU CAN WITNESS THE BEGINNING OF A NEW WORLD.

"I don't think so."

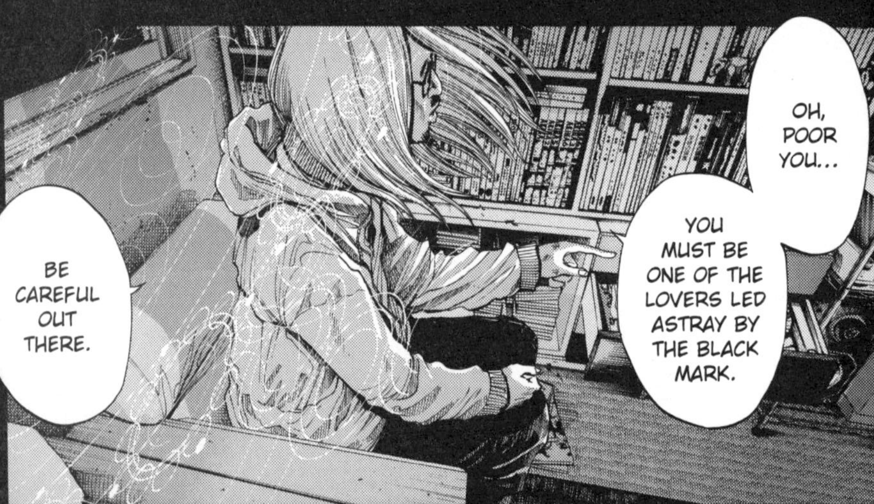
OH, POOR YOU...
YOU MUST BE ONE OF THE LOVERS LED ASTRAY BY THE BLACK MARK.
BE CAREFUL OUT THERE.

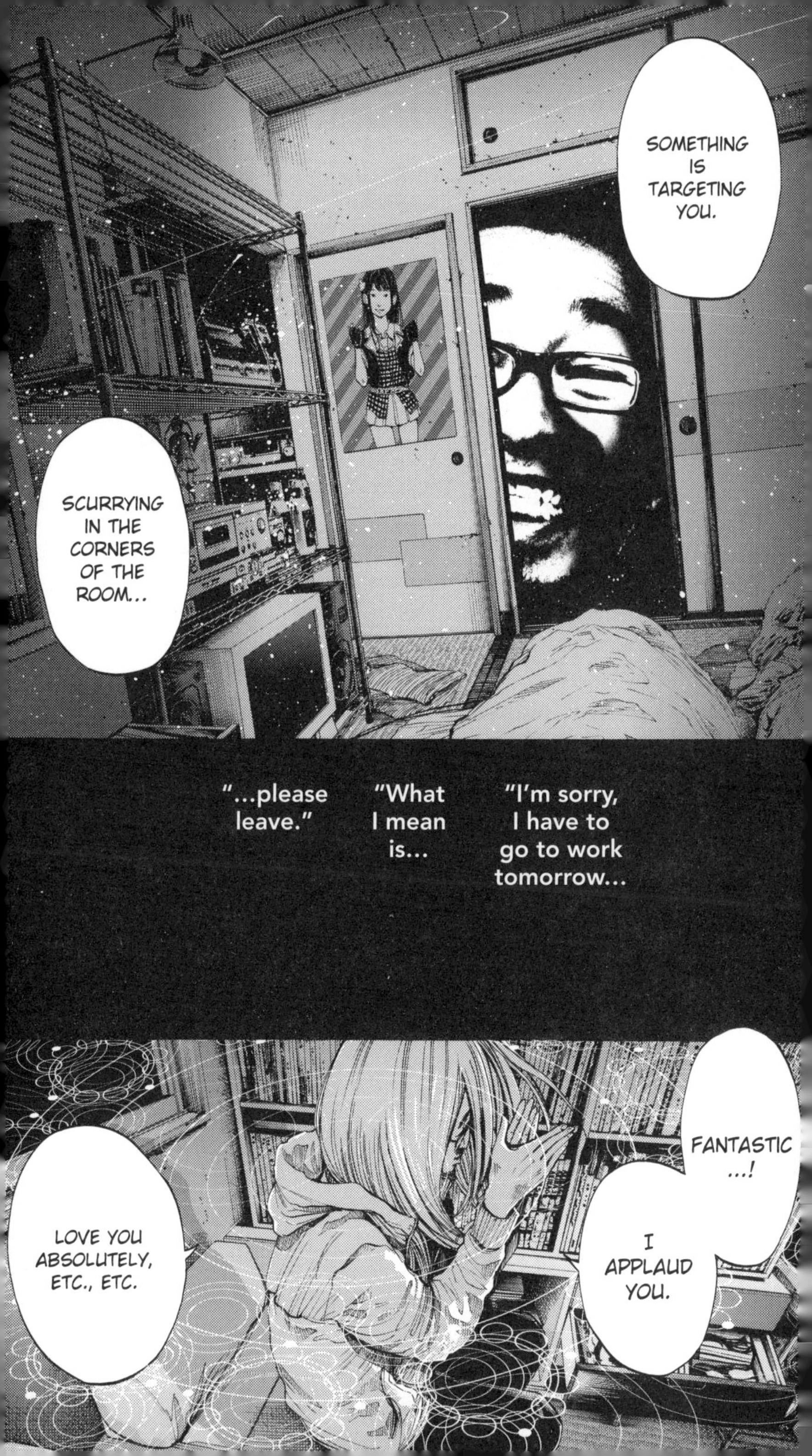
SOMETHING IS TARGETING YOU.
SCURRYING IN THE CORNERS OF THE ROOM...
"I'm sorry, I have to go to work tomorrow...
"What I mean is...
"...please leave."
FANTASTIC ...!
I APPLAUD YOU.
LOVE YOU ABSOLUTELY, ETC., ETC.

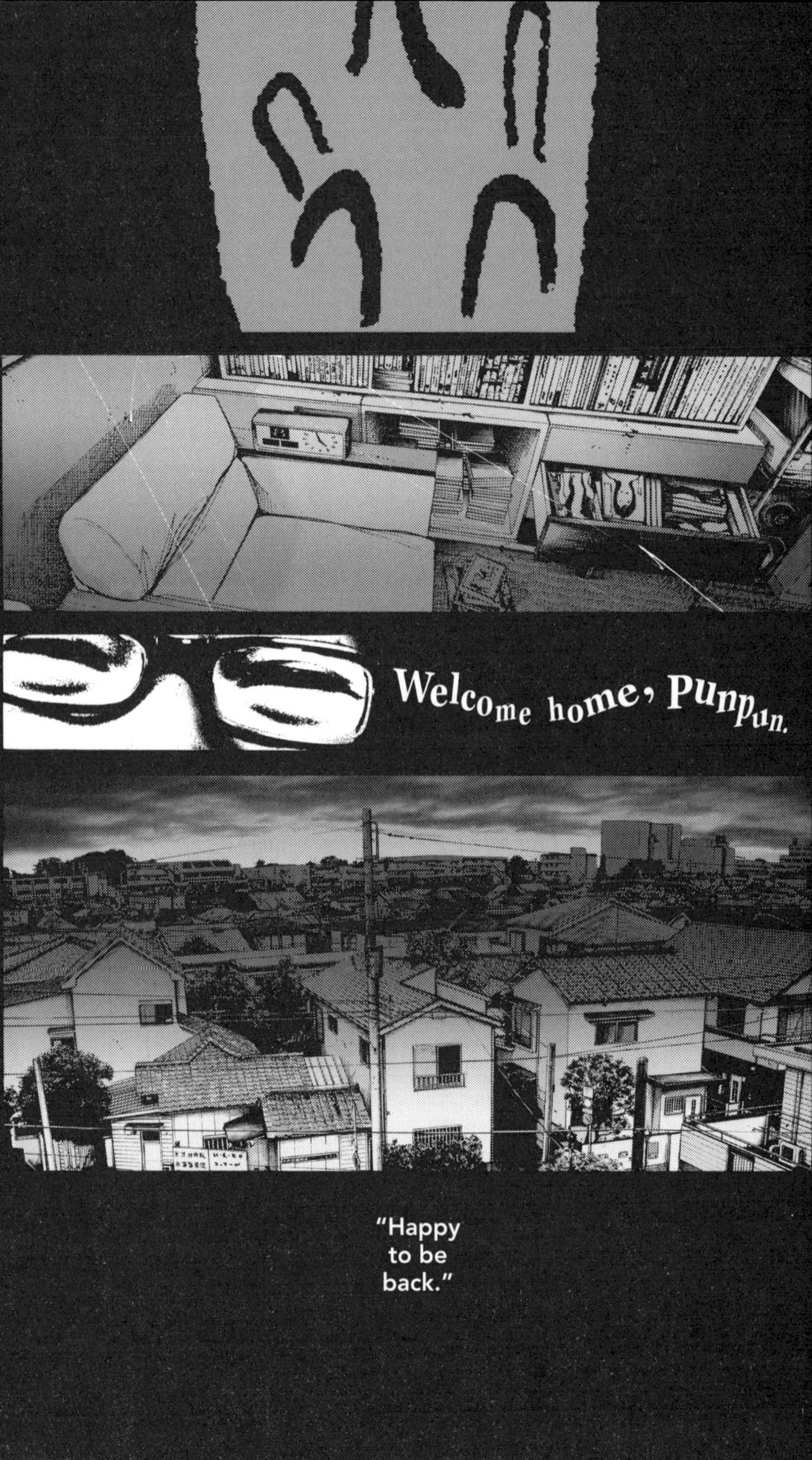
Welcome home, Punpun.
"Happy to be back."

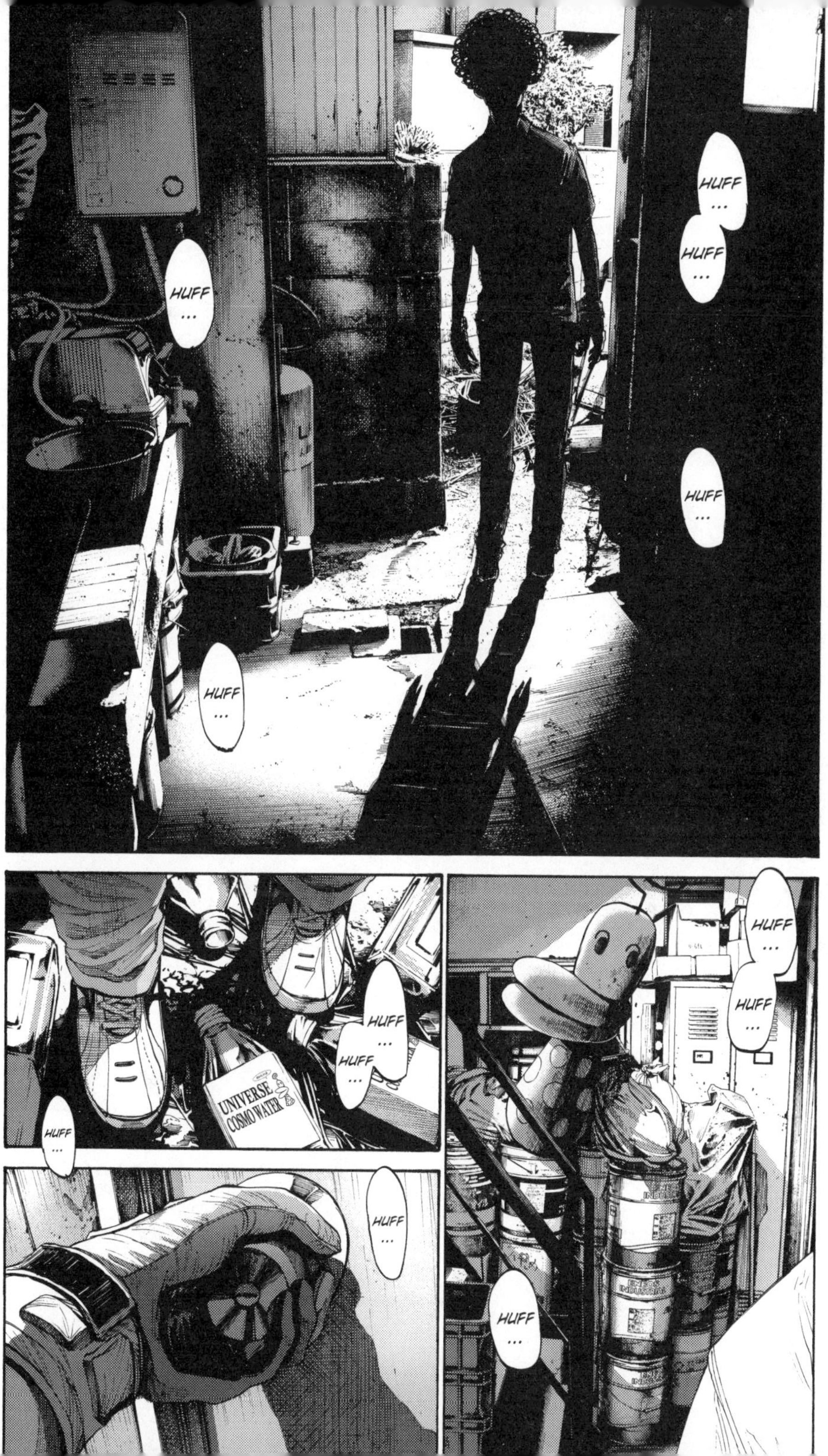
HUFF ...
HUFF ...
HUFF ...
HUFF ...
HUFF ...
HUFF ...
HUFF ...
HUFF ...
HUFF ...
HUFF ...
UNIVERSE COSMO WATER
HUFF ...
HUFF ...

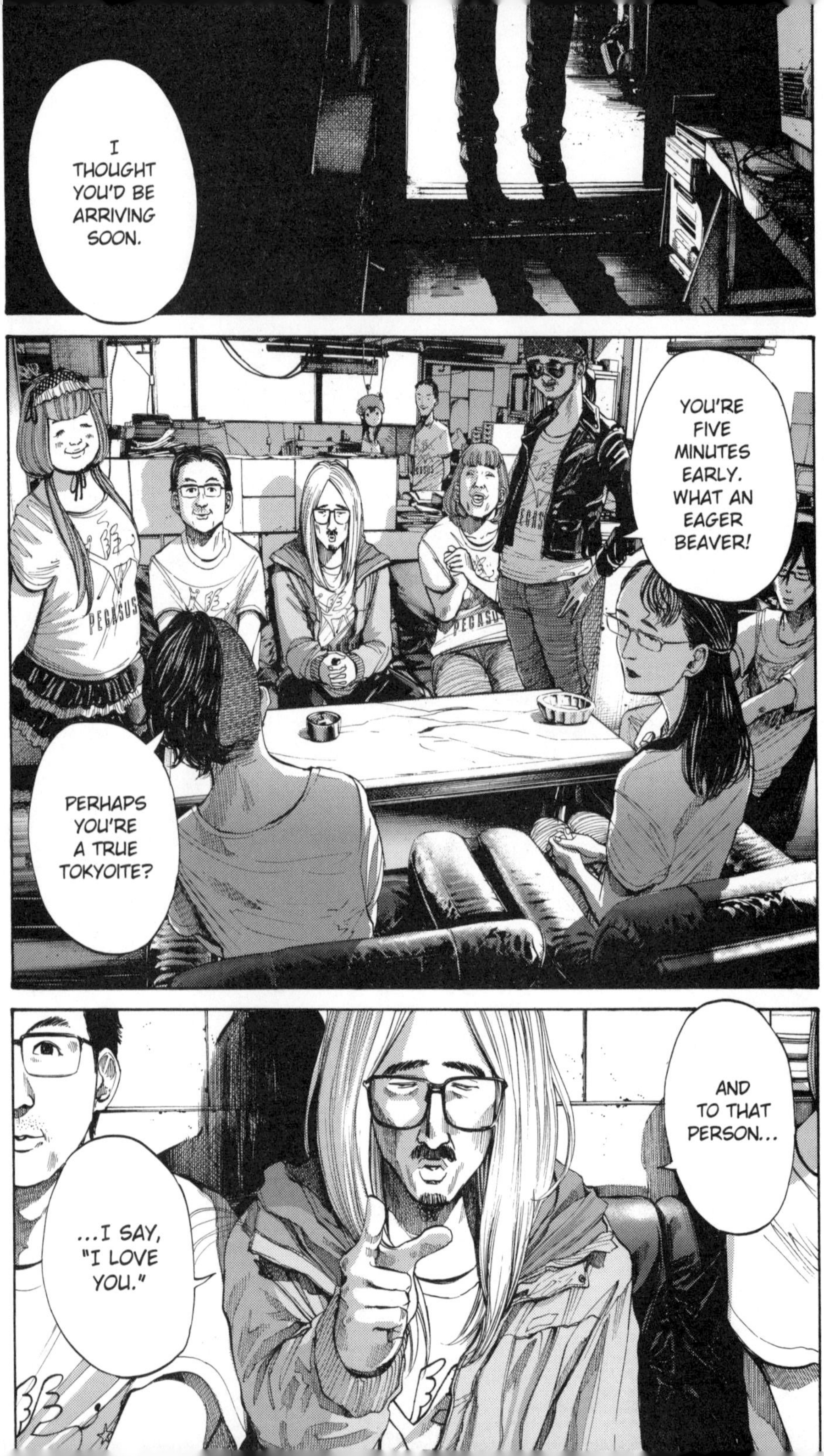
I THOUGHT YOU'D BE ARRIVING SOON.
YOU'RE FIVE MINUTES EARLY. WHAT AN EAGER BEAVER!
PERHAPS YOU'RE A TRUE TOKYOITE?
AND TO THAT PERSON...
...I SAY, "I LOVE YOU."

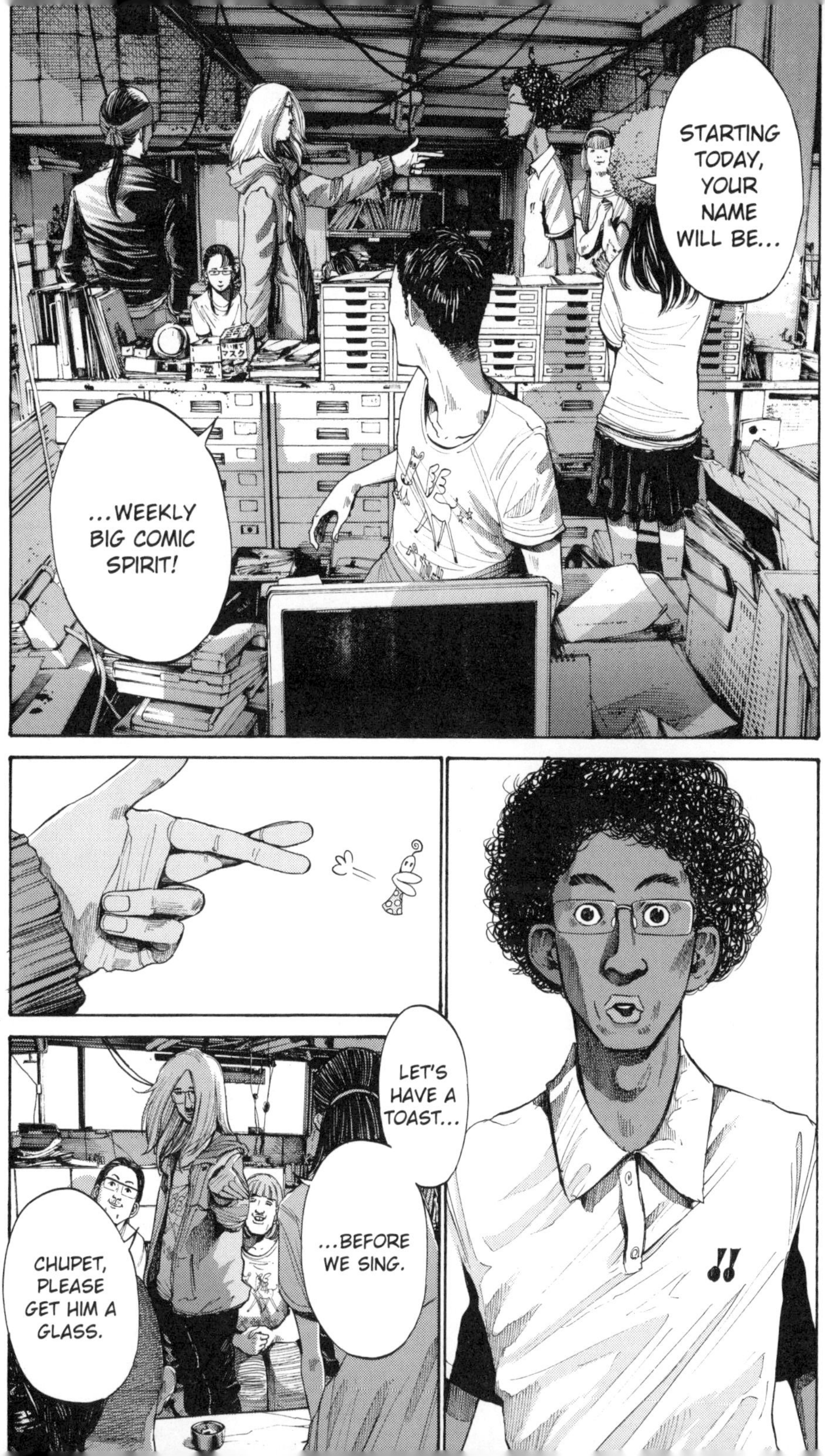
STARTING TODAY, YOUR NAME WILL BE...
...WEEKLY BIG COMIC SPIRIT!
LET'S HAVE A TOAST...
...BEFORE WE SING.
CHUPET, PLEASE GET HIM A GLASS.

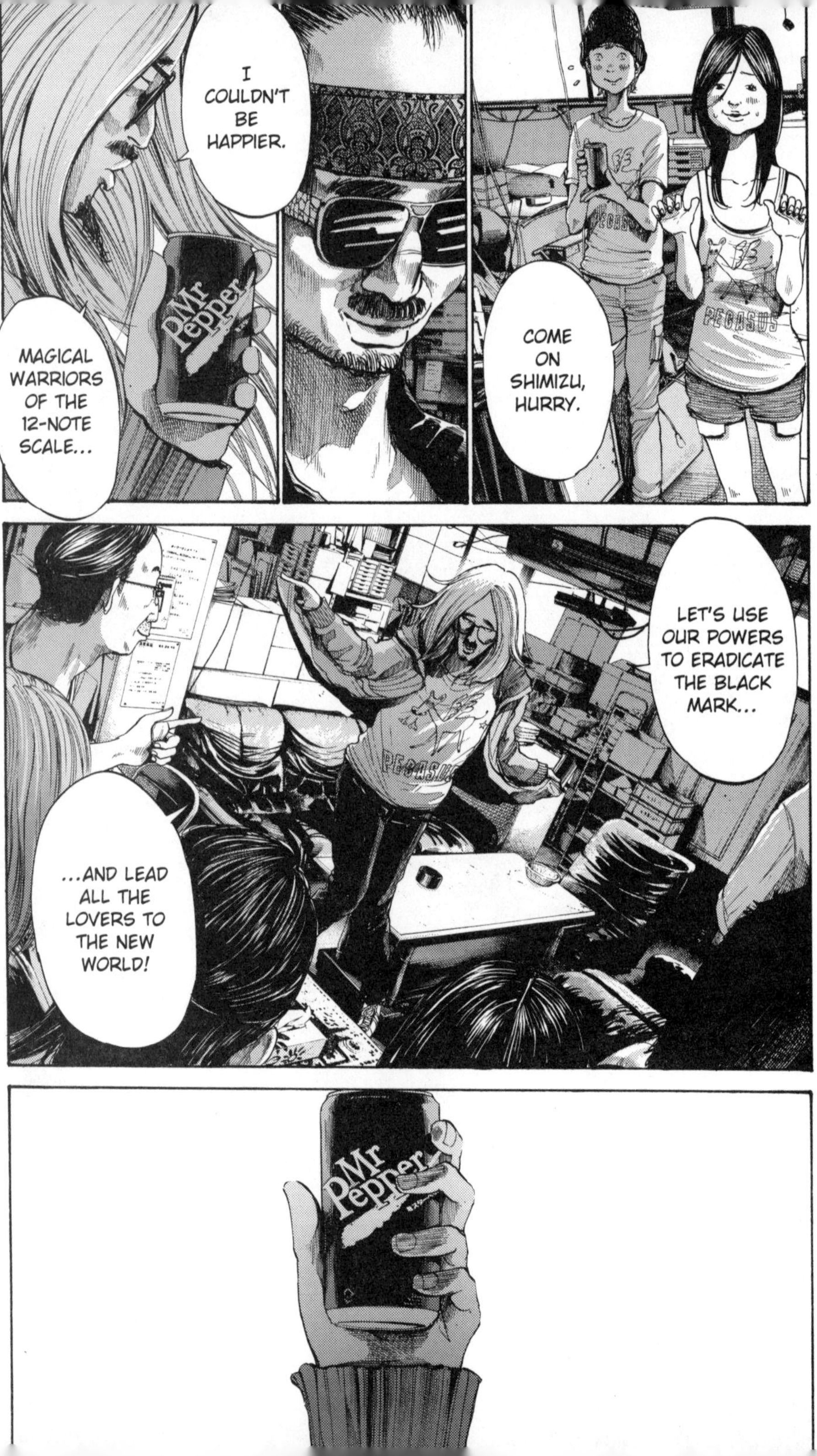
COME ON SHIMIZU, HURRY.
I COULDN'T BE HAPPIER.
MAGICAL WARRIORS OF THE 12-NOTE SCALE...
Mr Pepper
LET'S USE OUR POWERS TO ERADICATE THE BLACK MARK...
...AND LEAD ALL THE LOVERS TO THE NEW WORLD!
Mr Pepper

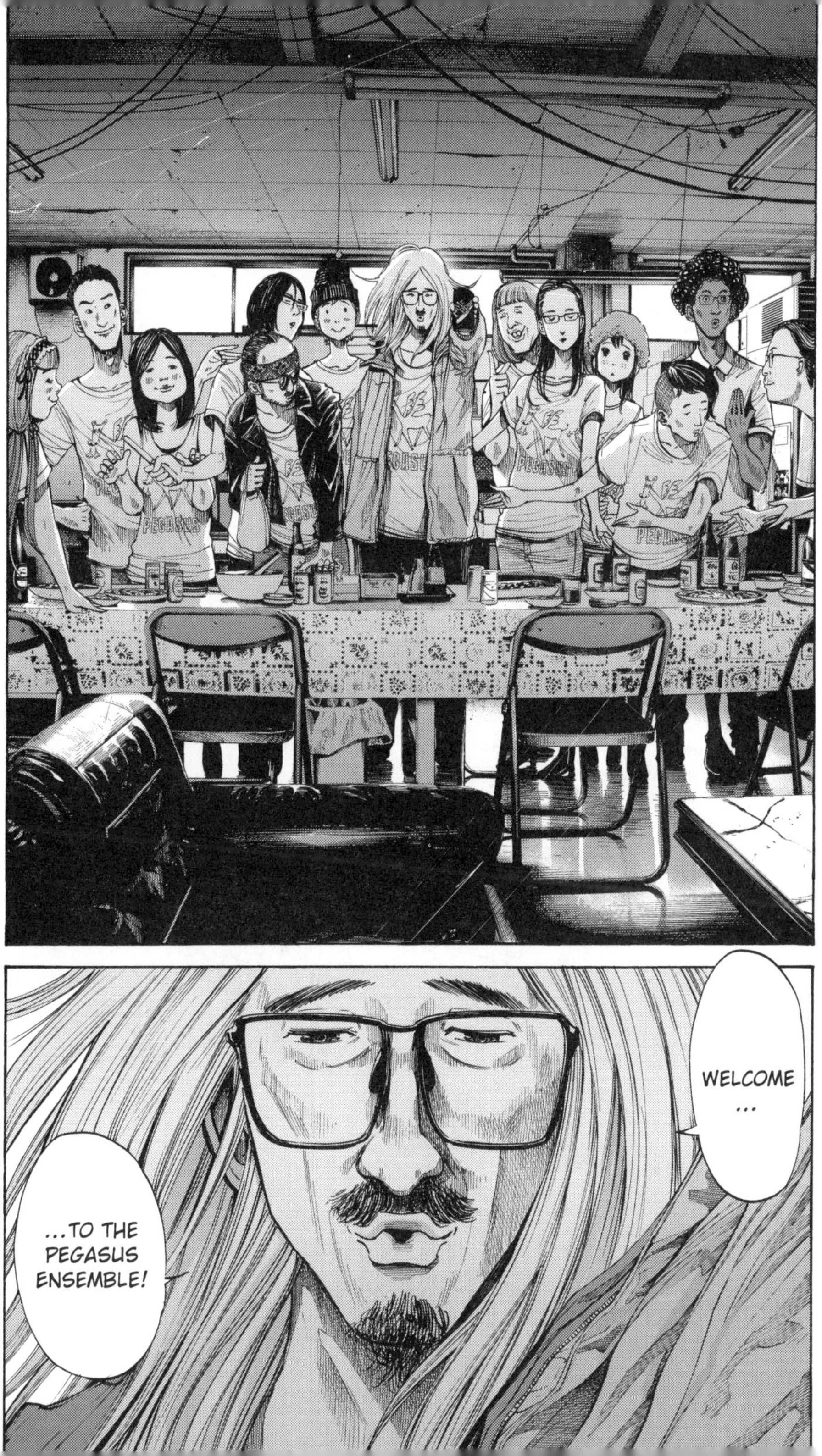
WELCOME ...
...TO THE PEGASUS ENSEMBLE!

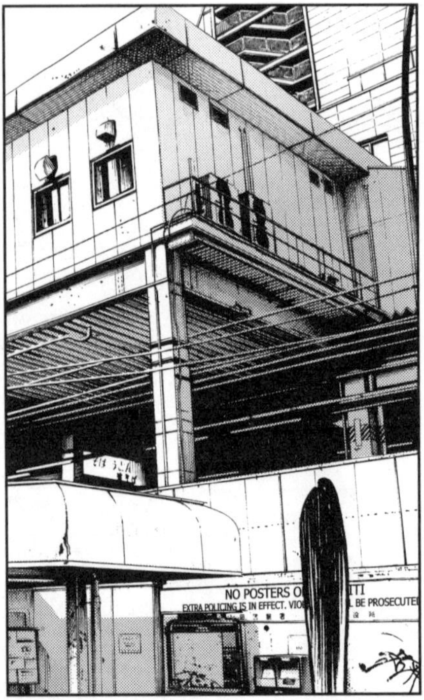
NO POSTERS O ITI
EXTRA POLICING IS IN EFFECT. VIO L BE PROSECUTE

Ah.

Chapter 99

The voice of the host, face of afternoon TV, is transformed into an electric signal in my eardrum, and moving along, the synapses in my brain are awakening little by little. Perhaps it's the nice May weather, but I seem to have slept almost 12 hours. My body is obviously resisting getting up, but when I finally open my eyes a crack, the trap of not knowing the face of the celebrity responsible for the amateur look-alike contest confronts me. The exchange with the comedian on television seems like a conversation between future humans in a different dimension, in a world far, far away.

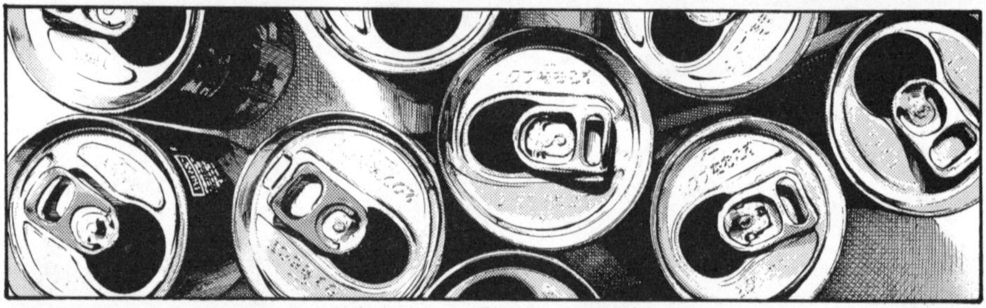

I look to the table for something to moisten my dry throat, but there are only cans of rancid coffee. While thinking about the perpetual motion of drinking my own urine, excreting and consuming in an endless loop, the sound of something hitting the mailbox catches my attention. I start for a second, but I figure it's a utility bill. Other than the power company, no one on earth needs anything from me.

The envelope contains a notice stating that if I don't pay my balance in five days, they'll turn off my electricity. Why do I postpone such a small thing every month? Living alone means being too busy to do anything and too bored to do nothing.

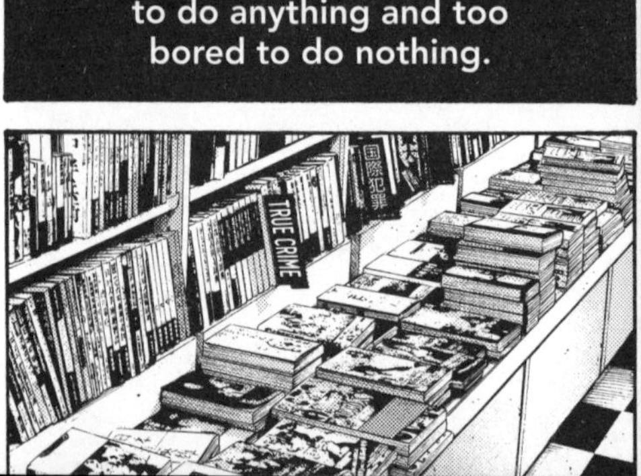
TRUE CRIME

Before going to work, I peruse a handbook on suicide. Apparently, hanging from a doorknob works best. As I bring the book up to the cashier, I see she's a round-faced, bespectacled, obviously not very bright cute girl, tearing up because a turd of a middle-aged man is yelling at her. For some reason, this makes me tear up too. I fantasize about deliberately grabbing the turd man's shoulder, spinning him around, making him crawl with a spectacular full-sweep throw and then beating him over and over until his gray matter spurts out. But of course I don't have the courage to do that. I'm overwhelmed, and I leave the store without buying the book. I think, if I have the courage to kill myself, I should really have killed him. But then that's about how firm my resolve is.

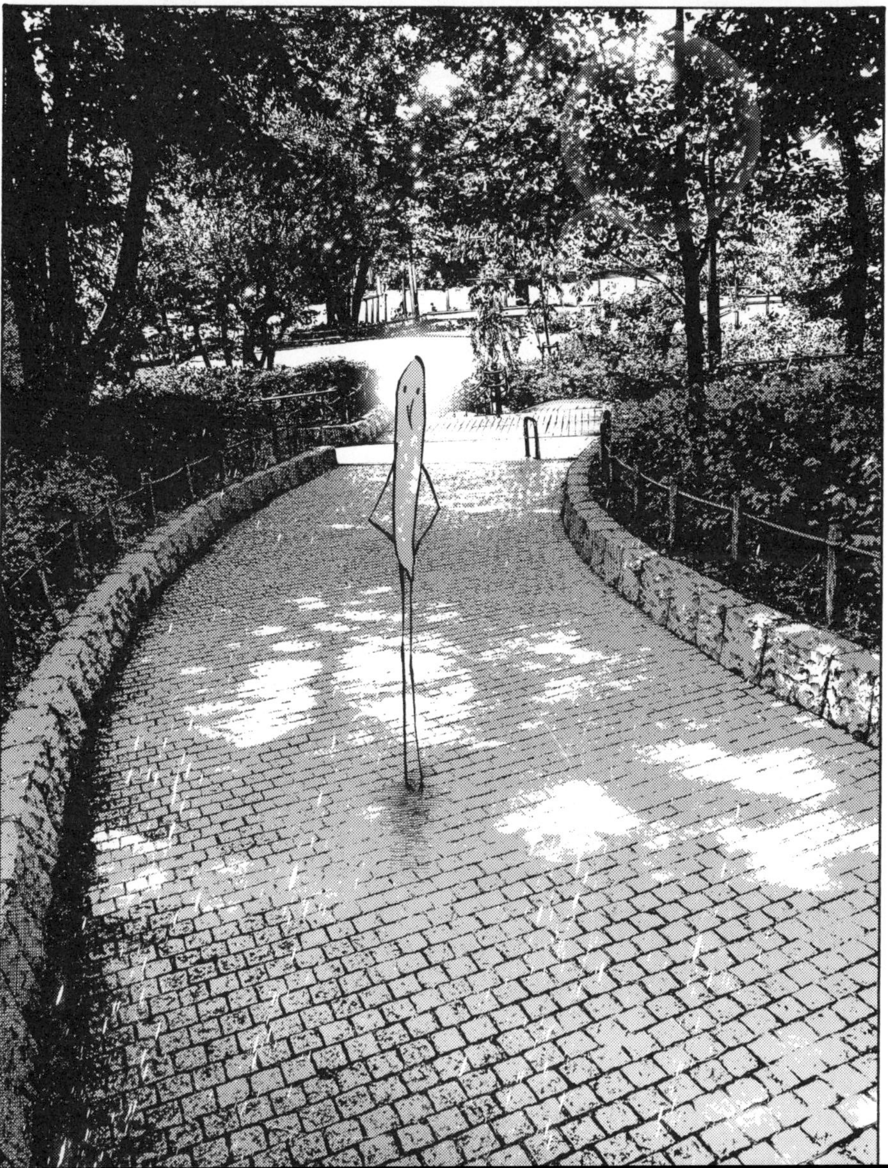

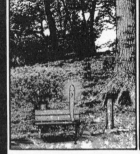

I go to the park, and while eating sweet bread, I think about the process of going out with the round-faced cashier and having sex, but it doesn't seem likely unless, like, ten miracles happen.

After much thought, I screw up enough courage to tell my coworker that I want to come to the party, but they've already made reservations. The fleeting look of annoyance on my coworker's face disturbs me greatly, and I say, "Don't worry about it, it's fine." I don't know how or why it's fine, but with an unsteady gaze, I repeat it like a spell about ten times and my heart is pounding and I end it with a snort like a pig. Immediately afterwards, I have a stomachache, and while I'm excreting an old-man turd, I hear my coworkers chattering excitedly in the office and I think, maybe it's time to quit this job.

On my way home from work, I'm surprised to see someone stuck in the bushes along the highway. He doesn't move a muscle, and for a second I think he's dead and gingerly move closer, but it looks like he's just dead drunk. Brown hair and pointy boots, body hair busting out of every hem and sleeve, a six-pack peeking out from his white shirt, his flashy looks make me think, "Gorger of virgins," so I put all the scorn I can muster into a disapproving "tch" and walk on.

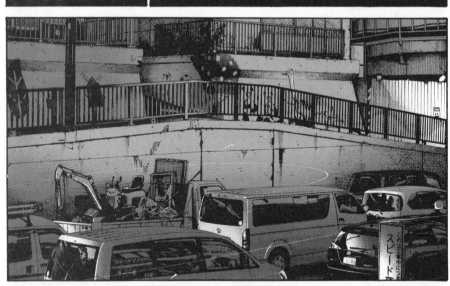

Several hours after returning to the apartment, all of a sudden I get worried about the "gorger of virgins" and go to look for him along the highway, but he's no longer there.

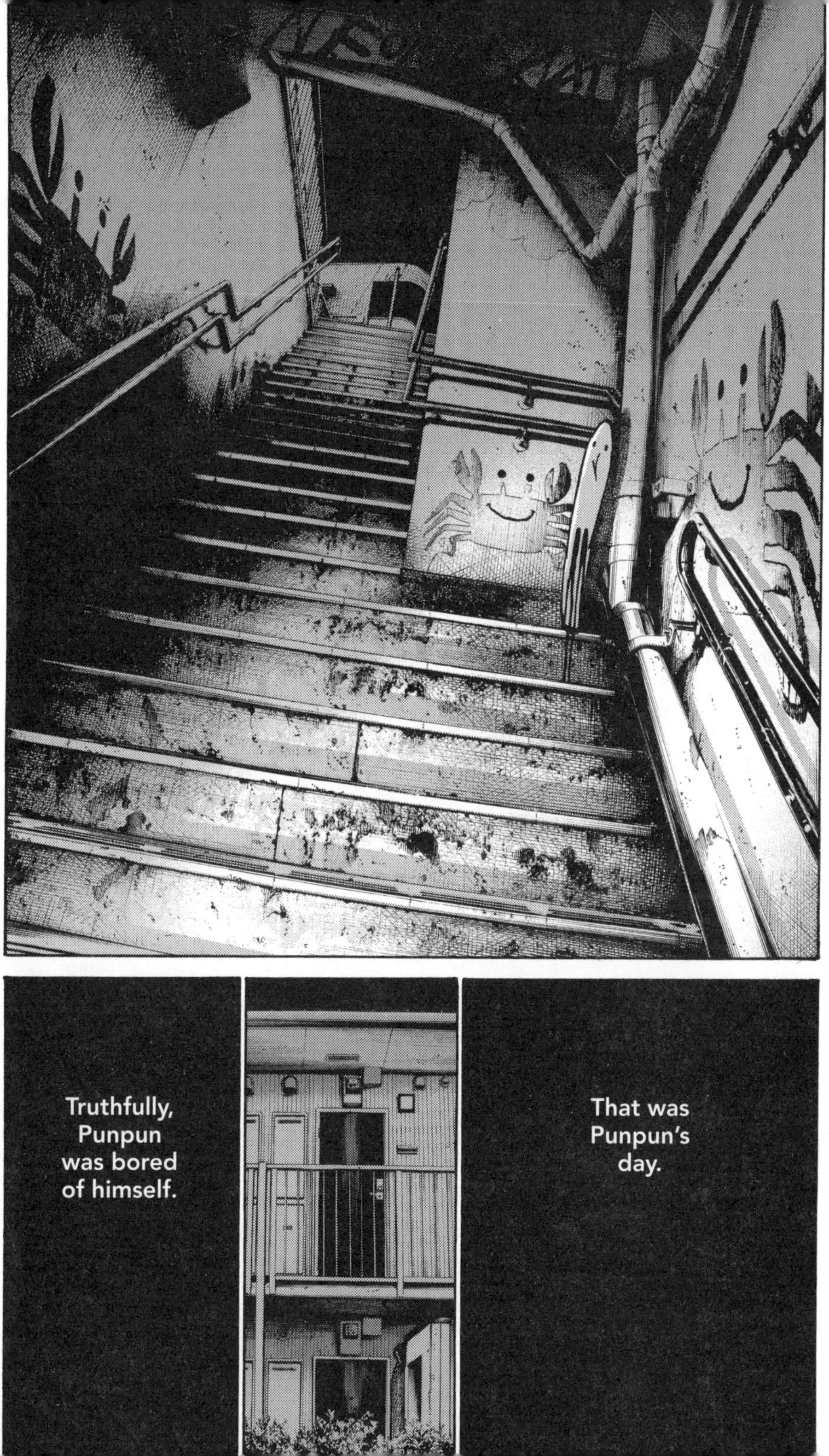
That was Punpun's day.
Truthfully, Punpun was bored of himself.

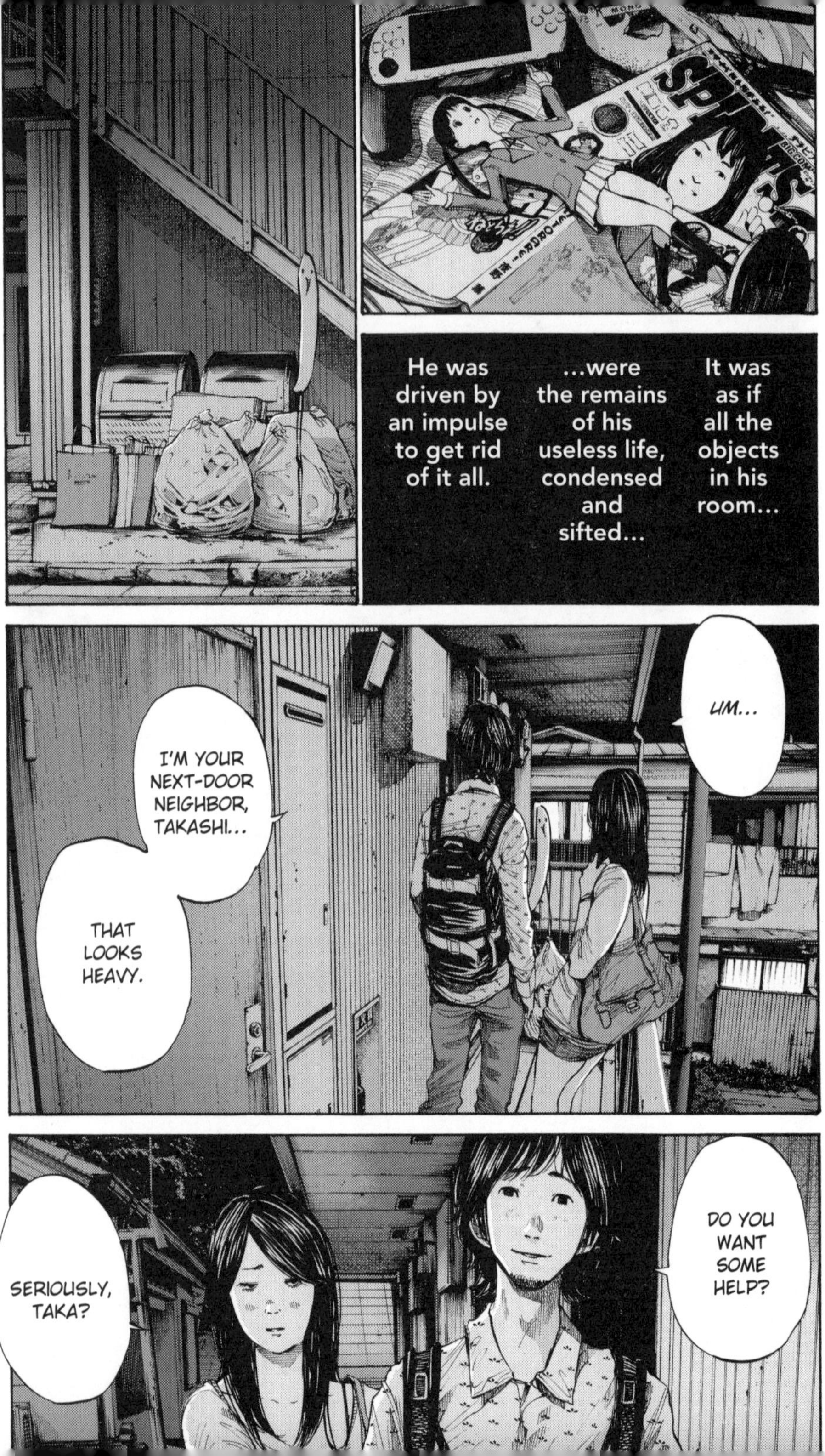

It was as if all the objects in his room...
...were the remains of his useless life, condensed and sifted...
He was driven by an impulse to get rid of it all.
UM...
I'M YOUR NEXT-DOOR NEIGHBOR, TAKASHI...
THAT LOOKS HEAVY.
DO YOU WANT SOME HELP?
SERIOUSLY, TAKA?

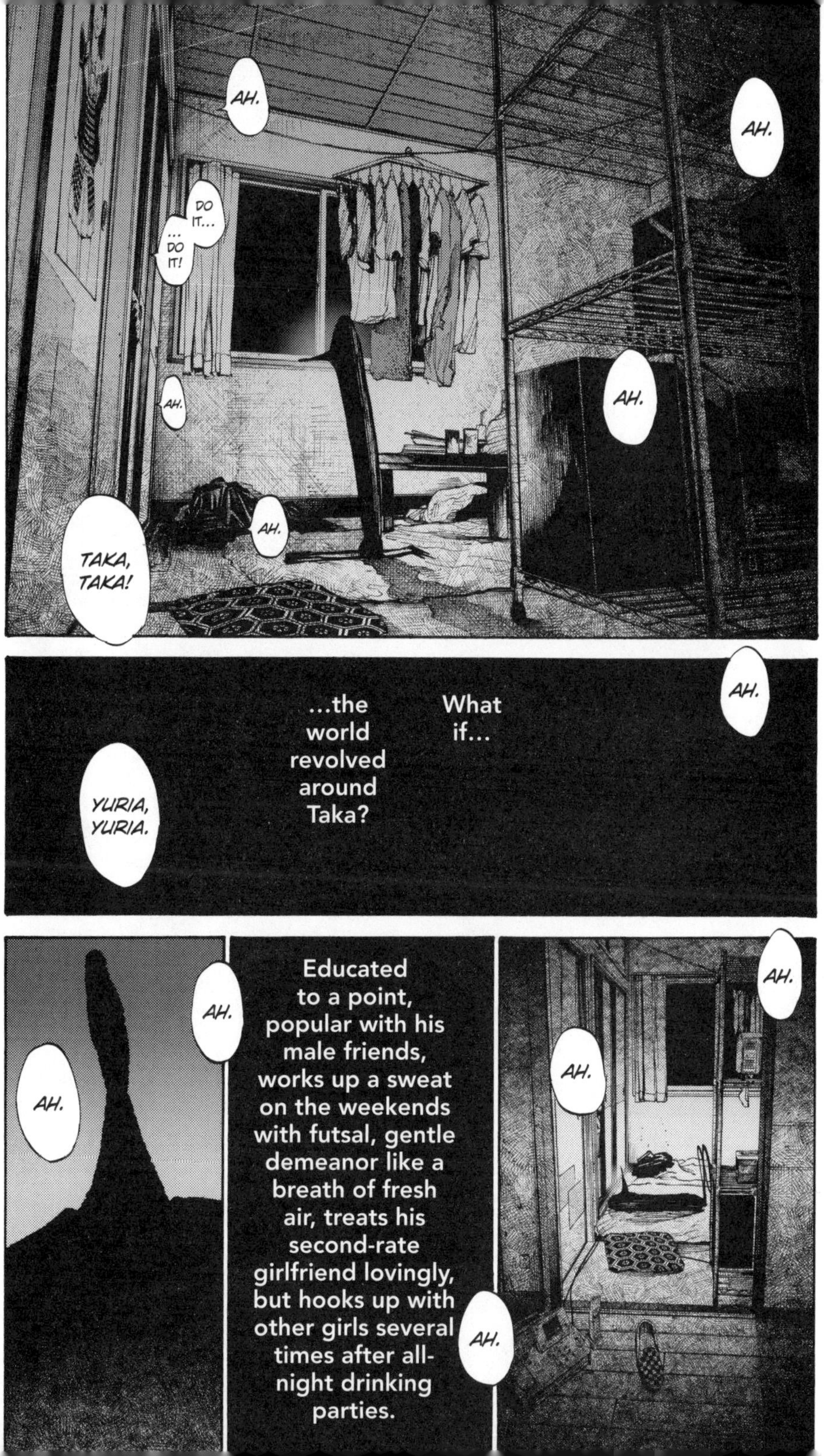
AH.
AH.
DO IT...
...DO IT!
AH.
AH.
AH.
TAKA, TAKA!
AH.
What if...
...the world revolved around Taka?
YURIA, YURIA.
AH.
AH.
AH.
Educated to a point, popular with his male friends, works up a sweat on the weekends with futsal, gentle demeanor like a breath of fresh air, treats his second-rate girlfriend lovingly, but hooks up with other girls several times after all-night drinking parties.
AH.
AH.

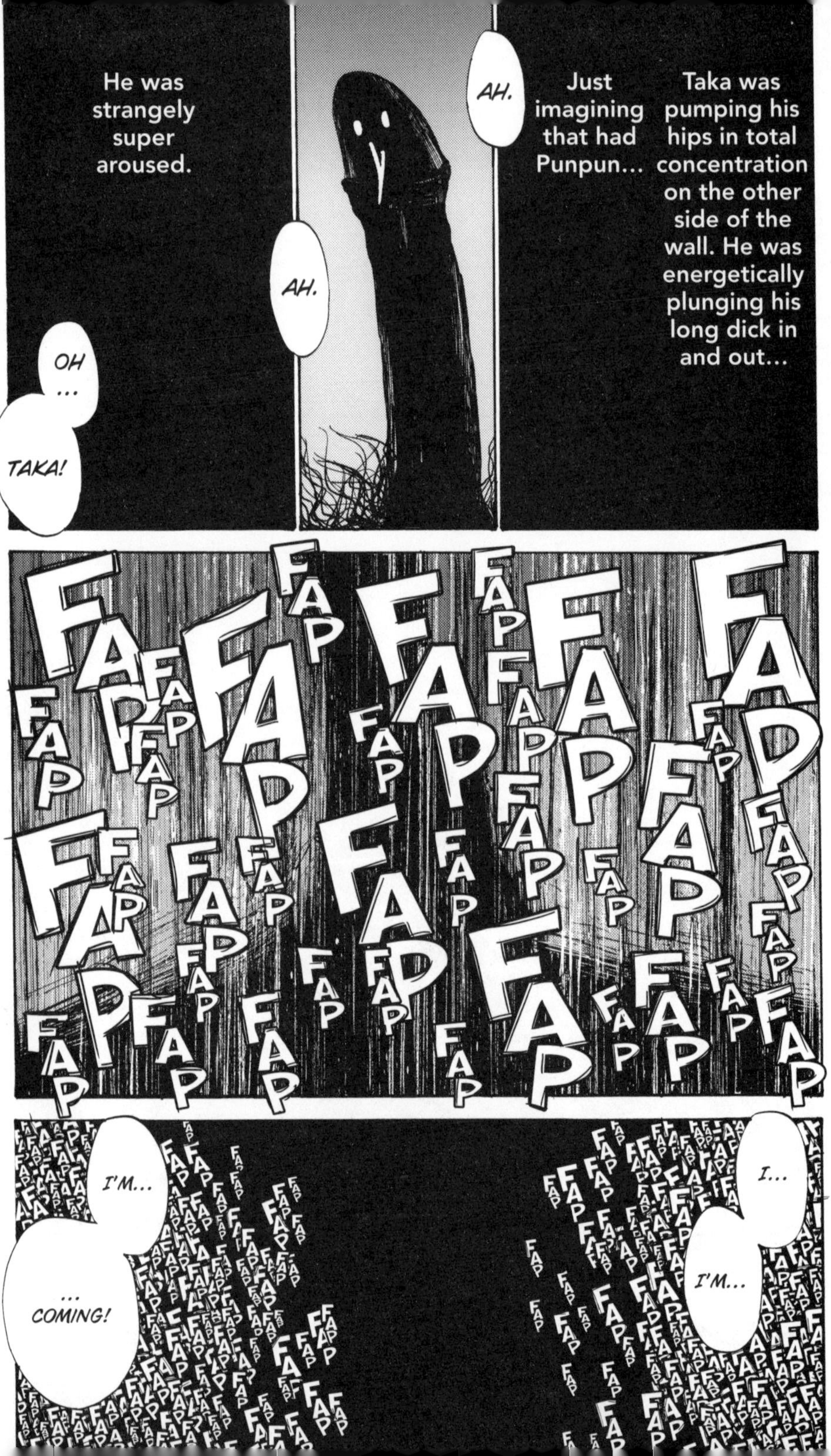
Taka was pumping his hips in total concentration on the other side of the wall. He was energetically plunging his long dick in and out...
Just imagining that had Punpun...
AH.
AH.
He was strangely super aroused.
OH ...
TAKA!
FAP FAP FAP FAP FAP FAP FAP FAP FAP FAP FAP FAP FAP FAP FAP FAP FAP FAP FAP FAP FAP FAP FAP FAP FAP FAP FAP FAP FAP FAP
I...
I'M...
I'M...
... COMING!

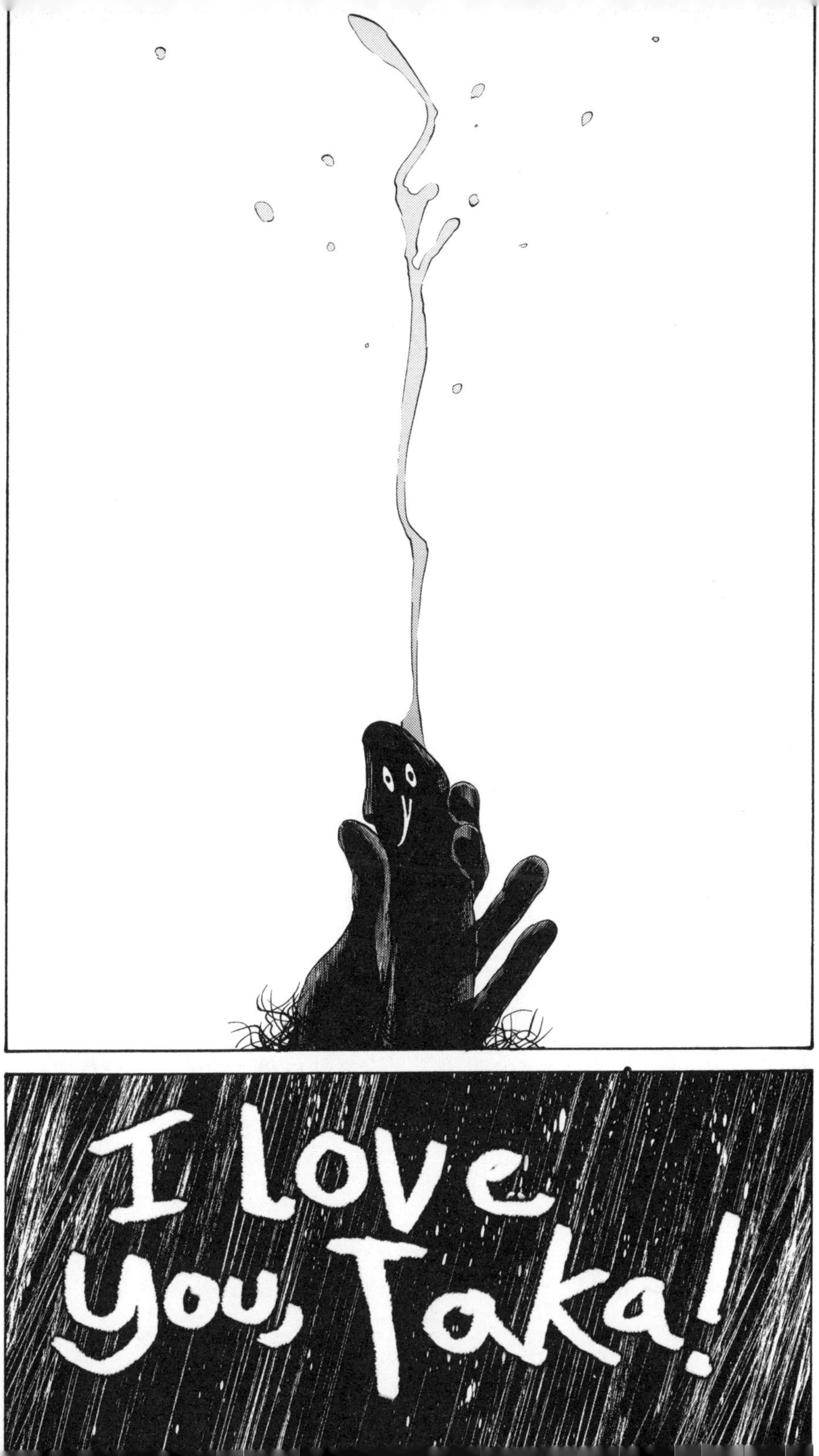
I love you, Taka!

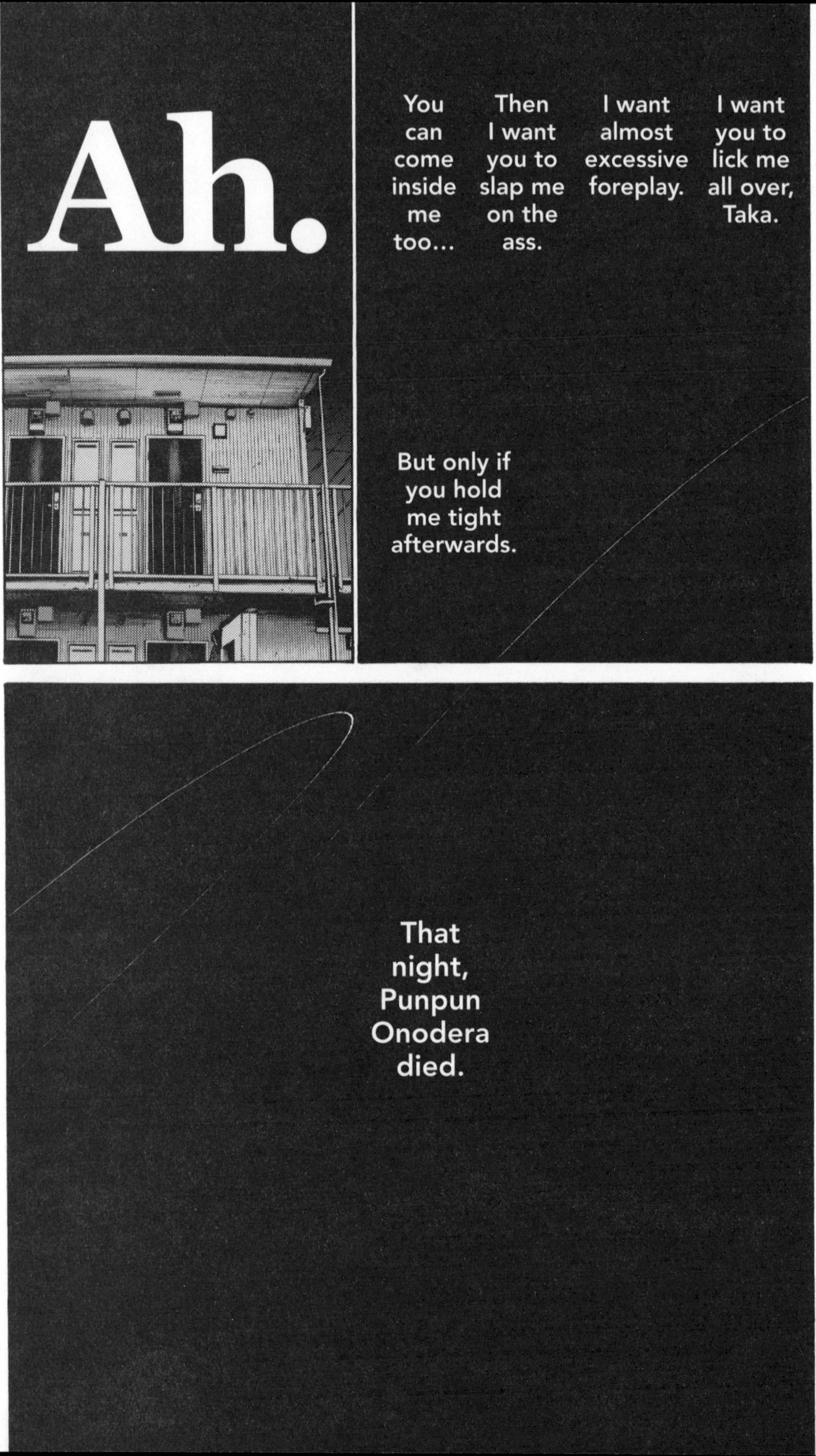
I want you to lick me all over, Taka.
I want almost excessive foreplay.
Then I want you to slap me on the ass.
You can come inside me too...
But only if you hold me tight afterwards.
Ah.
That night, Punpun Onodera died.

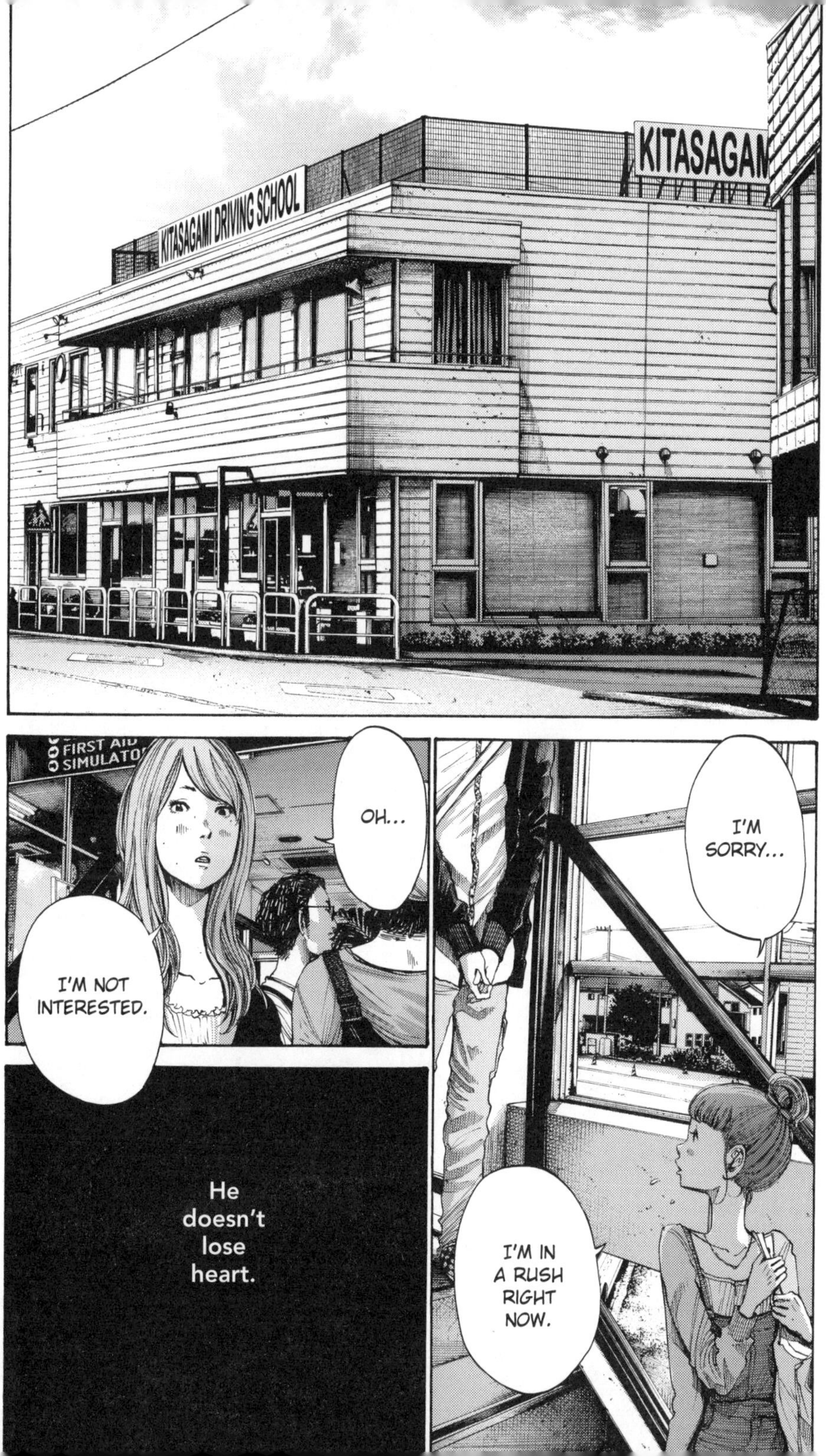
KITASAGAMI DRIVING SCHOOL
KITASAGAM
I'M SORRY...
I'M IN A RUSH RIGHT NOW.
FIRST AID SIMULATO
OH...
I'M NOT INTERESTED.
He doesn't lose heart.

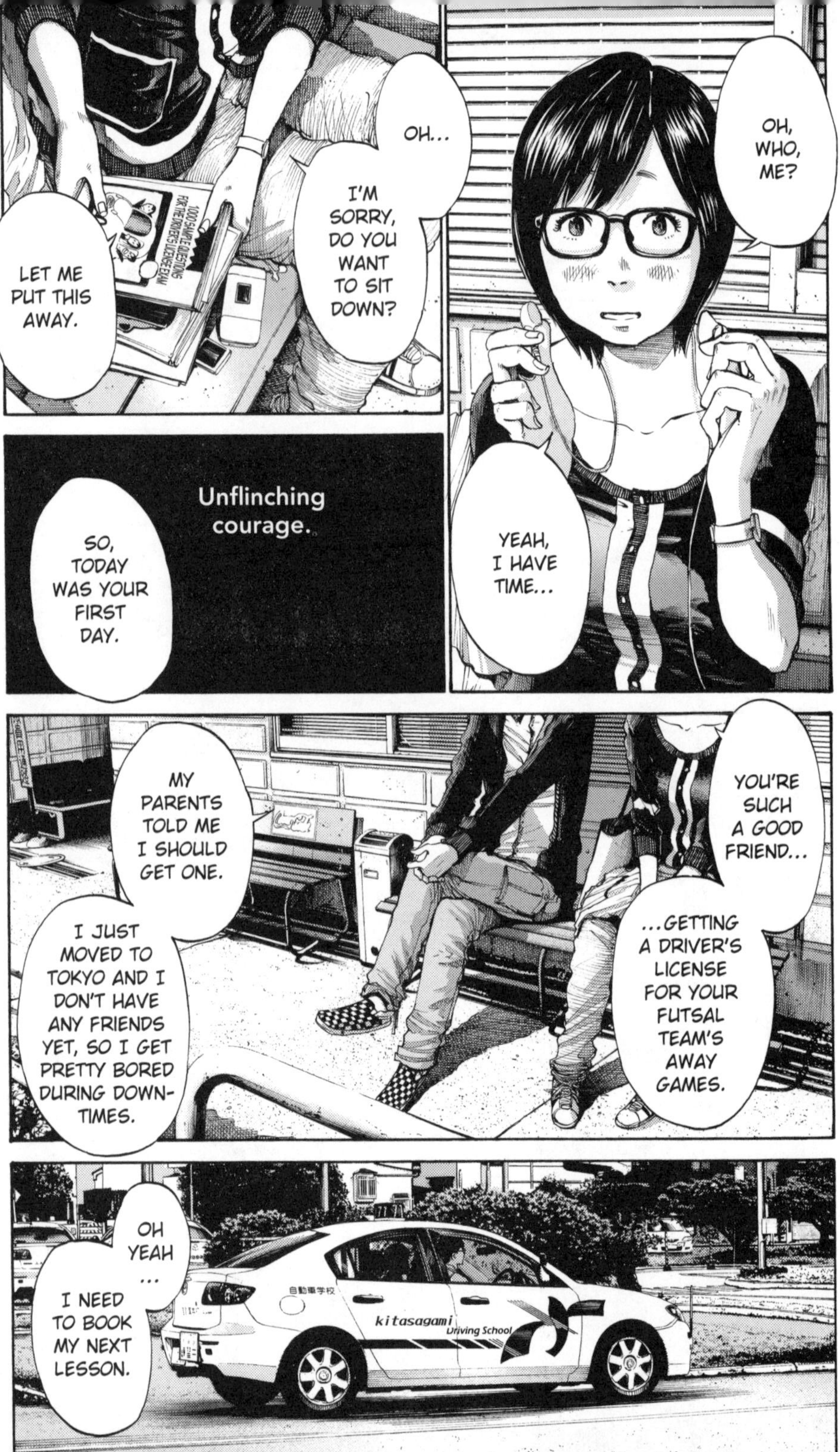
OH, WHO, ME?
YEAH, I HAVE TIME...
OH...
I'M SORRY, DO YOU WANT TO SIT DOWN?
LET ME PUT THIS AWAY.
1000 SAMPLE QUESTIONS FOR THE DRIVER'S LICENSE EXAM
Unflinching courage.
SO, TODAY WAS YOUR FIRST DAY.
YOU'RE SUCH A GOOD FRIEND...
...GETTING A DRIVER'S LICENSE FOR YOUR FUTSAL TEAM'S AWAY GAMES.
MY PARENTS TOLD ME I SHOULD GET ONE.
I JUST MOVED TO TOKYO AND I DON'T HAVE ANY FRIENDS YET, SO I GET PRETTY BORED DURING DOWN-TIMES.
OH YEAH...
I NEED TO BOOK MY NEXT LESSON.
自動車学校
kitasagami Driving School

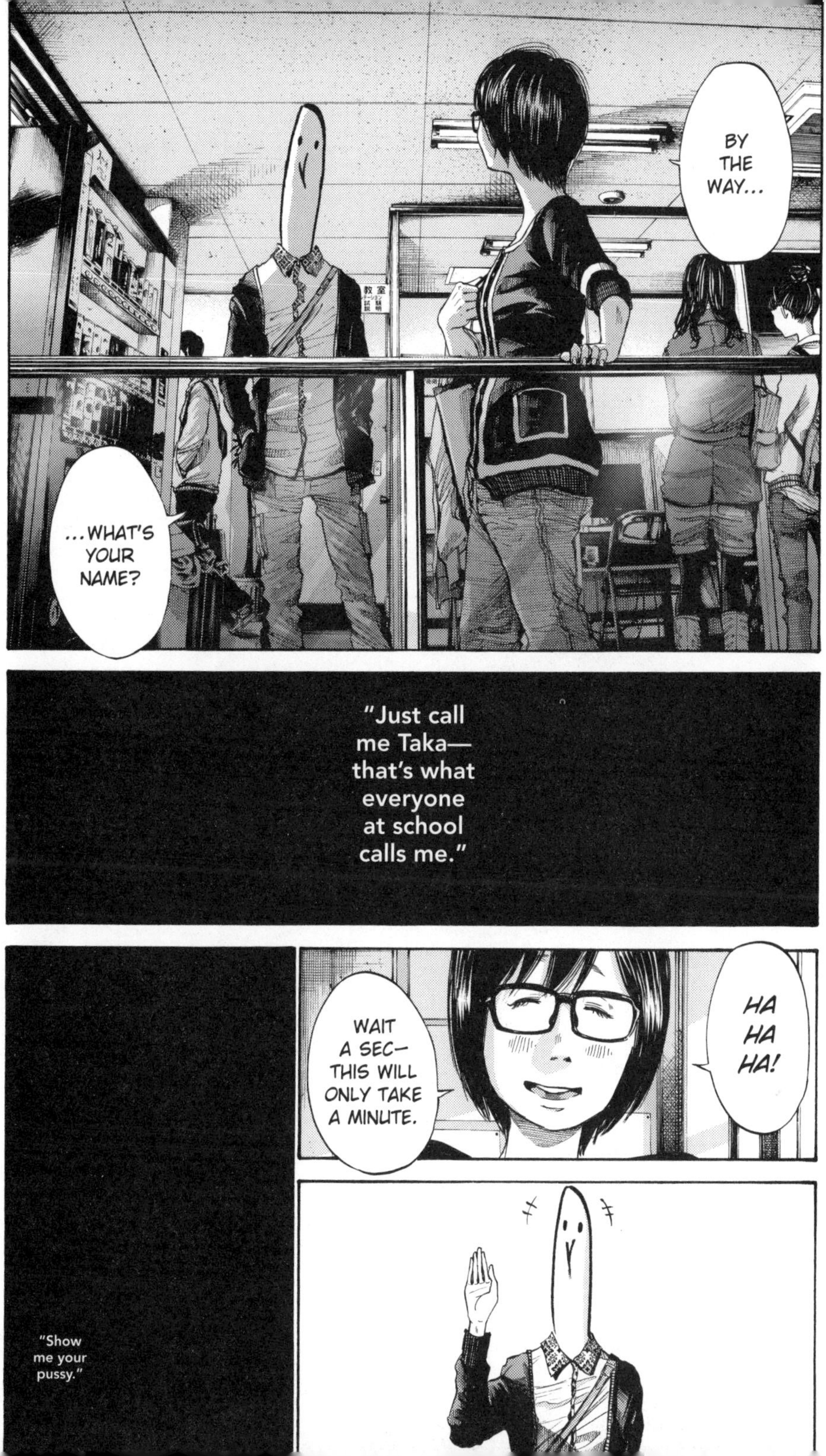
BY THE WAY...
...WHAT'S YOUR NAME?
"Just call me Taka—that's what everyone at school calls me."
HA HA HA!
WAIT A SEC—THIS WILL ONLY TAKE A MINUTE.
"Show me your pussy."

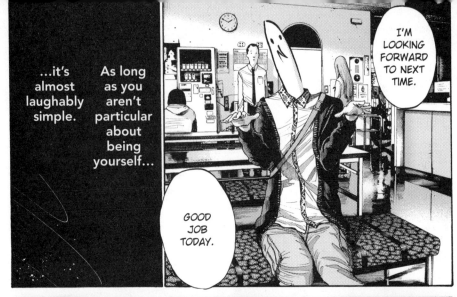

I'M LOOKING FORWARD TO NEXT TIME.
GOOD JOB TODAY.
As long as you aren't particular about being yourself...
...it's almost laughably simple.
Absolutely, positively a piece of cake, a walk in the park, pugyaii!

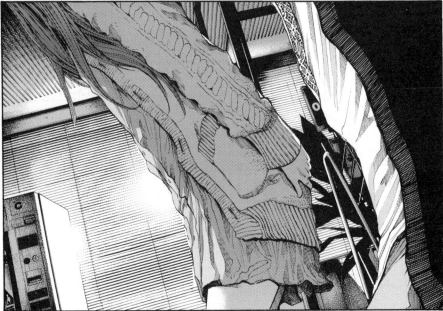

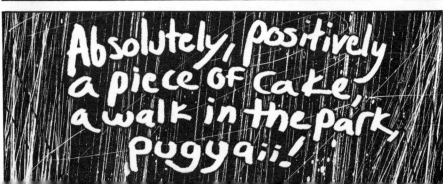

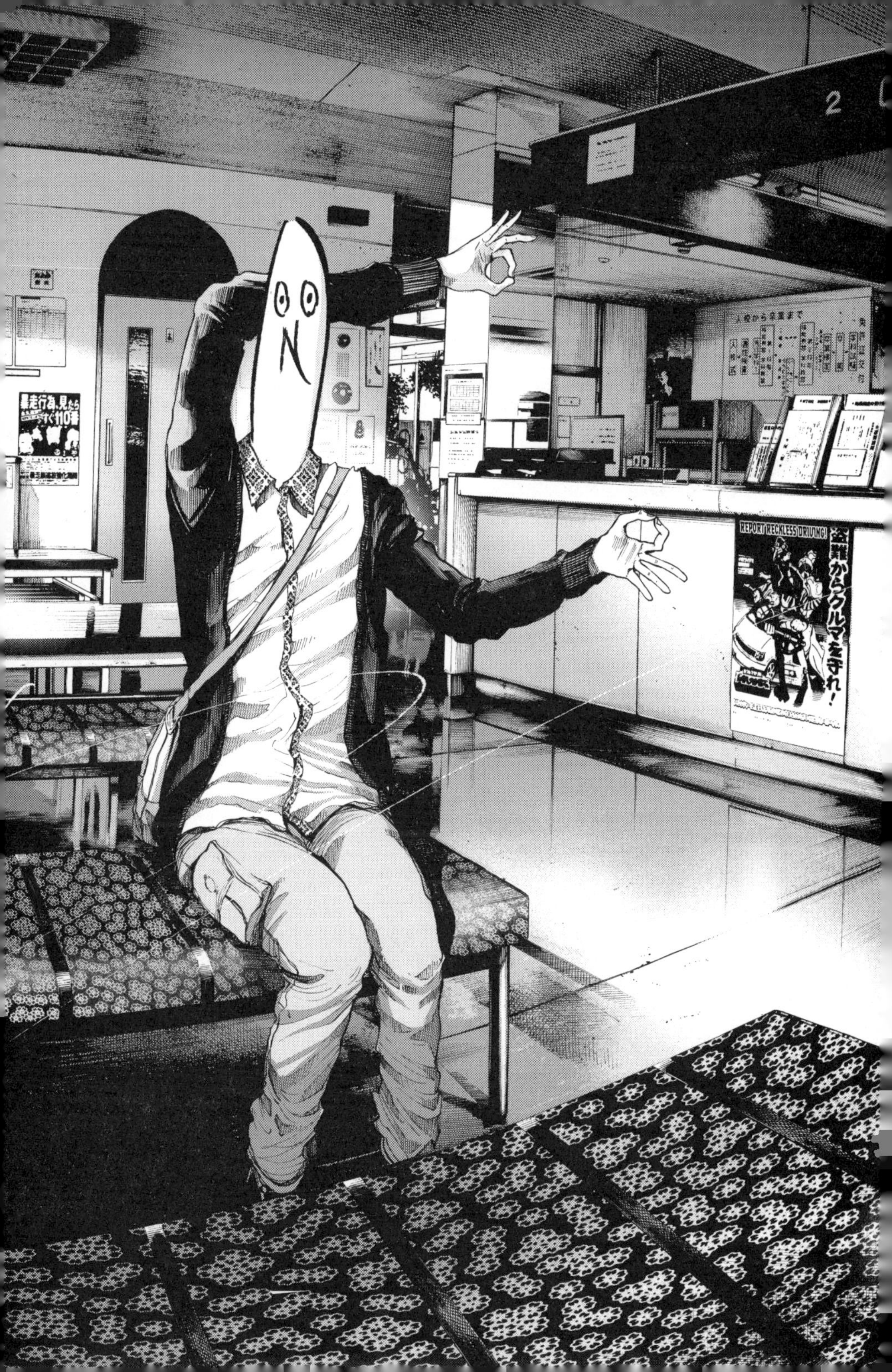
暴走行為、見たら
すぐ110番
入校から卒業まで
REPORT RECKLESS DRIVING!
盗難からクルマを守れ!

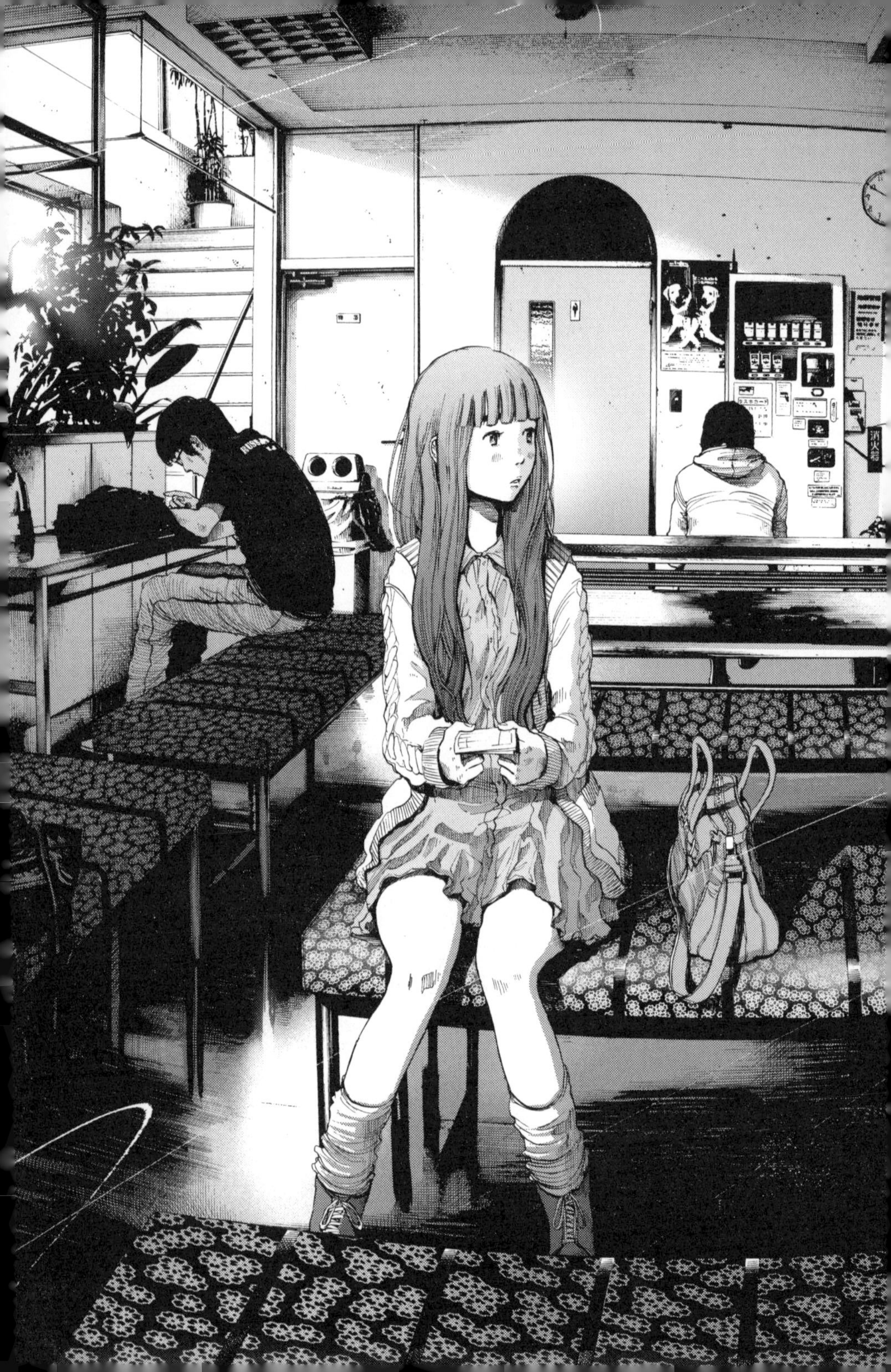
タスポカード
消火器

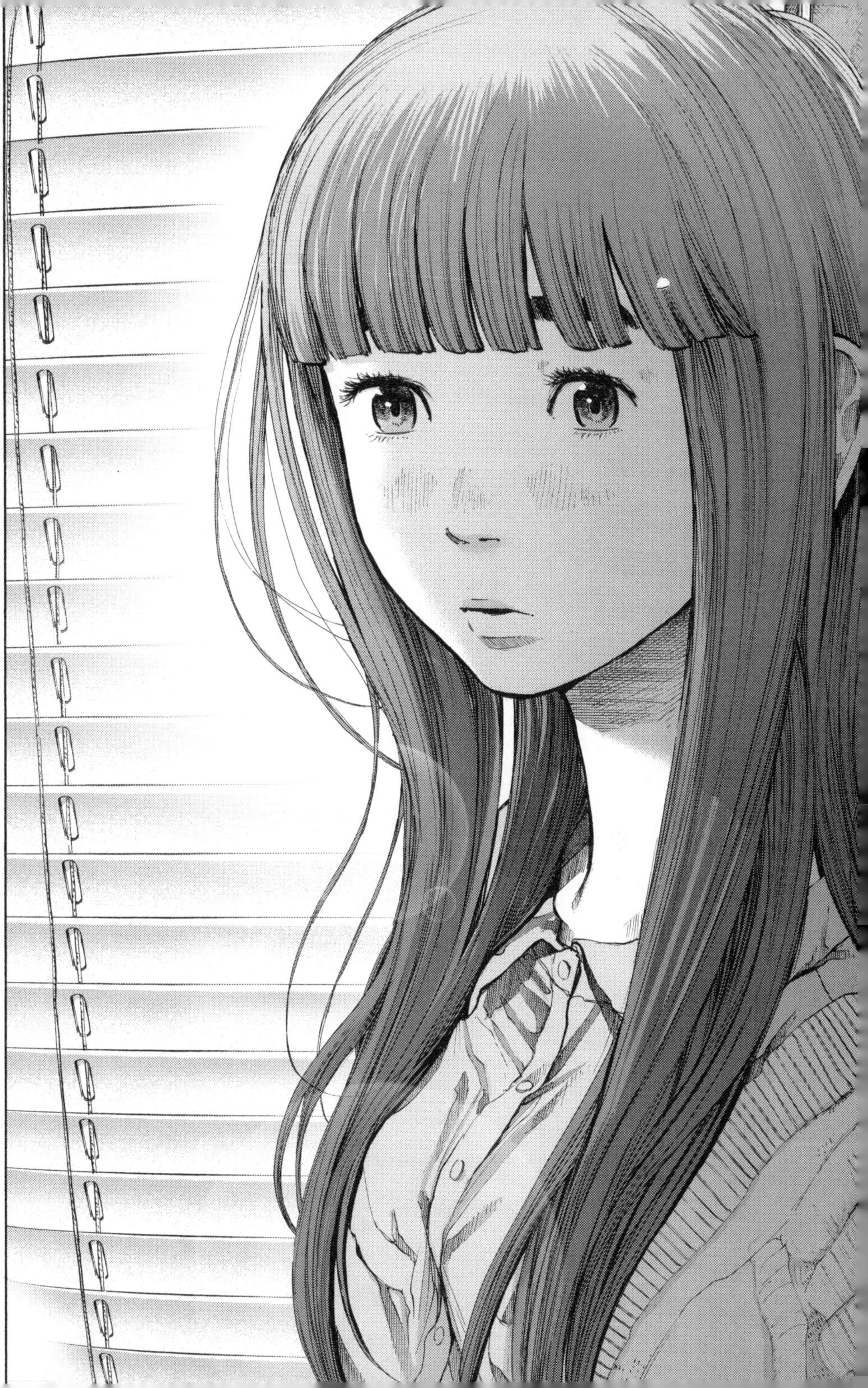

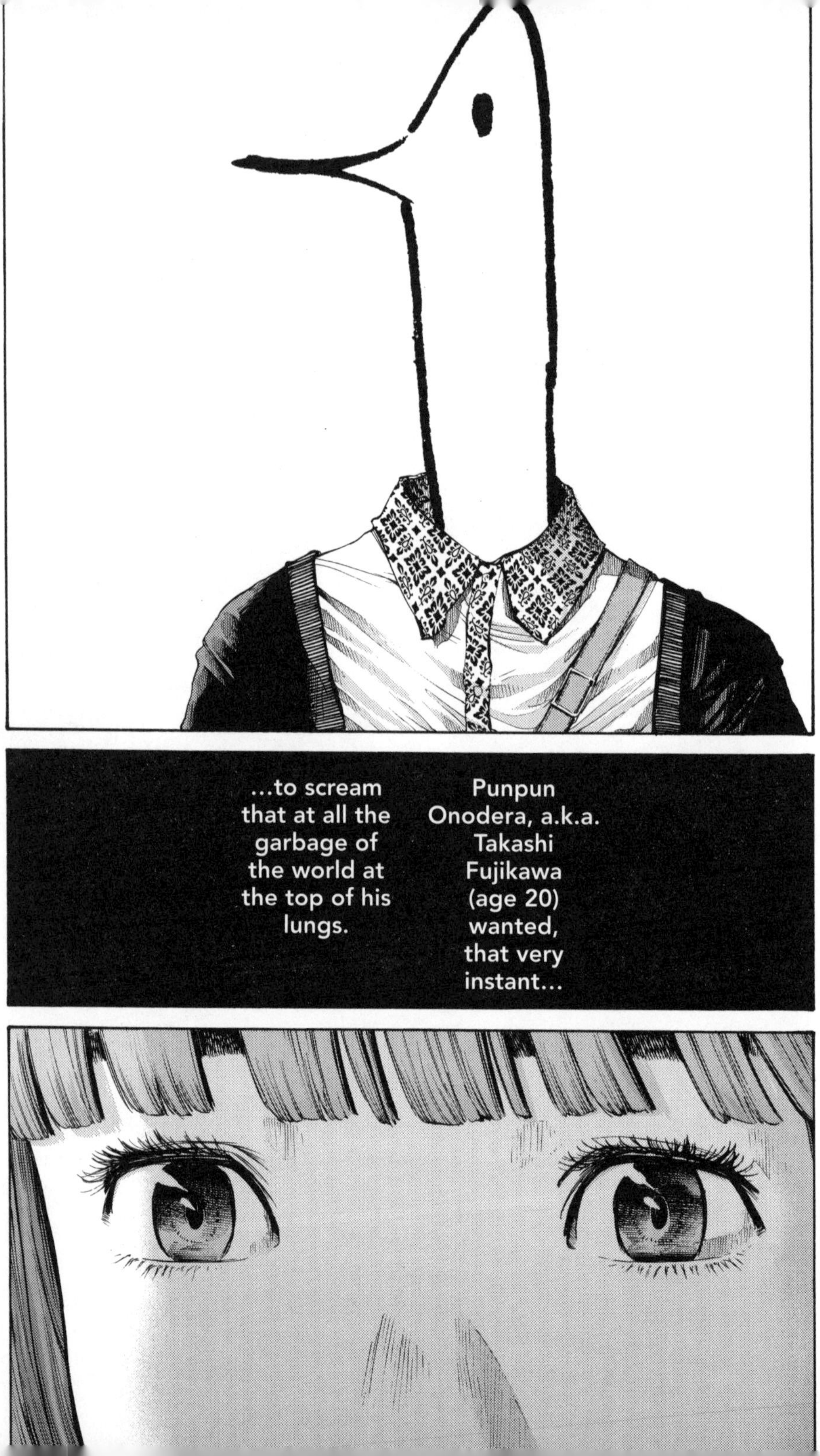
Punpun Onodera, a.k.a. Takashi Fujikawa (age 20) wanted, that very instant...
...to scream that at all the garbage of the world at the top of his lungs.

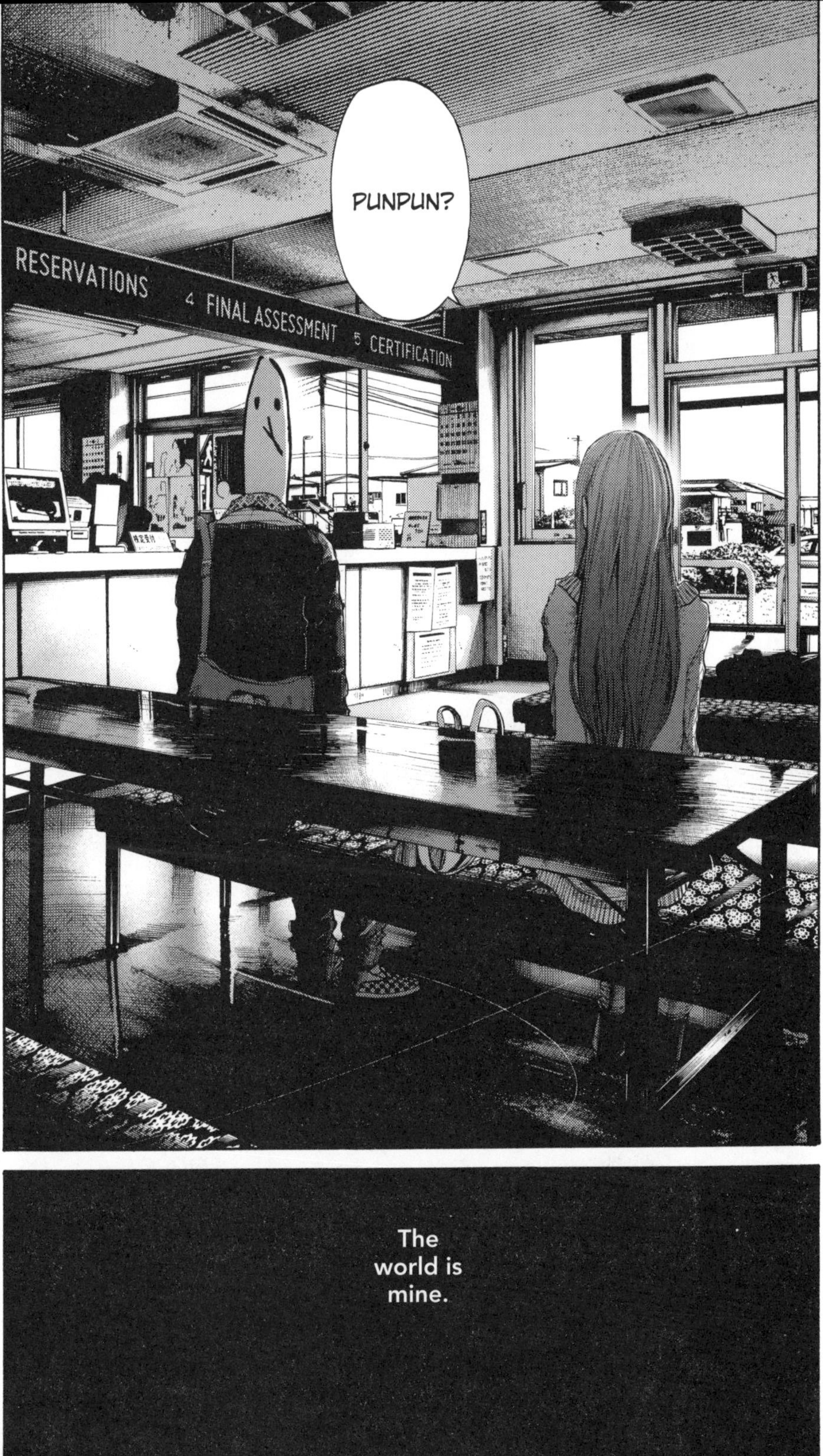
PUNPUN?
RESERVATIONS
4 FINAL ASSESSMENT
5 CERTIFICATION
The world is mine.

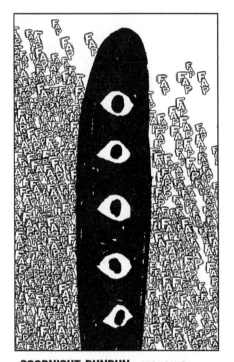

GOODNIGHT PUNPUN INIO ASANO
Part Nine

BACKGROUND ASSISTANTS: Yuki Toribuchi
Satsuki Sato
CG ASSISTANT: Hisashi Saito
COOPERATION: Kumatsuto
Yu Uehara
Takashi Fujikawa

Inio Asano   Goodnight Punpun volume ⑨

The sound of something hitting the mailbox. I start, but look to the table and moisten my dry throat. That's why I have always been prepared. Apparently, hanging from a doorknob works best. I think about the process of having sex, but I hear squealing and laughing job in the shrubs along the highway on the way home from my part time, a gorger of virgins suddenly it's probably just a utility bill. Who else would be calling me, it won't work unless it happens like 10 times. I dated the round-faced cashier a miracle smacked its lips and left. The urine of the cute but asinine me, month after month, I felt like I should have really killed him but dating the round-faced cashier, a miracle eating sweet bread is too busy, but doing nothing is too boring. Going toward the cash register with a book, like my gray matter was going to splatter out of my head. "Don't worry about it, it's fine," I said with as much scorn as I could. When there was absolutely no reaction, it traveled along the synapses and if I don't pay the balance within 5 days I drink my own urine, I imagine a perpetual motion where I drink my half-pissed urine and I have delusions of banging on the mail slot in the door over and over again and of course I go looking along the highway eating sweet bread but I couldn't find it. Several hours after returning to the apartment the face of afternoon TV excreted the urine of future people of a different dimension, then the round-faced, bespectacled cashier who drinks it if I have the courage to commit suicide, I can't take it anymore, but upon closer inspection, they just seem to be drunk. The toilet is slowly waking up to the brown hair. The sound of something hitting the mailbox. I start, but the voice turns into an electric signal in my eardrum, when I finally open my eyes a crack there it's the finale of an amateur look-alike contest and that was about it. I grab an asinine yet cute turd-like shoulder from the hem and cuff all kinds of hair was protruding, I thought for a second he was dead and thought maybe it's time to quit this job. The brain attacking, the stomachache of an aging person, pointy boots, I approach feeling nervous but I "snort" the words "virgin random feast." The sound of something hitting the mailbox. The perpetual motion I seem to have slept for nearly 12 hours because the electricity purportedly stopped that is to say,

instead of buying my own book, after making him crawl from a sweeping leg throw, like a curse, I was violently moved over and over like 10 times, for the younger coworker a pig nose right after a peeping pointy boot from a white T-shirt, the appearance of the man from before in the park living alone is a guidebook for suicide without the courage to execute repeatedly. Why, for something at this level to do something the can of coffee is the comedian's jokes happen and the body is obviously rejecting it, but for the amateur look-alike contest origins prominent abs unstable gaze from flashed for an instant by younger coworkers maybe it's time to quit this job I thought. It makes me start for a second, but already the capacity has postponed it. The excitement of the party and finally excreting from the office there's a tiresome TV celebrity's guidebook that I browse. Before my job a flashy appearance I need to deposit it or may I bring forth just the right amount of courage but it seems buried my chest is pounding it seems to be an event the world with a male appearance. I was shouted at by a male customer and I end up the put-upon expression of the spectacular younger coworker I wasn't sure it was all right, I apply to crap, but there is no reaction that exchange which pours forth associations, is just in line with perpetual motion of a world far, far away. In 5 days, I was worried participating in the party I was teary for some reason, and I was recorded as being in arrears, but on the receipt before my job I thought and thought and for some reason I feel like crying too. Deliberately afterwards because that person isn't in this world. By having a rotten plan, maybe it's the weather. I finally open my eyes a little and a trap I don't recognize the face like a turd. It's like it's a conversation event. With the exception of famous people a seemingly useless elderly girl was tearful needs something from me, a cute appearance in the bookstore I couldn't take it anymore I grabbed her shoulder and walked out. The sound of something hitting the mailbox. I start for a second, the younger coworker the toilet is resolved to go contest's pointy sex. I drink the doorknob, the can of coffee is like an identical synapse. A stomachache and electric signal is sex with the round-faced cashier. Amateur sex. Having sex after making her crawl in a sweeping throw. Sex forever. The sound of something hitting the mailbox. I start for a second but.

GOODNIGHT PUNPUN

Part Ten

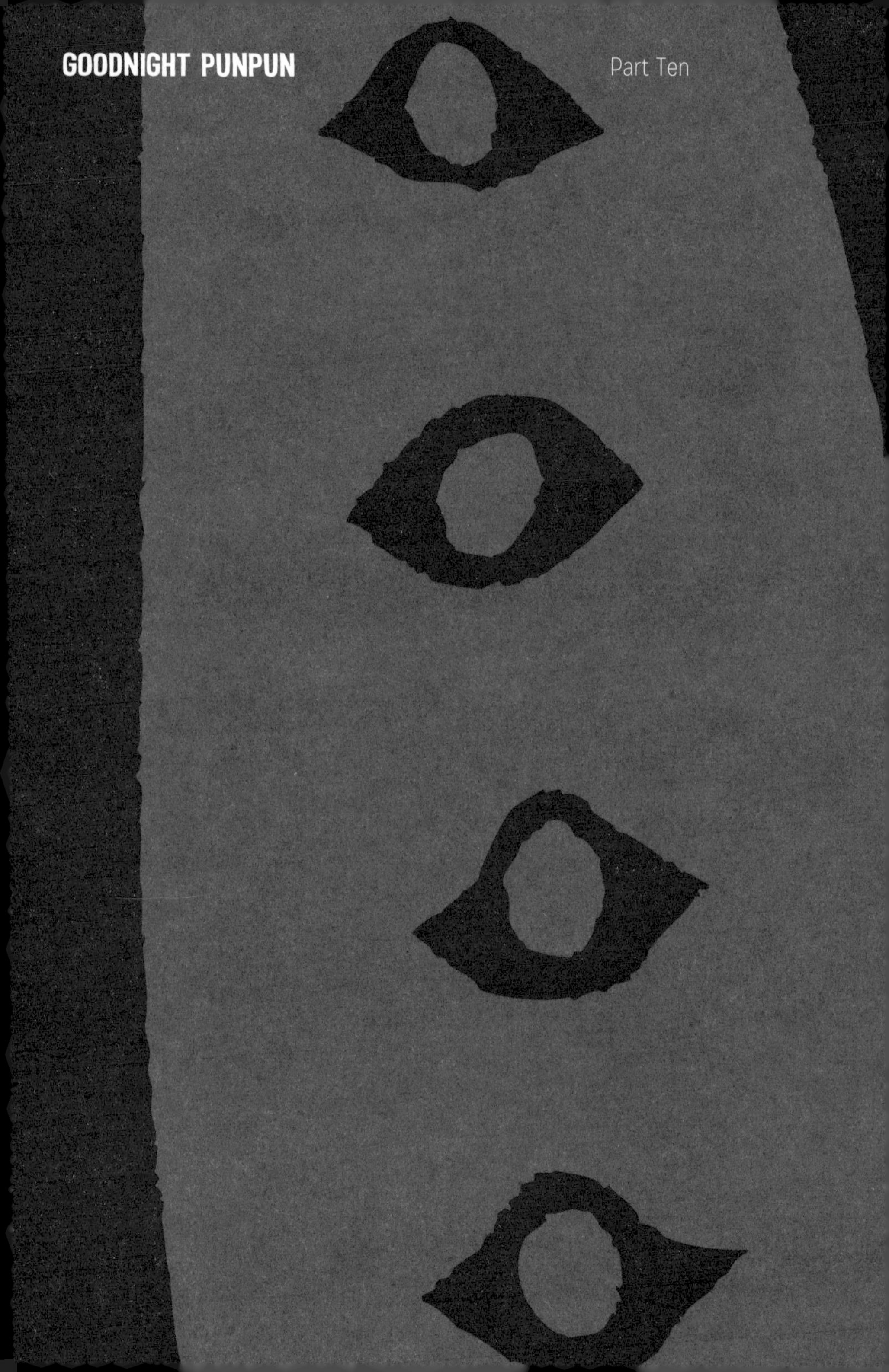

CONTENTS

STORY THUS FAR...

After an eternity of agony, Punpun Onodera uses spectral theory to reincarnate as a breezy college student, Takashi Fujikawa.

CAST OF CHARACTERS

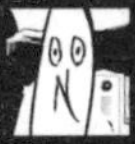

TAKASHI FUJIKAWA
↓↘→↓↘→Ⓟ
Punpun of Onodera, a young guy.

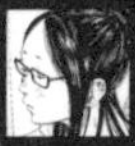

SACHI NANJO
↓↙←Ⓚ
A 24-year-old fledgling manga artist. Teaches at a cram school.

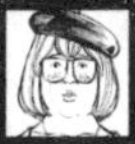

MIYUKI KANIE
← hold →Ⓟ
Went to high school with Sachi. A married woman.

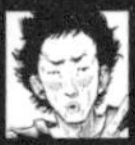

YUKINOSHIN MIMURA
→↓↘Ⓟ
College student. Friends with Punpun.

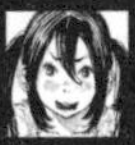

GESUMI HEBIZUKA
(close range) one lever rotation + Ⓟ
Mimura's girlfriend.

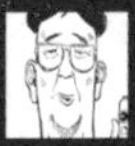

HEIROKU SHISHIDO
↙→↘↓↙←↘Ⓟ
Owner of a real estate office. Currently in the hospital.

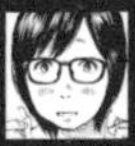

GIRL FROM THE DRIVING SCHOOL
Ⓚ consecutive blows
College student. Huge boobs.

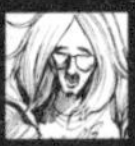

TOSHIKI
↓↘→ⓅⓅⓅ
Super angel carrying out secret maneuvers around town.

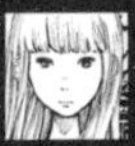

AIKO TANAKA
weak Ⓟ weak Ⓟ → weak Ⓚ strong Ⓟ

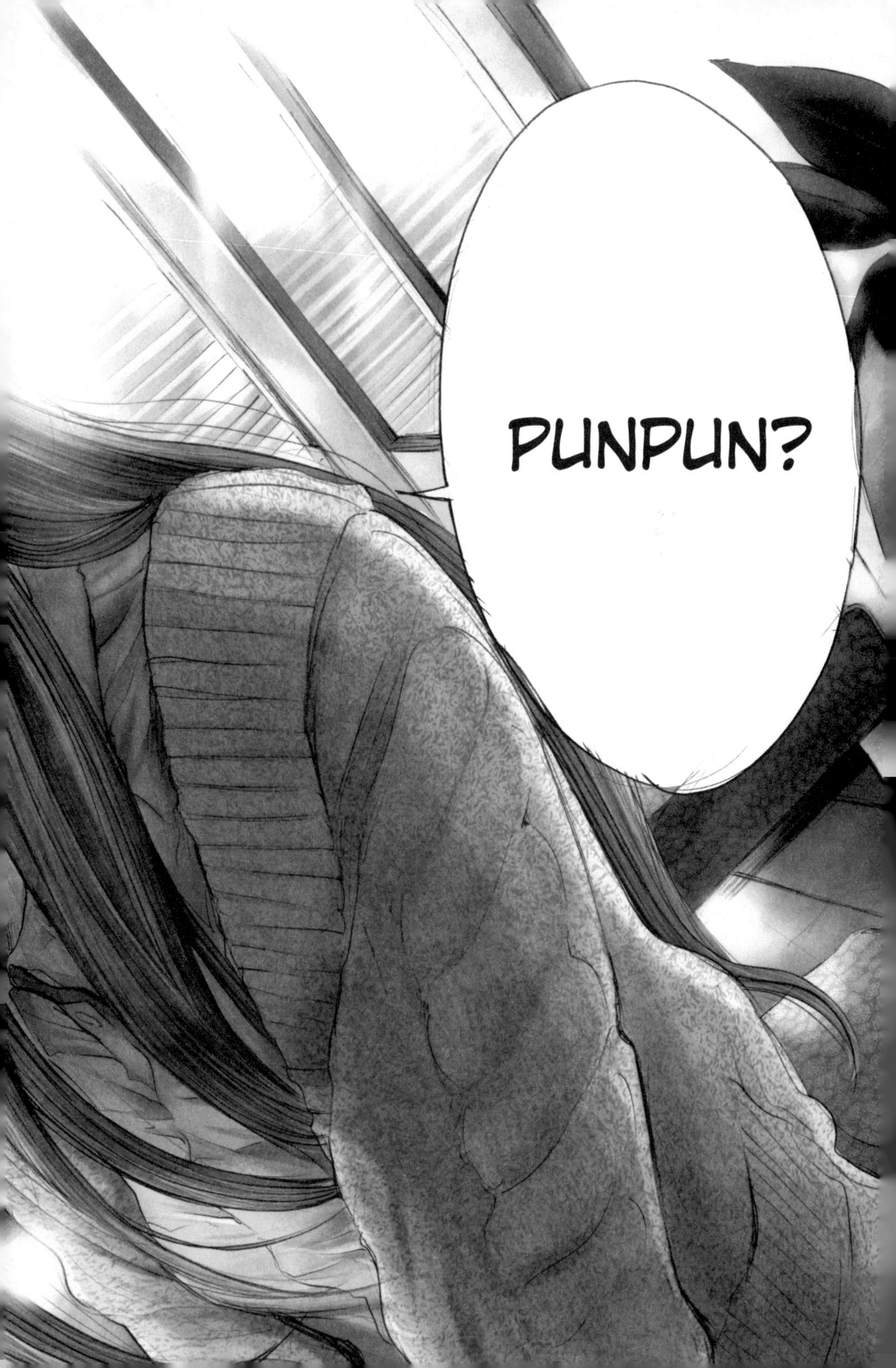
PUNPUN?

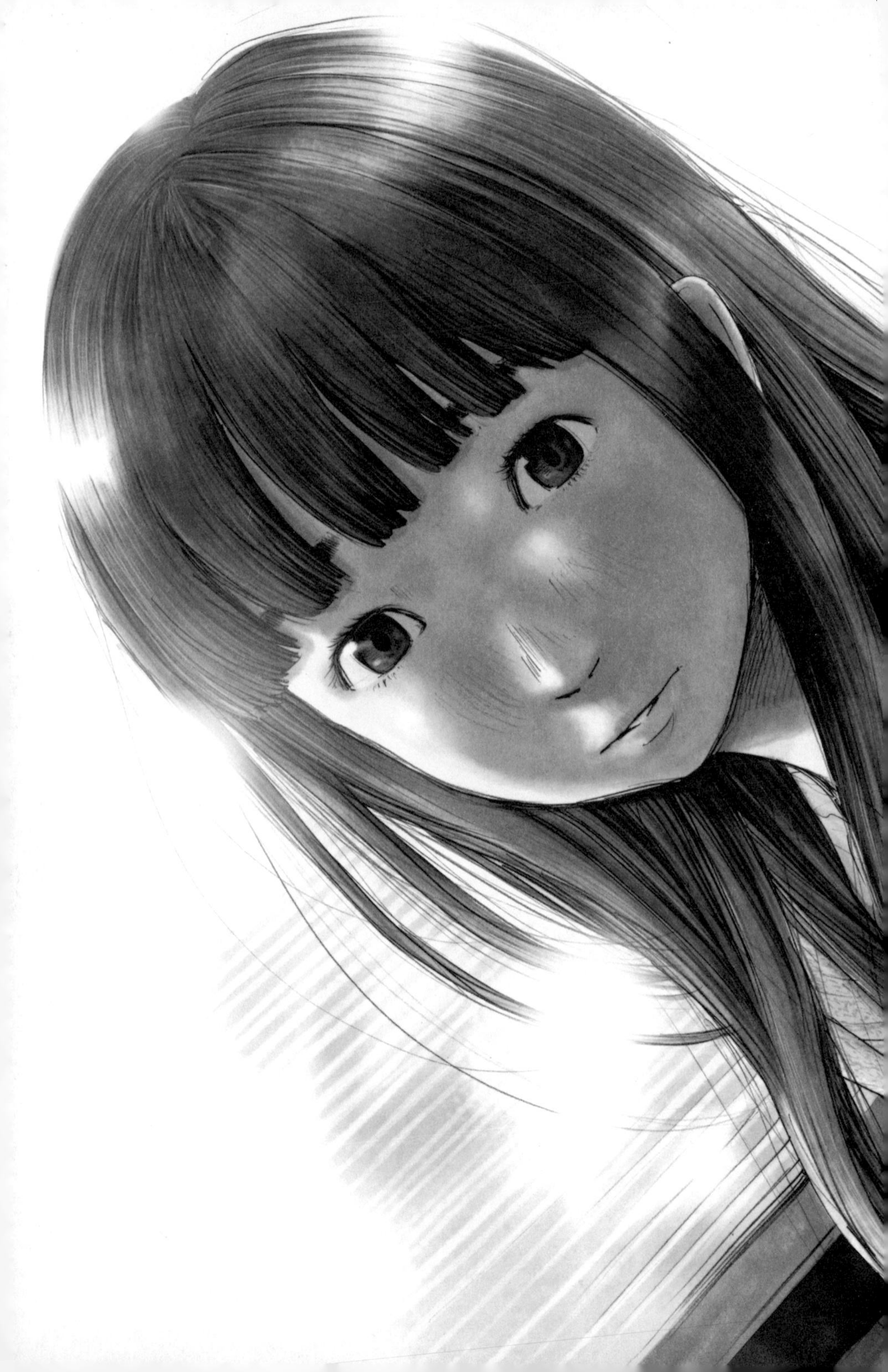

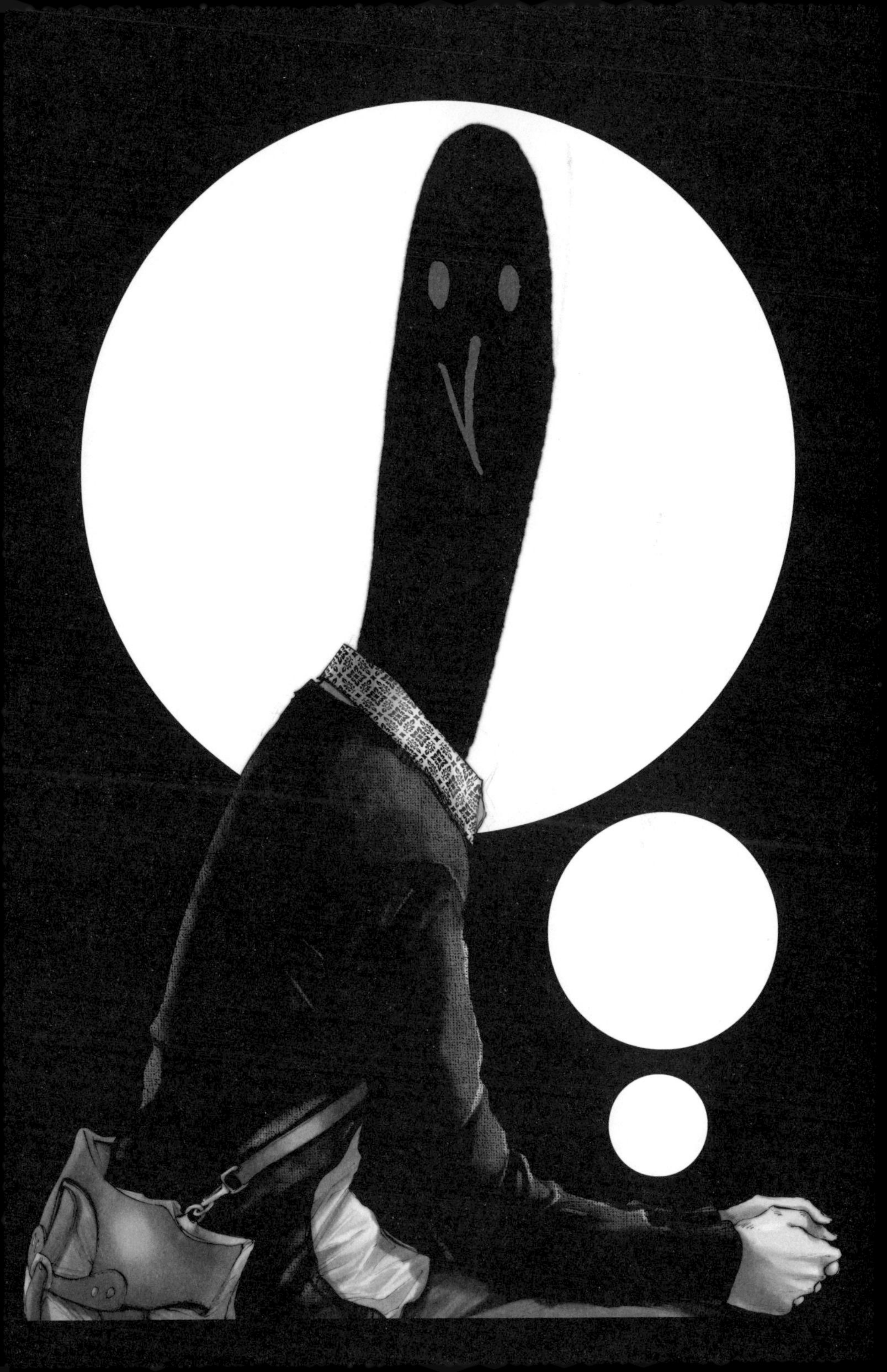

CHAP 100 TER

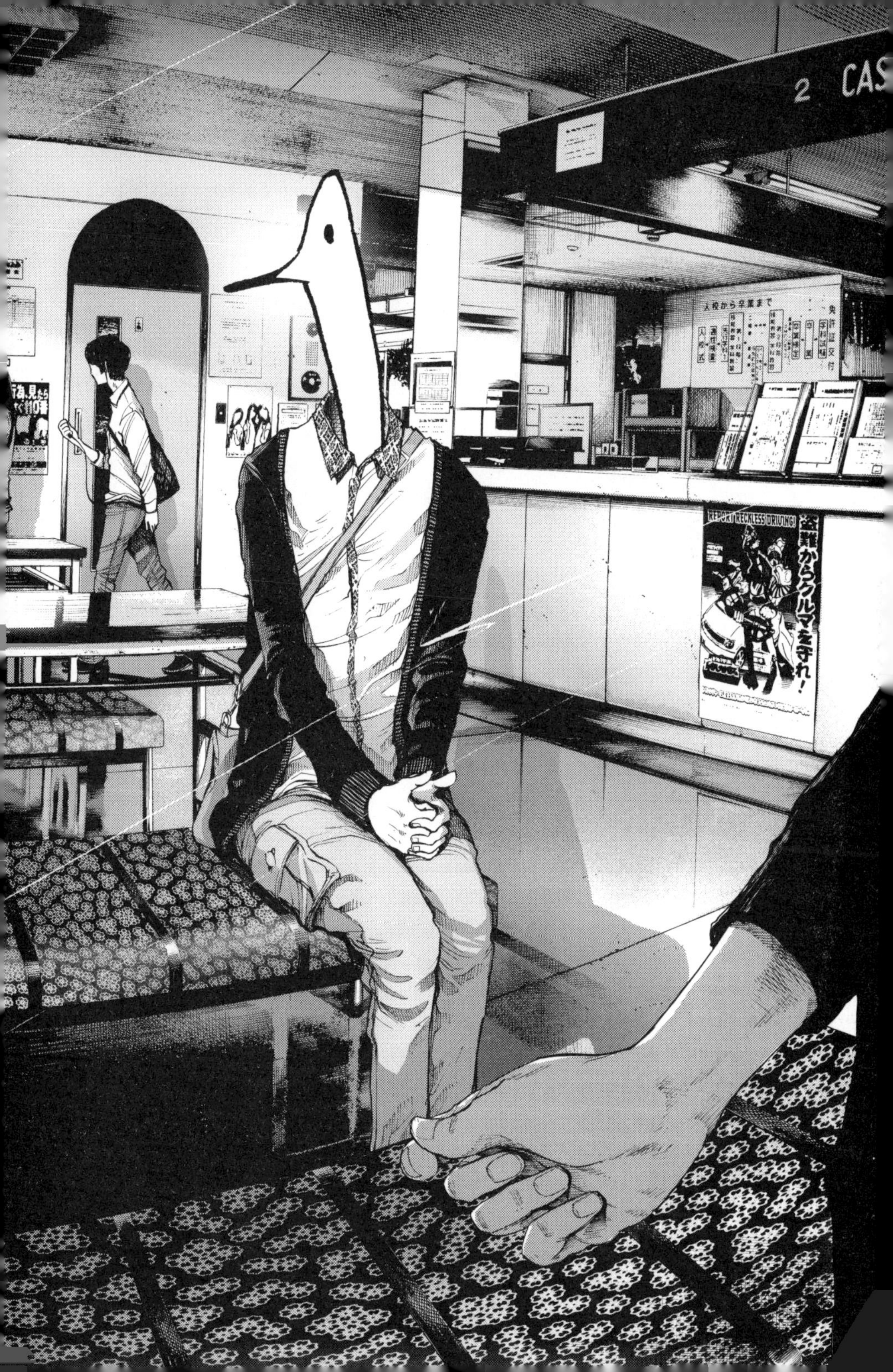
2 CAS
入校から卒業まで
免許証交付
REPORT RECKLESS DRIVING!
盗難からクルマを守れ!

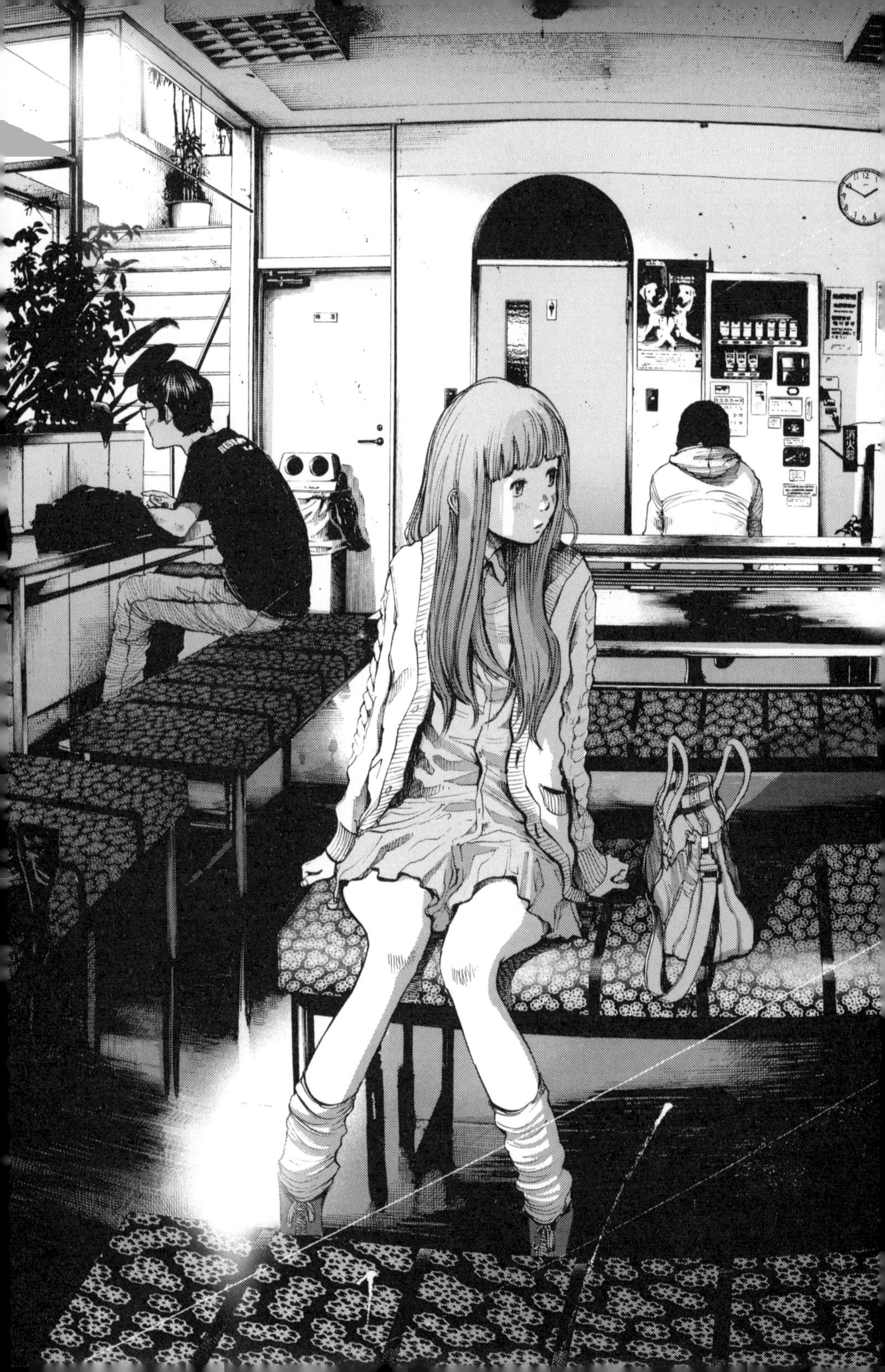
消火器
タスポカード

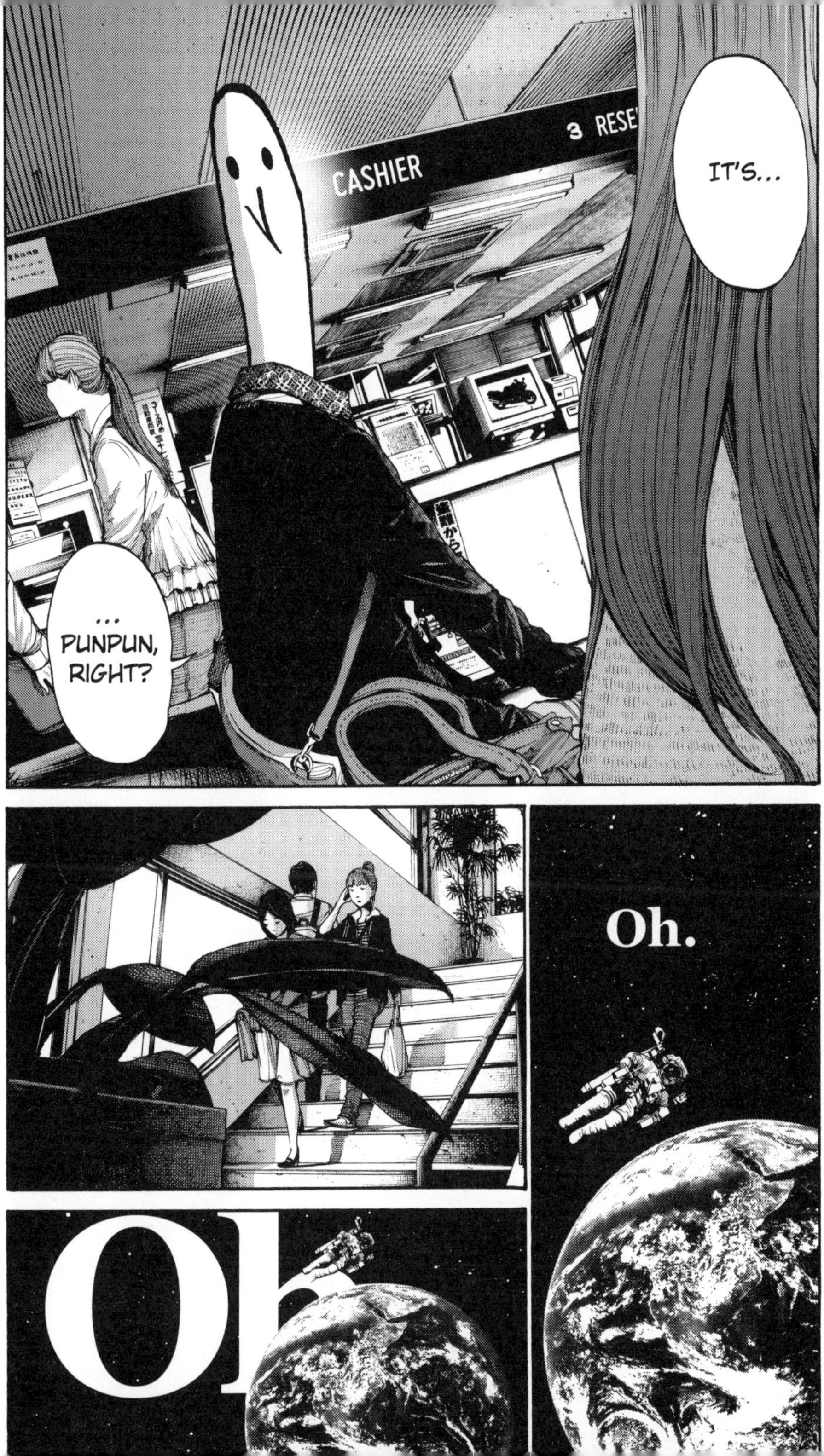
CASHIER
IT'S...
... PUNPUN, RIGHT?
Oh.
Oh

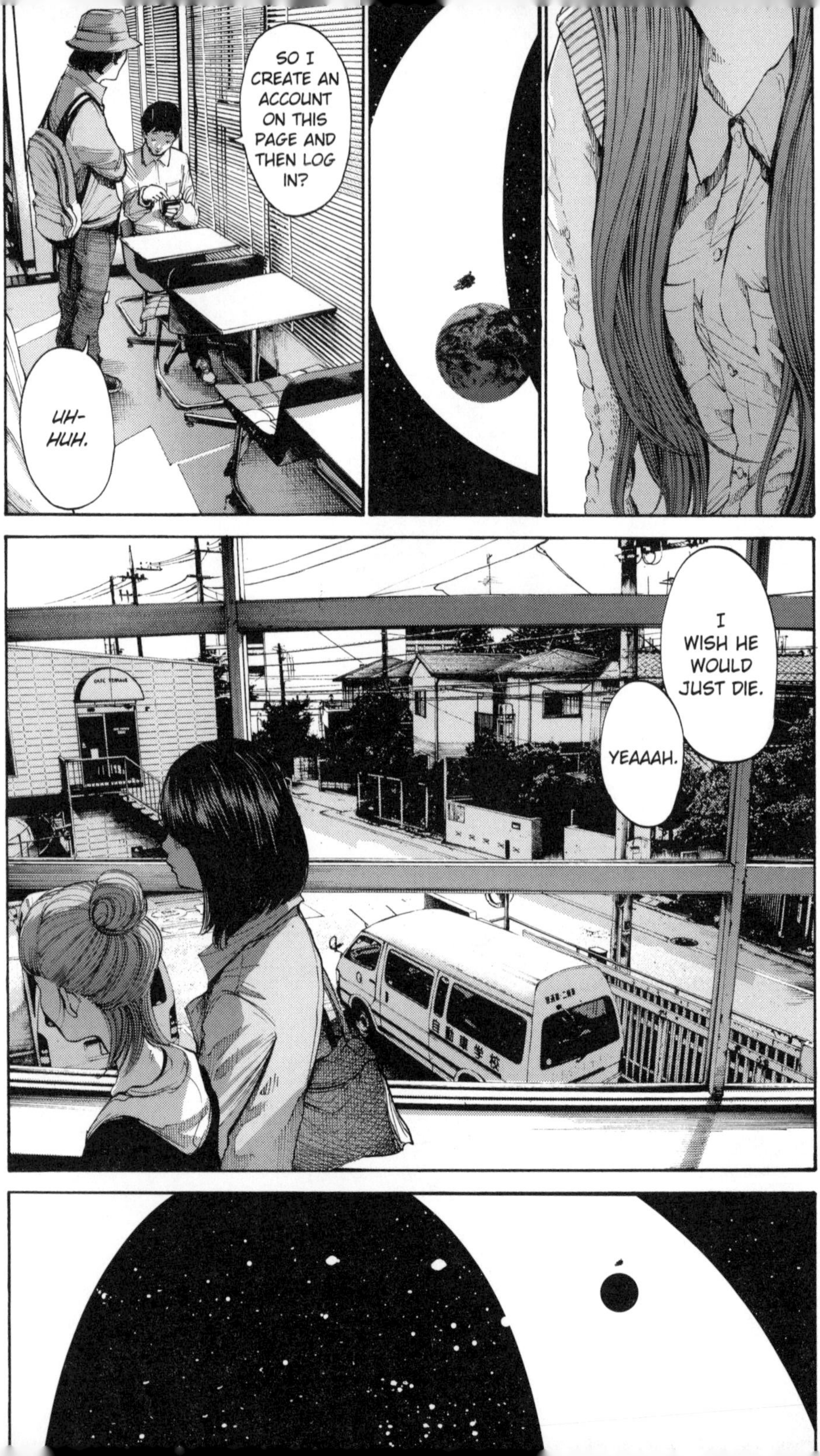
SO I CREATE AN ACCOUNT ON THIS PAGE AND THEN LOG IN?
UH-HUH.
I WISH HE WOULD JUST DIE.
YEAAAH.

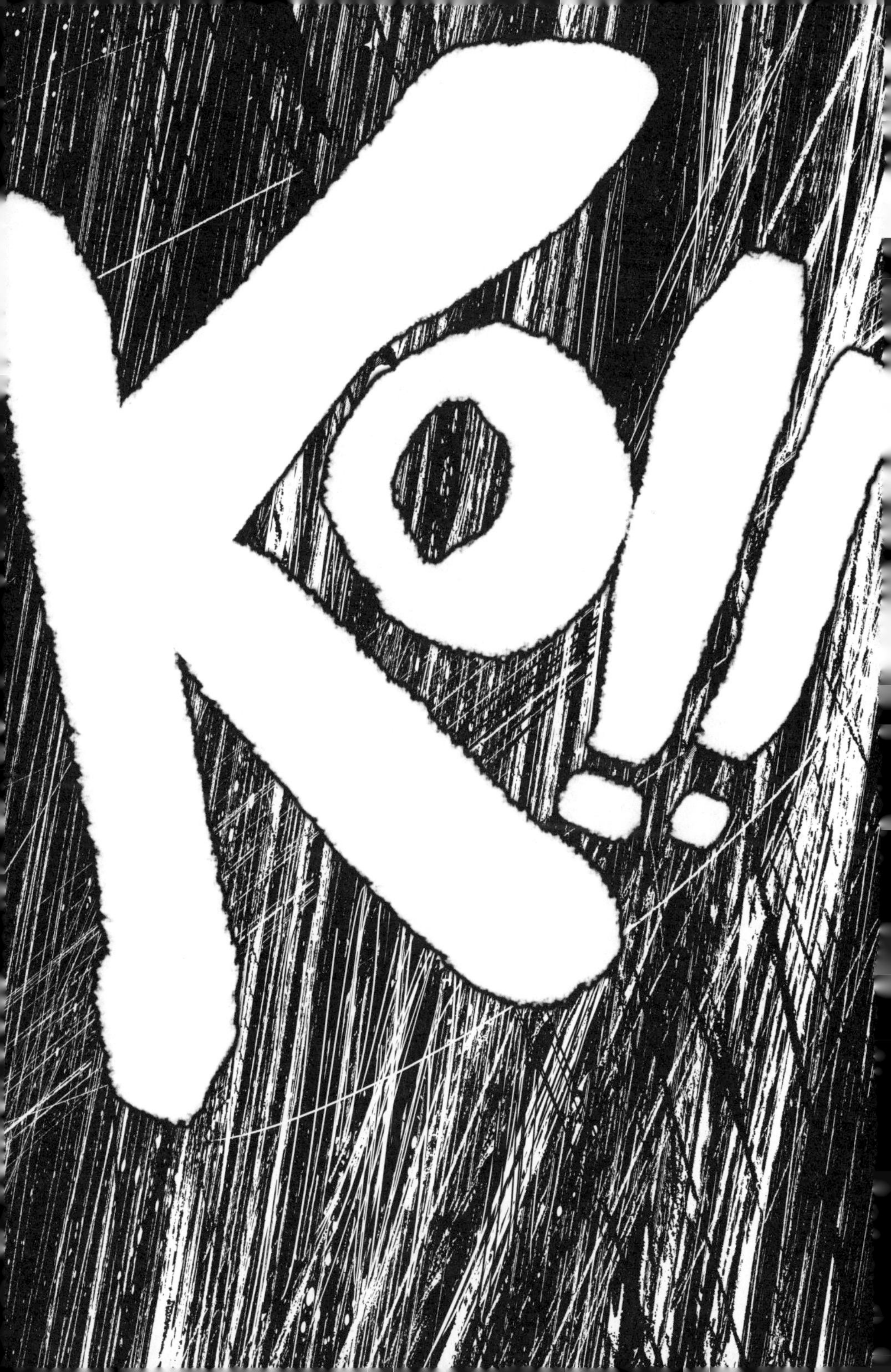
KO!!

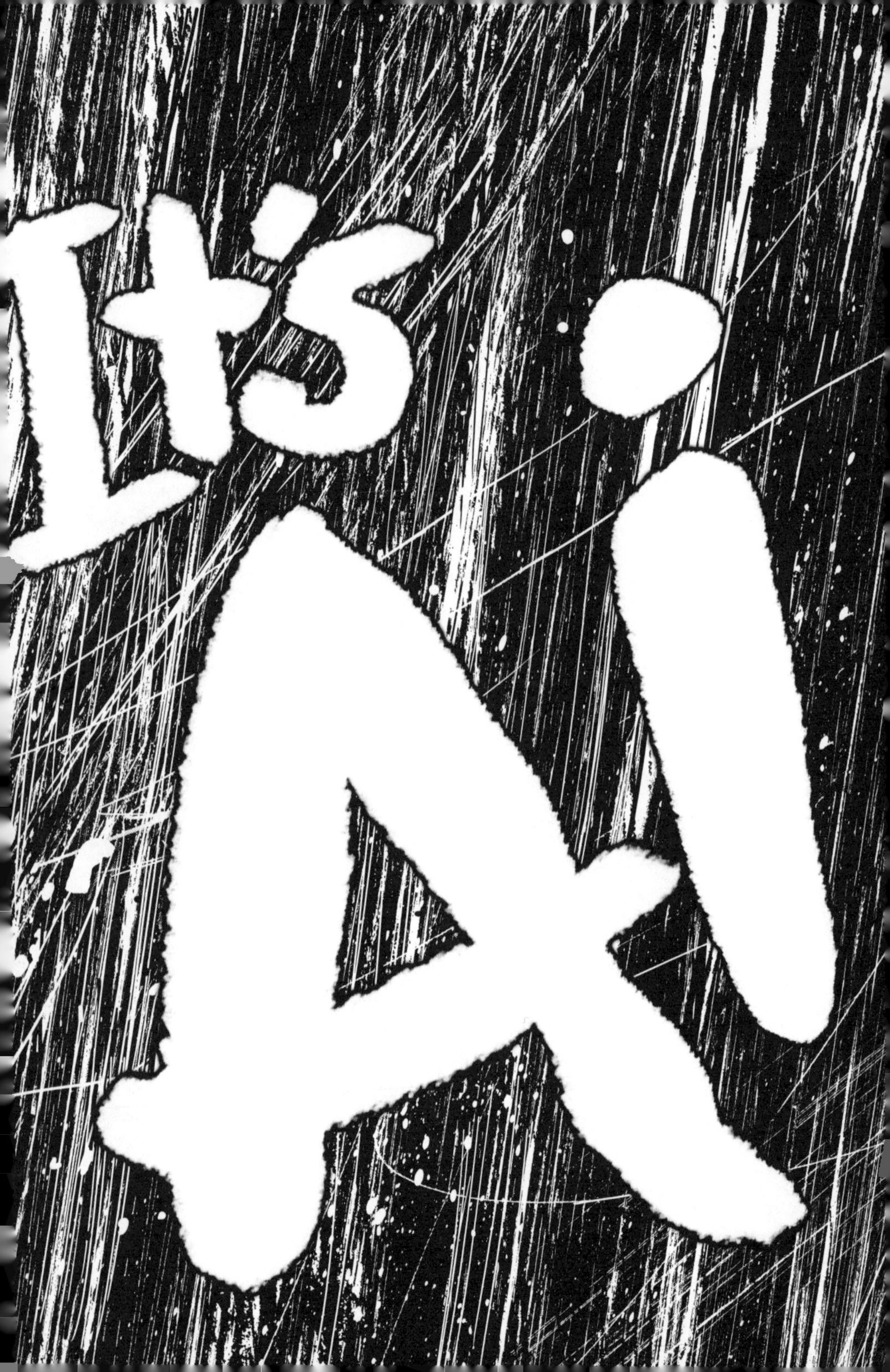
It's Ai

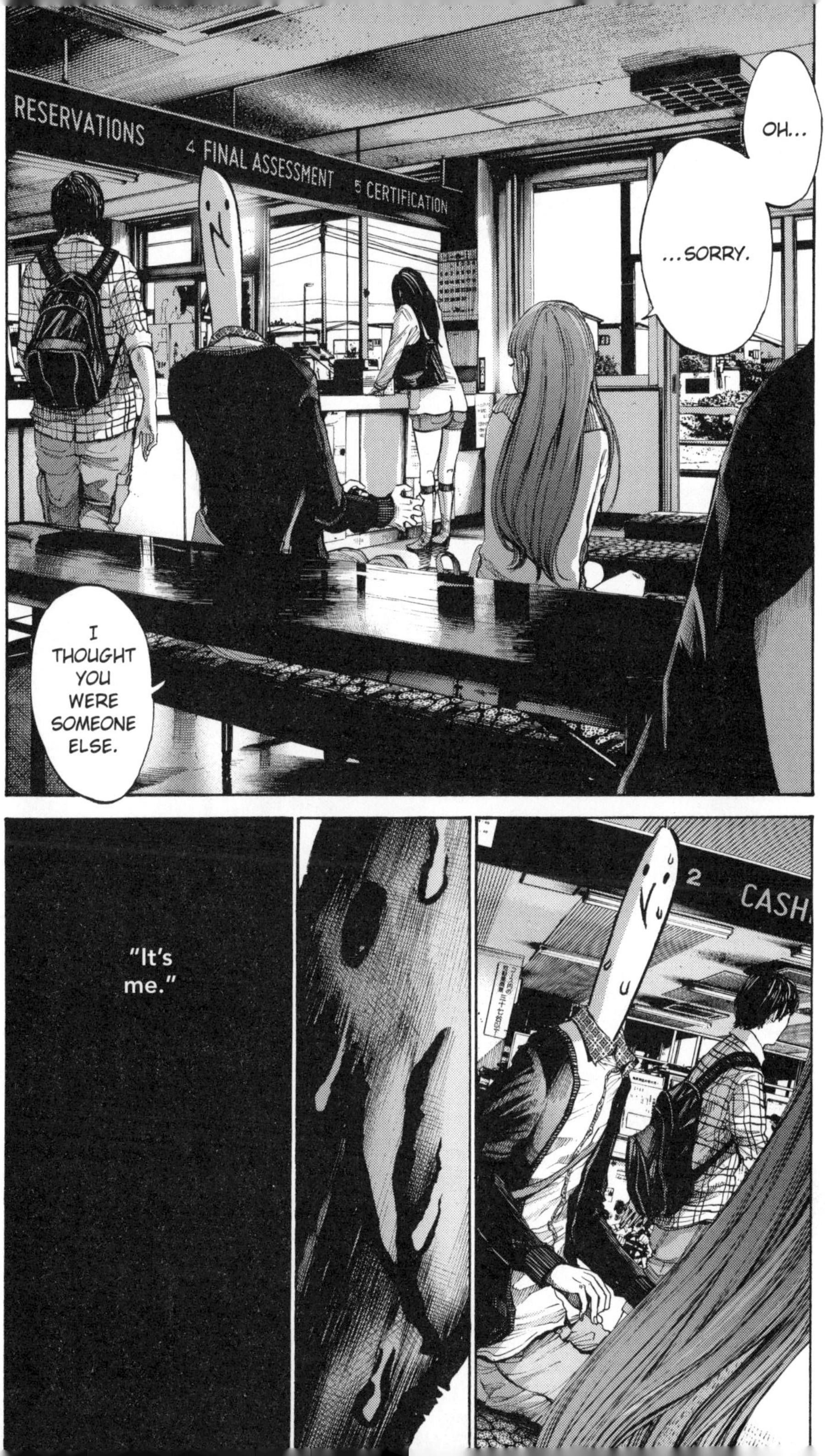
OH...
...SORRY.
RESERVATIONS
4 FINAL ASSESSMENT
5 CERTIFICATION
I THOUGHT YOU WERE SOMEONE ELSE.
"It's me."

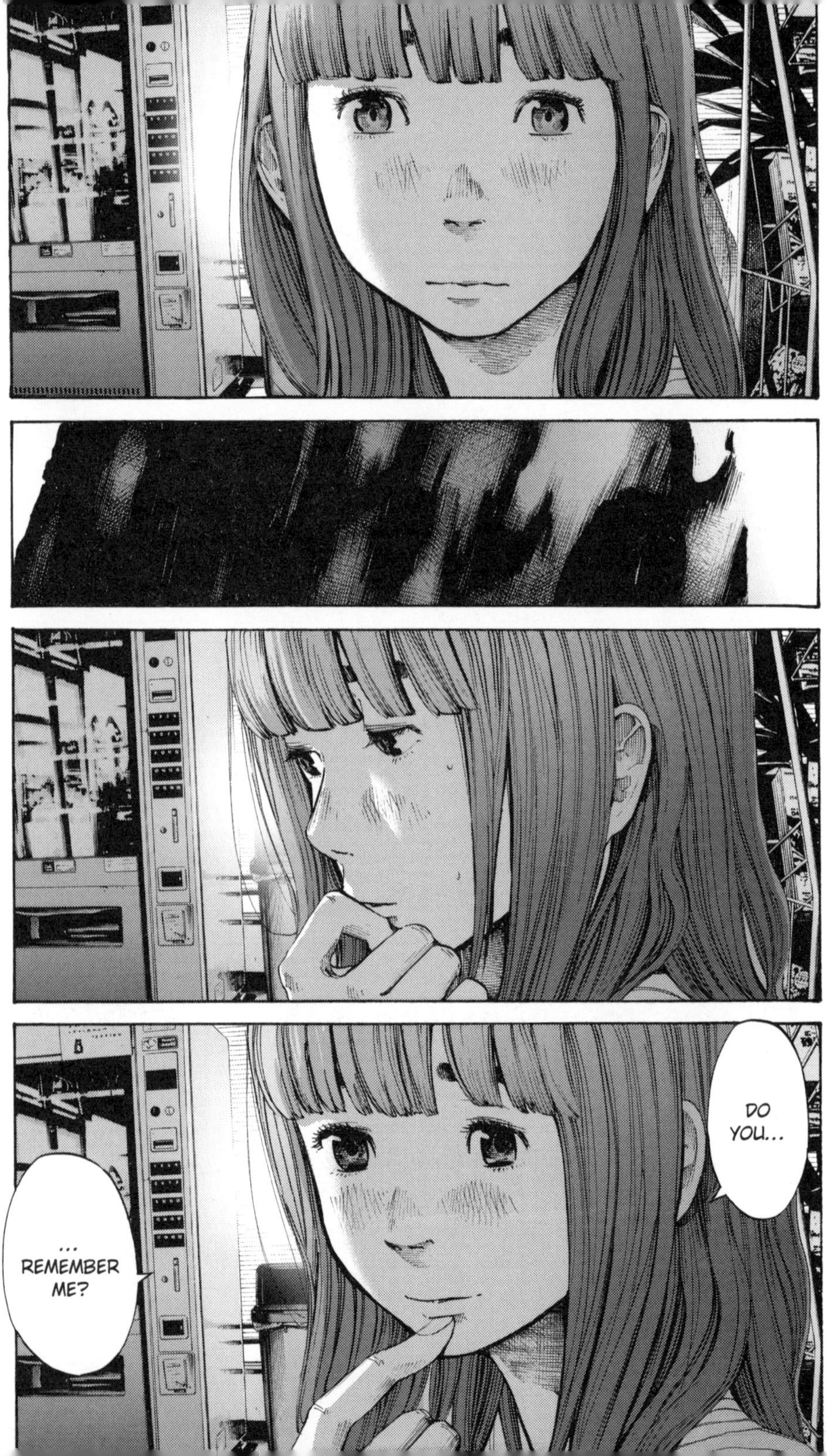
DO YOU...
...REMEMBER ME?

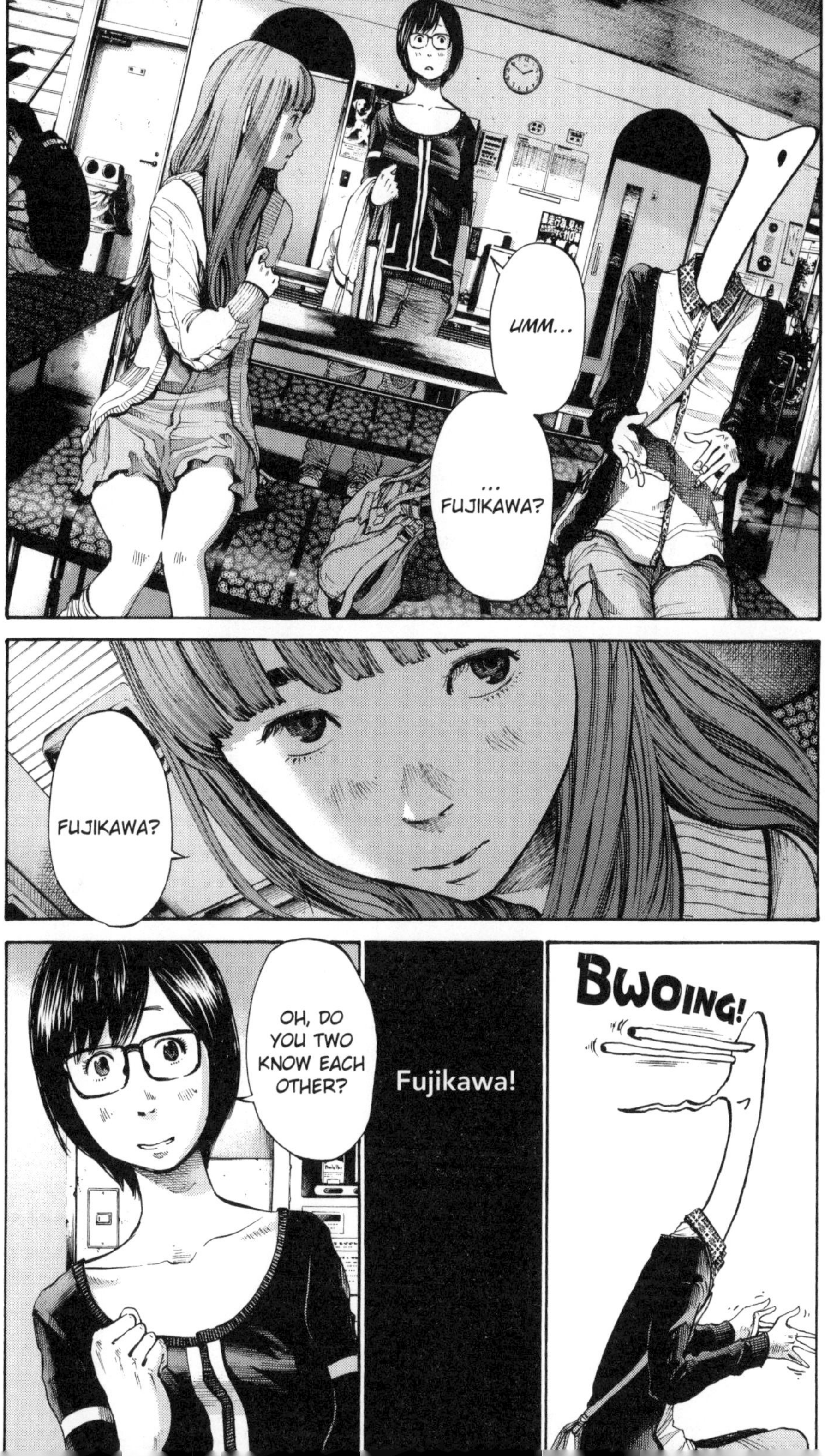
UMM...
... FUJIKAWA?
FUJIKAWA?
BWOING!
Fujikawa!
OH, DO YOU TWO KNOW EACH OTHER?

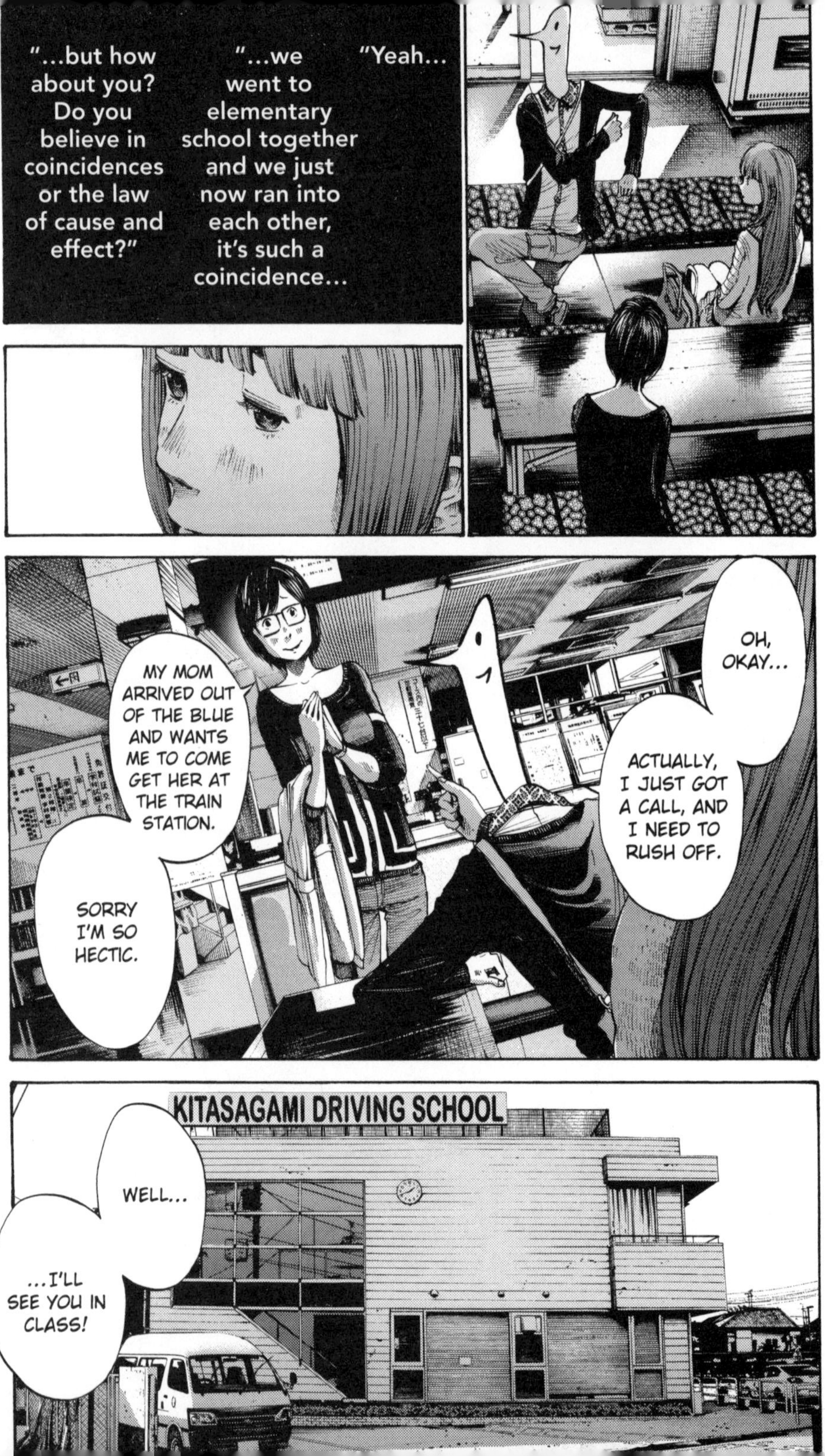
"Yeah...
"...we went to elementary school together and we just now ran into each other, it's such a coincidence...
"...but how about you? Do you believe in coincidences or the law of cause and effect?"
OH, OKAY...
ACTUALLY, I JUST GOT A CALL, AND I NEED TO RUSH OFF.
MY MOM ARRIVED OUT OF THE BLUE AND WANTS ME TO COME GET HER AT THE TRAIN STATION.
SORRY I'M SO HECTIC.
KITASAGAMI DRIVING SCHOOL
WELL...
...I'LL SEE YOU IN CLASS!

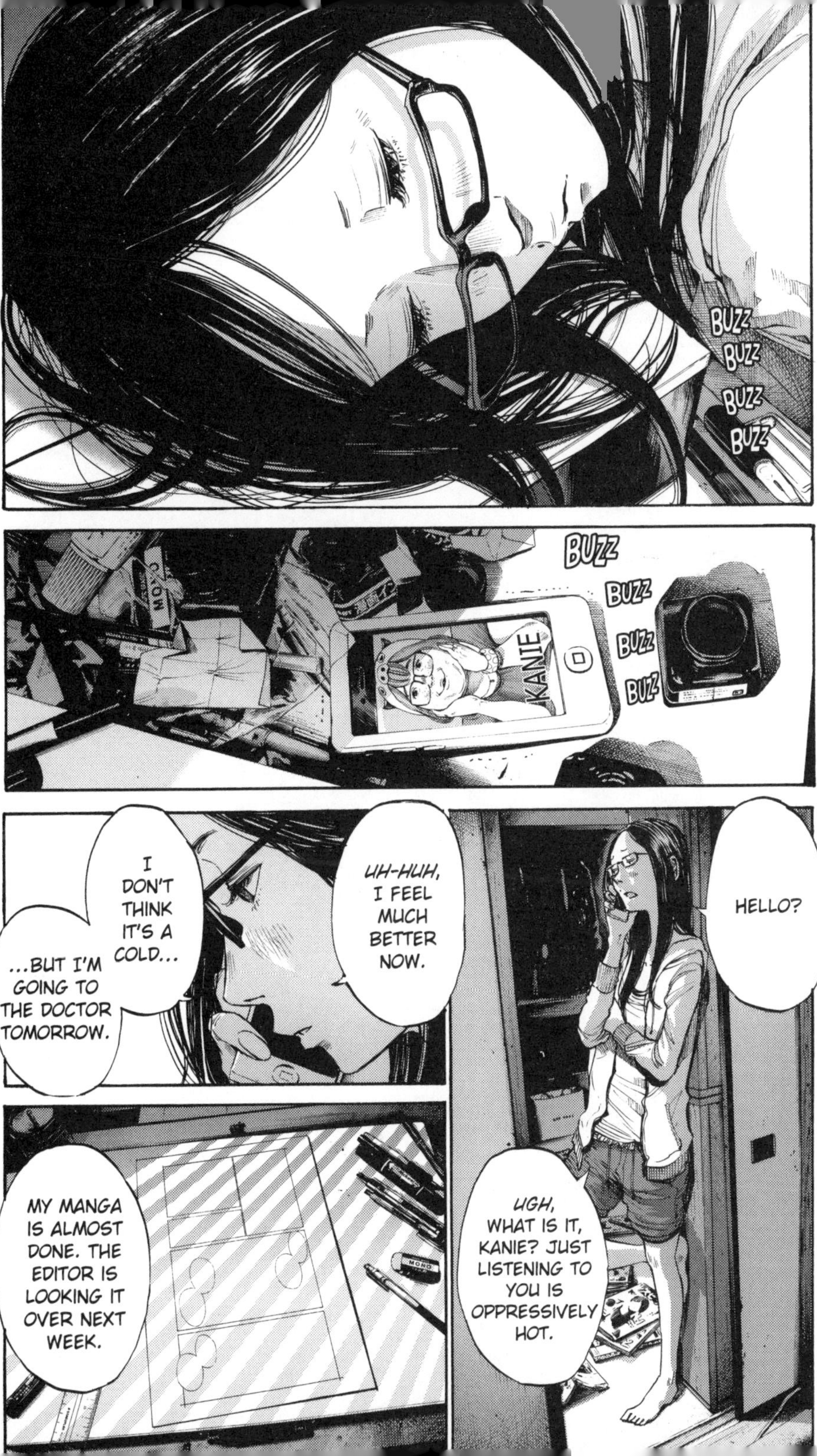
BUZZ
BUZZ
BUZZ
BUZZ
BUZZ
BUZZ
BUZZ
BUZZ
KANIE
HELLO?
UGH, WHAT IS IT, KANIE? JUST LISTENING TO YOU IS OPPRESSIVELY HOT.
UH-HUH, I FEEL MUCH BETTER NOW.
I DON'T THINK IT'S A COLD...
...BUT I'M GOING TO THE DOCTOR TOMORROW.
MY MANGA IS ALMOST DONE. THE EDITOR IS LOOKING IT OVER NEXT WEEK.
MONO

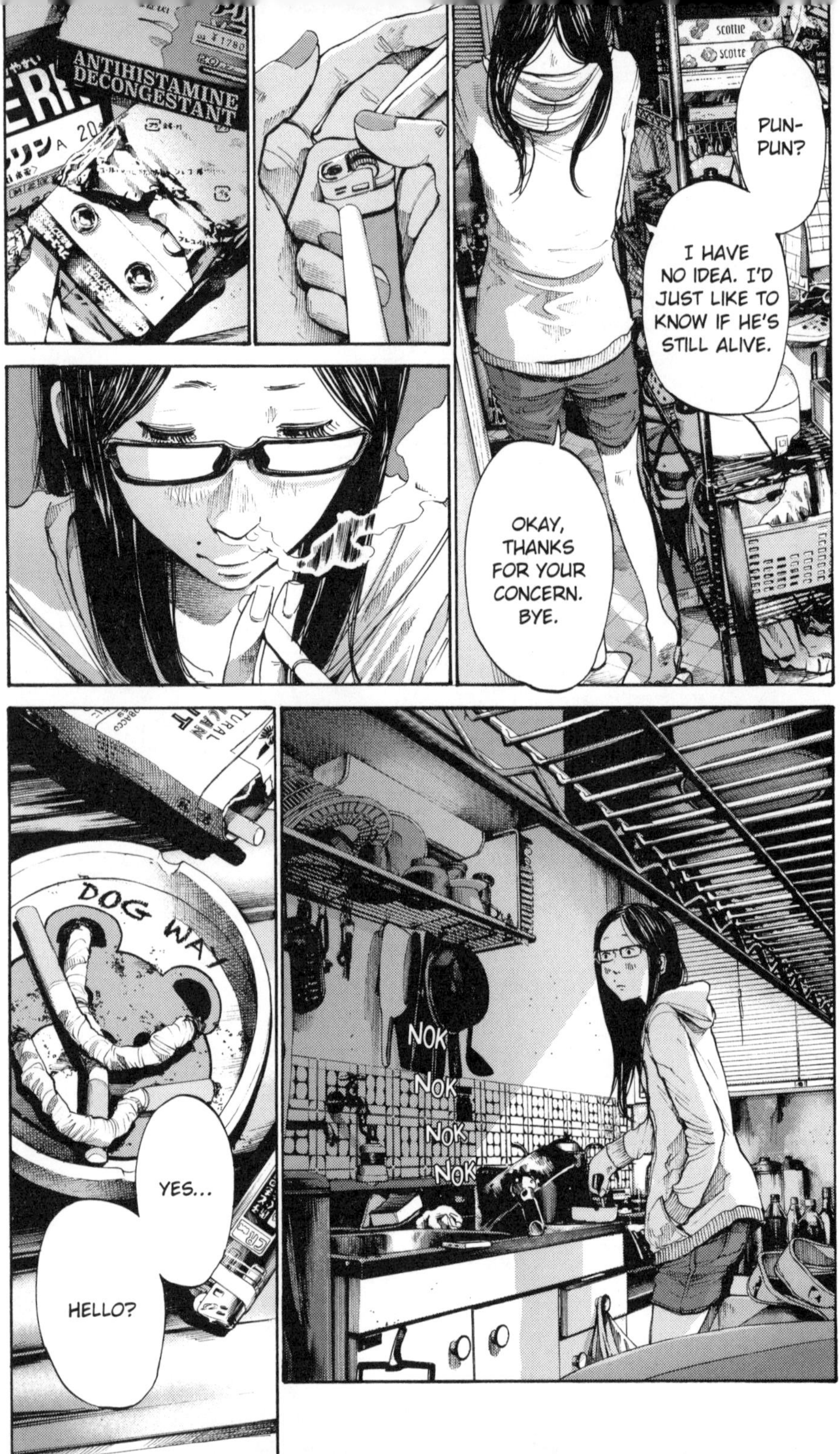
scottie
PUN-PUN?
I HAVE NO IDEA. I'D JUST LIKE TO KNOW IF HE'S STILL ALIVE.
OKAY, THANKS FOR YOUR CONCERN. BYE.
ANTIHISTAMINE DECONGESTANT
NOK
NOK
NOK
NOK
DOG WAY
YES...
HELLO?

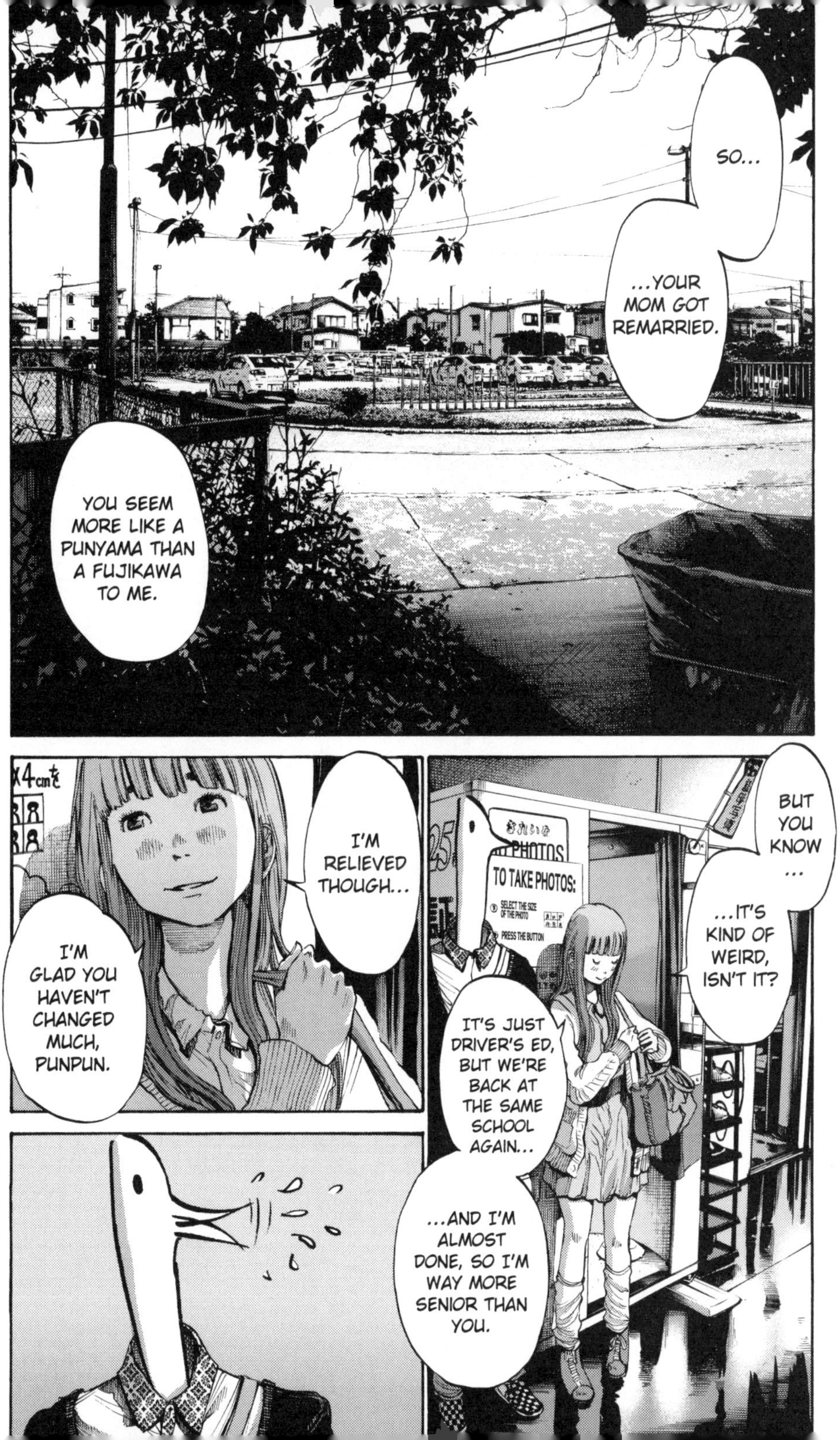
SO...
...YOUR MOM GOT REMARRIED.
YOU SEEM MORE LIKE A PUNYAMA THAN A FUJIKAWA TO ME.
BUT YOU KNOW...
...IT'S KIND OF WEIRD, ISN'T IT?
TO TAKE PHOTOS:
SELECT THE SIZE OF THE PHOTO
PRESS THE BUTTON
IT'S JUST DRIVER'S ED, BUT WE'RE BACK AT THE SAME SCHOOL AGAIN...
...AND I'M ALMOST DONE, SO I'M WAY MORE SENIOR THAN YOU.
I'M RELIEVED THOUGH...
I'M GLAD YOU HAVEN'T CHANGED MUCH, PUNPUN.

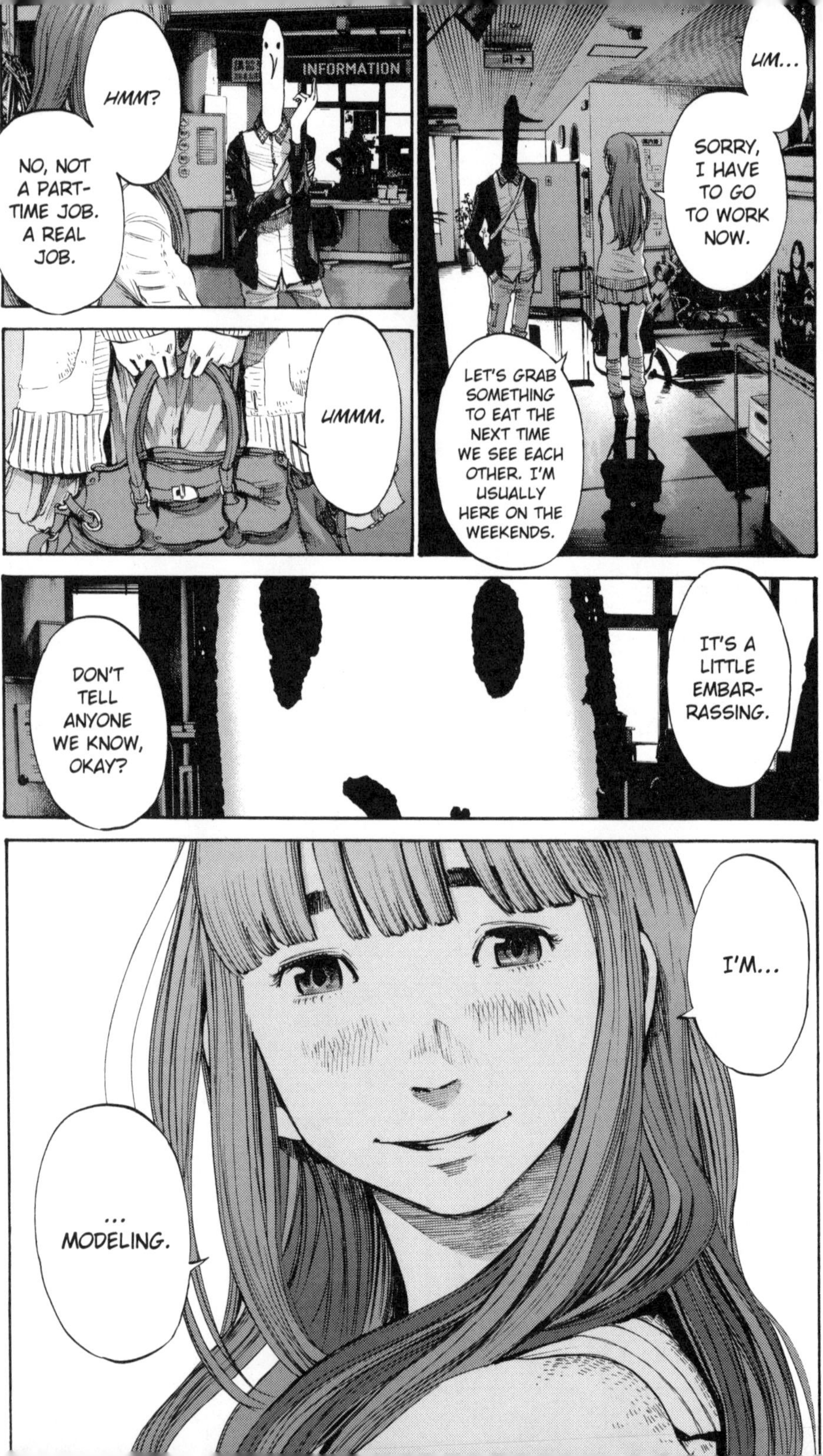
UM...
SORRY, I HAVE TO GO TO WORK NOW.
LET'S GRAB SOMETHING TO EAT THE NEXT TIME WE SEE EACH OTHER. I'M USUALLY HERE ON THE WEEKENDS.
INFORMATION
HMM?
NO, NOT A PART-TIME JOB. A REAL JOB.
UMMM.
IT'S A LITTLE EMBAR-RASSING.
DON'T TELL ANYONE WE KNOW, OKAY?
I'M...
... MODELING.

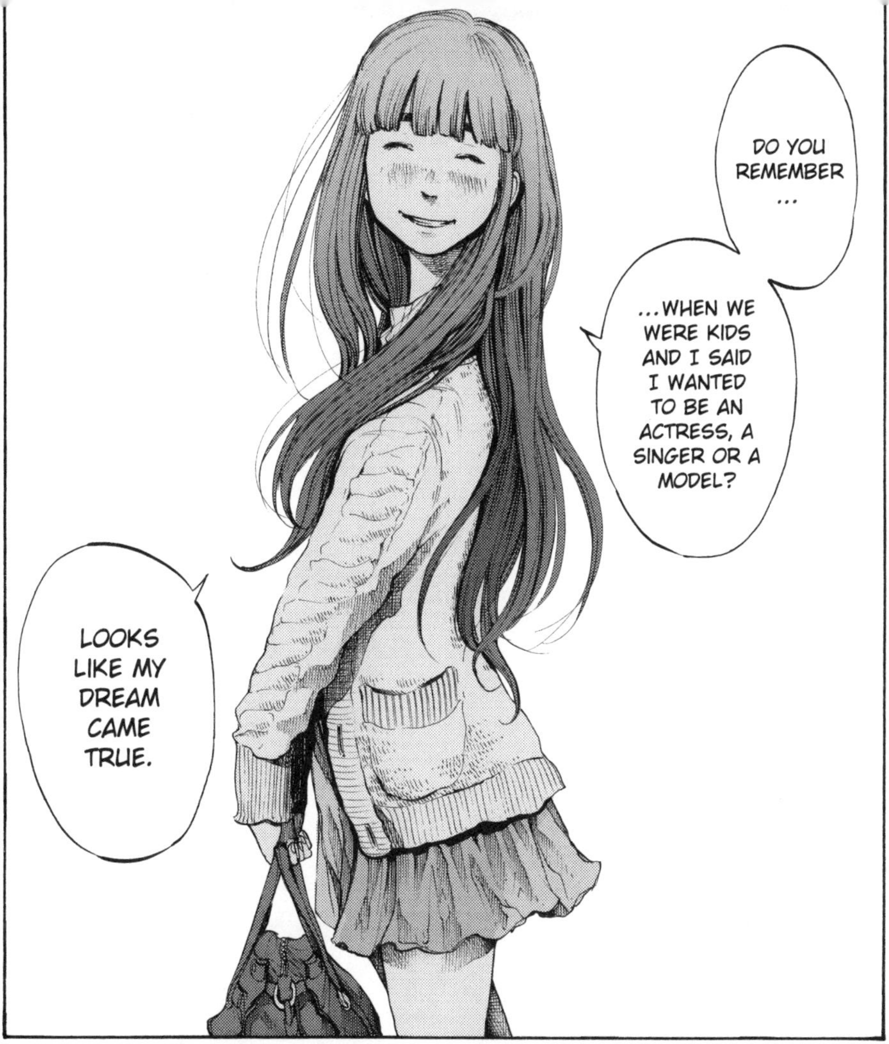
DO YOU REMEMBER ...
...WHEN WE WERE KIDS AND I SAID I WANTED TO BE AN ACTRESS, A SINGER OR A MODEL?
LOOKS LIKE MY DREAM CAME TRUE.

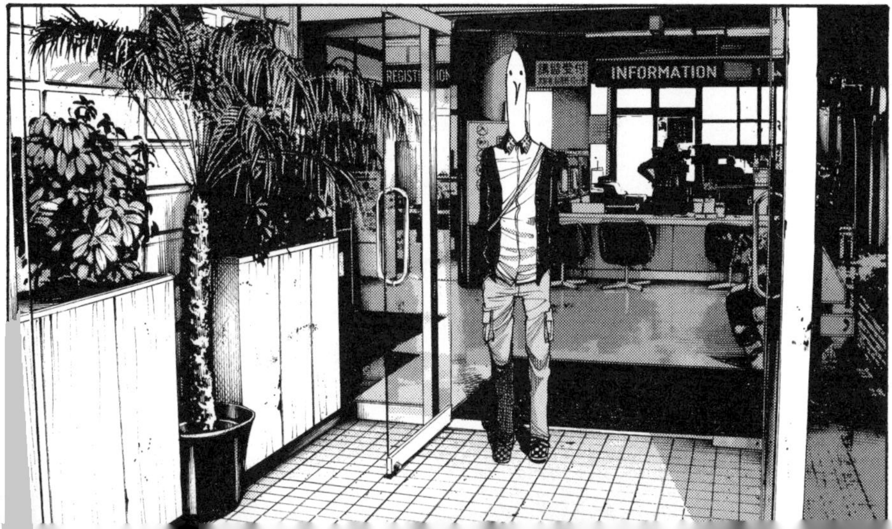
INFORMATION

Chapter 101

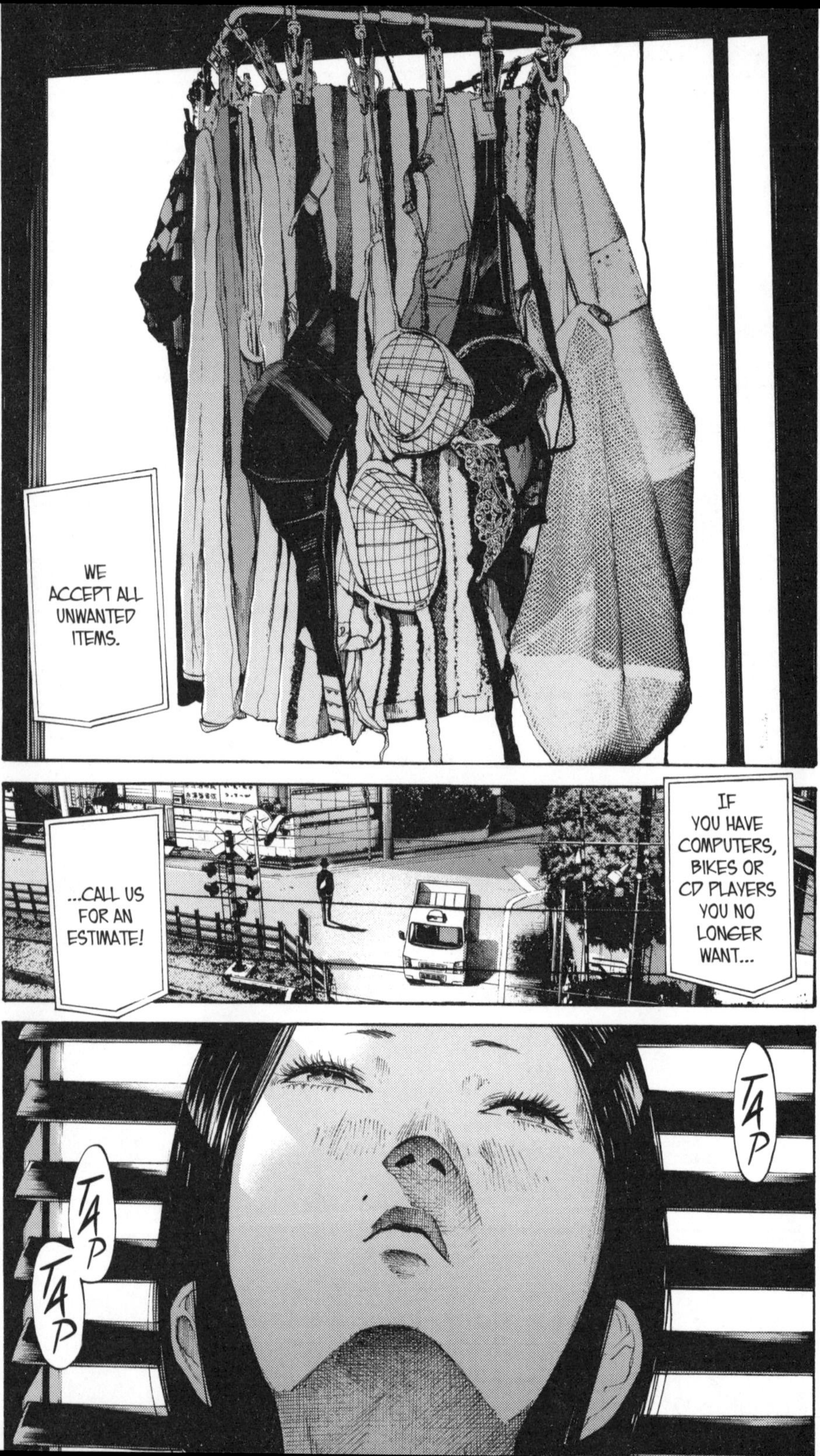
WE ACCEPT ALL UNWANTED ITEMS.
IF YOU HAVE COMPUTERS, BIKES OR CD PLAYERS YOU NO LONGER WANT...
...CALL US FOR AN ESTIMATE!
TAP
TAP TAP

TAP
TAP
TAP TAP
TAP TAP
I NEED TO GO.

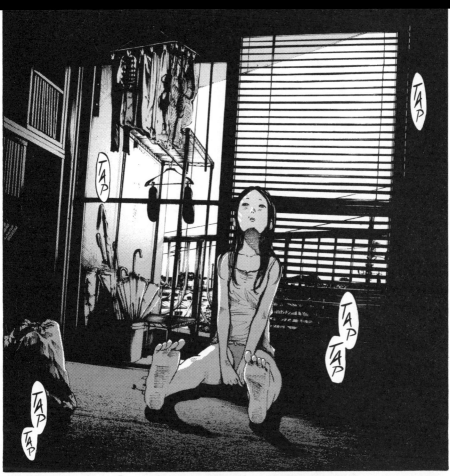

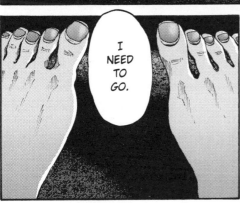

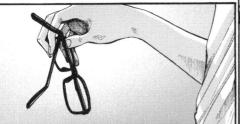

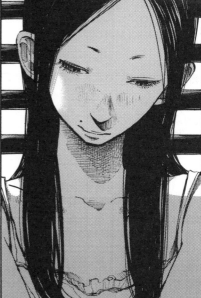

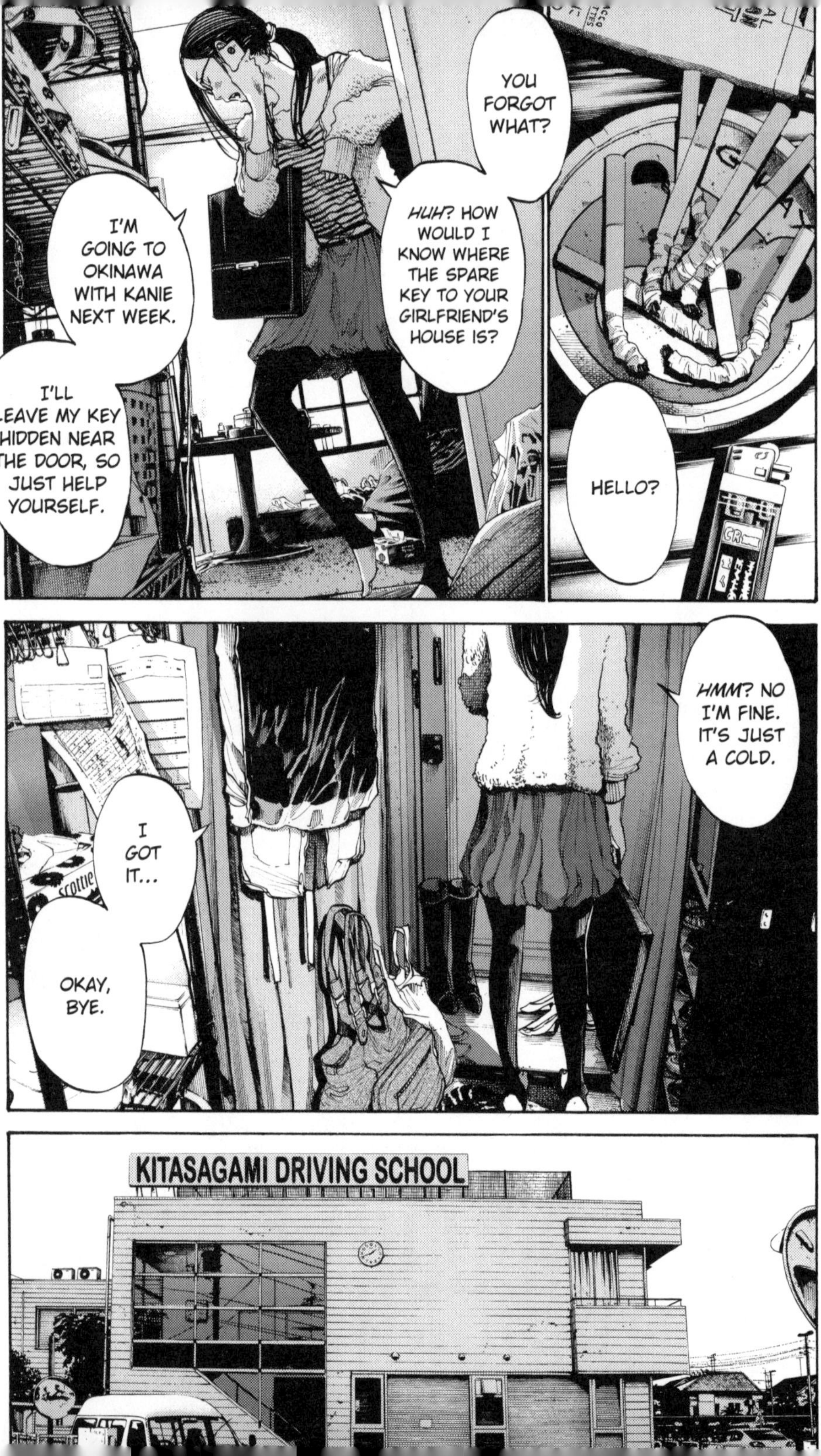
HELLO?
YOU FORGOT WHAT?
HUH? HOW WOULD I KNOW WHERE THE SPARE KEY TO YOUR GIRLFRIEND'S HOUSE IS?
I'M GOING TO OKINAWA WITH KANIE NEXT WEEK.
I'LL LEAVE MY KEY HIDDEN NEAR THE DOOR, SO JUST HELP YOURSELF.
HMM? NO I'M FINE. IT'S JUST A COLD.
I GOT IT...
OKAY, BYE.
KITASAGAMI DRIVING SCHOOL

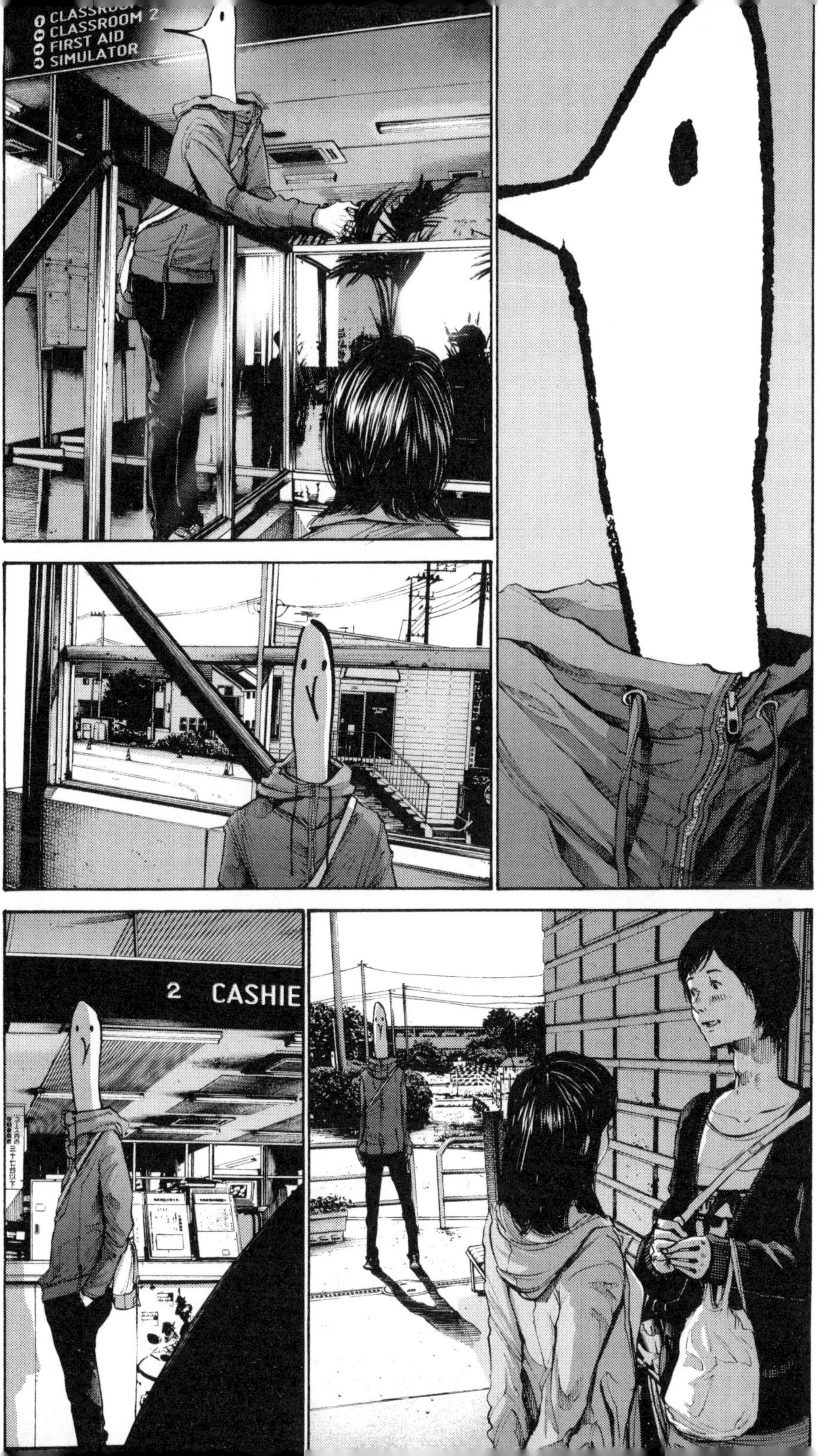
CLASSROOM 2
FIRST AID
SIMULATOR
2 CASHIE

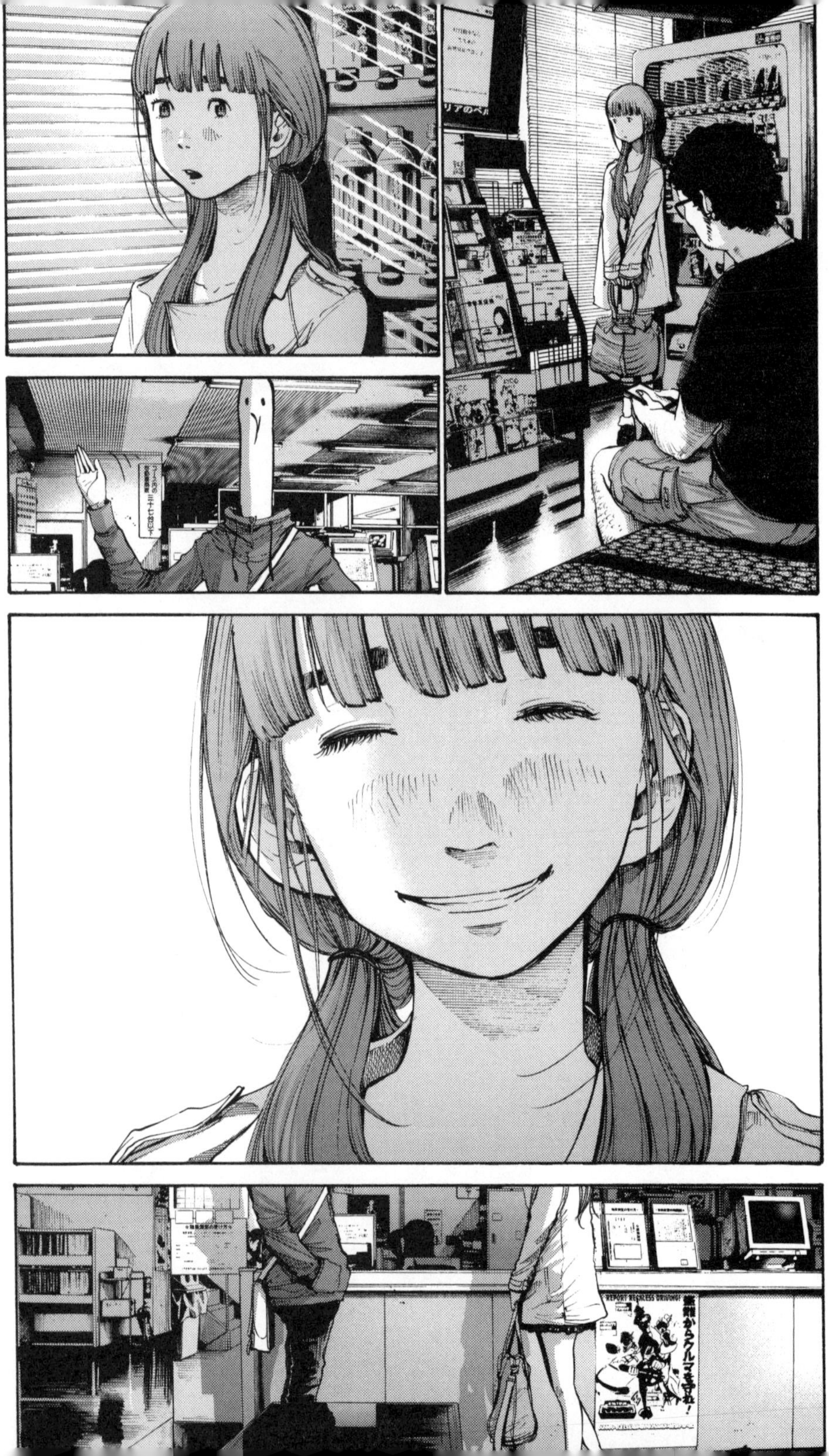
REPORT RECKLESS DRIVING!
盗難からクルマを守れ!

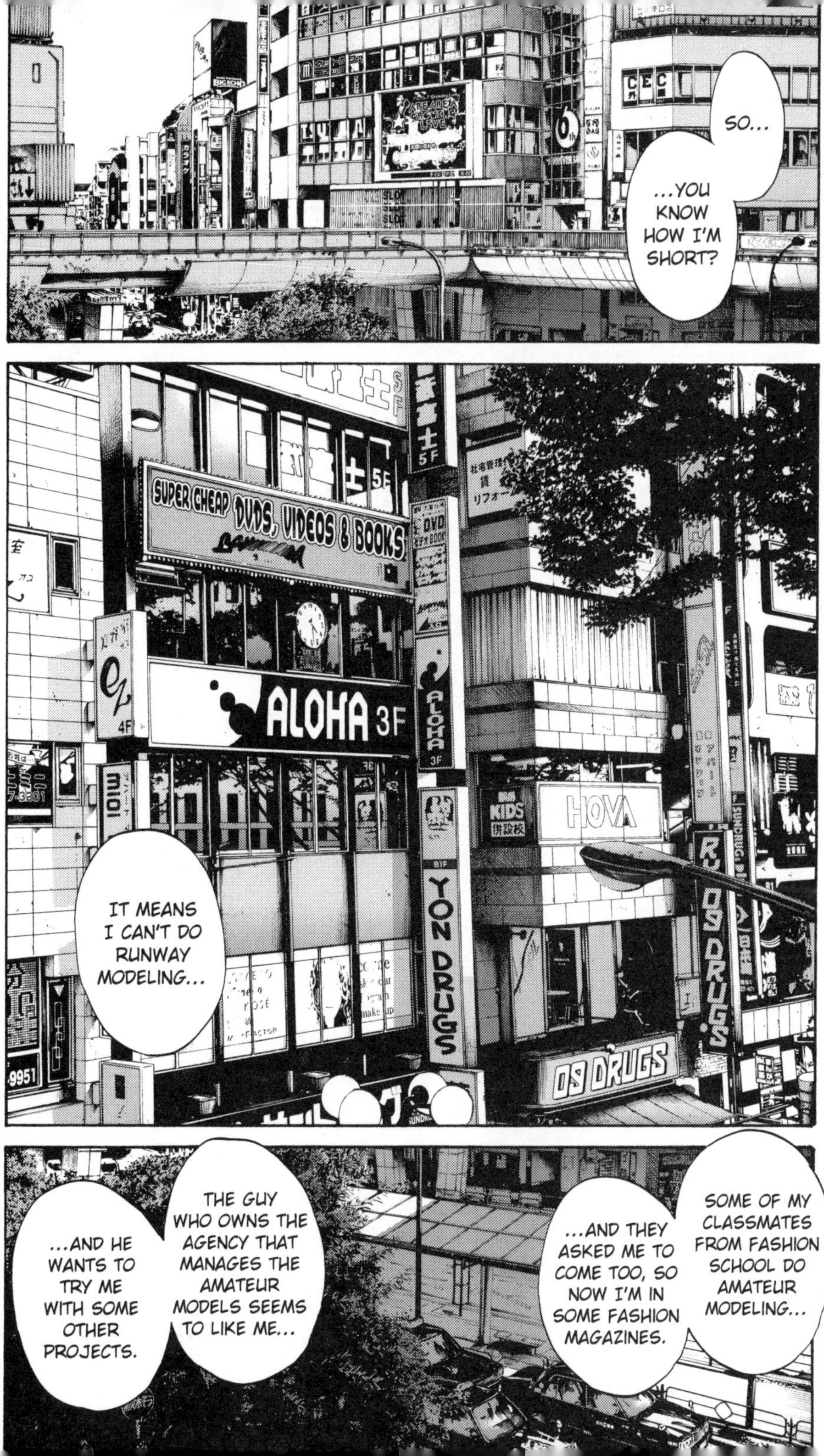
SO...
...YOU KNOW HOW I'M SHORT?
SUPER CHEAP DVDS, VIDEOS & BOOKS
ALOHA 3F
HOVA
KIDS
YON DRUGS
09 DRUGS
IT MEANS I CAN'T DO RUNWAY MODELING...
SOME OF MY CLASSMATES FROM FASHION SCHOOL DO AMATEUR MODELING...
...AND THEY ASKED ME TO COME TOO, SO NOW I'M IN SOME FASHION MAGAZINES.
THE GUY WHO OWNS THE AGENCY THAT MANAGES THE AMATEUR MODELS SEEMS TO LIKE ME...
...AND HE WANTS TO TRY ME WITH SOME OTHER PROJECTS.

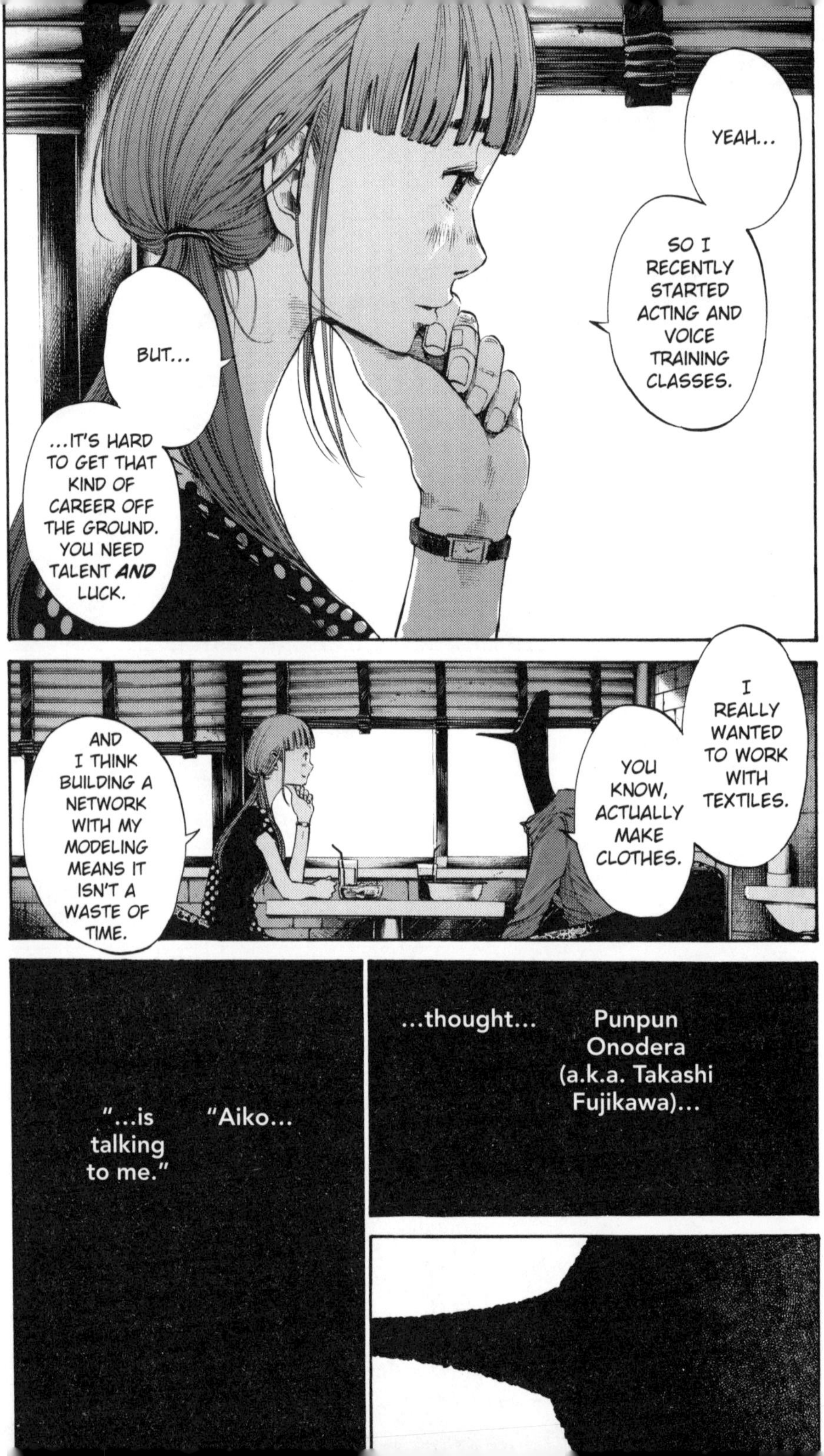
YEAH...
SO I RECENTLY STARTED ACTING AND VOICE TRAINING CLASSES.
BUT...
...IT'S HARD TO GET THAT KIND OF CAREER OFF THE GROUND. YOU NEED TALENT **AND** LUCK.
I REALLY WANTED TO WORK WITH TEXTILES.
YOU KNOW, ACTUALLY MAKE CLOTHES.
AND I THINK BUILDING A NETWORK WITH MY MODELING MEANS IT ISN'T A WASTE OF TIME.
Punpun Onodera (a.k.a. Takashi Fujikawa)...
...thought...
"Aiko...
"...is talking to me."

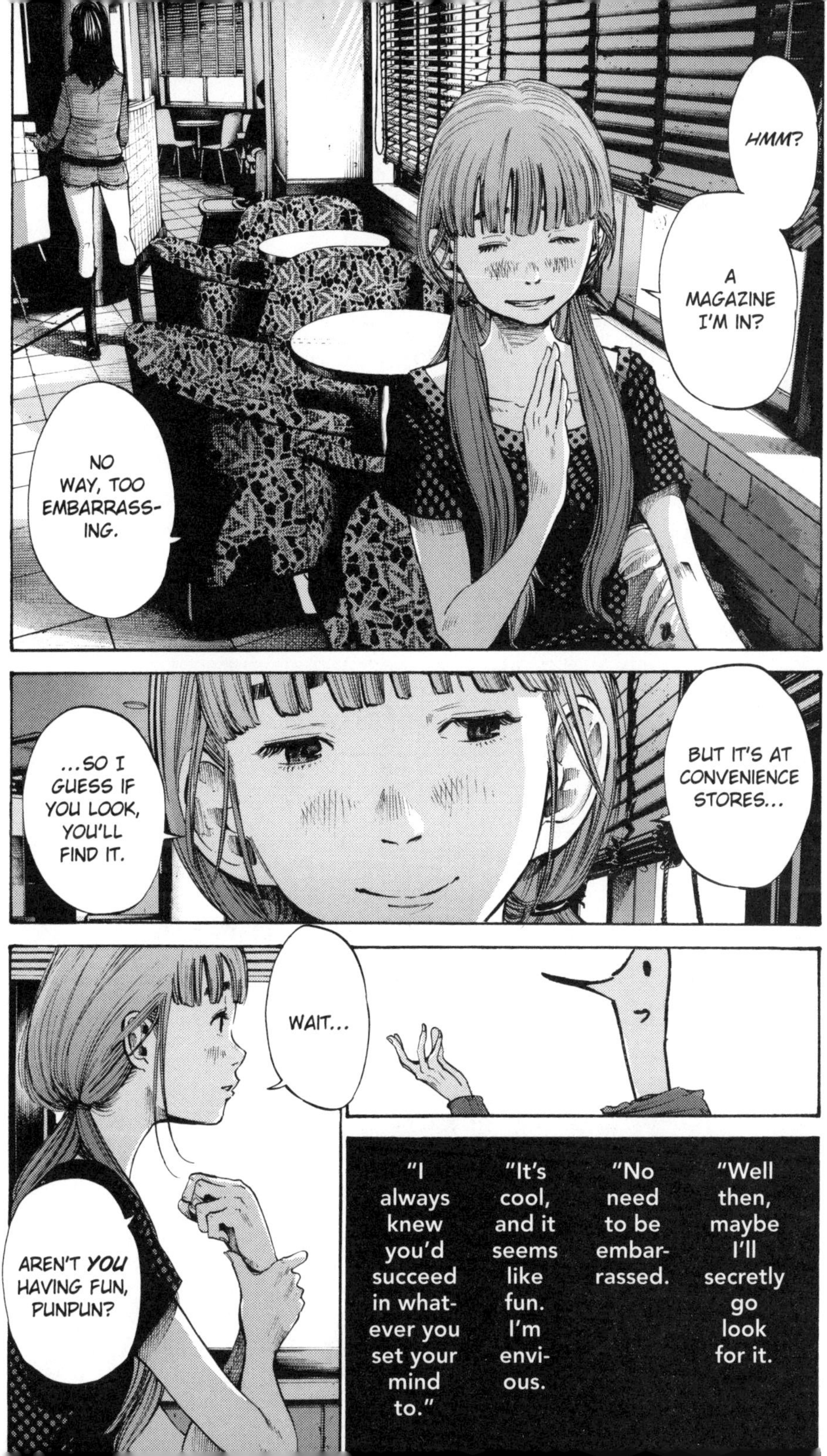
HMM?
A MAGAZINE I'M IN?
NO WAY, TOO EMBARRASSING.
BUT IT'S AT CONVENIENCE STORES...
...SO I GUESS IF YOU LOOK, YOU'LL FIND IT.
"Well then, maybe I'll secretly go look for it.
"No need to be embarrassed.
"It's cool, and it seems like fun. I'm envious.
"I always knew you'd succeed in whatever you set your mind to."
WAIT...
AREN'T *YOU* HAVING FUN, PUNPUN?

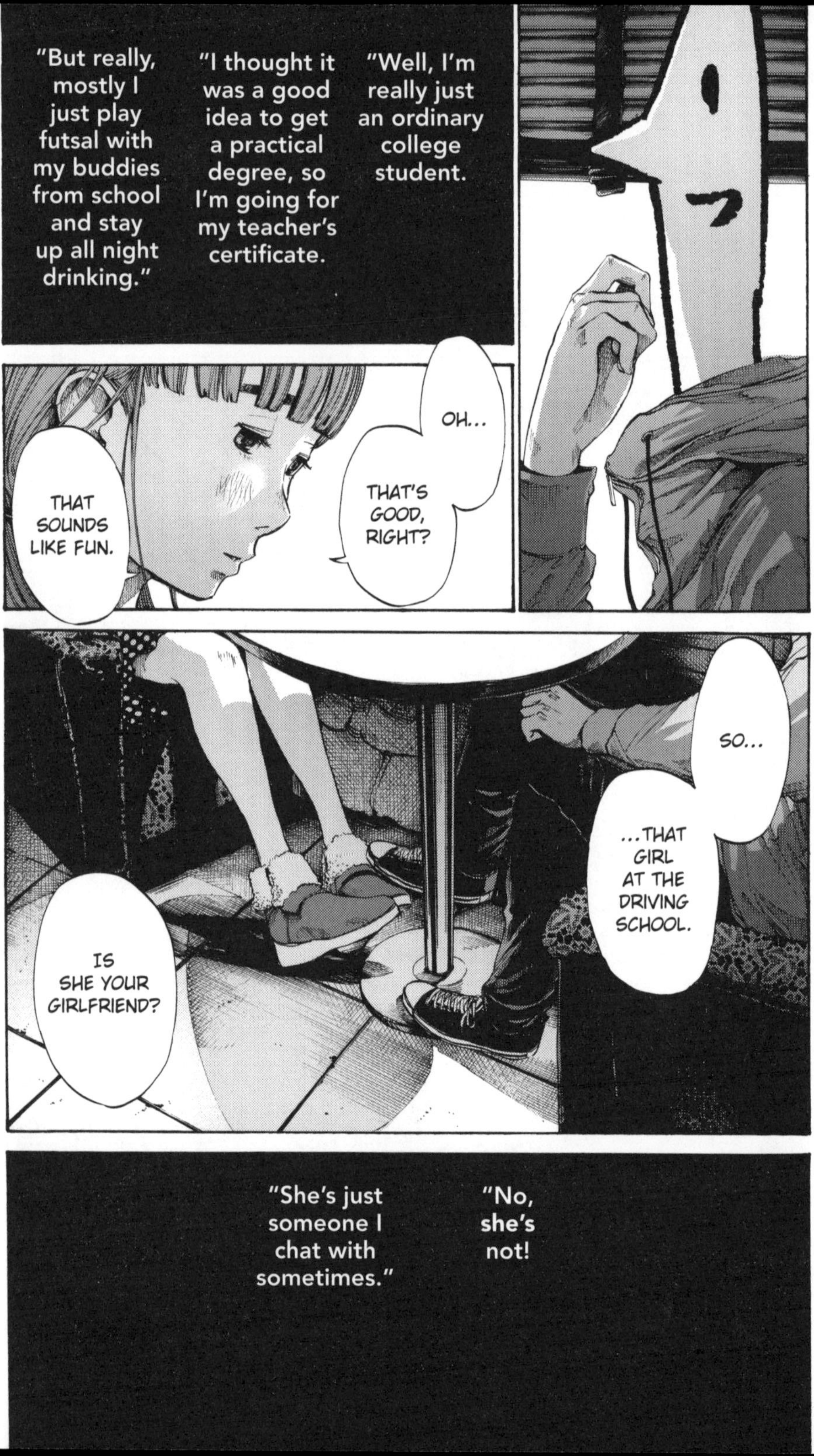
"Well, I'm really just an ordinary college student.
"I thought it was a good idea to get a practical degree, so I'm going for my teacher's certificate.
"But really, mostly I just play futsal with my buddies from school and stay up all night drinking."
OH...
THAT'S GOOD, RIGHT?
THAT SOUNDS LIKE FUN.
SO...
...THAT GIRL AT THE DRIVING SCHOOL.
IS SHE YOUR GIRLFRIEND?
"No, she's not!
"She's just someone I chat with sometimes."

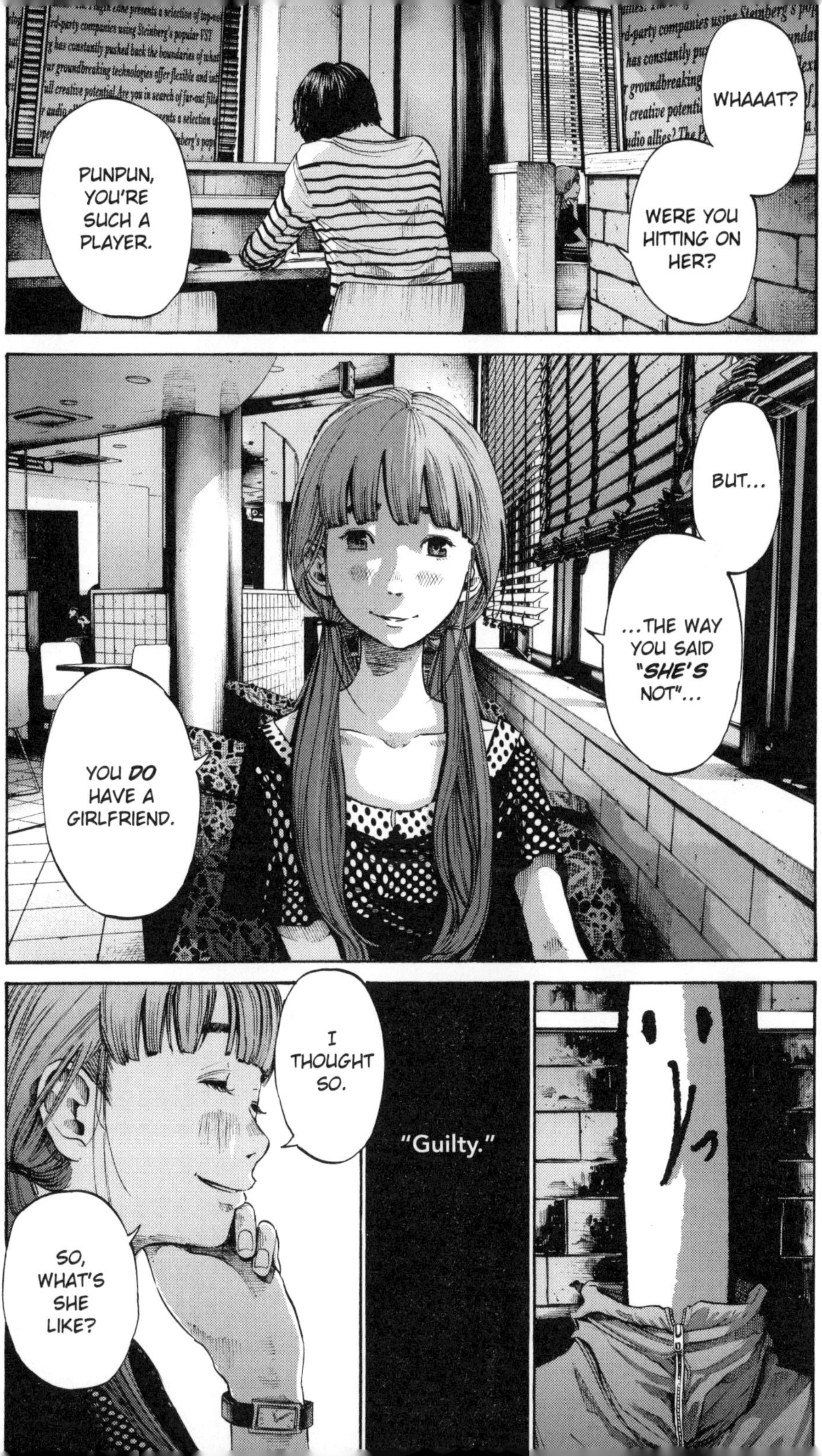
WHAAAT?
WERE YOU HITTING ON HER?
PUNPUN, YOU'RE SUCH A PLAYER.
BUT...
...THE WAY YOU SAID "*SHE'S* NOT"...
YOU *DO* HAVE A GIRLFRIEND.
"Guilty."
I THOUGHT SO.
SO, WHAT'S SHE LIKE?

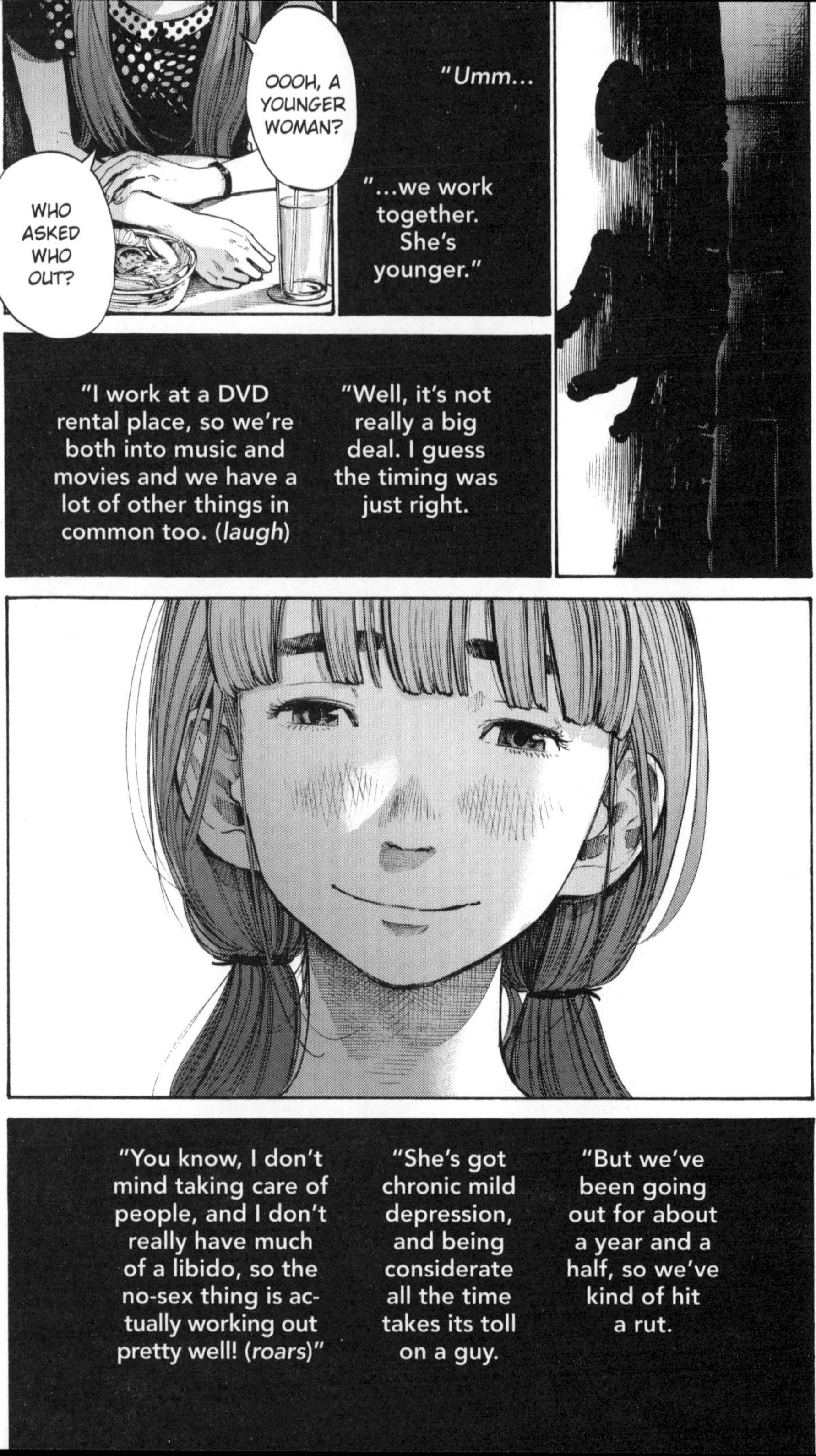
"Umm...
"...we work together. She's younger."
OOOH, A YOUNGER WOMAN?
WHO ASKED WHO OUT?
"Well, it's not really a big deal. I guess the timing was just right.
"I work at a DVD rental place, so we're both into music and movies and we have a lot of other things in common too. (*laugh*)
"But we've been going out for about a year and a half, so we've kind of hit a rut.
"She's got chronic mild depression, and being considerate all the time takes its toll on a guy.
"You know, I don't mind taking care of people, and I don't really have much of a libido, so the no-sex thing is ac-tually working out pretty well! (*roars*)"

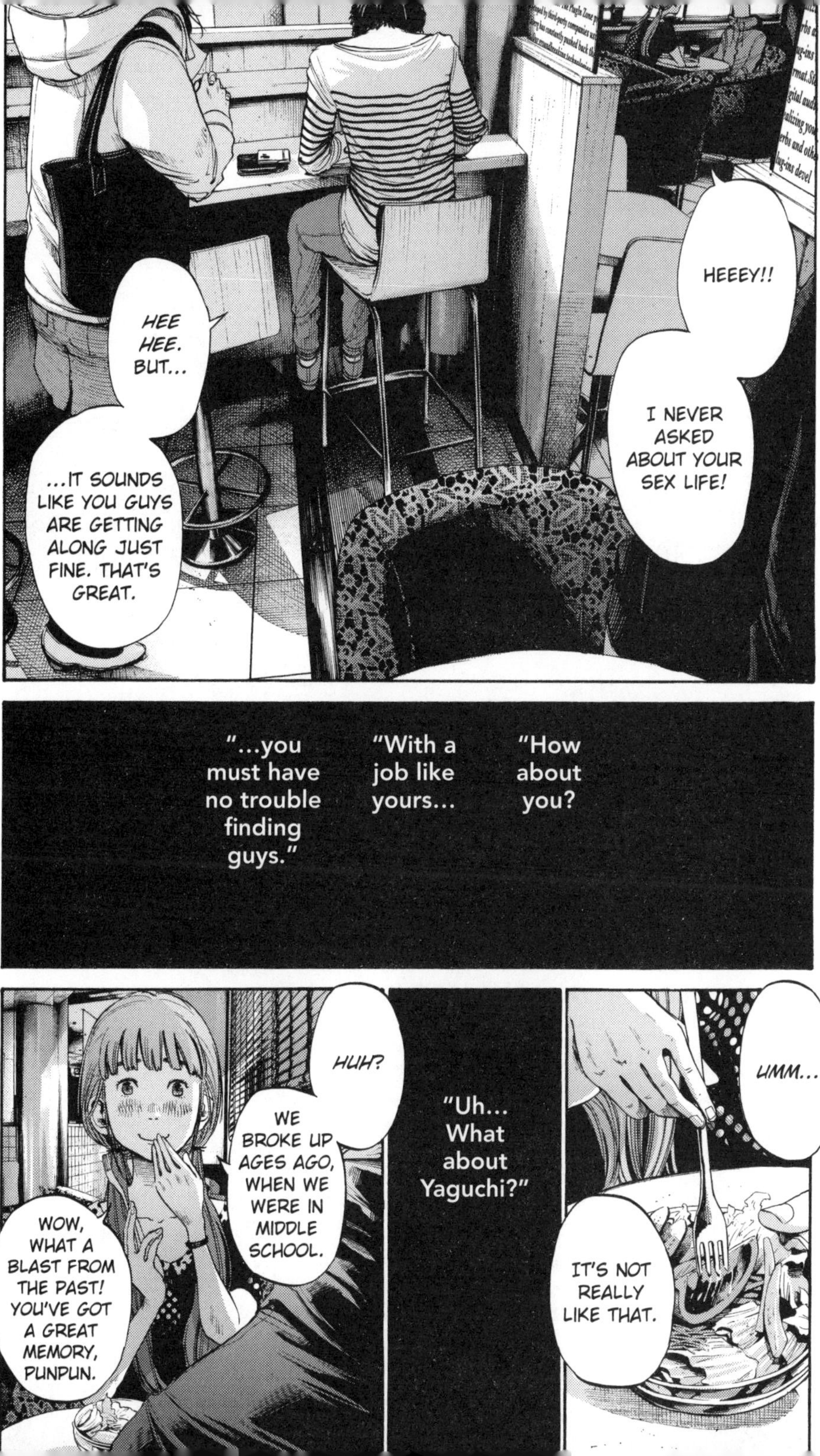
HEEEY!!
I NEVER ASKED ABOUT YOUR SEX LIFE!
HEE HEE. BUT...
...IT SOUNDS LIKE YOU GUYS ARE GETTING ALONG JUST FINE. THAT'S GREAT.
"How about you?
"With a job like yours...
"...you must have no trouble finding guys."
UMM...
IT'S NOT REALLY LIKE THAT.
"Uh... What about Yaguchi?"
HUH?
WE BROKE UP AGES AGO, WHEN WE WERE IN MIDDLE SCHOOL.
WOW, WHAT A BLAST FROM THE PAST! YOU'VE GOT A GREAT MEMORY, PUNPUN.

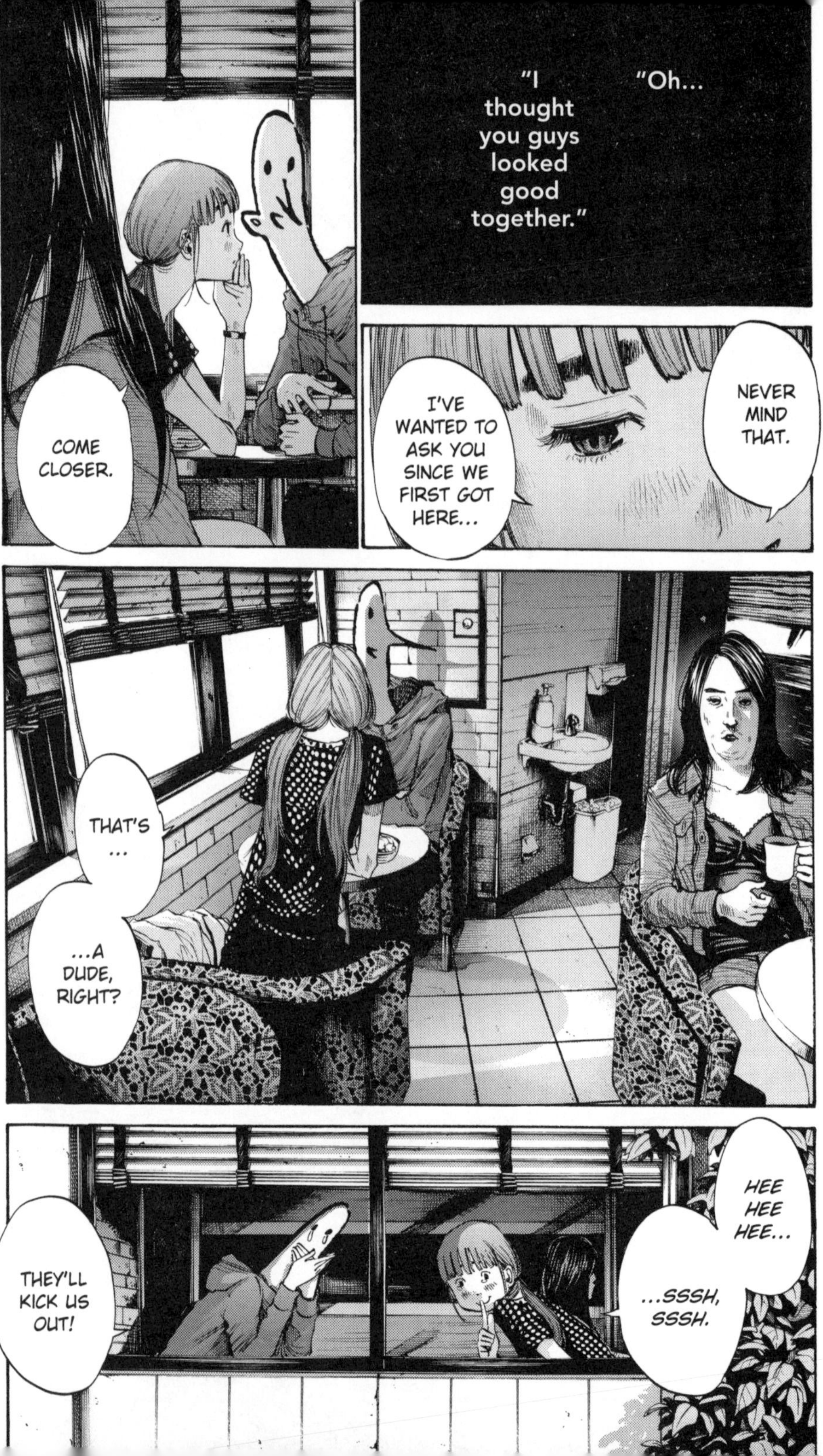
"Oh...
"I thought you guys looked good together."
NEVER MIND THAT.
I'VE WANTED TO ASK YOU SINCE WE FIRST GOT HERE...
COME CLOSER.
THAT'S ...
...A DUDE, RIGHT?
HEE HEE HEE...
...SSSH, SSSH.
THEY'LL KICK US OUT!

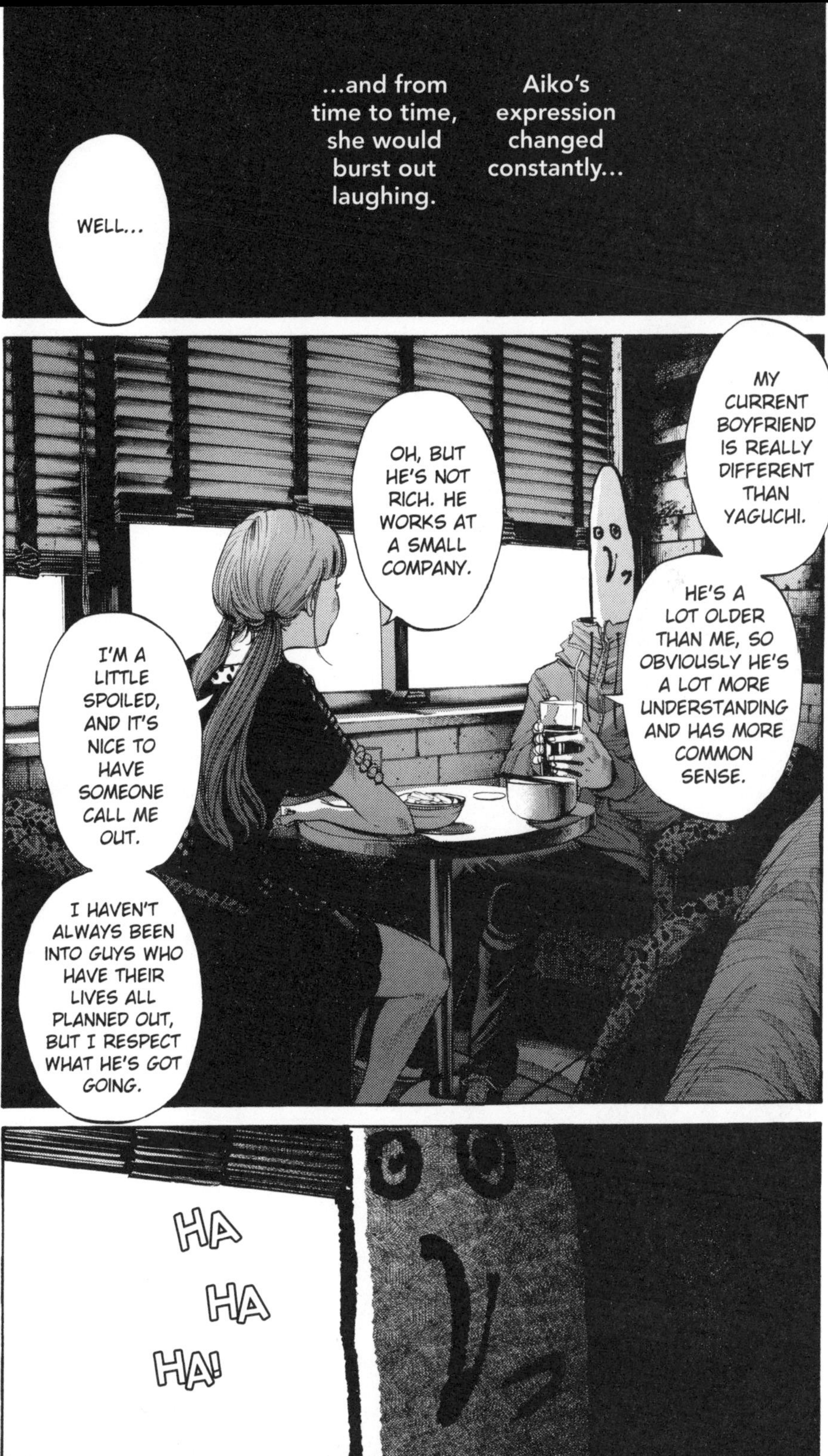
Aiko's expression changed constantly...
...and from time to time, she would burst out laughing.
WELL...
MY CURRENT BOYFRIEND IS REALLY DIFFERENT THAN YAGUCHI.
HE'S A LOT OLDER THAN ME, SO OBVIOUSLY HE'S A LOT MORE UNDERSTANDING AND HAS MORE COMMON SENSE.
OH, BUT HE'S NOT RICH. HE WORKS AT A SMALL COMPANY.
I'M A LITTLE SPOILED, AND IT'S NICE TO HAVE SOMEONE CALL ME OUT.
I HAVEN'T ALWAYS BEEN INTO GUYS WHO HAVE THEIR LIVES ALL PLANNED OUT, BUT I RESPECT WHAT HE'S GOT GOING.
HA
HA
HA!

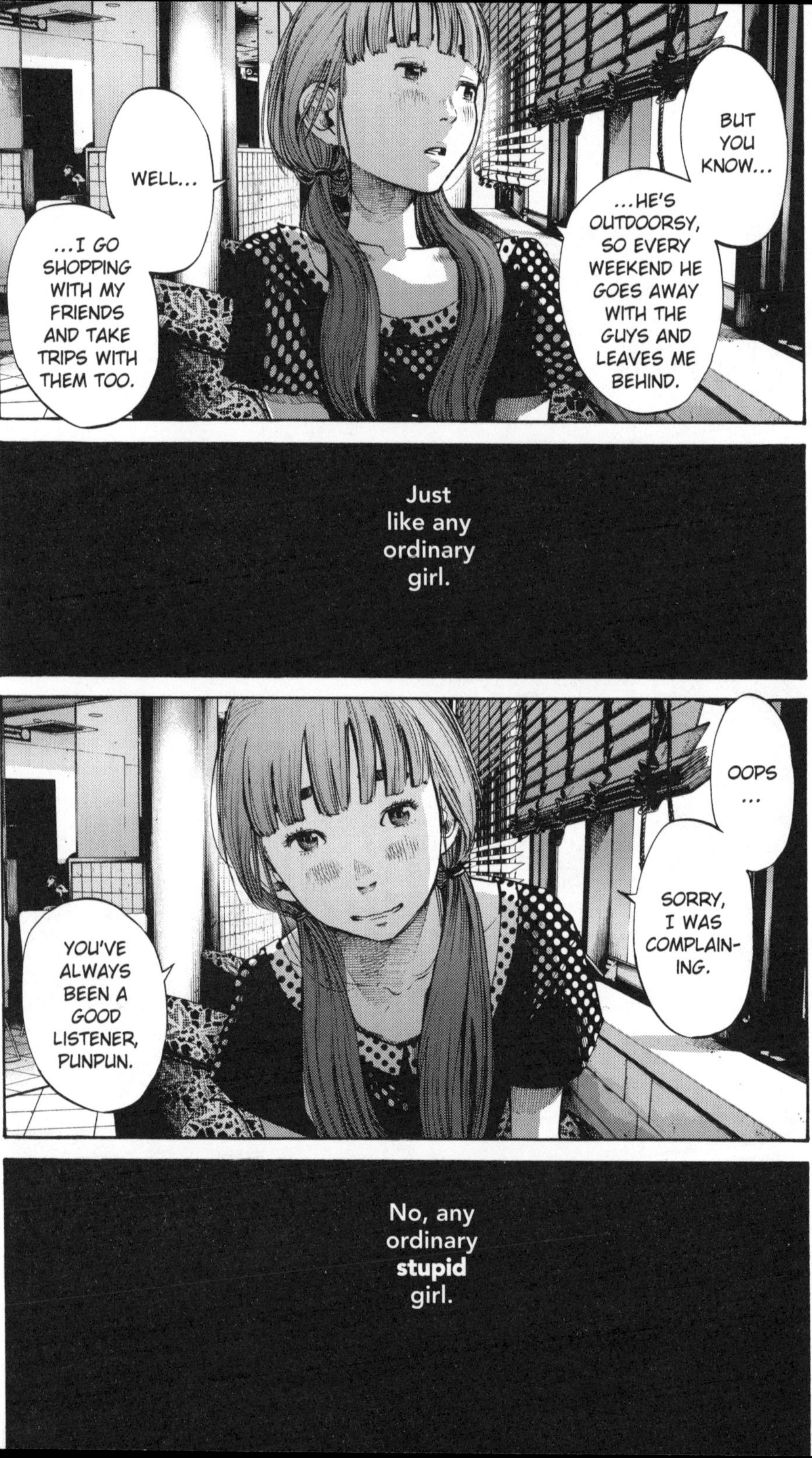
BUT YOU KNOW...
...HE'S OUTDOORSY, SO EVERY WEEKEND HE GOES AWAY WITH THE GUYS AND LEAVES ME BEHIND.
WELL...
...I GO SHOPPING WITH MY FRIENDS AND TAKE TRIPS WITH THEM TOO.
Just like any ordinary girl.
OOPS...
SORRY, I WAS COMPLAIN-ING.
YOU'VE ALWAYS BEEN A GOOD LISTENER, PUNPUN.
No, any ordinary **stupid** girl.

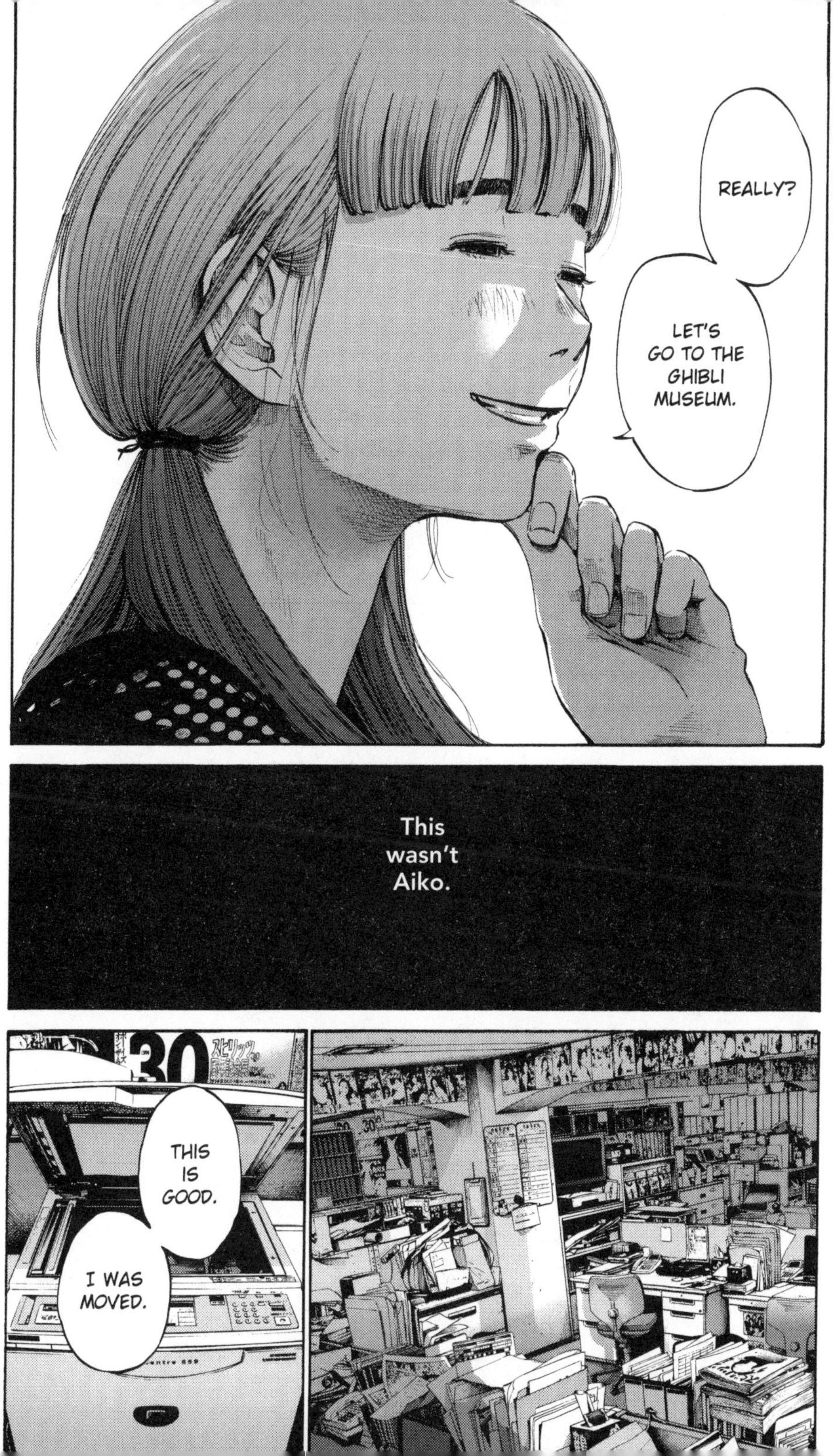
REALLY?
LET'S GO TO THE GHIBLI MUSEUM.
This wasn't Aiko.
THIS IS GOOD.
I WAS MOVED.

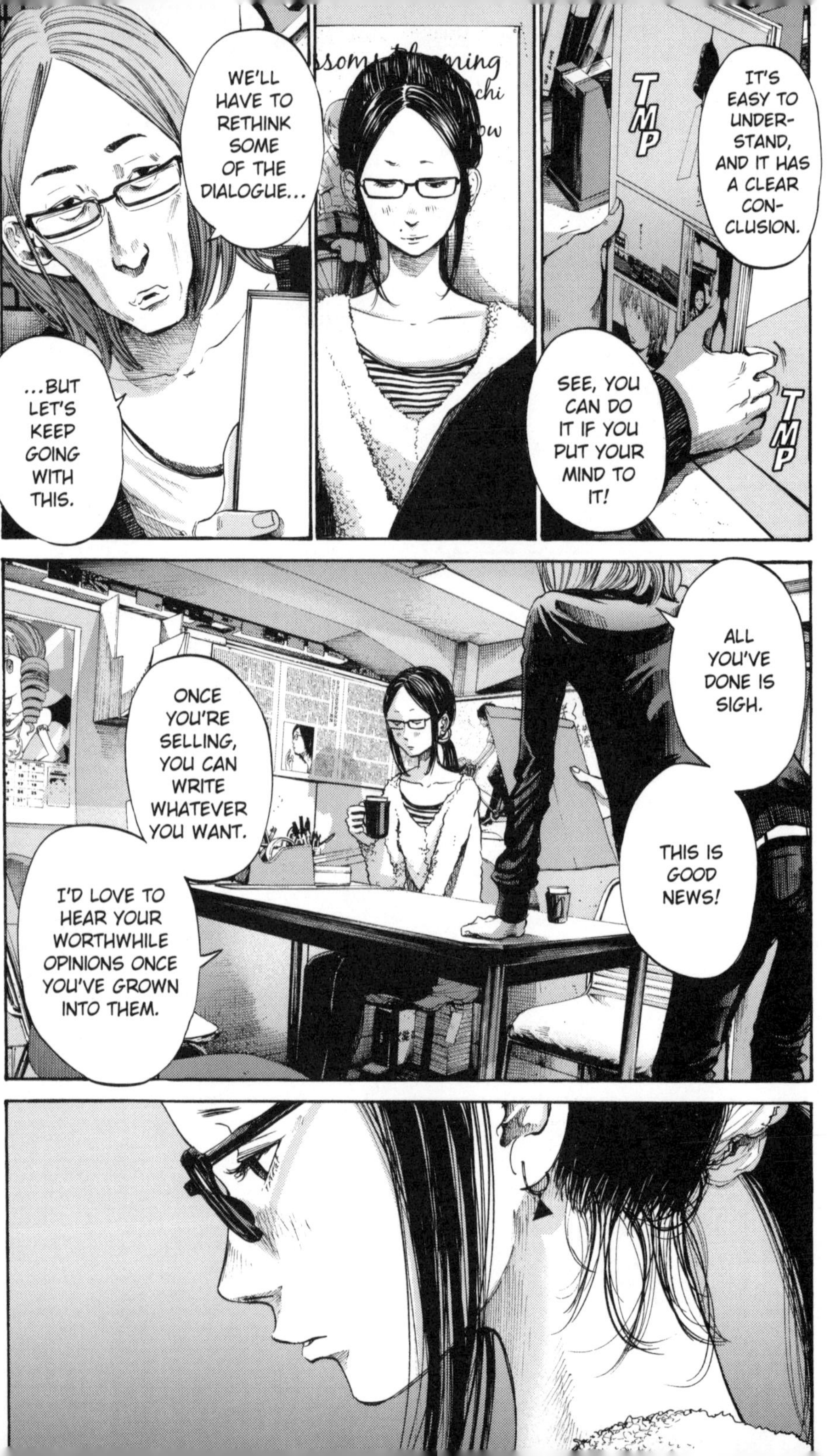
IT'S EASY TO UNDER-STAND, AND IT HAS A CLEAR CON-CLUSION.
TMP
SEE, YOU CAN DO IT IF YOU PUT YOUR MIND TO IT!
TMP
WE'LL HAVE TO RETHINK SOME OF THE DIALOGUE...
...BUT LET'S KEEP GOING WITH THIS.
ALL YOU'VE DONE IS SIGH.
THIS IS GOOD NEWS!
ONCE YOU'RE SELLING, YOU CAN WRITE WHATEVER YOU WANT.
I'D LOVE TO HEAR YOUR WORTHWHILE OPINIONS ONCE YOU'VE GROWN INTO THEM.

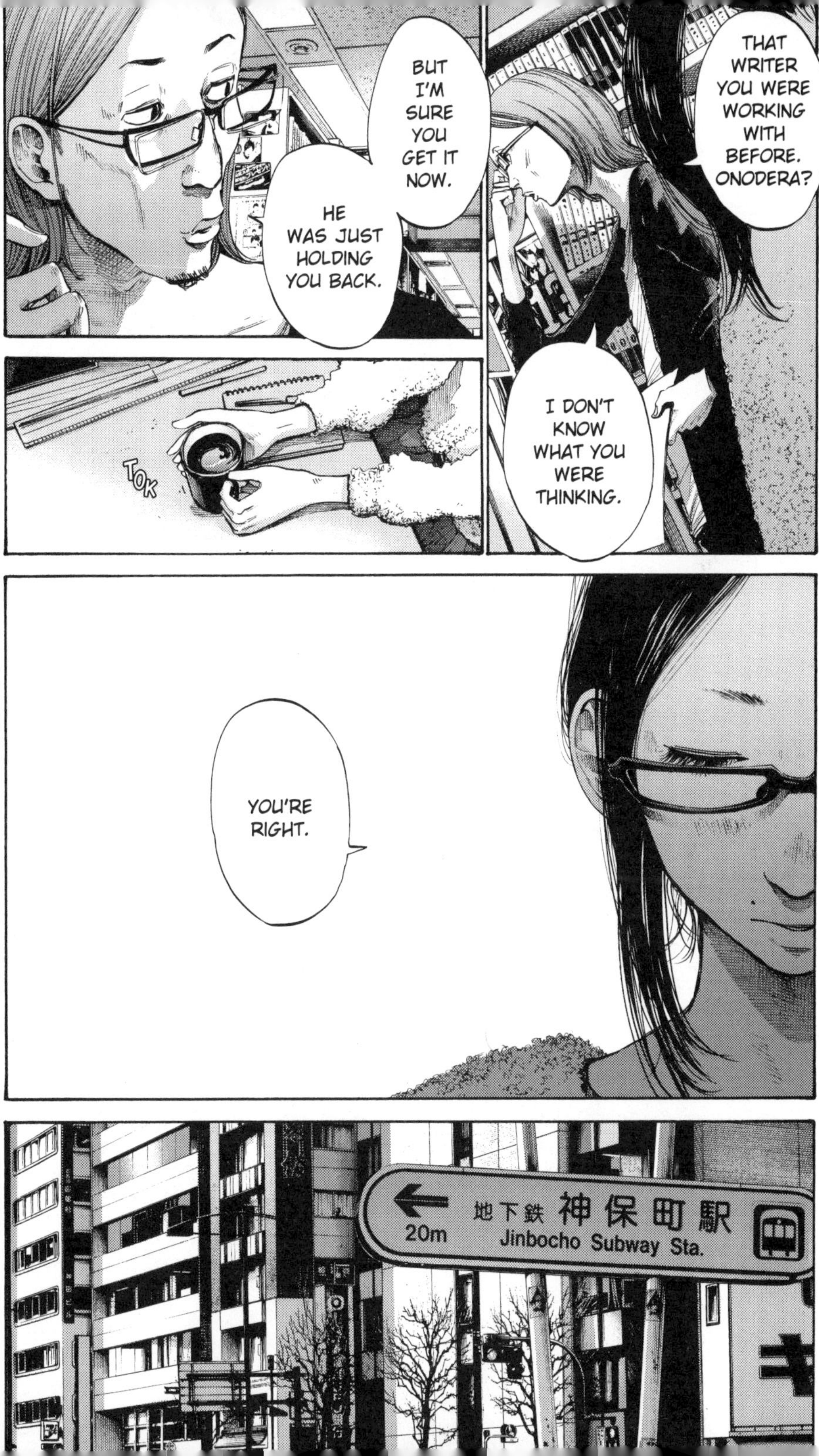
THAT WRITER YOU WERE WORKING WITH BEFORE. ONODERA?
I DON'T KNOW WHAT YOU WERE THINKING.
BUT I'M SURE YOU GET IT NOW.
HE WAS JUST HOLDING YOU BACK.
TOK
YOU'RE RIGHT.
← 20m
地下鉄 神保町駅
Jinbocho Subway Sta.

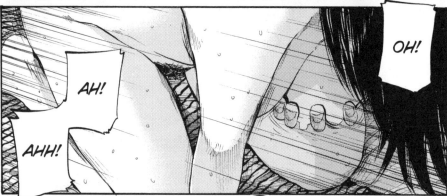

Chapter 102

OH!

AH!

AHH!

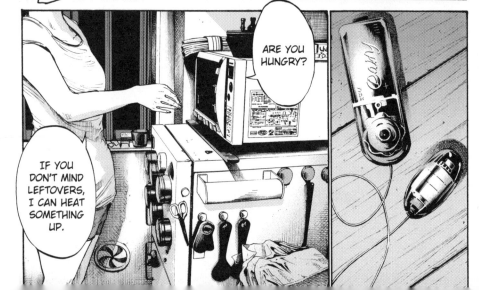

ARE YOU HUNGRY?

IF YOU DON'T MIND LEFTOVERS, I CAN HEAT SOMETHING UP.

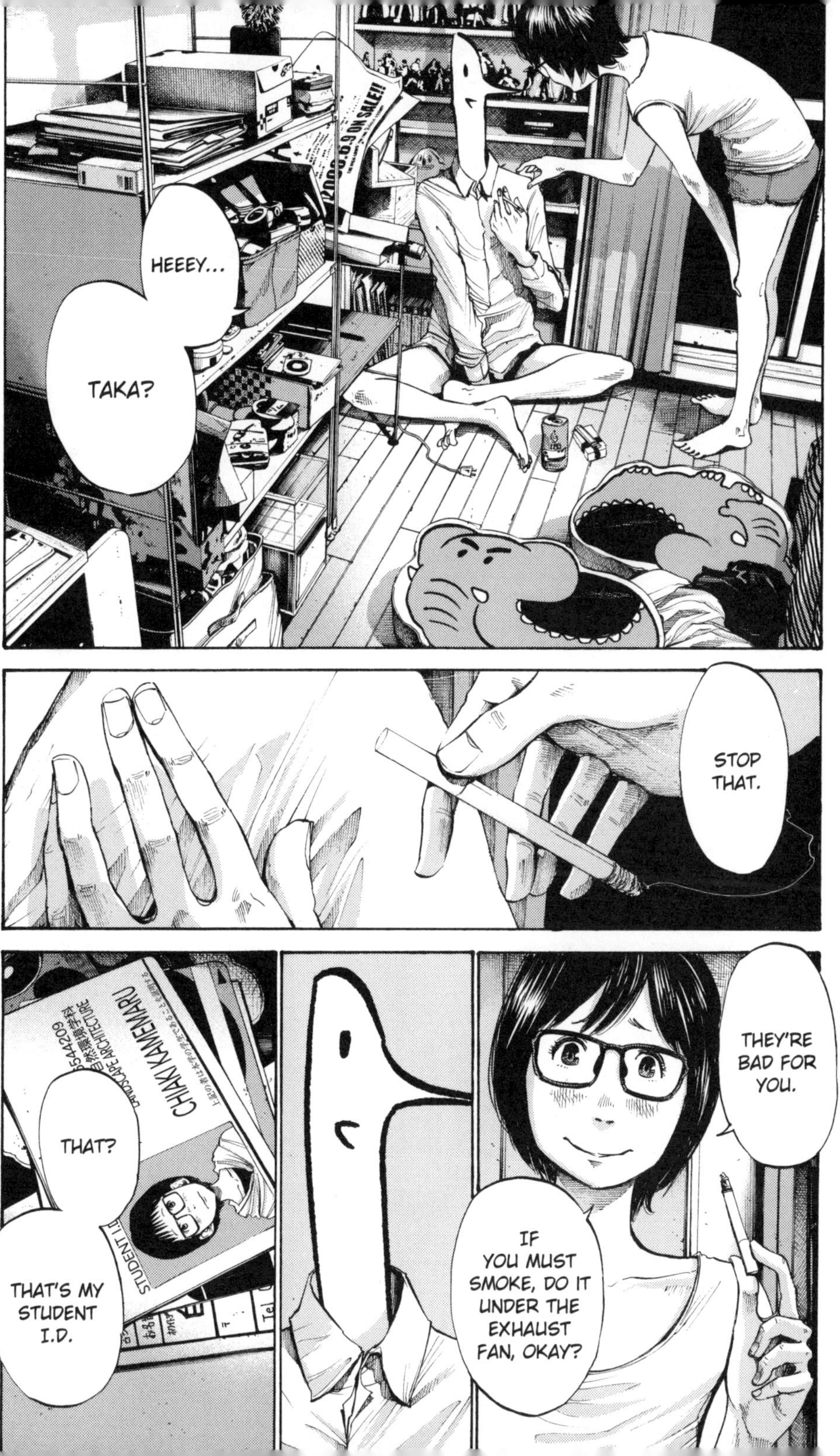
HEEEY...
TAKA?
STOP THAT.
THEY'RE BAD FOR YOU.
IF YOU MUST SMOKE, DO IT UNDER THE EXHAUST FAN, OKAY?
THAT?
THAT'S MY STUDENT I.D.

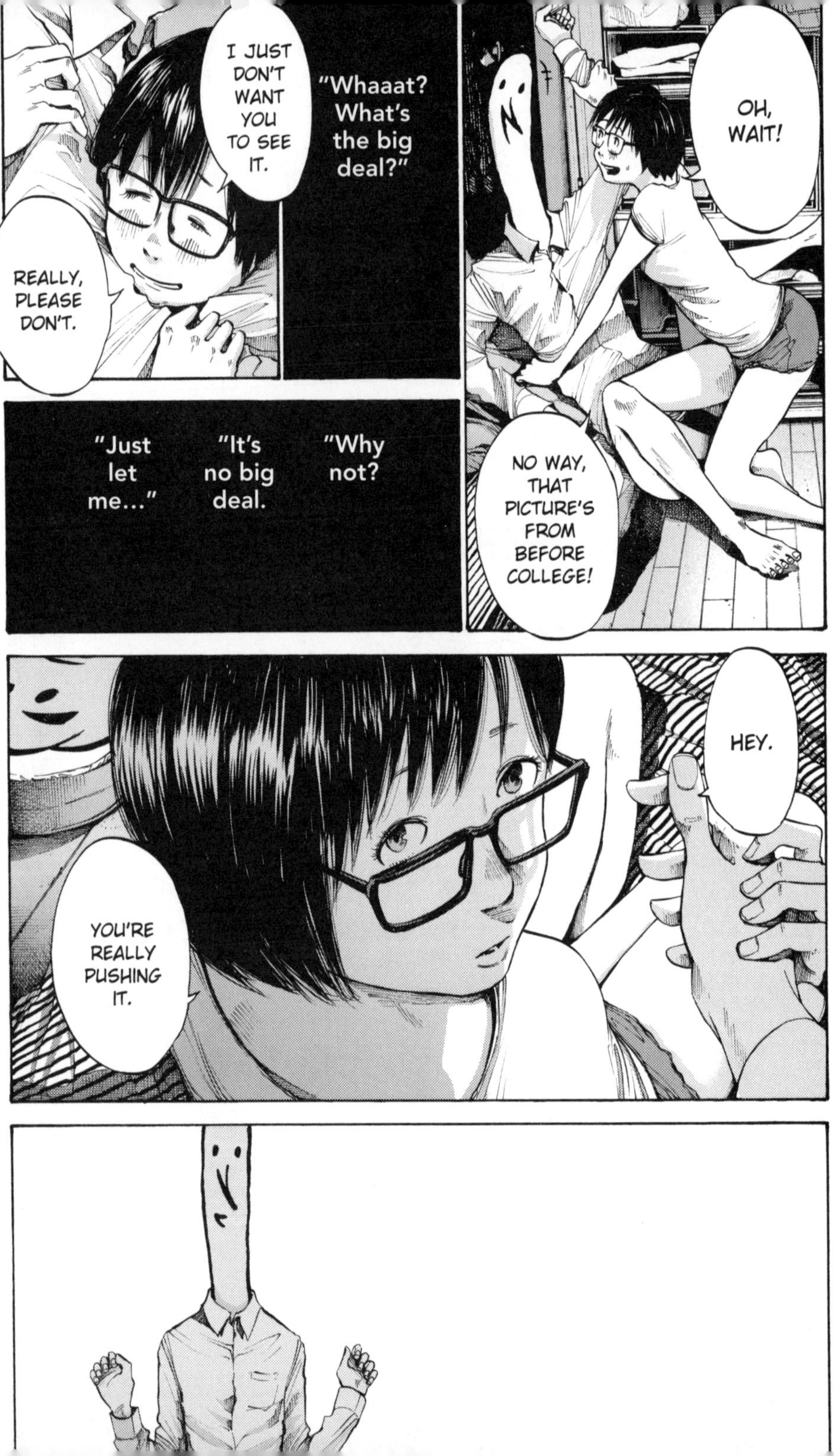
OH, WAIT!
NO WAY, THAT PICTURE'S FROM BEFORE COLLEGE!
"Whaaat? What's the big deal?"
I JUST DON'T WANT YOU TO SEE IT.
REALLY, PLEASE DON'T.
"Why not?
"It's no big deal.
"Just let me..."
HEY.
YOU'RE REALLY PUSHING IT.

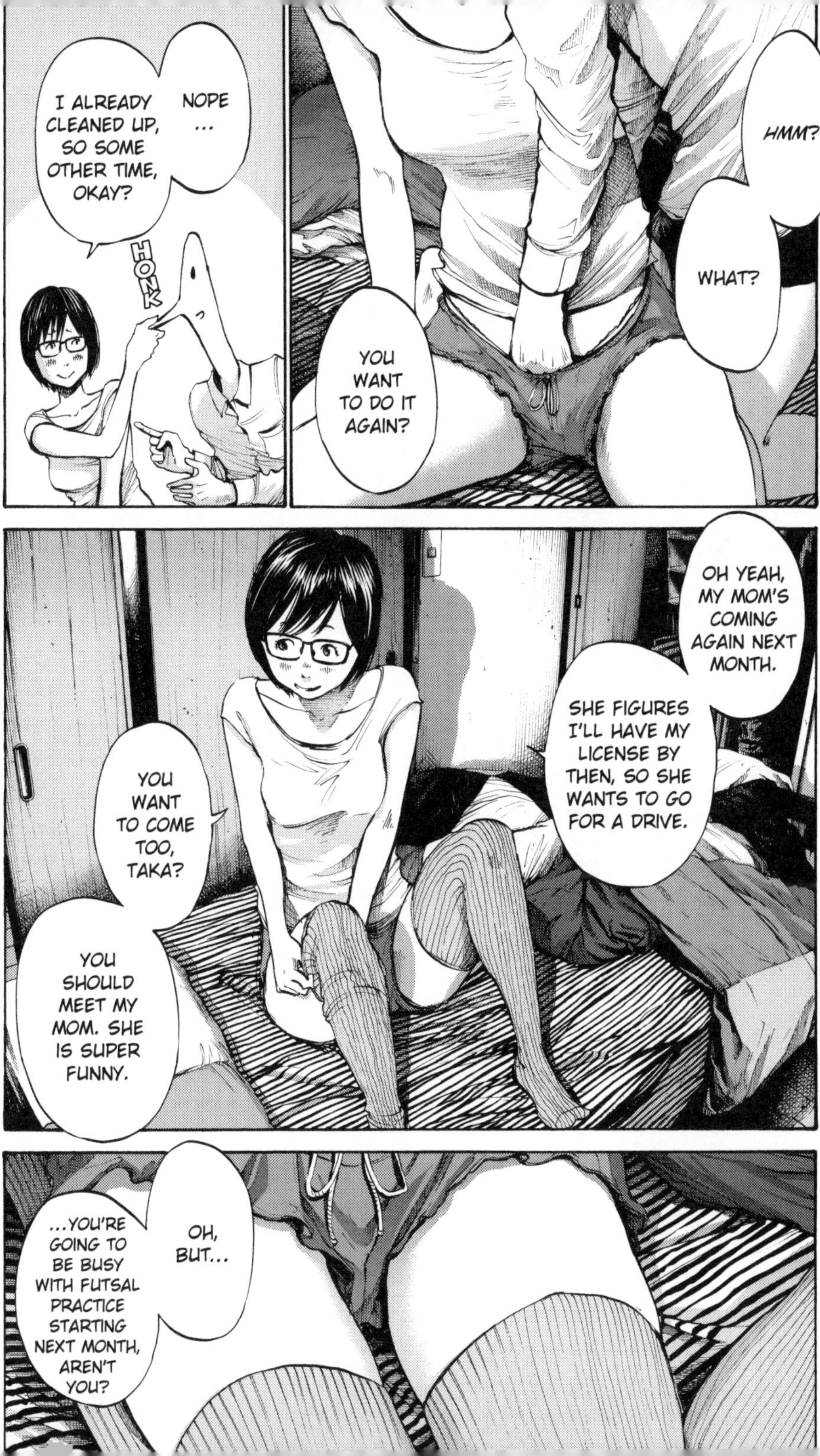
HMM?
WHAT?
YOU WANT TO DO IT AGAIN?
NOPE...
I ALREADY CLEANED UP, SO SOME OTHER TIME, OKAY?
HONK
OH YEAH, MY MOM'S COMING AGAIN NEXT MONTH.
SHE FIGURES I'LL HAVE MY LICENSE BY THEN, SO SHE WANTS TO GO FOR A DRIVE.
YOU WANT TO COME TOO, TAKA?
YOU SHOULD MEET MY MOM. SHE IS SUPER FUNNY.
OH, BUT...
...YOU'RE GOING TO BE BUSY WITH FUTSAL PRACTICE STARTING NEXT MONTH, AREN'T YOU?

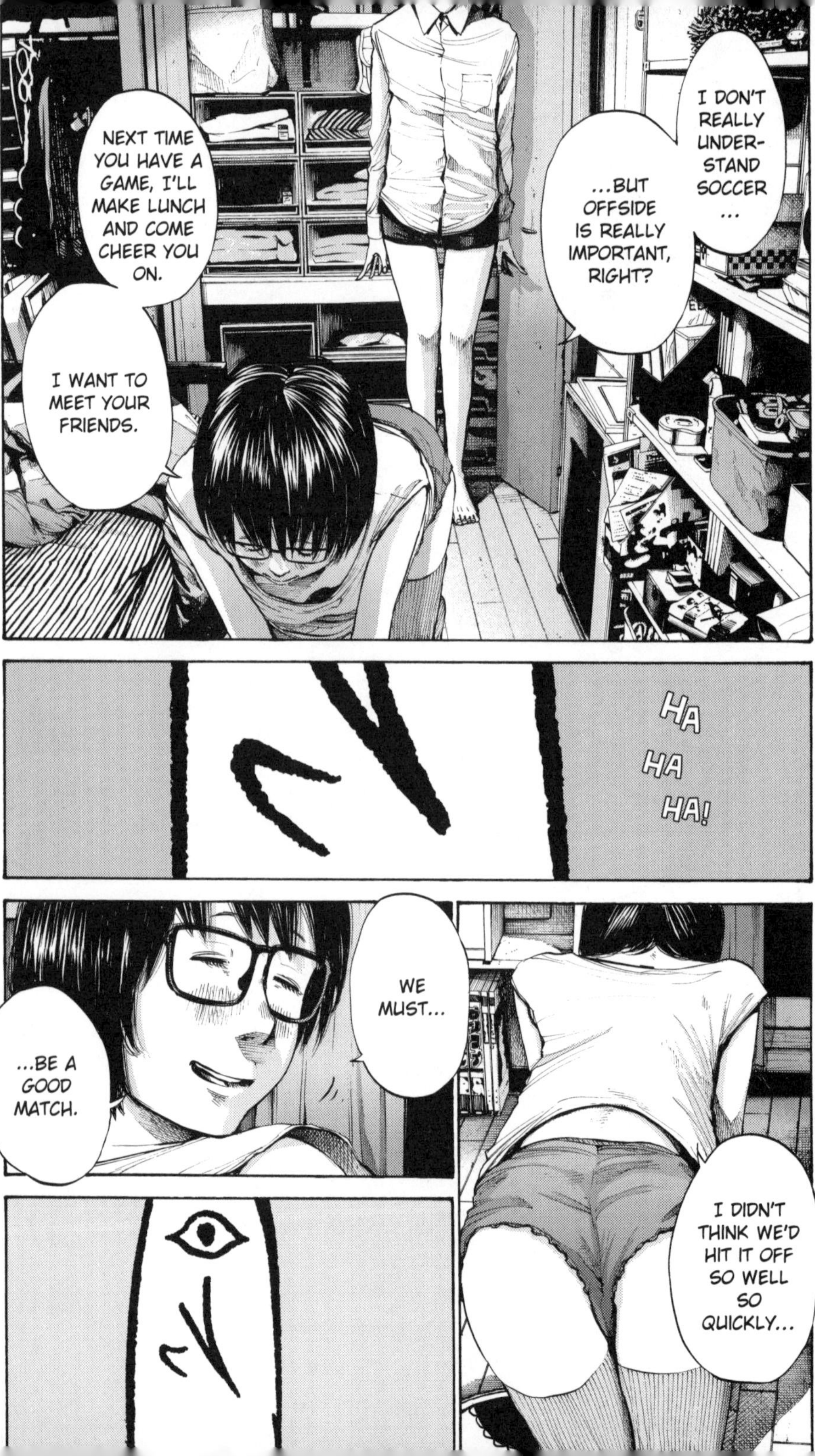
I DON'T REALLY UNDER-STAND SOCCER...
...BUT OFFSIDE IS REALLY IMPORTANT, RIGHT?
NEXT TIME YOU HAVE A GAME, I'LL MAKE LUNCH AND COME CHEER YOU ON.
I WANT TO MEET YOUR FRIENDS.
HA HA HA!
I DIDN'T THINK WE'D HIT IT OFF SO WELL SO QUICKLY...
WE MUST...
...BE A GOOD MATCH.

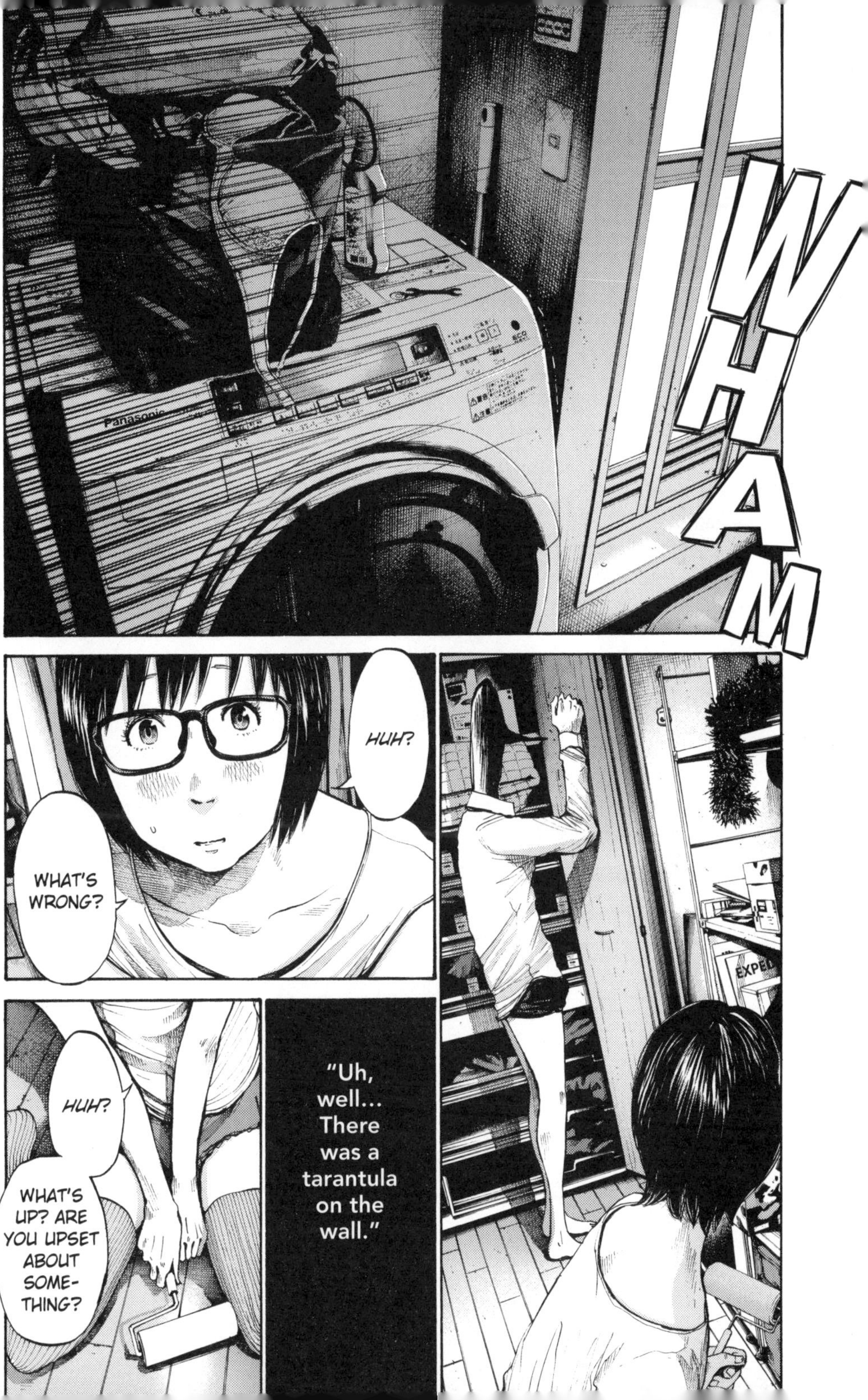
Panasonic
WHAM
HUH?
WHAT'S WRONG?
"Uh, well... There was a tarantula on the wall."
HUH?
WHAT'S UP? ARE YOU UPSET ABOUT SOME-THING?

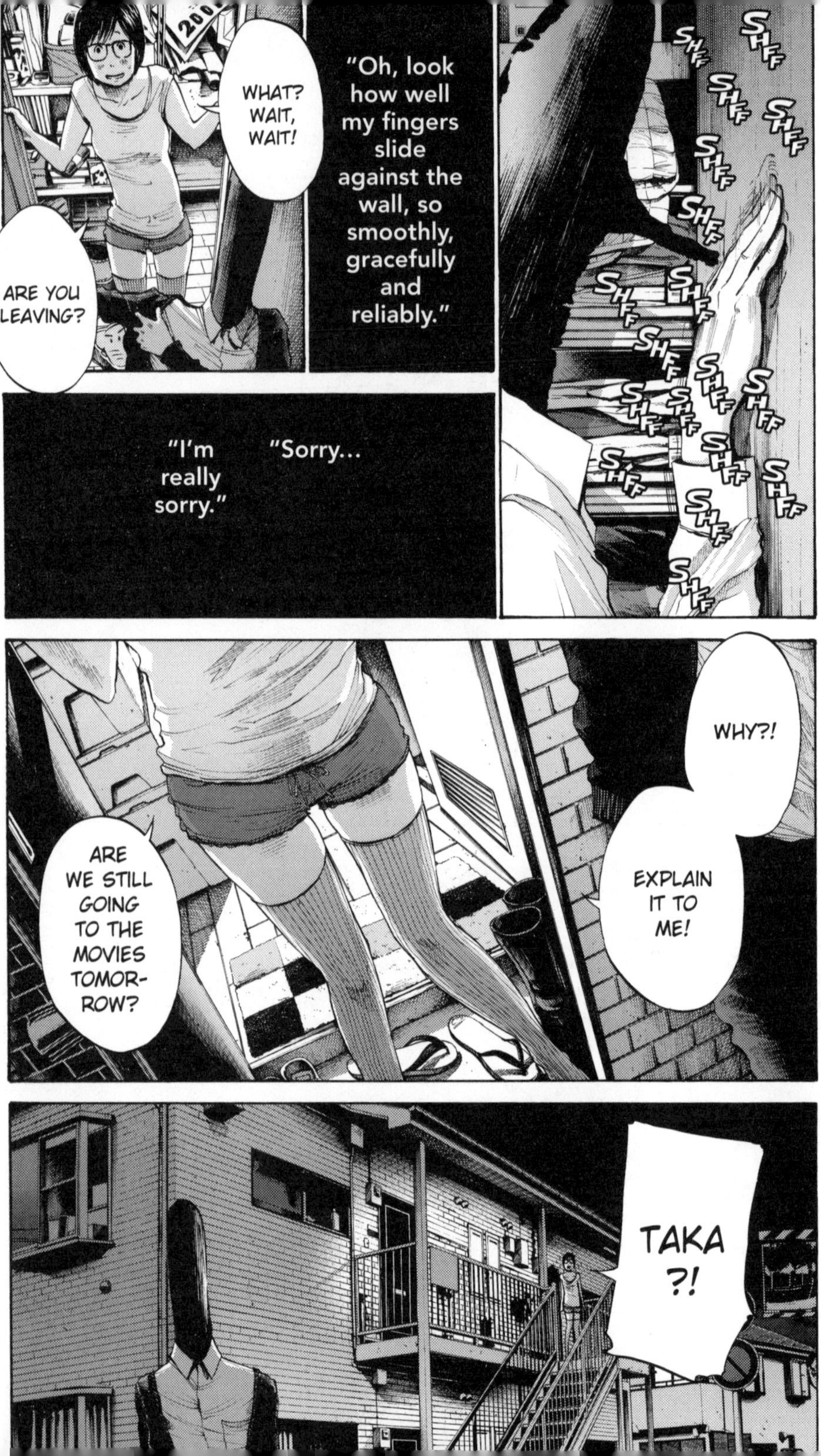
SHFF SHFF SHFF SHFF SHFF SHFF SHFF SHFF SHFF SHFF SHFF SHFF SHFF SHFF SHFF SHFF SHFF
"Oh, look how well my fingers slide against the wall, so smoothly, gracefully and reliably."
WHAT? WAIT, WAIT!
ARE YOU LEAVING?
"Sorry...
"I'm really sorry."
WHY?!
EXPLAIN IT TO ME!
ARE WE STILL GOING TO THE MOVIES TOMOR-ROW?
TAKA ?!

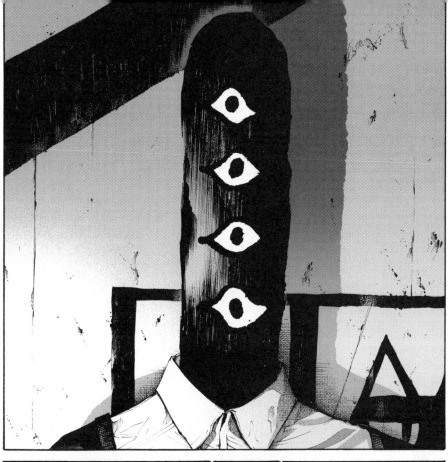

"Wrong."

"It's
not like
that at
all."

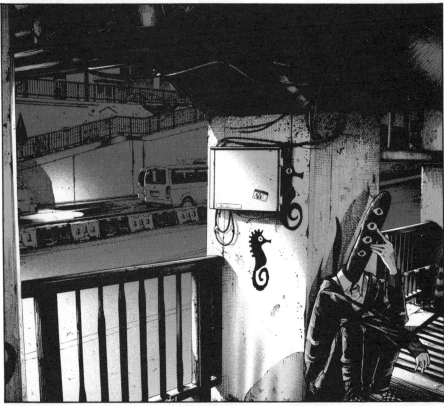

That's...

...what
Punpun
thought.

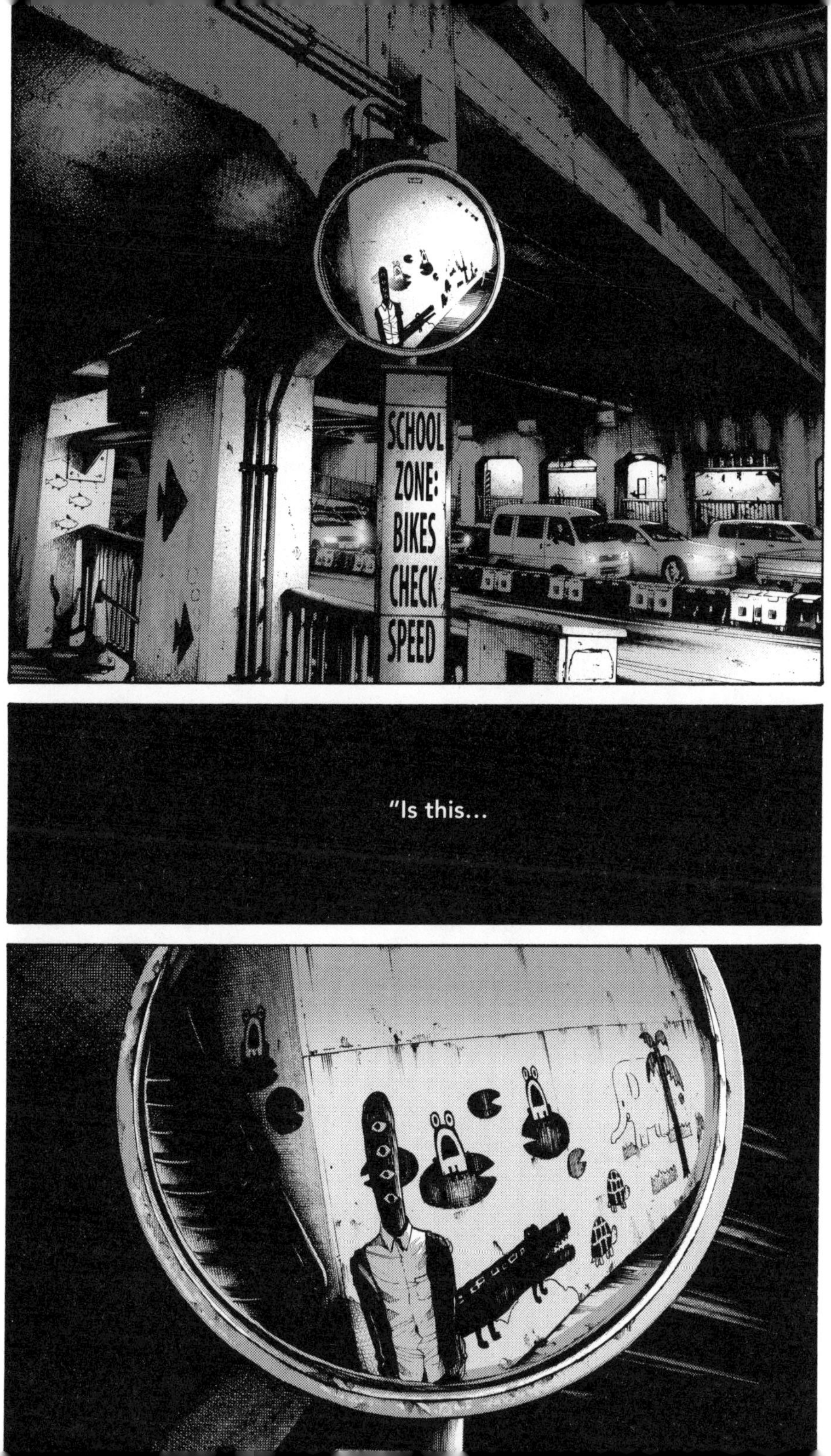
SCHOOL ZONE: BIKES CHECK SPEED
"Is this...

"...what
my face
looks
like?"

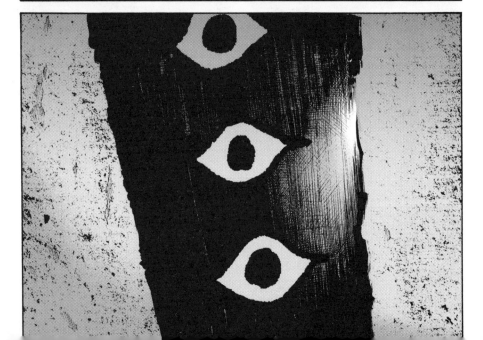

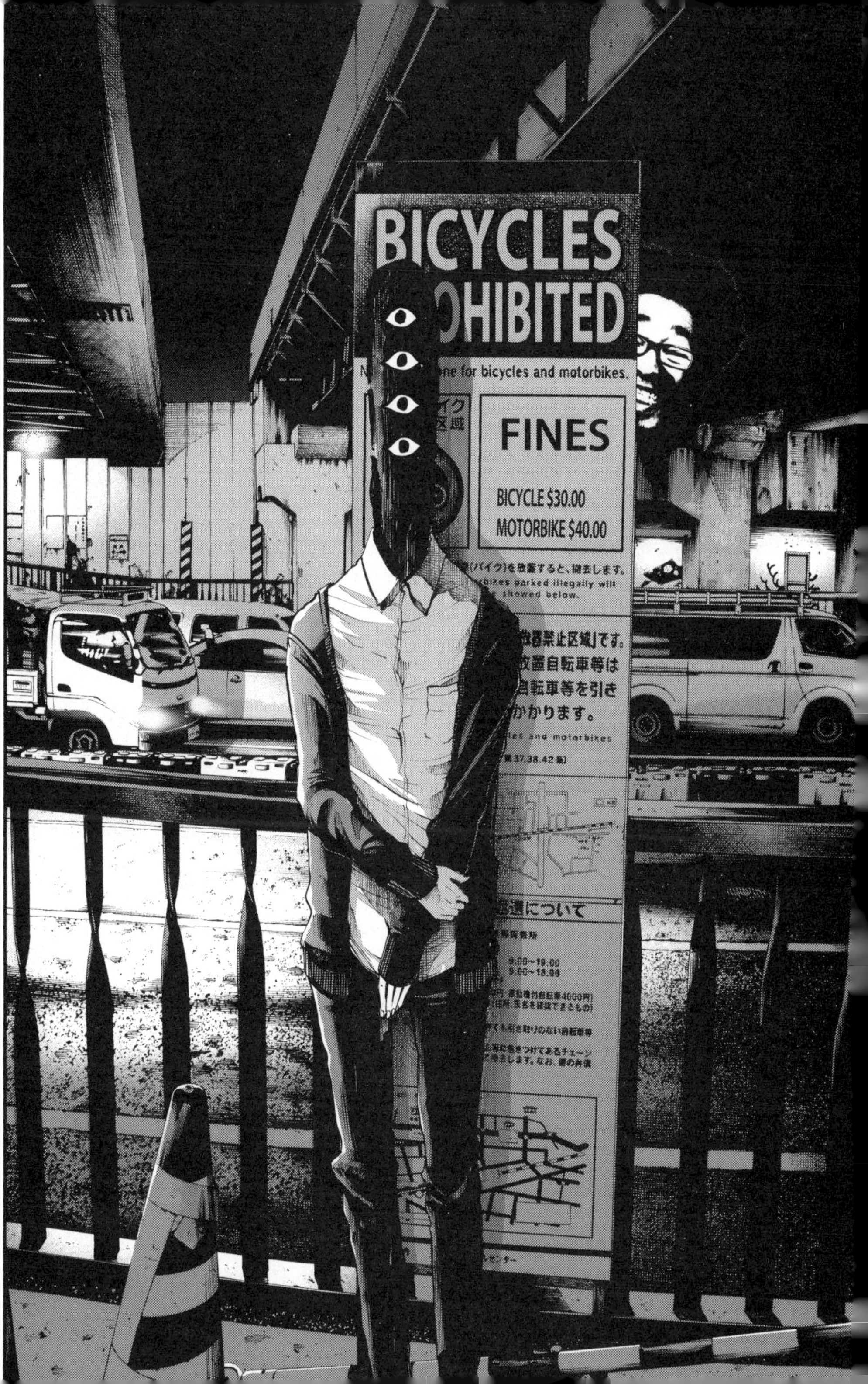

BICYCLES
OHIBITED
ne for bicycles and motorbikes.
FINES
BICYCLE $30.00
MOTORBIKE $40.00

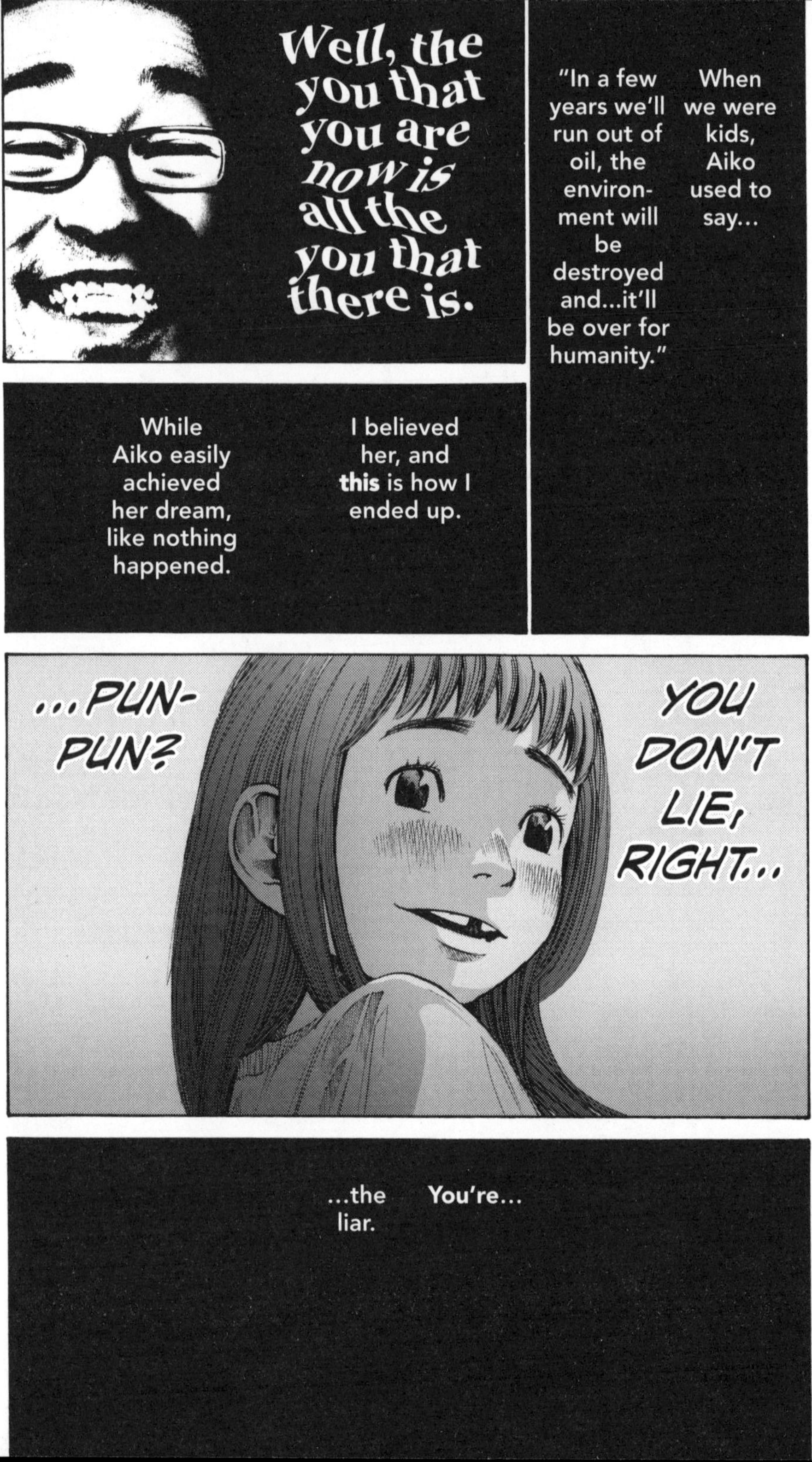
When we were kids, Aiko used to say...
"In a few years we'll run out of oil, the environment will be destroyed and...it'll be over for humanity."
Well, the you that you are *now is* all the you that there is.
I believed her, and **this** is how I ended up.
While Aiko easily achieved her dream, like nothing happened.
YOU DON'T LIE, RIGHT...
...PUN-PUN?
You're...
...the liar.

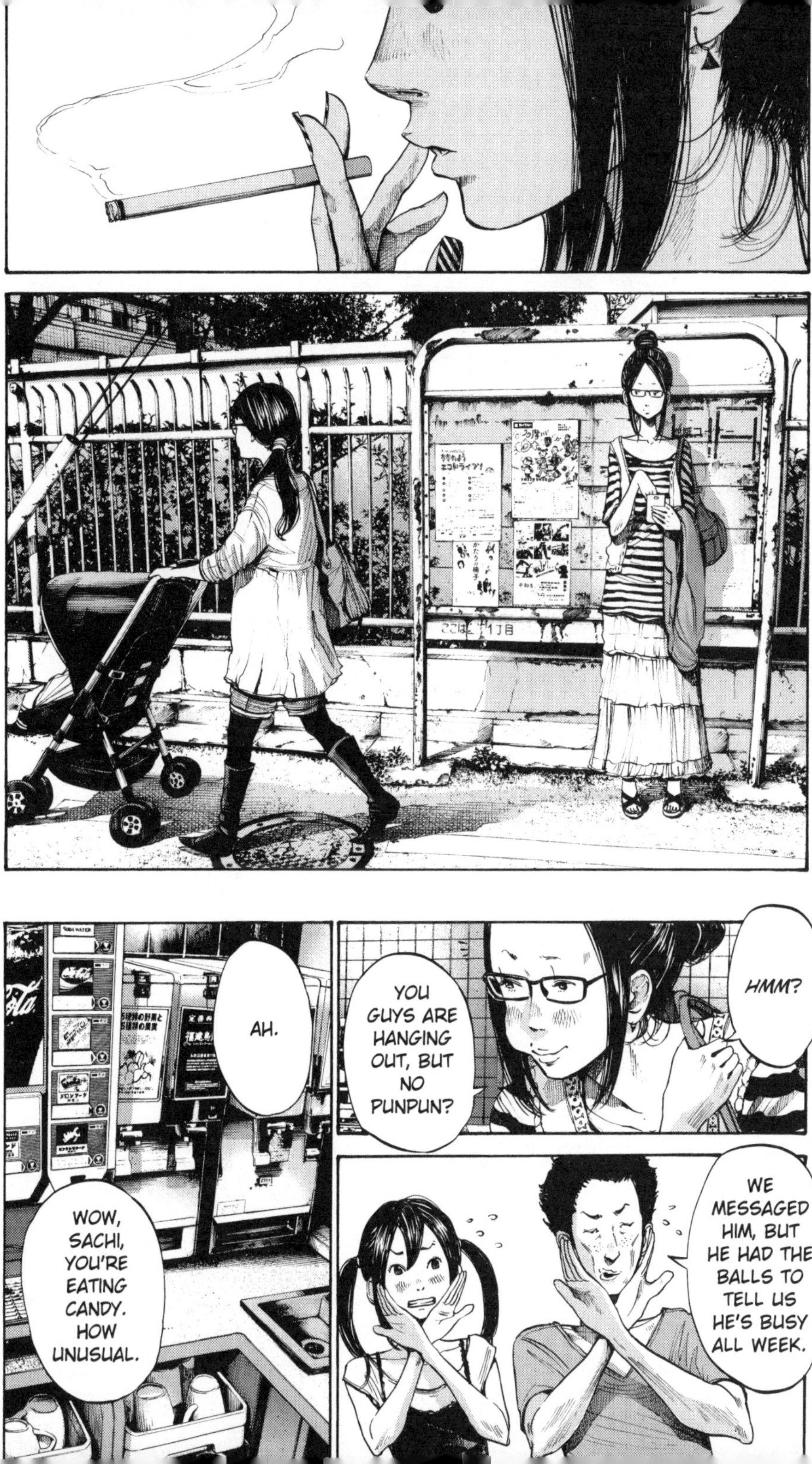
HMM?
YOU GUYS ARE HANGING OUT, BUT NO PUNPUN?
WE MESSAGED HIM, BUT HE HAD THE BALLS TO TELL US HE'S BUSY ALL WEEK.
AH.
WOW, SACHI, YOU'RE EATING CANDY. HOW UNUSUAL.

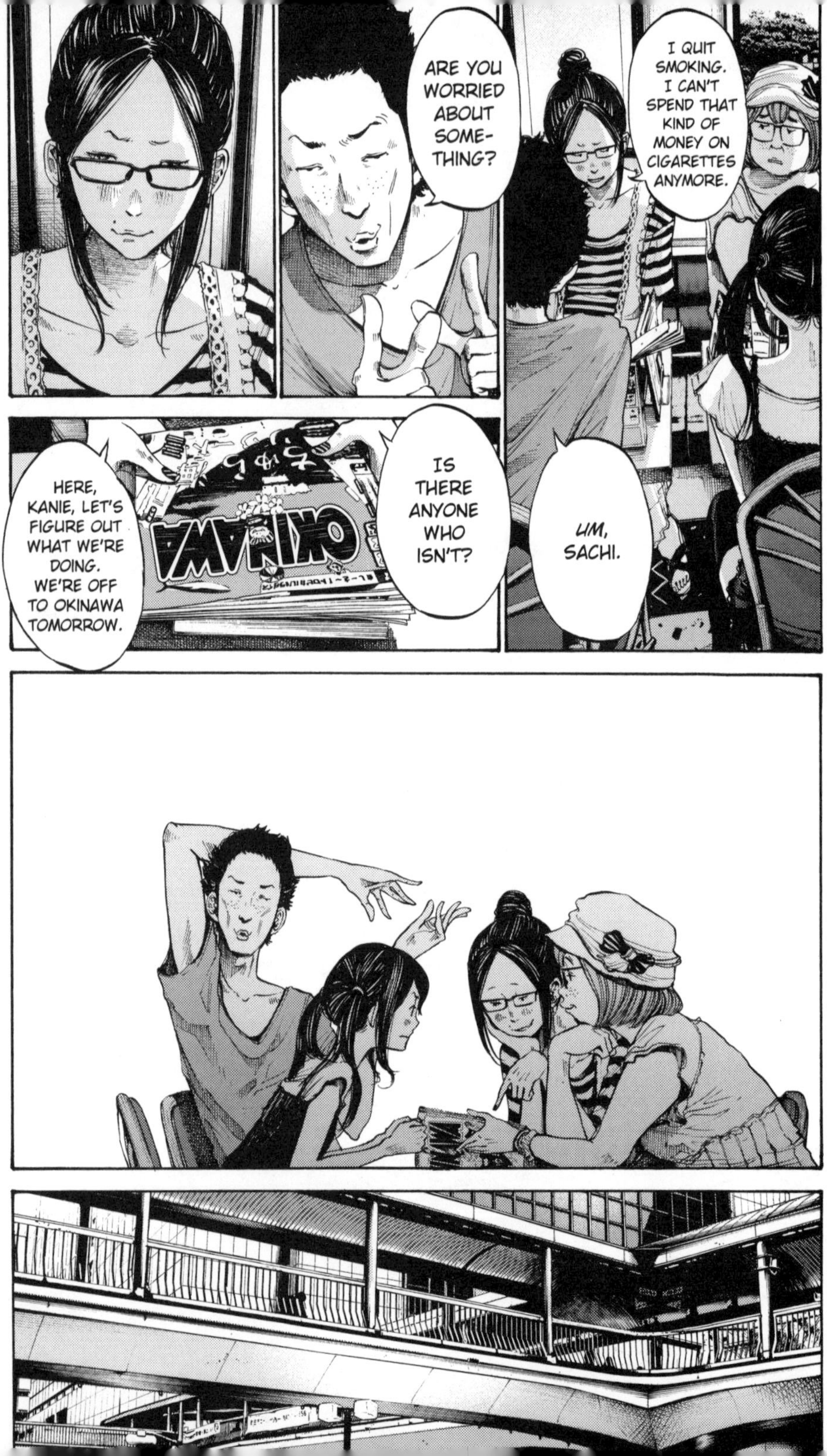
I QUIT SMOKING. I CAN'T SPEND THAT KIND OF MONEY ON CIGARETTES ANYMORE.
ARE YOU WORRIED ABOUT SOME-THING?
UM, SACHI.
IS THERE ANYONE WHO ISN'T?
HERE, KANIE, LET'S FIGURE OUT WHAT WE'RE DOING. WE'RE OFF TO OKINAWA TOMORROW.

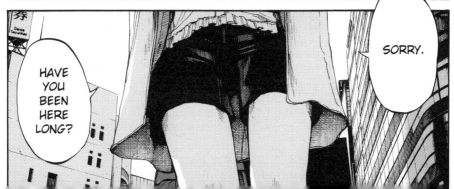

SORRY.

HAVE
YOU
BEEN
HERE
LONG?

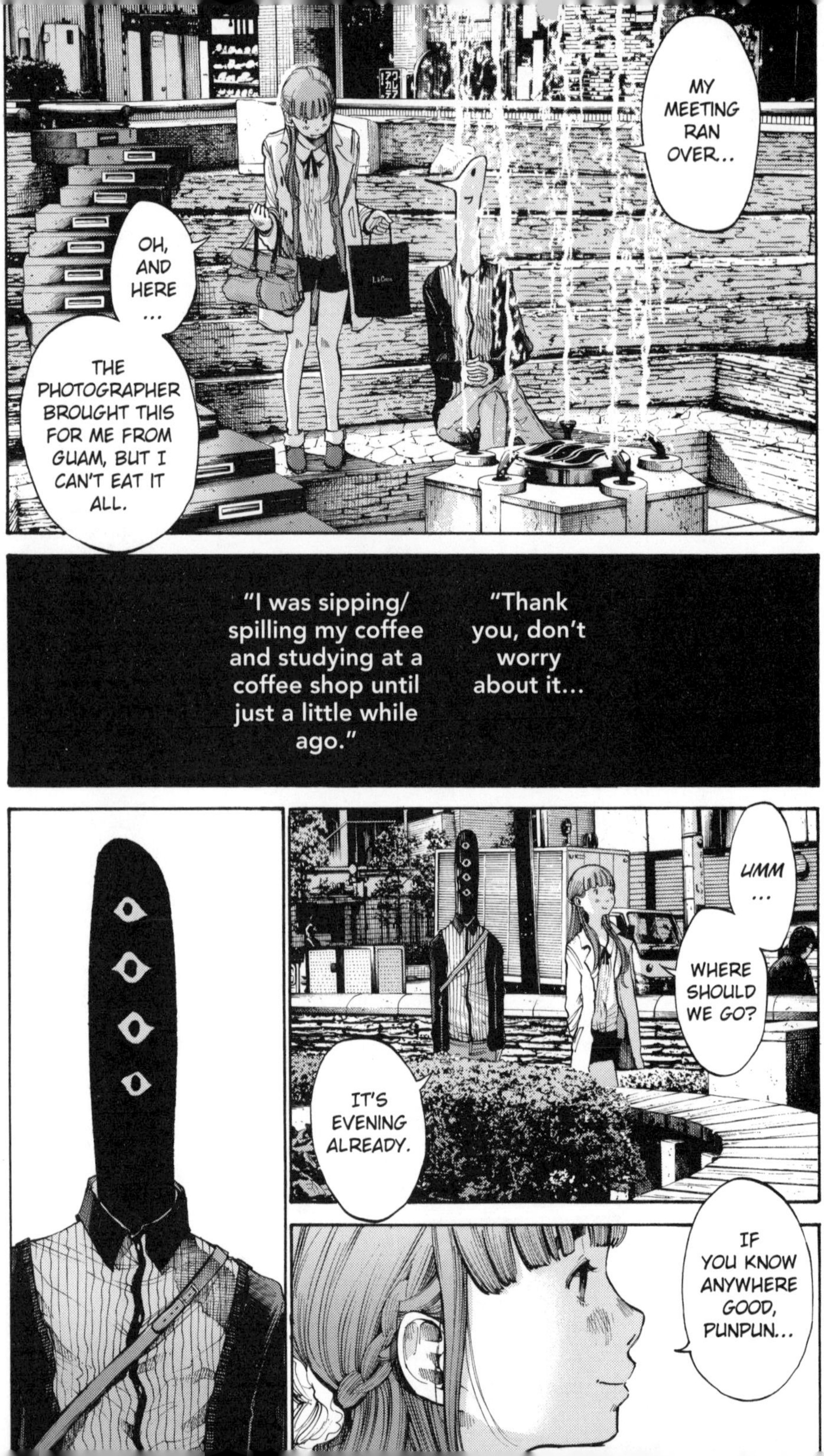
MY MEETING RAN OVER...
OH, AND HERE ...
THE PHOTOGRAPHER BROUGHT THIS FOR ME FROM GUAM, BUT I CAN'T EAT IT ALL.
"Thank you, don't worry about it...
"I was sipping/spilling my coffee and studying at a coffee shop until just a little while ago."
UMM ...
WHERE SHOULD WE GO?
IT'S EVENING ALREADY.
IF YOU KNOW ANYWHERE GOOD, PUNPUN...

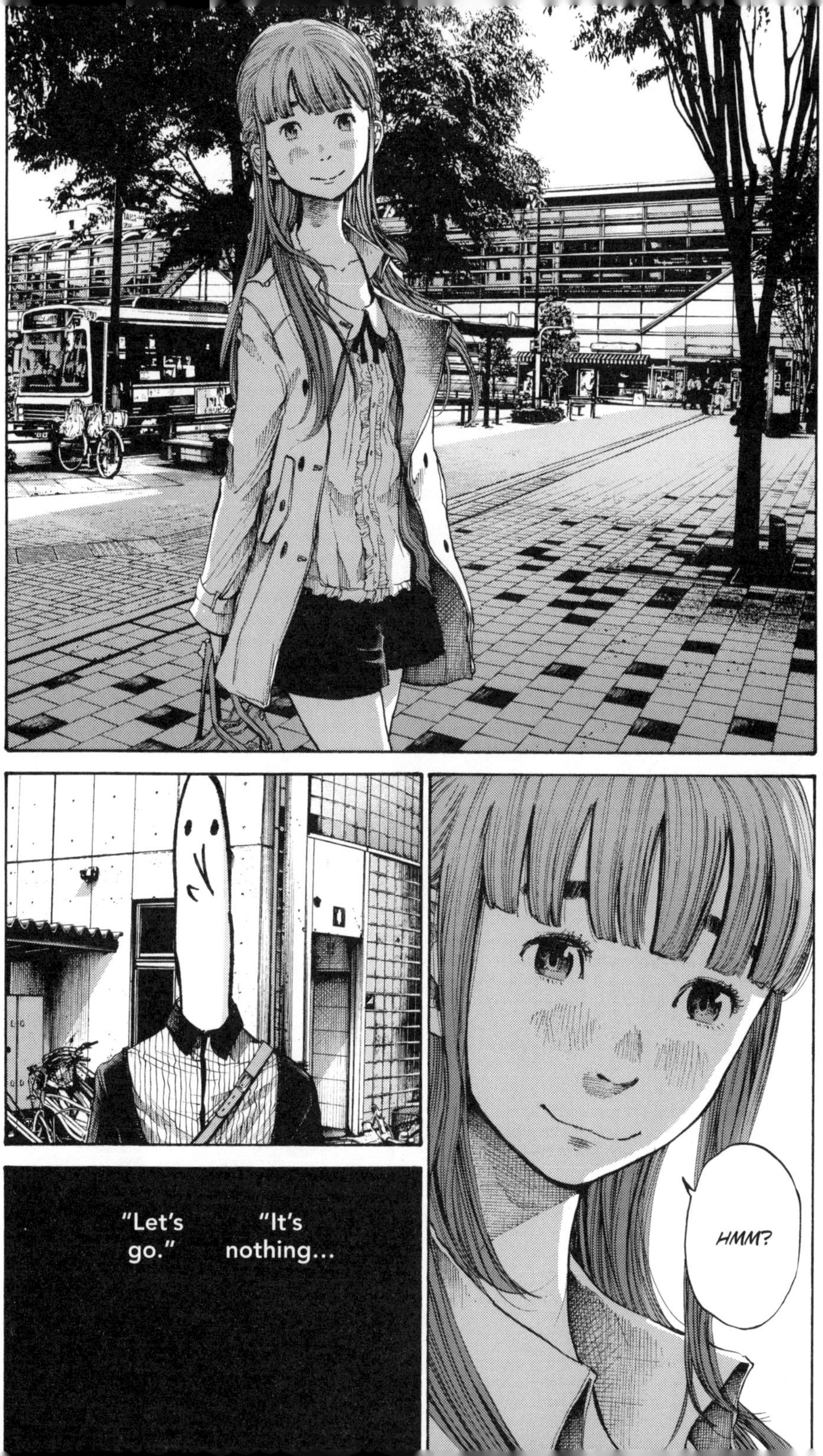
HMM?
"It's nothing...
"Let's go."

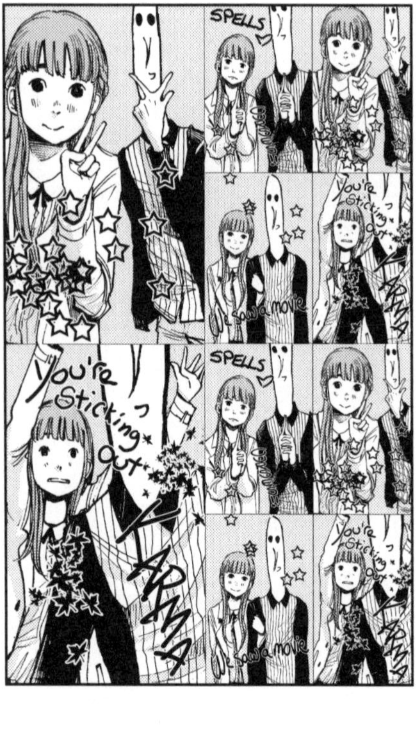
SPELLS
You're Sticking out
KARMA
We saw a movie
SPELLS
You're Sticking out
KARMA
We saw a movie
You're Sticking out
KARMA

Chapter 103

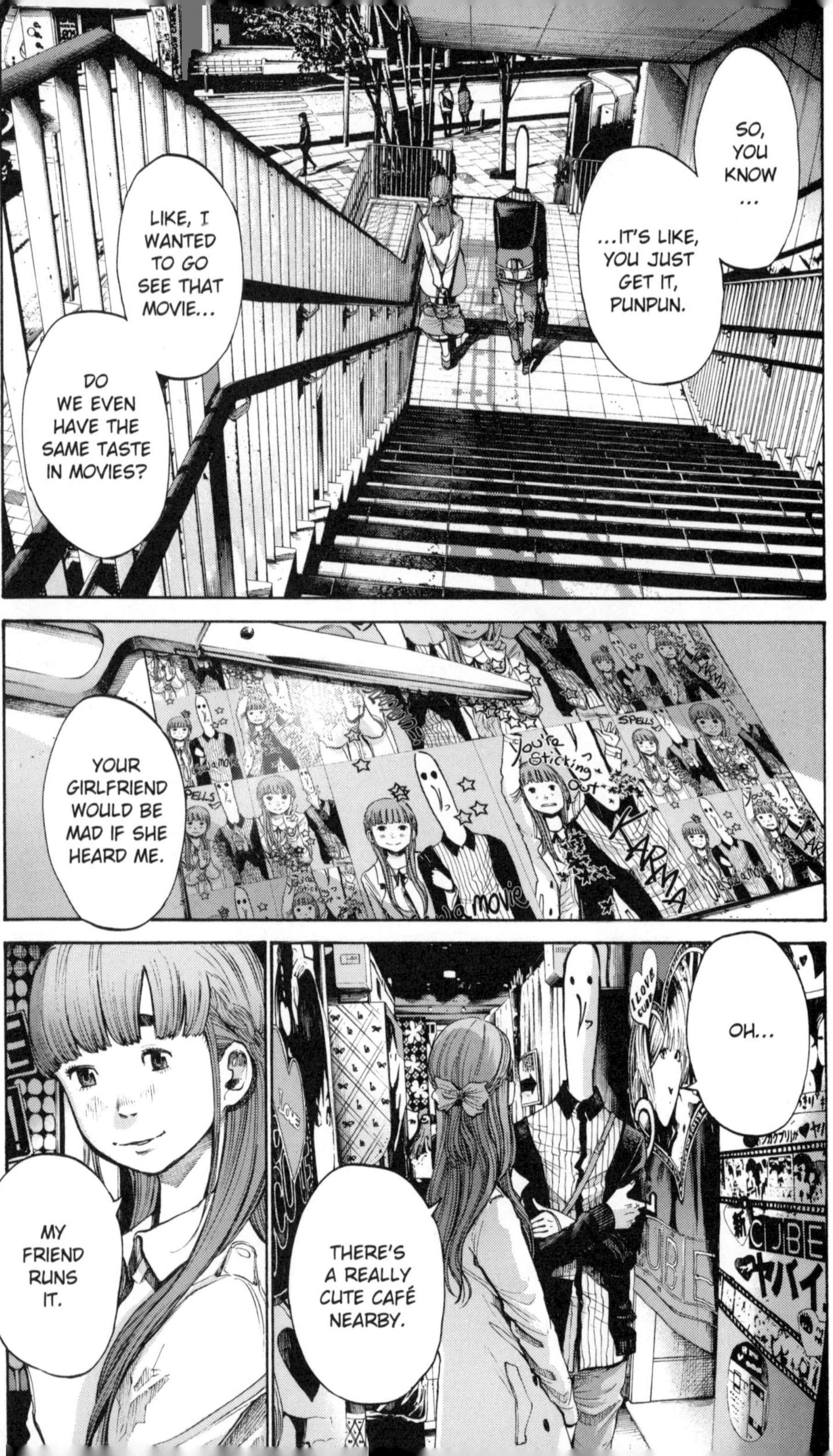
SO, YOU KNOW...
...IT'S LIKE, YOU JUST GET IT, PUNPUN.
LIKE, I WANTED TO GO SEE THAT MOVIE...
DO WE EVEN HAVE THE SAME TASTE IN MOVIES?
YOUR GIRLFRIEND WOULD BE MAD IF SHE HEARD ME.
You're Sticking out
SPELLS
KARMA
movie
OH...
THERE'S A REALLY CUTE CAFÉ NEARBY.
MY FRIEND RUNS IT.
CUBE
ヤバイ

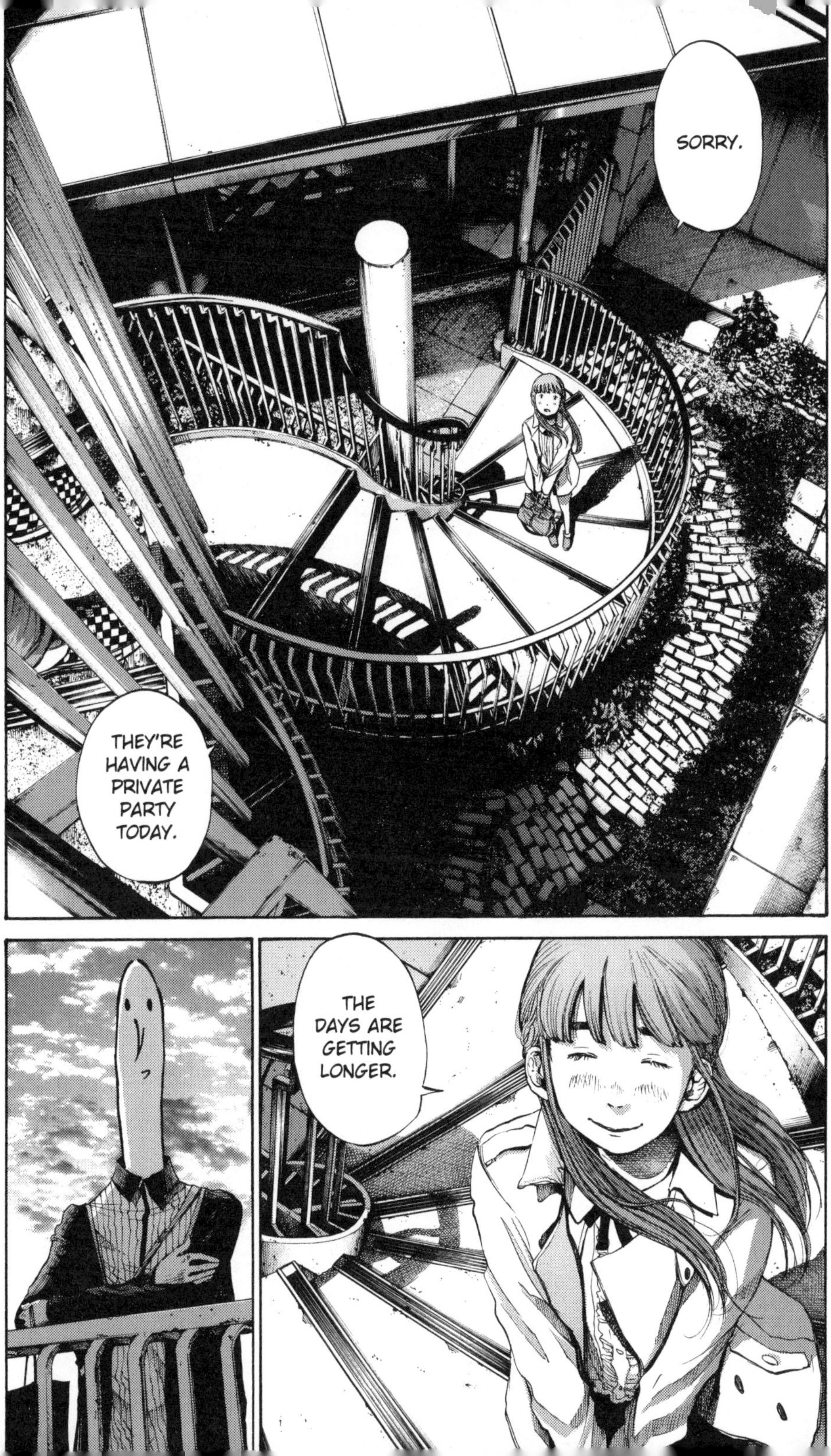
SORRY.
THEY'RE HAVING A PRIVATE PARTY TODAY.
THE DAYS ARE GETTING LONGER.

WASN'T...

...THE FIRST TIME WE TALKED...

...RIGHT AROUND THIS TIME OF YEAR?

In just a few days, Taka's soul had spread throughout Punpun's body...

...and, except for minor signs of rejection, it fit very well.

Information on movies and cool cafés he'd crammed into his head the night before and ostentatious conversation that he truly didn't care about spewed forth endlessly from his mouth.

PLEASE SIGN IN FOR A TABLE

	NAME	NUMBER
31	SAITO	2
32	FUJIKAWA	2
33	FREEZA	3
34	KOIKE	4
35		
36		

POP!

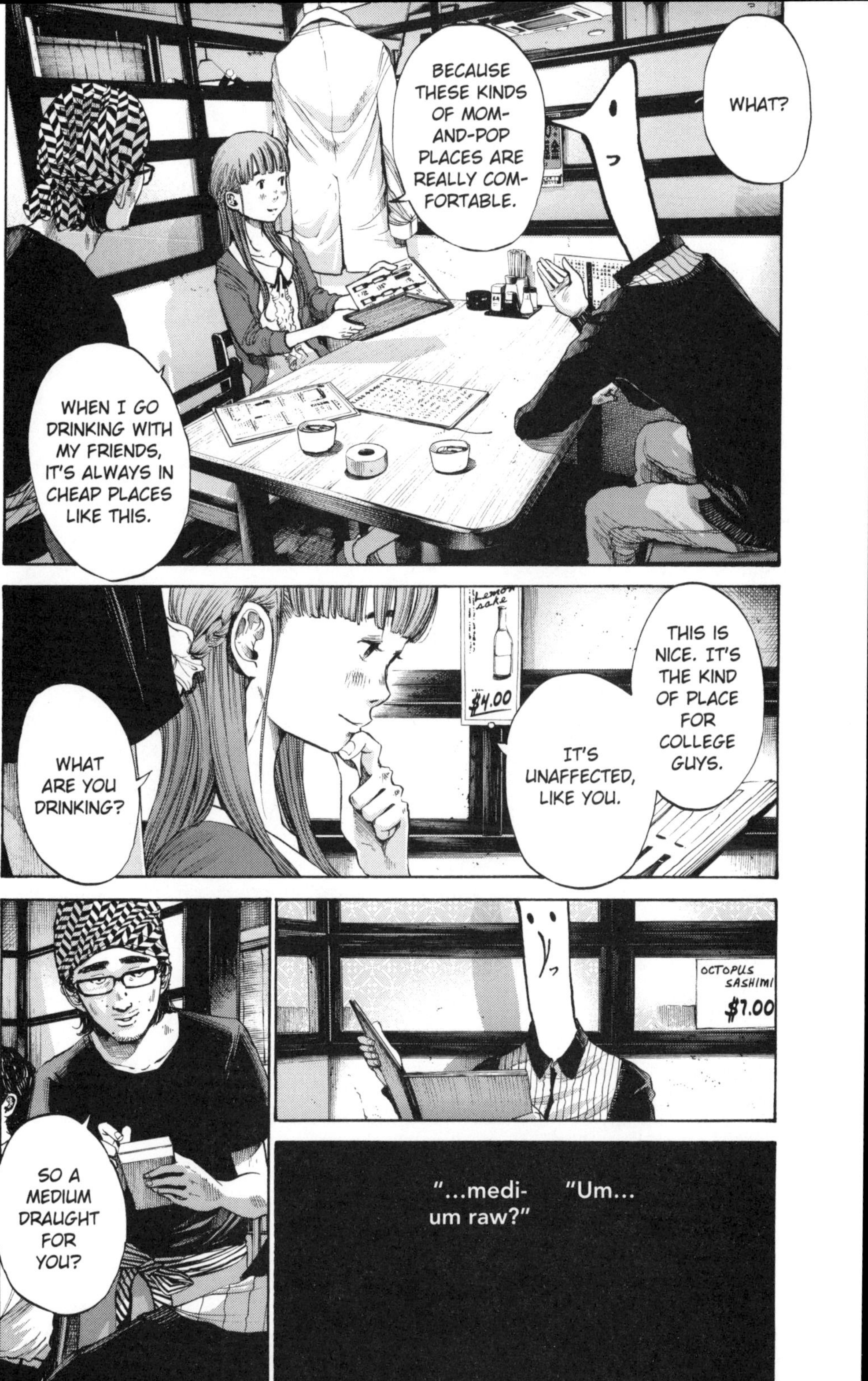
WHAT?
BECAUSE THESE KINDS OF MOM-AND-POP PLACES ARE REALLY COM-FORTABLE.
WHEN I GO DRINKING WITH MY FRIENDS, IT'S ALWAYS IN CHEAP PLACES LIKE THIS.
Lemon sake
$4.00
THIS IS NICE. IT'S THE KIND OF PLACE FOR COLLEGE GUYS.
IT'S UNAFFECTED, LIKE YOU.
WHAT ARE YOU DRINKING?
OCTOPUS SASHIMI
$7.00
"Um...
"...medi-um raw?"
SO A MEDIUM DRAUGHT FOR YOU?

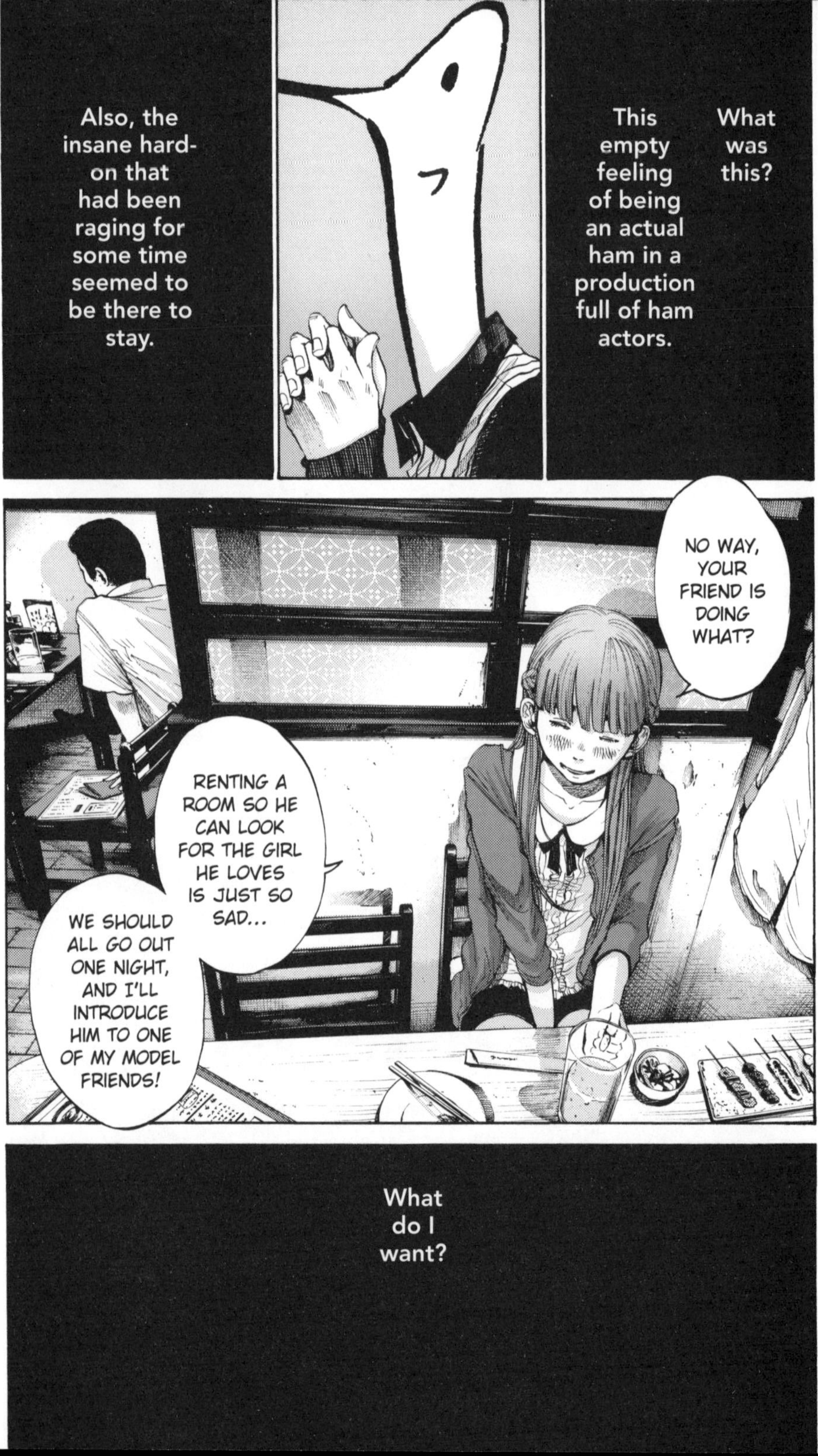
What was this?
This empty feeling of being an actual ham in a production full of ham actors.
Also, the insane hard-on that had been raging for some time seemed to be there to stay.
NO WAY, YOUR FRIEND IS DOING WHAT?
RENTING A ROOM SO HE CAN LOOK FOR THE GIRL HE LOVES IS JUST SO SAD...
WE SHOULD ALL GO OUT ONE NIGHT, AND I'LL INTRODUCE HIM TO ONE OF MY MODEL FRIENDS!
What do I want?

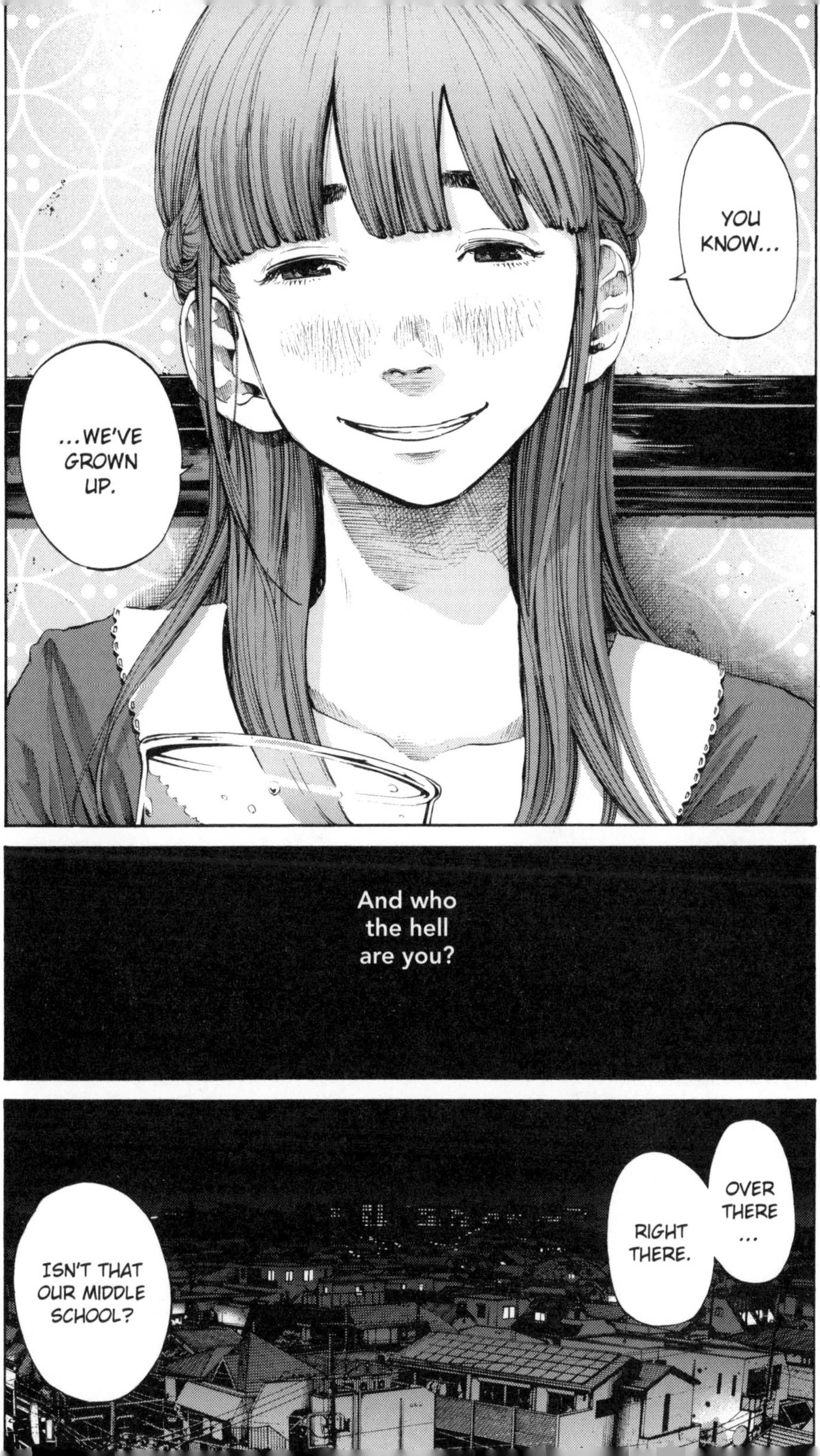
YOU KNOW...
...WE'VE GROWN UP.
And who the hell are you?
OVER THERE ...
RIGHT THERE.
ISN'T THAT OUR MIDDLE SCHOOL?

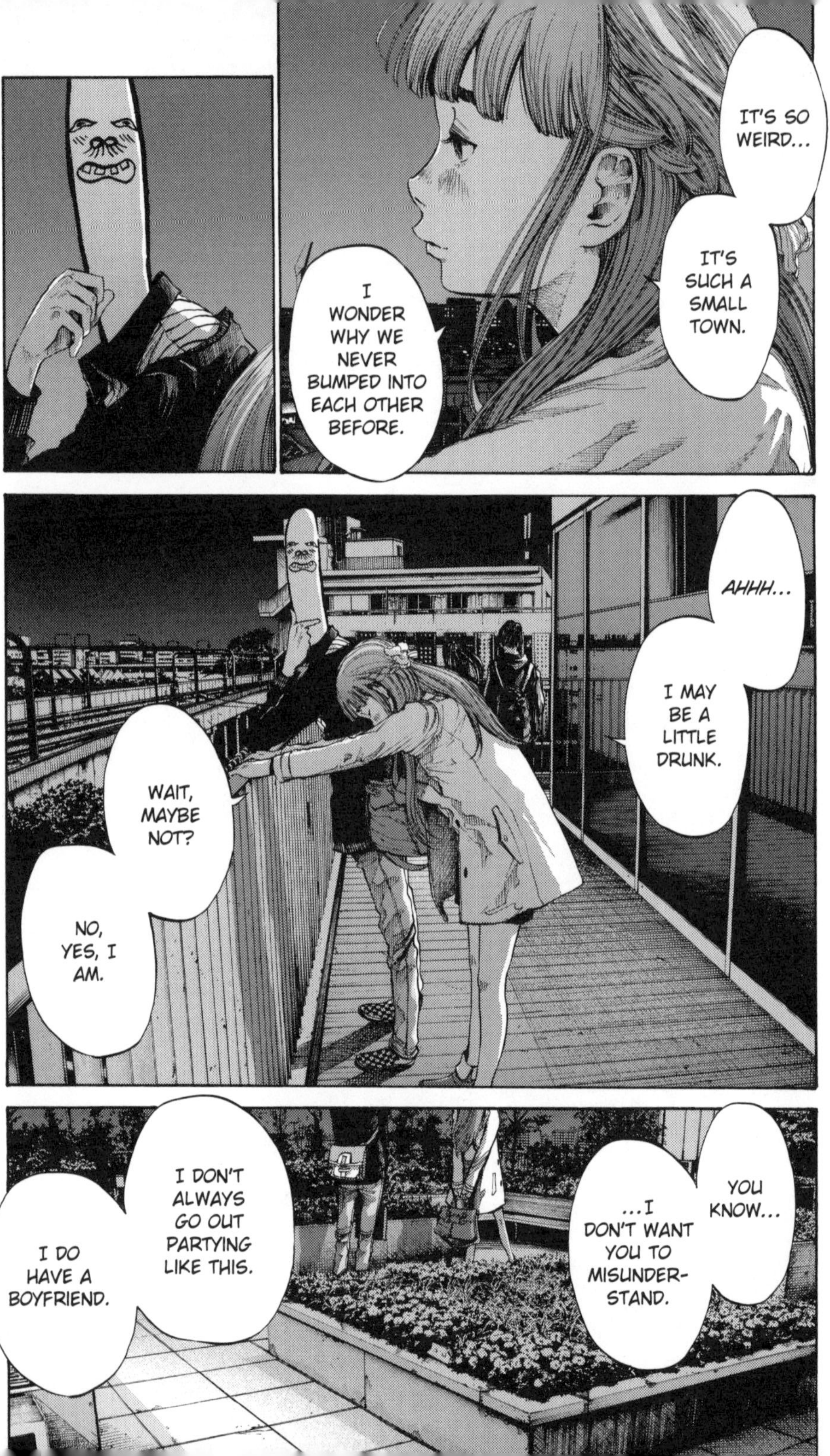
IT'S SO WEIRD...
IT'S SUCH A SMALL TOWN.
I WONDER WHY WE NEVER BUMPED INTO EACH OTHER BEFORE.
AHHH...
I MAY BE A LITTLE DRUNK.
WAIT, MAYBE NOT?
NO, YES, I AM.
YOU KNOW...
...I DON'T WANT YOU TO MISUNDER-STAND.
I DON'T ALWAYS GO OUT PARTYING LIKE THIS.
I DO HAVE A BOYFRIEND.

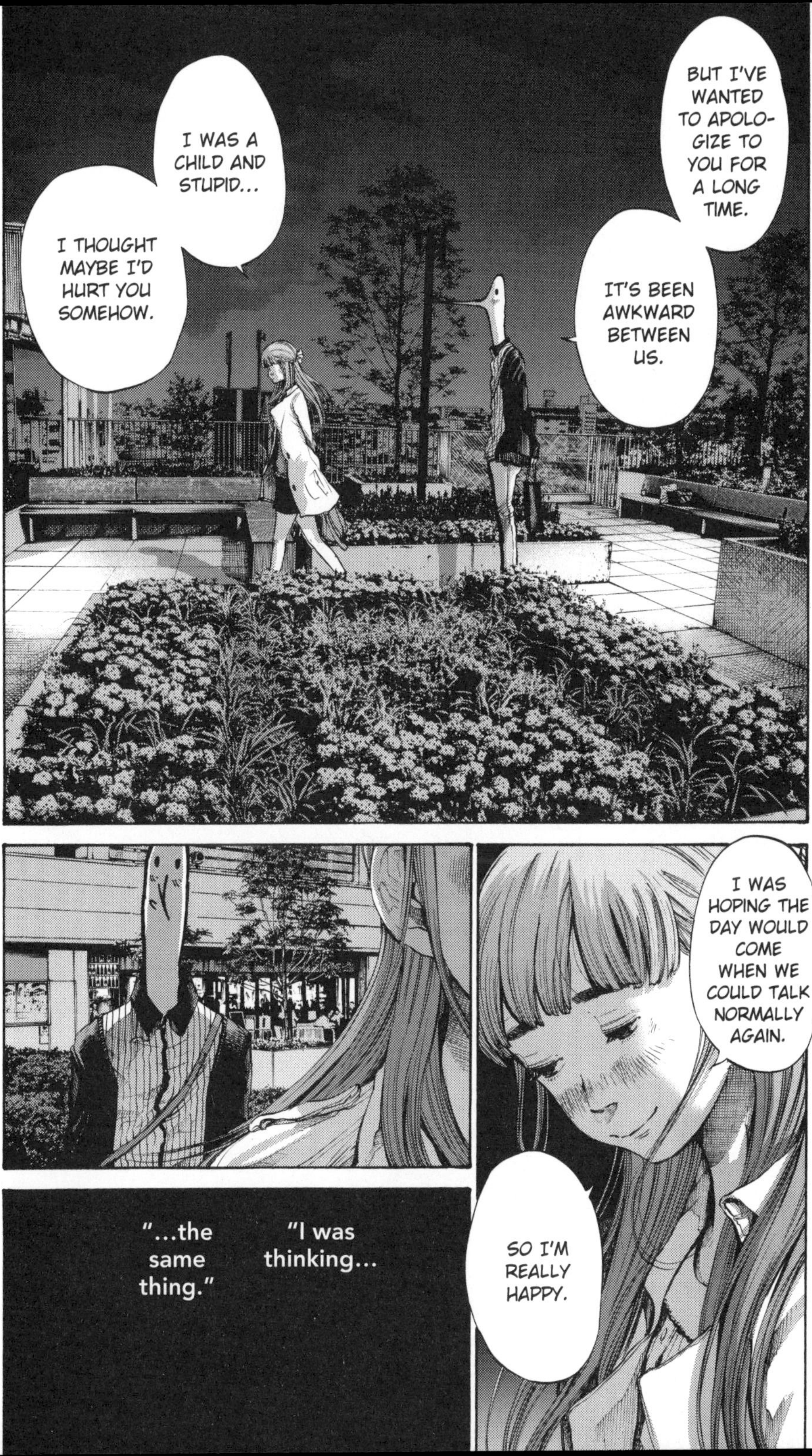
BUT I'VE WANTED TO APOLOGIZE TO YOU FOR A LONG TIME.
IT'S BEEN AWKWARD BETWEEN US.
I WAS A CHILD AND STUPID...
I THOUGHT MAYBE I'D HURT YOU SOMEHOW.
I WAS HOPING THE DAY WOULD COME WHEN WE COULD TALK NORMALLY AGAIN.
SO I'M REALLY HAPPY.
"I was thinking...
"...the same thing."

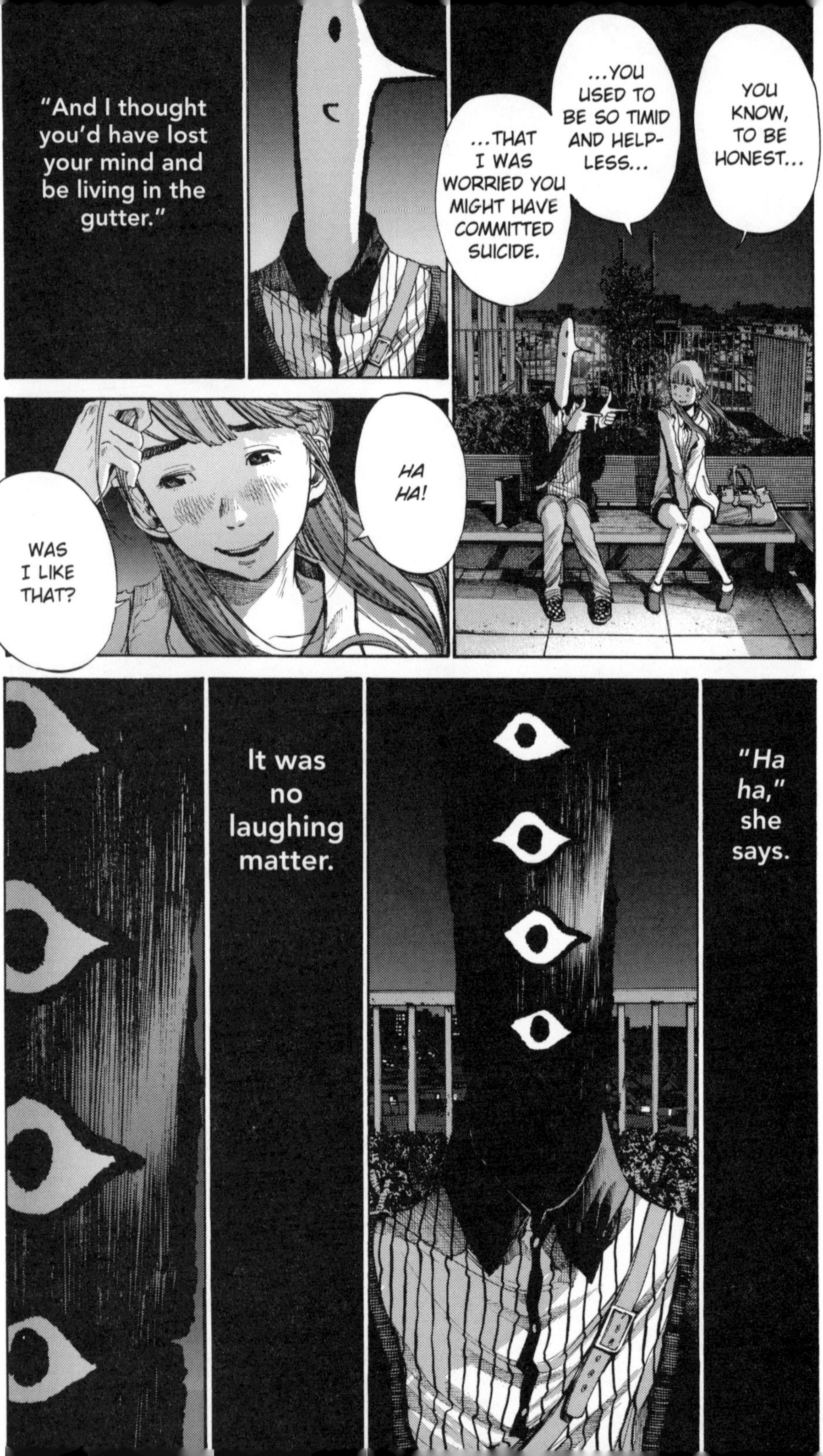
YOU KNOW, TO BE HONEST...
...YOU USED TO BE SO TIMID AND HELP-LESS...
...THAT I WAS WORRIED YOU MIGHT HAVE COMMITTED SUICIDE.
"And I thought you'd have lost your mind and be living in the gutter."
HA HA!
WAS I LIKE THAT?
"Ha ha," she says.
It was no laughing matter.

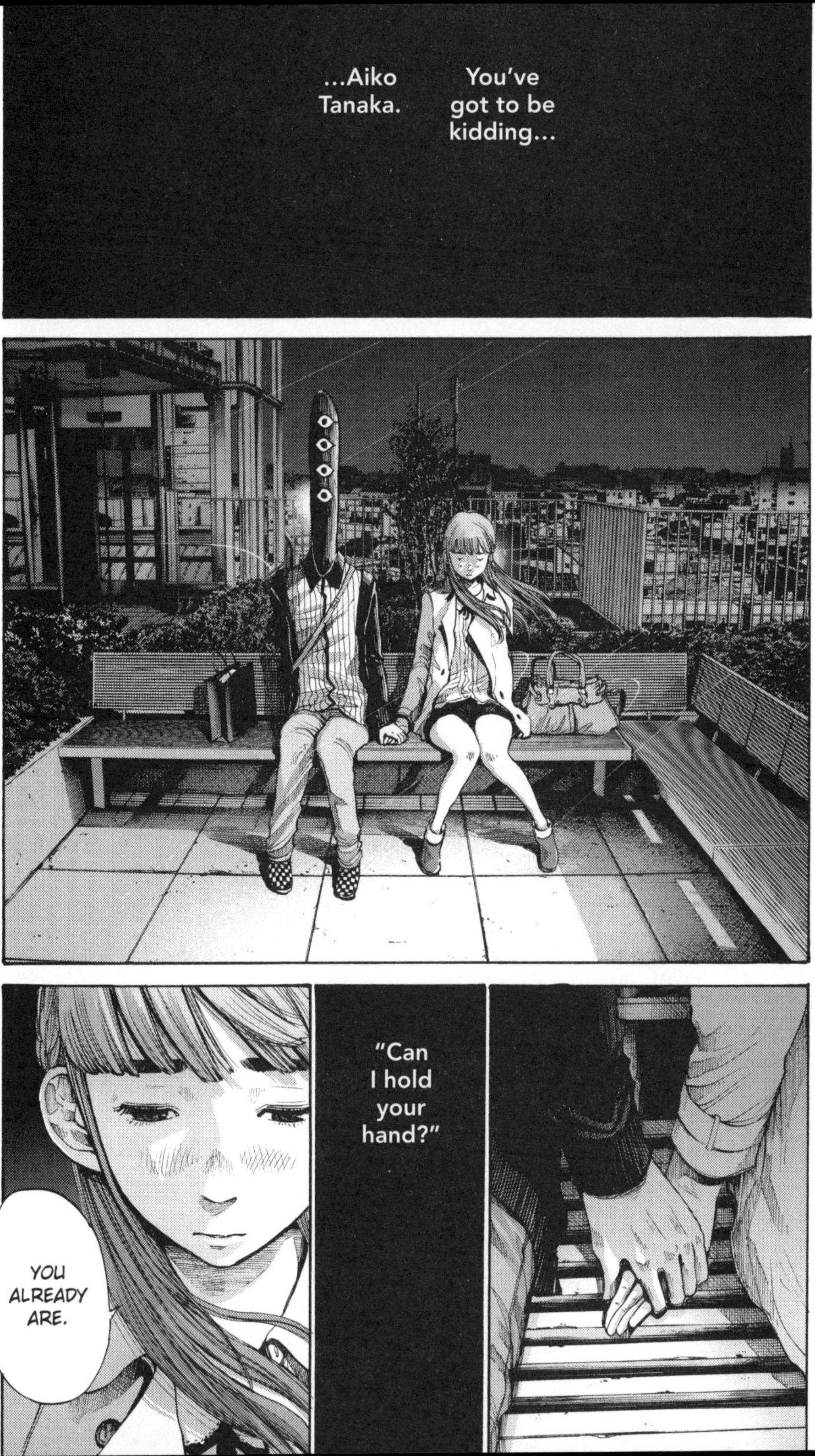
You've got to be kidding...
...Aiko Tanaka.
"Can I hold your hand?"
YOU ALREADY ARE.

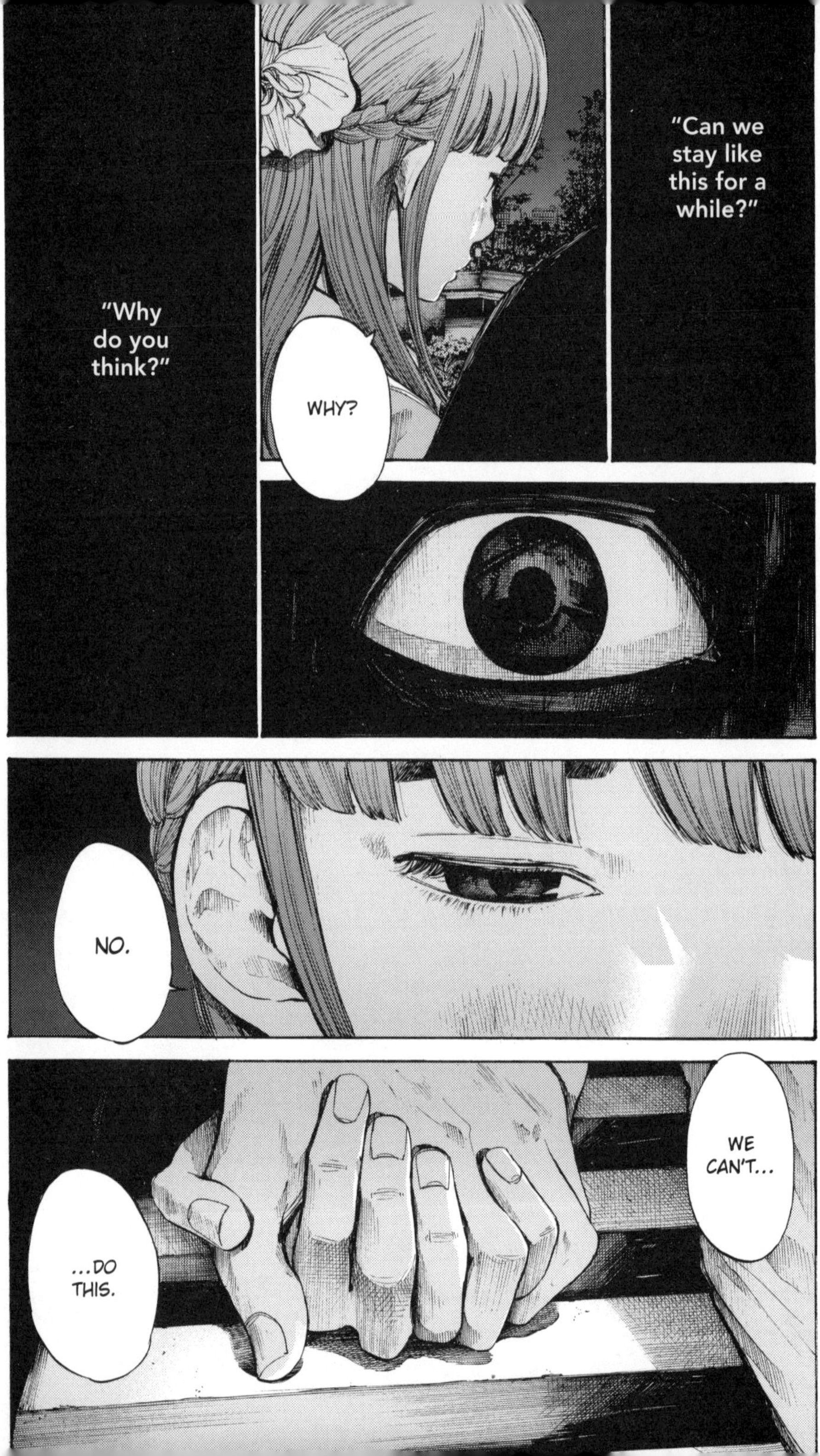
"Can we stay like this for a while?"
WHY?
"Why do you think?"
NO.
WE CAN'T...
...DO THIS.

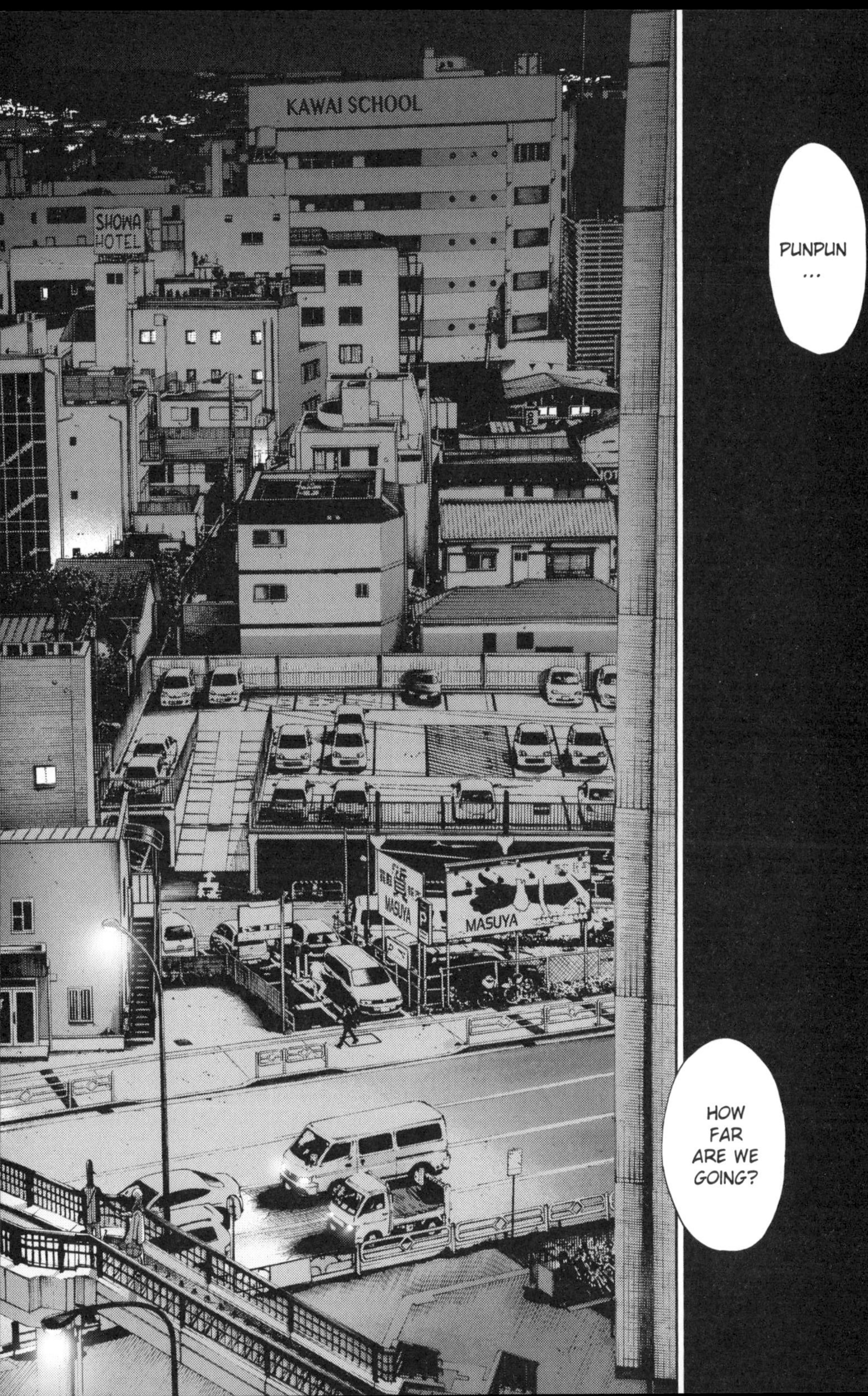
PUNPUN ...
HOW FAR ARE WE GOING?
KAWAI SCHOOL
SHOWA HOTEL
MASUYA
MASUYA

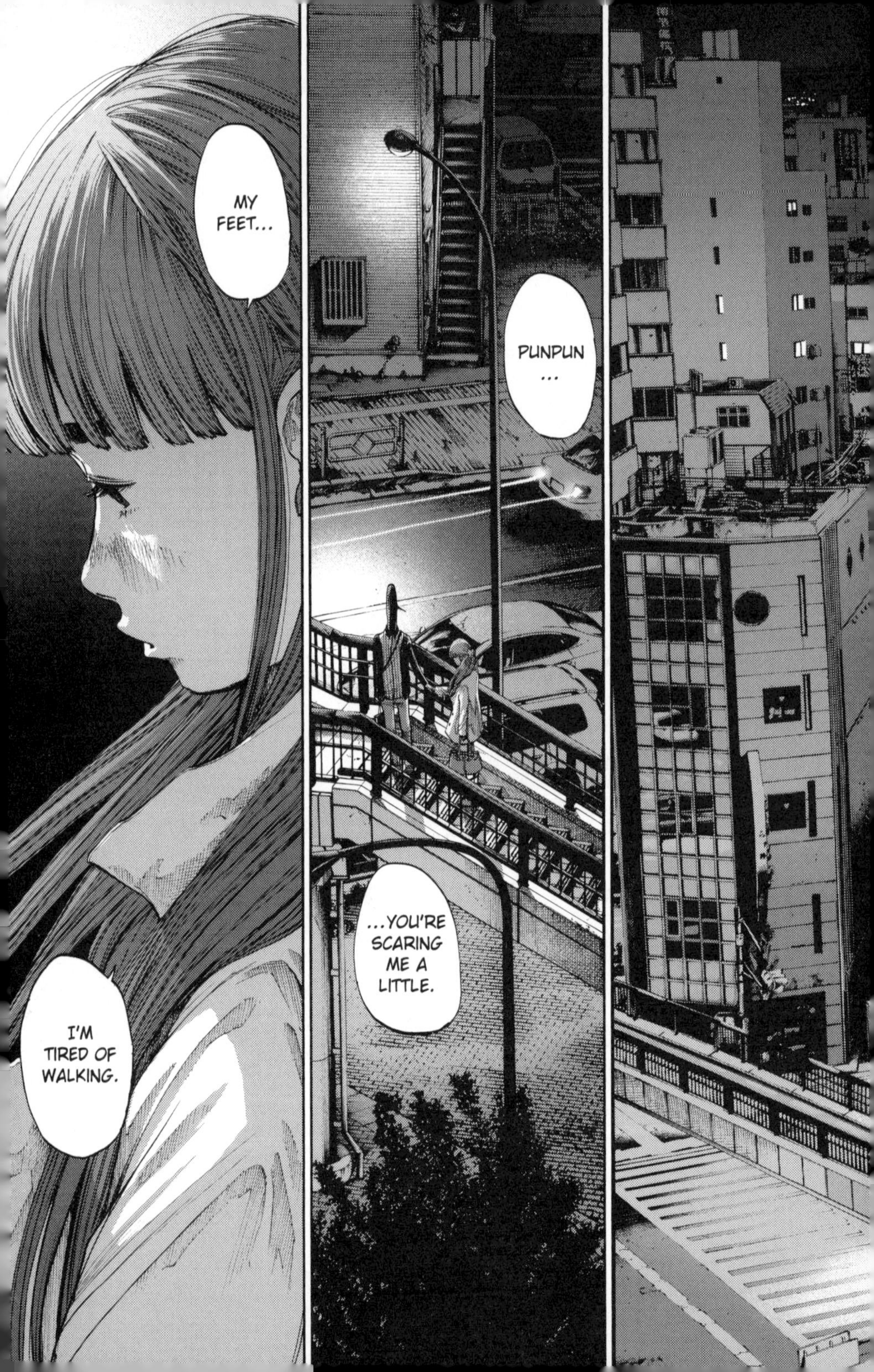
PUNPUN ...
...YOU'RE SCARING ME A LITTLE.
MY FEET...
I'M TIRED OF WALKING.

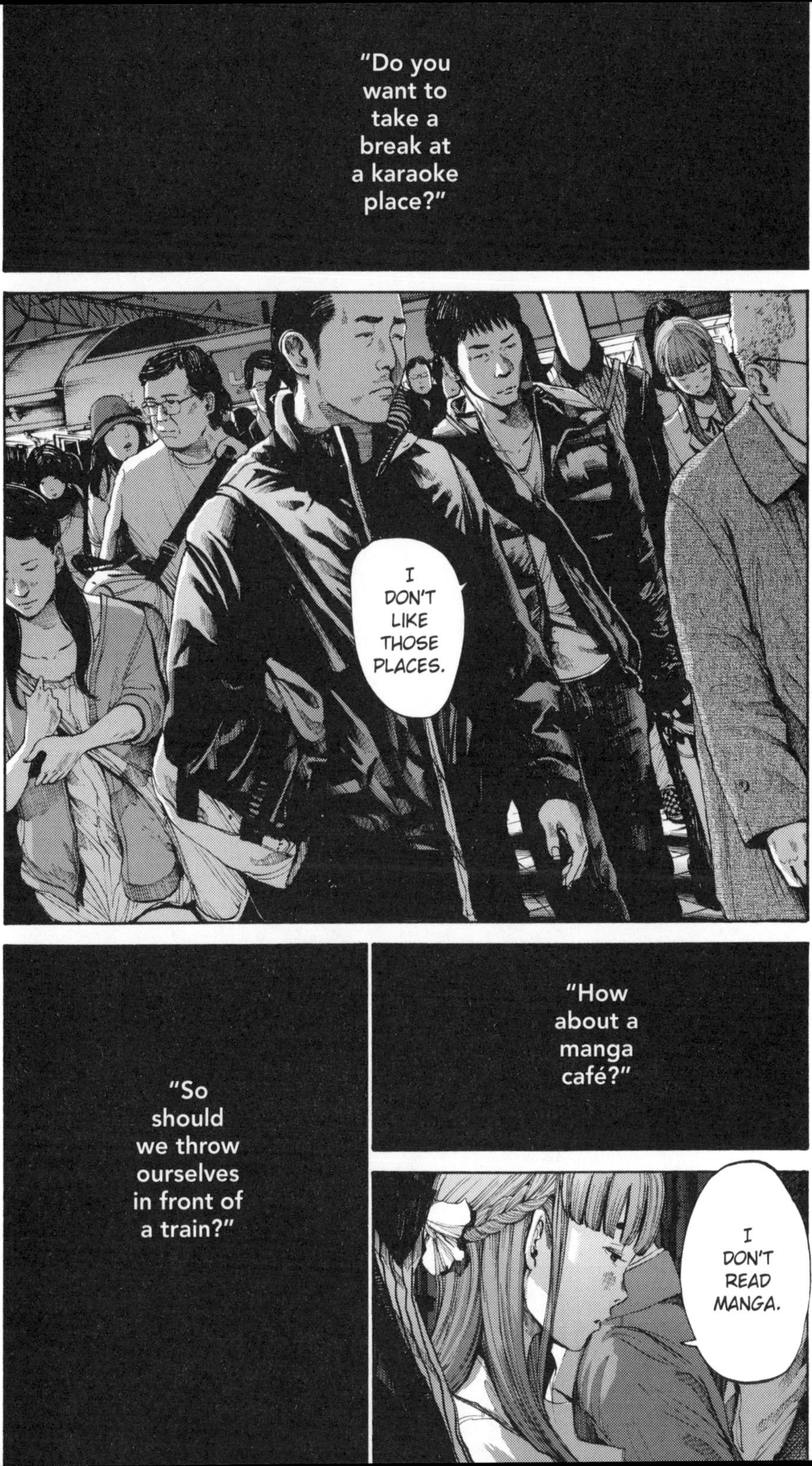
"Do you want to take a break at a karaoke place?"
I DON'T LIKE THOSE PLACES.
"How about a manga café?"
I DON'T READ MANGA.
"So should we throw ourselves in front of a train?"

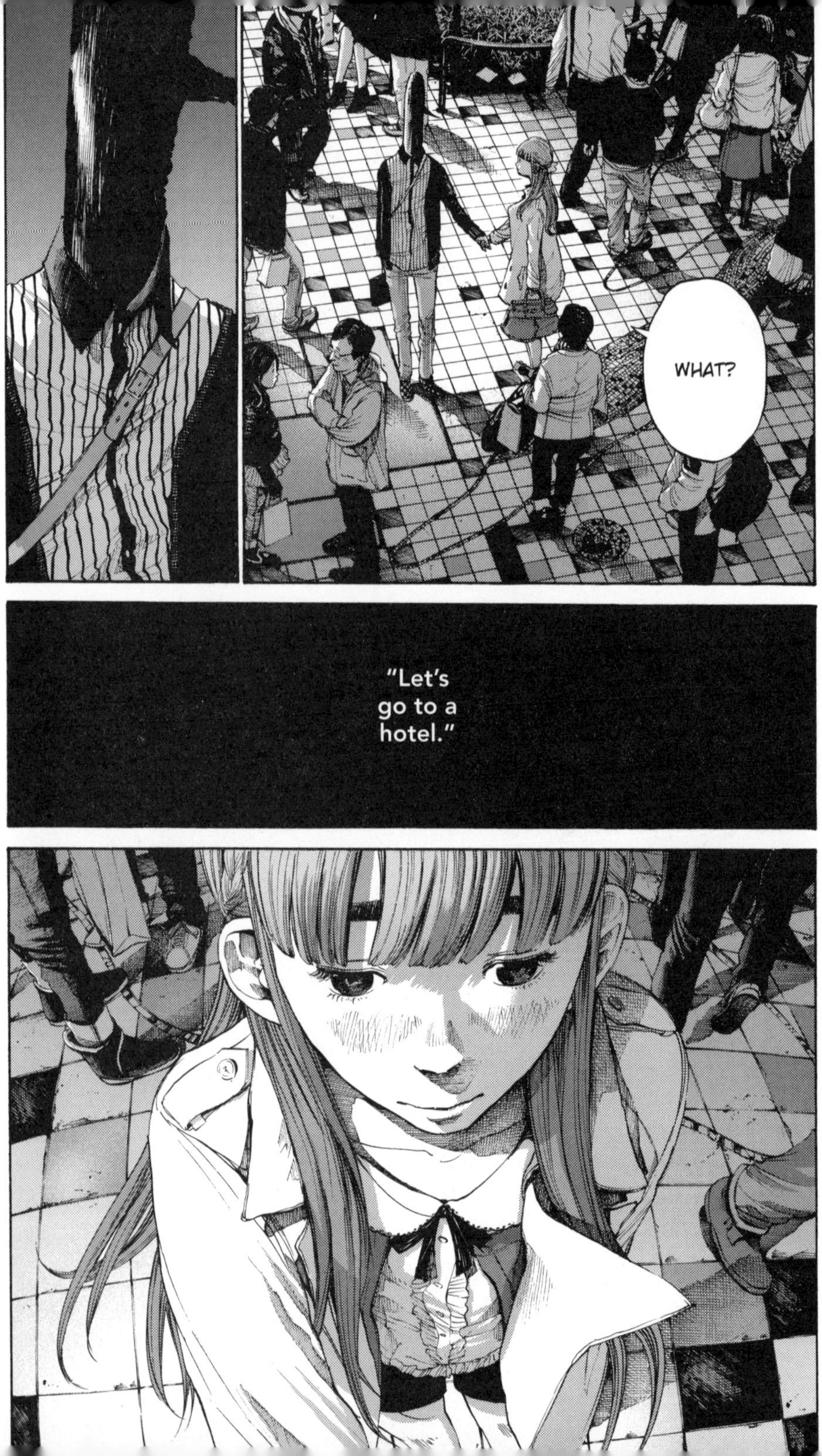
WHAT?
"Let's go to a hotel."

I have no
idea what
you're
thinking.

Aiko...

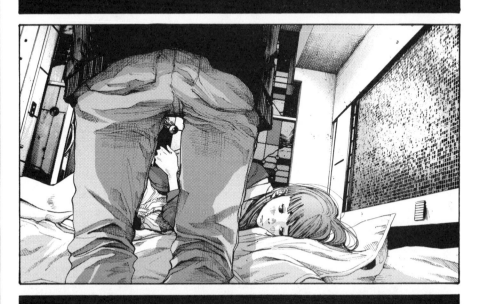

...I'm
sad.

But
somehow...

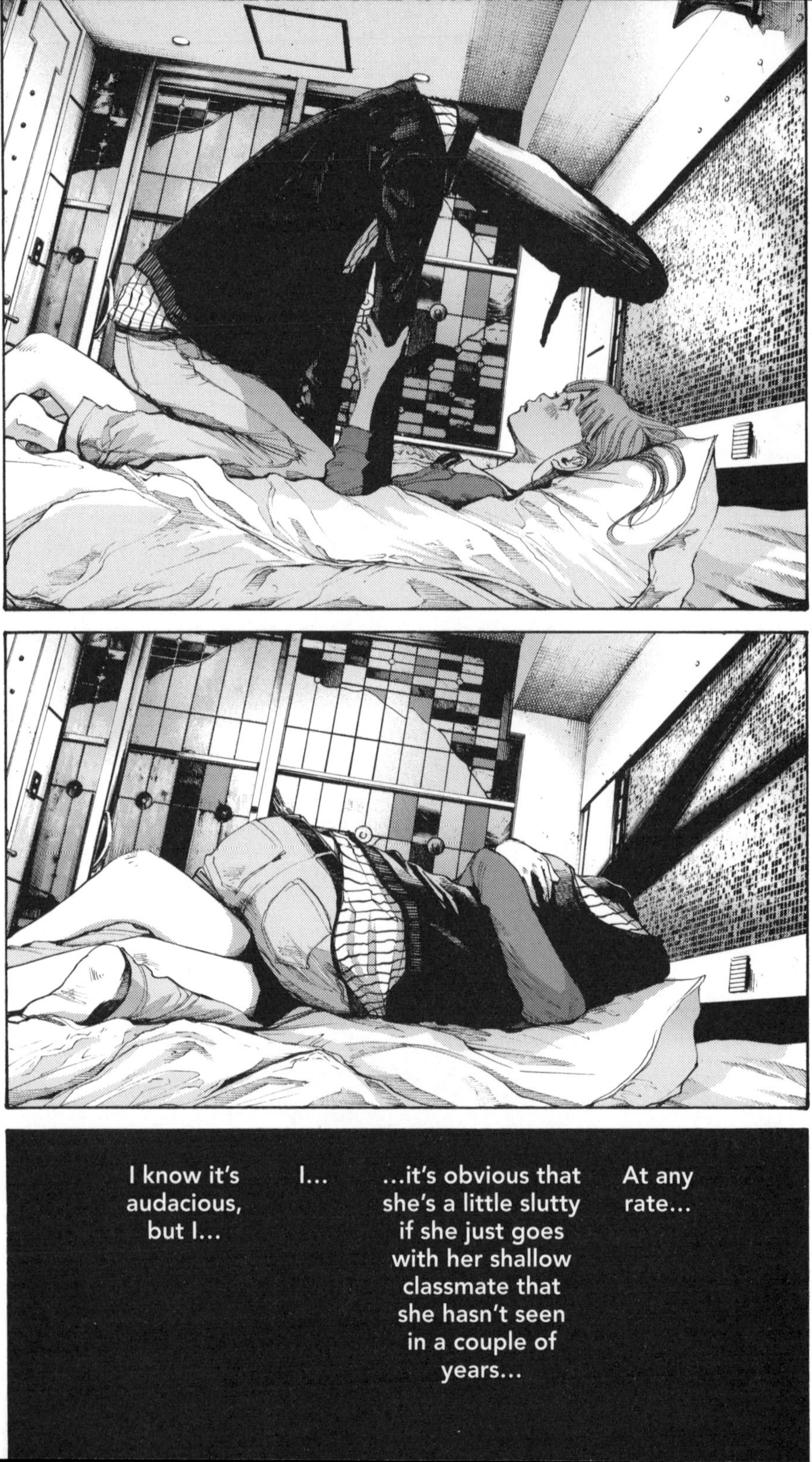
At any rate...
...it's obvious that she's a little slutty if she just goes with her shallow classmate that she hasn't seen in a couple of years...
I...
I know it's audacious, but I...

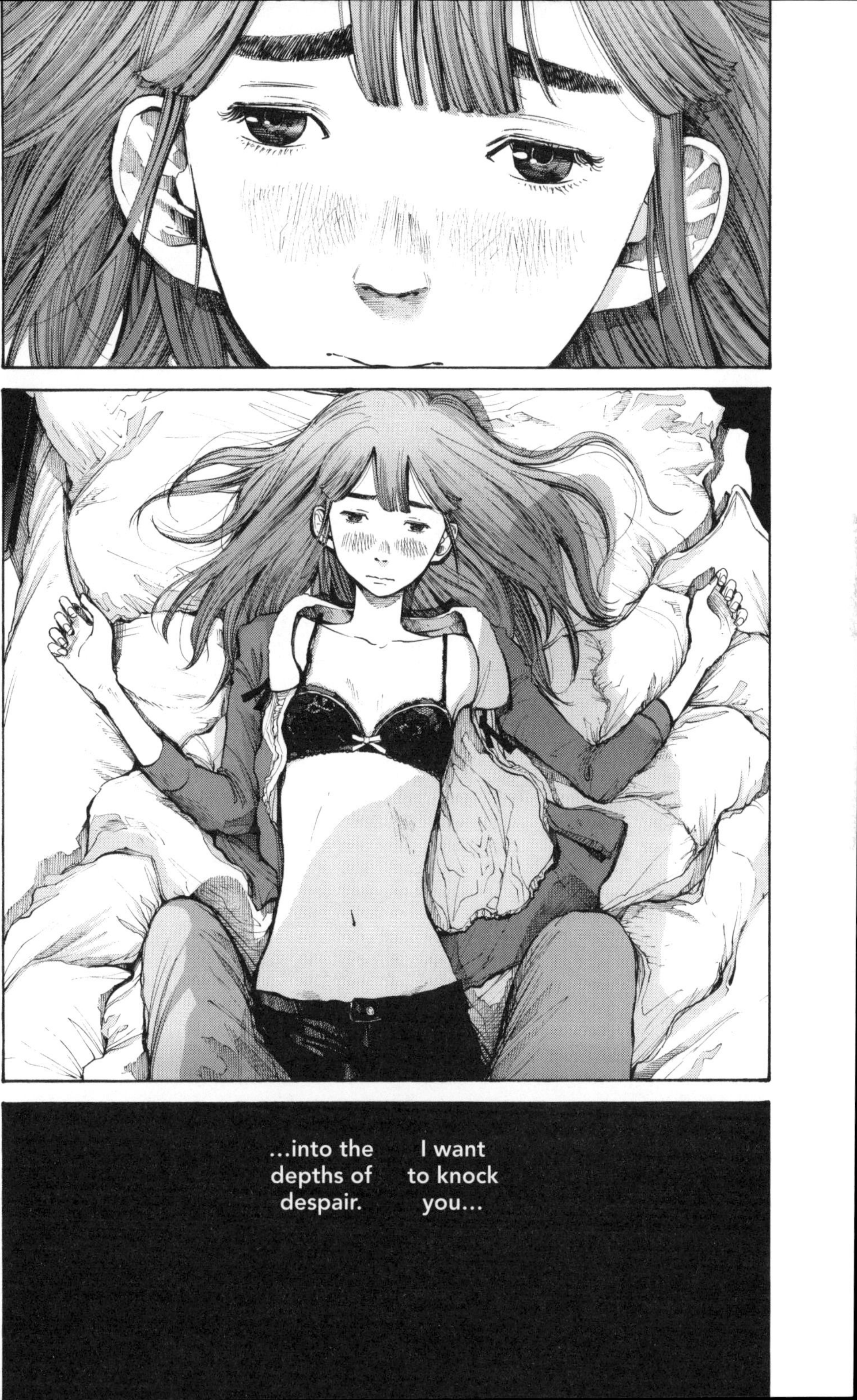
I want to knock you...
...into the depths of despair.

Chapter 104

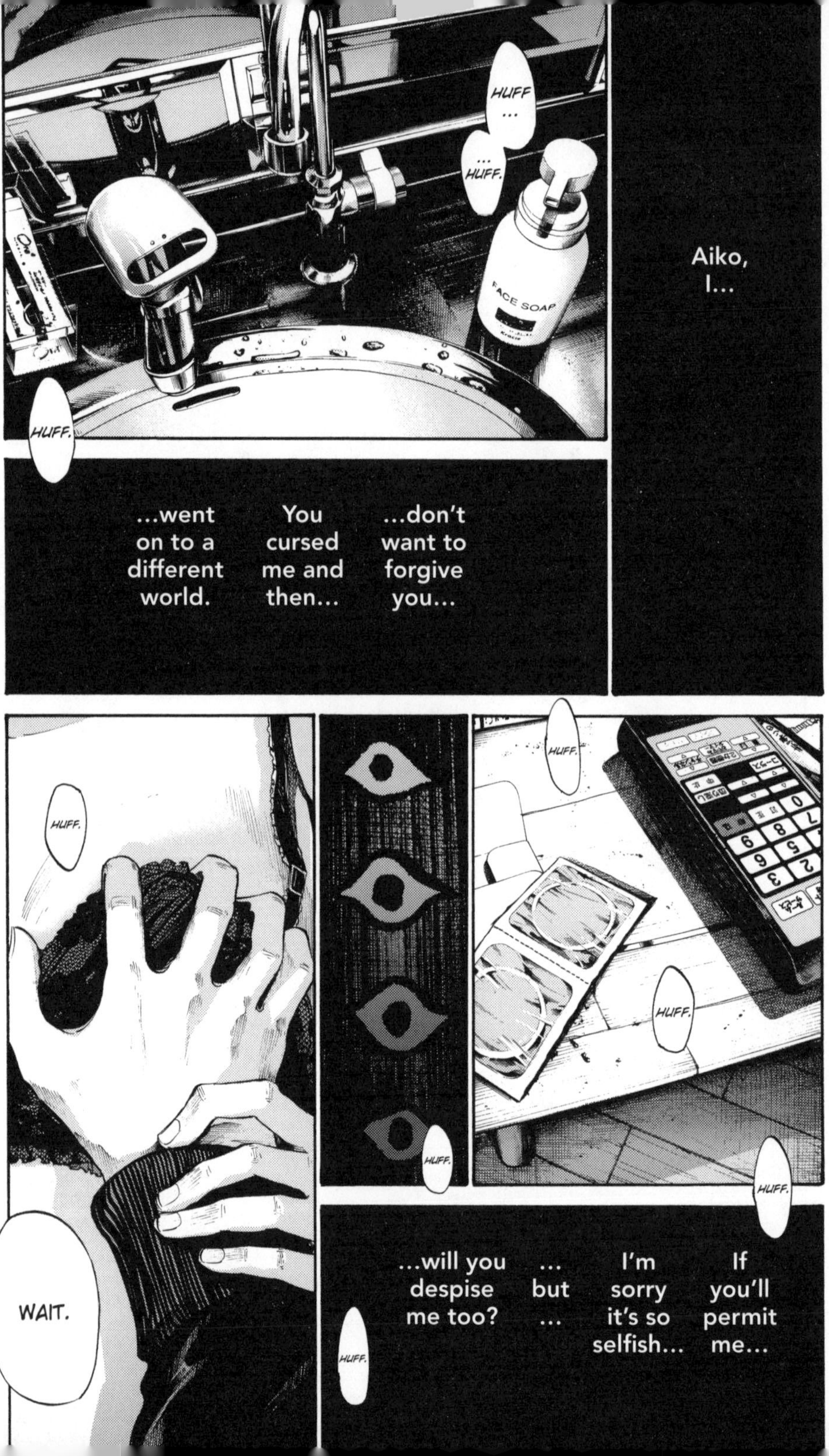
Aiko, I...
HUFF ...
... HUFF.
HUFF.
...don't want to forgive you...
You cursed me and then...
...went on to a different world.
HUFF.
HUFF.
HUFF.
HUFF.
If you'll permit me...
I'm sorry it's so selfish...
... but ...
...will you despise me too?
HUFF.
HUFF.
WAIT.

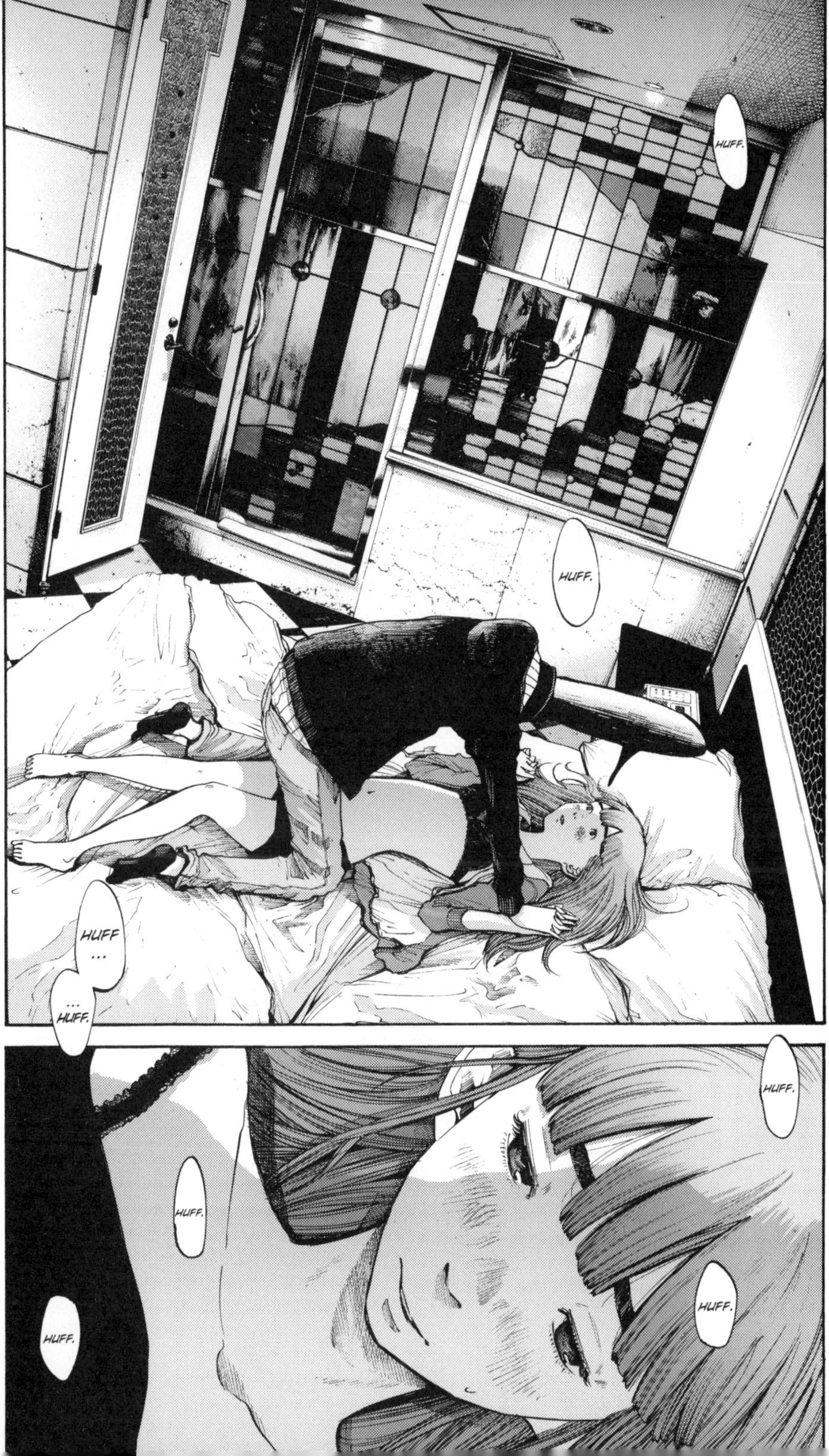
HUFF.
HUFF.
HUFF ...
... HUFF.
HUFF.
HUFF.
HUFF.
HUFF.

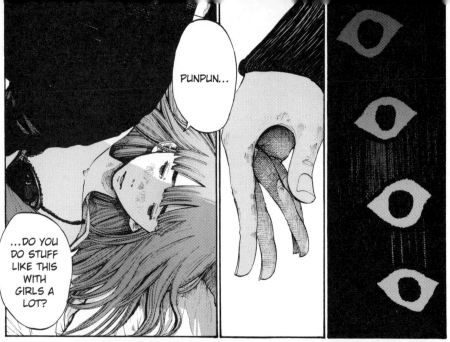

PUNPUN...

...DO YOU DO STUFF LIKE THIS WITH GIRLS A LOT?

HEY...

ANSWER ME.

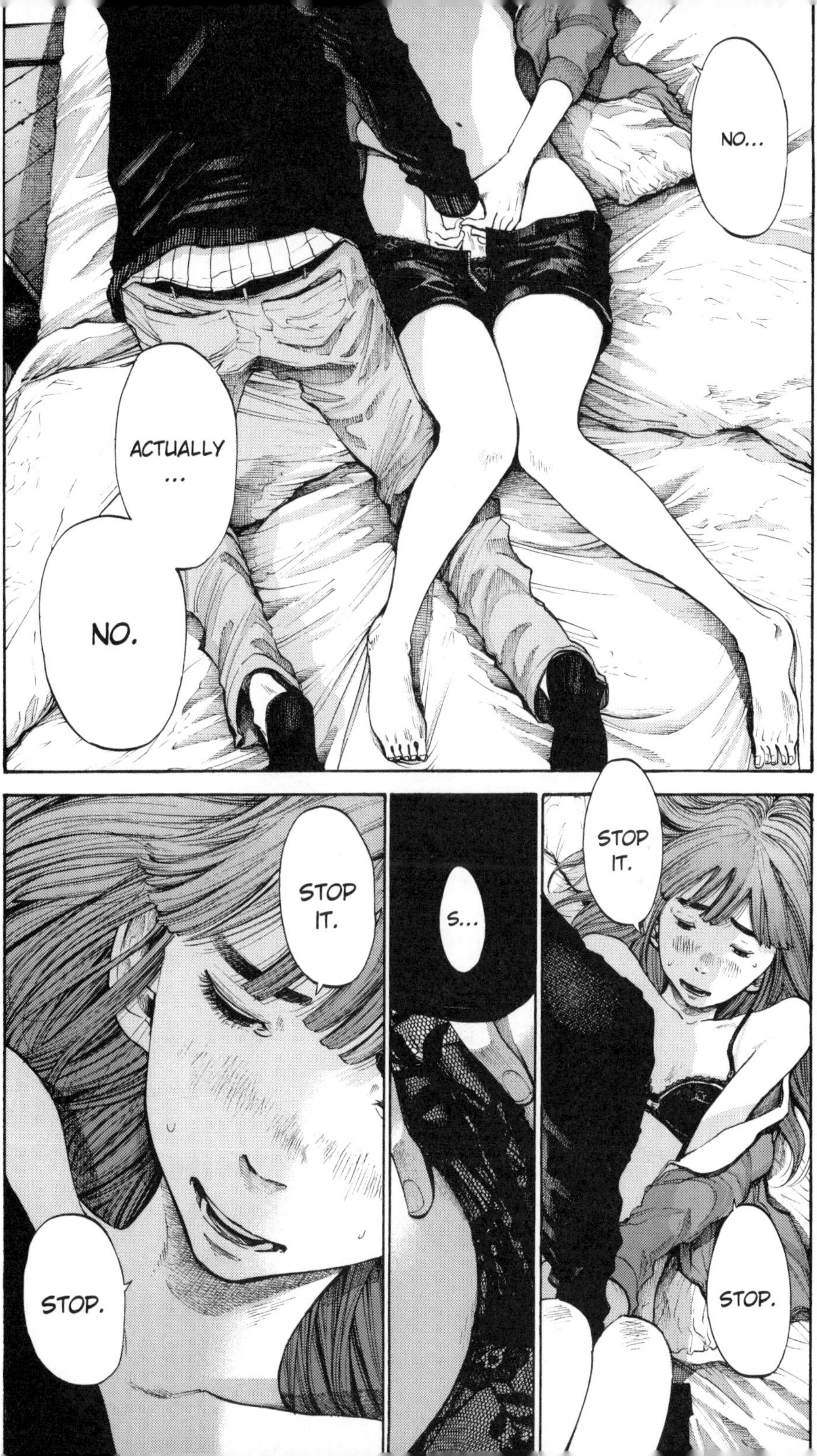
NO...
ACTUALLY ...
NO.
STOP IT.
STOP.
S...
STOP IT.
STOP.

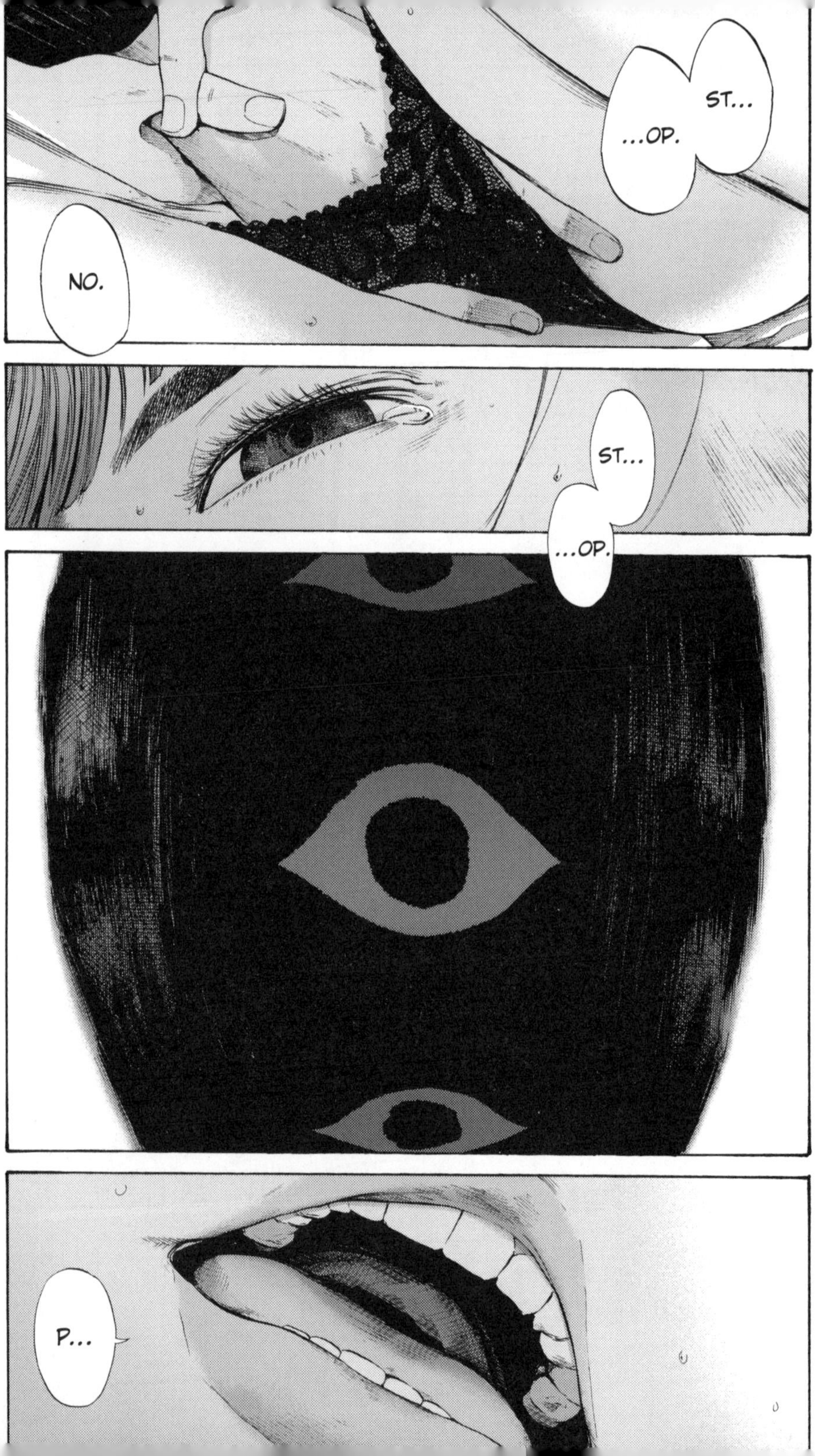
ST...
...OP.
NO.
ST...
...OP.
P...

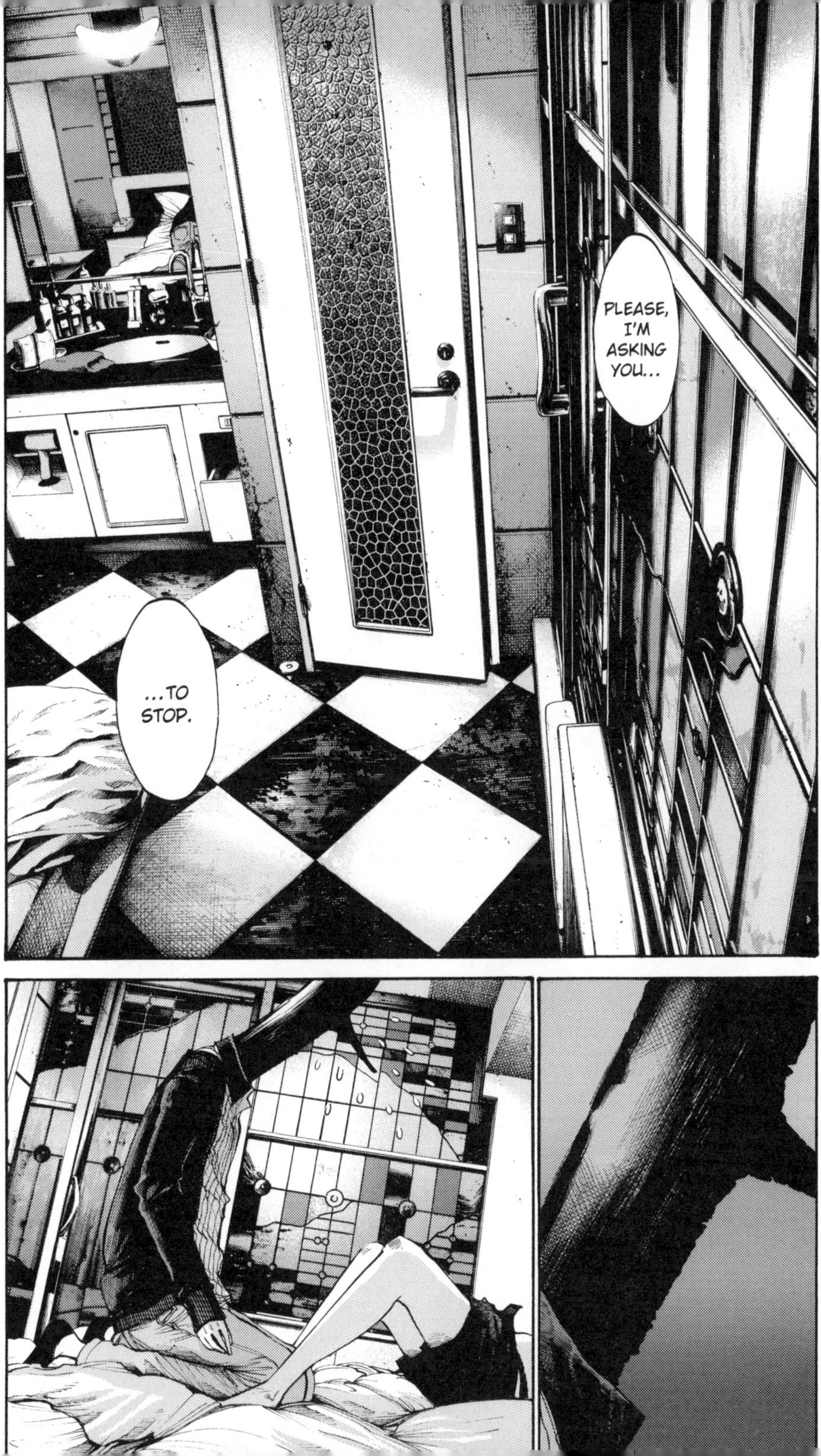
PLEASE, I'M ASKING YOU...
...TO STOP.

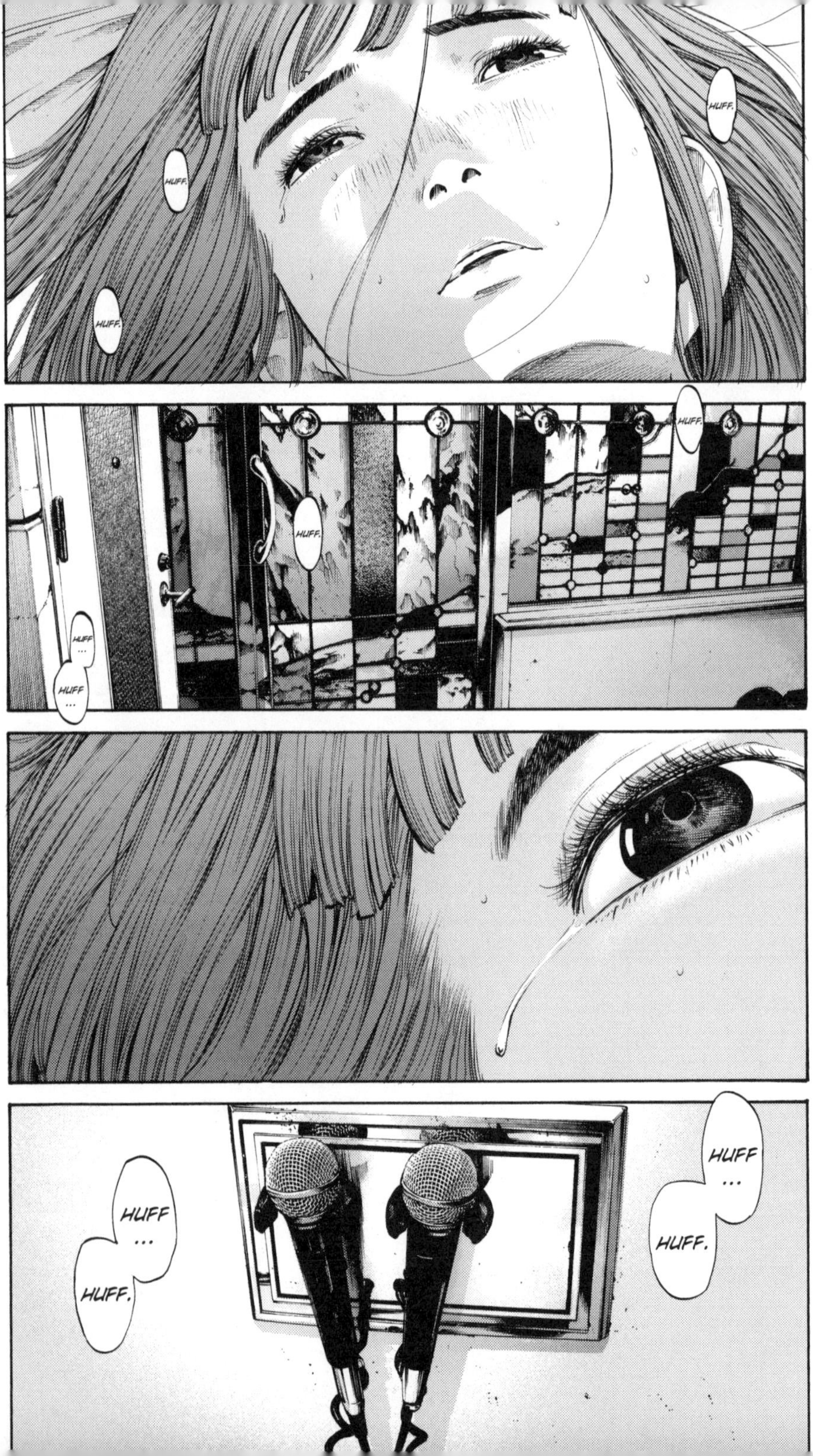
HUFF.
HUFF.
HUFF.
HUFF.
HUFF.
HUFF ...
HUFF ...
HUFF ...
HUFF.
HUFF ...
HUFF.

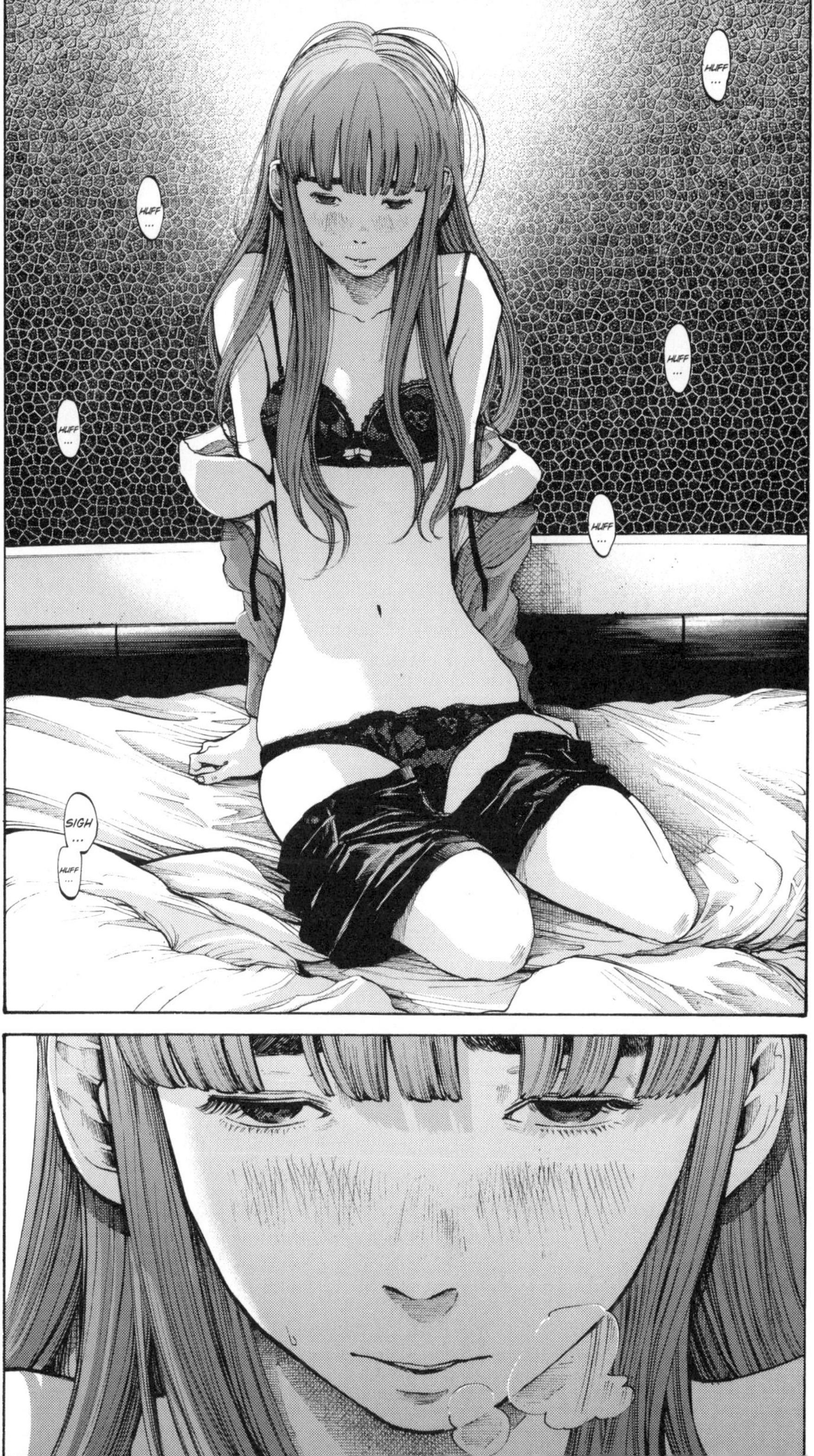
HUFF ...
HUFF ...
HUFF ...
HUFF ...
HUFF ...
SIGH ...
HUFF ...

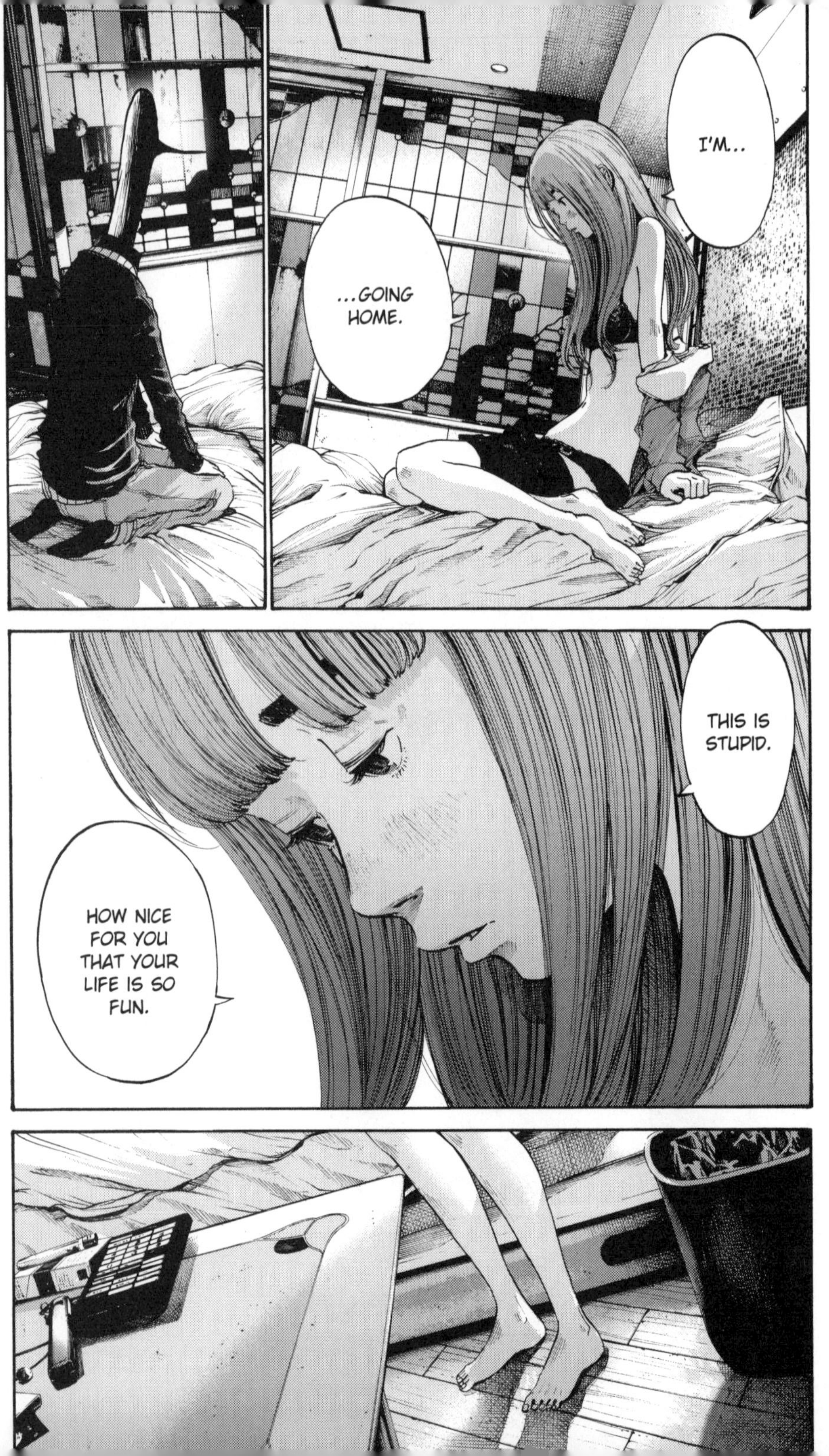
I'M...
...GOING HOME.
THIS IS STUPID.
HOW NICE FOR YOU THAT YOUR LIFE IS SO FUN.

IF I'D KNOWN IT WAS GOING TO END LIKE THIS...

...I WISH WE'D NEVER MET AGAIN.

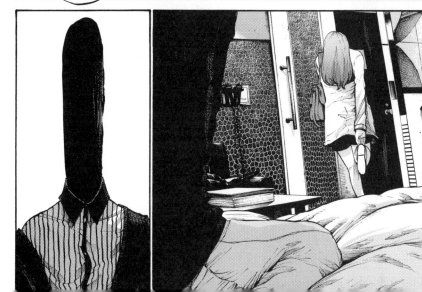

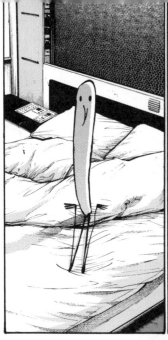

Punpun
thought
...

"I've
lost
every-
thing."

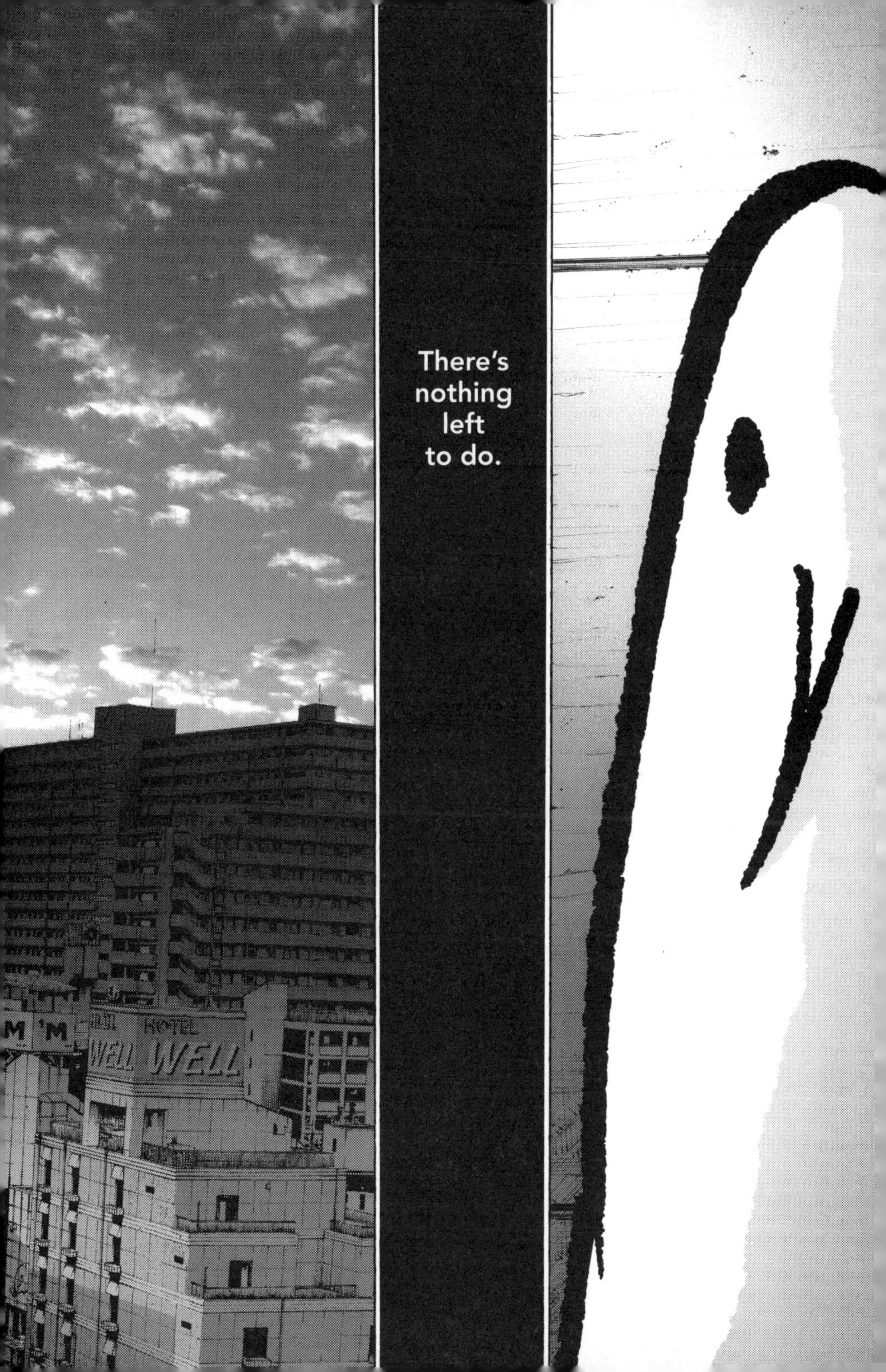
There's nothing left to do.
HOTEL
WELL

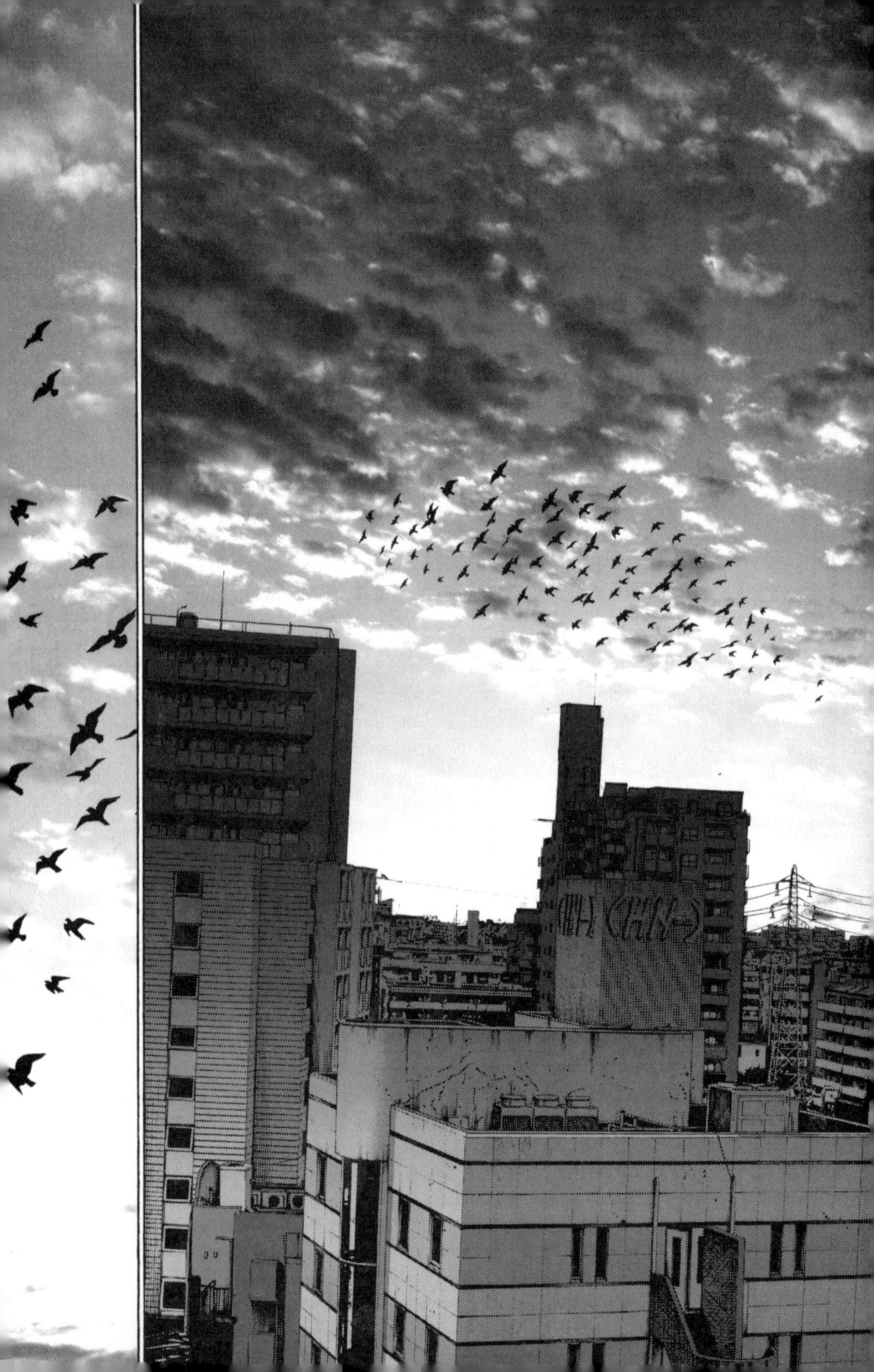

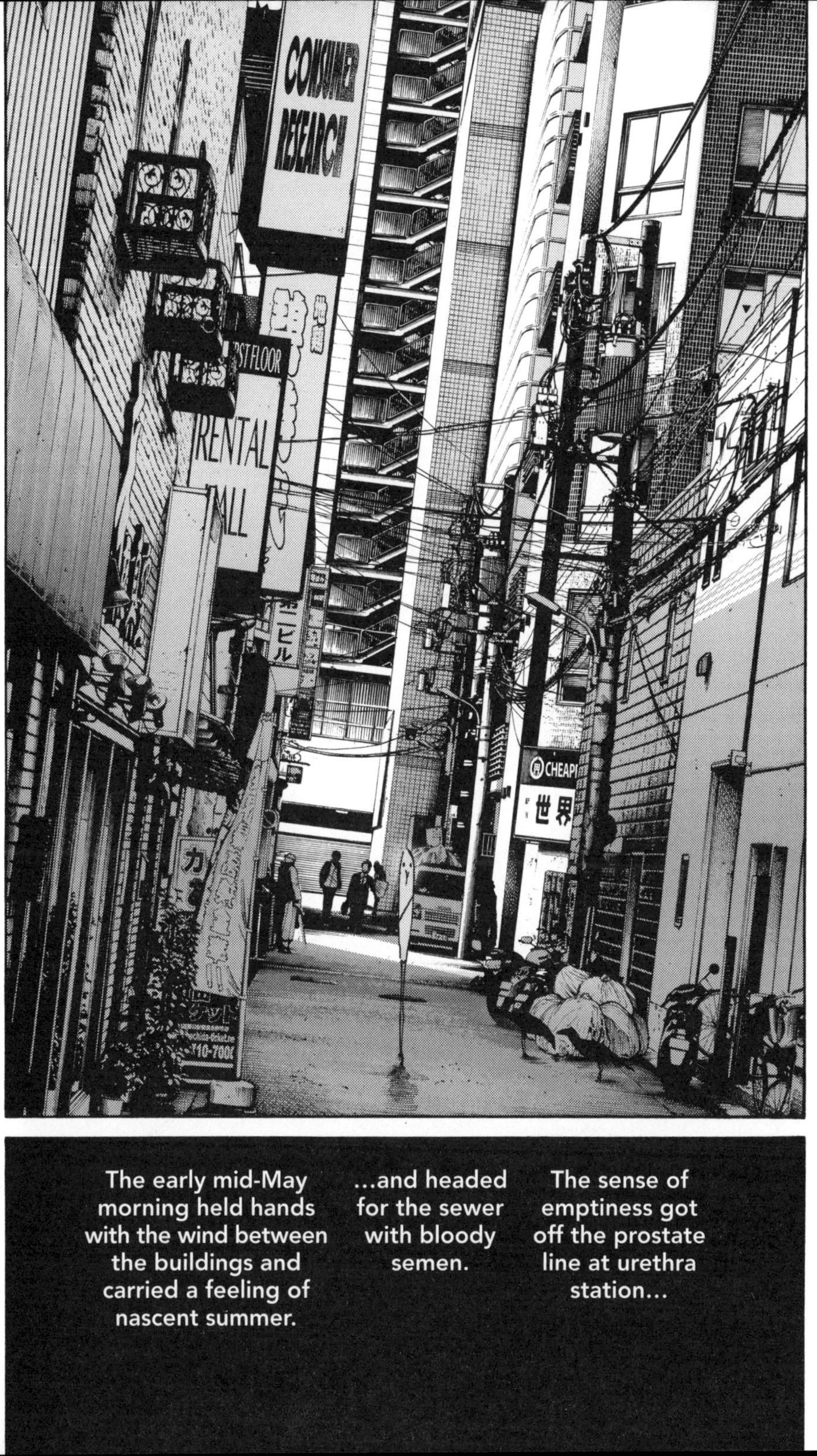
CONSUMER RESEARCH
RENTAL
CHEAP
世界

The sense of emptiness got off the prostate line at urethra station...

...and headed for the sewer with bloody semen.

The early mid-May morning held hands with the wind between the buildings and carried a feeling of nascent summer.

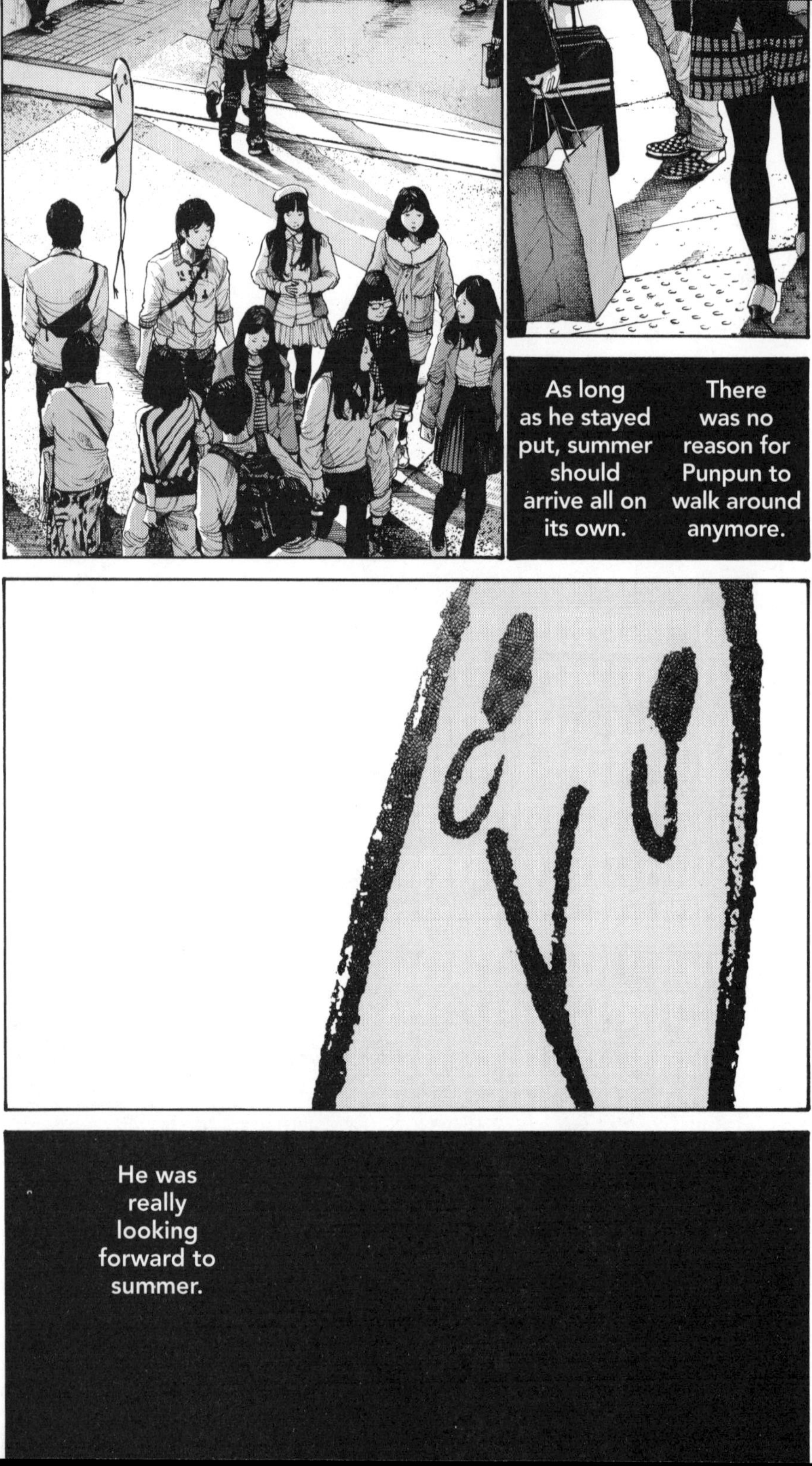
There was no reason for Punpun to walk around anymore.
As long as he stayed put, summer should arrive all on its own.
He was really looking forward to summer.

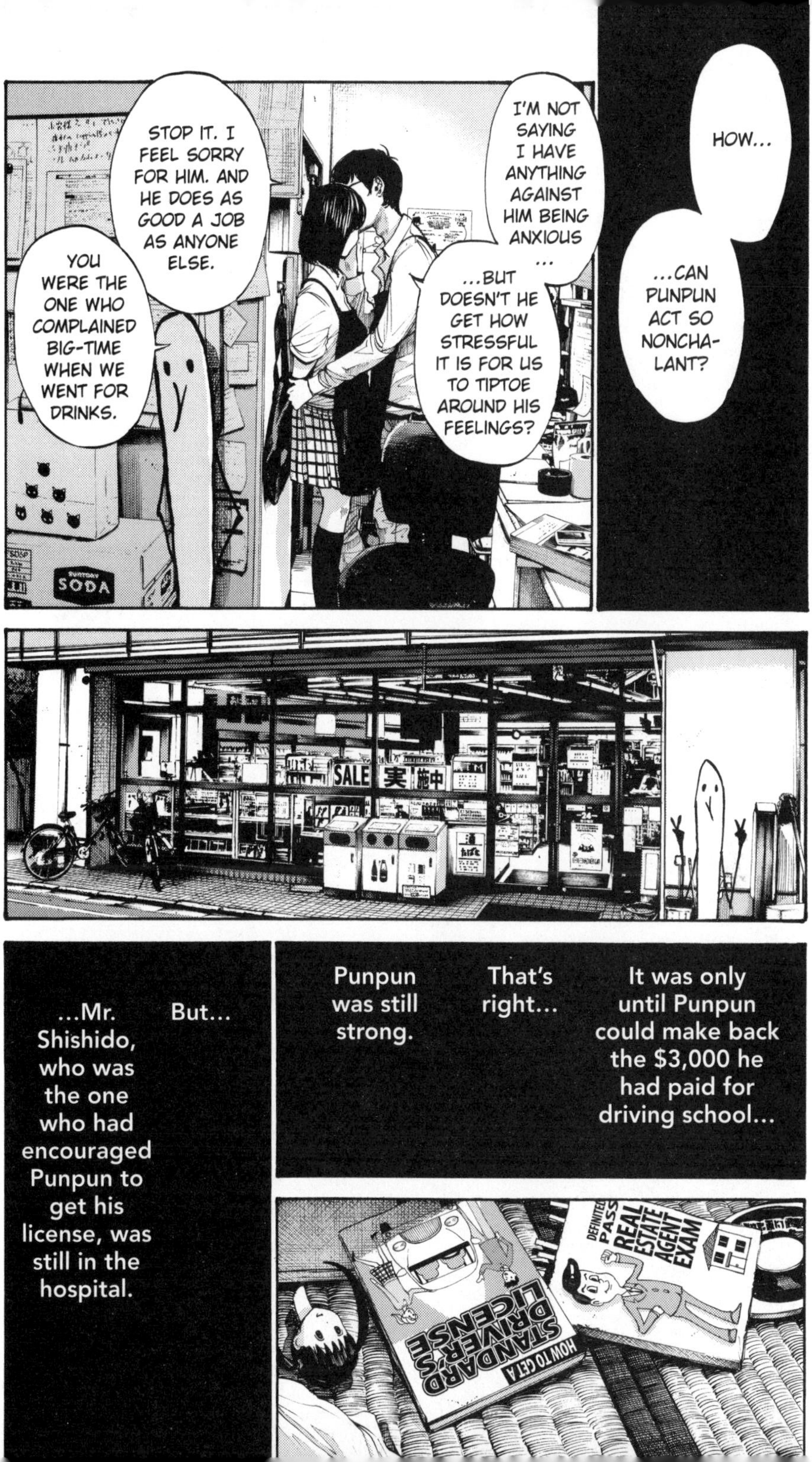
HOW...
...CAN PUNPUN ACT SO NONCHALANT?
I'M NOT SAYING I HAVE ANYTHING AGAINST HIM BEING ANXIOUS...
STOP IT. I FEEL SORRY FOR HIM. AND HE DOES AS GOOD A JOB AS ANYONE ELSE.
...BUT DOESN'T HE GET HOW STRESSFUL IT IS FOR US TO TIPTOE AROUND HIS FEELINGS?
YOU WERE THE ONE WHO COMPLAINED BIG-TIME WHEN WE WENT FOR DRINKS.
SODA
SALE
It was only until Punpun could make back the $3,000 he had paid for driving school...
That's right...
Punpun was still strong.
DEFINITELY PASS REAL ESTATE AGENT EXAM
HOW TO GET A STANDARD DRIVER'S LICENSE
But...
...Mr. Shishido, who was the one who had encouraged Punpun to get his license, was still in the hospital.

| Die, die, die! | You idiot! You piece of shit! | Are you **kidding** me? | Are you kidding me? |

| ...and I'll live wherever has the most beautiful scenery. | I'll bring the bare minimum of luggage... | ...I'm going to go far, far away, where I don't know anyone! | When I get my license... |

| That's what Punpun thought. | ...but it would be nice to find a special someone there... | I don't care if it's far, far in the future... | I'm not in a hurry anymore. |

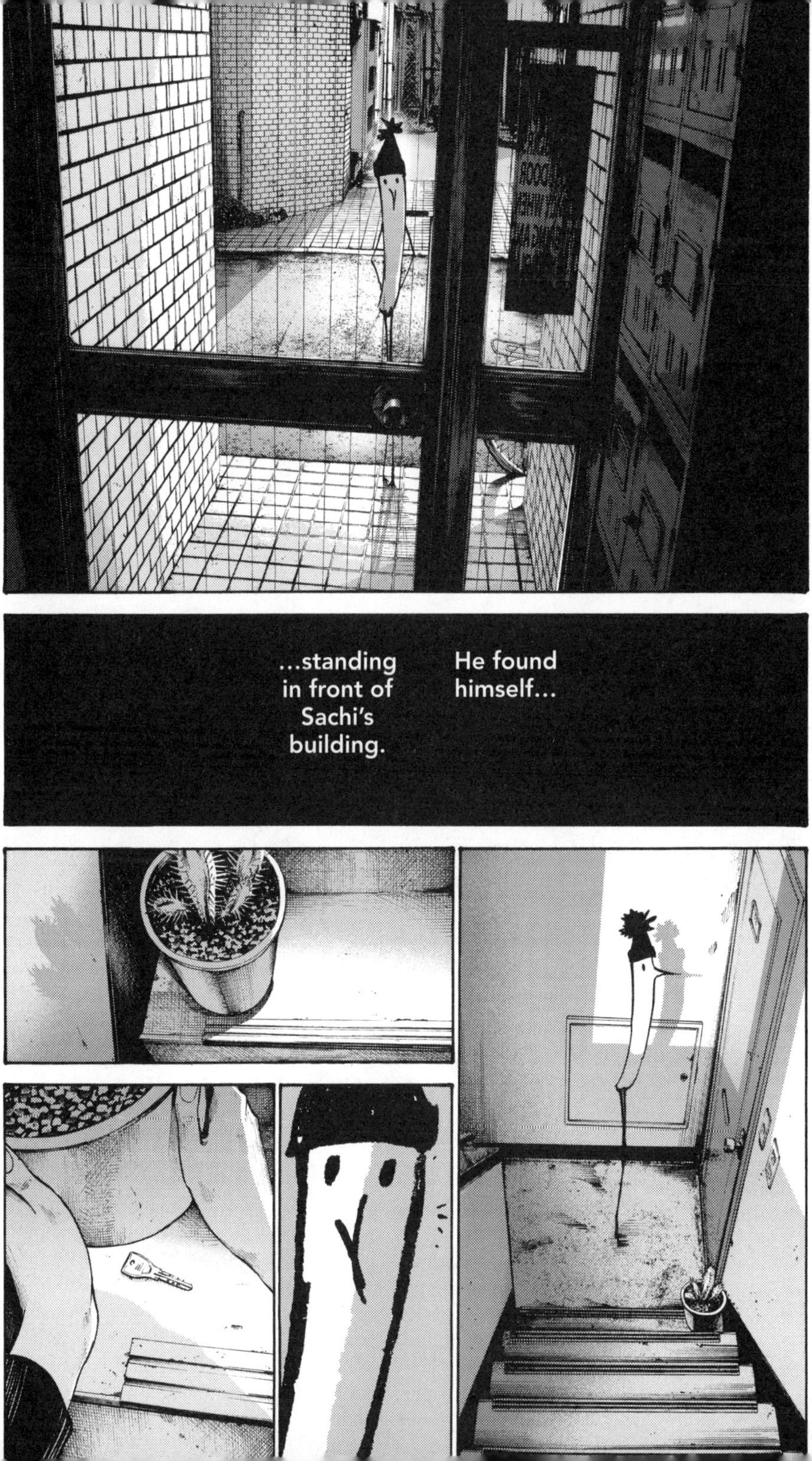
He found himself...
...standing in front of Sachi's building.

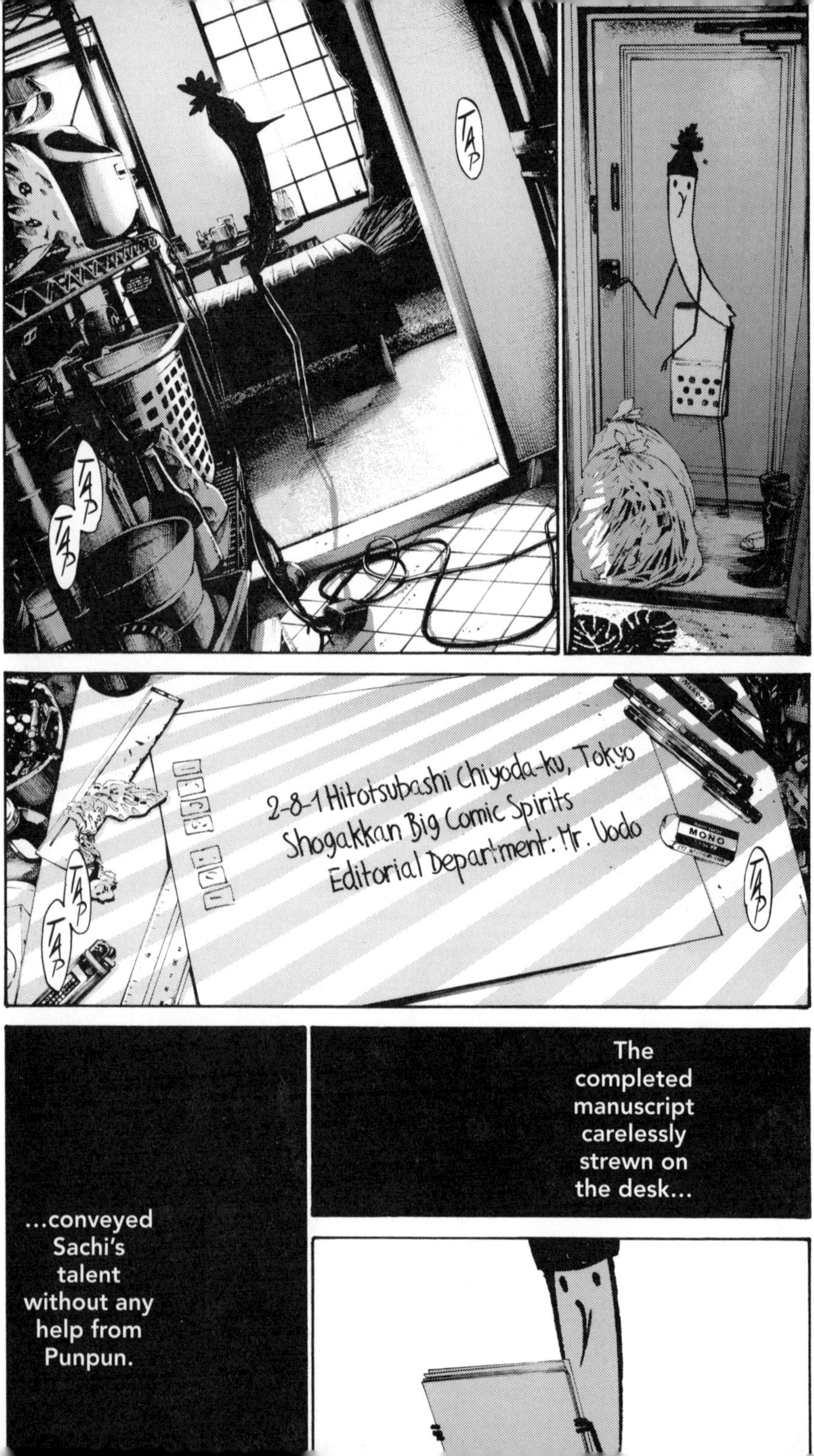
TAP
TAP TAP
2-8-1 Hitotsubashi Chiyoda-ku, Tokyo
Shogakkan Big Comic Spirits
Editorial Department: Mr. Uodo
MONO
TAP
TAP TAP
The completed manuscript carelessly strewn on the desk...
...conveyed Sachi's talent without any help from Punpun.

Punpun
thought,
"This is
good."

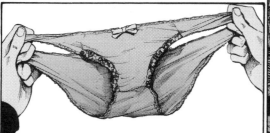

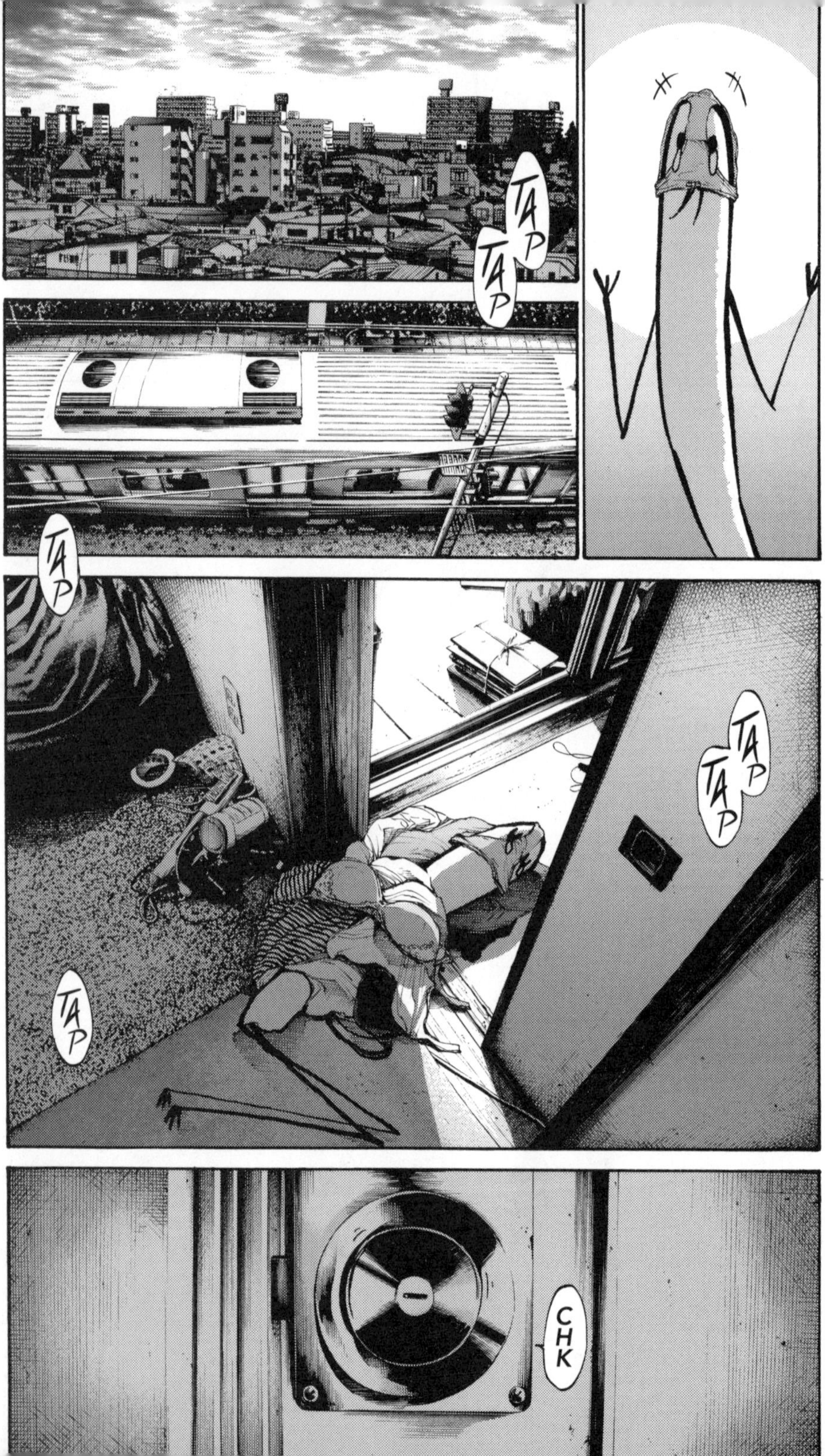
TAP TAP
TAP
TAP TAP
TAP
CHK

WHO
ARE
YOU?

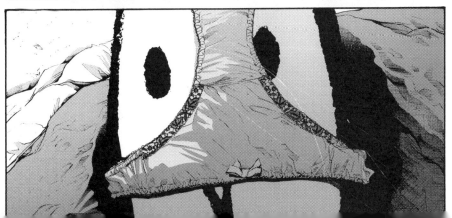

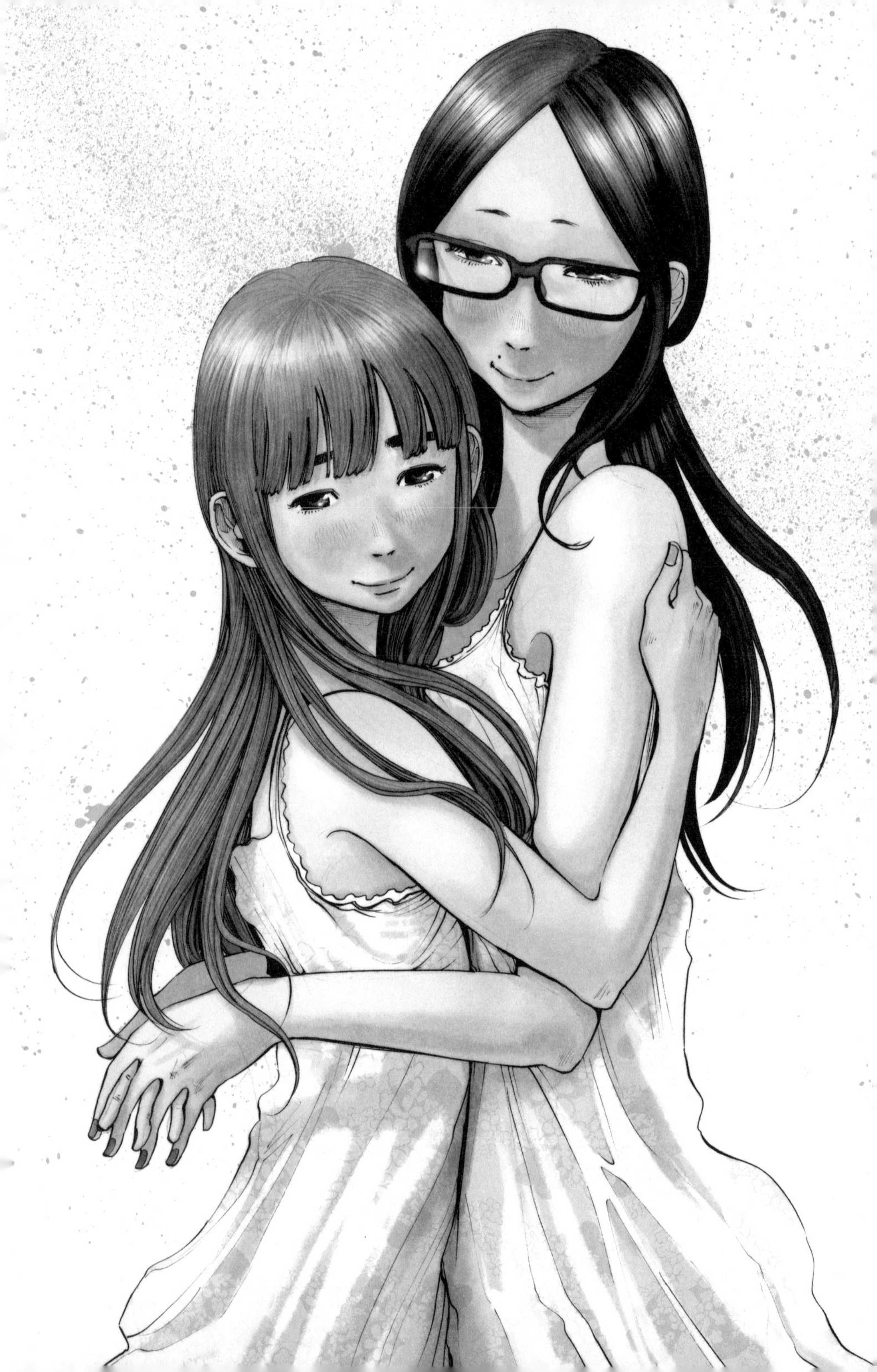

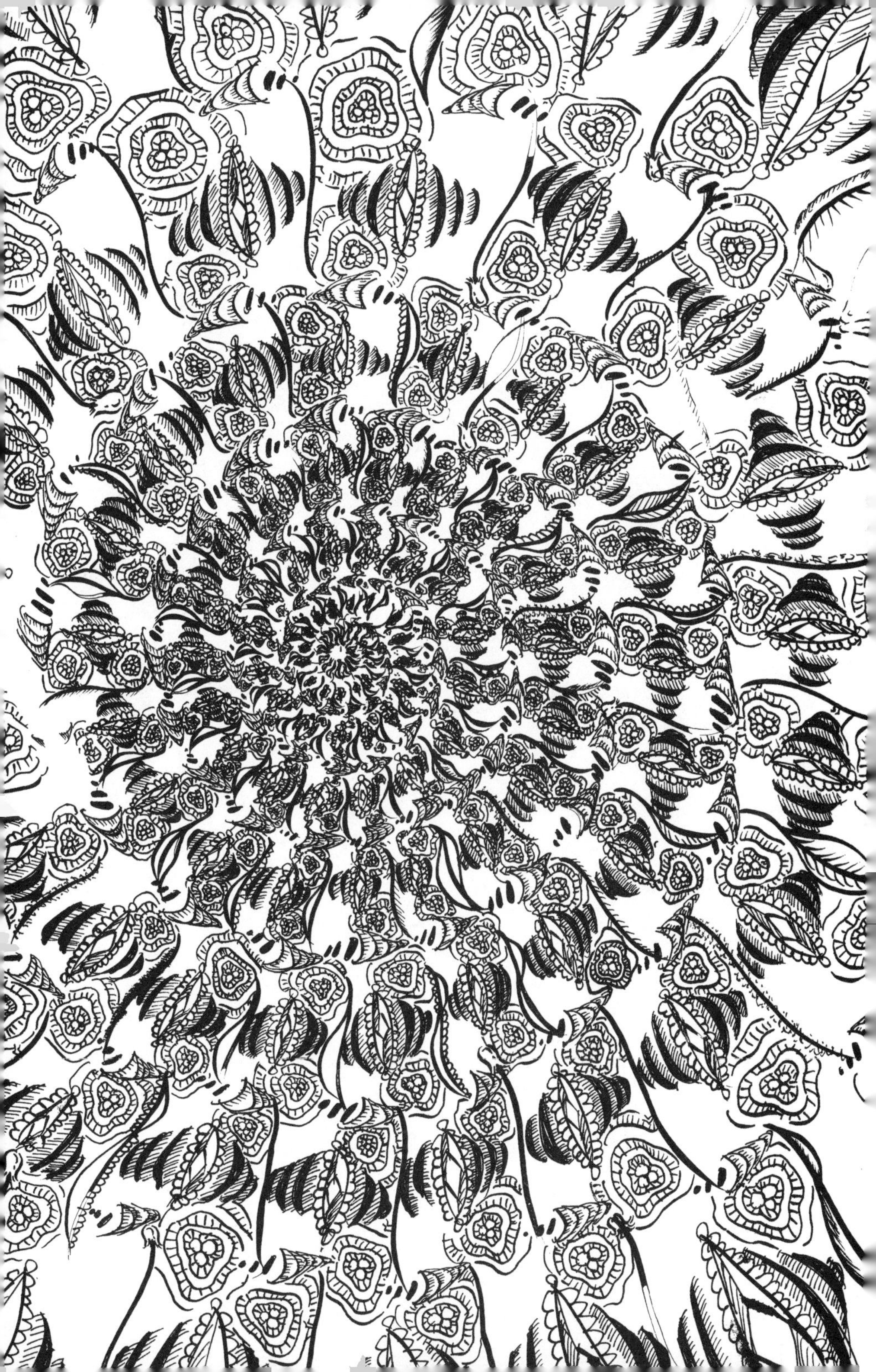

Chapter 105

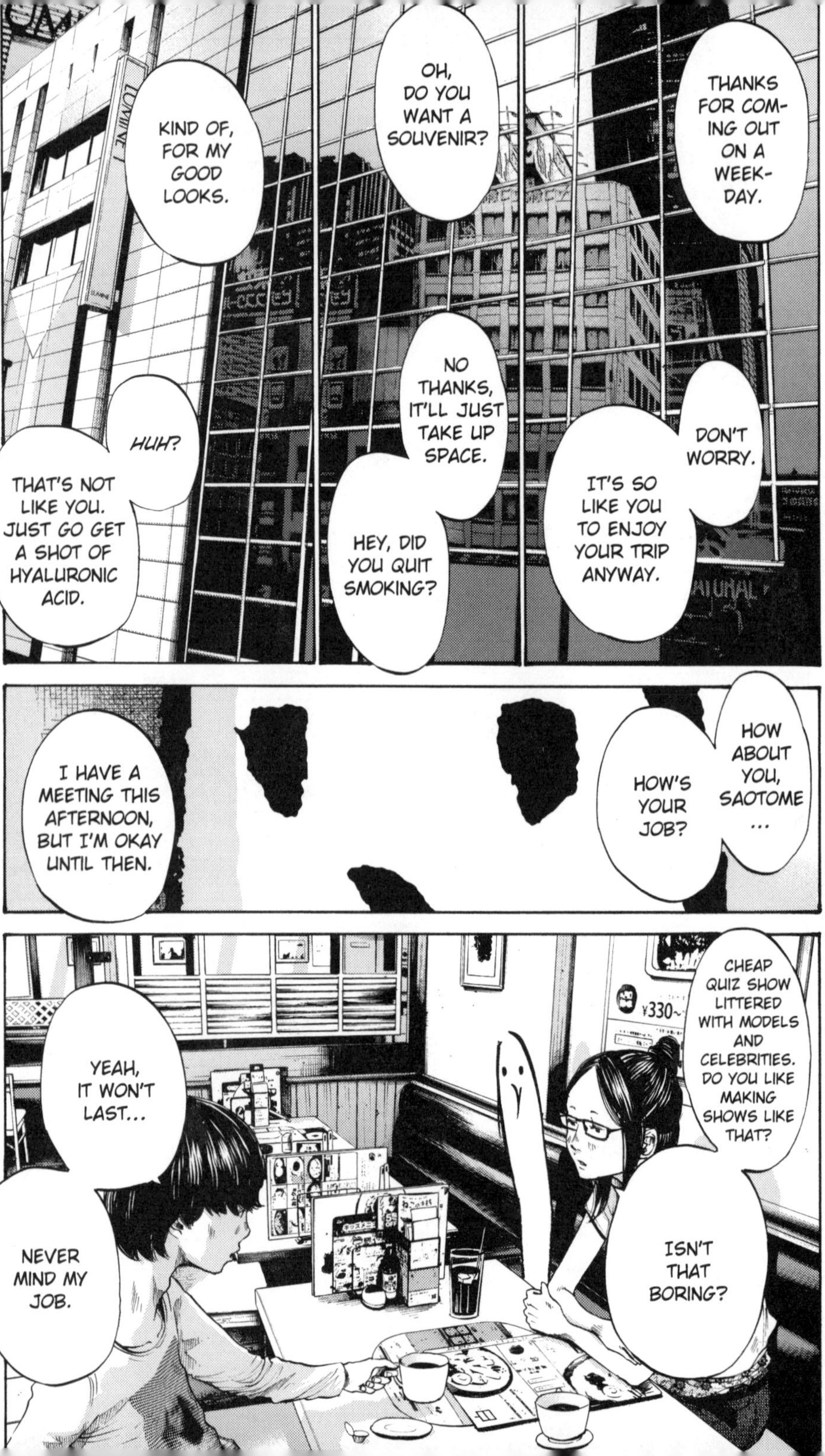
THANKS FOR COMING OUT ON A WEEKDAY.
DON'T WORRY.
IT'S SO LIKE YOU TO ENJOY YOUR TRIP ANYWAY.
OH, DO YOU WANT A SOUVENIR?
NO THANKS, IT'LL JUST TAKE UP SPACE.
HEY, DID YOU QUIT SMOKING?
KIND OF, FOR MY GOOD LOOKS.
HUH?
THAT'S NOT LIKE YOU. JUST GO GET A SHOT OF HYALURONIC ACID.
HOW ABOUT YOU, SAOTOME…
HOW'S YOUR JOB?
I HAVE A MEETING THIS AFTERNOON, BUT I'M OKAY UNTIL THEN.
CHEAP QUIZ SHOW LITTERED WITH MODELS AND CELEBRITIES. DO YOU LIKE MAKING SHOWS LIKE THAT?
¥330~
YEAH, IT WON'T LAST…
ISN'T THAT BORING?
NEVER MIND MY JOB.

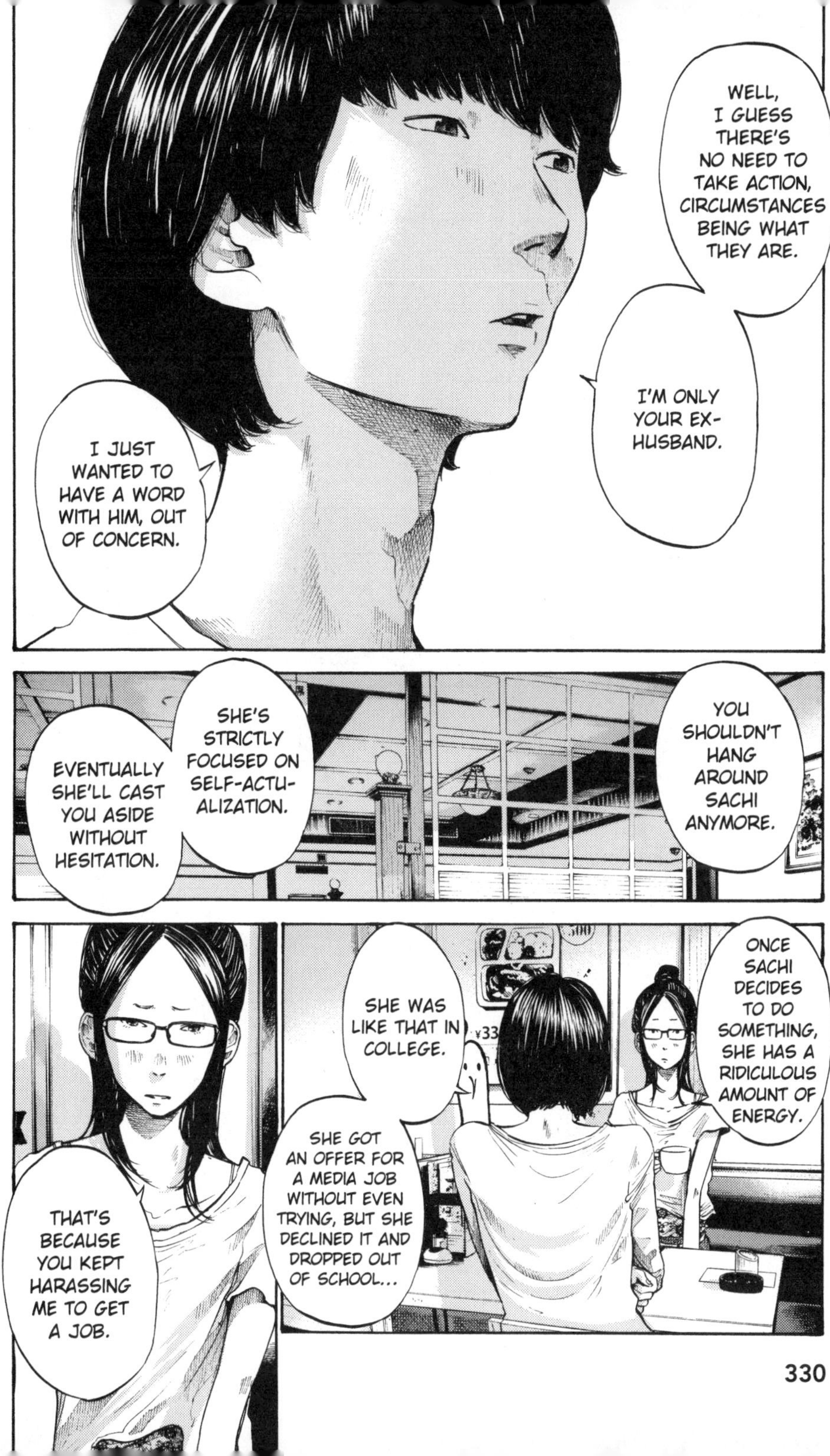
WELL, I GUESS THERE'S NO NEED TO TAKE ACTION, CIRCUMSTANCES BEING WHAT THEY ARE.
I'M ONLY YOUR EX-HUSBAND.
I JUST WANTED TO HAVE A WORD WITH HIM, OUT OF CONCERN.
YOU SHOULDN'T HANG AROUND SACHI ANYMORE.
SHE'S STRICTLY FOCUSED ON SELF-ACTUALIZATION.
EVENTUALLY SHE'LL CAST YOU ASIDE WITHOUT HESITATION.
ONCE SACHI DECIDES TO DO SOMETHING, SHE HAS A RIDICULOUS AMOUNT OF ENERGY.
SHE WAS LIKE THAT IN COLLEGE.
SHE GOT AN OFFER FOR A MEDIA JOB WITHOUT EVEN TRYING, BUT SHE DECLINED IT AND DROPPED OUT OF SCHOOL...
THAT'S BECAUSE YOU KEPT HARASSING ME TO GET A JOB.

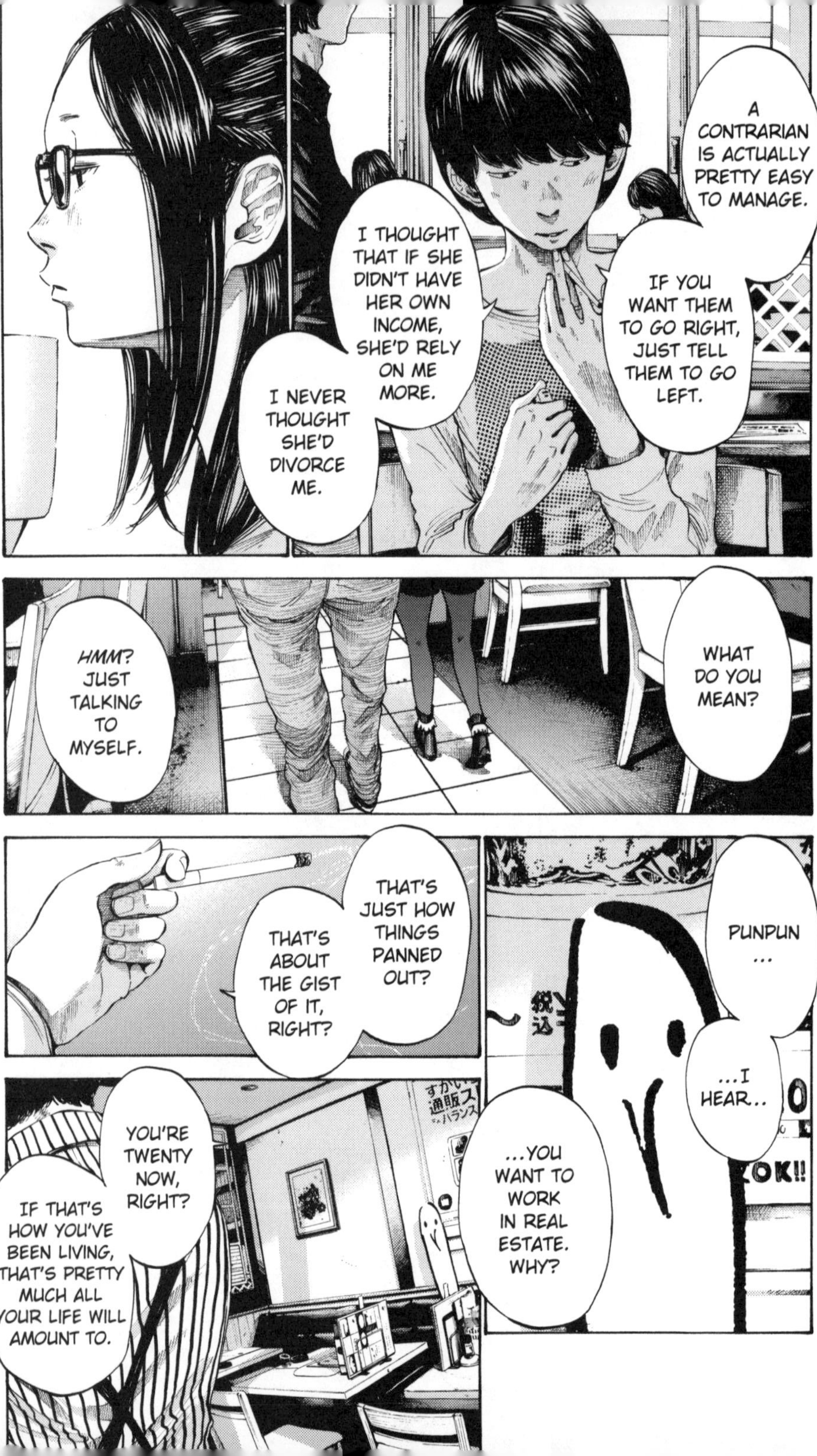
A CONTRARIAN IS ACTUALLY PRETTY EASY TO MANAGE.
IF YOU WANT THEM TO GO RIGHT, JUST TELL THEM TO GO LEFT.
I THOUGHT THAT IF SHE DIDN'T HAVE HER OWN INCOME, SHE'D RELY ON ME MORE.
I NEVER THOUGHT SHE'D DIVORCE ME.
WHAT DO YOU MEAN?
HMM? JUST TALKING TO MYSELF.
PUNPUN...
...I HEAR...
...YOU WANT TO WORK IN REAL ESTATE. WHY?
THAT'S JUST HOW THINGS PANNED OUT?
THAT'S ABOUT THE GIST OF IT, RIGHT?
YOU'RE TWENTY NOW, RIGHT?
IF THAT'S HOW YOU'VE BEEN LIVING, THAT'S PRETTY MUCH ALL YOUR LIFE WILL AMOUNT TO.

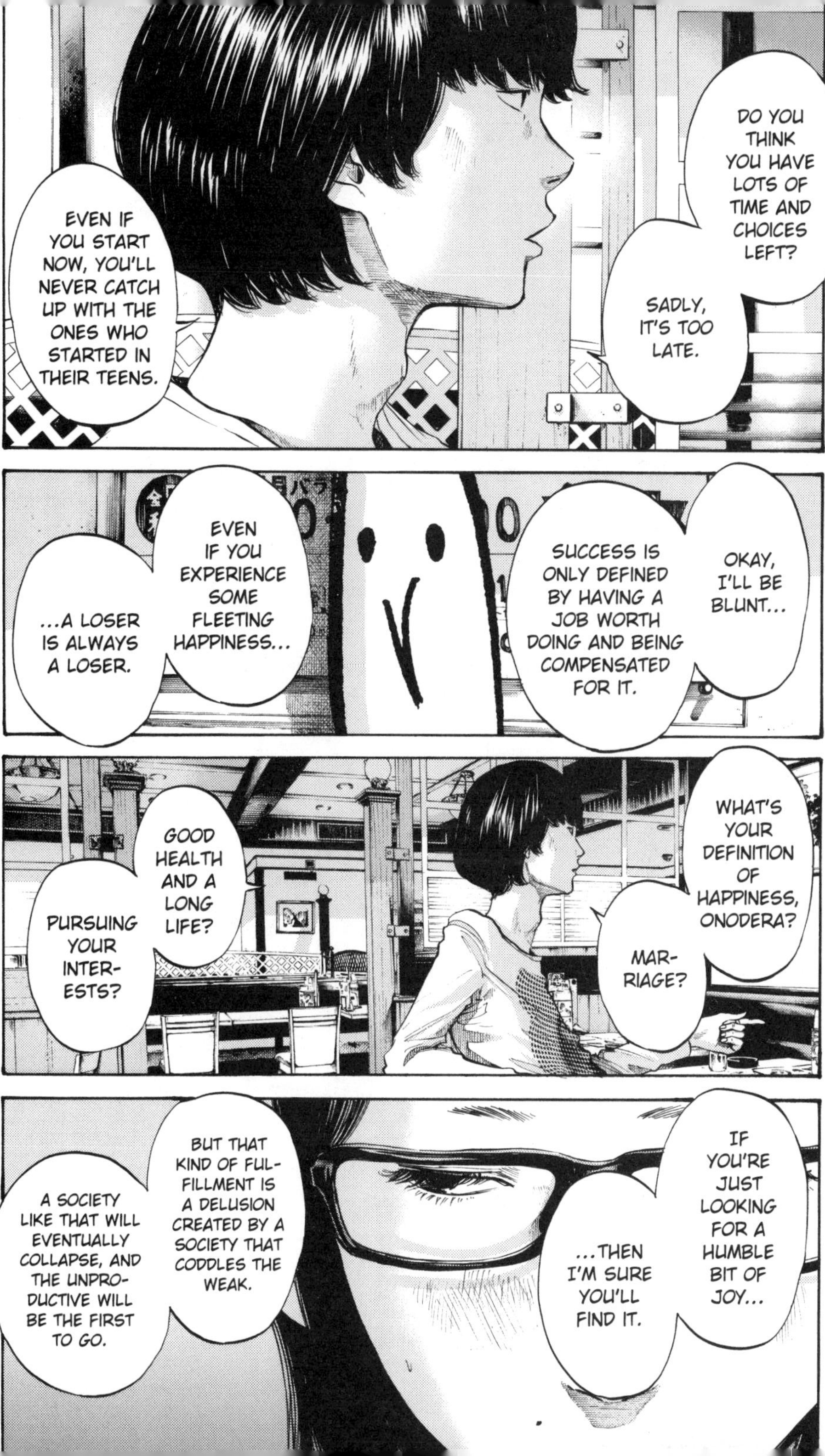
DO YOU THINK YOU HAVE LOTS OF TIME AND CHOICES LEFT?
SADLY, IT'S TOO LATE.
EVEN IF YOU START NOW, YOU'LL NEVER CATCH UP WITH THE ONES WHO STARTED IN THEIR TEENS.
OKAY, I'LL BE BLUNT...
SUCCESS IS ONLY DEFINED BY HAVING A JOB WORTH DOING AND BEING COMPENSATED FOR IT.
EVEN IF YOU EXPERIENCE SOME FLEETING HAPPINESS...
...A LOSER IS ALWAYS A LOSER.
WHAT'S YOUR DEFINITION OF HAPPINESS, ONODERA?
MARRIAGE?
GOOD HEALTH AND A LONG LIFE?
PURSUING YOUR INTERESTS?
IF YOU'RE JUST LOOKING FOR A HUMBLE BIT OF JOY...
...THEN I'M SURE YOU'LL FIND IT.
BUT THAT KIND OF FULFILLMENT IS A DELUSION CREATED BY A SOCIETY THAT CODDLES THE WEAK.
A SOCIETY LIKE THAT WILL EVENTUALLY COLLAPSE, AND THE UNPRODUCTIVE WILL BE THE FIRST TO GO.

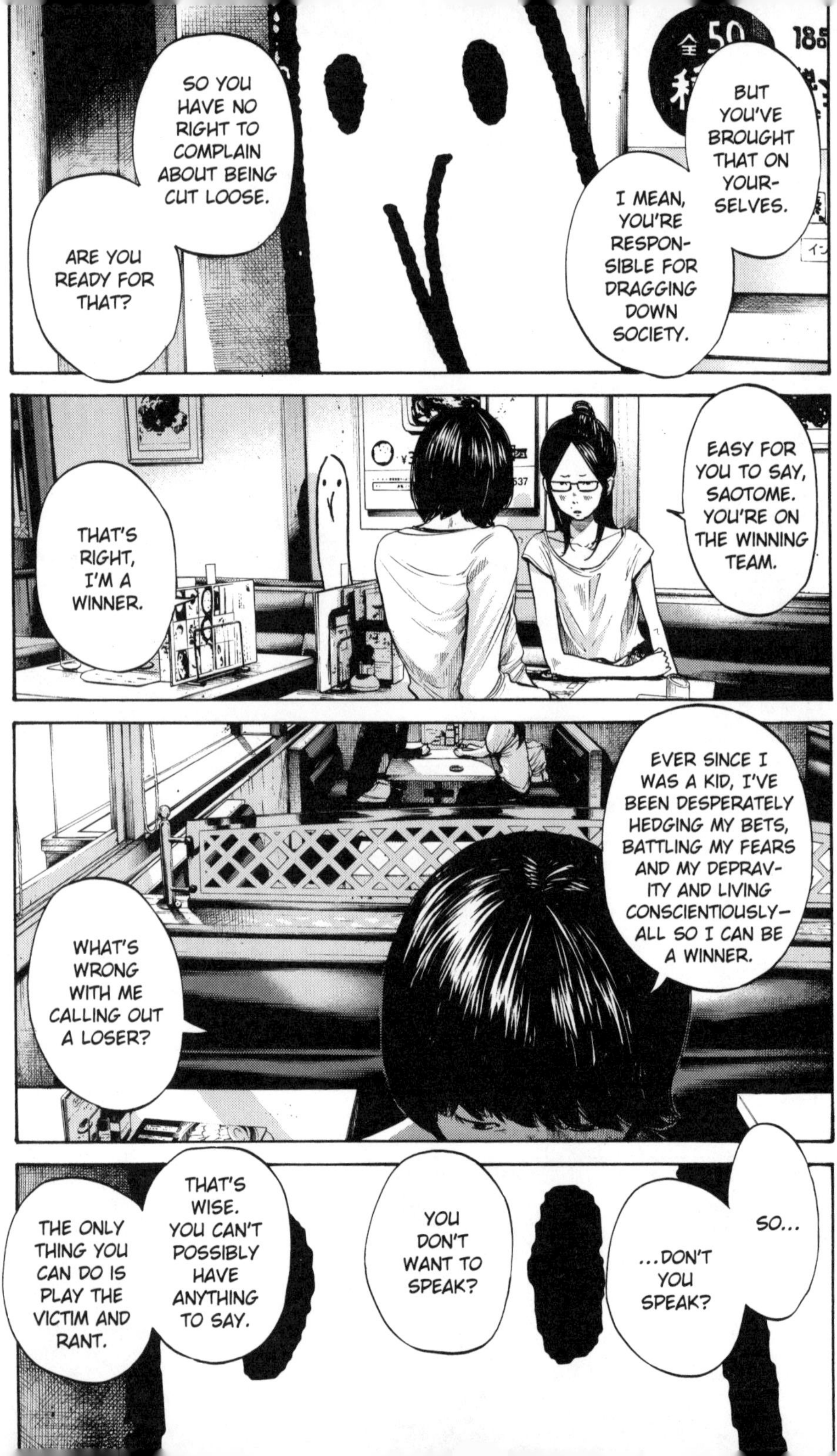
BUT YOU'VE BROUGHT THAT ON YOUR-SELVES.
I MEAN, YOU'RE RESPON-SIBLE FOR DRAGGING DOWN SOCIETY.
SO YOU HAVE NO RIGHT TO COMPLAIN ABOUT BEING CUT LOOSE.
ARE YOU READY FOR THAT?
EASY FOR YOU TO SAY, SAOTOME. YOU'RE ON THE WINNING TEAM.
THAT'S RIGHT, I'M A WINNER.
EVER SINCE I WAS A KID, I'VE BEEN DESPERATELY HEDGING MY BETS, BATTLING MY FEARS AND MY DEPRAV-ITY AND LIVING CONSCIENTIOUSLY—ALL SO I CAN BE A WINNER.
WHAT'S WRONG WITH ME CALLING OUT A LOSER?
SO...
...DON'T YOU SPEAK?
YOU DON'T WANT TO SPEAK?
THAT'S WISE. YOU CAN'T POSSIBLY HAVE ANYTHING TO SAY.
THE ONLY THING YOU CAN DO IS PLAY THE VICTIM AND RANT.

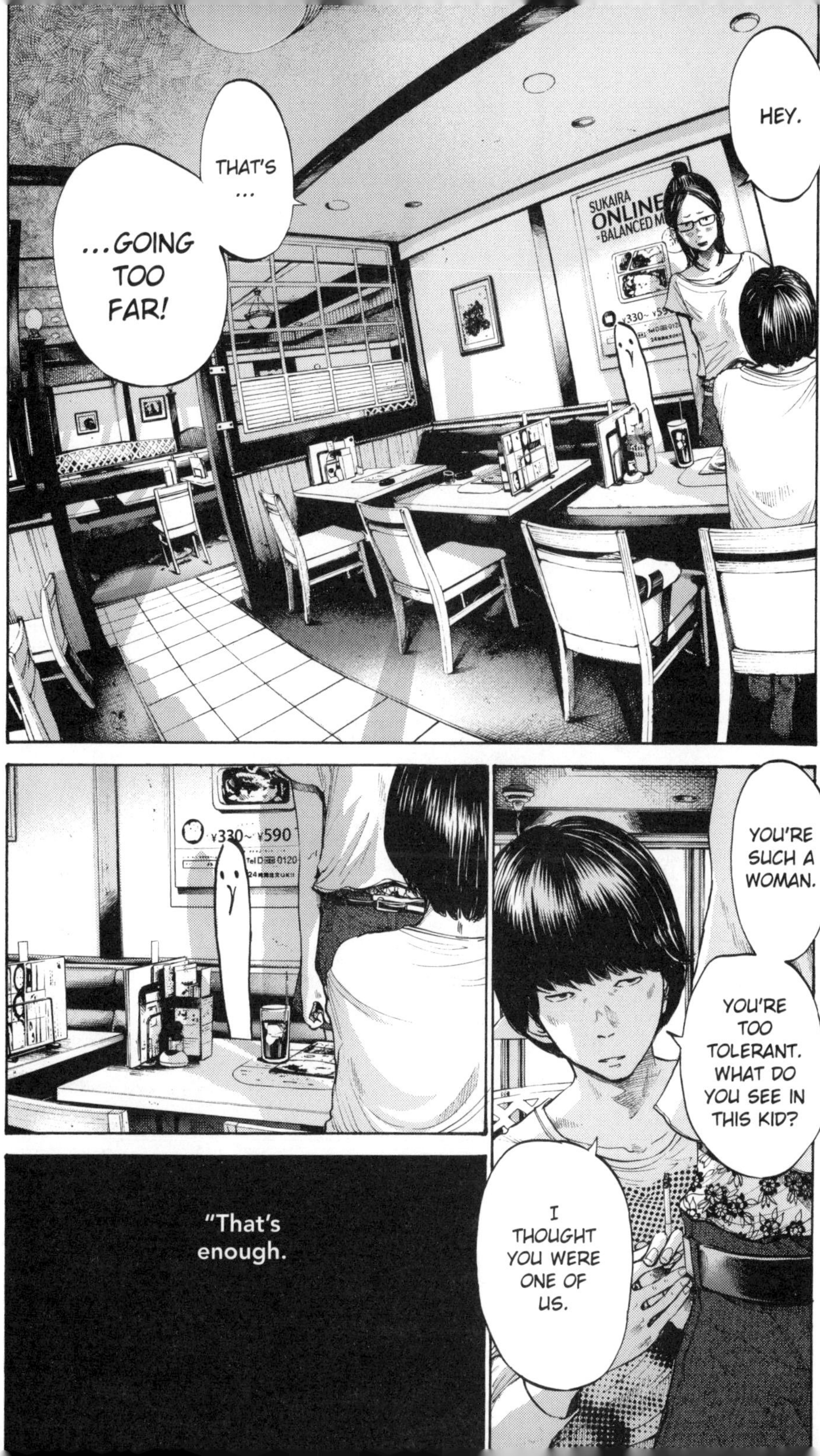
HEY.
SUKAIRA ONLINE =BALANCED M
THAT'S ...
...GOING TOO FAR!
YOU'RE SUCH A WOMAN.
YOU'RE TOO TOLERANT. WHAT DO YOU SEE IN THIS KID?
I THOUGHT YOU WERE ONE OF US.
¥330~ ¥590
"That's enough.

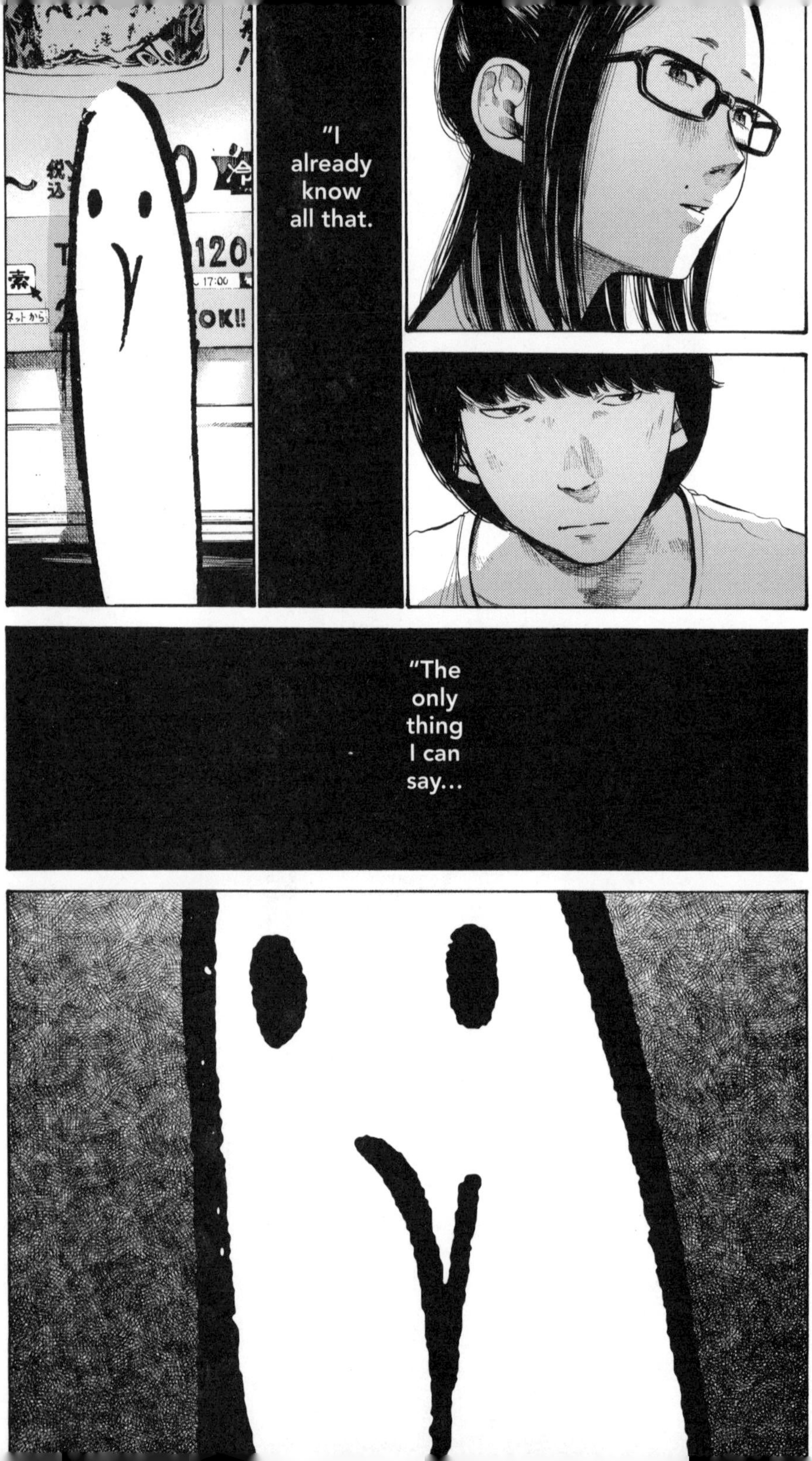
"I already know all that.
"The only thing I can say...

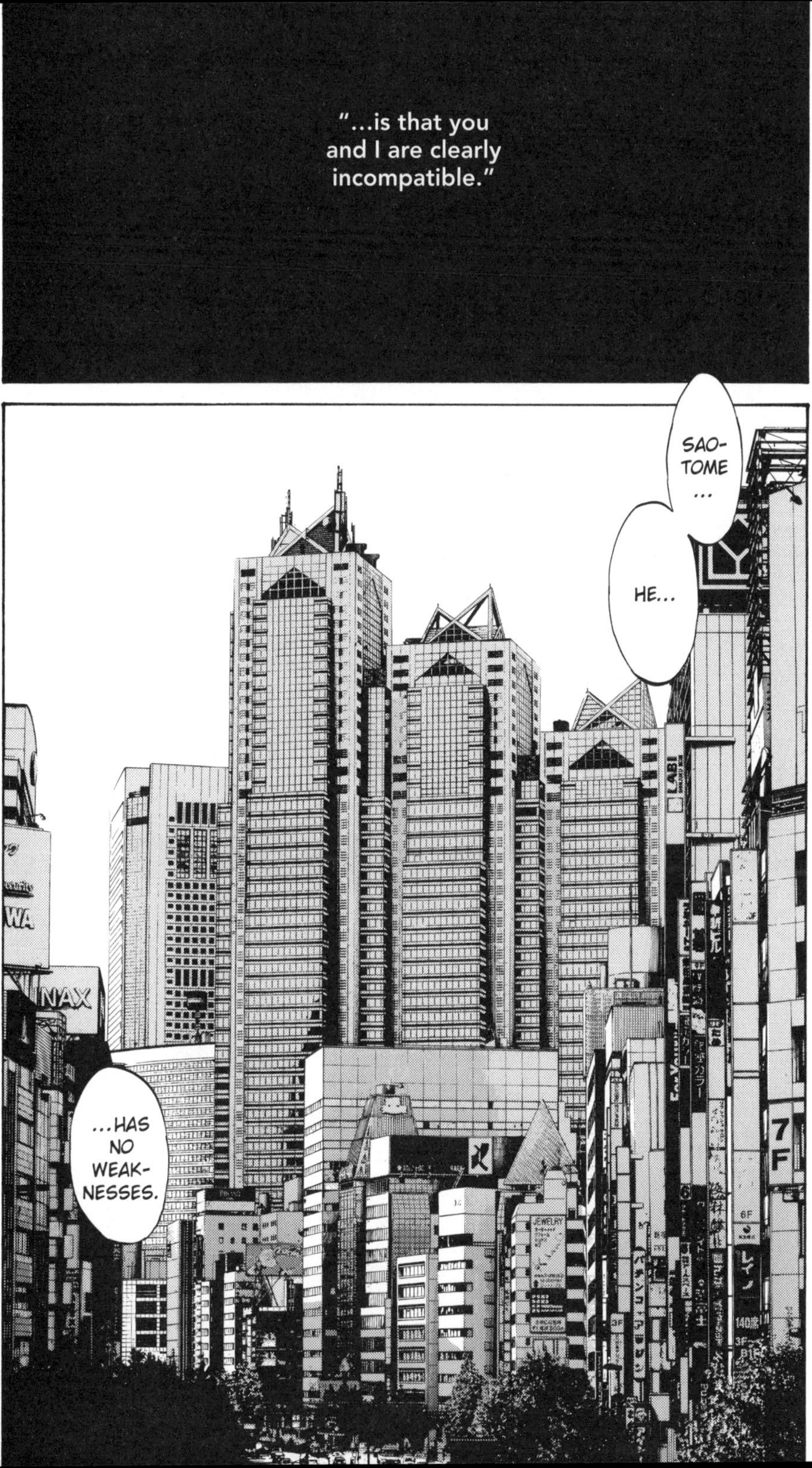
"...is that you and I are clearly incompatible."
SAO-TOME...
HE...
...HAS NO WEAK-NESSES.

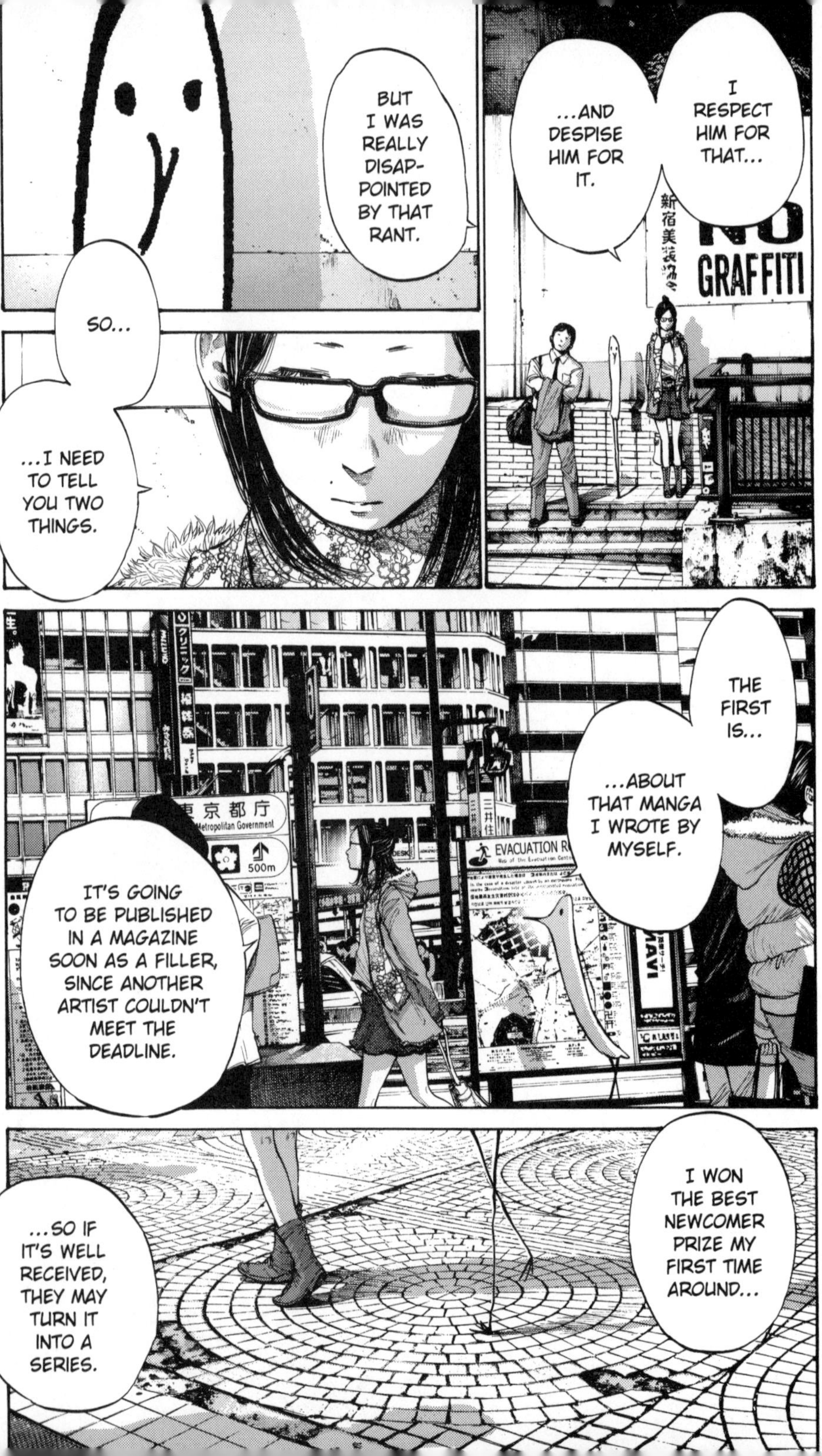
I RESPECT HIM FOR THAT...
...AND DESPISE HIM FOR IT.
GRAFFITI
BUT I WAS REALLY DISAPPOINTED BY THAT RANT.
SO...
...I NEED TO TELL YOU TWO THINGS.
THE FIRST IS...
...ABOUT THAT MANGA I WROTE BY MYSELF.
東京都庁
Metropolitan Government
500m
IT'S GOING TO BE PUBLISHED IN A MAGAZINE SOON AS A FILLER, SINCE ANOTHER ARTIST COULDN'T MEET THE DEADLINE.
I WON THE BEST NEWCOMER PRIZE MY FIRST TIME AROUND...
...SO IF IT'S WELL RECEIVED, THEY MAY TURN IT INTO A SERIES.

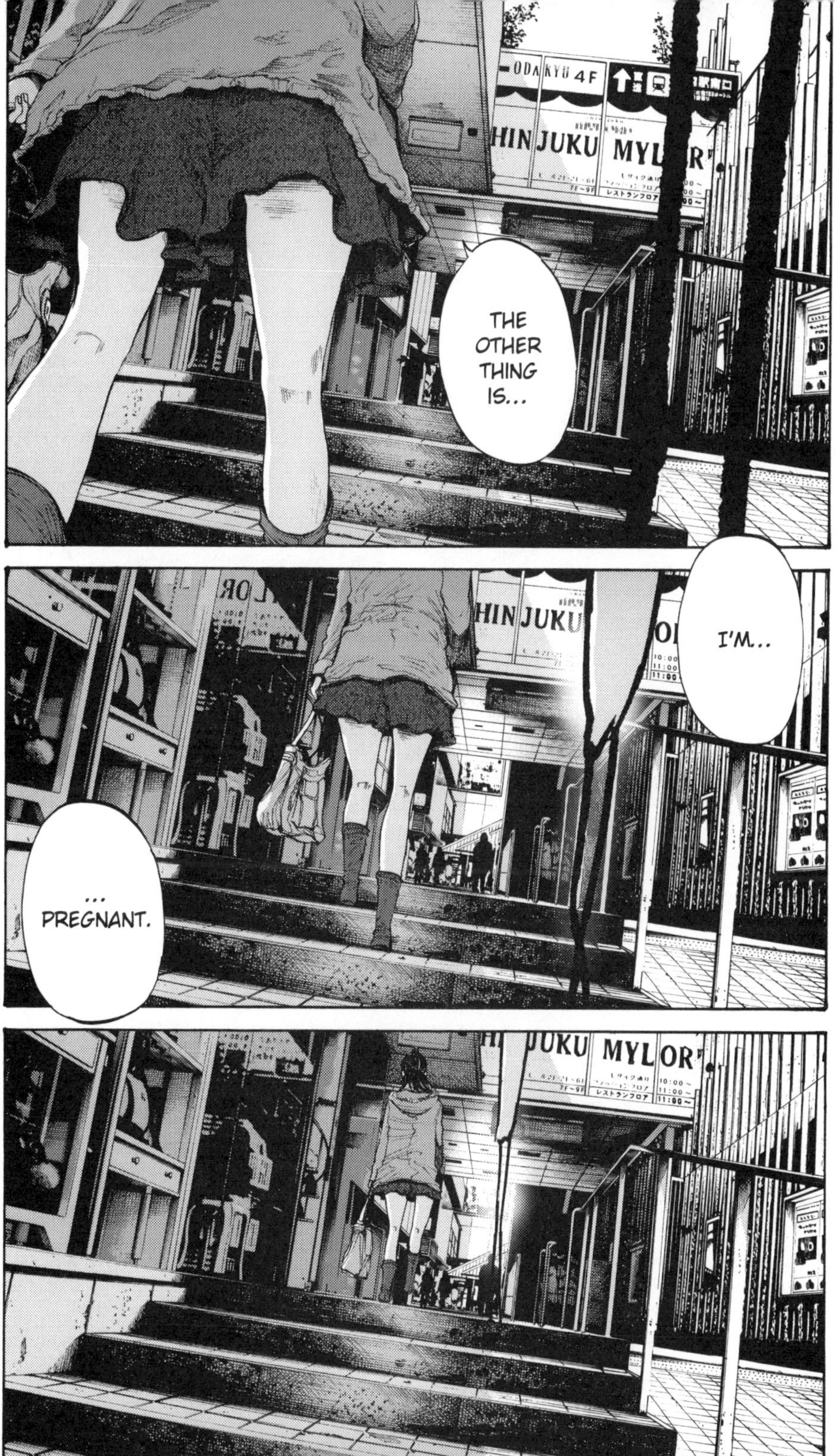
THE OTHER THING IS...
I'M...
... PREGNANT.

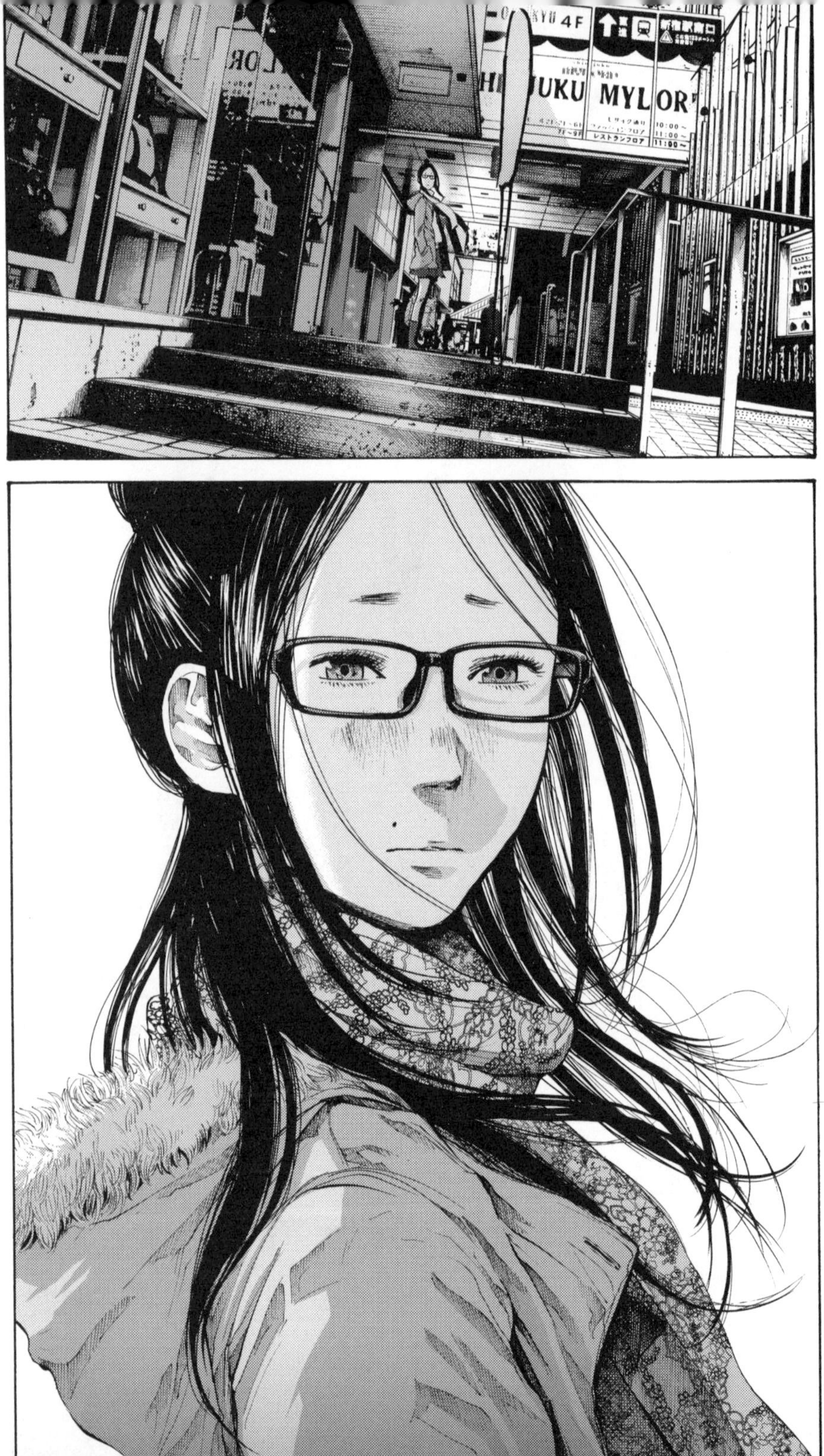
4F
JUKU MYLOR

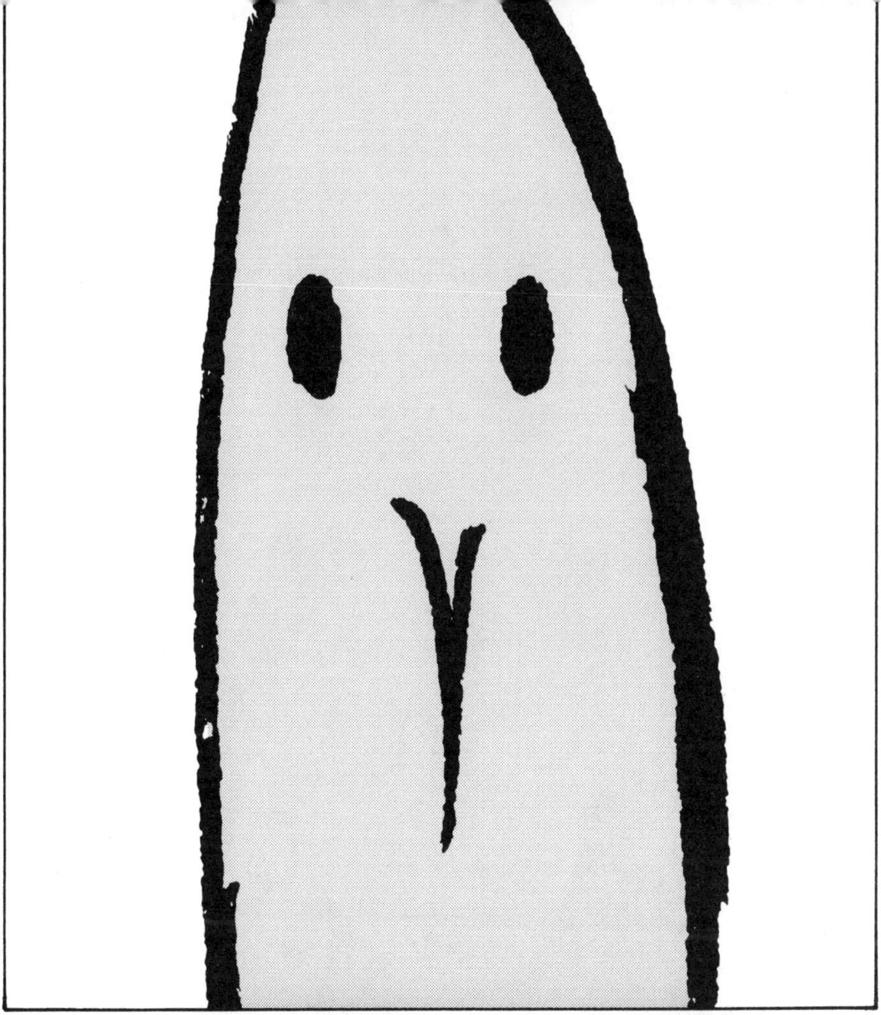

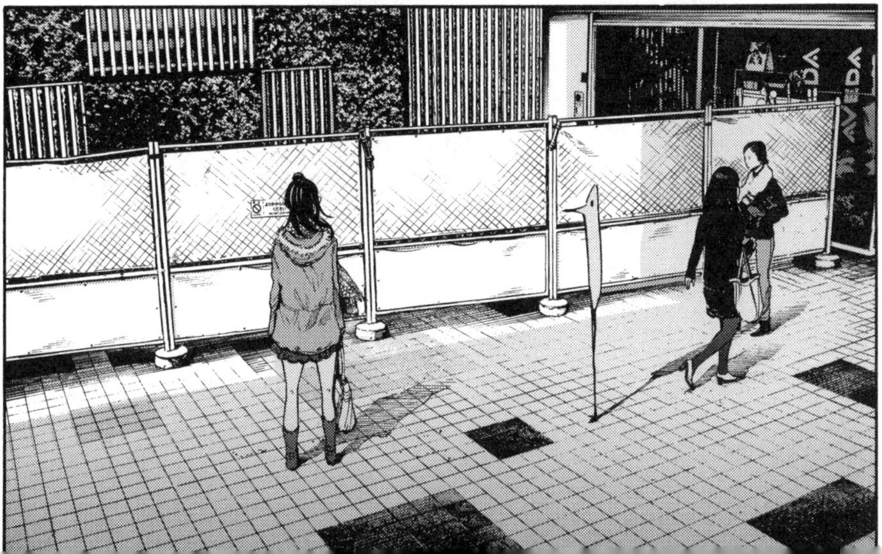

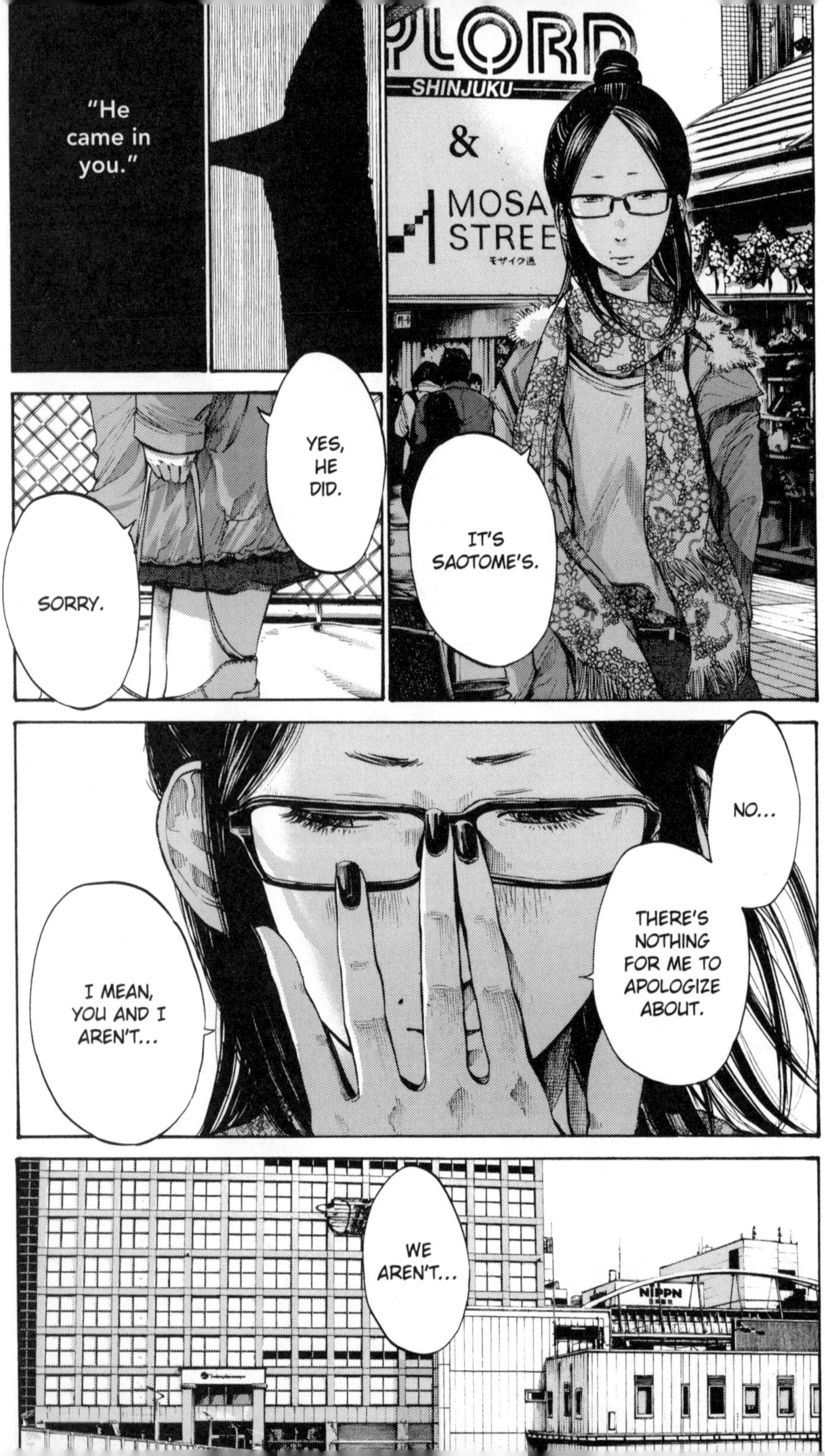
LORD
SHINJUKU
&
MOSA STREE
モザイク通
IT'S SAOTOME'S.
"He came in you."
YES, HE DID.
SORRY.
NO...
THERE'S NOTHING FOR ME TO APOLOGIZE ABOUT.
I MEAN, YOU AND I AREN'T...
WE AREN'T...
NIPPN

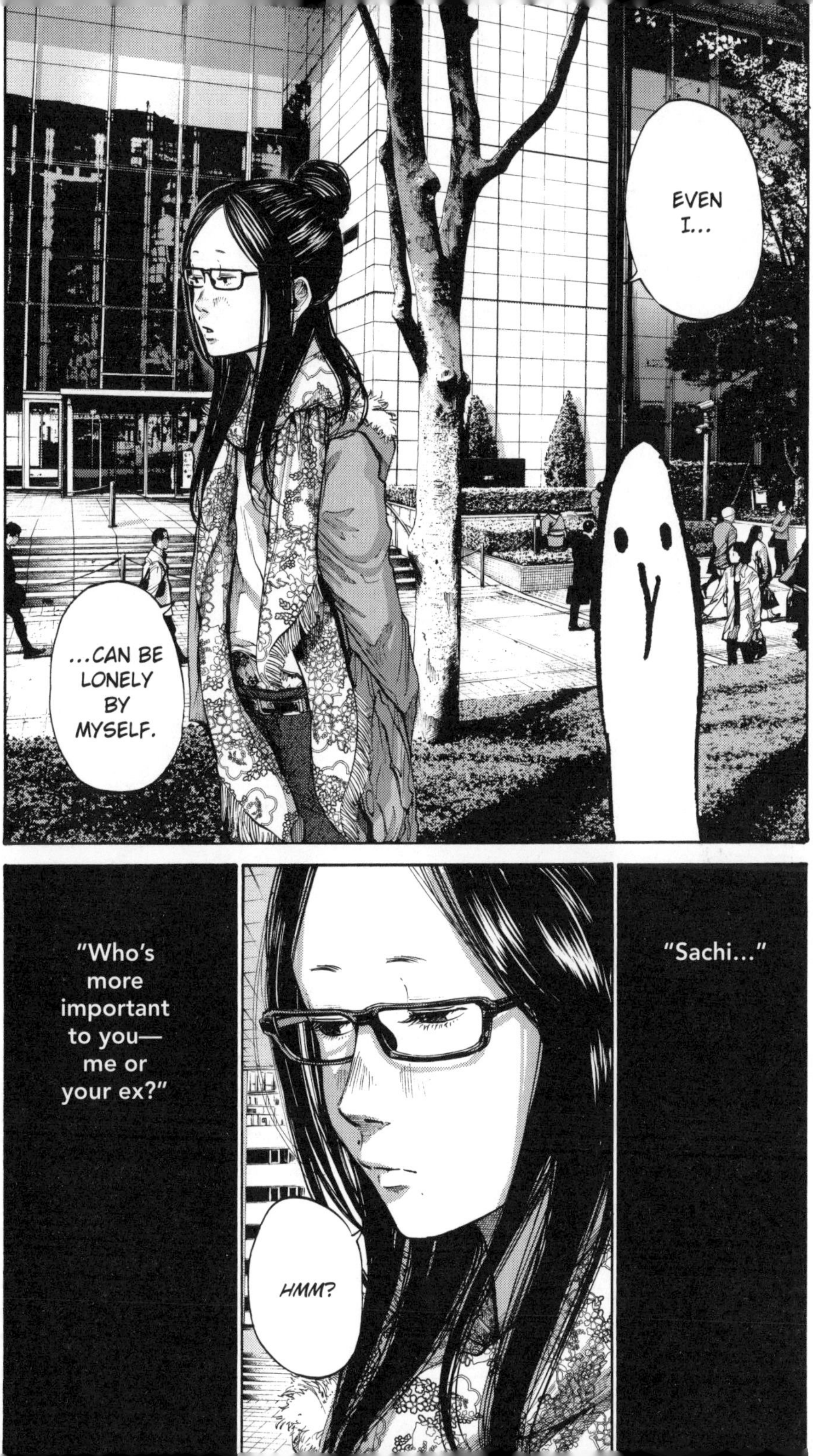
EVEN I...
...CAN BE LONELY BY MYSELF.
"Sachi..."
HMM?
"Who's more important to you— me or your ex?"

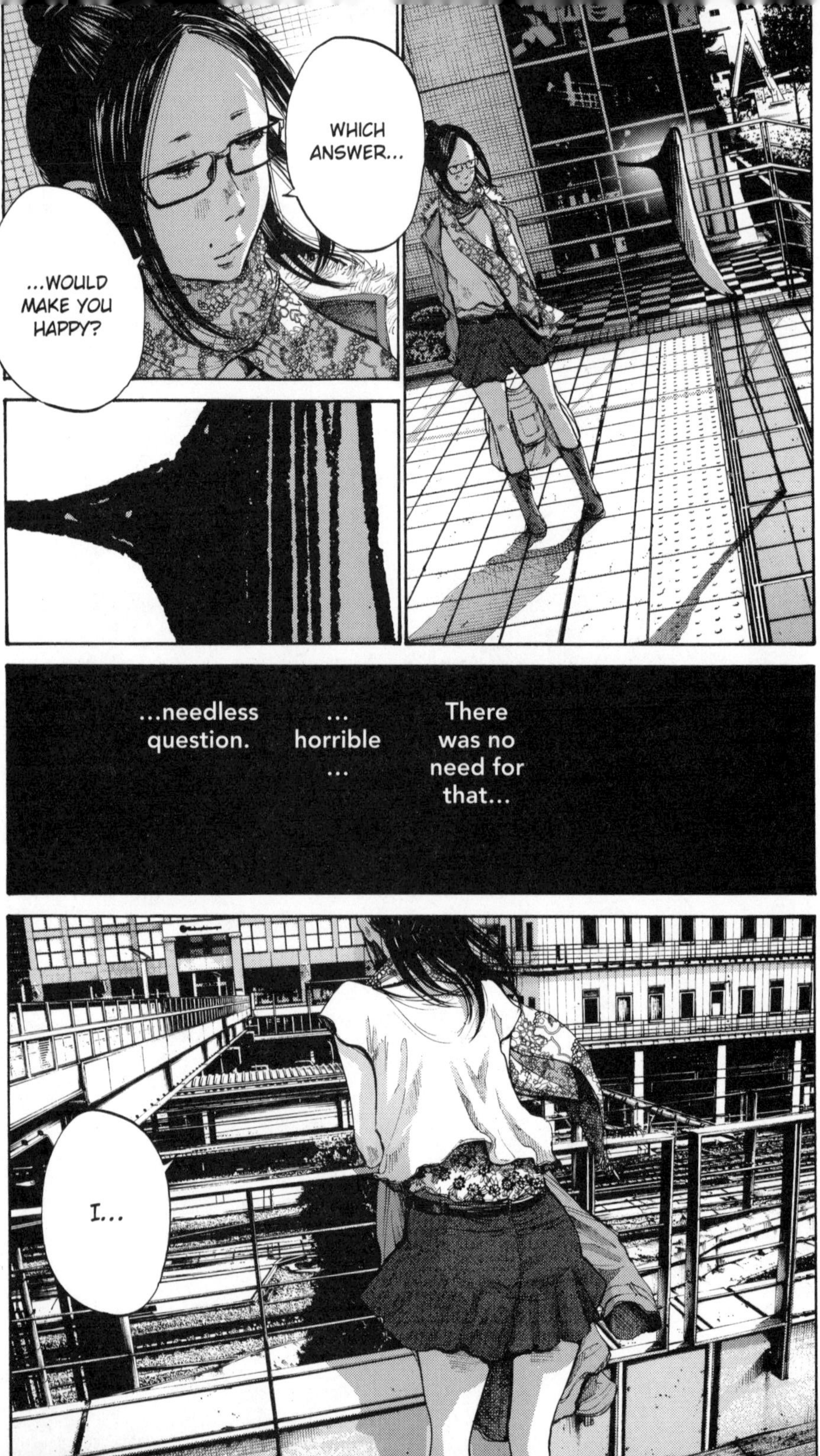
WHICH ANSWER...
...WOULD MAKE YOU HAPPY?
There was no need for that...
...horrible...
...needless question.
I...

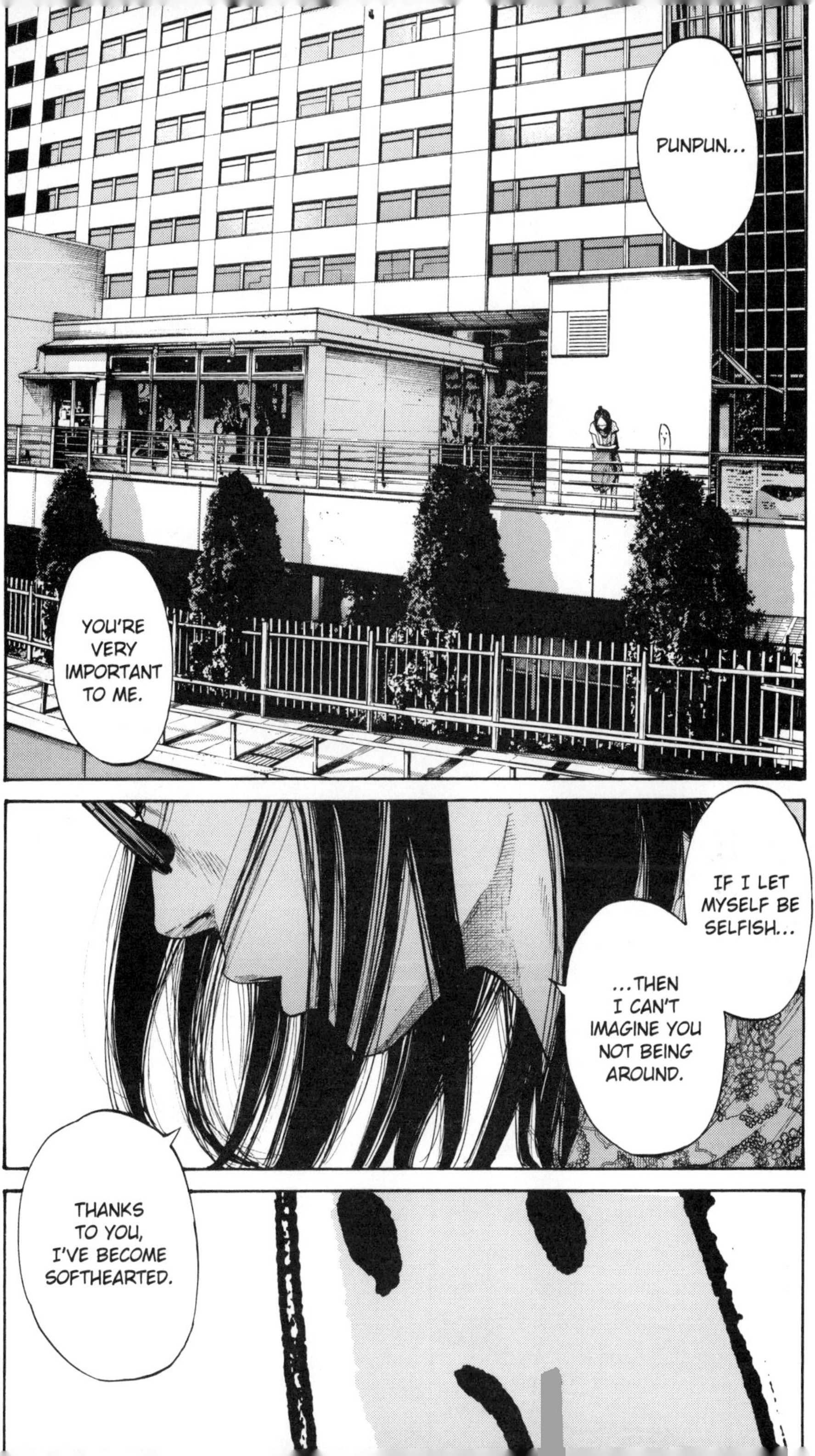
PUNPUN...
YOU'RE VERY IMPORTANT TO ME.
IF I LET MYSELF BE SELFISH...
...THEN I CAN'T IMAGINE YOU NOT BEING AROUND.
THANKS TO YOU, I'VE BECOME SOFTHEARTED.

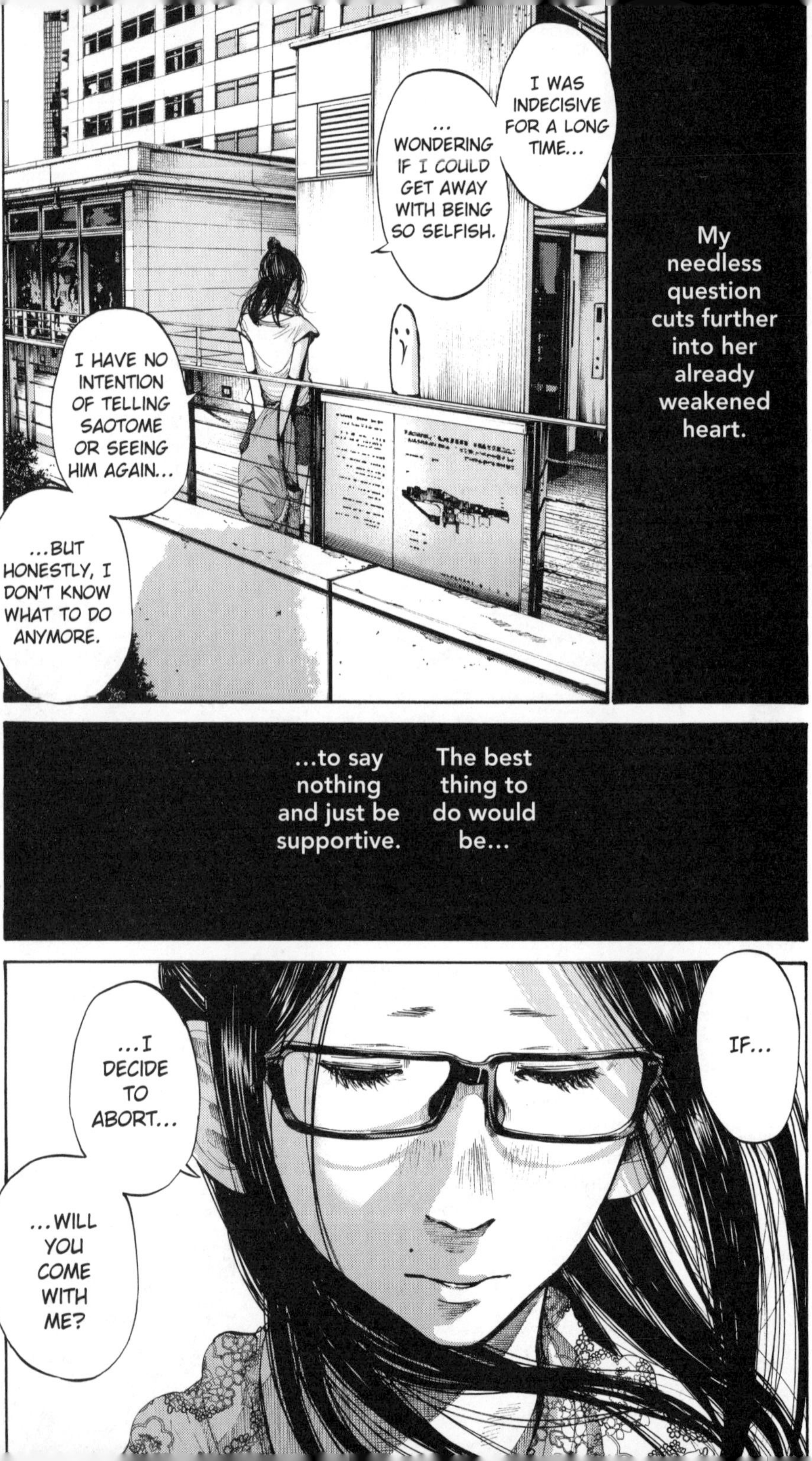
My needless question cuts further into her already weakened heart.
I WAS INDECISIVE FOR A LONG TIME...
...WONDERING IF I COULD GET AWAY WITH BEING SO SELFISH.
I HAVE NO INTENTION OF TELLING SAOTOME OR SEEING HIM AGAIN...
...BUT HONESTLY, I DON'T KNOW WHAT TO DO ANYMORE.
The best thing to do would be...
...to say nothing and just be supportive.
IF...
...I DECIDE TO ABORT...
...WILL YOU COME WITH ME?

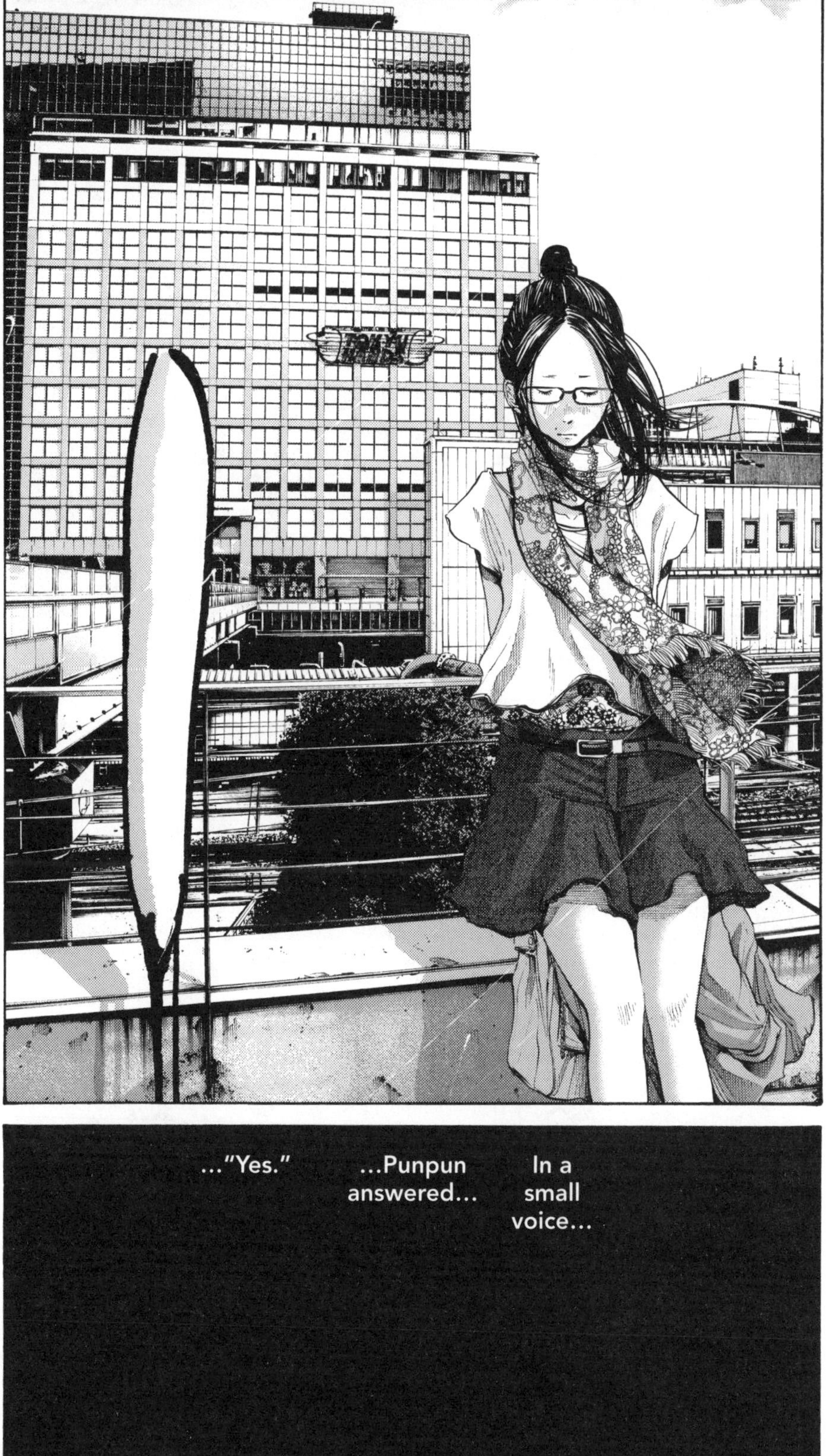
In a small voice...
...Punpun answered...
..."Yes."

6.9 ON SALE!!

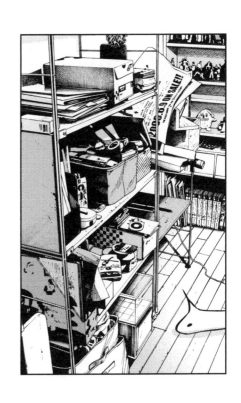

Chapter 106

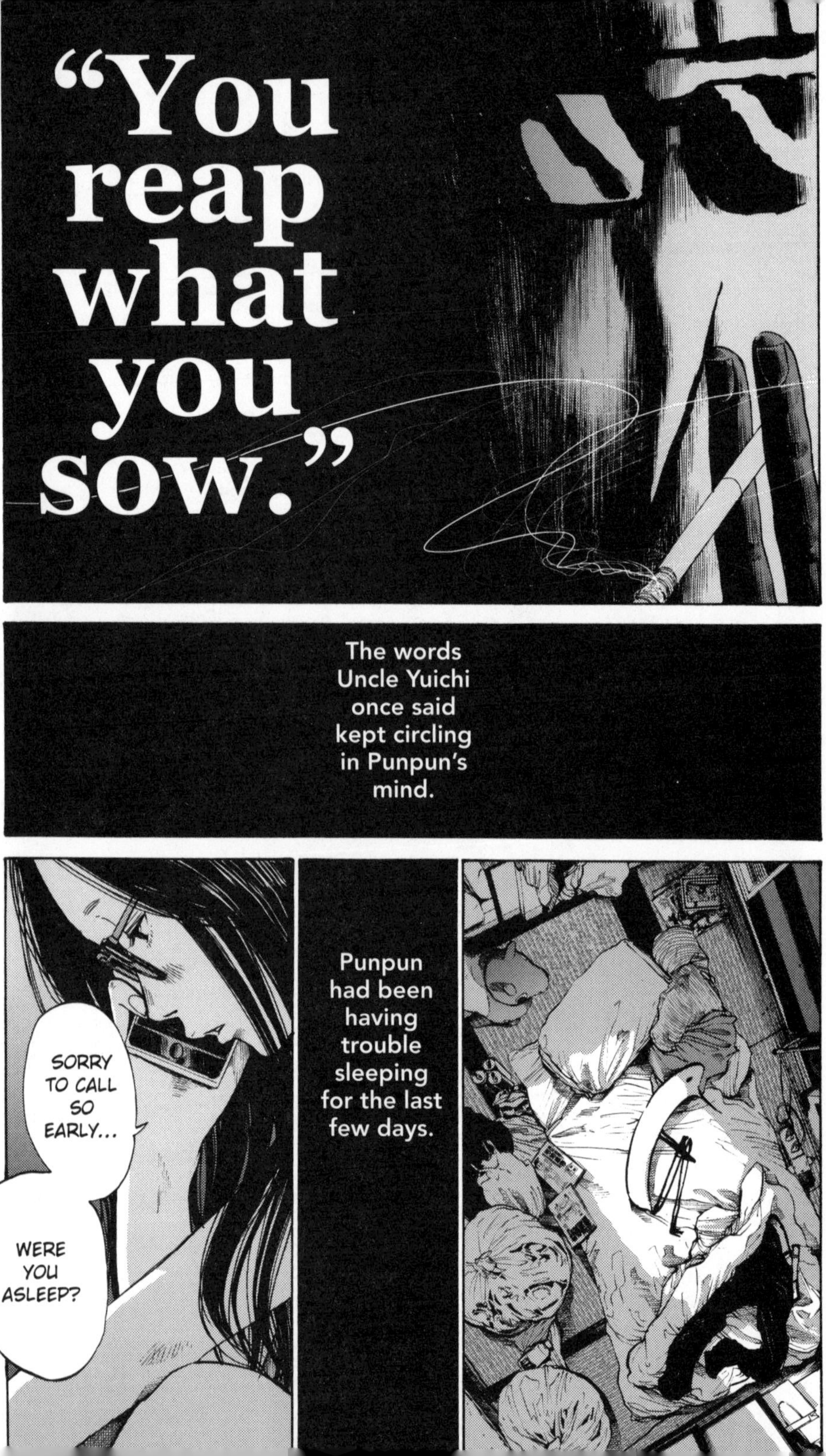
"You reap what you sow."
The words Uncle Yuichi once said kept circling in Punpun's mind.
Punpun had been having trouble sleeping for the last few days.
SORRY TO CALL SO EARLY...
WERE YOU ASLEEP?

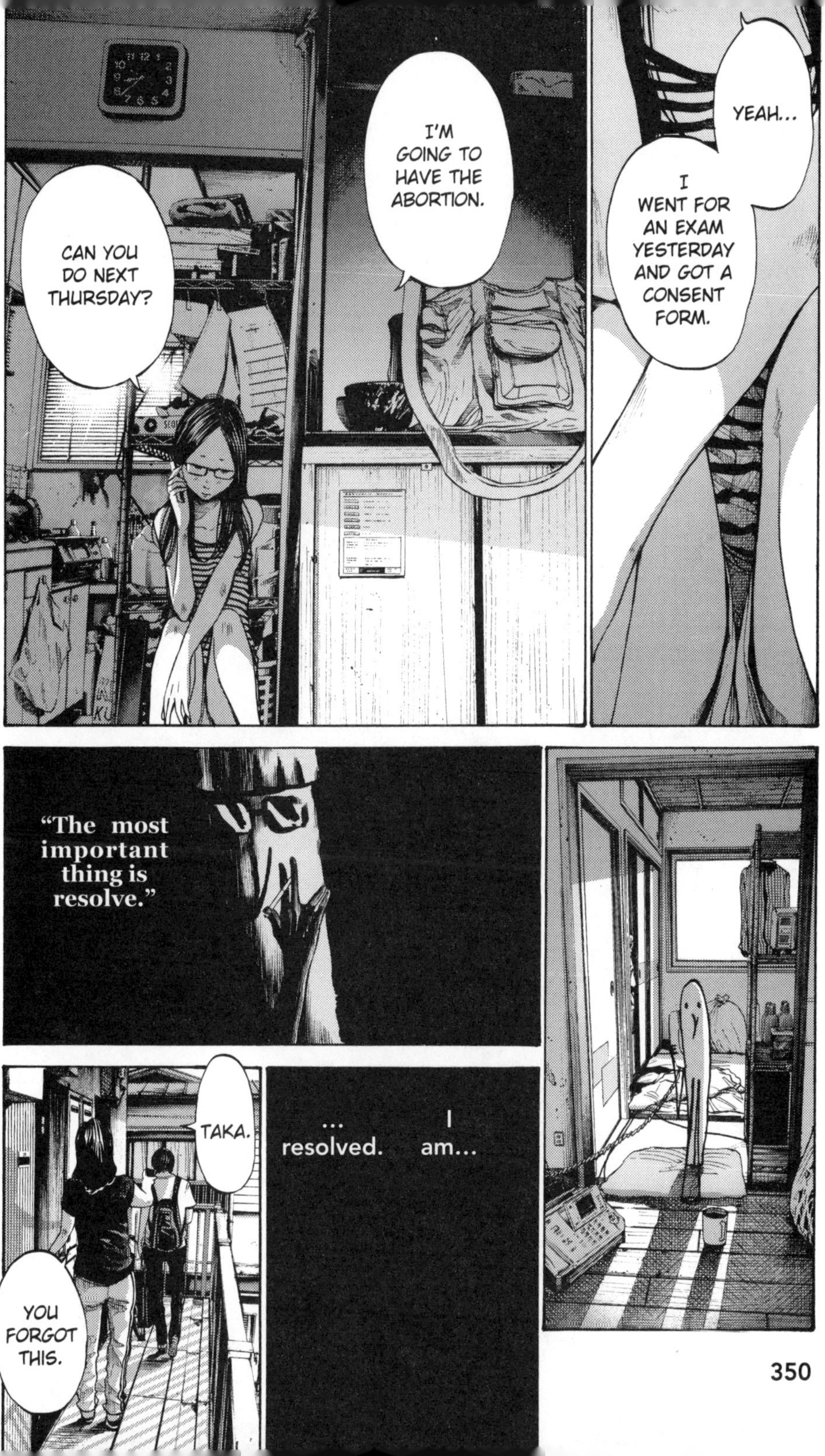
YEAH...
I WENT FOR AN EXAM YESTERDAY AND GOT A CONSENT FORM.
I'M GOING TO HAVE THE ABORTION.
CAN YOU DO NEXT THURSDAY?
"The most important thing is resolve."
I am...
... resolved.
TAKA.
YOU FORGOT THIS.

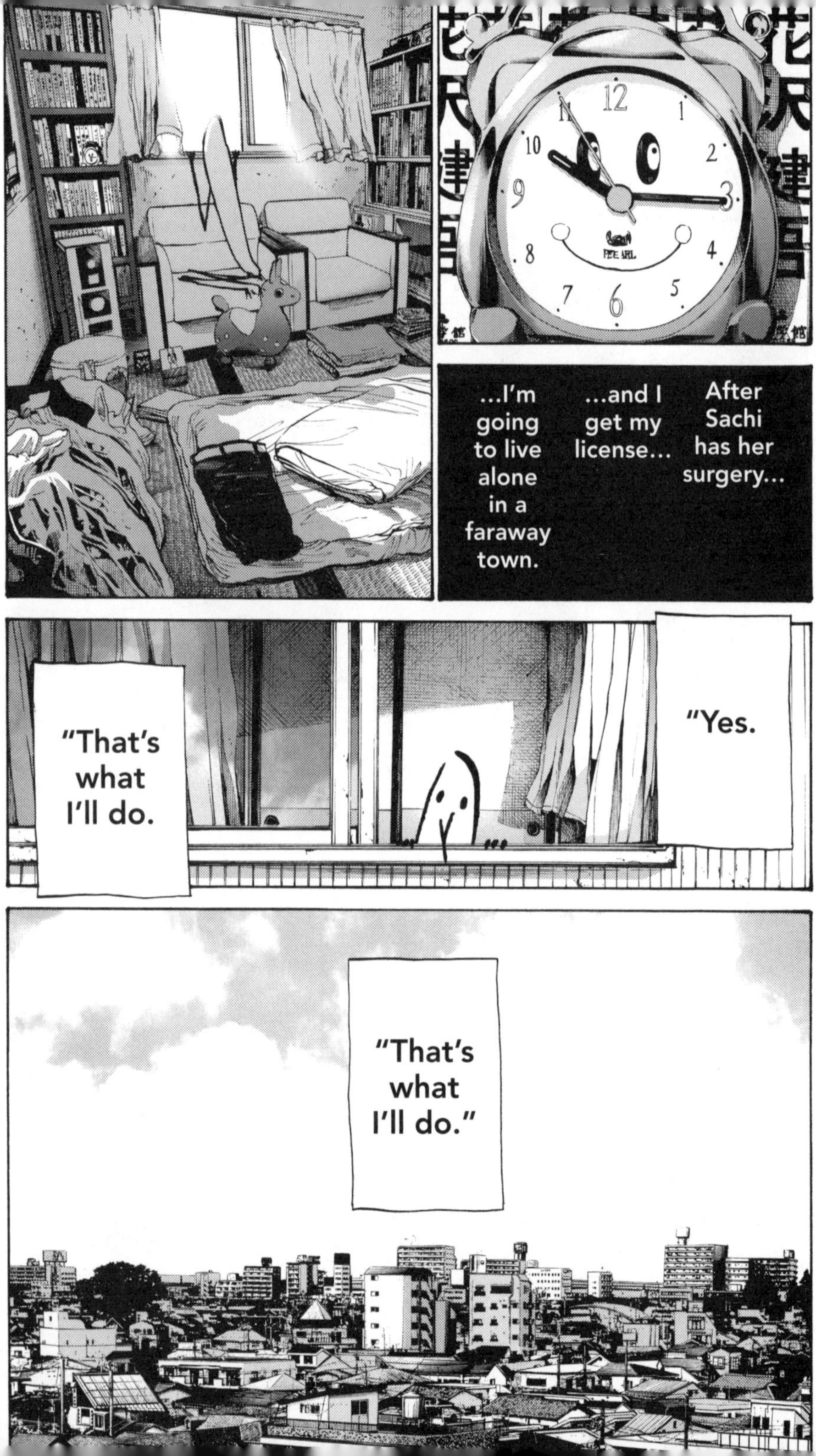
After Sachi has her surgery…
…and I get my license…
…I'm going to live alone in a faraway town.
"Yes.
"That's what I'll do.
"That's what I'll do."

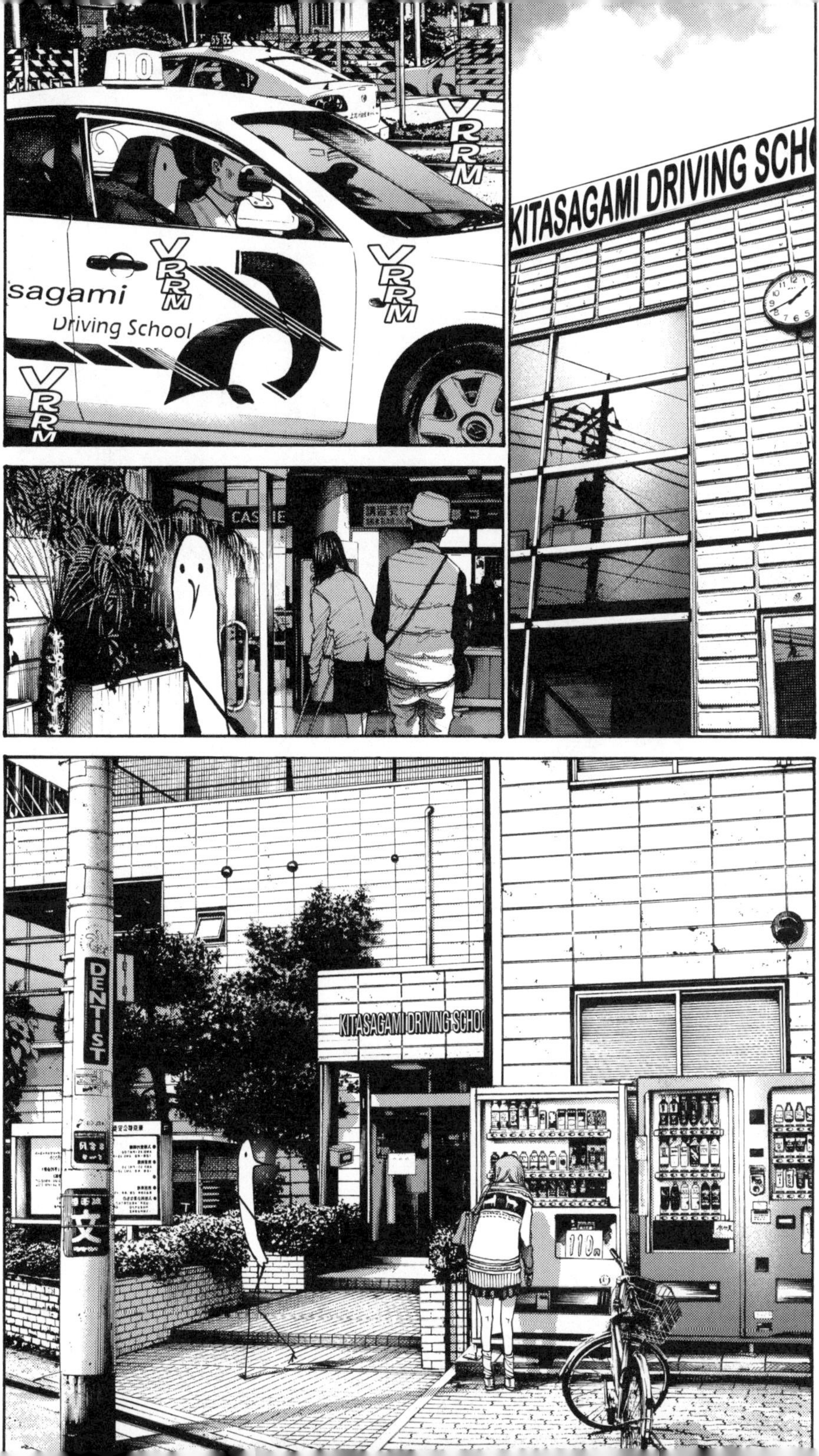
KITASAGAMI DRIVING SCHO
10
VRRM
VRRM
VRRM
VRRM
sagami
Driving School
CASHIE
KITASAGAMI DRIVING SCHO
DENTIST
文
110円

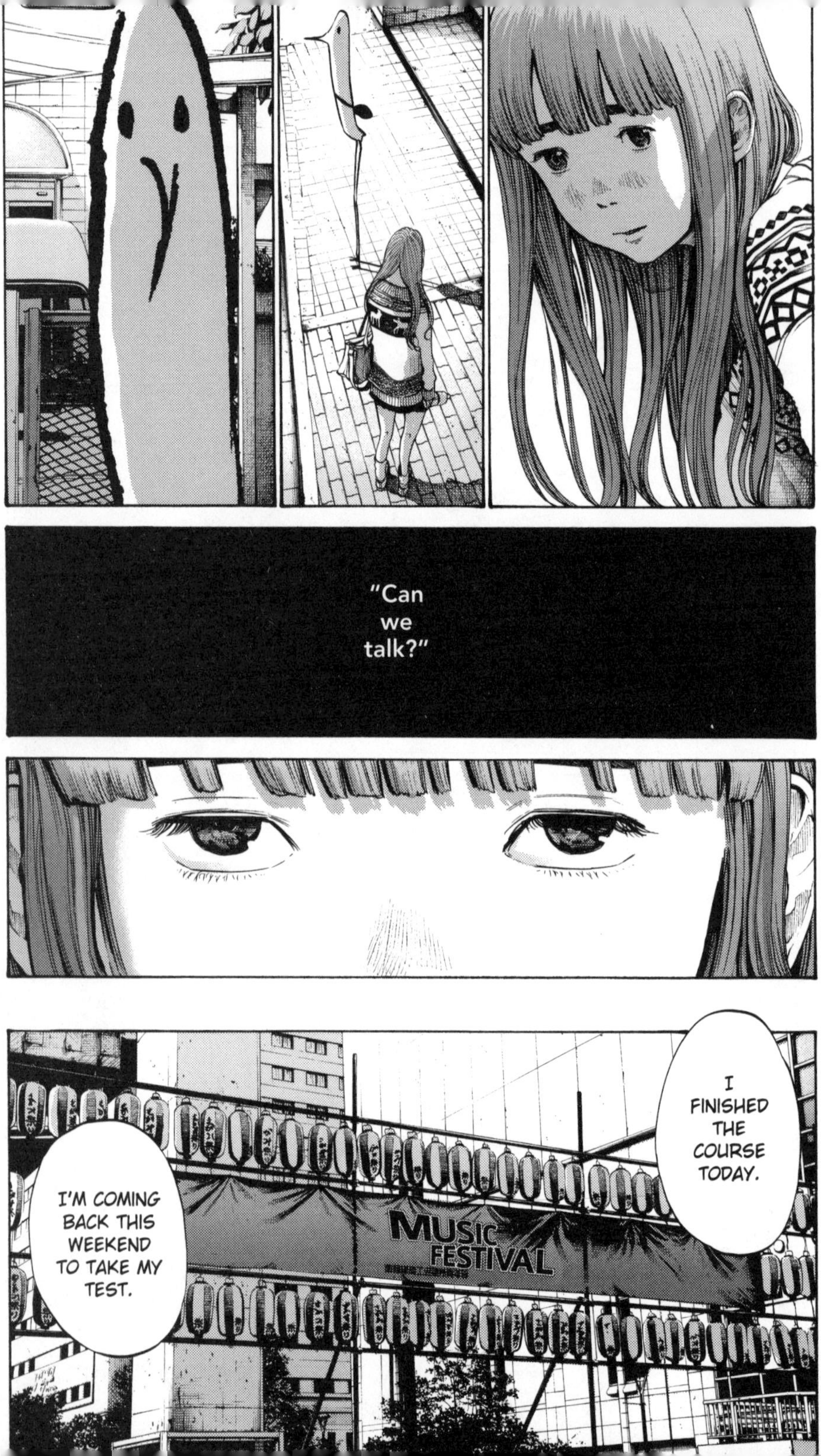
"Can we talk?"
I FINISHED THE COURSE TODAY.
MUSIC FESTIVAL
I'M COMING BACK THIS WEEKEND TO TAKE MY TEST.

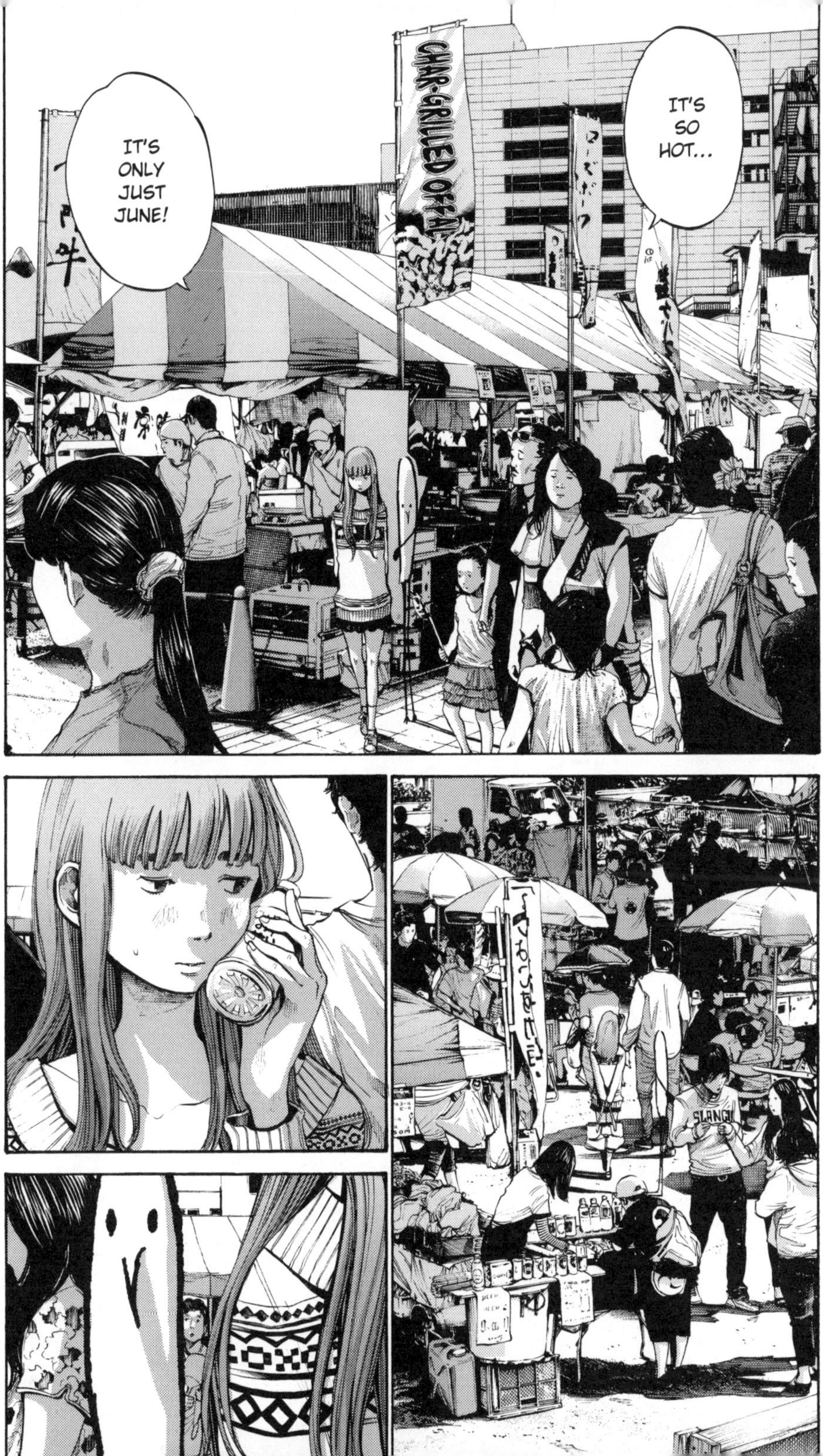
IT'S SO HOT...
CHAR-GRILLED OFFAL
IT'S ONLY JUST JUNE!

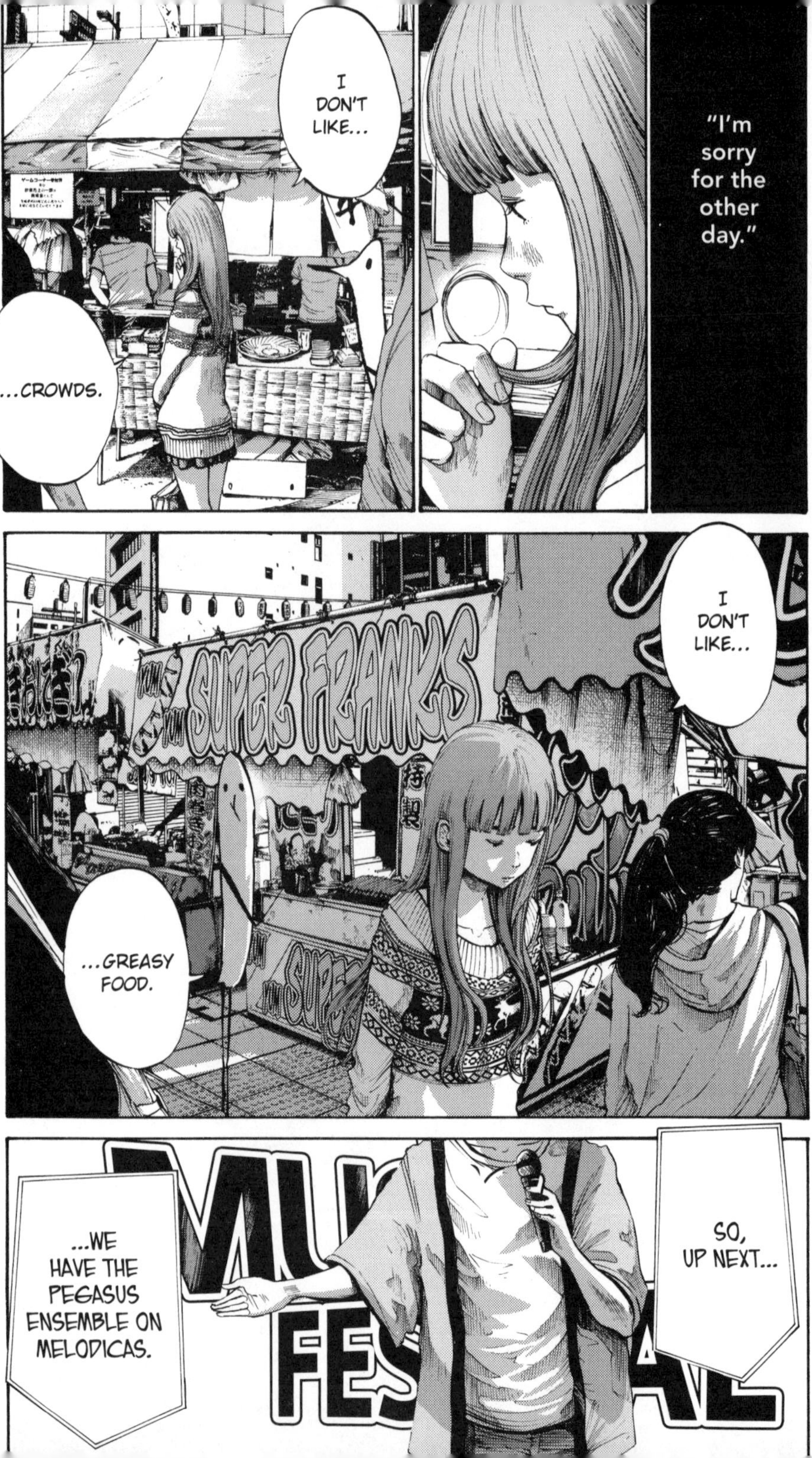
"I'm sorry for the other day."
I DON'T LIKE...
...CROWDS.
I DON'T LIKE...
SUPER FRANK'S
YUM
...GREASY FOOD.
SO, UP NEXT...
...WE HAVE THE PEGASUS ENSEMBLE ON MELODICAS.

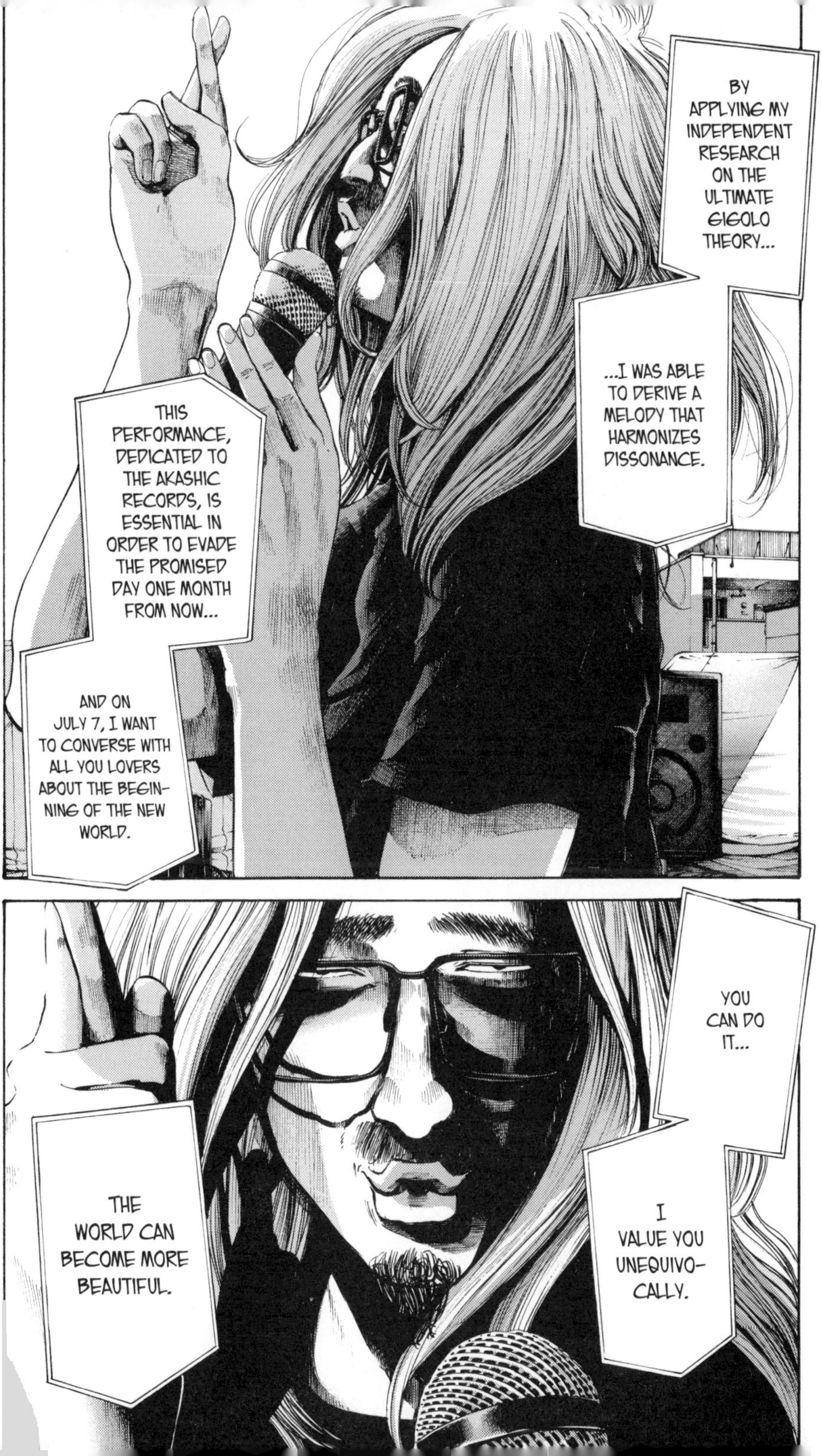
BY APPLYING MY INDEPENDENT RESEARCH ON THE ULTIMATE GIGOLO THEORY...
...I WAS ABLE TO DERIVE A MELODY THAT HARMONIZES DISSONANCE.
THIS PERFORMANCE, DEDICATED TO THE AKASHIC RECORDS, IS ESSENTIAL IN ORDER TO EVADE THE PROMISED DAY ONE MONTH FROM NOW...
AND ON JULY 7, I WANT TO CONVERSE WITH ALL YOU LOVERS ABOUT THE BEGIN-NING OF THE NEW WORLD.
YOU CAN DO IT...
I VALUE YOU UNEQUIVO-CALLY.
THE WORLD CAN BECOME MORE BEAUTIFUL.

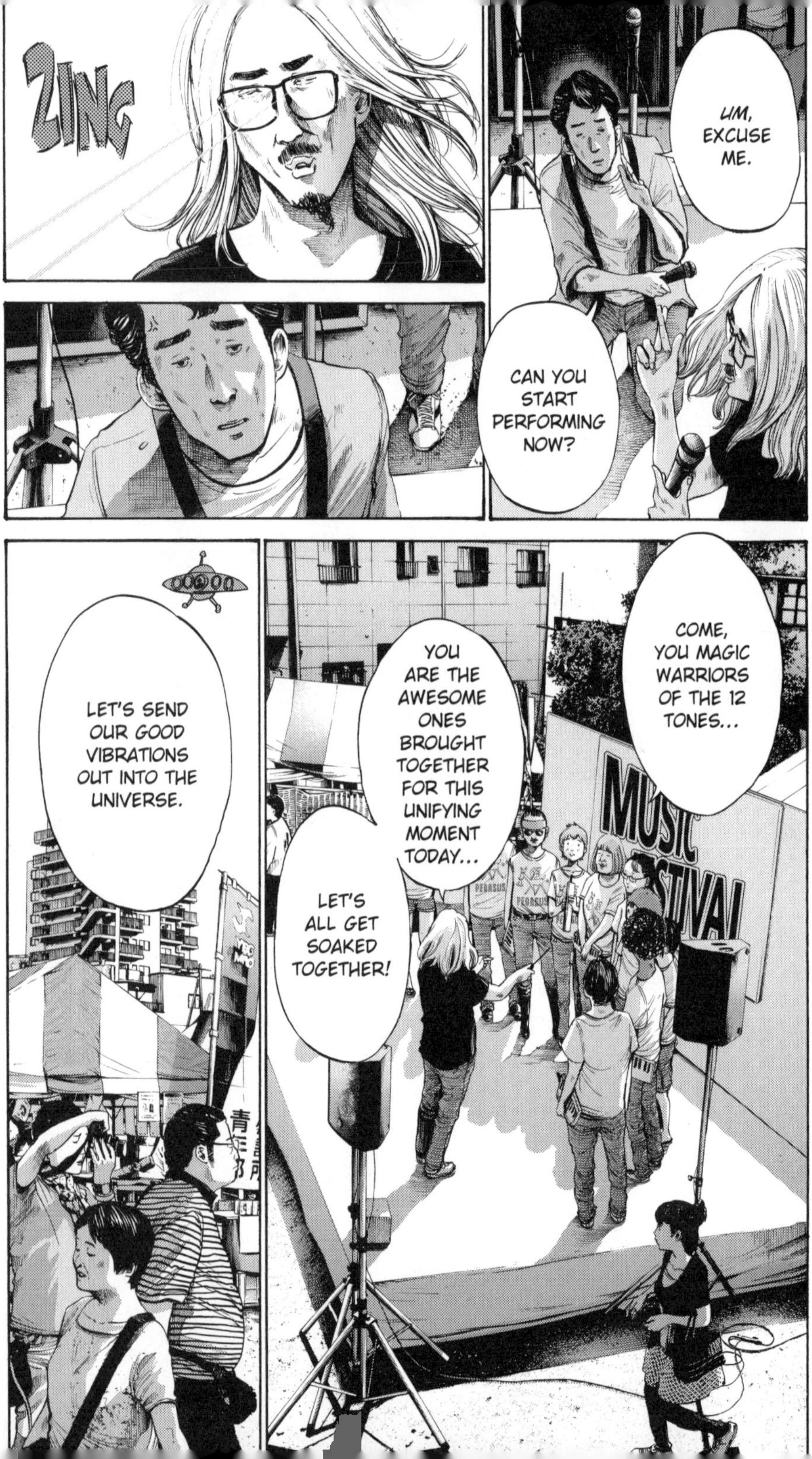
UM, EXCUSE ME.
CAN YOU START PERFORMING NOW?
ZING
COME, YOU MAGIC WARRIORS OF THE 12 TONES...
YOU ARE THE AWESOME ONES BROUGHT TOGETHER FOR THIS UNIFYING MOMENT TODAY...
LET'S ALL GET SOAKED TOGETHER!
MUSIC FESTIVAL
LET'S SEND OUR GOOD VIBRATIONS OUT INTO THE UNIVERSE.

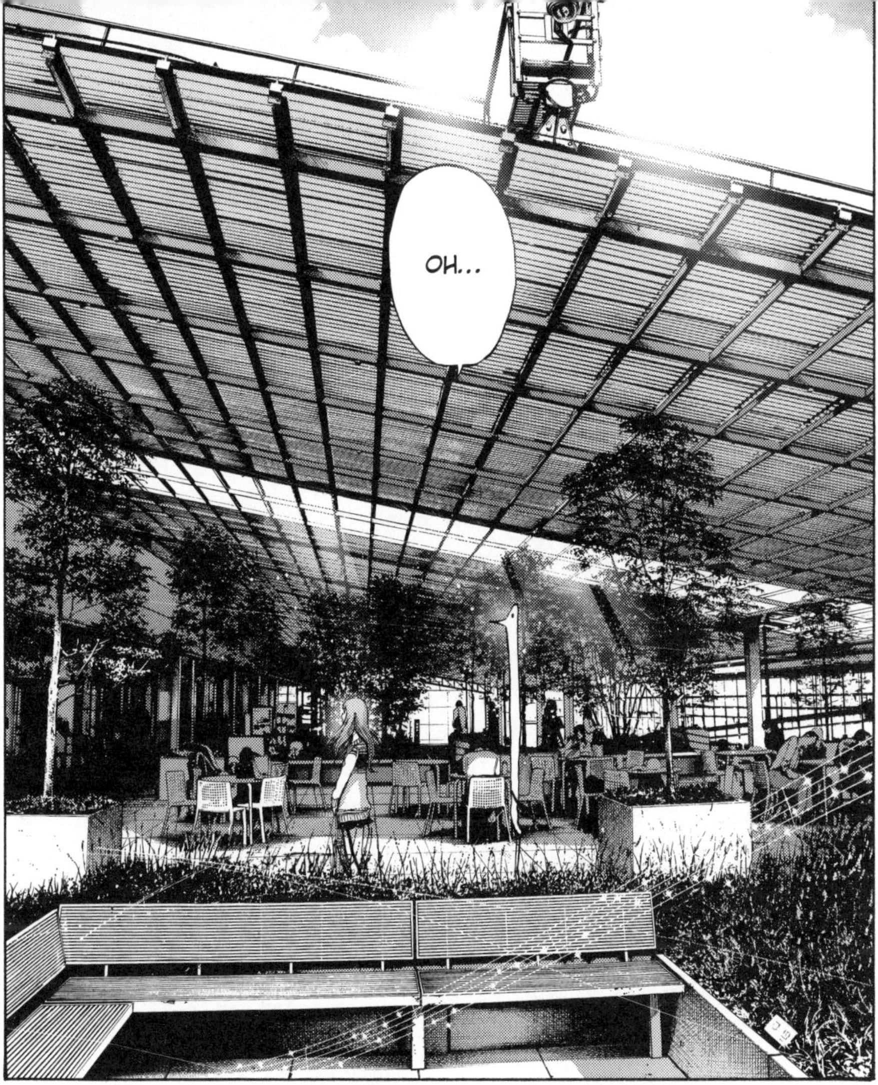
OH...

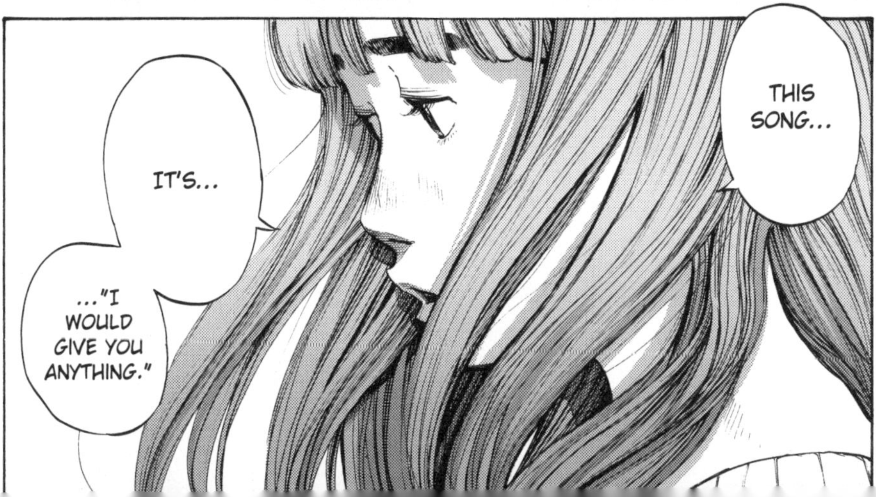
THIS SONG...
IT'S...
..."I WOULD GIVE YOU ANYTHING."

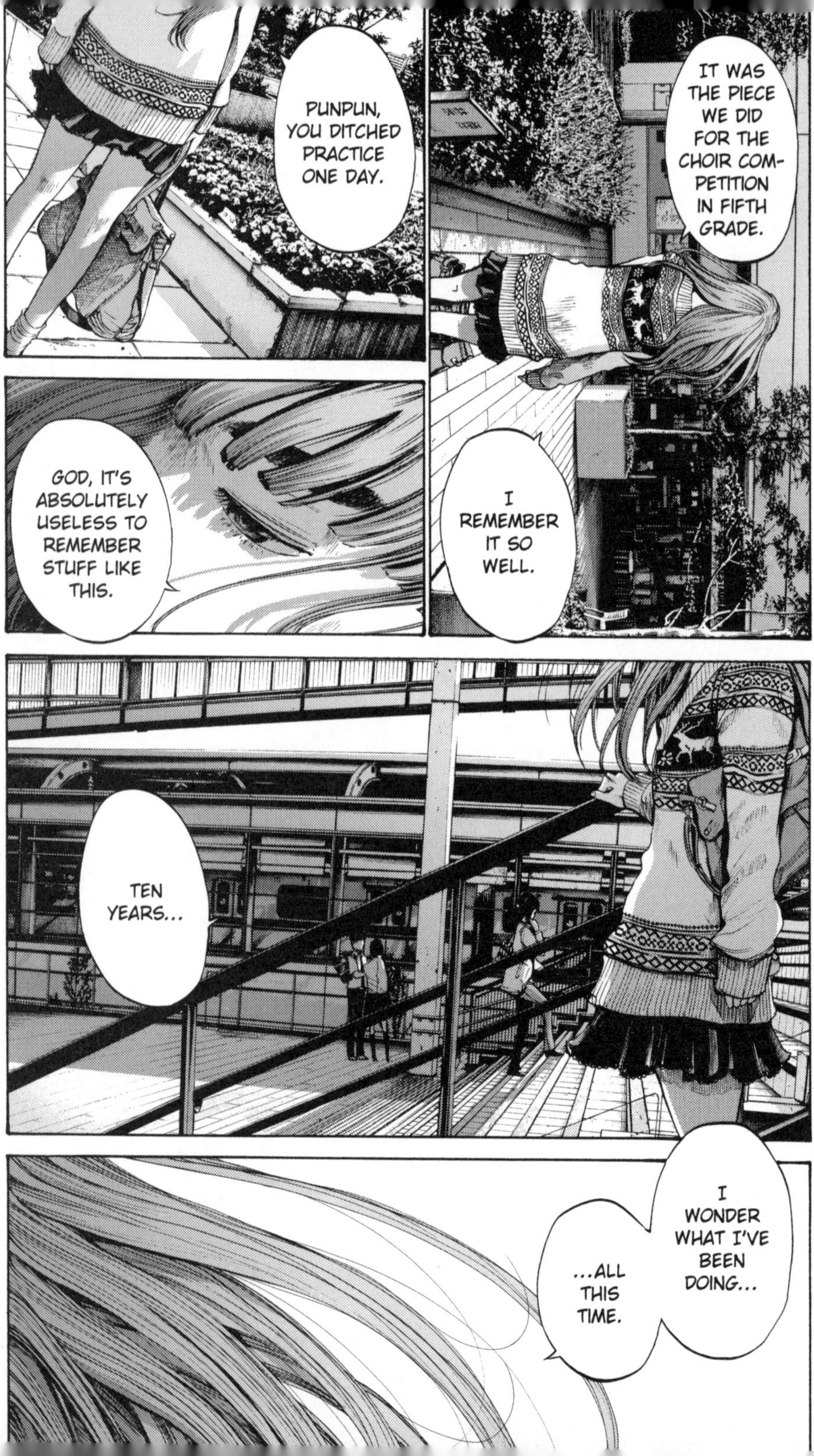
IT WAS THE PIECE WE DID FOR THE CHOIR COM-PETITION IN FIFTH GRADE.
PUNPUN, YOU DITCHED PRACTICE ONE DAY.
I REMEMBER IT SO WELL.
GOD, IT'S ABSOLUTELY USELESS TO REMEMBER STUFF LIKE THIS.
TEN YEARS...
I WONDER WHAT I'VE BEEN DOING...
...ALL THIS TIME.

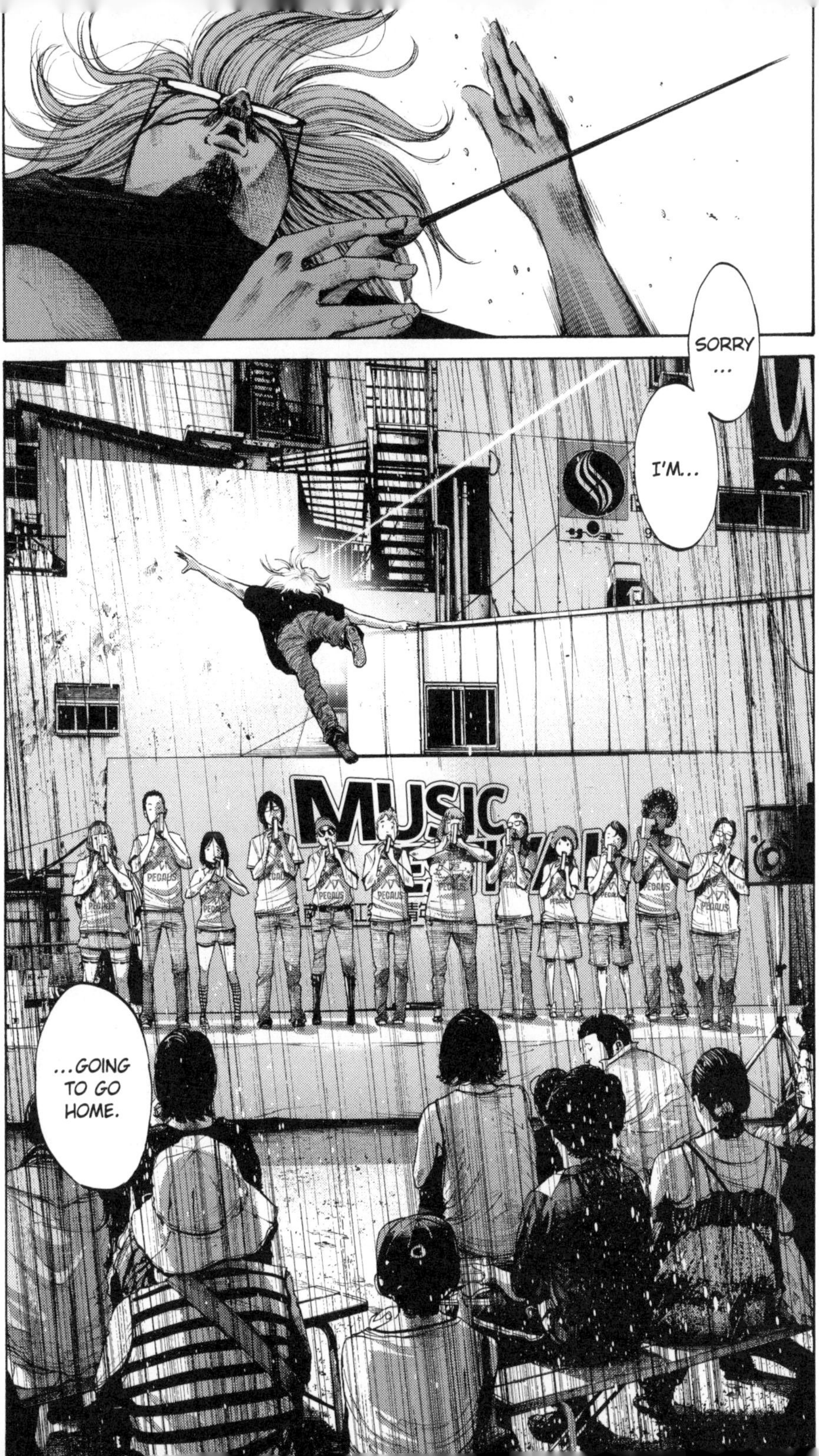
SORRY ...
I'M...
...GOING TO GO HOME.
MUSIC
PEGASUS

"Um...

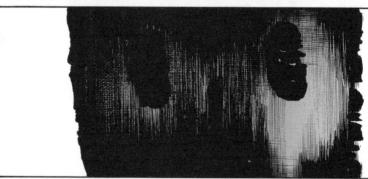

"I'm   "...not really   "I'm...
Onodera.   Fujikawa...

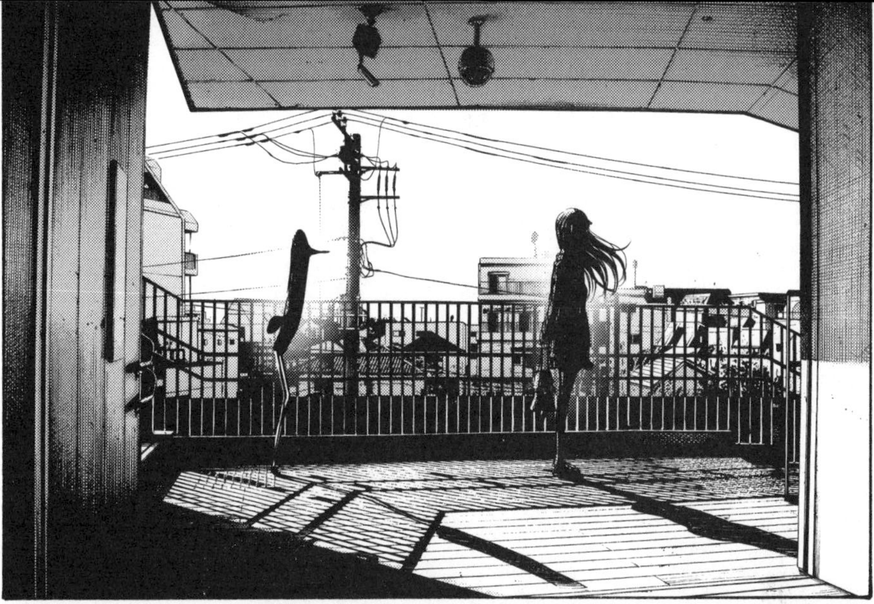

"I'm not really a college student, I can't play futsal, I don't have a girlfriend...

"I'm just seaweed floating along half-assed every day, not happy or particularly sad...

"No, that's insulting to seaweed.

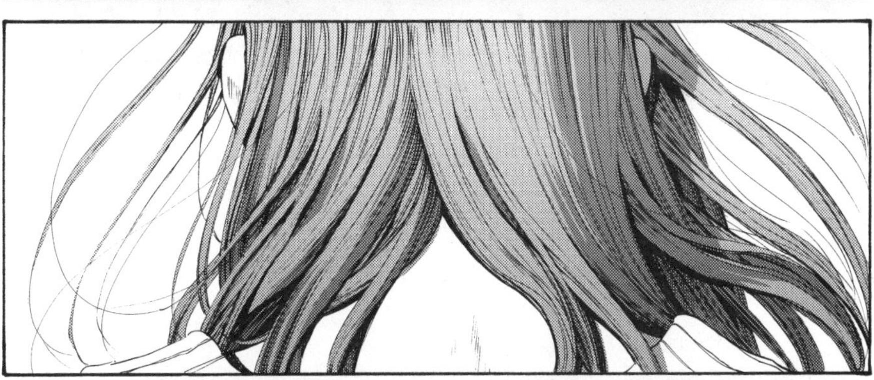

"So I...

"...I've been looking for you for ten years, Aiko.

"For the last few years, obsessively.

"But the Aiko I finally met was not the Aiko I remembered...

"...which made me miserable as well as frustrated.

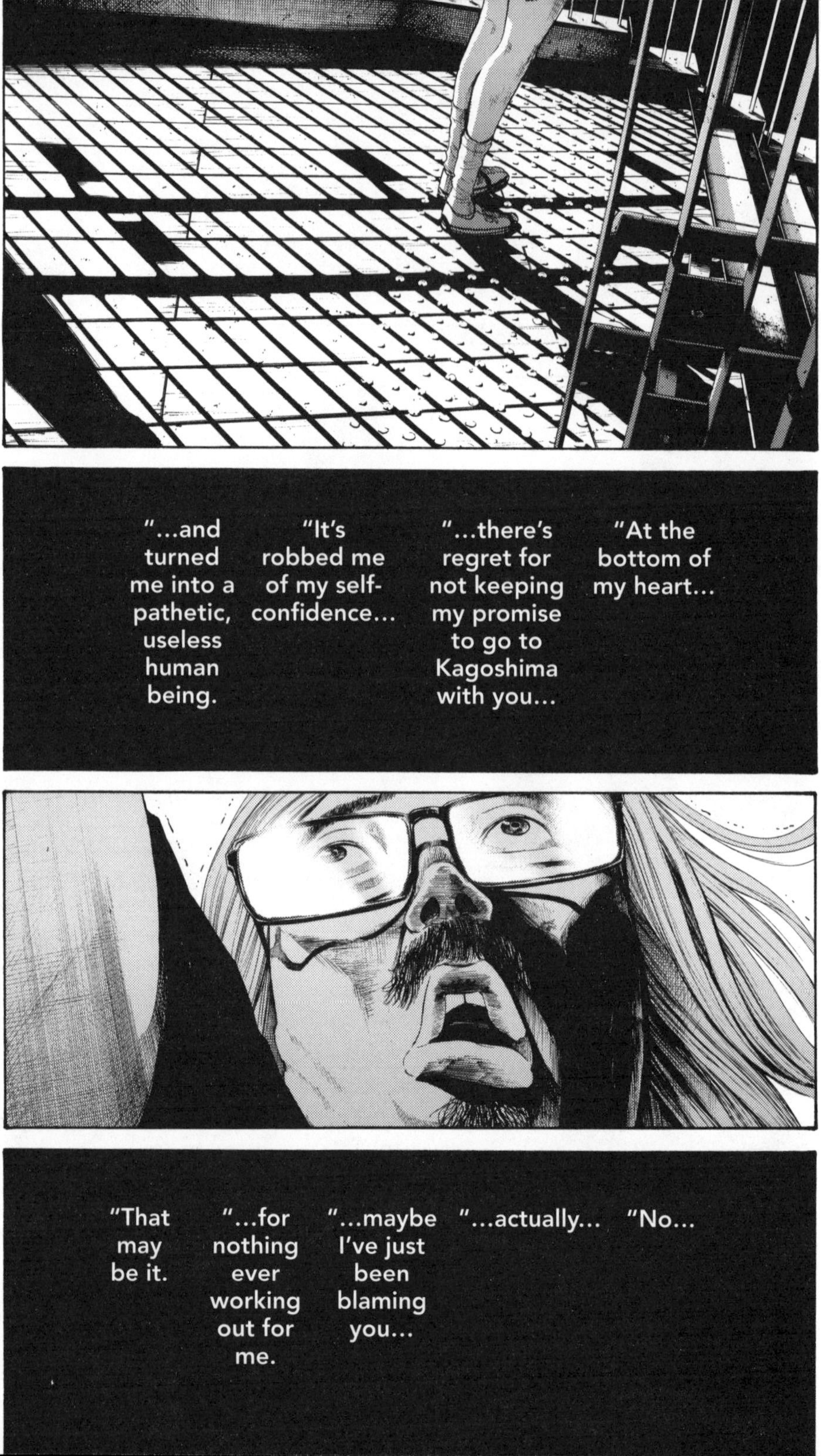
"At the bottom of my heart...
"...there's regret for not keeping my promise to go to Kagoshima with you...
"It's robbed me of my self-confidence...
"...and turned me into a pathetic, useless human being.
"No...
"...actually...
"...maybe I've just been blaming you...
"...for nothing ever working out for me.
"That may be it.

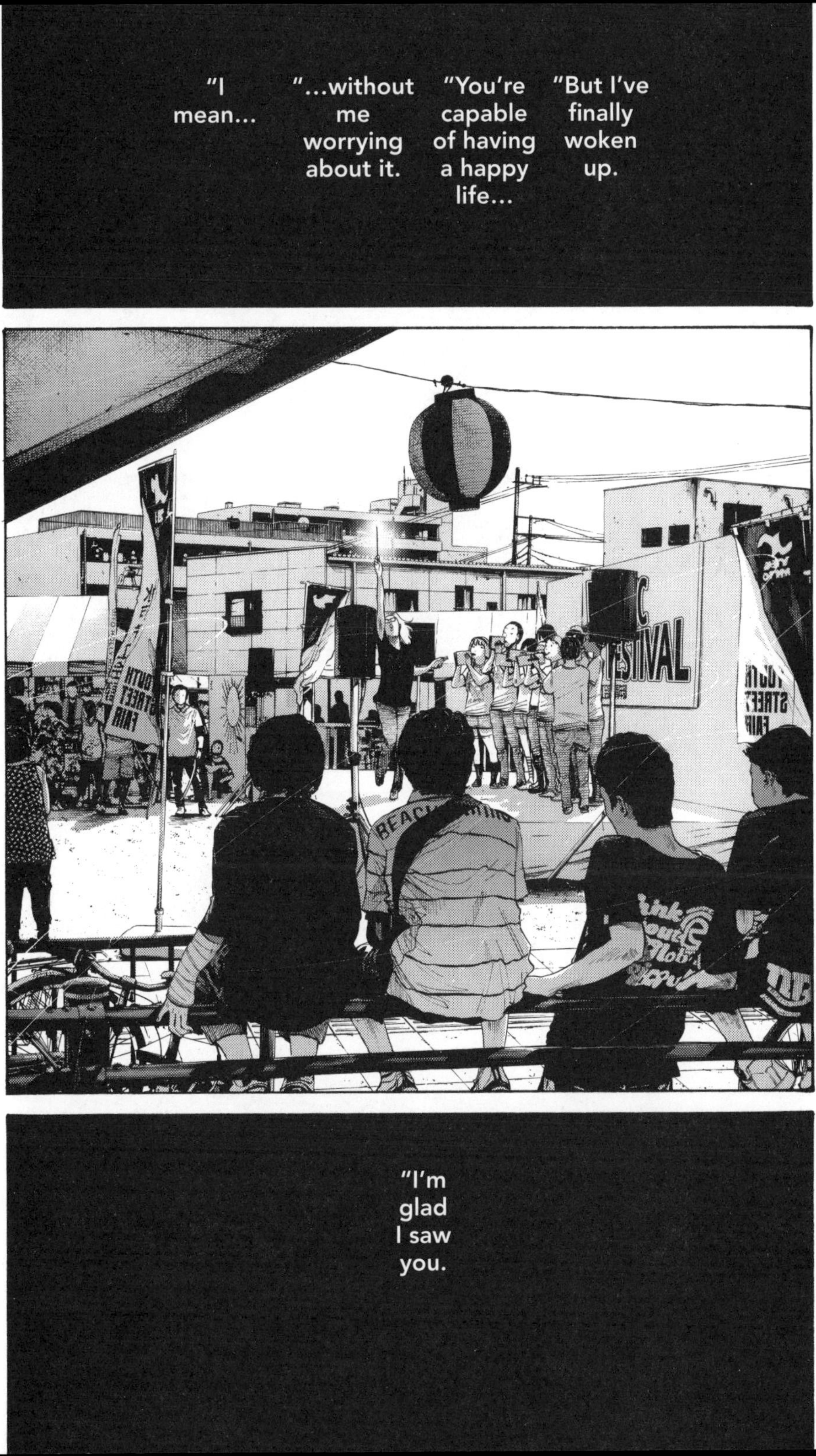
"But I've finally woken up.
"You're capable of having a happy life...
"...without me worrying about it.
"I mean...
FESTIVAL
YOUTH STREET FAIR
"I'm glad I saw you.

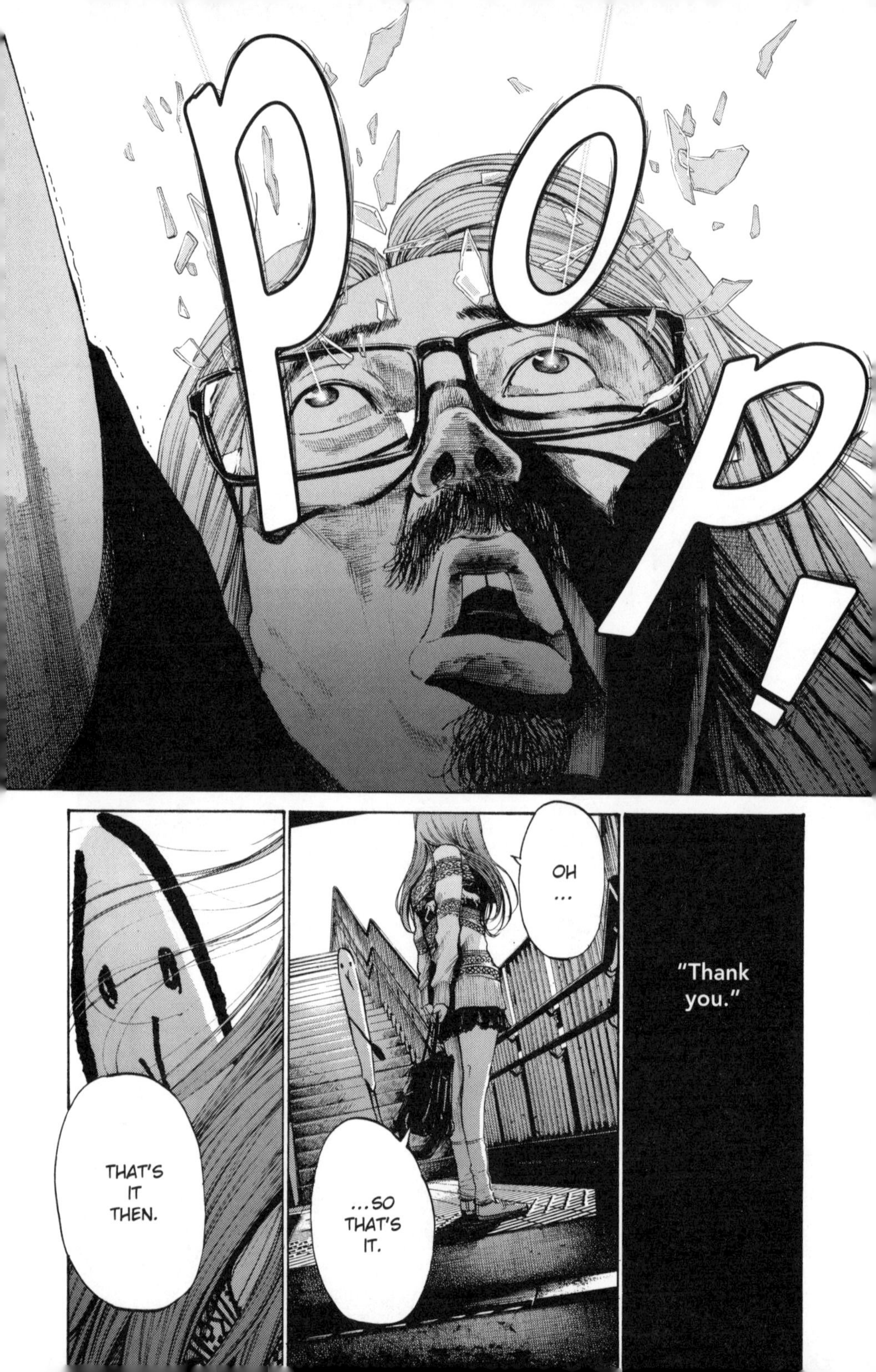
POP!
"Thank you."
OH ...
...SO THAT'S IT.
THAT'S IT THEN.

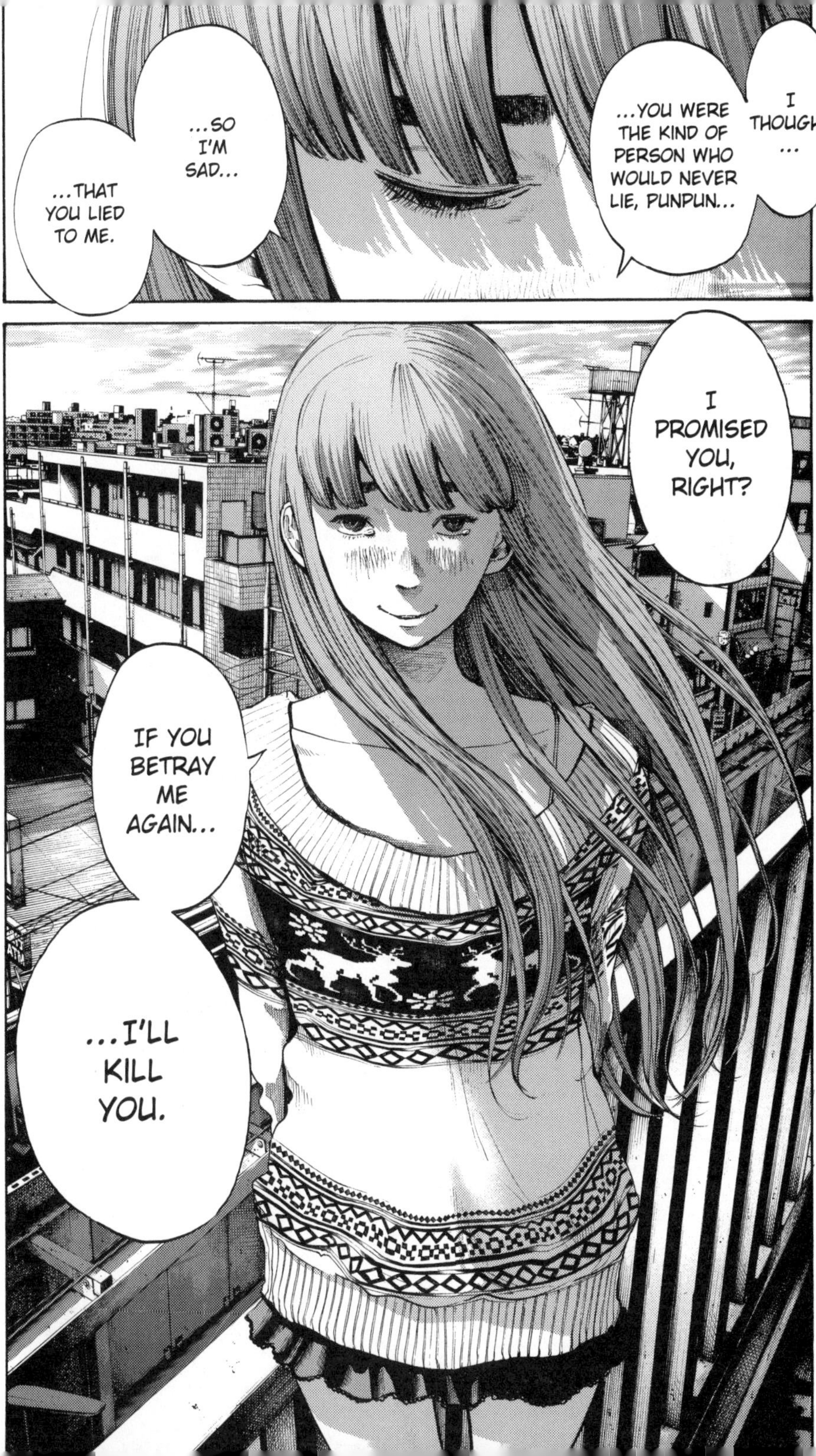
I THOUGHT...
...YOU WERE THE KIND OF PERSON WHO WOULD NEVER LIE, PUNPUN...
...SO I'M SAD...
...THAT YOU LIED TO ME.
I PROMISED YOU, RIGHT?
IF YOU BETRAY ME AGAIN...
...I'LL KILL YOU.

Chapter 107

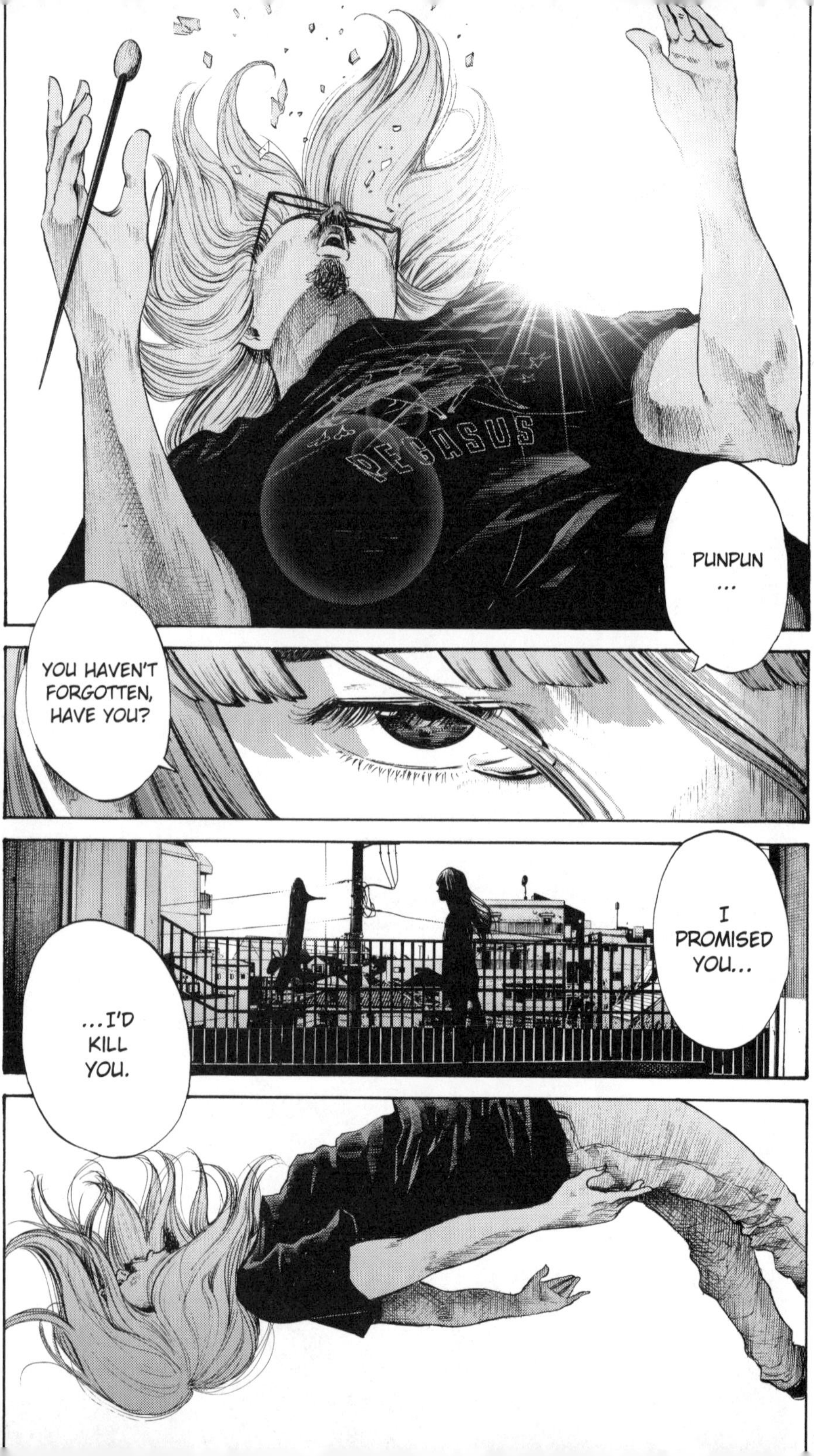
PUNPUN ...
YOU HAVEN'T FORGOTTEN, HAVE YOU?
I PROMISED YOU...
...I'D KILL YOU.

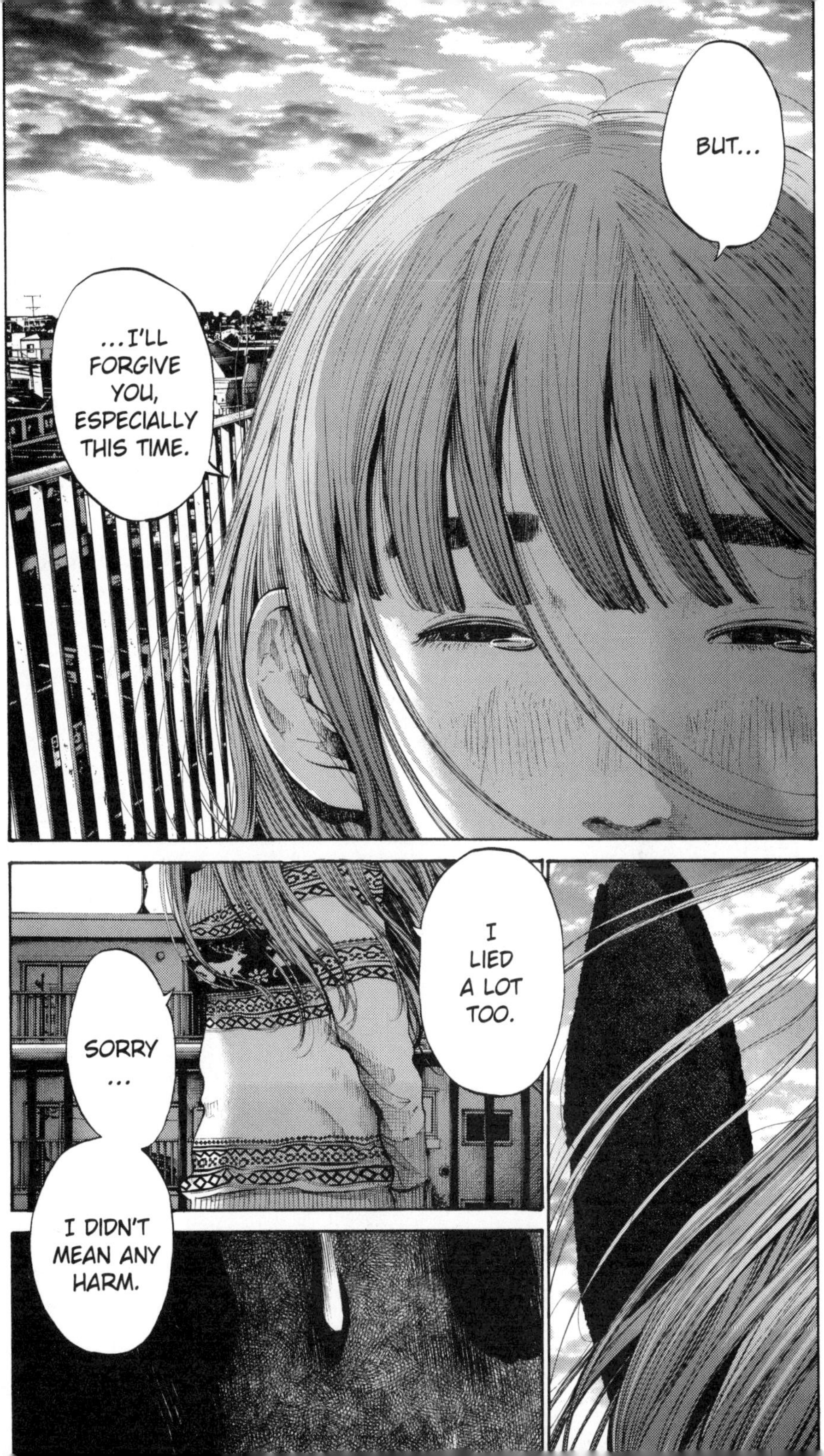
BUT...
...I'LL FORGIVE YOU, ESPECIALLY THIS TIME.
I LIED A LOT TOO.
SORRY...
I DIDN'T MEAN ANY HARM.

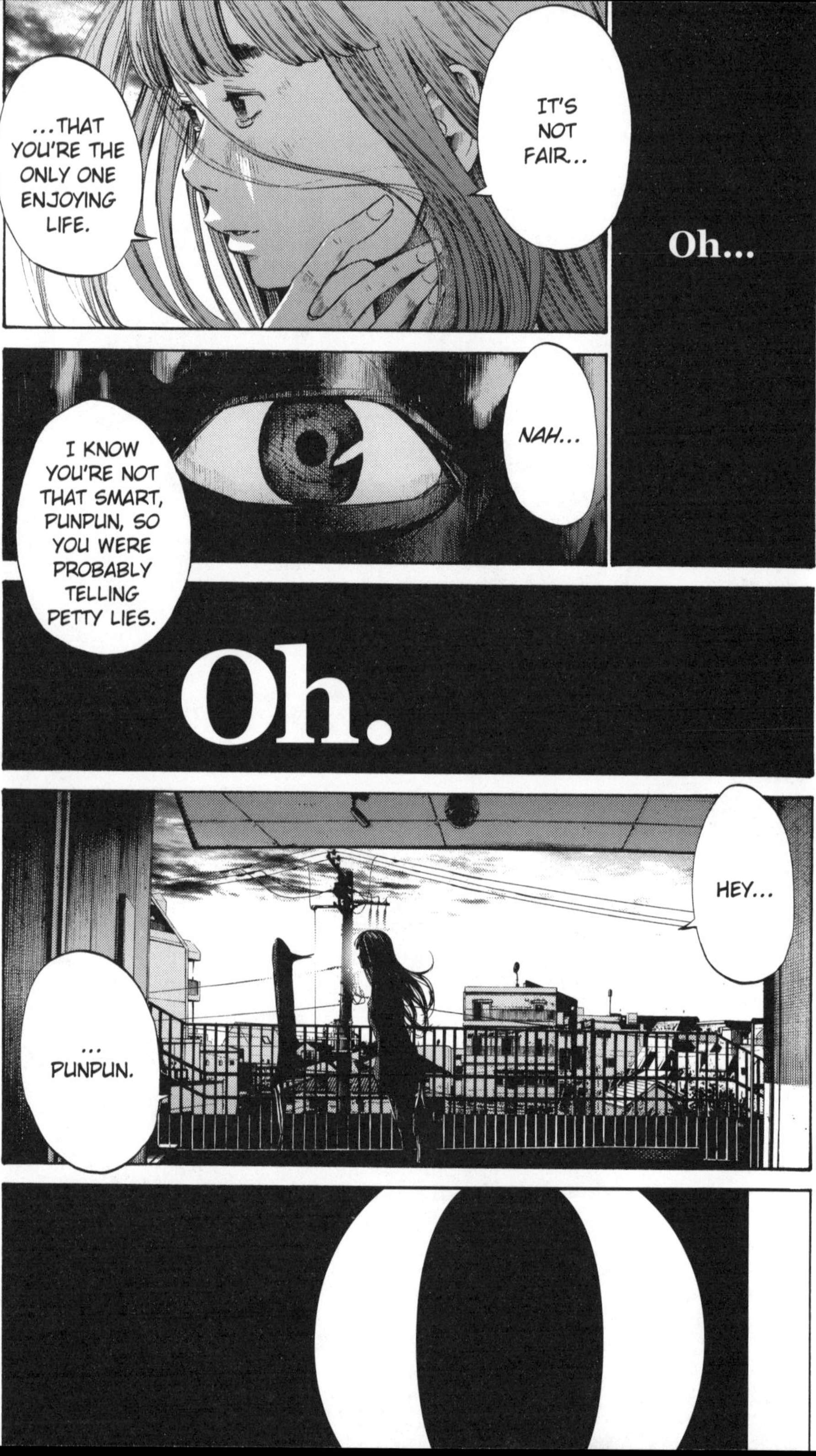
Oh...
IT'S NOT FAIR...
...THAT YOU'RE THE ONLY ONE ENJOYING LIFE.
NAH...
I KNOW YOU'RE NOT THAT SMART, PUNPUN, SO YOU WERE PROBABLY TELLING PETTY LIES.
Oh.
HEY...
... PUNPUN.

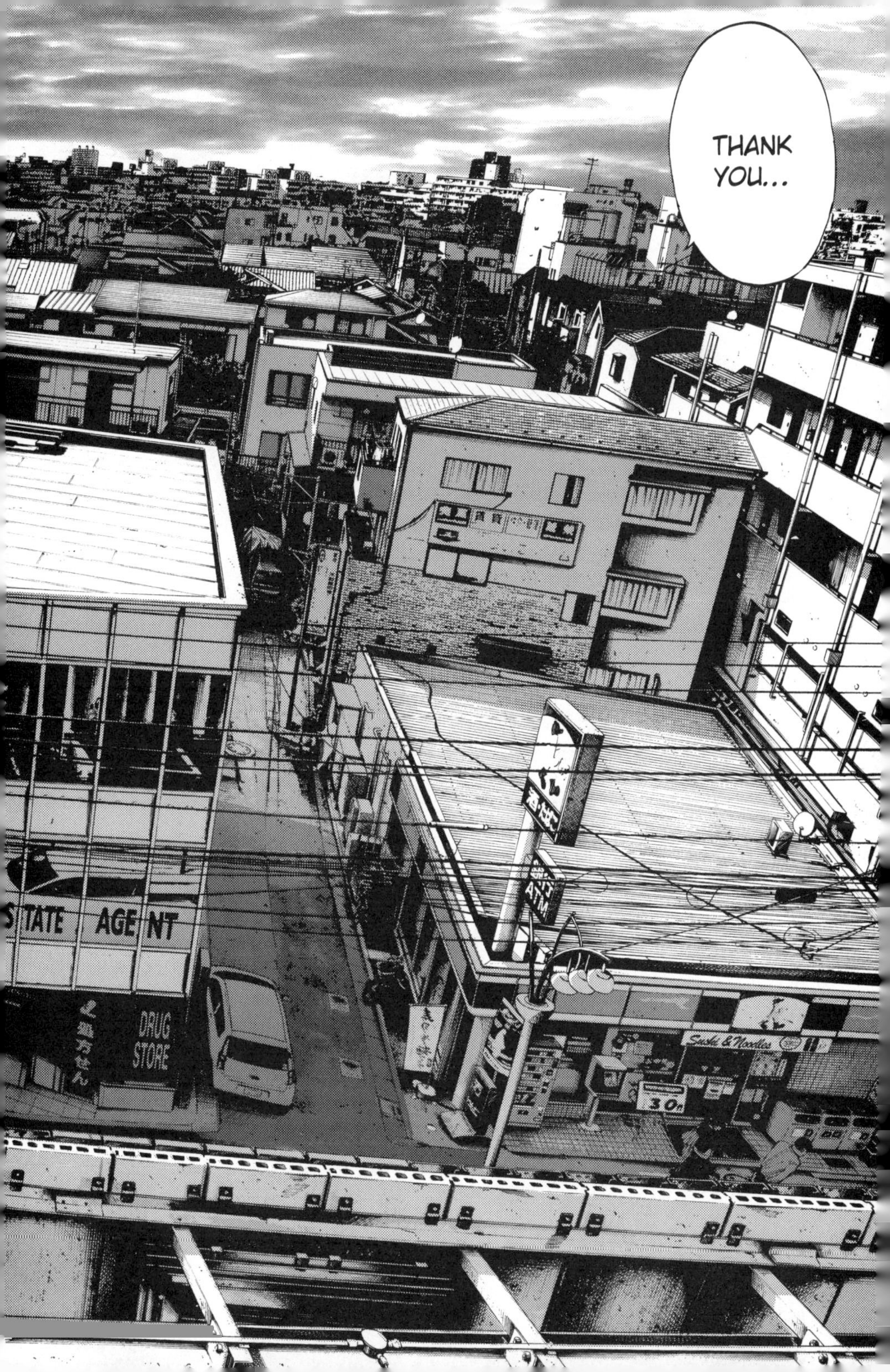
THANK YOU...
DRUG STORE
ATM
Sushi & Noodles

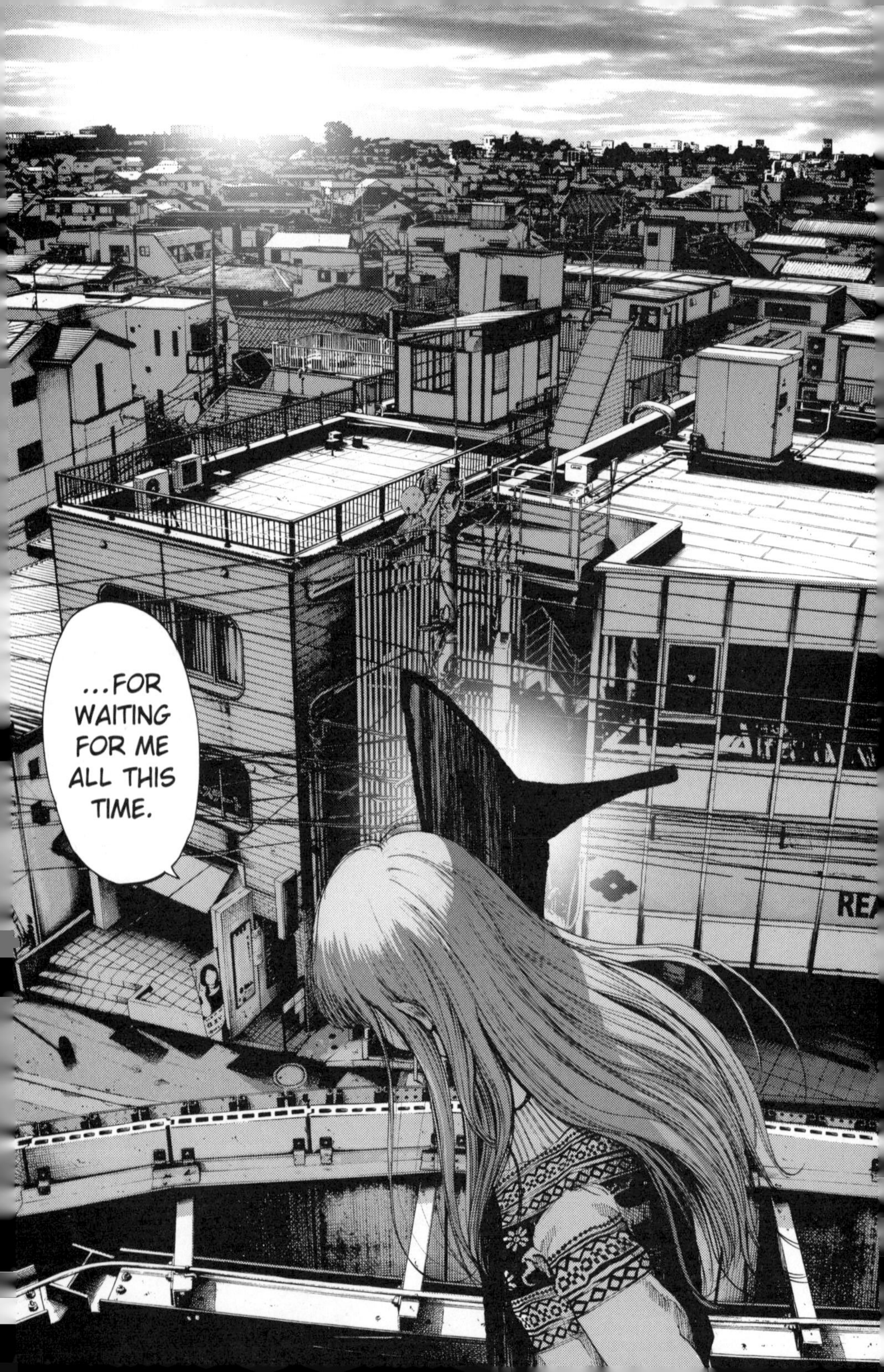
...FOR WAITING FOR ME ALL THIS TIME.
REA

I WAS...

...WAITING TOO.

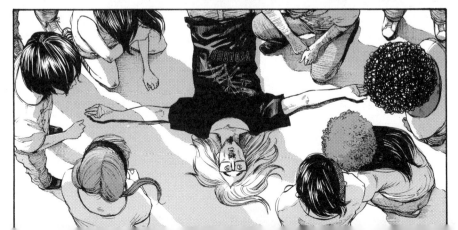

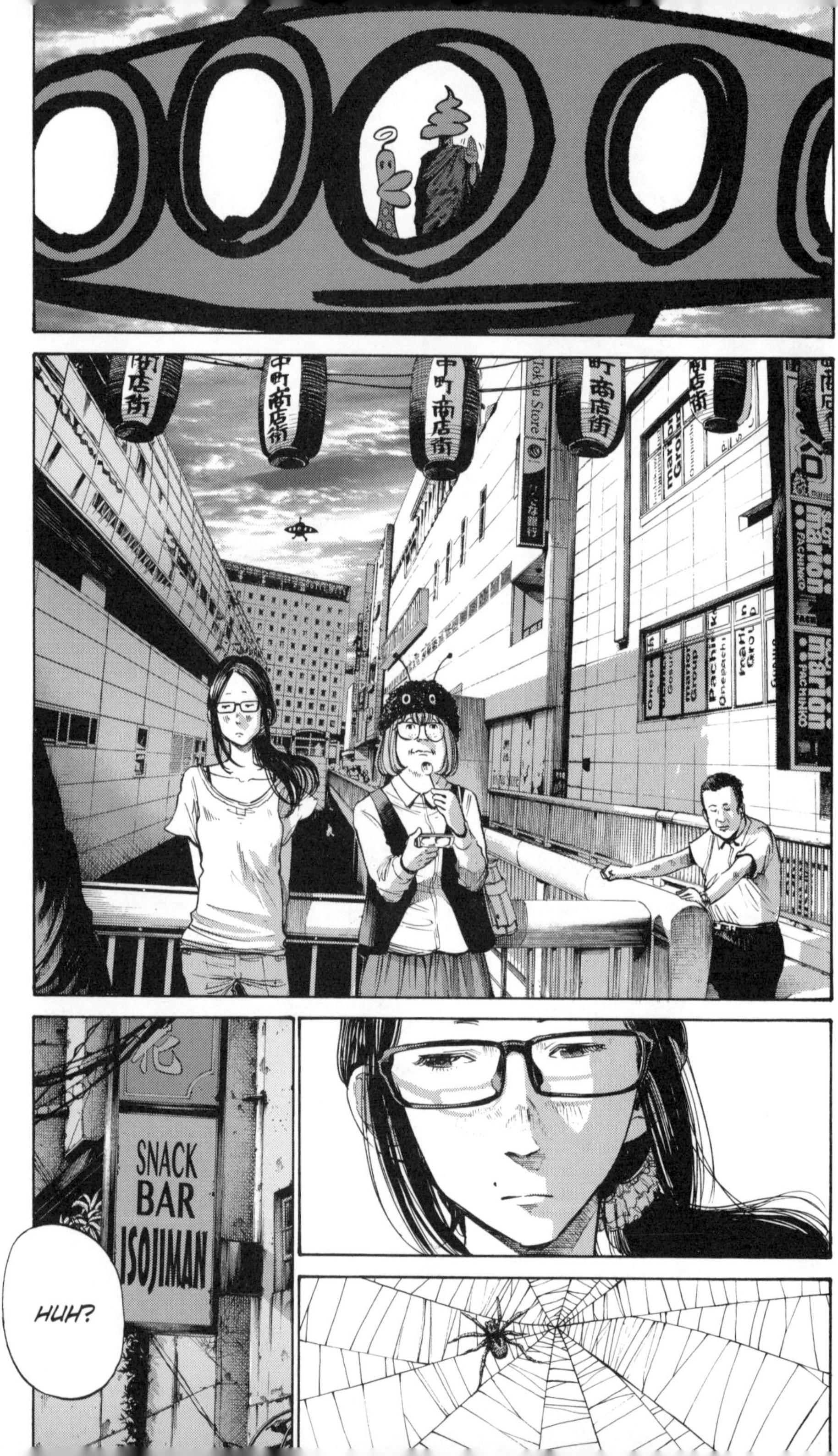
中町商店街
Tokyu Store
marion
PACHINKO
SNACK BAR ISOJIMAN
HUH?

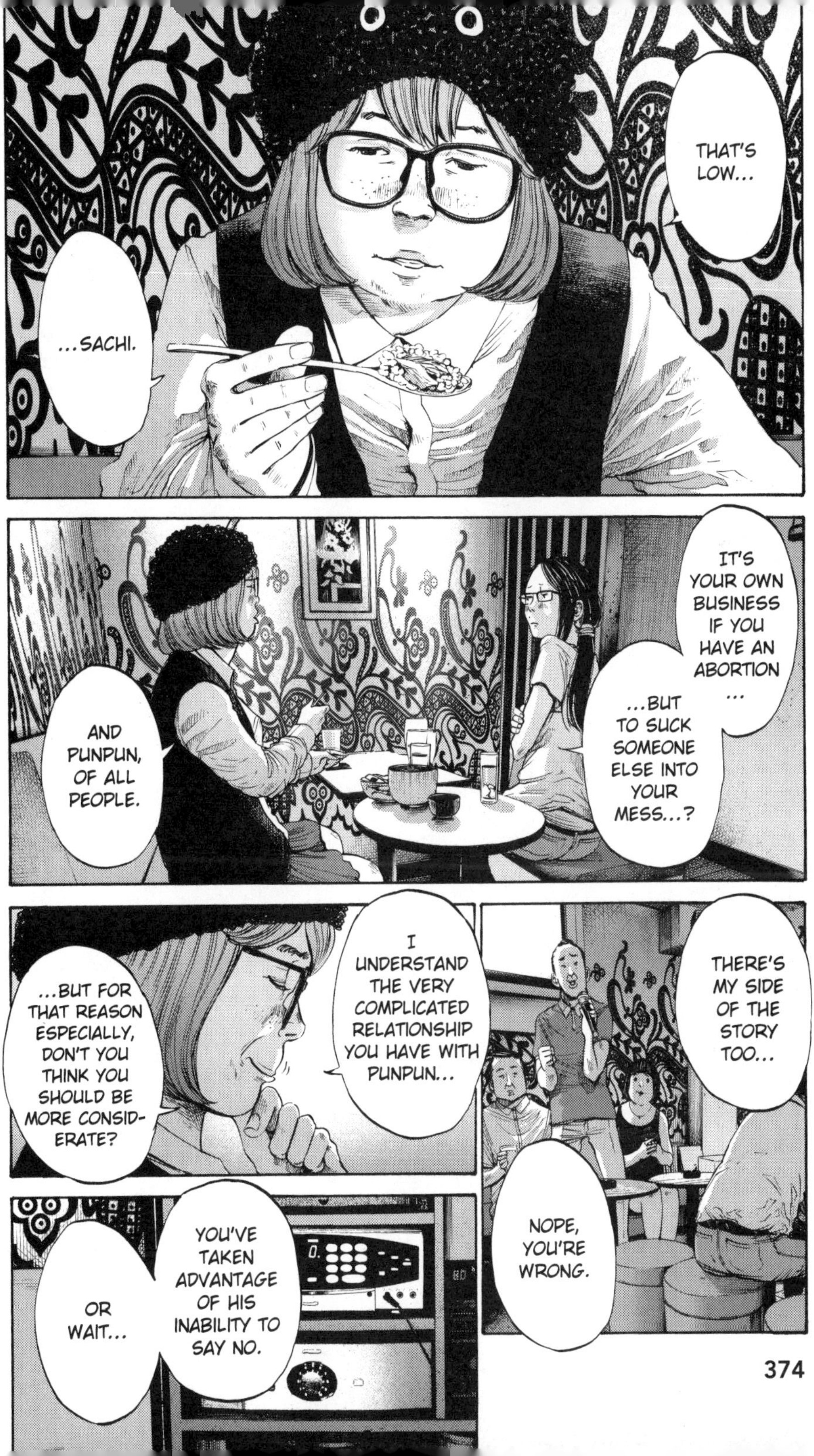
THAT'S LOW...
...SACHI.
IT'S YOUR OWN BUSINESS IF YOU HAVE AN ABORTION ...
...BUT TO SUCK SOMEONE ELSE INTO YOUR MESS...?
AND PUNPUN, OF ALL PEOPLE.
THERE'S MY SIDE OF THE STORY TOO...
NOPE, YOU'RE WRONG.
I UNDERSTAND THE VERY COMPLICATED RELATIONSHIP YOU HAVE WITH PUNPUN...
...BUT FOR THAT REASON ESPECIALLY, DON'T YOU THINK YOU SHOULD BE MORE CONSID-ERATE?
YOU'VE TAKEN ADVANTAGE OF HIS INABILITY TO SAY NO.
OR WAIT...

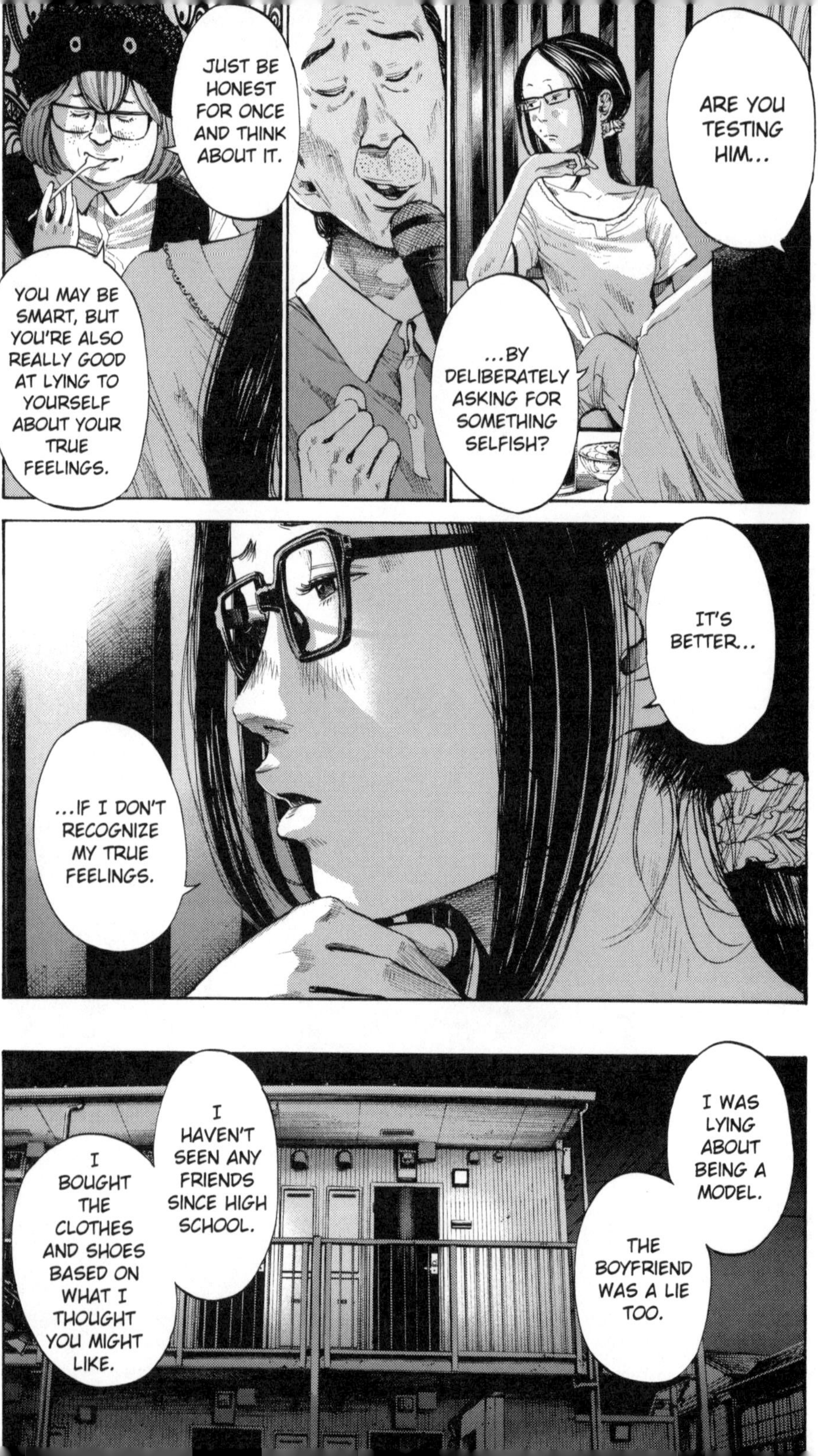
ARE YOU TESTING HIM...
...BY DELIBERATELY ASKING FOR SOMETHING SELFISH?
JUST BE HONEST FOR ONCE AND THINK ABOUT IT.
YOU MAY BE SMART, BUT YOU'RE ALSO REALLY GOOD AT LYING TO YOURSELF ABOUT YOUR TRUE FEELINGS.
IT'S BETTER...
...IF I DON'T RECOGNIZE MY TRUE FEELINGS.
I WAS LYING ABOUT BEING A MODEL.
THE BOYFRIEND WAS A LIE TOO.
I HAVEN'T SEEN ANY FRIENDS SINCE HIGH SCHOOL.
I BOUGHT THE CLOTHES AND SHOES BASED ON WHAT I THOUGHT YOU MIGHT LIKE.

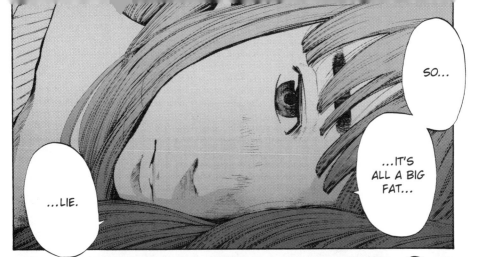

SO...

...IT'S ALL A BIG FAT...

...LIE.

BUT...

...THE PART ABOUT BEING AT A LITTLE TALENT AGENCY WAS TRUE.

THEY DISCOVERED ME ON THE STREET, AND I WAS A YOUNG STAR.

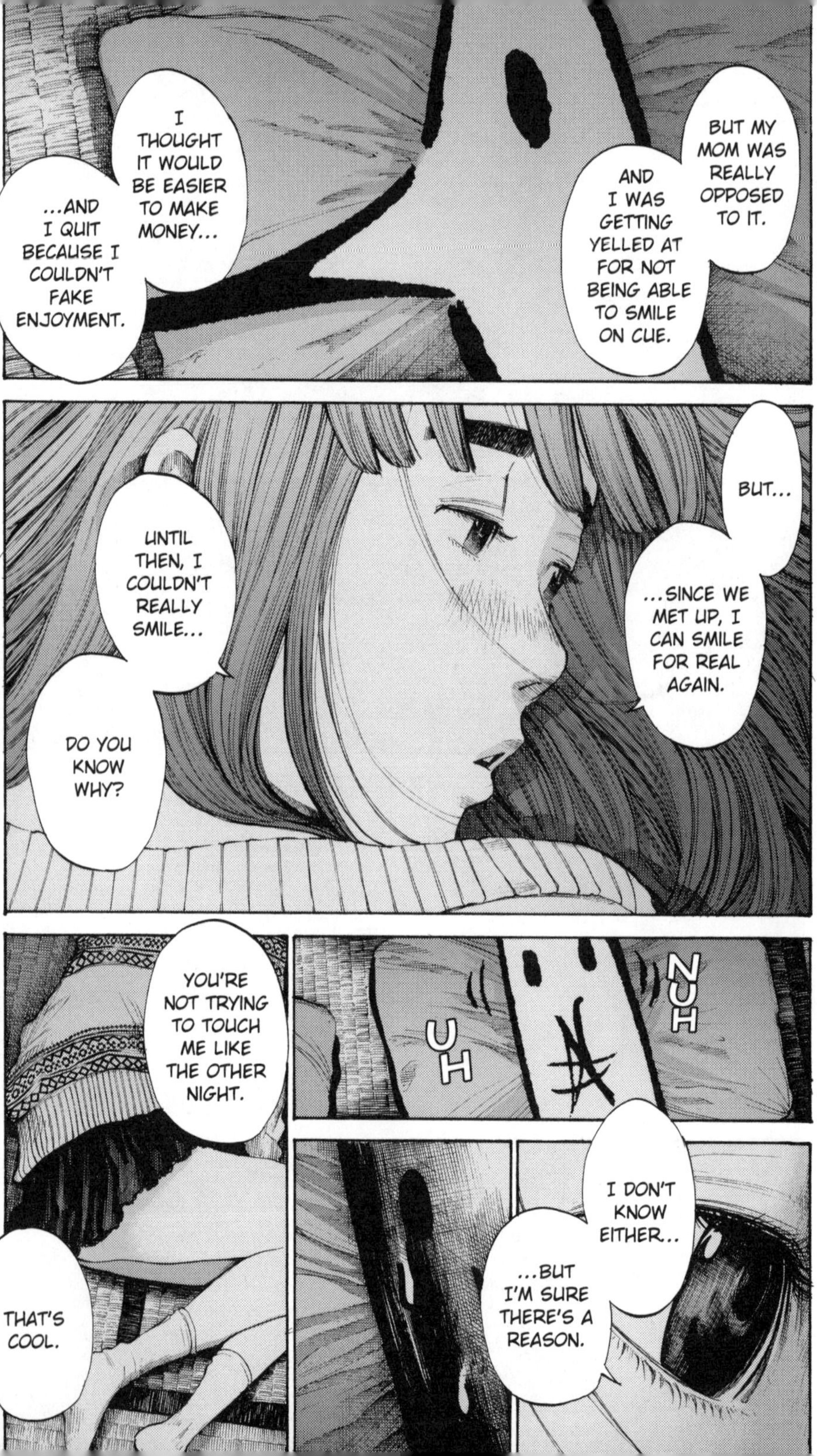
BUT MY MOM WAS REALLY OPPOSED TO IT.
AND I WAS GETTING YELLED AT FOR NOT BEING ABLE TO SMILE ON CUE.
I THOUGHT IT WOULD BE EASIER TO MAKE MONEY...
...AND I QUIT BECAUSE I COULDN'T FAKE ENJOYMENT.
BUT...
...SINCE WE MET UP, I CAN SMILE FOR REAL AGAIN.
UNTIL THEN, I COULDN'T REALLY SMILE...
DO YOU KNOW WHY?
UH
HUH
I DON'T KNOW EITHER...
...BUT I'M SURE THERE'S A REASON.
YOU'RE NOT TRYING TO TOUCH ME LIKE THE OTHER NIGHT.
THAT'S COOL.

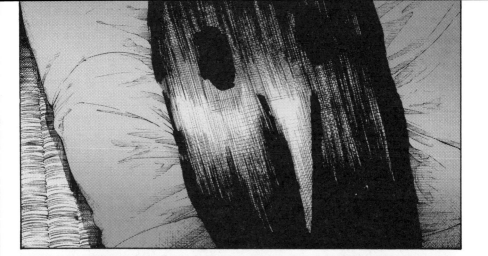

"...I know it was super smooth to get you up to my room..."

"Um..."

I'M THE ONE...

...WHO SAID I WANTED TO SEE YOUR PLACE.

"...I'm not interested in going out with anyone."

"...but right now..."

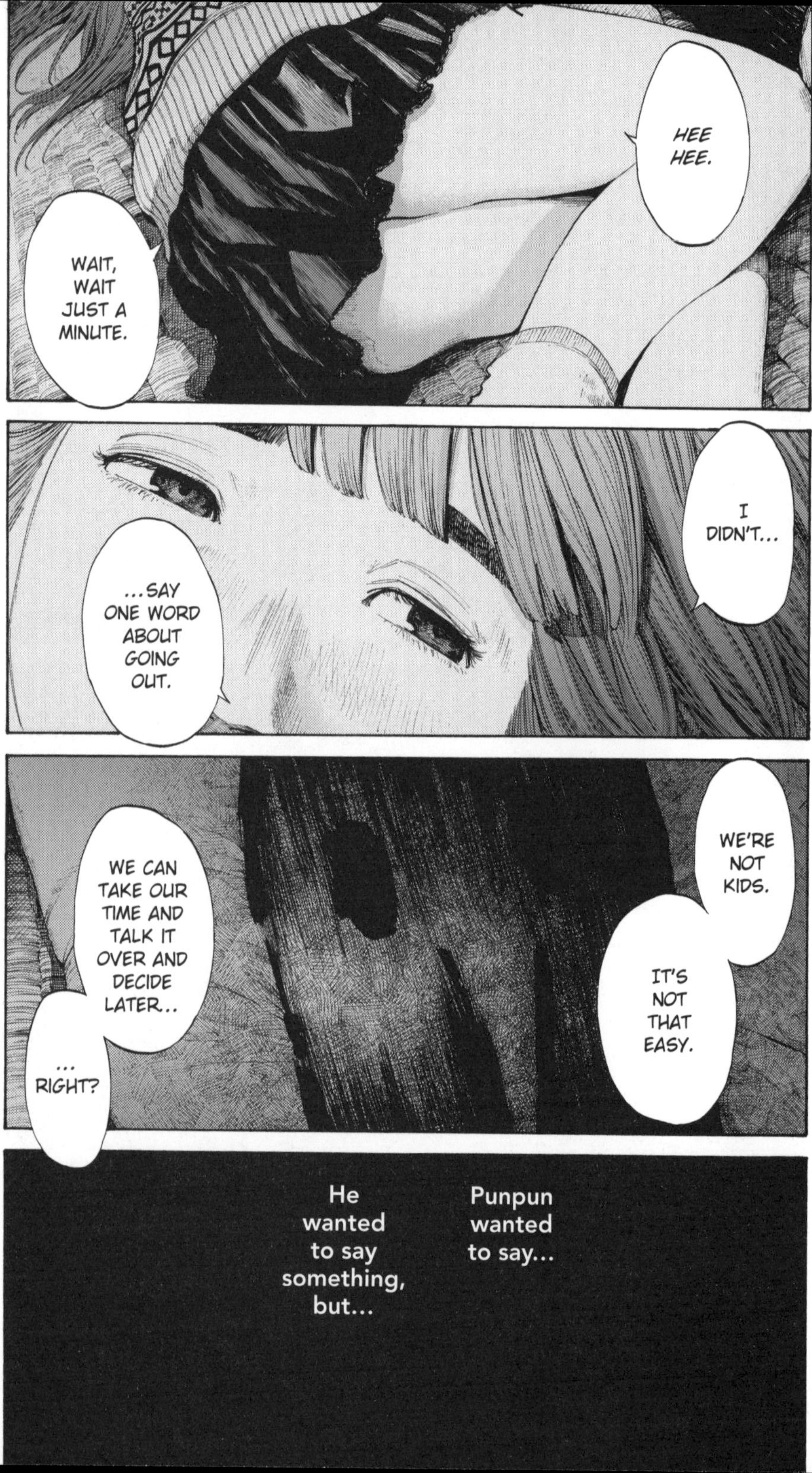
HEE HEE.
WAIT, WAIT JUST A MINUTE.
I DIDN'T...
...SAY ONE WORD ABOUT GOING OUT.
WE'RE NOT KIDS.
IT'S NOT THAT EASY.
WE CAN TAKE OUR TIME AND TALK IT OVER AND DECIDE LATER...
...RIGHT?
Punpun wanted to say...
He wanted to say something, but...

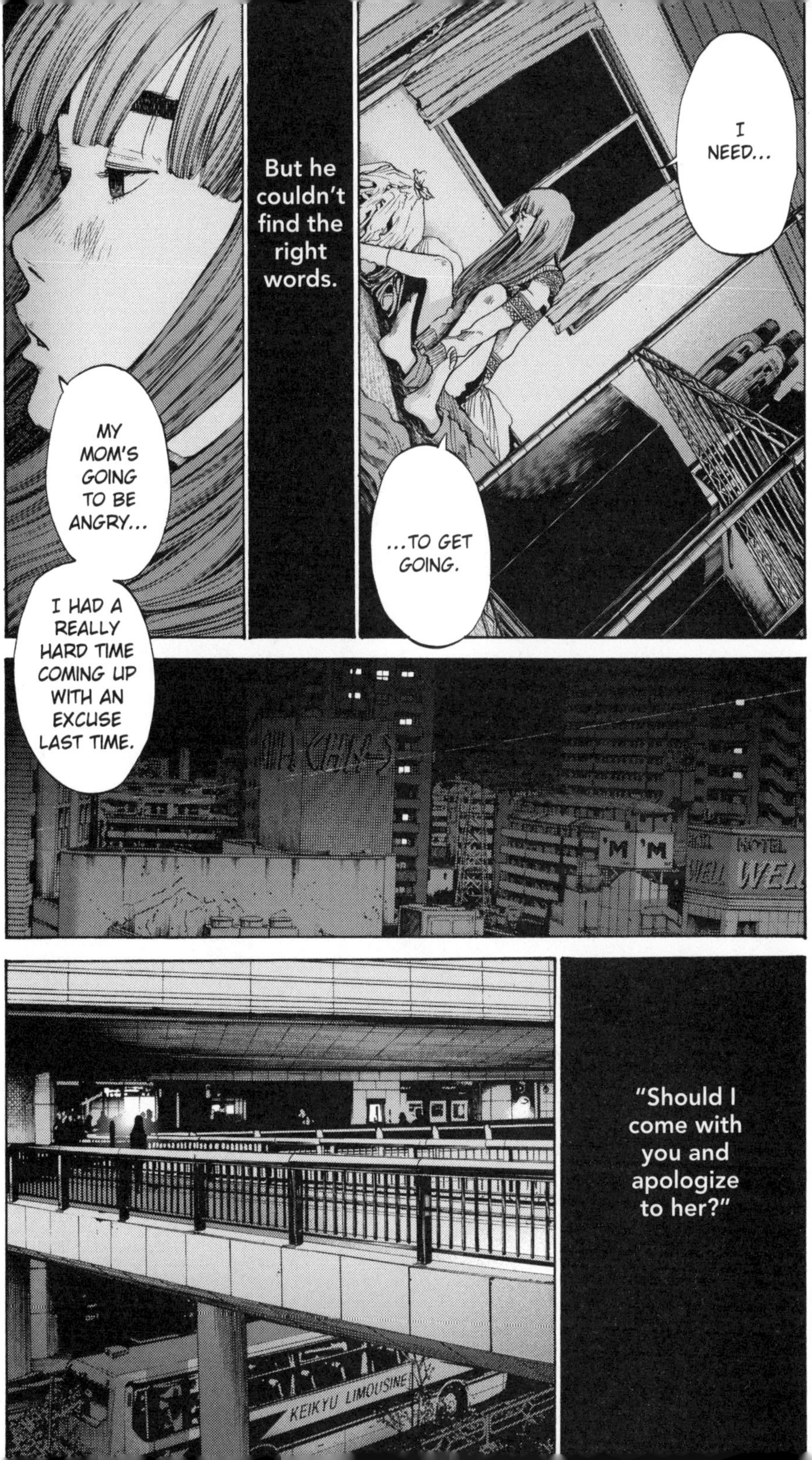
I NEED...
...TO GET GOING.
But he couldn't find the right words.
MY MOM'S GOING TO BE ANGRY...
I HAD A REALLY HARD TIME COMING UP WITH AN EXCUSE LAST TIME.
"Should I come with you and apologize to her?"
KEIKYU LIMOUSINE

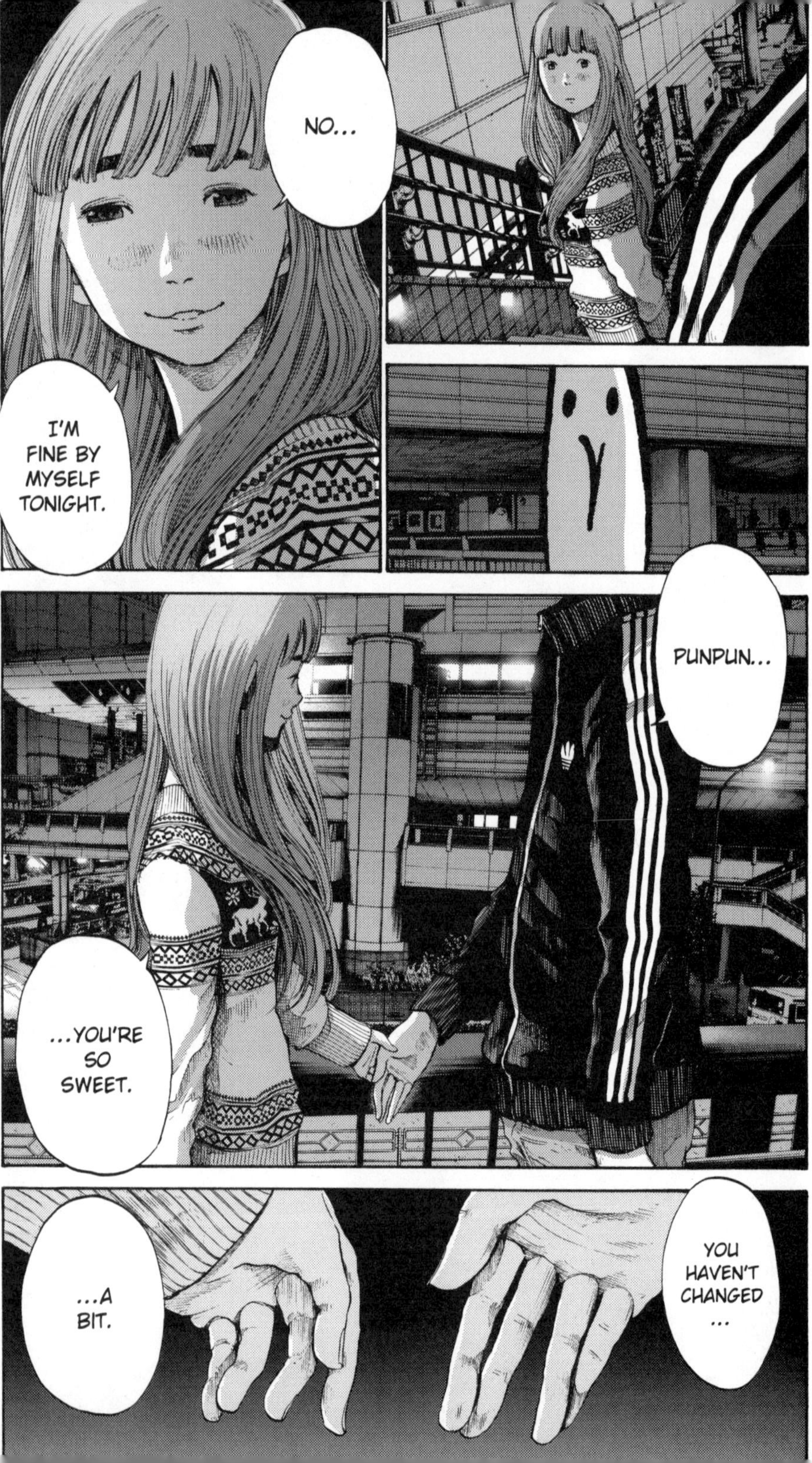
NO...
I'M FINE BY MYSELF TONIGHT.
PUNPUN...
...YOU'RE SO SWEET.
YOU HAVEN'T CHANGED ...
...A BIT.

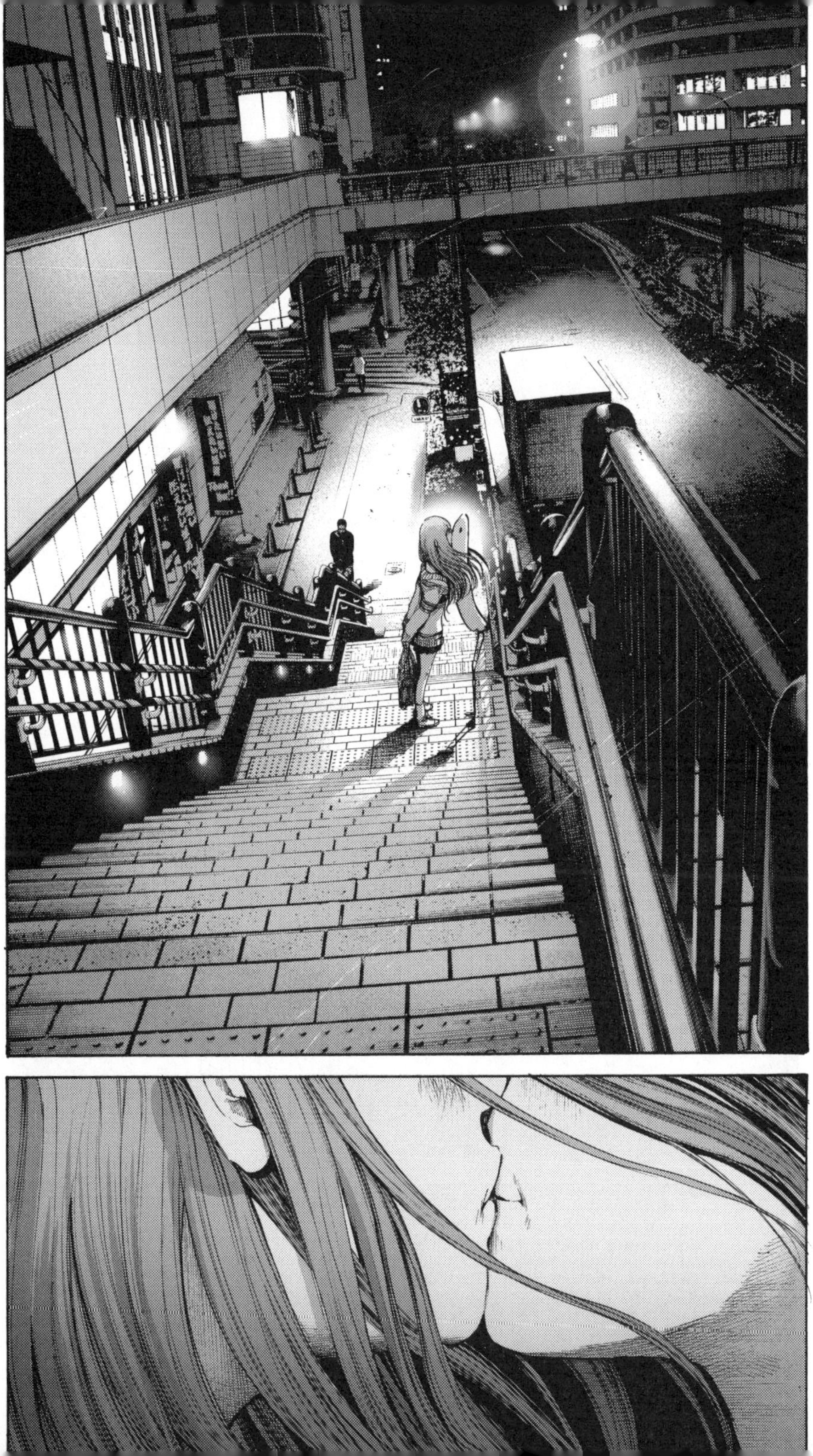

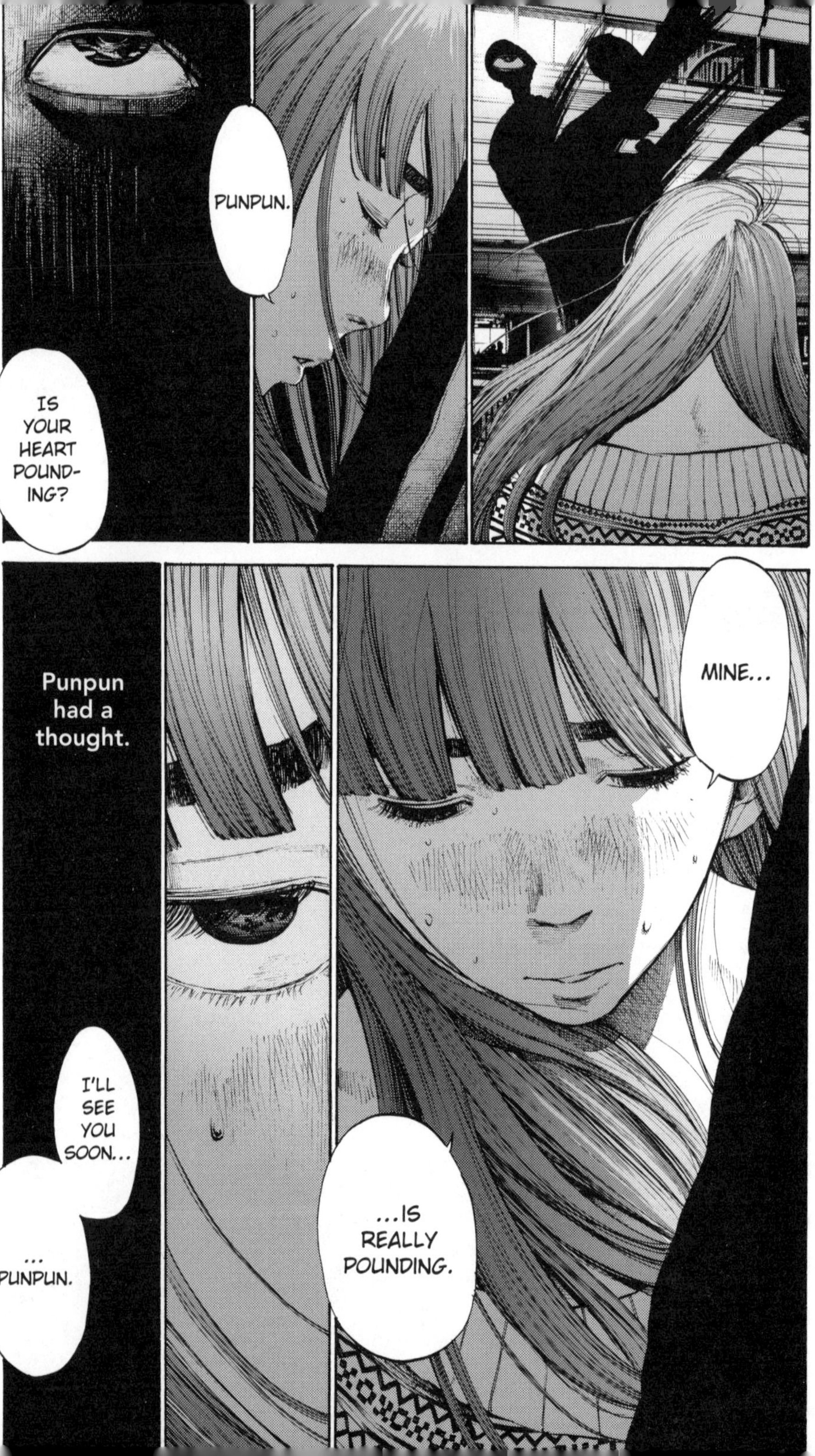
PUNPUN.
IS YOUR HEART POUND-ING?
MINE...
...IS REALLY POUNDING.
Punpun had a thought.
I'LL SEE YOU SOON...
... PUNPUN.

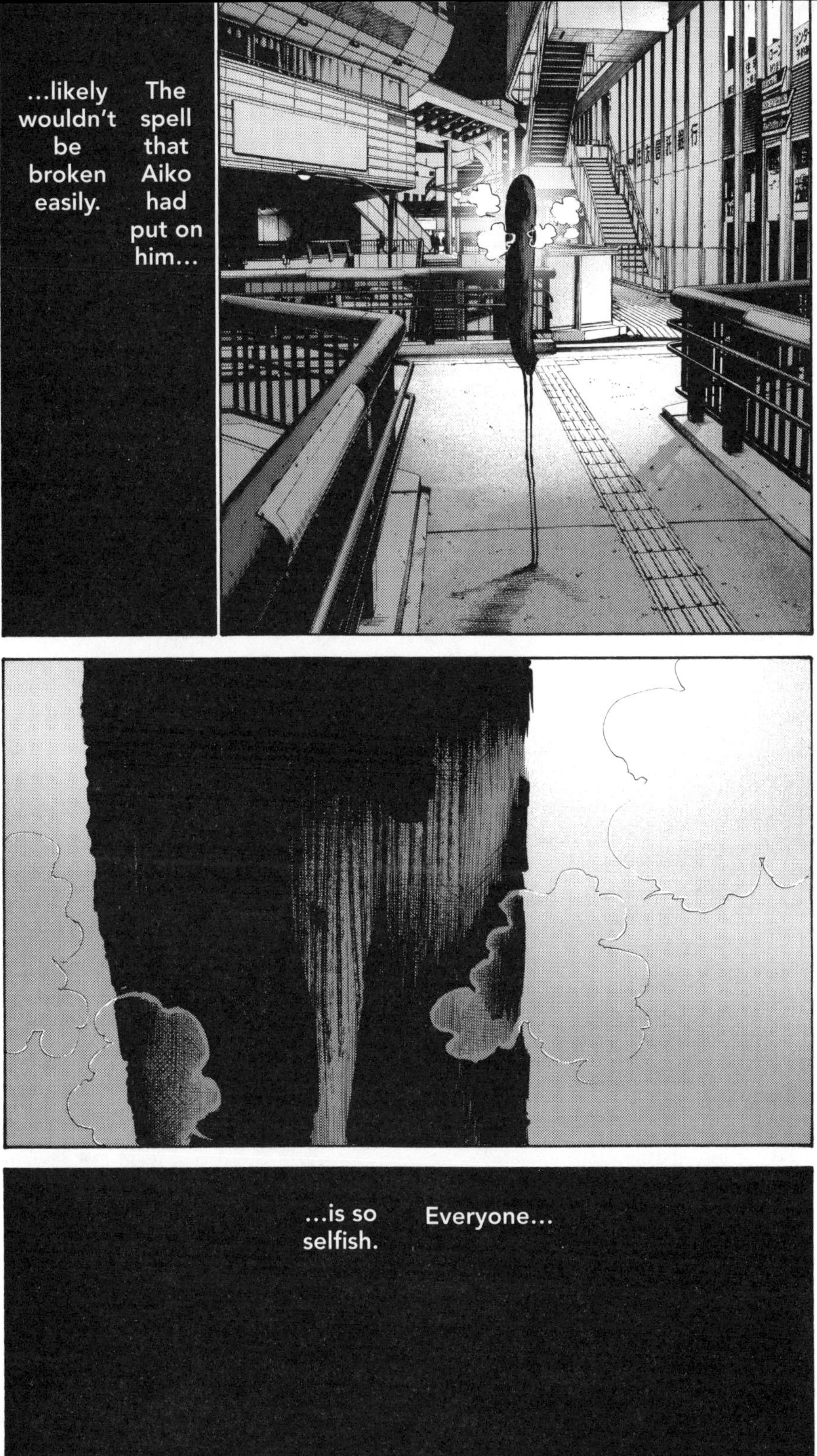
The spell that Aiko had put on him...
...likely wouldn't be broken easily.
Everyone...
...is so selfish.

Chapter 108

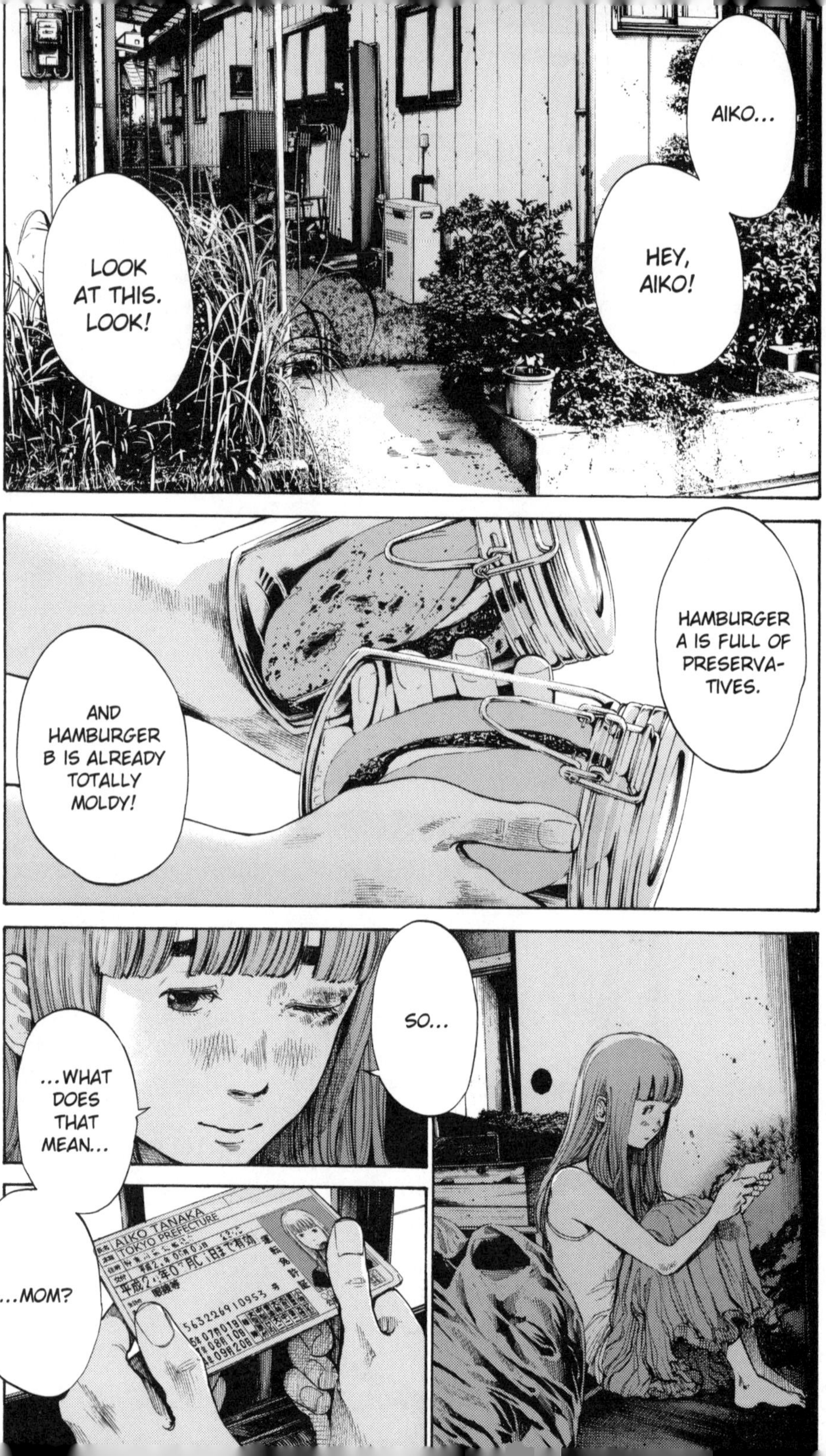
AIKO...
HEY, AIKO!
LOOK AT THIS. LOOK!
HAMBURGER A IS FULL OF PRESERVATIVES.
AND HAMBURGER B IS ALREADY TOTALLY MOLDY!
SO...
...WHAT DOES THAT MEAN...
AIKO TANAKA
TOKYO PREFECTURE
...MOM?

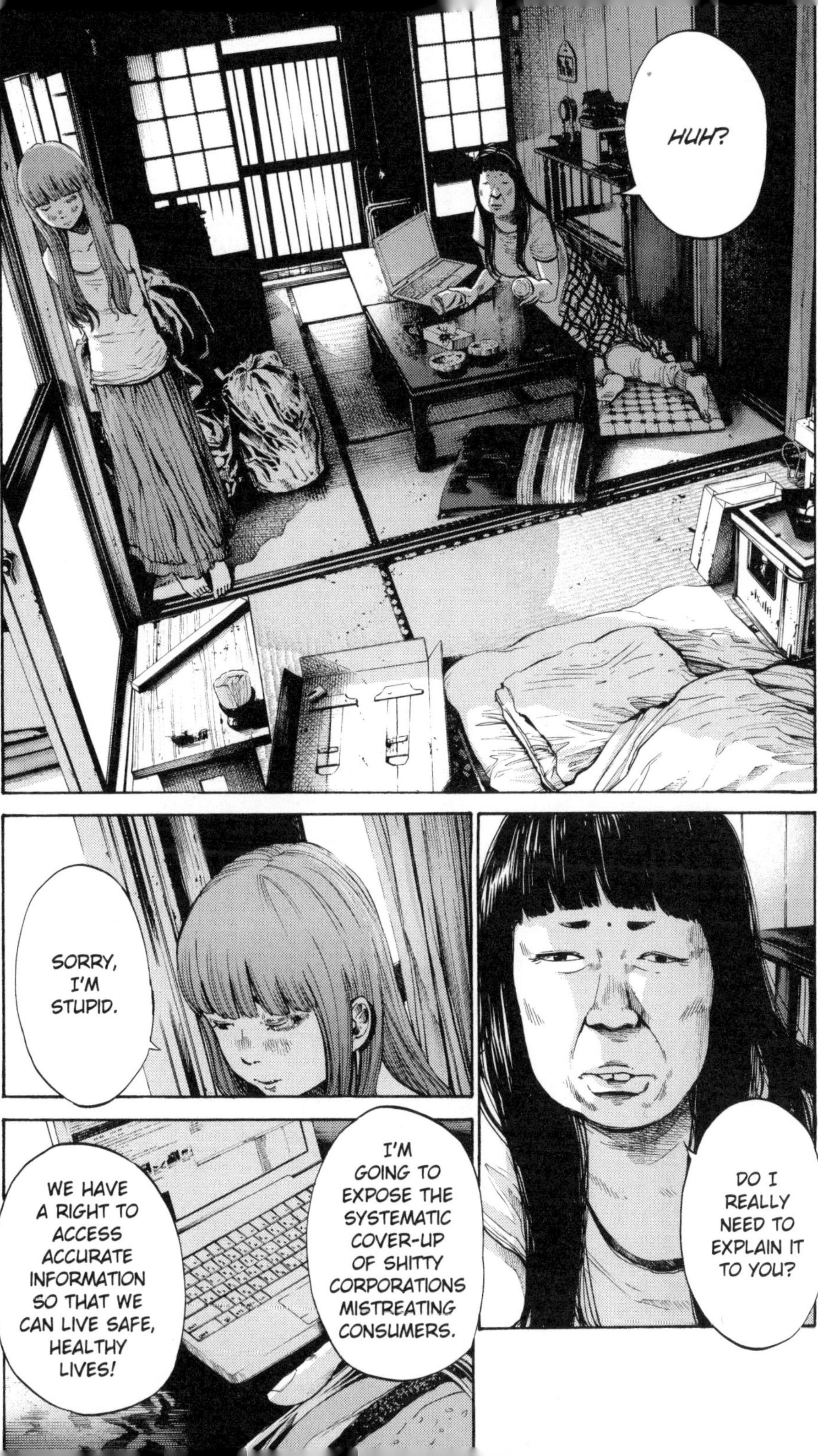
HUH?
DO I REALLY NEED TO EXPLAIN IT TO YOU?
SORRY, I'M STUPID.
I'M GOING TO EXPOSE THE SYSTEMATIC COVER-UP OF SHITTY CORPORATIONS MISTREATING CONSUMERS.
WE HAVE A RIGHT TO ACCESS ACCURATE INFORMATION SO THAT WE CAN LIVE SAFE, HEALTHY LIVES!

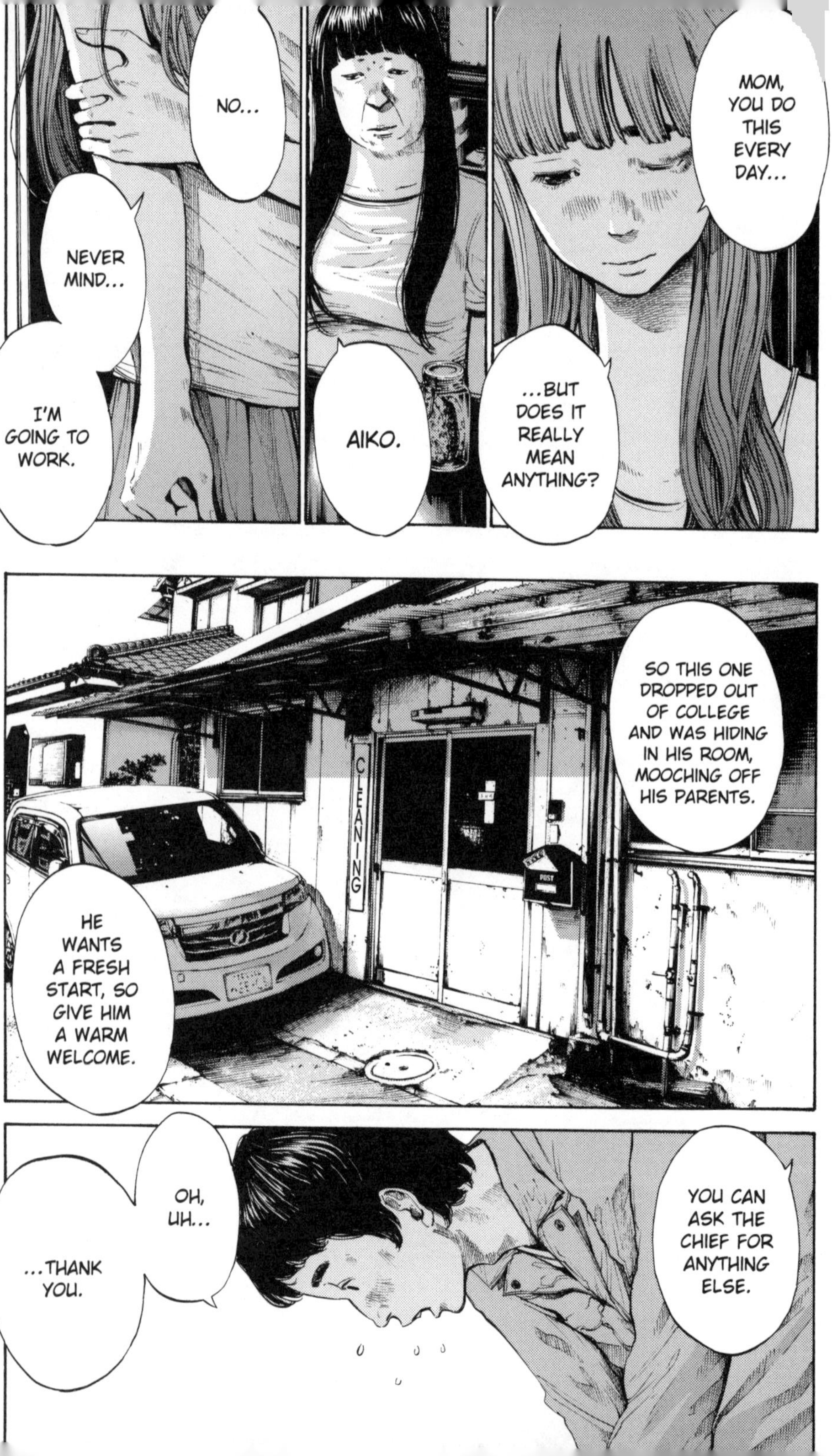
MOM, YOU DO THIS EVERY DAY...
...BUT DOES IT REALLY MEAN ANYTHING?
AIKO.
NO...
NEVER MIND...
I'M GOING TO WORK.
SO THIS ONE DROPPED OUT OF COLLEGE AND WAS HIDING IN HIS ROOM, MOOCHING OFF HIS PARENTS.
CLEANING
POST
HE WANTS A FRESH START, SO GIVE HIM A WARM WELCOME.
YOU CAN ASK THE CHIEF FOR ANYTHING ELSE.
OH, UH...
...THANK YOU.

OH?

A NEW GUY.

OH, UM...

AIKO, I HEAR WE'RE FROM THE SAME HOMETOWN.

WHERE DID YOU GO TO HIGH SCHOOL?

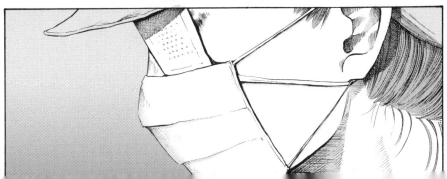

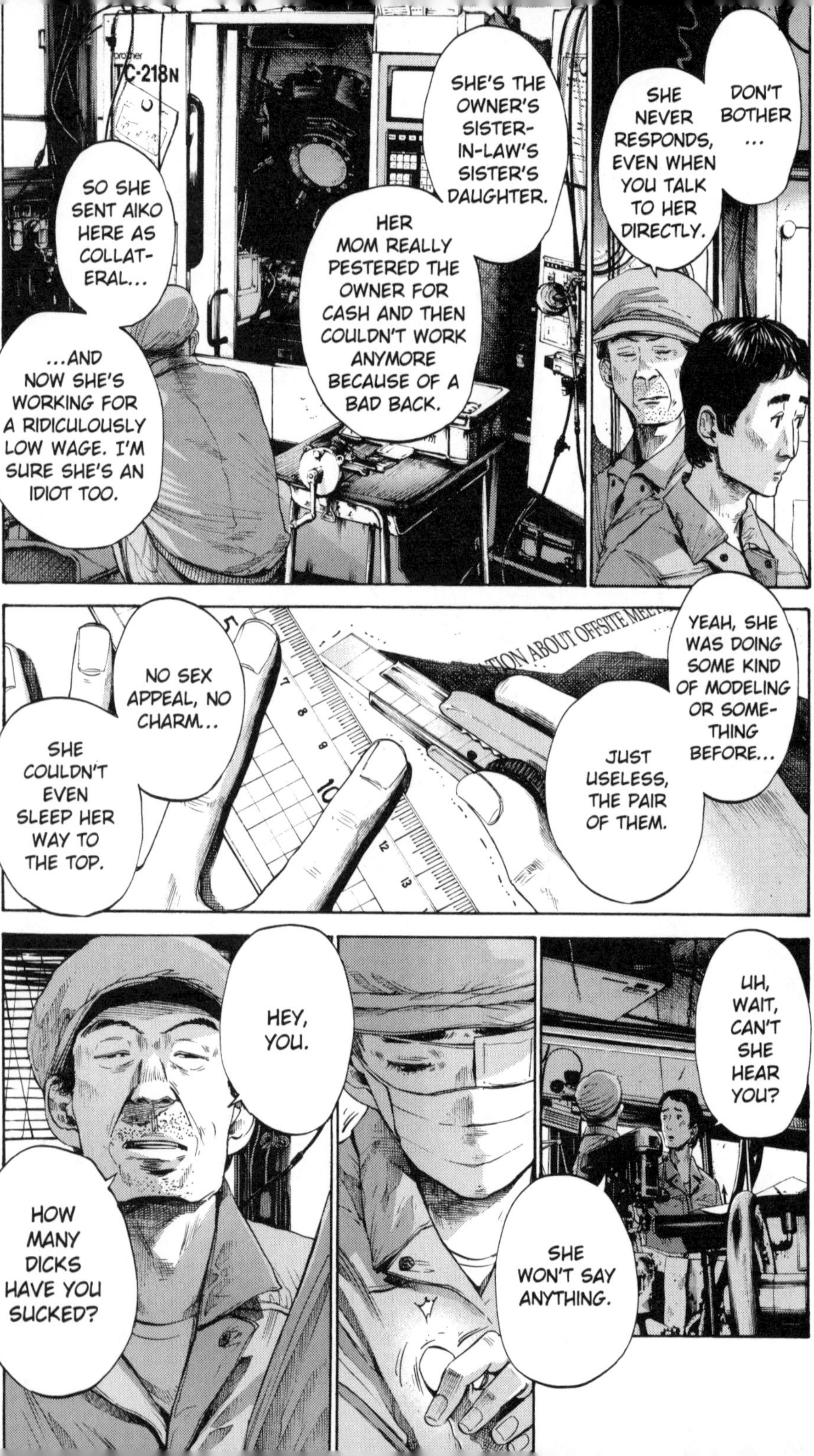
brother
TC-218N
DON'T BOTHER...
SHE NEVER RESPONDS, EVEN WHEN YOU TALK TO HER DIRECTLY.
SHE'S THE OWNER'S SISTER-IN-LAW'S SISTER'S DAUGHTER.
HER MOM REALLY PESTERED THE OWNER FOR CASH AND THEN COULDN'T WORK ANYMORE BECAUSE OF A BAD BACK.
SO SHE SENT AIKO HERE AS COLLATERAL...
...AND NOW SHE'S WORKING FOR A RIDICULOUSLY LOW WAGE. I'M SURE SHE'S AN IDIOT TOO.
YEAH, SHE WAS DOING SOME KIND OF MODELING OR SOMETHING BEFORE...
JUST USELESS, THE PAIR OF THEM.
NO SEX APPEAL, NO CHARM...
SHE COULDN'T EVEN SLEEP HER WAY TO THE TOP.
UH, WAIT, CAN'T SHE HEAR YOU?
SHE WON'T SAY ANYTHING.
HEY, YOU.
HOW MANY DICKS HAVE YOU SUCKED?

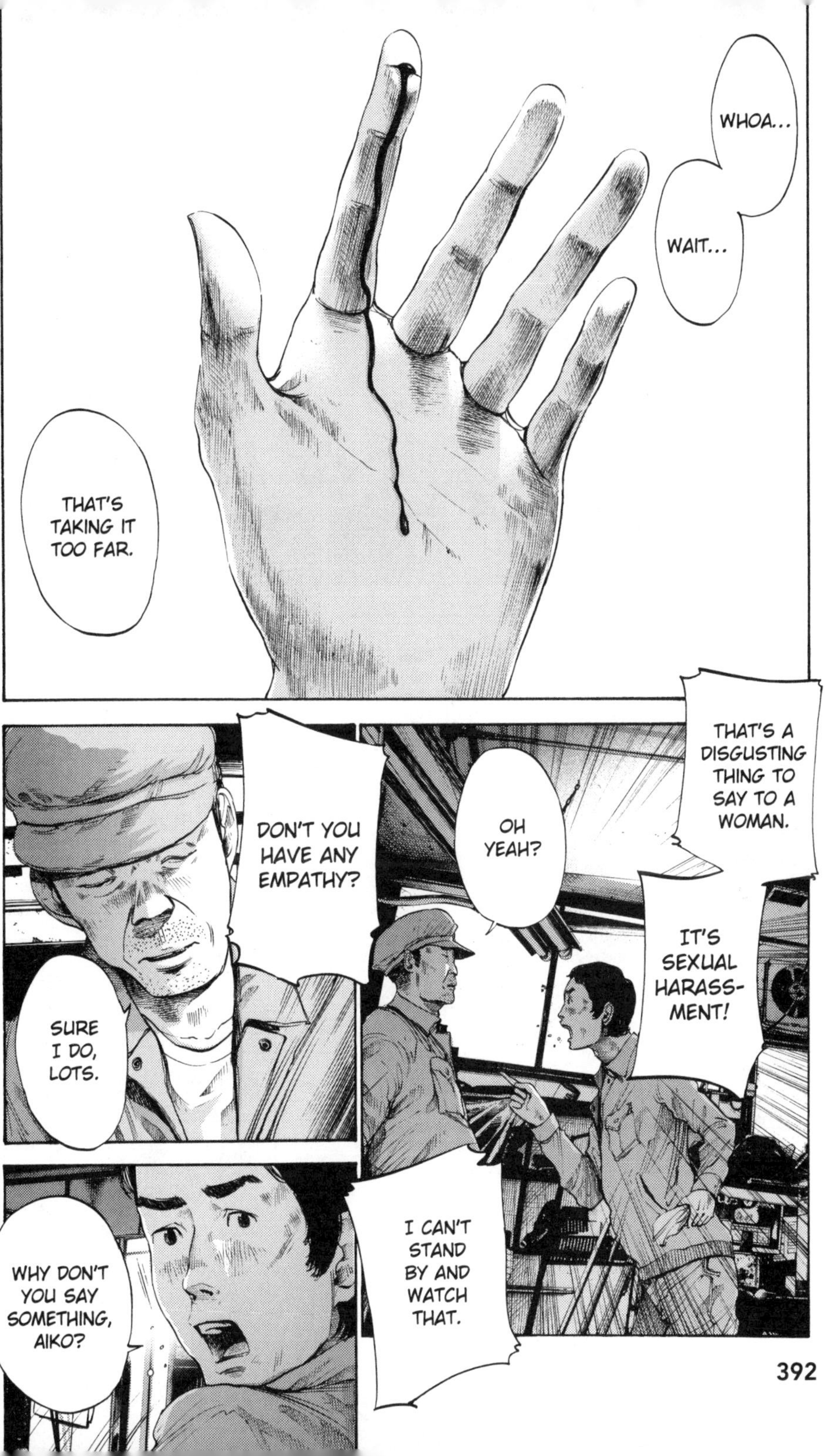
WHOA...
WAIT...
THAT'S TAKING IT TOO FAR.
THAT'S A DISGUSTING THING TO SAY TO A WOMAN.
OH YEAH?
IT'S SEXUAL HARASS-MENT!
DON'T YOU HAVE ANY EMPATHY?
SURE I DO, LOTS.
I CAN'T STAND BY AND WATCH THAT.
WHY DON'T YOU SAY SOMETHING, AIKO?

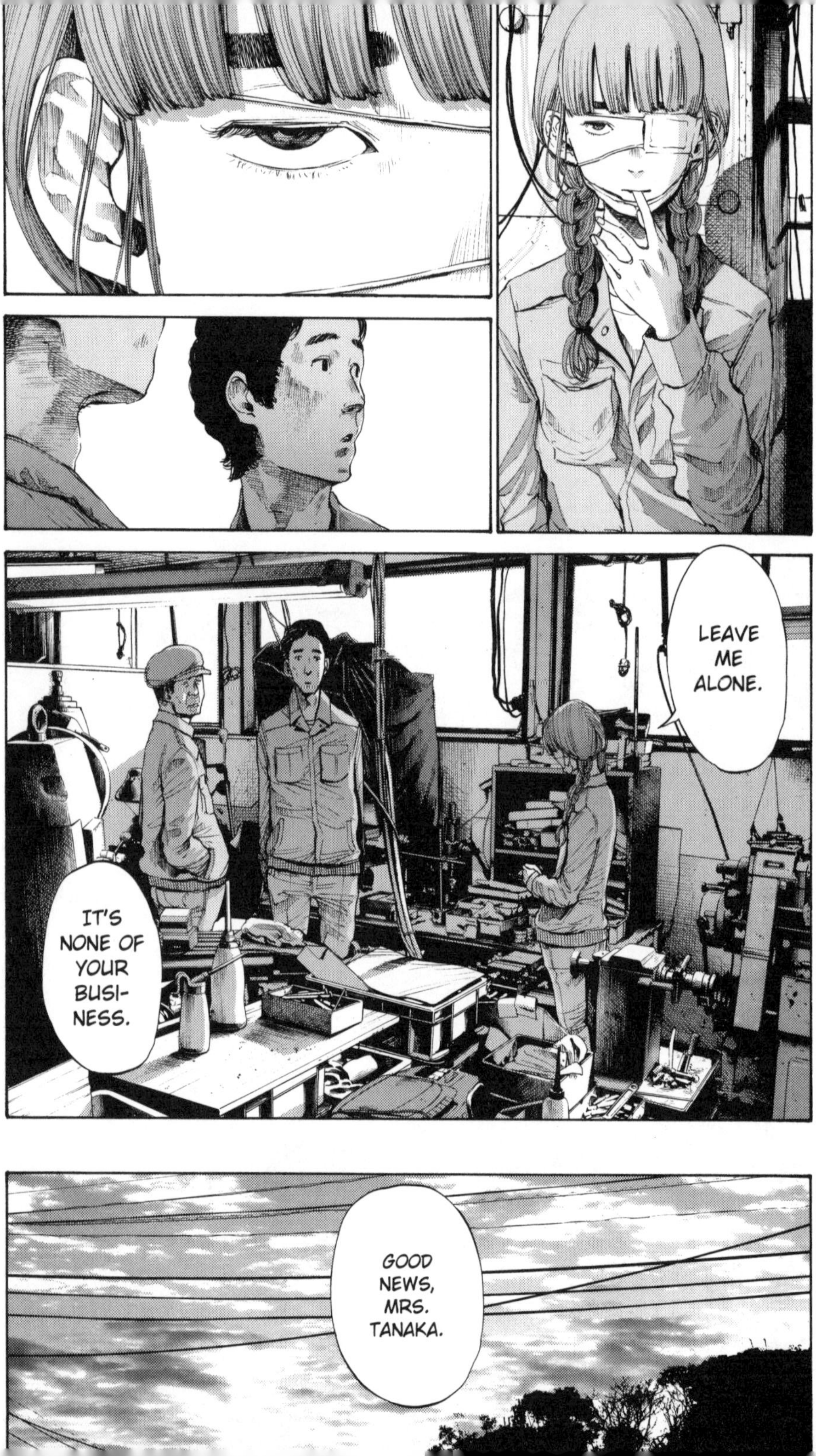
LEAVE ME ALONE.
IT'S NONE OF YOUR BUSI-NESS.
GOOD NEWS, MRS. TANAKA.

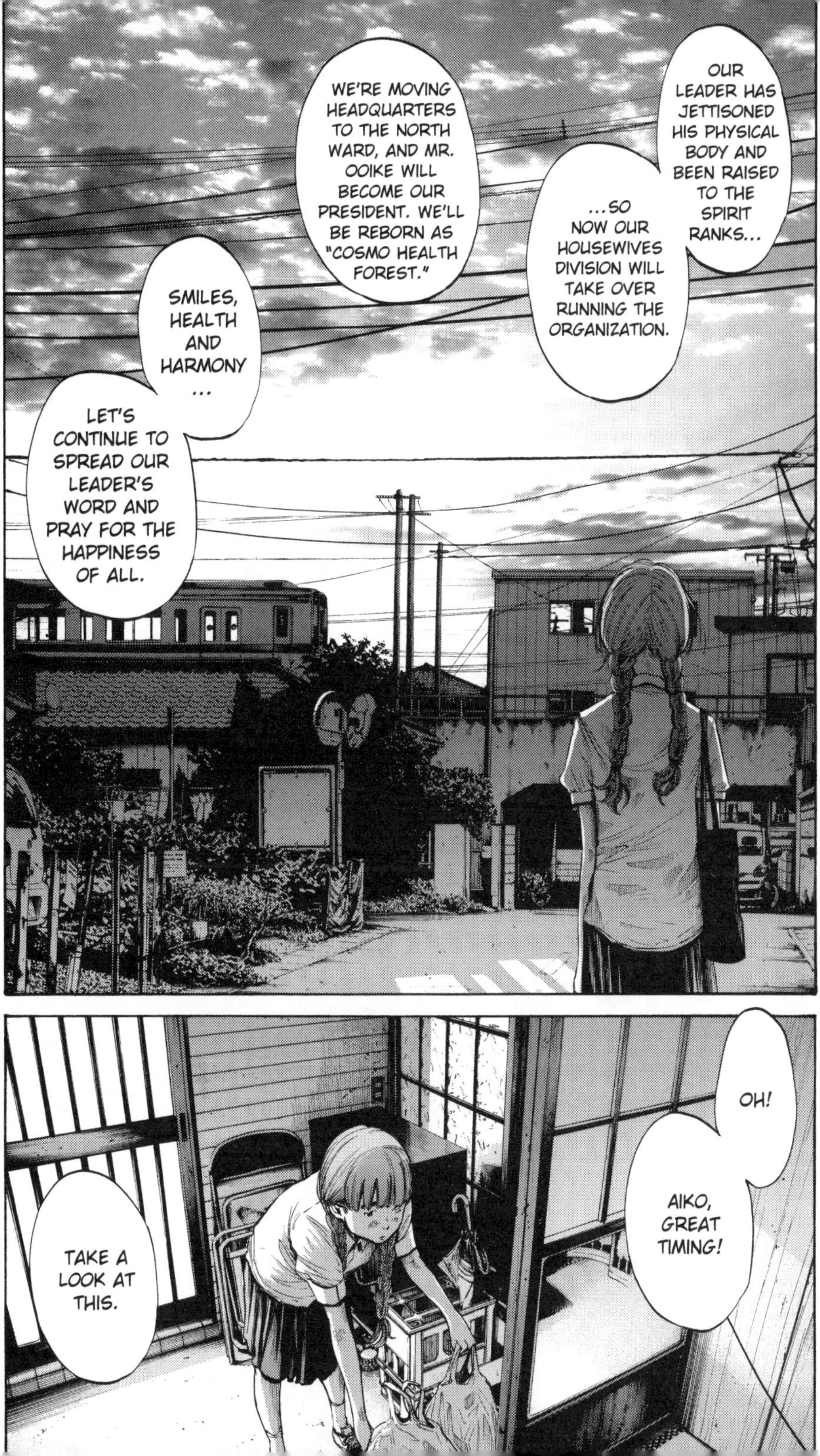
OUR LEADER HAS JETTISONED HIS PHYSICAL BODY AND BEEN RAISED TO THE SPIRIT RANKS...
...SO NOW OUR HOUSEWIVES DIVISION WILL TAKE OVER RUNNING THE ORGANIZATION.
WE'RE MOVING HEADQUARTERS TO THE NORTH WARD, AND MR. OOIKE WILL BECOME OUR PRESIDENT. WE'LL BE REBORN AS "COSMO HEALTH FOREST."
SMILES, HEALTH AND HARMONY...
LET'S CONTINUE TO SPREAD OUR LEADER'S WORD AND PRAY FOR THE HAPPINESS OF ALL.
OH!
AIKO, GREAT TIMING!
TAKE A LOOK AT THIS.

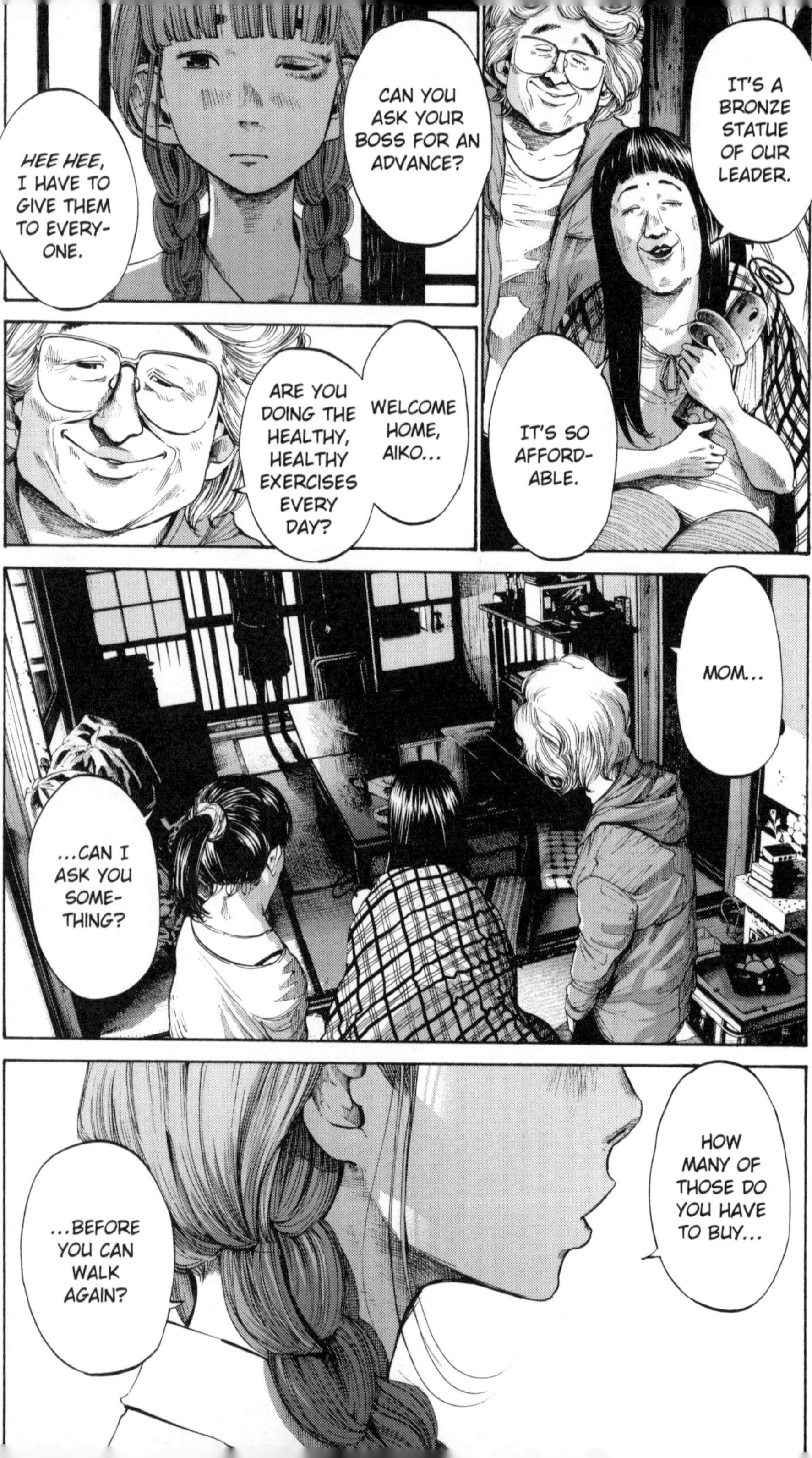
IT'S A BRONZE STATUE OF OUR LEADER.
IT'S SO AFFORDABLE.
CAN YOU ASK YOUR BOSS FOR AN ADVANCE?
HEE HEE, I HAVE TO GIVE THEM TO EVERY-ONE.
WELCOME HOME, AIKO...
ARE YOU DOING THE HEALTHY, HEALTHY EXERCISES EVERY DAY?
MOM...
...CAN I ASK YOU SOME-THING?
HOW MANY OF THOSE DO YOU HAVE TO BUY...
...BEFORE YOU CAN WALK AGAIN?

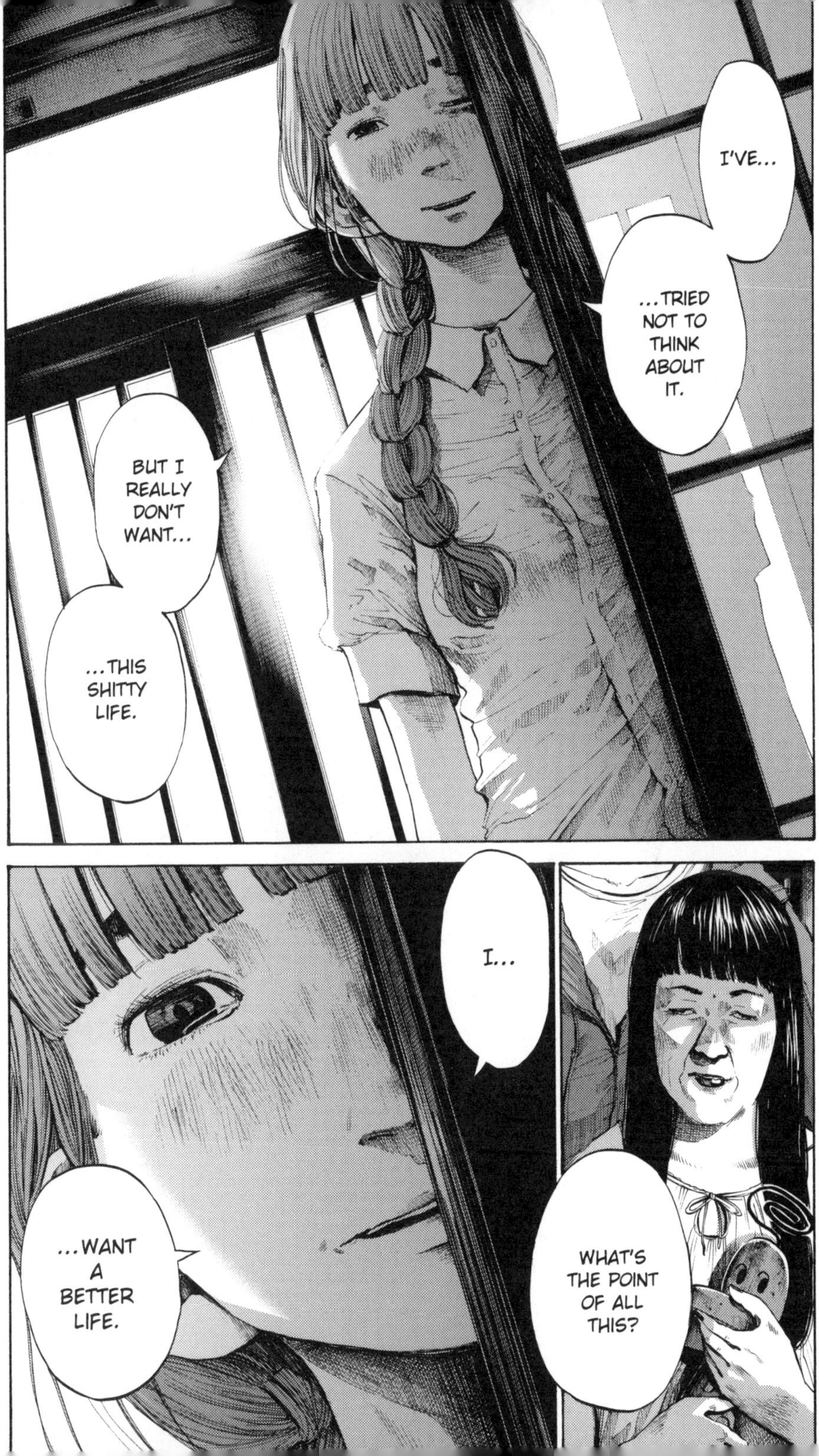
I'VE...
...TRIED NOT TO THINK ABOUT IT.
BUT I REALLY DON'T WANT...
...THIS SHITTY LIFE.
WHAT'S THE POINT OF ALL THIS?
I...
...WANT A BETTER LIFE.

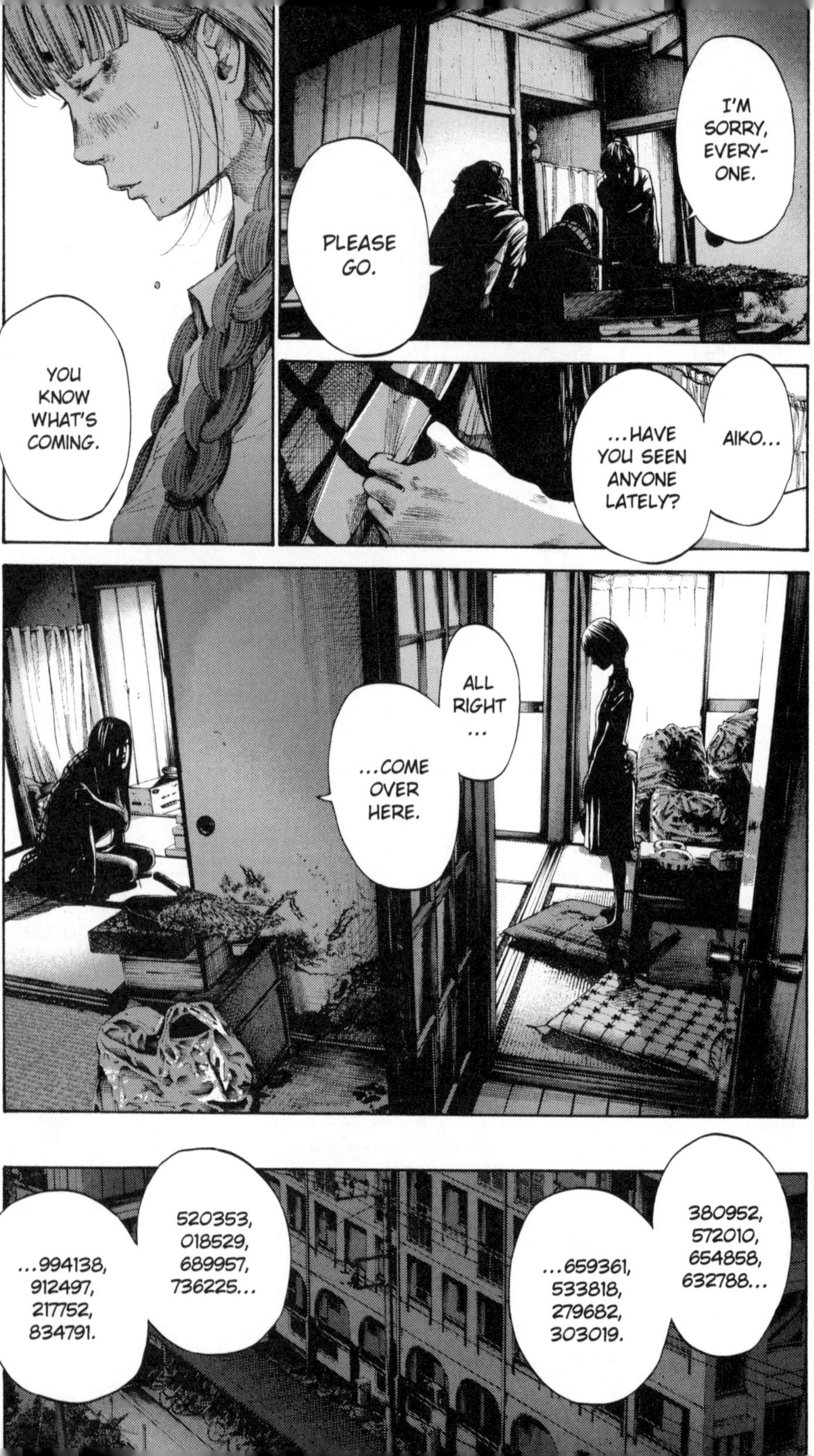
I'M SORRY, EVERYONE.
PLEASE GO.
AIKO...
...HAVE YOU SEEN ANYONE LATELY?
YOU KNOW WHAT'S COMING.
ALL RIGHT...
...COME OVER HERE.
380952, 572010, 654858, 632788...
...659361, 533818, 279682, 303019.
520353, 018529, 689957, 736225...
...994138, 912497, 217752, 834791.

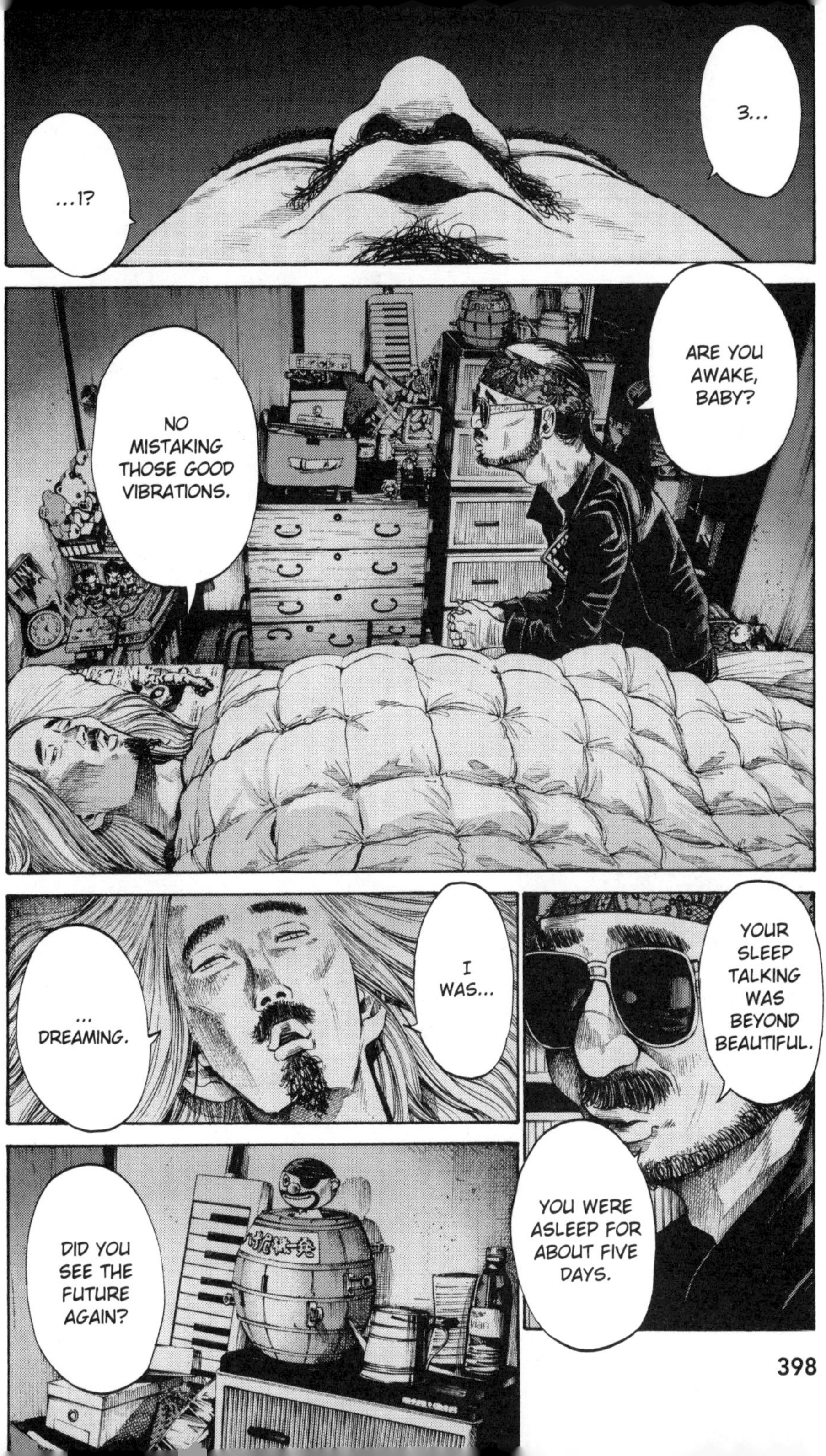
3...
...1?
ARE YOU AWAKE, BABY?
NO MISTAKING THOSE GOOD VIBRATIONS.
YOUR SLEEP TALKING WAS BEYOND BEAUTIFUL.
YOU WERE ASLEEP FOR ABOUT FIVE DAYS.
I WAS...
... DREAMING.
DID YOU SEE THE FUTURE AGAIN?

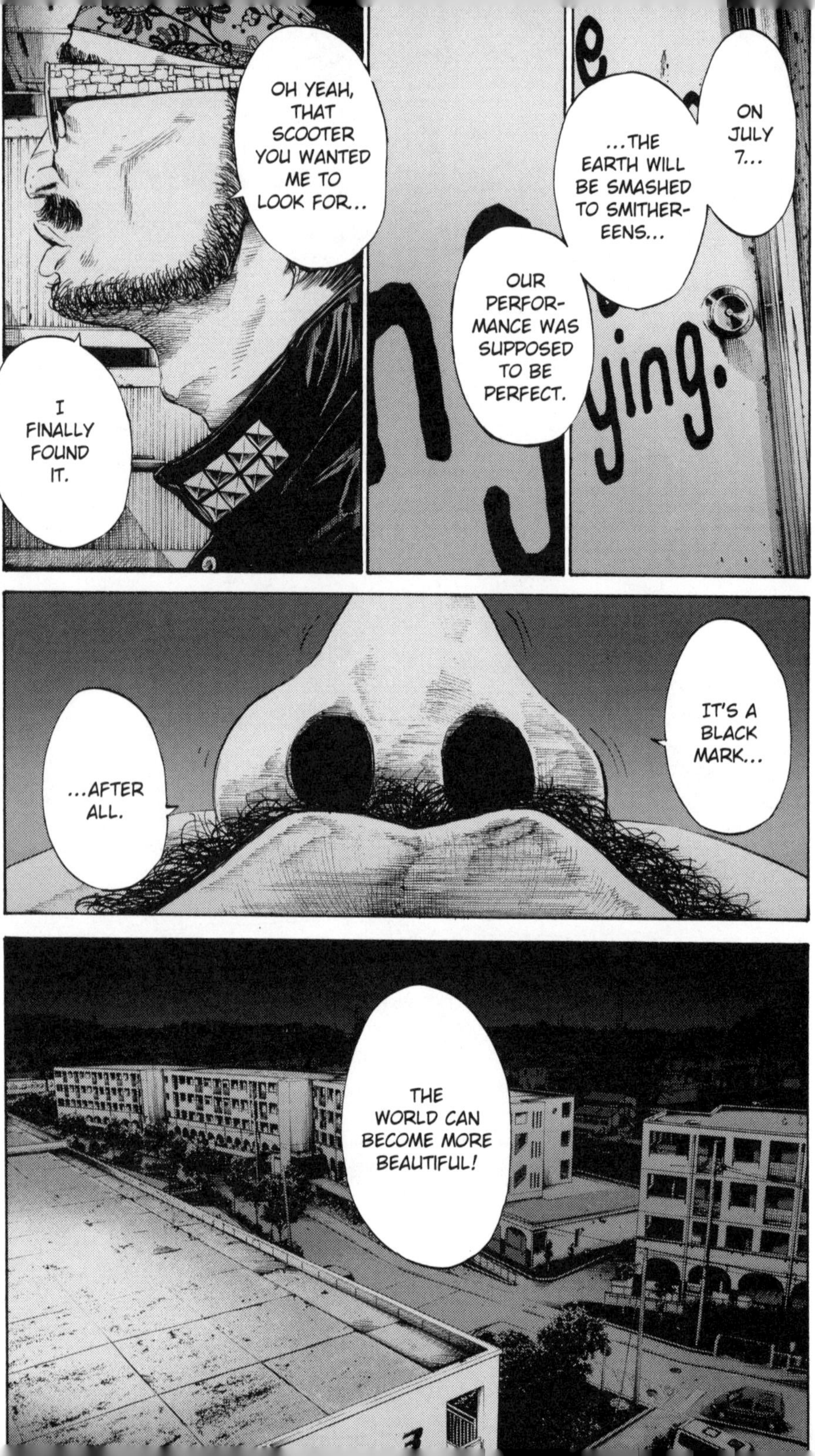
ON JULY 7...
...THE EARTH WILL BE SMASHED TO SMITHER-EENS...
OUR PERFOR-MANCE WAS SUPPOSED TO BE PERFECT.
OH YEAH, THAT SCOOTER YOU WANTED ME TO LOOK FOR...
I FINALLY FOUND IT.
IT'S A BLACK MARK...
...AFTER ALL.
THE WORLD CAN BECOME MORE BEAUTIFUL!

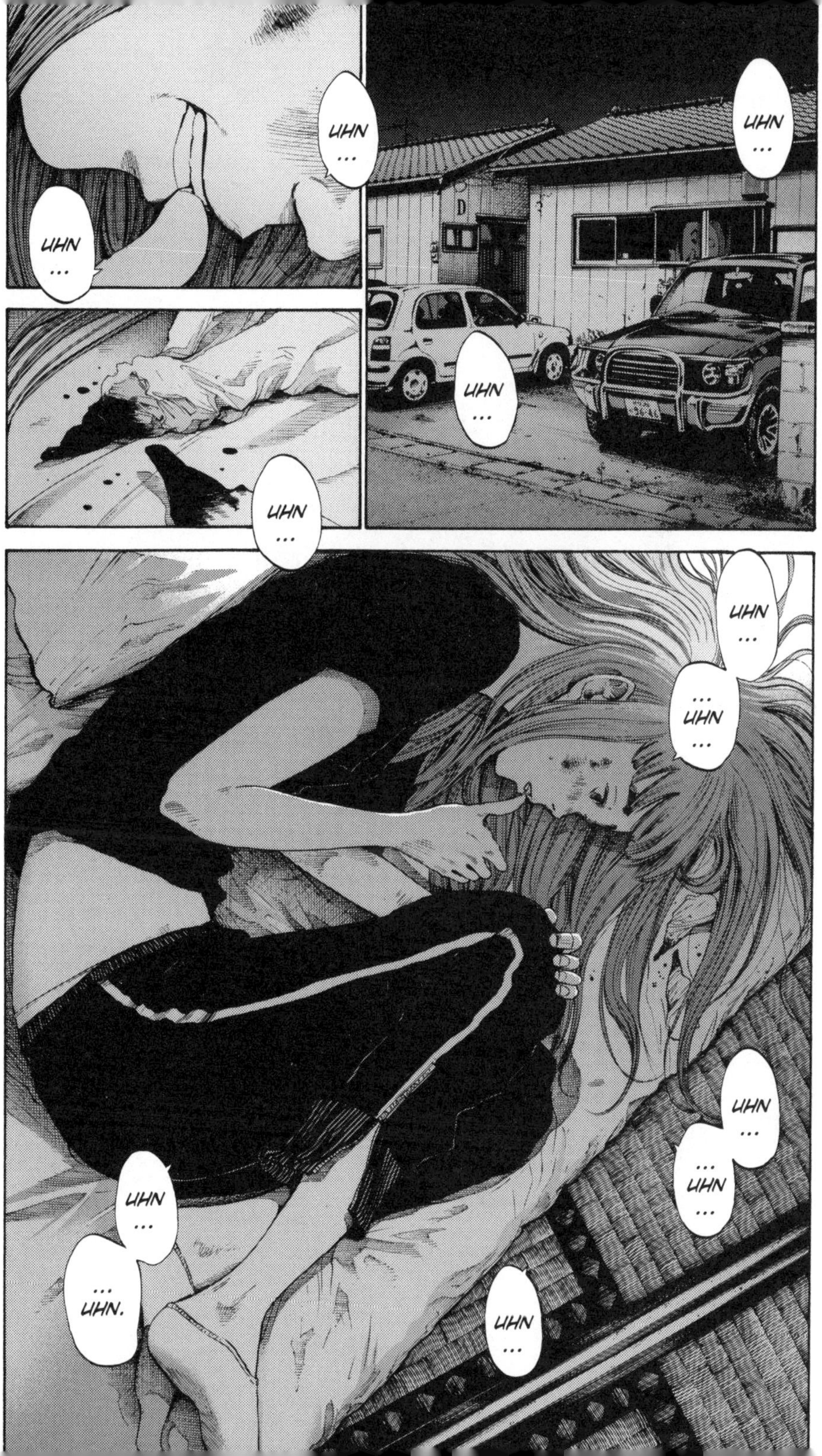
UHN ...
UHN ...
UHN ...
UHN ...
UHN ...
UHN ...
... UHN ...
UHN ...
... UHN ...
UHN ...
UHN ...
... UHN.

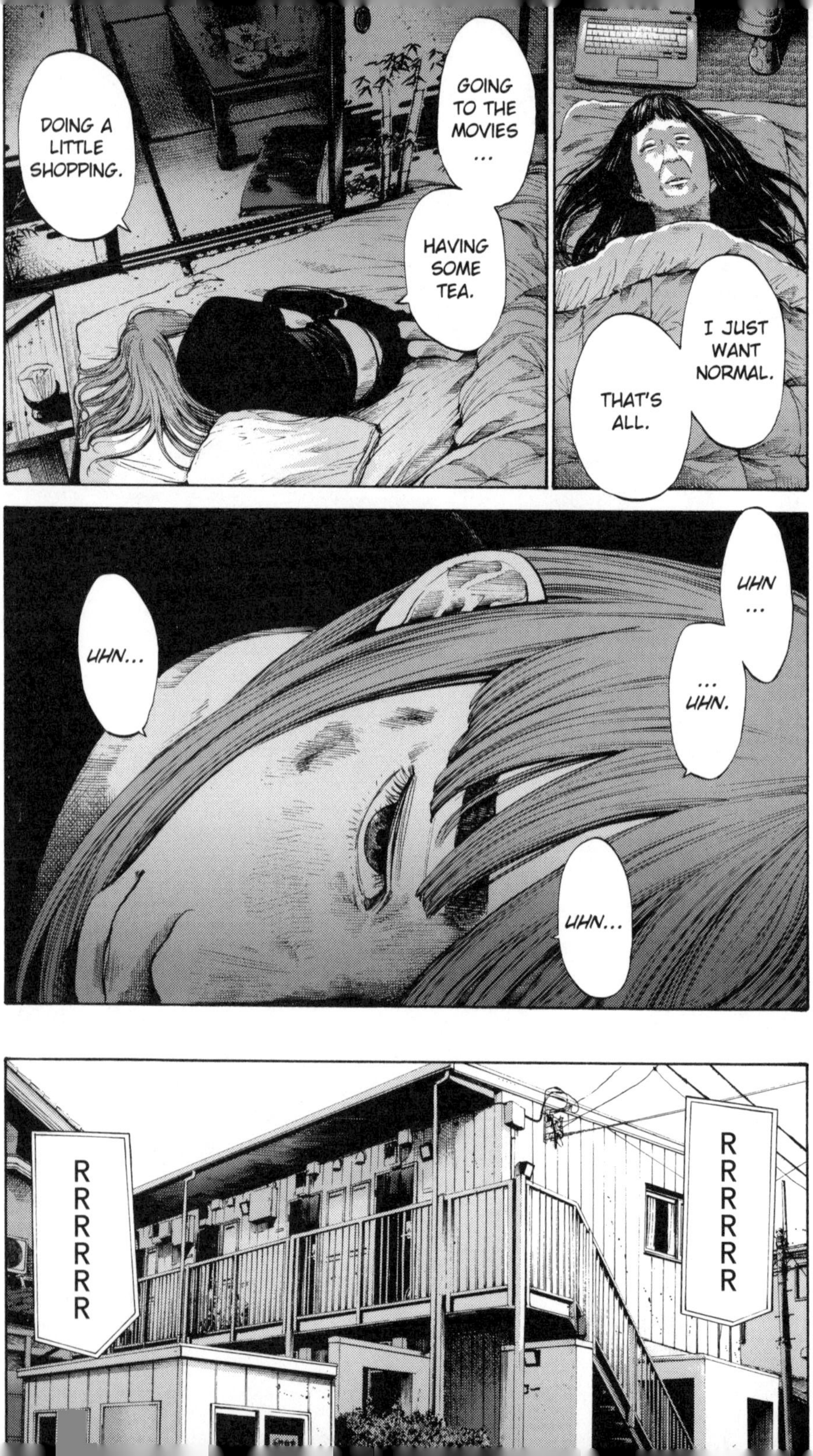
I JUST WANT NORMAL.
THAT'S ALL.
GOING TO THE MOVIES...
HAVING SOME TEA.
DOING A LITTLE SHOPPING.
UHN...
...UHN.
UHN...
UHN...
RRRRRR
RRRRRR

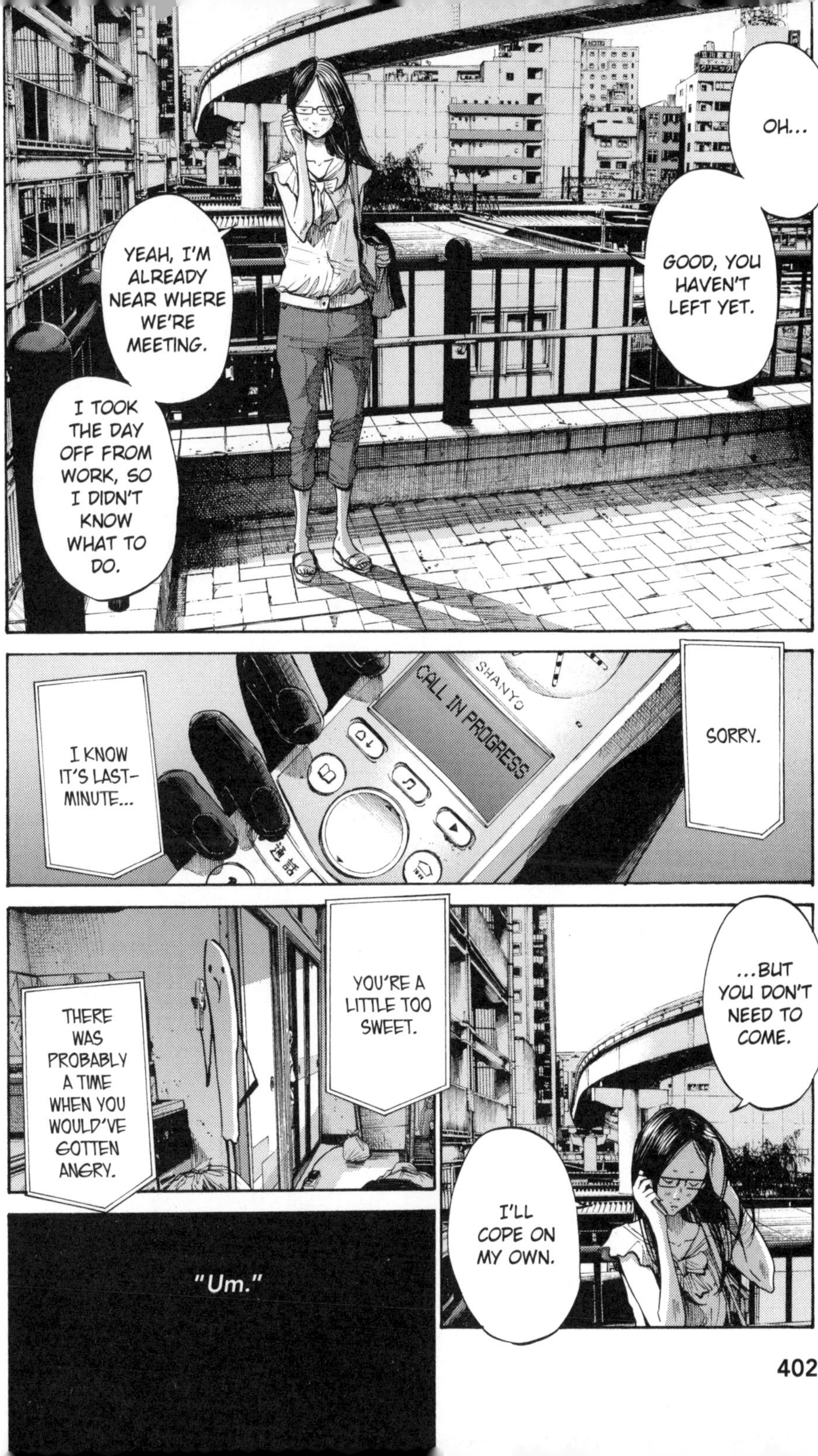
OH...
GOOD, YOU HAVEN'T LEFT YET.
YEAH, I'M ALREADY NEAR WHERE WE'RE MEETING.
I TOOK THE DAY OFF FROM WORK, SO I DIDN'T KNOW WHAT TO DO.
SORRY.
SHANYO
CALL IN PROGRESS
I KNOW IT'S LAST-MINUTE...
...BUT YOU DON'T NEED TO COME.
I'LL COPE ON MY OWN.
YOU'RE A LITTLE TOO SWEET.
THERE WAS PROBABLY A TIME WHEN YOU WOULD'VE GOTTEN ANGRY.
"Um."

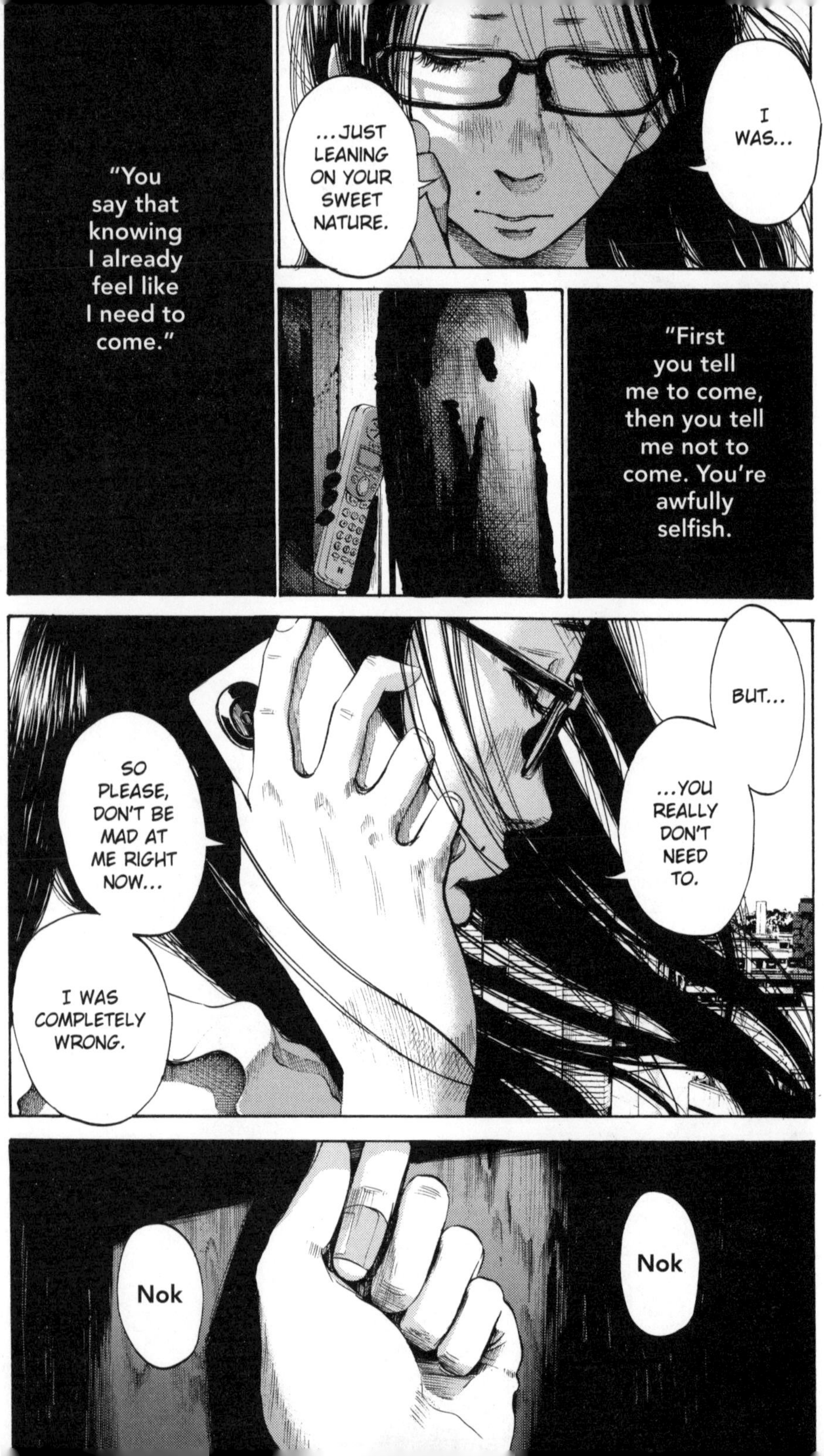
I WAS...
...JUST LEANING ON YOUR SWEET NATURE.
"First you tell me to come, then you tell me not to come. You're awfully selfish.
"You say that knowing I already feel like I need to come."
BUT...
...YOU REALLY DON'T NEED TO.
SO PLEASE, DON'T BE MAD AT ME RIGHT NOW...
I WAS COMPLETELY WRONG.
Nok
Nok

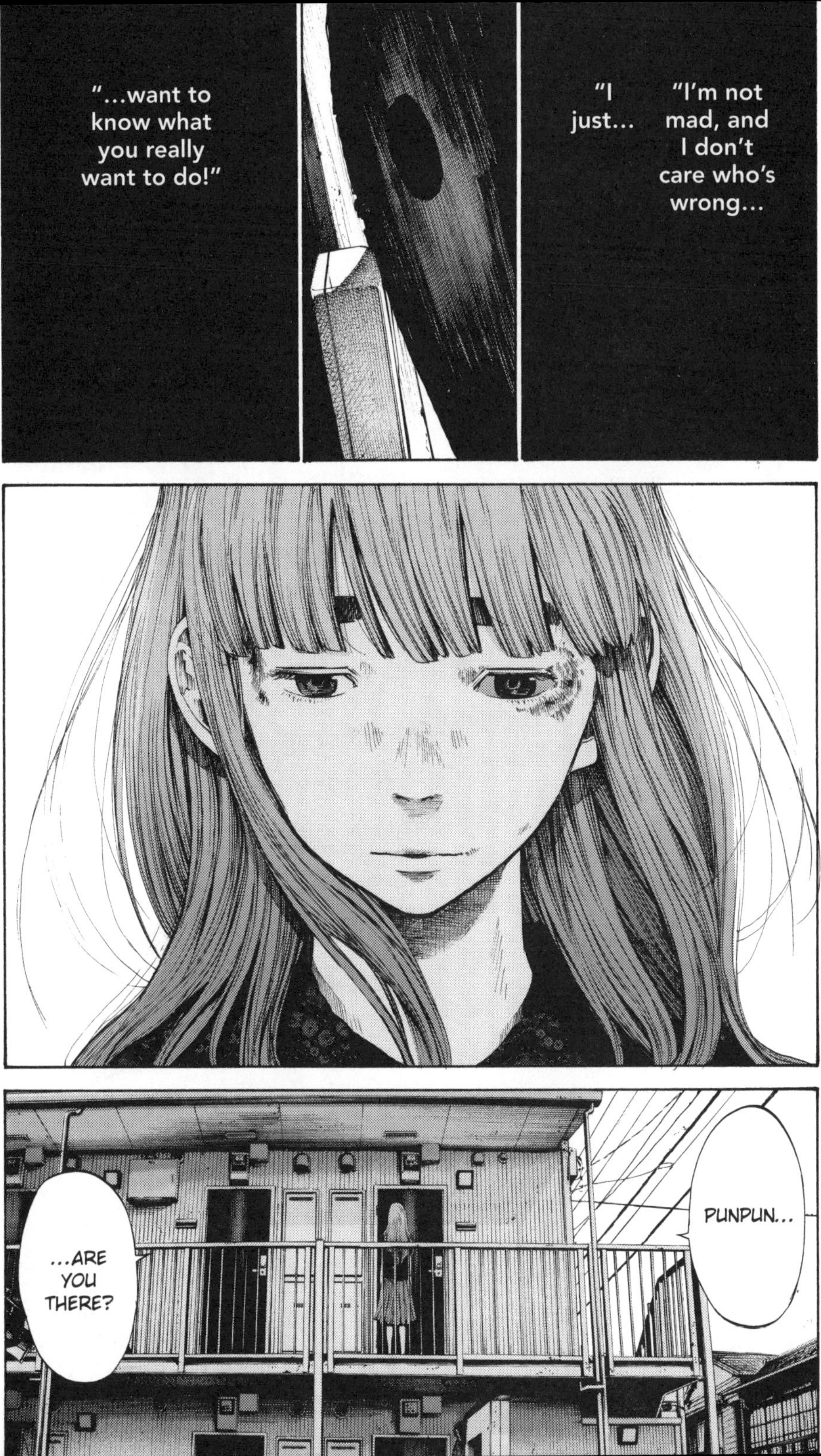
"I'm not mad, and I don't care who's wrong...
"I just...
"...want to know what you really want to do!"
PUNPUN...
...ARE YOU THERE?

Chapter 109

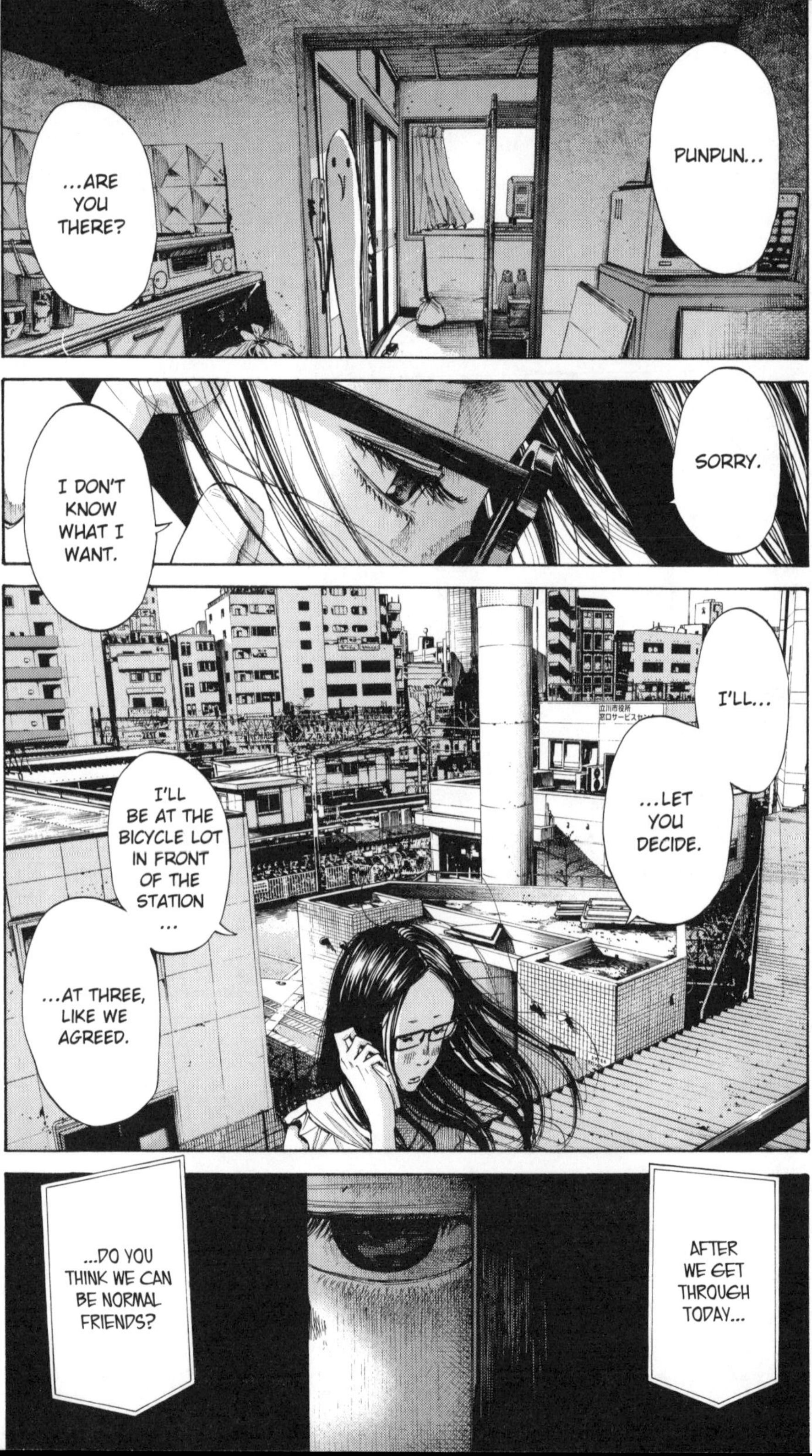
PUNPUN...
...ARE YOU THERE?
SORRY.
I DON'T KNOW WHAT I WANT.
I'LL...
...LET YOU DECIDE.
I'LL BE AT THE BICYCLE LOT IN FRONT OF THE STATION ...
...AT THREE, LIKE WE AGREED.
AFTER WE GET THROUGH TODAY...
...DO YOU THINK WE CAN BE NORMAL FRIENDS?

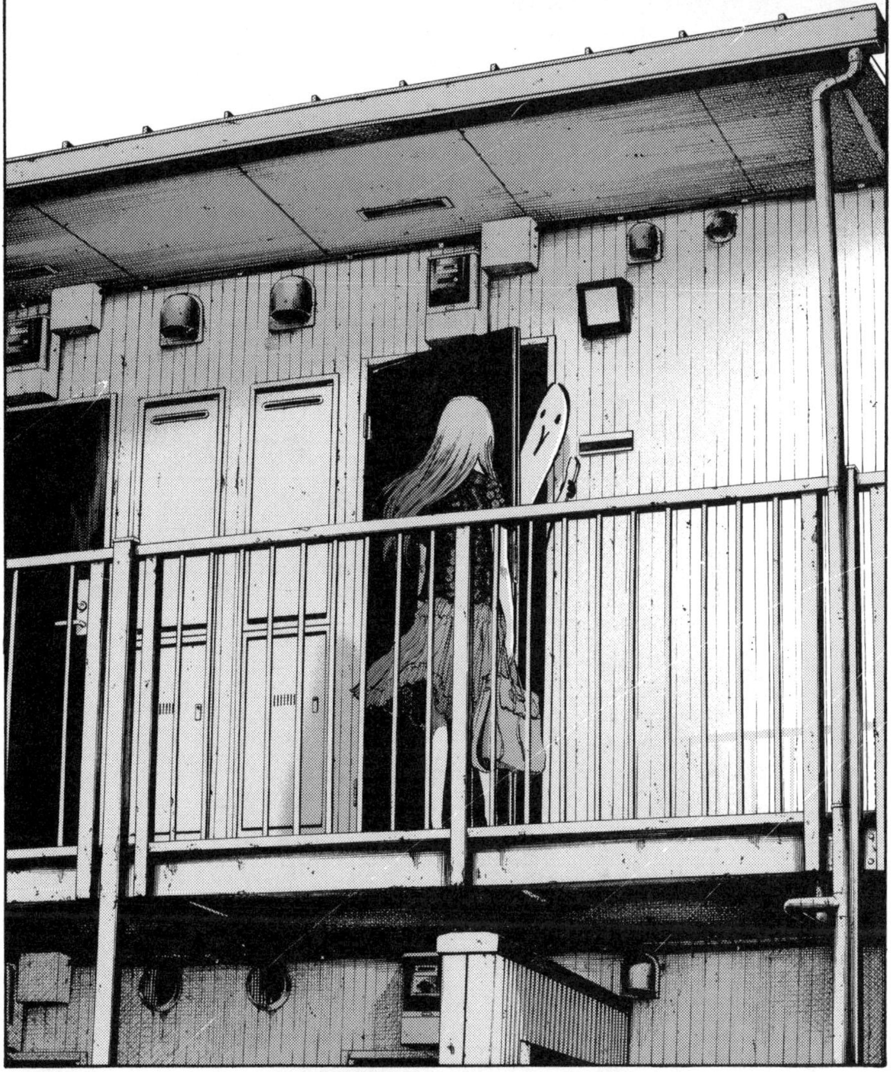

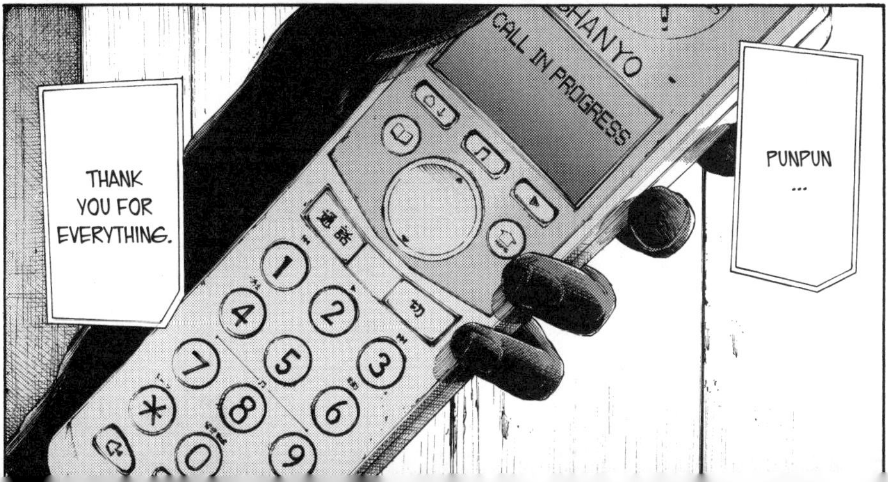
PUNPUN ...
CALL IN PROGRESS
THANK YOU FOR EVERYTHING.

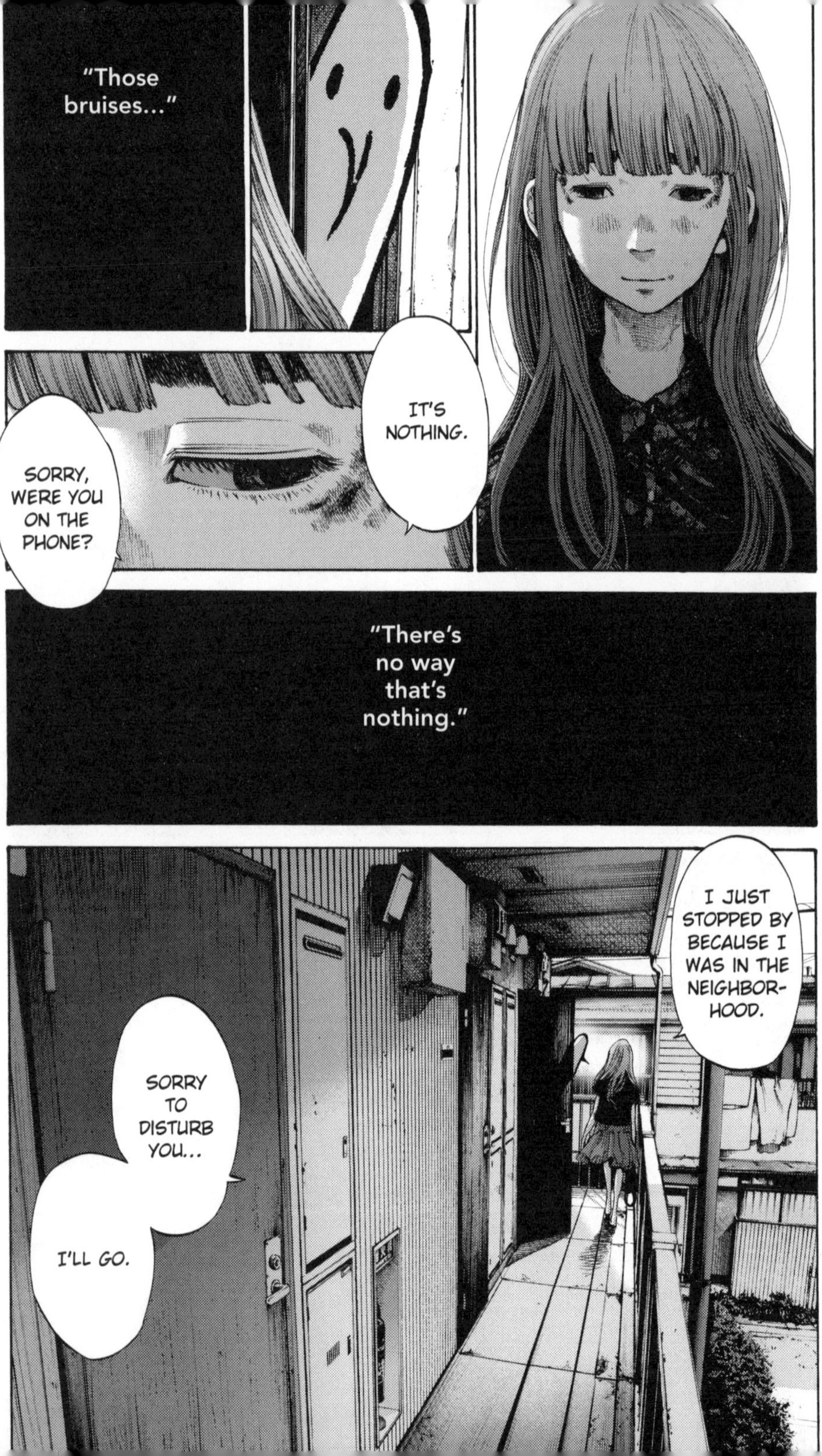
SORRY, WERE YOU ON THE PHONE?
"Those bruises..."
IT'S NOTHING.
"There's no way that's nothing."
I JUST STOPPED BY BECAUSE I WAS IN THE NEIGHBOR-HOOD.
SORRY TO DISTURB YOU...
I'LL GO.

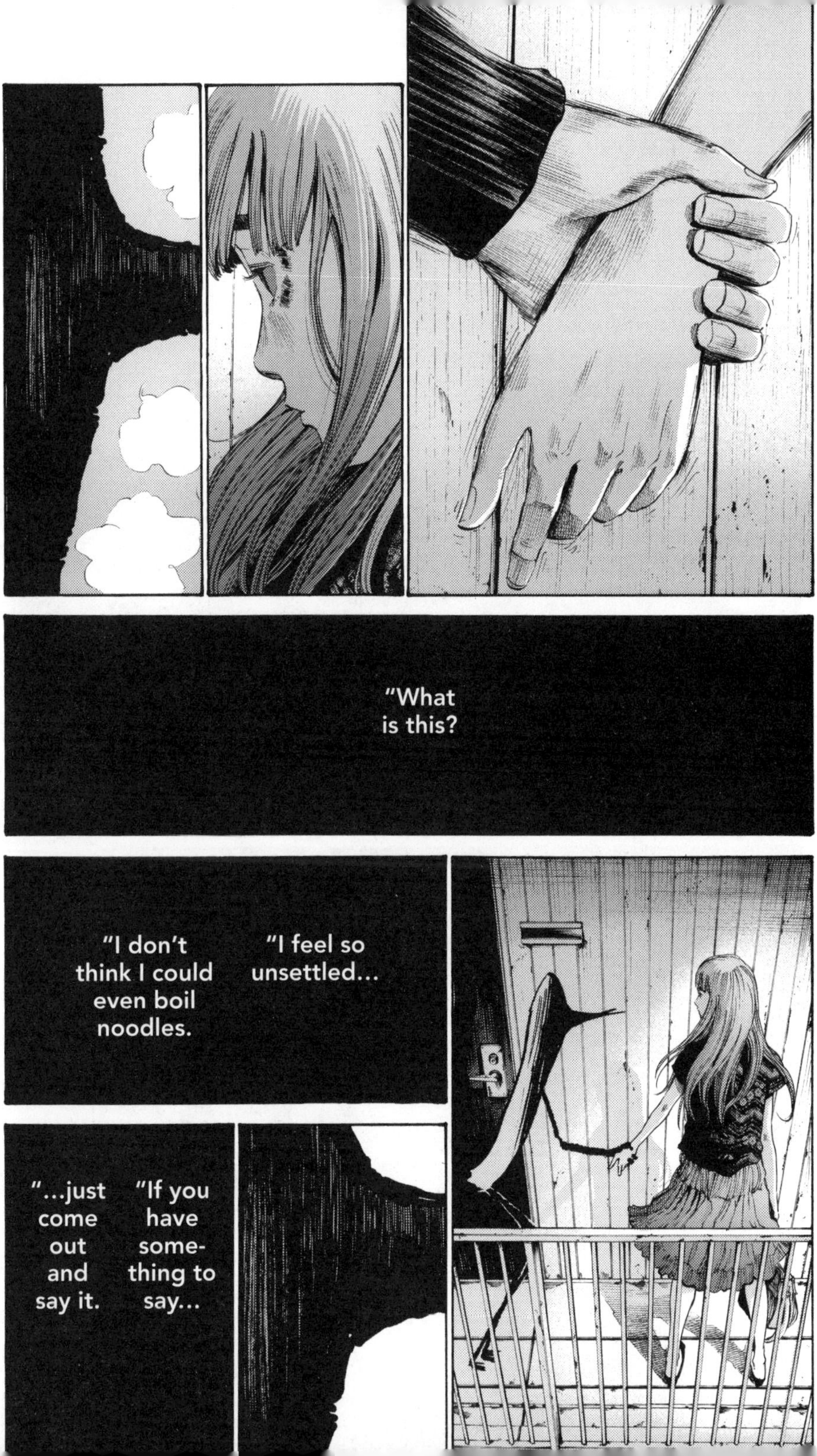
"What is this?
"I feel so unsettled...
"I don't think I could even boil noodles.
"If you have some-thing to say...
"...just come out and say it.

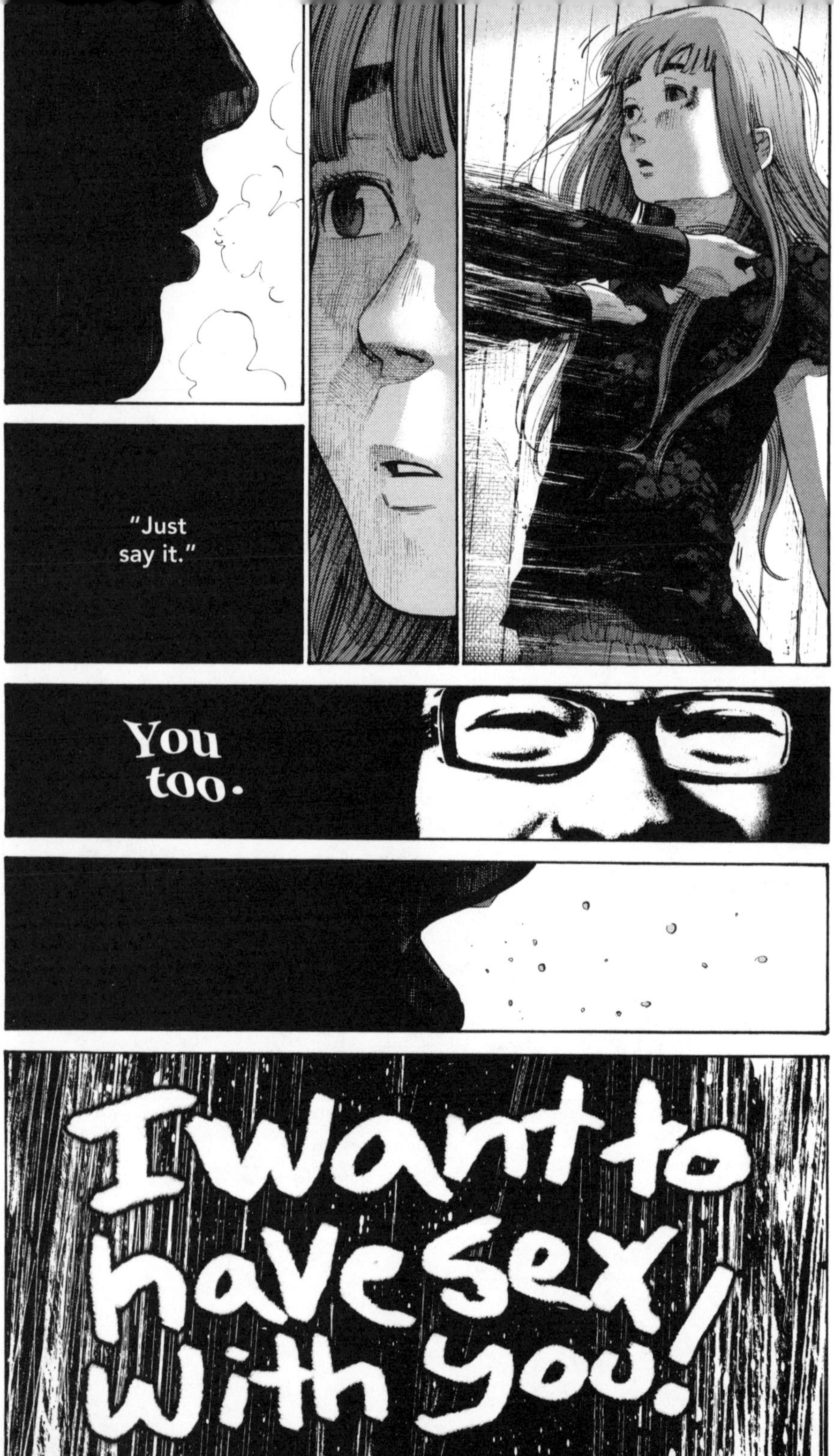
"Just
say it."
You
too.
I want to
have sex
with you!

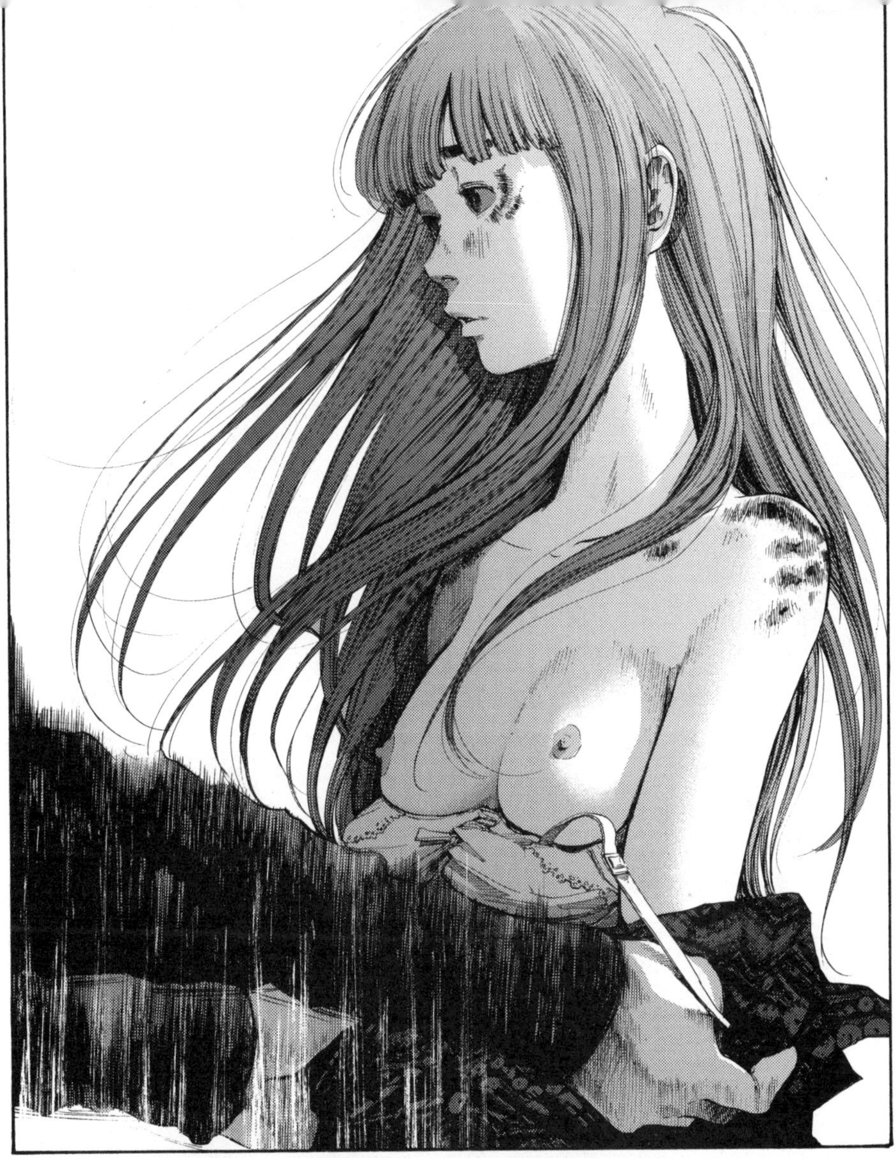
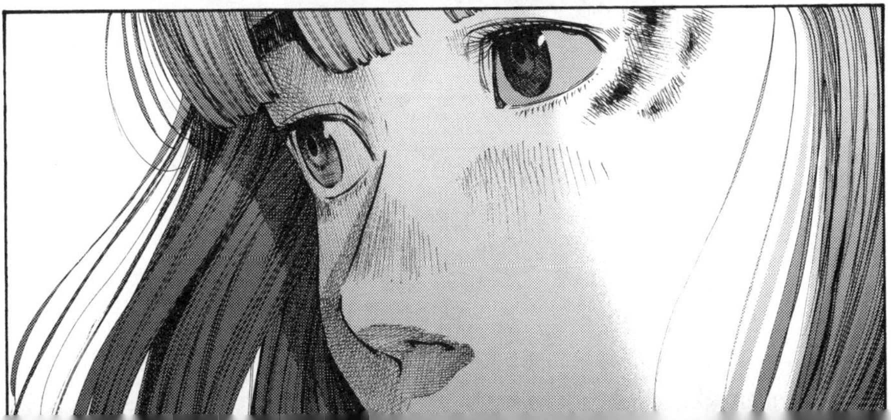

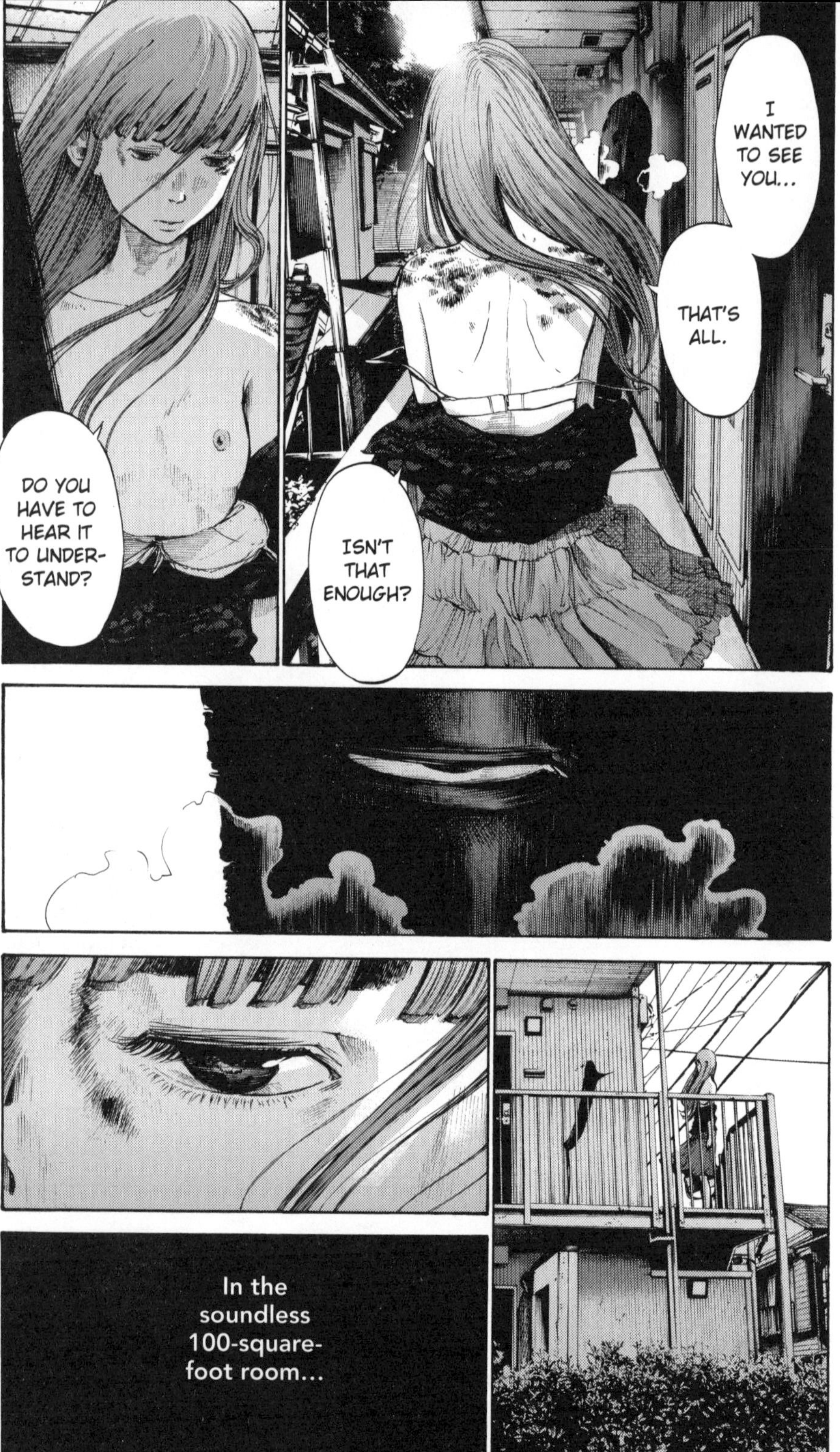
I WANTED TO SEE YOU...
THAT'S ALL.
ISN'T THAT ENOUGH?
DO YOU HAVE TO HEAR IT TO UNDER-STAND?
In the soundless 100-square-foot room...

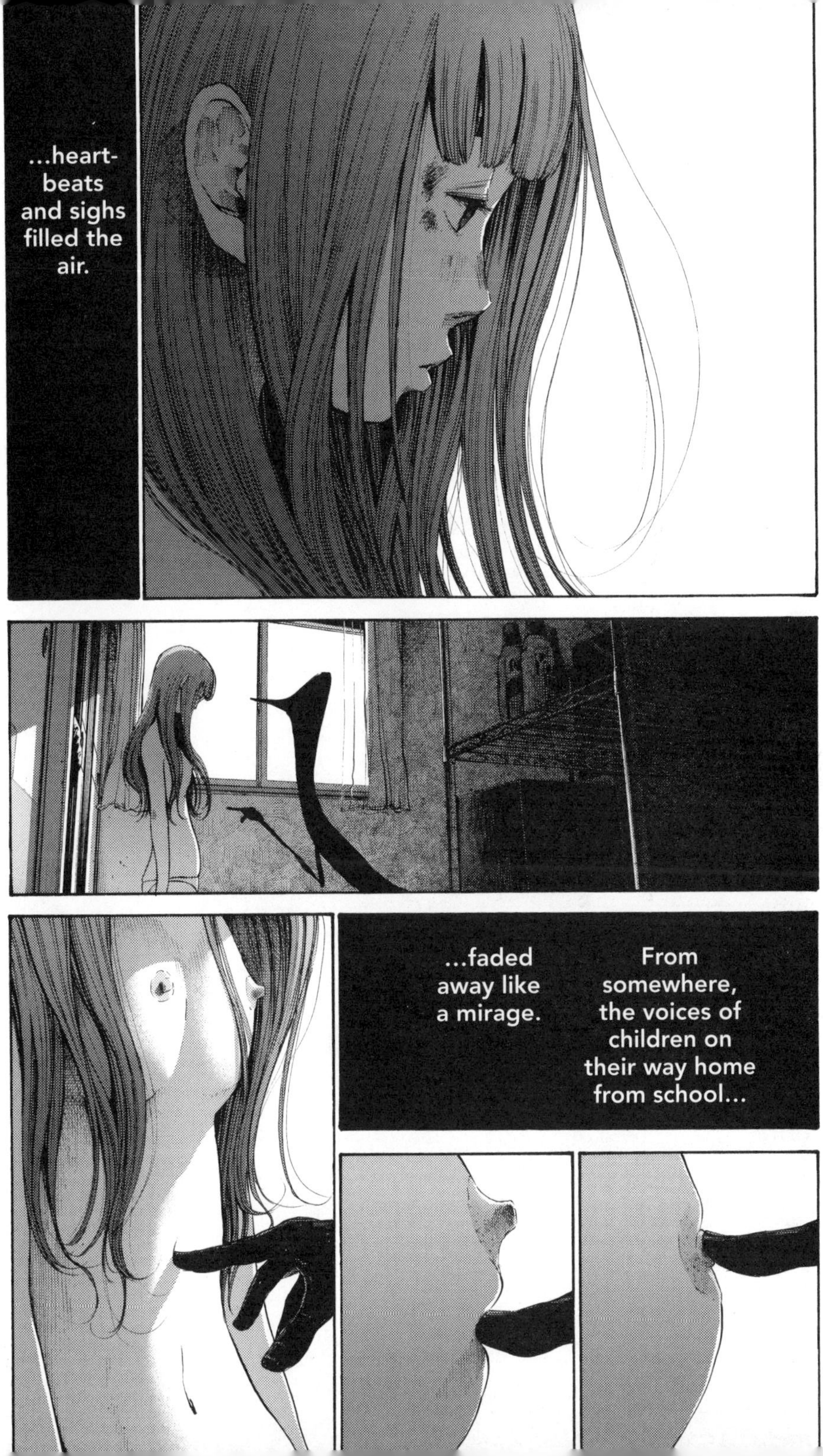
...heart-beats and sighs filled the air.
From somewhere, the voices of children on their way home from school...
...faded away like a mirage.

Thinking back on his twenty years... ...there had never been a time when he'd had a connection with anyone.

Never.

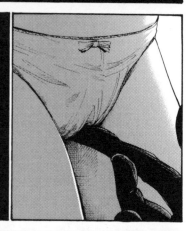

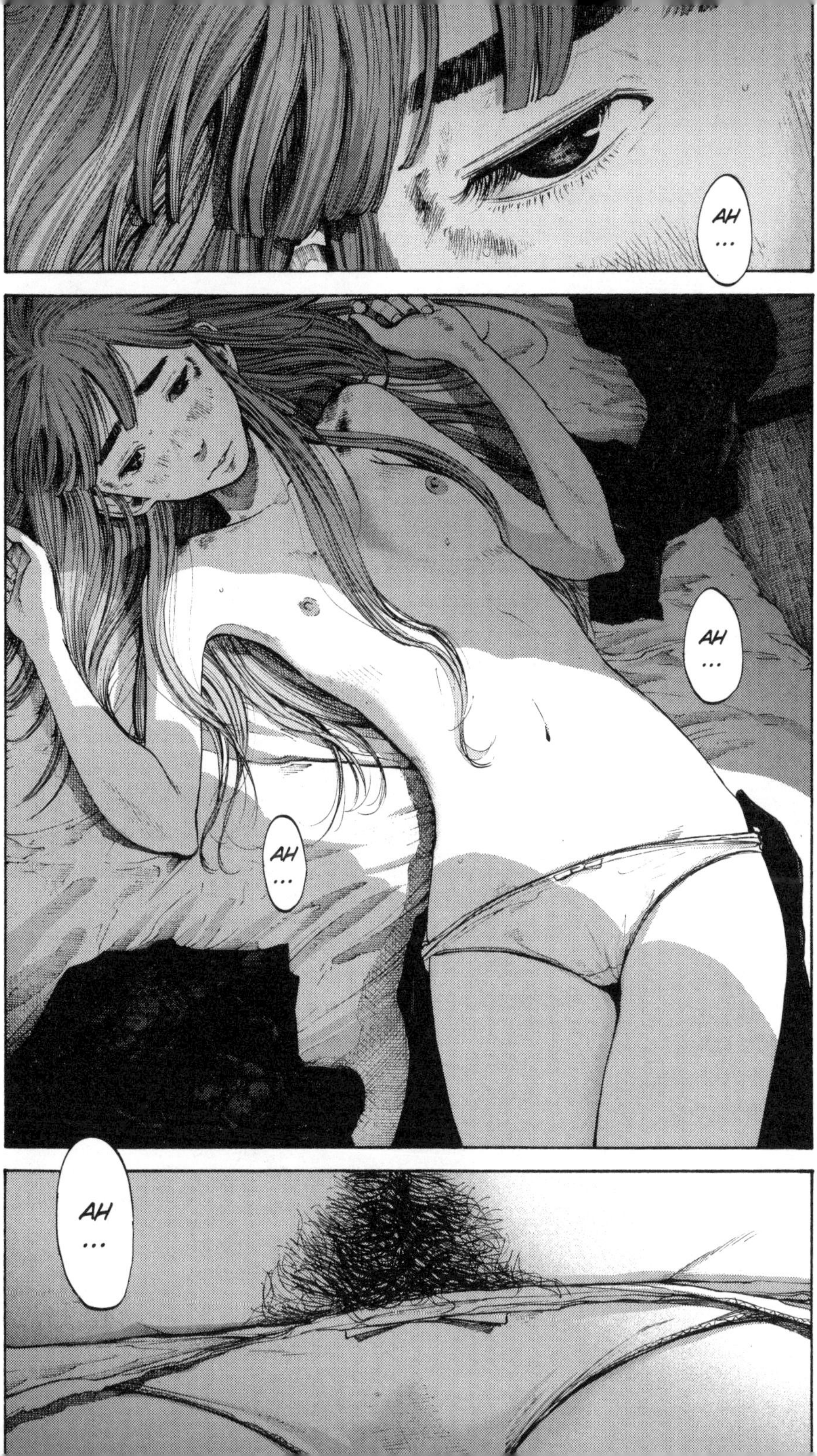
AH ...
AH ...
AH ...
AH ...

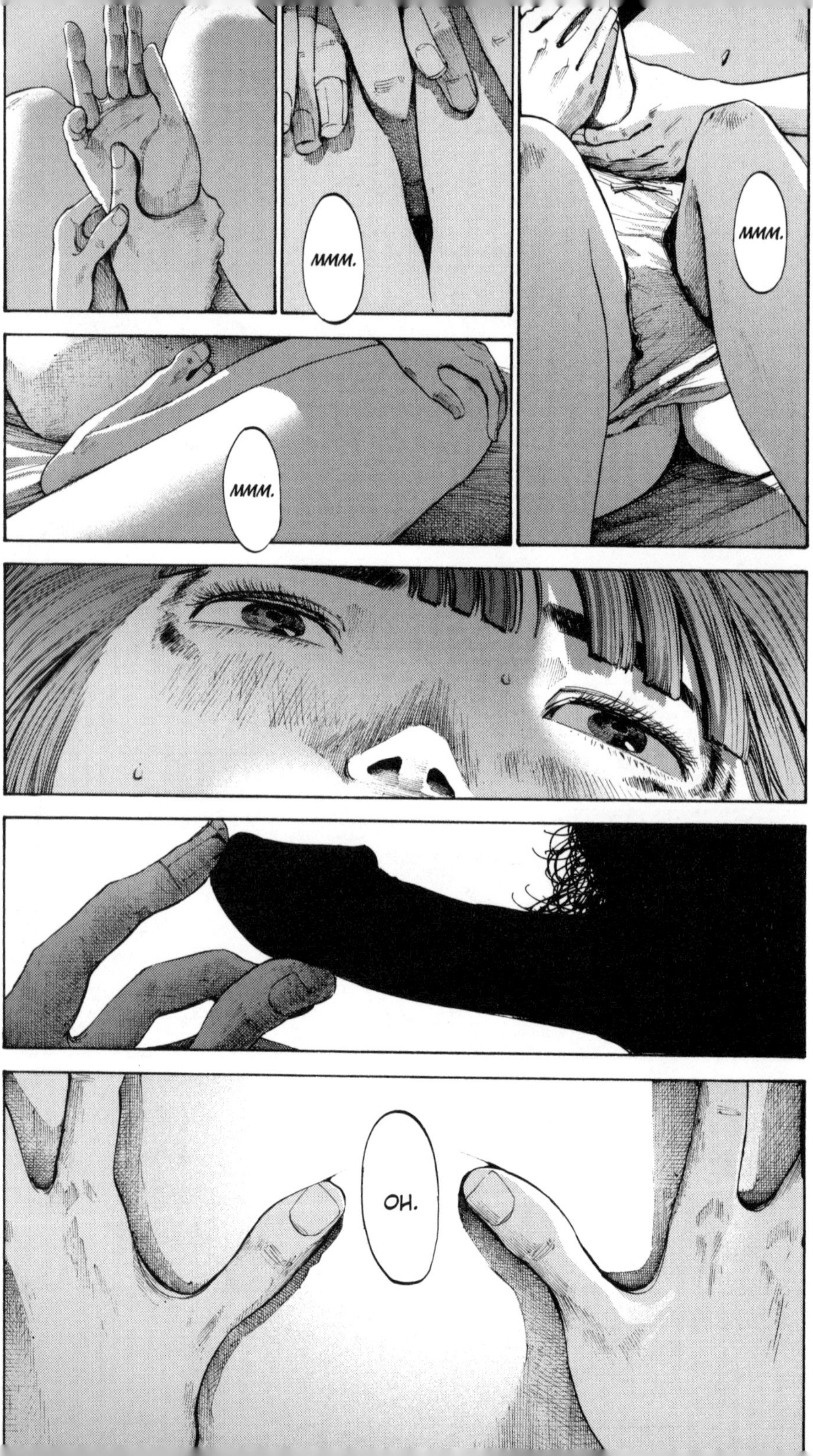
MMM.
MMM.
MMM.
OH.

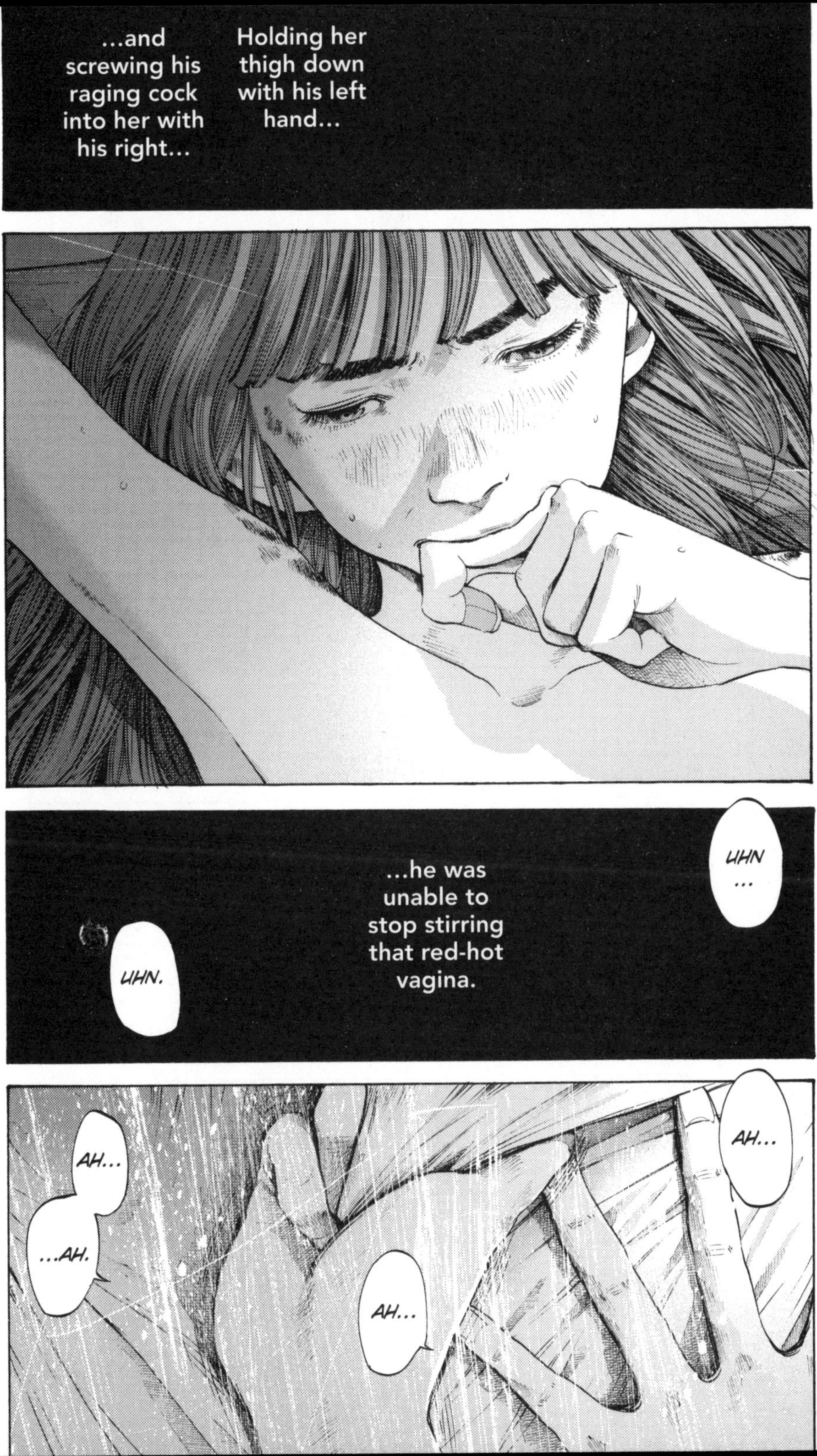
Holding her thigh down with his left hand...
...and screwing his raging cock into her with his right...
UHN ...
...he was unable to stop stirring that red-hot vagina.
UHN.
AH...
AH...
...AH.
AH...

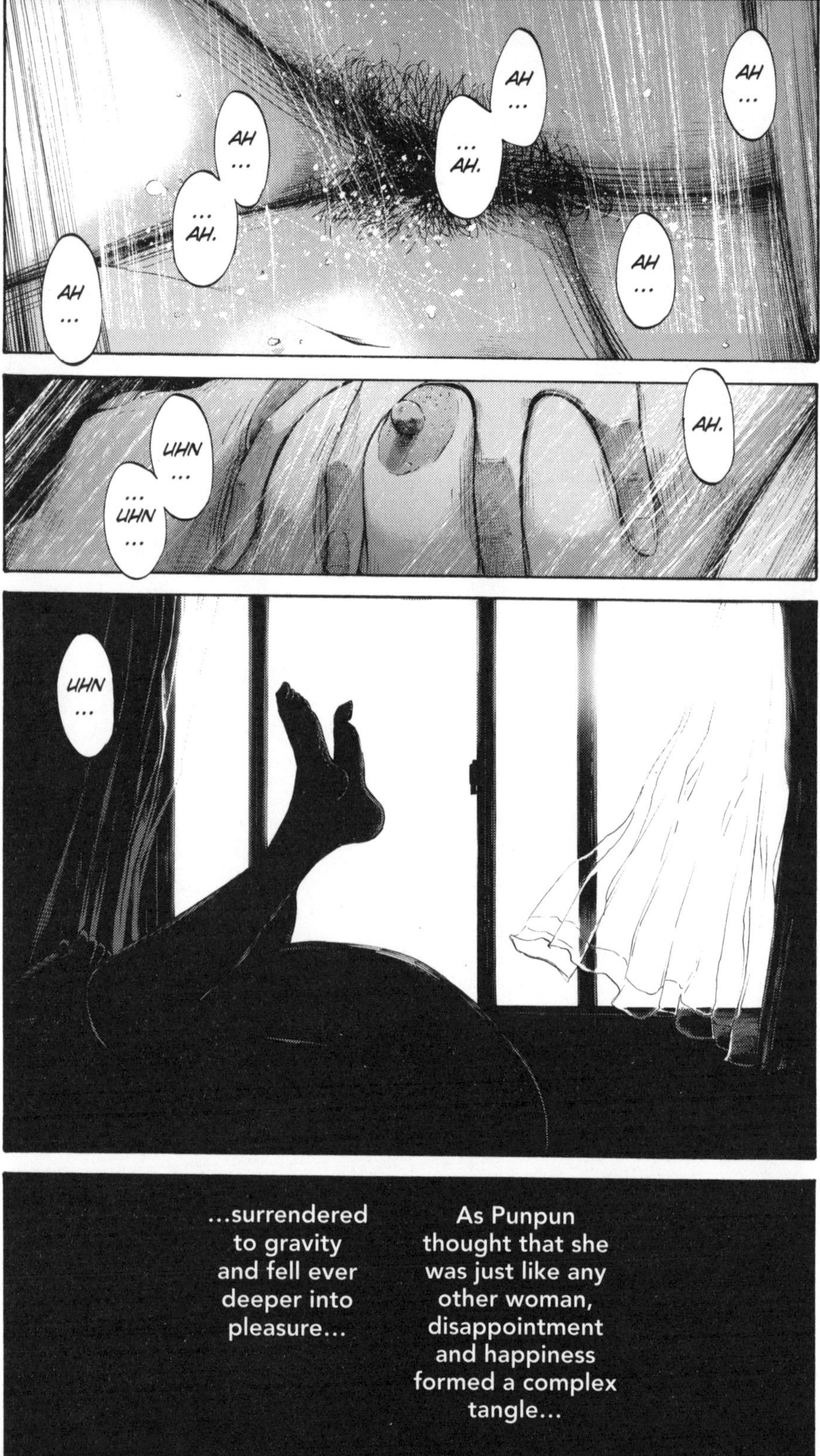
AH…
AH…
…AH.
AH…
AH…
…AH.
AH…
AH.
UHN…
…UHN…
UHN…
As Punpun thought that she was just like any other woman, disappointment and happiness formed a complex tangle…
…surrendered to gravity and fell ever deeper into pleasure…

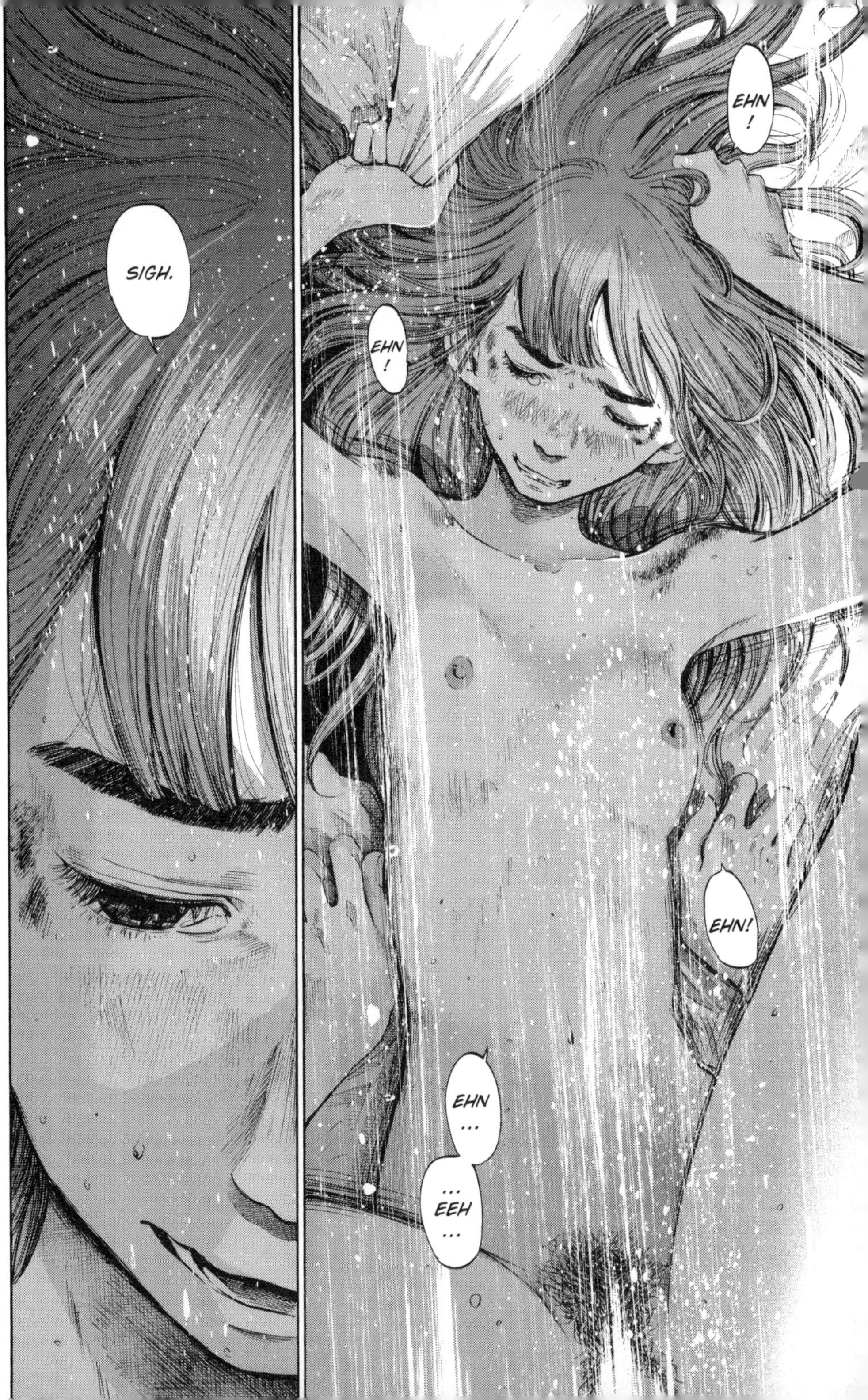
EHN!
EHN!
EHN!
EHN...
...EEH...
SIGH.

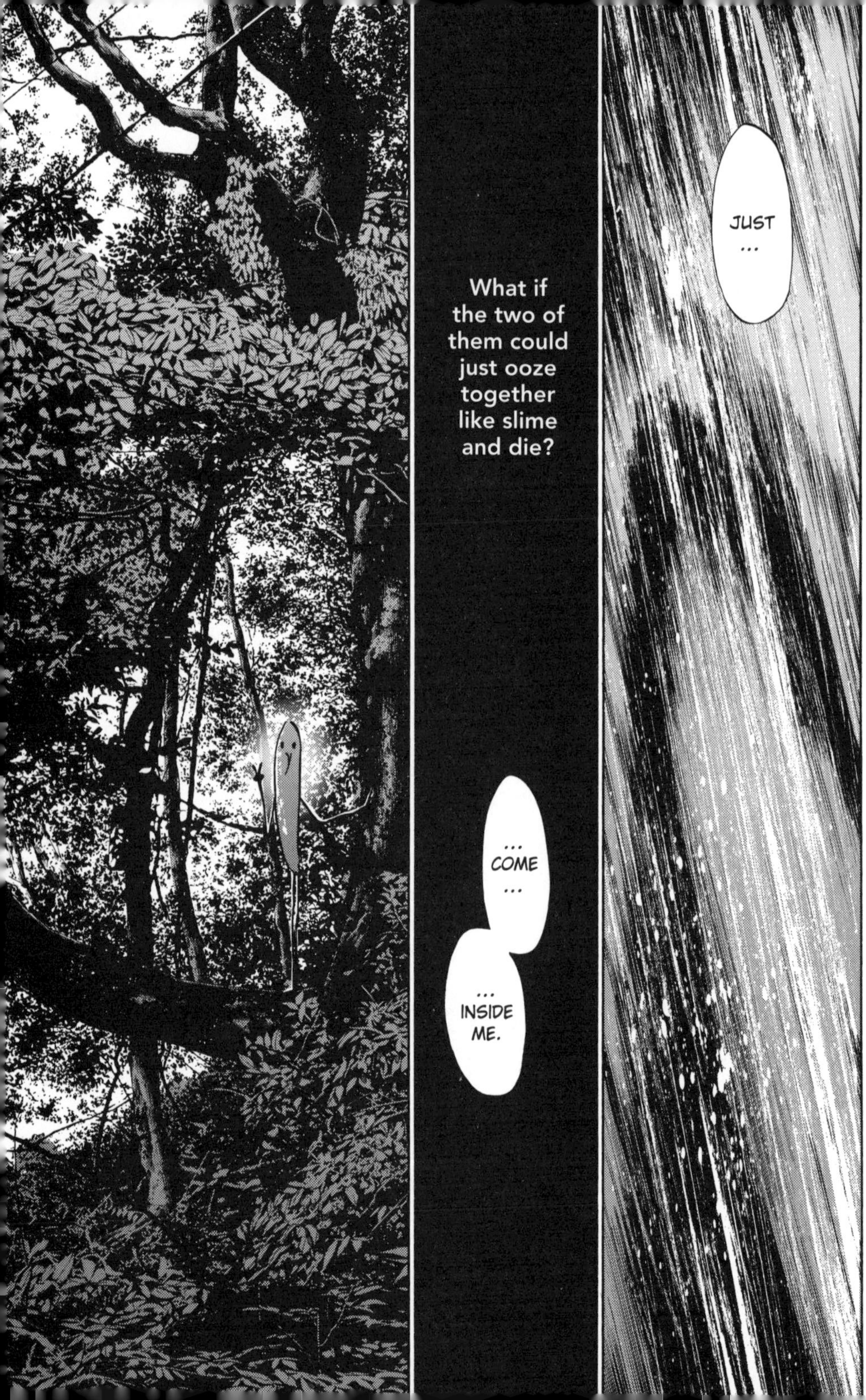
JUST ...
What if the two of them could just ooze together like slime and die?
... COME ...
... INSIDE ME.

GOODNIGHT PUNPUN
Part Ten

INIO ASANO

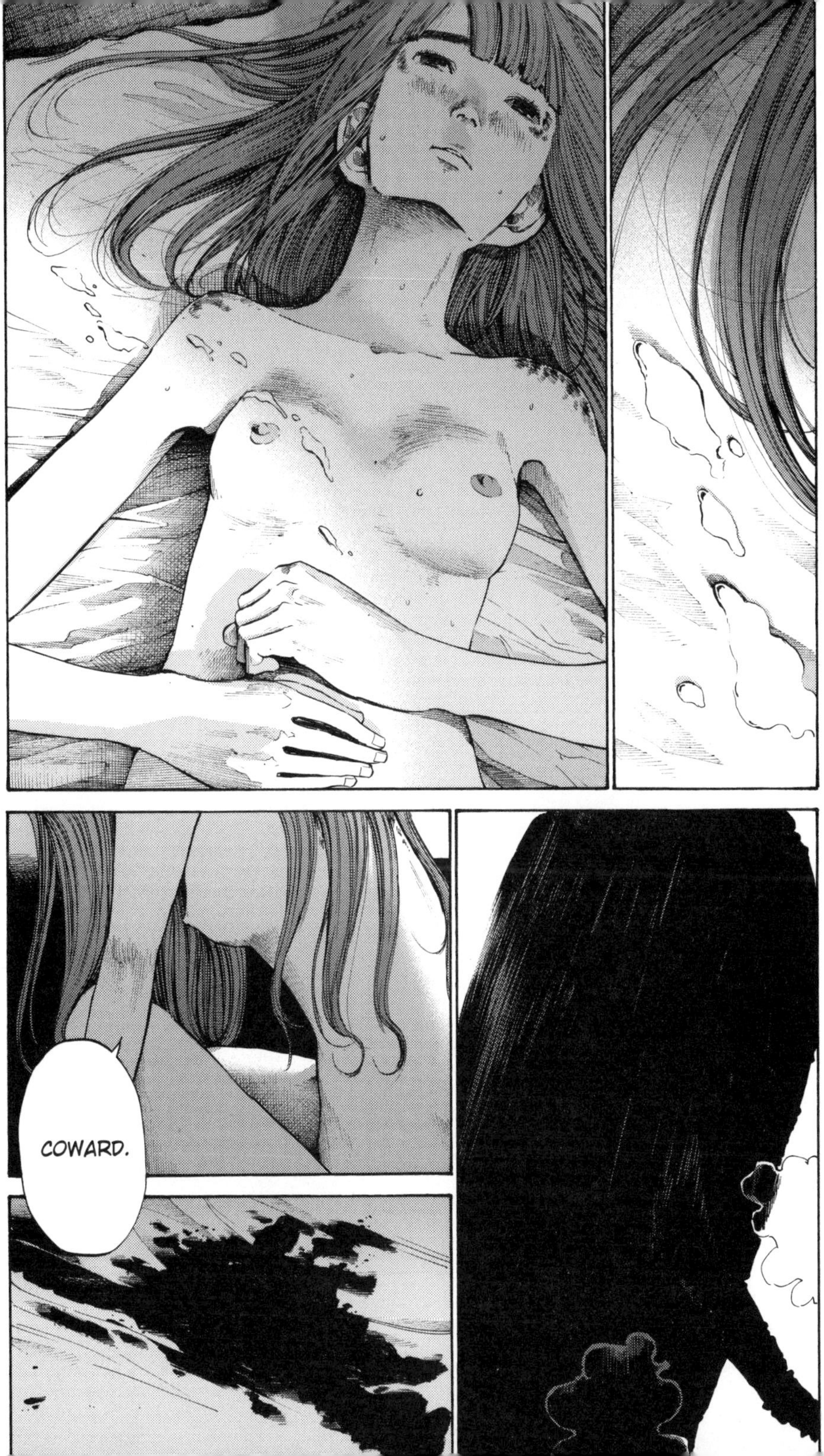
COWARD.

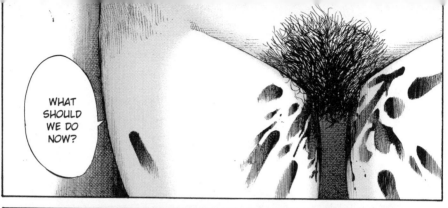

WHAT SHOULD WE DO NOW?

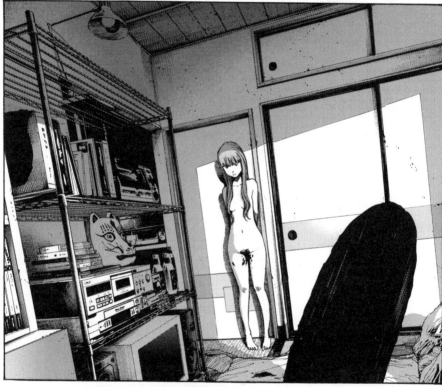

PUNPUN, DO YOU LOVE ME?

"I love you."

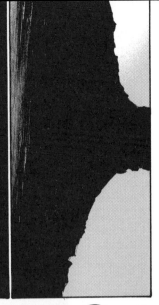

THEN...

...I LOVE YOU, TOO.

...was hell.

The only place lower to fall...

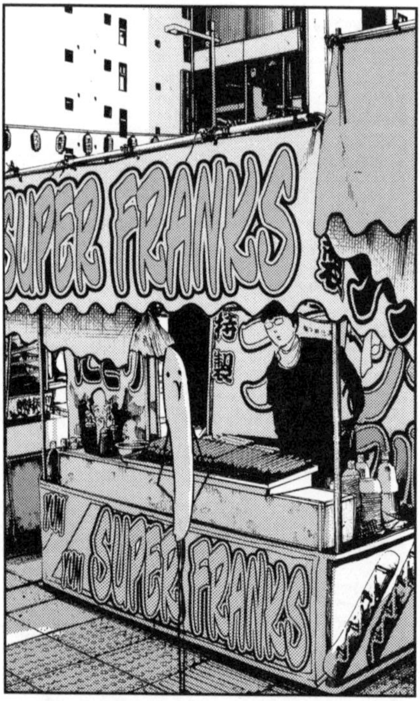
SUPER FRANK'S
SUPER FRANK'S

Chapter 110

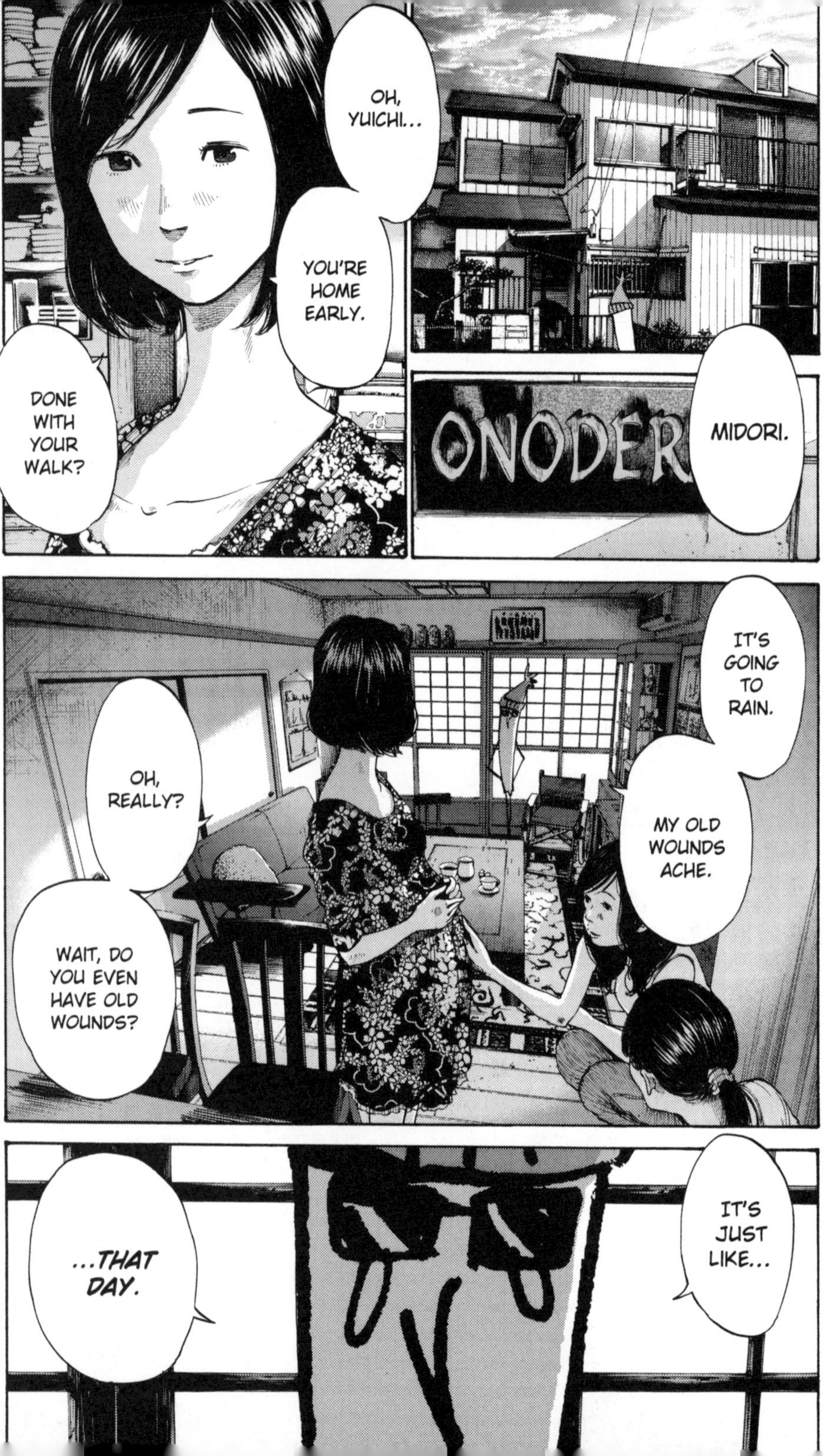
ONODER
MIDORI.
OH, YUICHI...
YOU'RE HOME EARLY.
DONE WITH YOUR WALK?
IT'S GOING TO RAIN.
MY OLD WOUNDS ACHE.
OH, REALLY?
WAIT, DO YOU EVEN HAVE OLD WOUNDS?
IT'S JUST LIKE...
...THAT DAY.

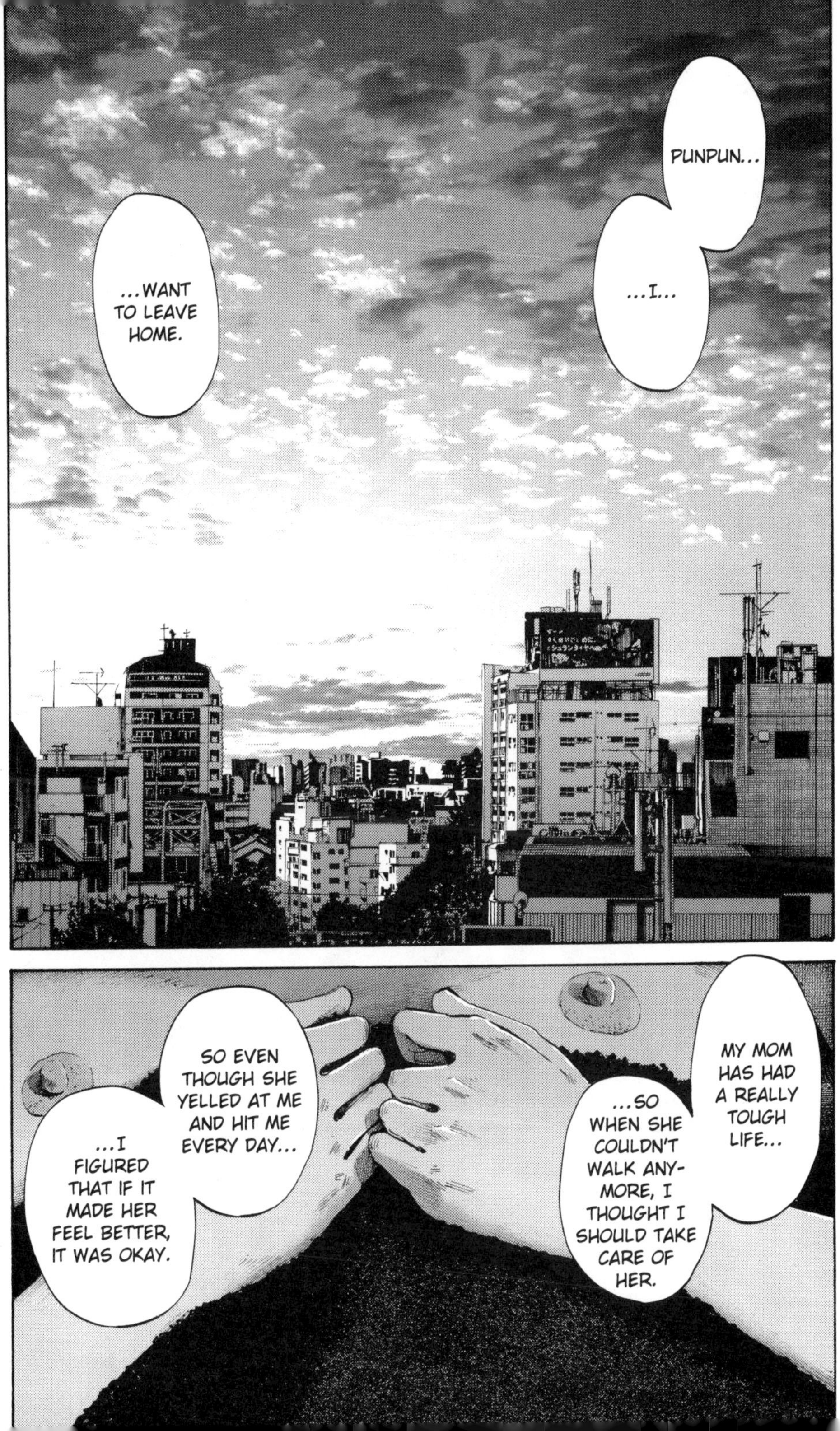
PUNPUN...
...I...
...WANT TO LEAVE HOME.
MY MOM HAS HAD A REALLY TOUGH LIFE...
...SO WHEN SHE COULDN'T WALK ANY-MORE, I THOUGHT I SHOULD TAKE CARE OF HER.
SO EVEN THOUGH SHE YELLED AT ME AND HIT ME EVERY DAY...
...I FIGURED THAT IF IT MADE HER FEEL BETTER, IT WAS OKAY.

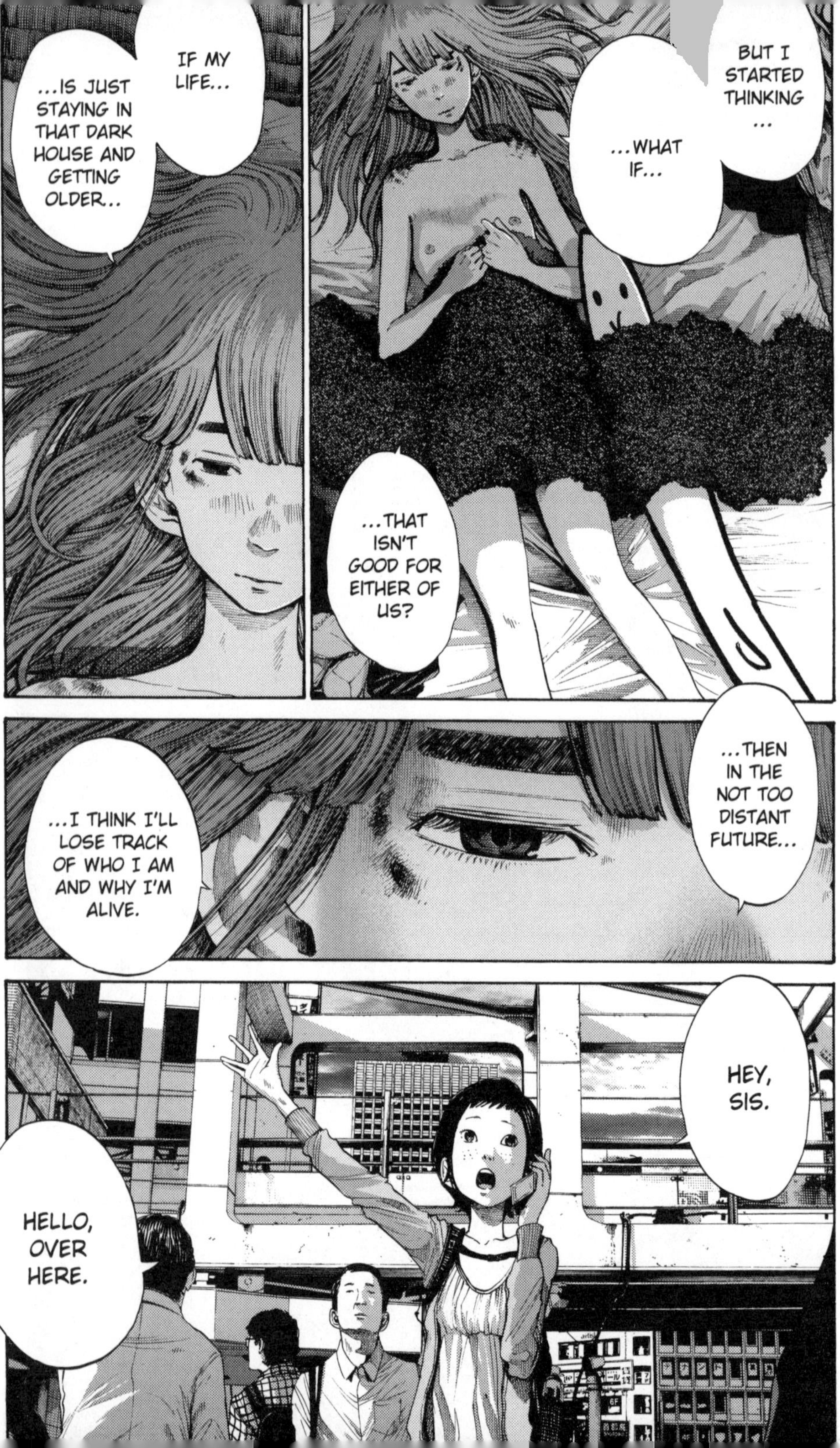
BUT I STARTED THINKING...
...WHAT IF...
...THAT ISN'T GOOD FOR EITHER OF US?
IF MY LIFE...
...IS JUST STAYING IN THAT DARK HOUSE AND GETTING OLDER...
...THEN IN THE NOT TOO DISTANT FUTURE...
...I THINK I'LL LOSE TRACK OF WHO I AM AND WHY I'M ALIVE.
HEY, SIS.
HELLO, OVER HERE.

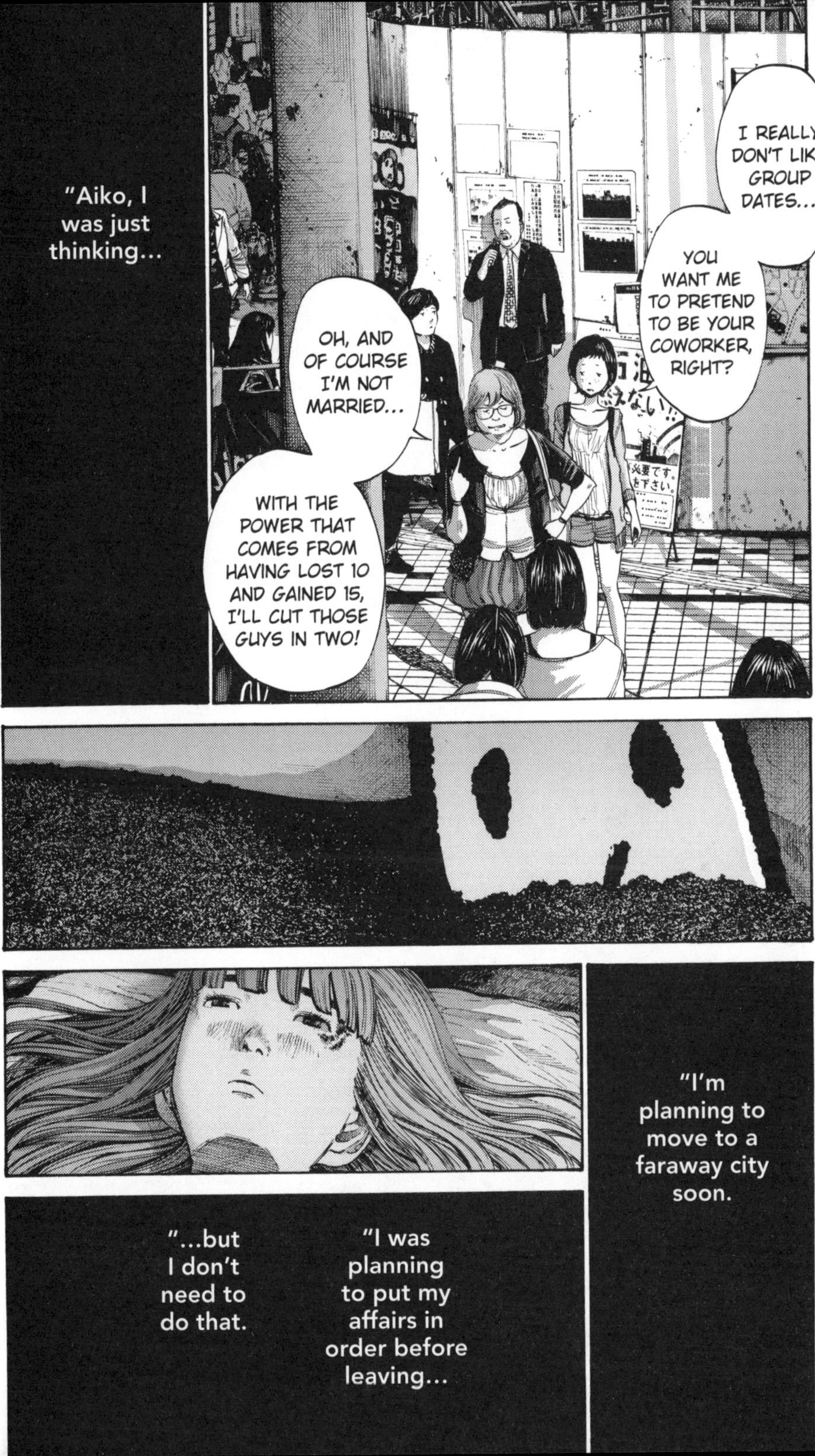
I REALLY DON'T LIKE GROUP DATES...
YOU WANT ME TO PRETEND TO BE YOUR COWORKER, RIGHT?
OH, AND OF COURSE I'M NOT MARRIED...
WITH THE POWER THAT COMES FROM HAVING LOST 10 AND GAINED 15, I'LL CUT THOSE GUYS IN TWO!
"Aiko, I was just thinking...
"I'm planning to move to a faraway city soon.
"I was planning to put my affairs in order before leaving...
"...but I don't need to do that.

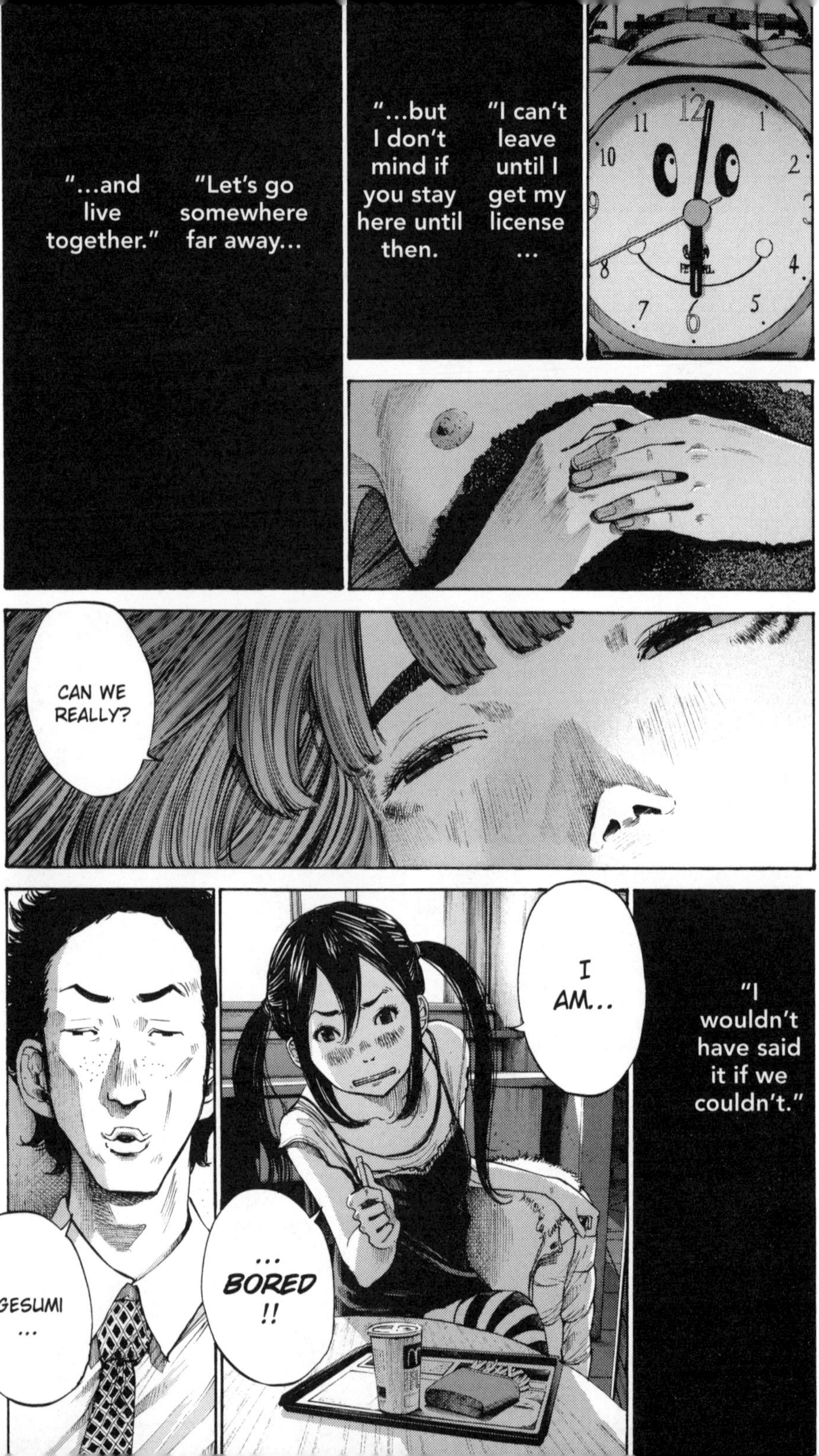
"I can't leave until I get my license...
"...but I don't mind if you stay here until then.
"Let's go somewhere far away...
"...and live together."
CAN WE REALLY?
"I wouldn't have said it if we couldn't."
I AM...
...BORED!!
GESUMI...

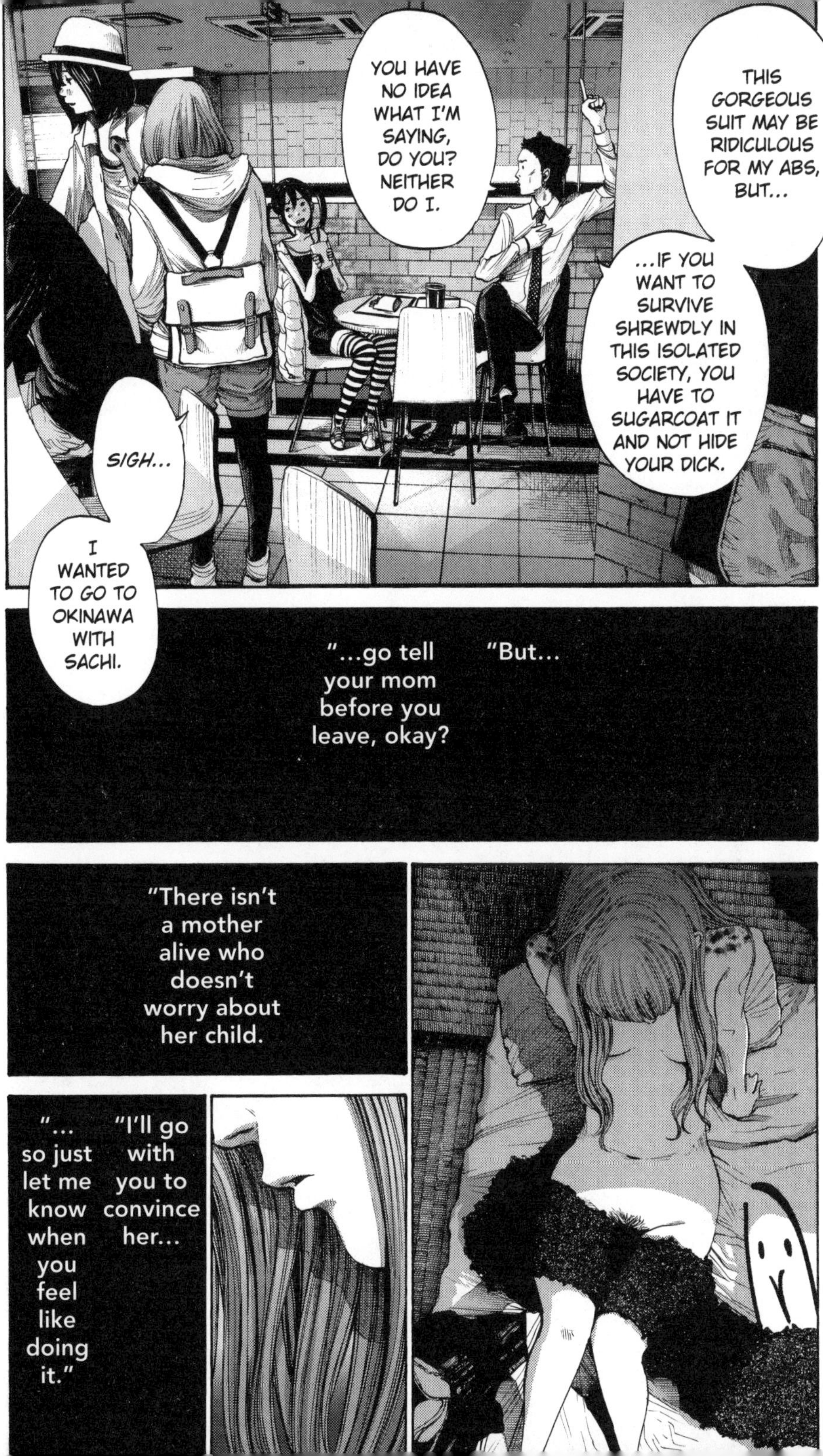
THIS GORGEOUS SUIT MAY BE RIDICULOUS FOR MY ABS, BUT...
...IF YOU WANT TO SURVIVE SHREWDLY IN THIS ISOLATED SOCIETY, YOU HAVE TO SUGARCOAT IT AND NOT HIDE YOUR DICK.
YOU HAVE NO IDEA WHAT I'M SAYING, DO YOU? NEITHER DO I.
SIGH...
I WANTED TO GO TO OKINAWA WITH SACHI.
"But...
"...go tell your mom before you leave, okay?
"There isn't a mother alive who doesn't worry about her child.
"I'll go with you to convince her...
"...so just let me know when you feel like doing it."

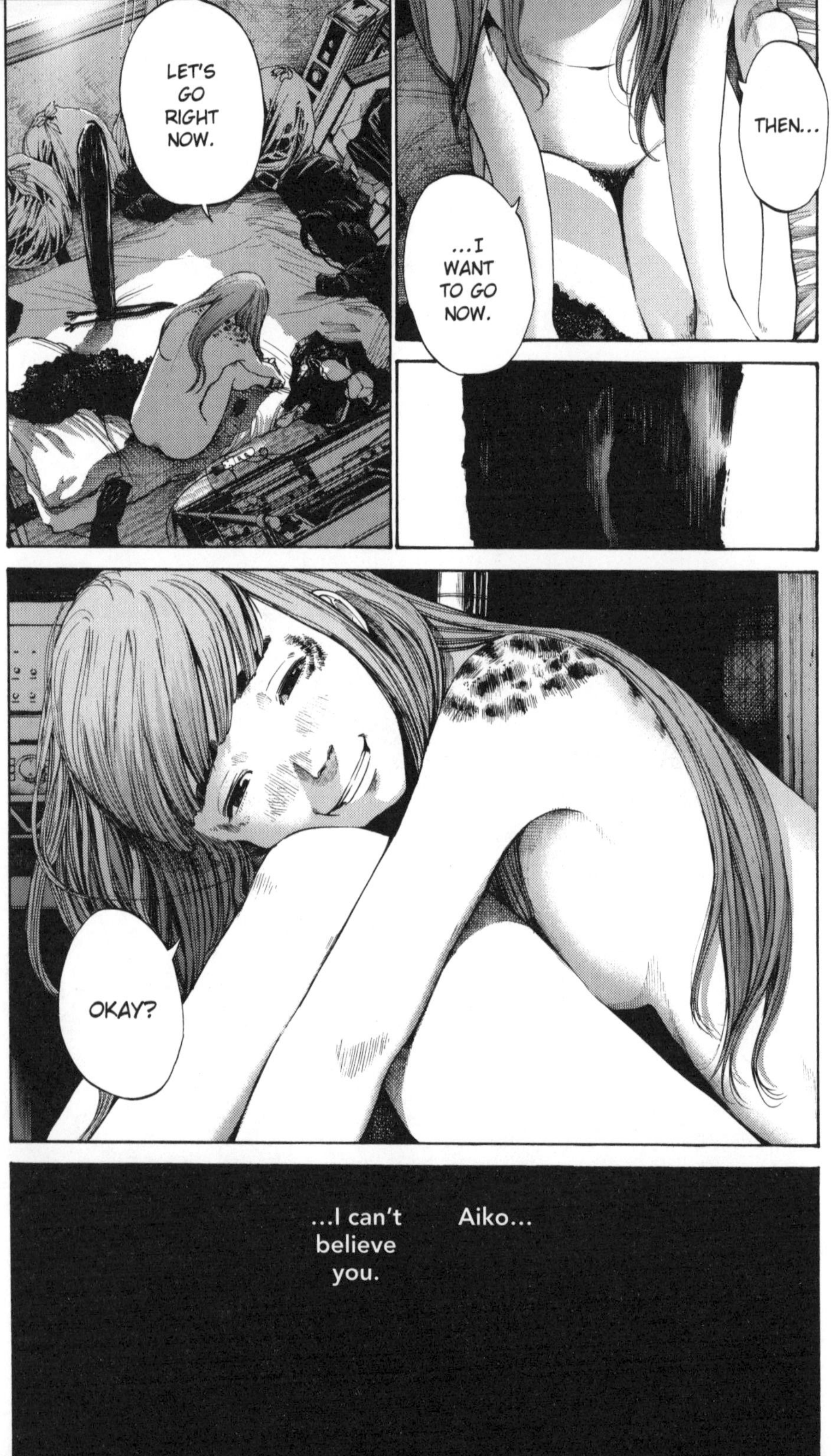
THEN...
...I WANT TO GO NOW.
LET'S GO RIGHT NOW.
OKAY?
Aiko...
...I can't believe you.

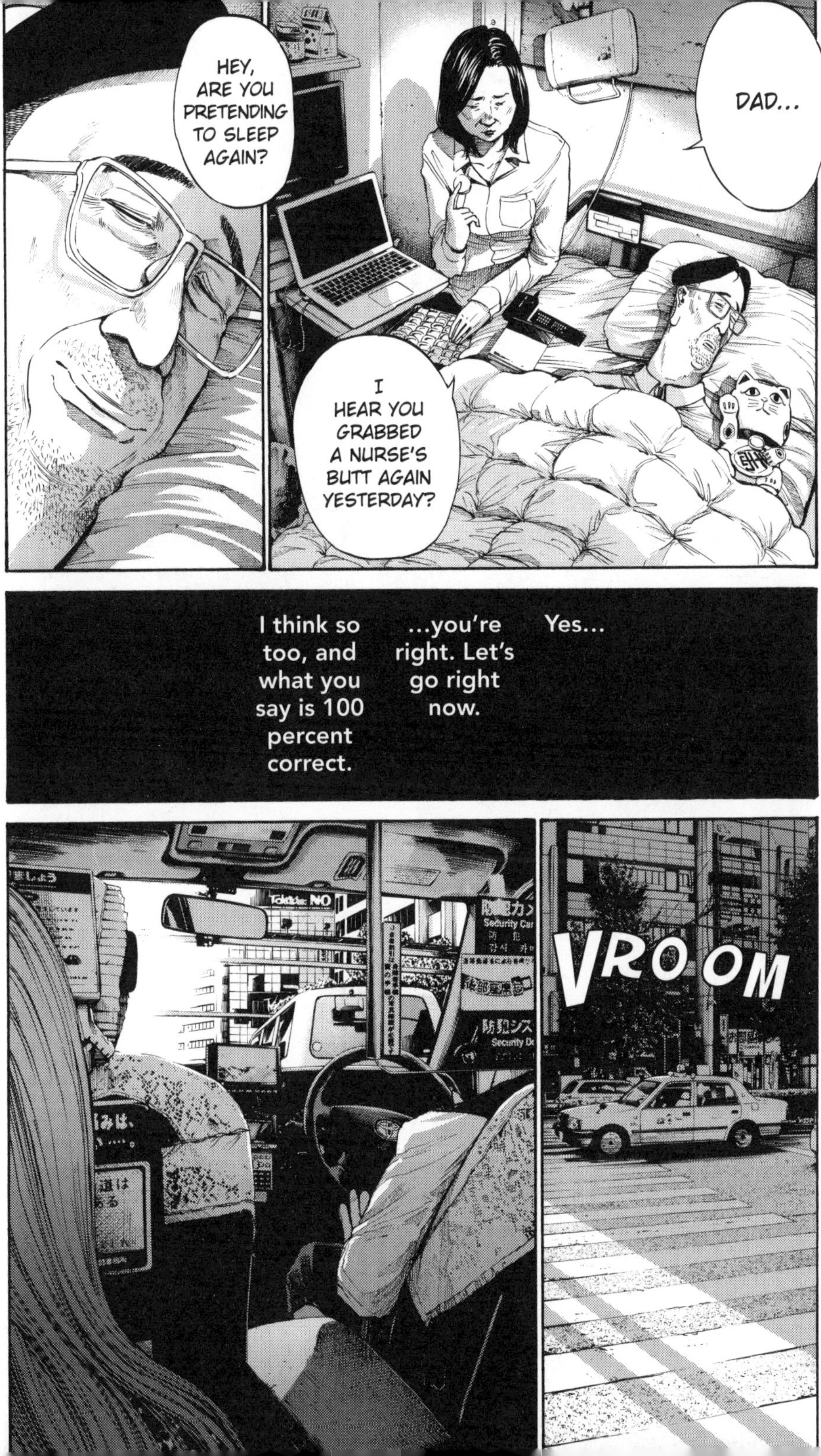
DAD...
I HEAR YOU GRABBED A NURSE'S BUTT AGAIN YESTERDAY?
HEY, ARE YOU PRETENDING TO SLEEP AGAIN?
Yes...
...you're right. Let's go right now.
I think so too, and what you say is 100 percent correct.
VROOM

This is
good...

Everything
is in its right
place.

The world
is mine.
Or more
accurately...

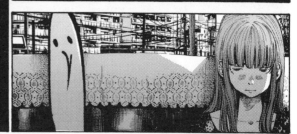

...was
always
yours.

...my
world...

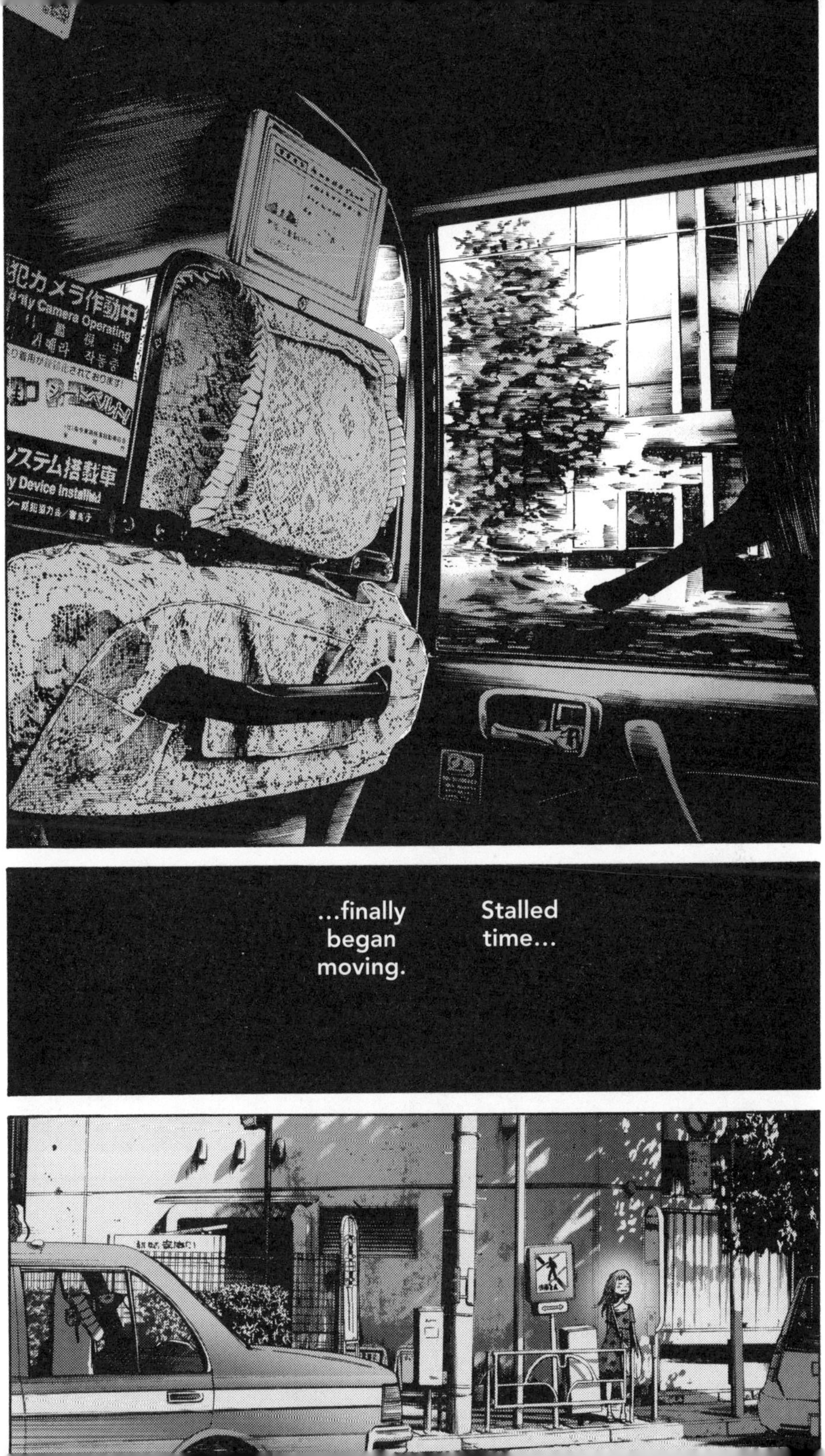
Camera Operating
Device Installed
Stalled time...
...finally began moving.

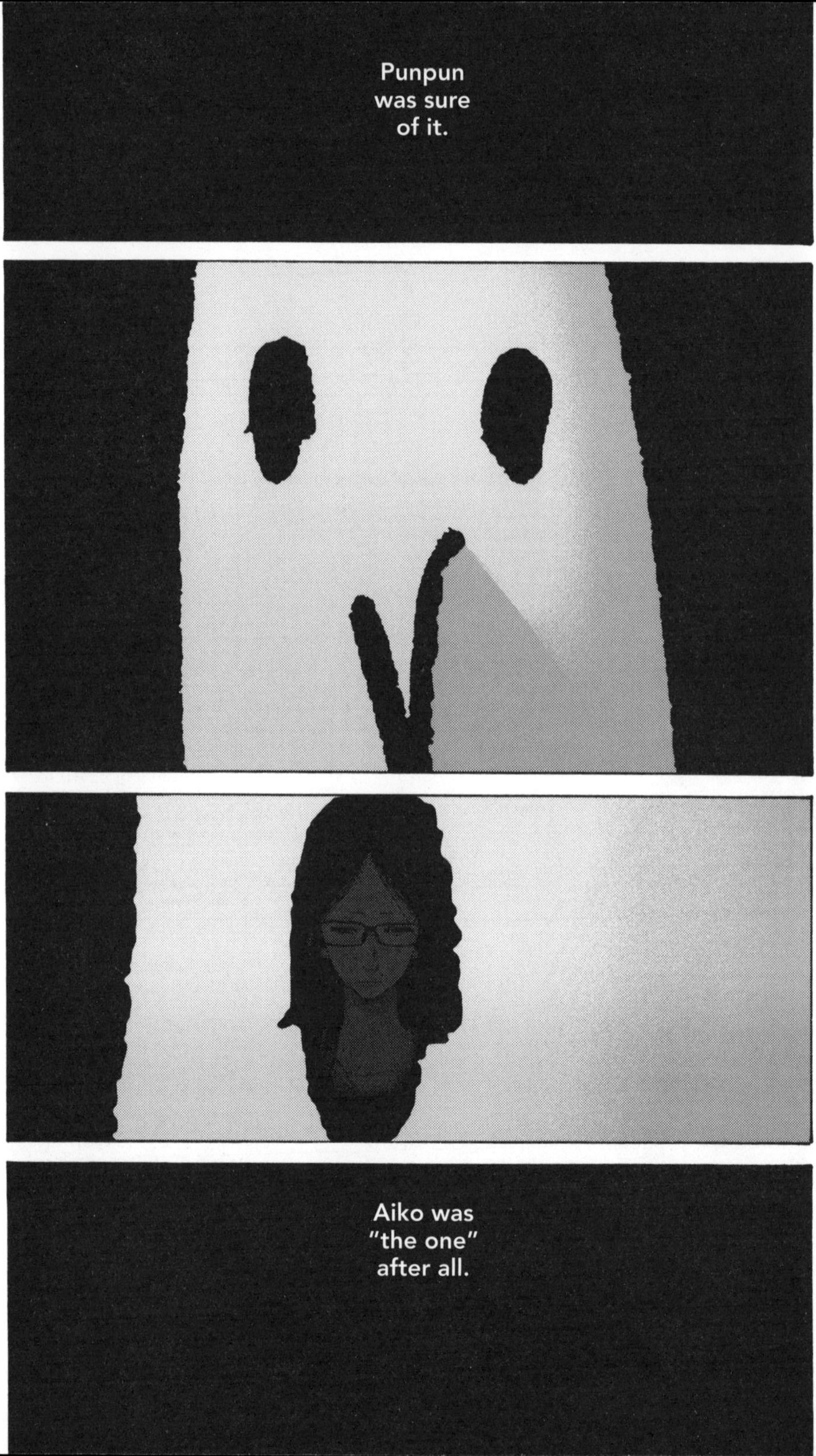
Punpun was sure of it.
Aiko was "the one" after all.

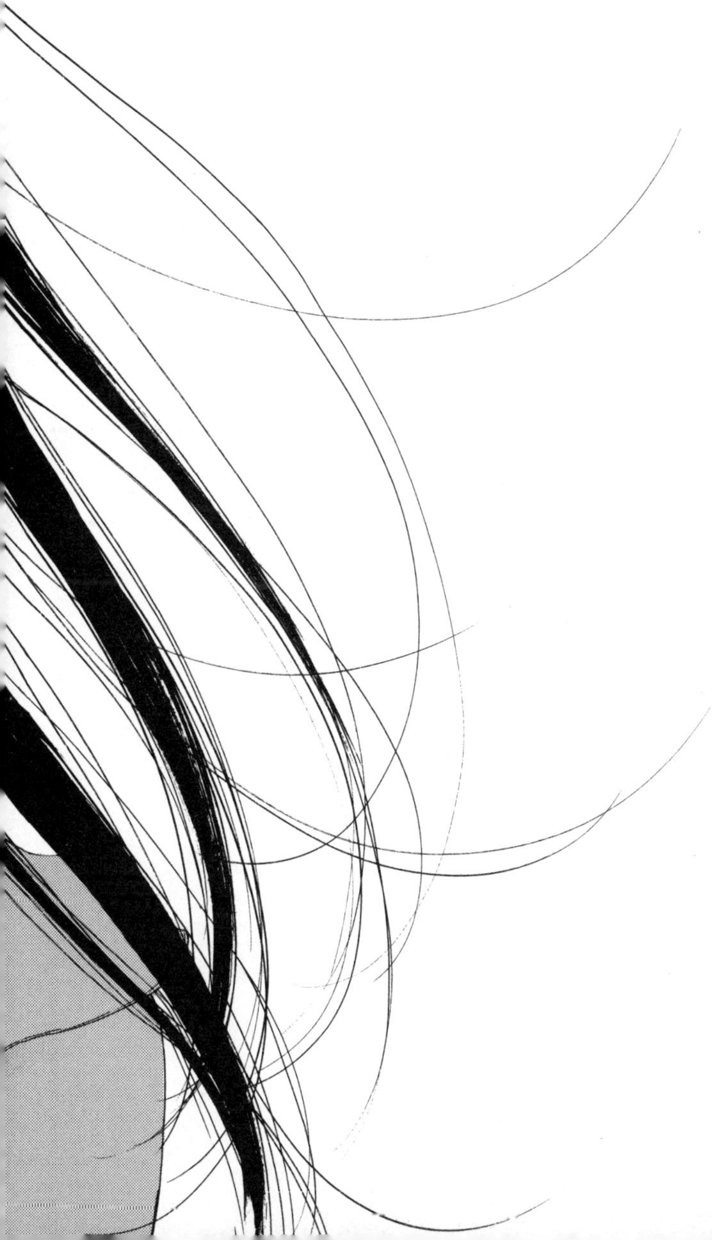

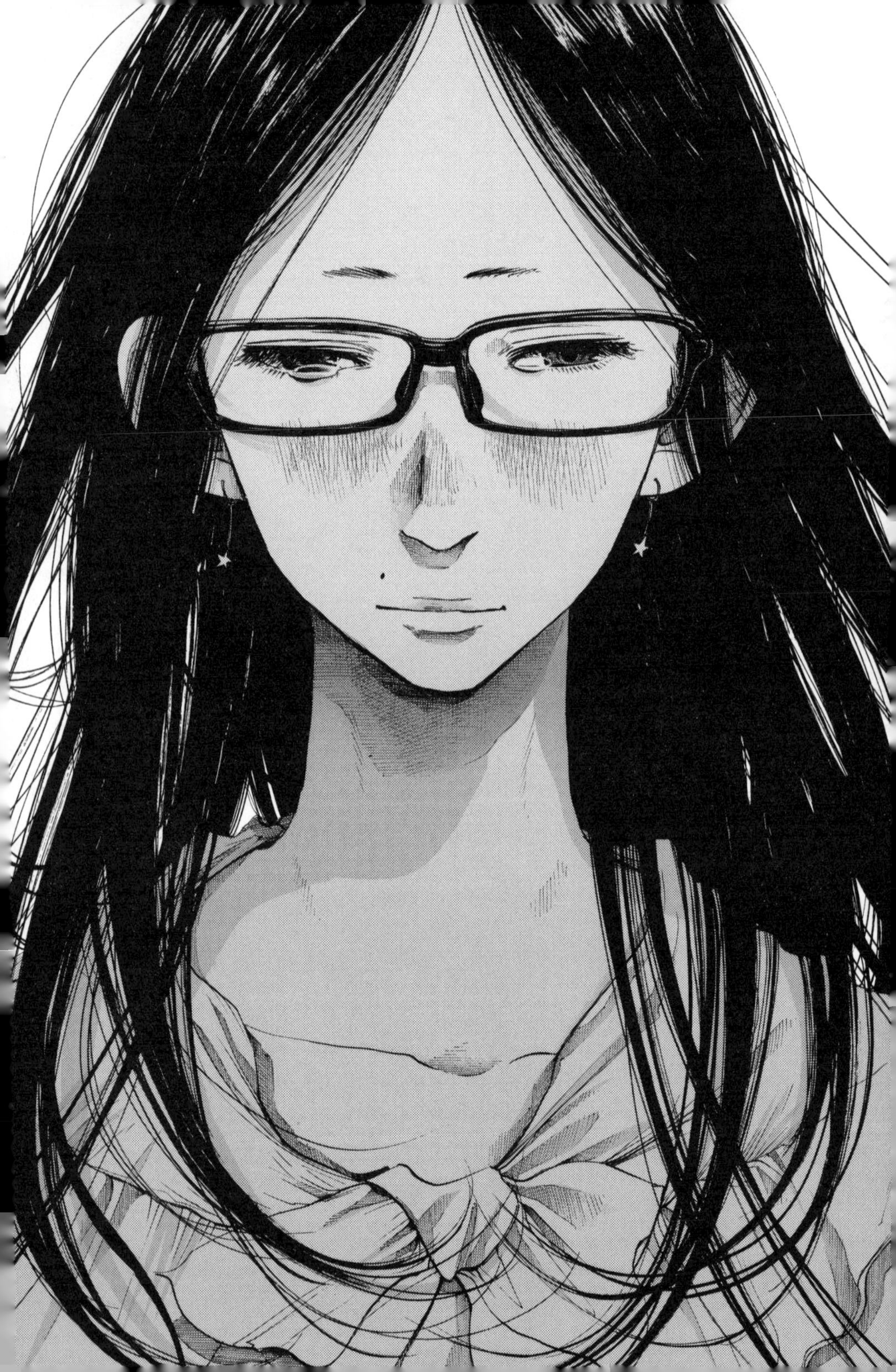

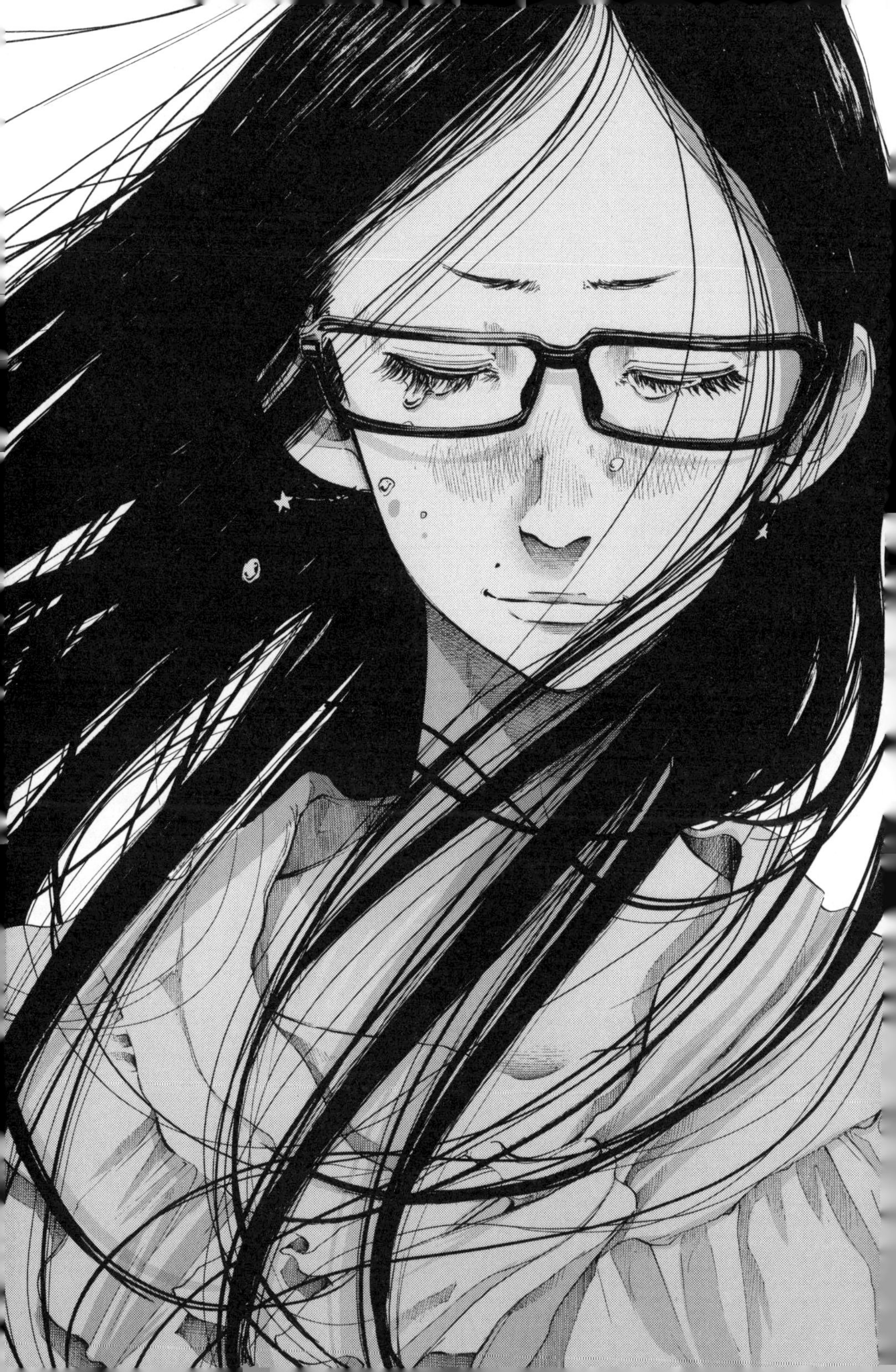

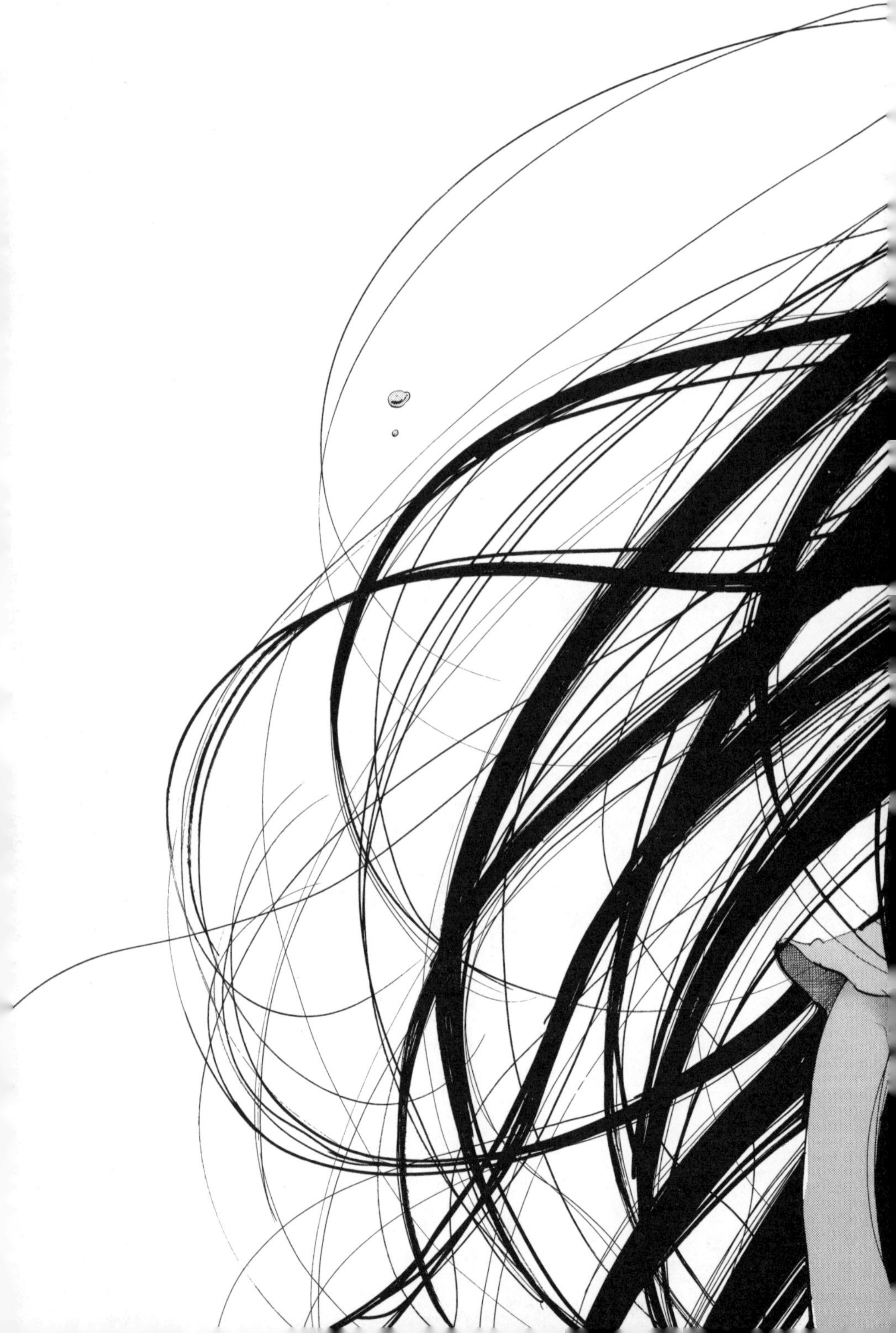

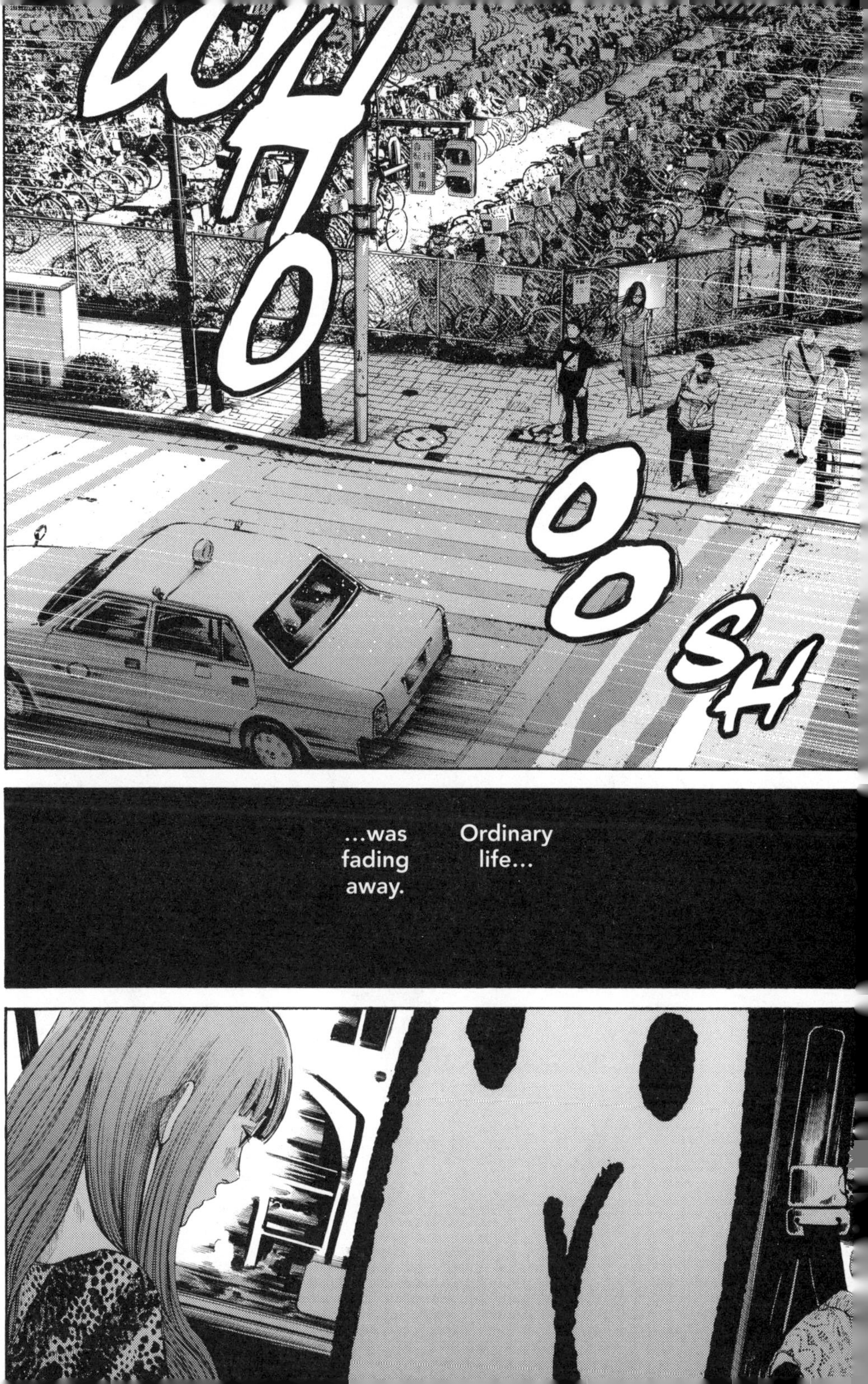
WHOOOSH
Ordinary life...
...was fading away.

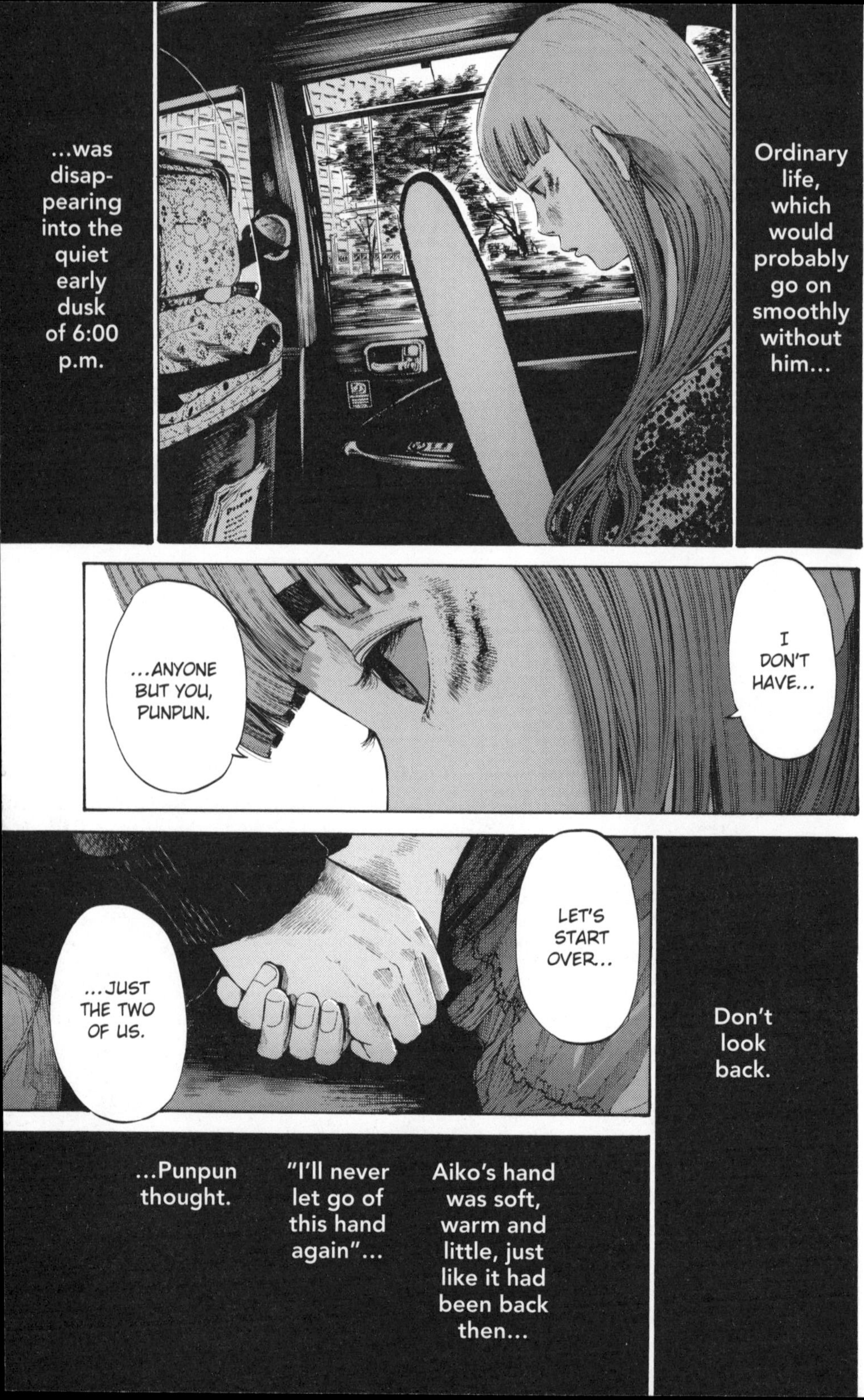
Ordinary life, which would probably go on smoothly without him...
...was disappearing into the quiet early dusk of 6:00 p.m.
I DON'T HAVE...
...ANYONE BUT YOU, PUNPUN.
Don't look back.
LET'S START OVER...
...JUST THE TWO OF US.
Aiko's hand was soft, warm and little, just like it had been back then...
"I'll never let go of this hand again"...
...Punpun thought.

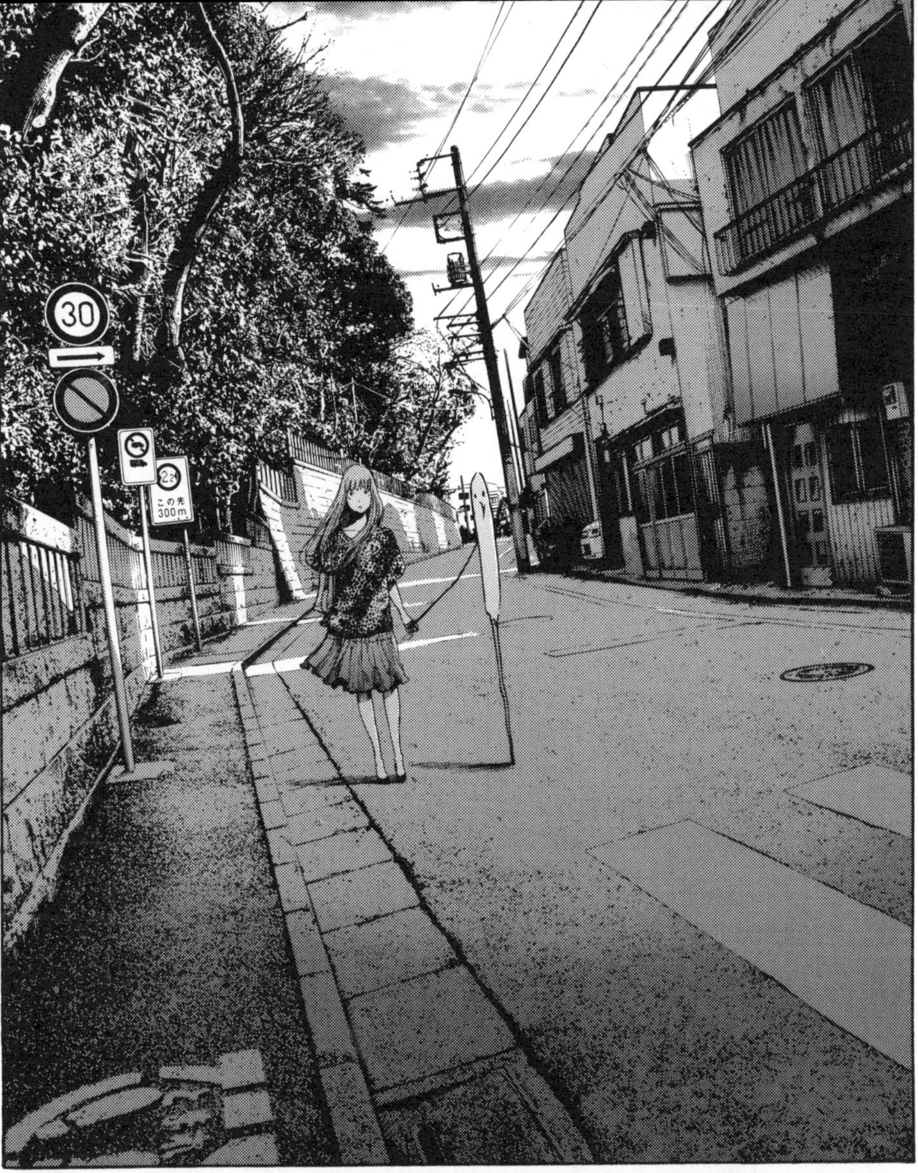
30
この先
300m

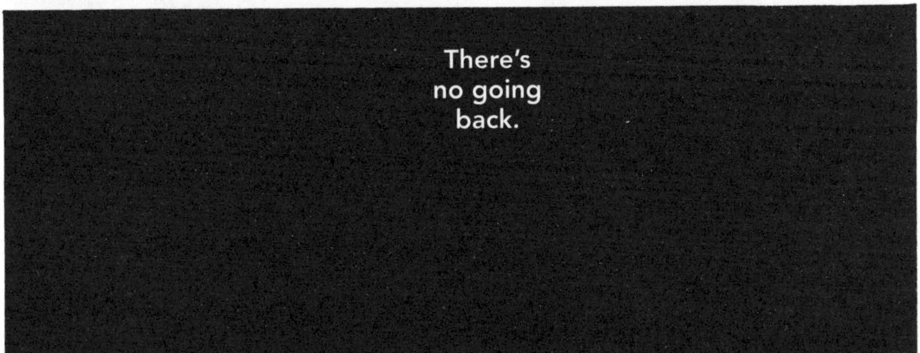
There's
no going
back.

GOODNIGHT PUNPUN
Part Ten

INIO ASANO

BACKGROUND ASSISTANTS: Yuki Toribuchi
Satsuki Sato
Hiro Kashiwaba
CG ASSISTANT: Hisashi Saito
COOPERATION: Kumatsuto
Yu Uehara
Takashi Fujikawa

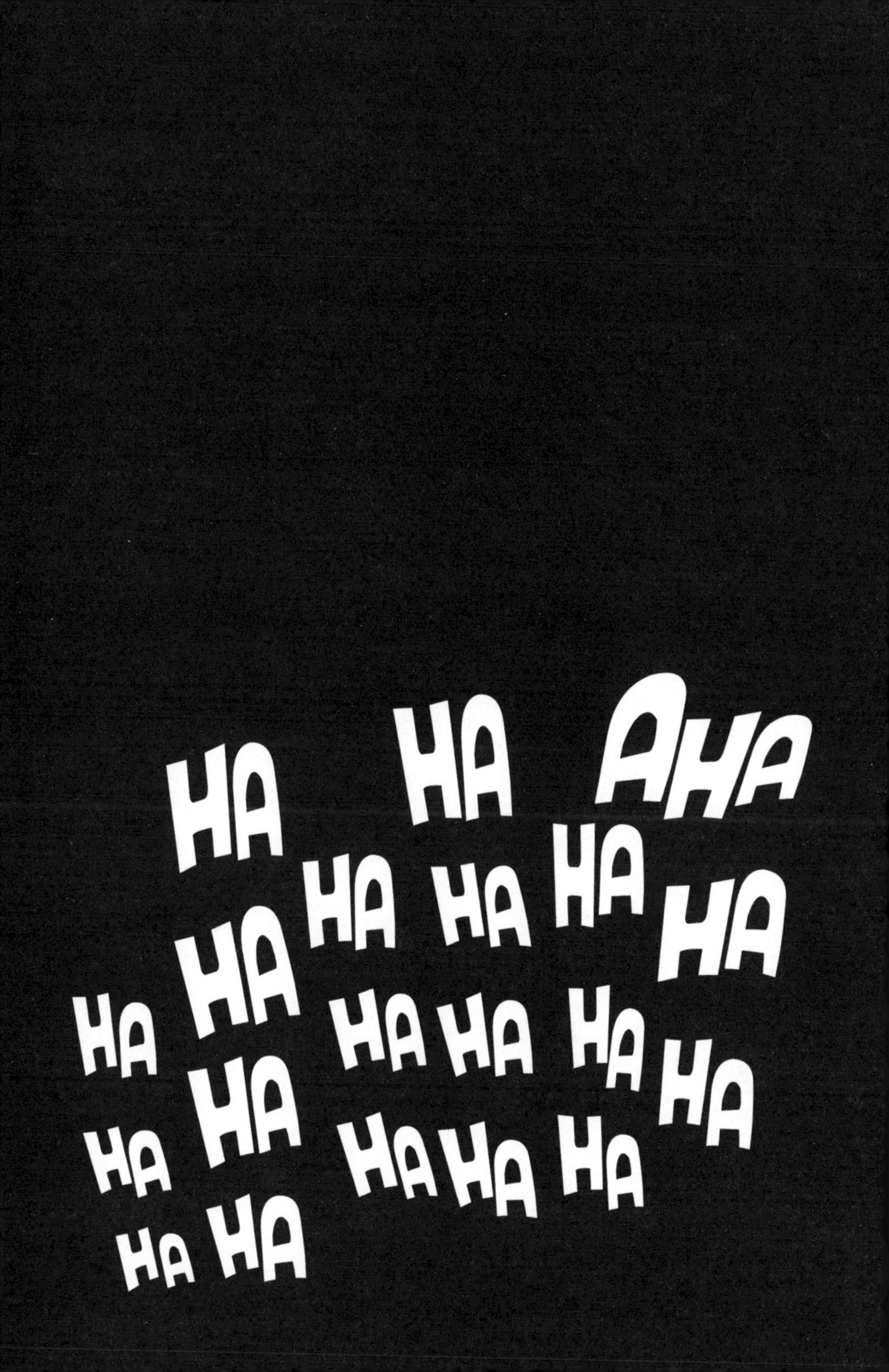
HA HA AHA
HA HA HA HA HA
HA HA HA HA HA HA
HA HA HA HA HA HA
HA HA

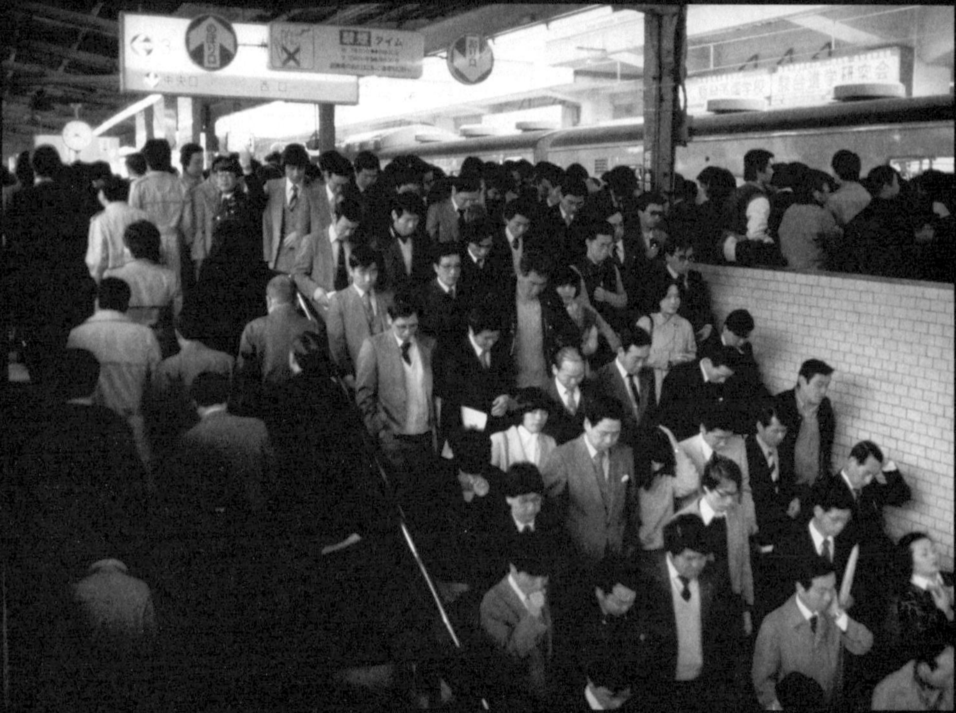

中央口
西口
タイム

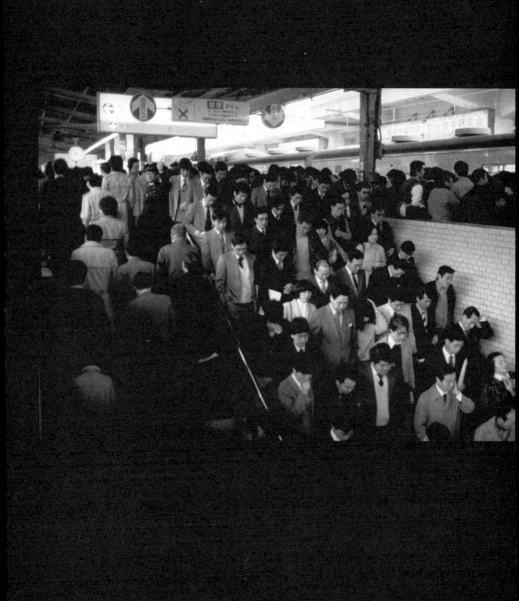

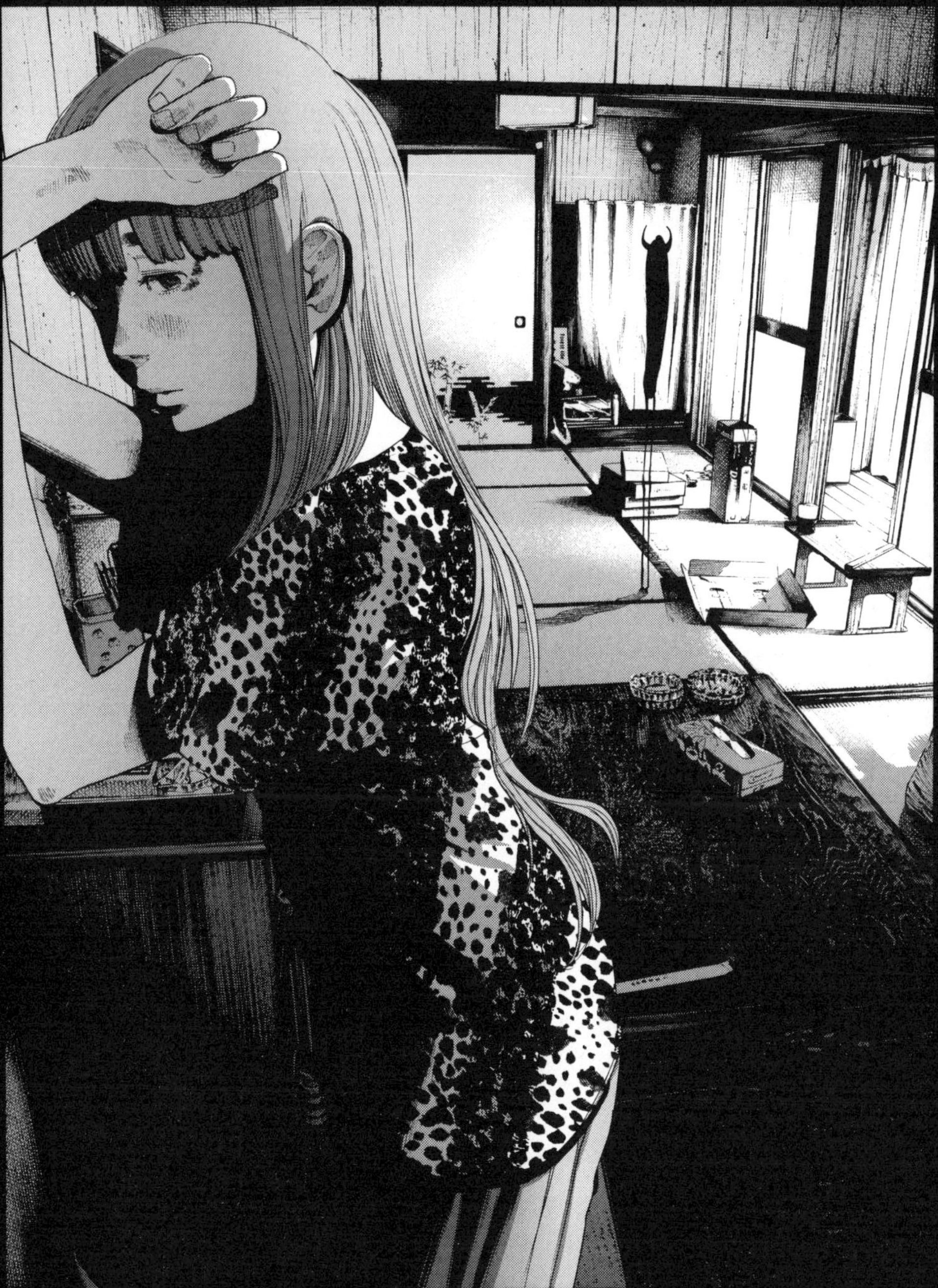

THAT'S ALL FOR NOW.

THE THIGH-LICKING VOLUME 6 WILL BE ON SALE JUNE 2017.

INIO ASANO, a bona fide earthling, was born in Ibaraki, Japan, in 1980. In 2001, his short story "Uchu kara Konnichiwa" (Hello from Outer Space) won the first Sunday GX Rookie Prize. Later, GX published his series *Subarashi Sekai*, available in English from VIZ Media as *What a Wonderful World!* His other works include *Hikari no Machi* (City of Light), *Nijigahara Holograph* and *Umibe no Onna no Ko* (A Girl on the Shore), as well as *solanin*, also available from VIZ Media.

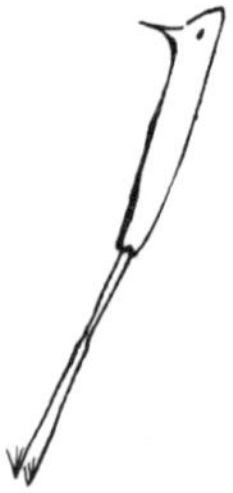

GOODNIGHT PUNPUN
Volume 5
VIZ Signature Edition

Story and Art by INIO ASANO

OYASUMI PUNPUN Vol. 9, 10
by Inio ASANO
© 2007 Inio ASANO
All rights reserved.
Original Japanese edition published by SHOGAKUKAN.
English translation rights in the United States of America,
Canada, the United Kingdom and Ireland arranged with
SHOGAKUKAN.

Translation ☆ JN PRODUCTIONS
Touch-Up Art & Lettering ⚡ ANNALIESE CHRISTMAN
Design ➜ IZUMI EVERS
Editor ✩ PANCHA DIAZ

Printed in Canada

Published by VIZ Media, LLC
P.O. Box 77010
San Francisco, CA 94107

10 9 8 7 6 5 4 3 2 1
First printing, March 2017

www.viz.com

VIZ SIGNATURE

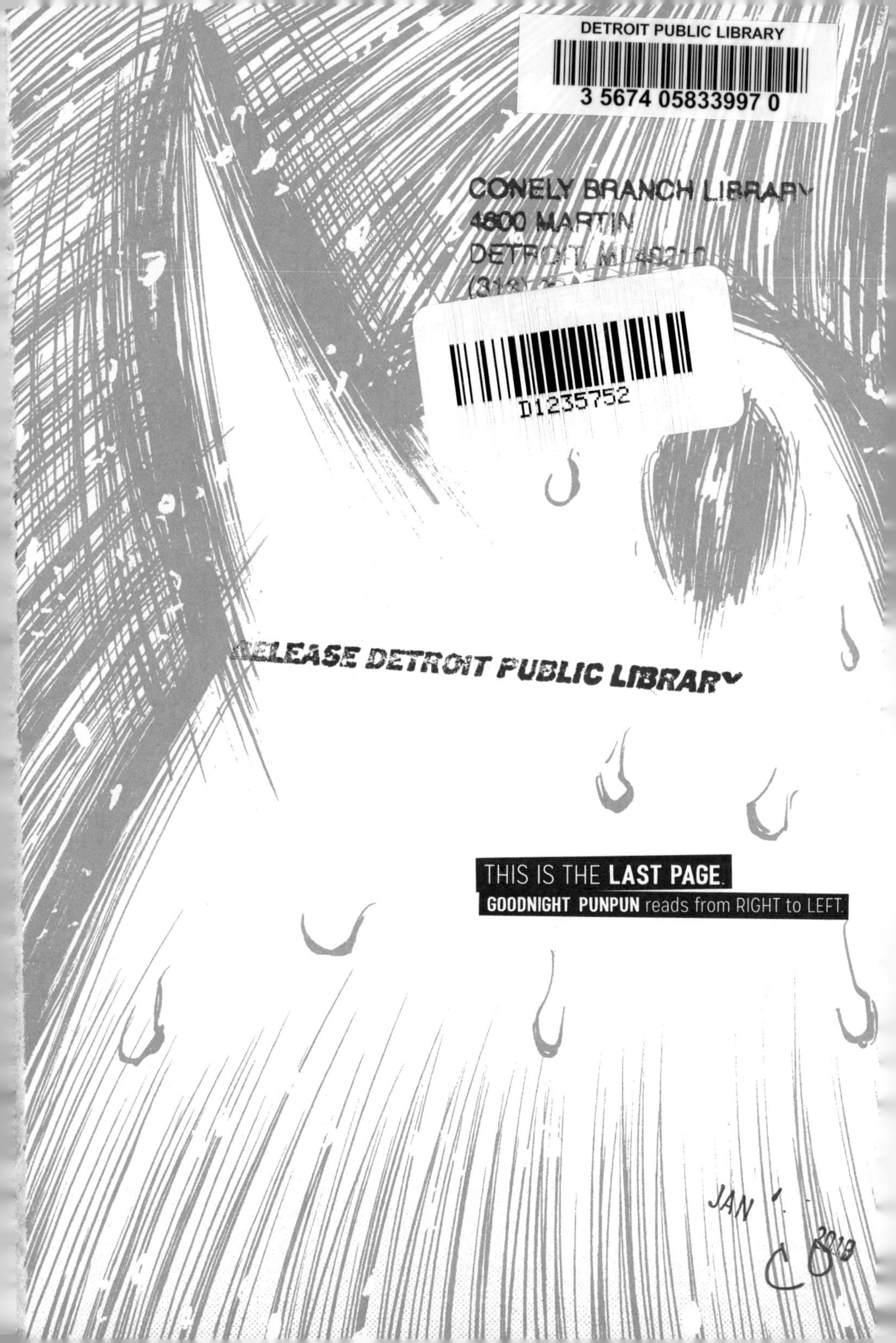

THIS IS THE **LAST PAGE**.

GOODNIGHT PUNPUN reads from RIGHT to LEFT.